Authoritative Guide
TO THE
KATALOPSI CONSTRUCTED LANGUAGE

AUTHORITATIVE GUIDE
TO THE
KATALOPSI CONSTRUCTED LANGUAGE

J. S. LING

AUTHORITATIVE GUIDE TO THE KATALOPSI CONSTRUCTED LANGUAGE

iUniverse books may be ordered through booksellers or by contacting:

iUniverse
1663 Liberty Drive
Bloomington, IN 47403
www.iuniverse.com
1-800-Authors (1-800-288-4677)

Because of the dynamic nature of the Internet, any web addresses or links contained in this book may have changed since publication and may no longer be valid. The views expressed in this work are solely those of the author and do not necessarily reflect the views of the publisher, and the publisher hereby disclaims any responsibility for them.

Any people depicted in stock imagery provided by Getty Images are models, and such images are being used for illustrative purposes only.
Certain stock imagery © Getty Images.

ISBN: 978-1-5320-6685-6 (sc)
ISBN: 978-1-5320-6686-3 (e)

Print information available on the last page.

iUniverse rev. date: 04/12/2019

CONTENTS

PREFACE

To create a language feels, to me, distinctly human—even instinctual. Noam Chomsky insists that what we humans do when we speak or sign is so closely linked to our humanness that to ask whether other animals have language is nonsensical.

Our creativity, though, also seems rather unique, and so why not engage both of these faculties at the same time? To say I thought that when I started this project would be misleading, but these thoughts were in the back of my mind when I created the language that is the subject of this book.

An interesting thing happens when you imagine the sounds of a language, the ordering of the words, and most importantly the words themselves. You cannot help but picture the people who speak the language, with all their culture, their interests, and the broad memetic environment they find themselves in. These flashes of a fictional ethnicity guided the process of building the lexicon. You think, *What do these people care about? What do they* talk *about?*

Of course I wanted to create a language that is functional, with a potential for use as a communicative medium at least as good as any natural language, but a good chunk of the vocabulary ended up being about that elusive, imaginary people.

The strangeness of language construction doesn't stop with the dictionary, however, because as I decided on the sounds the language will use and wrote out arbitrary rules for how the sounds should combine and mutually influence the realization of one another, a character began to emerge from that system, an unnamed quality. When I begin construction of a language, I feel myself psychologically perched on the edge of my seat, waiting to perceive the emergence of that elusive quality. There's really nothing to compare to that feeling.

I'm happy for anyone who wants to read this book for a love of studying constructed languages, but I'd especially like to encourage gamers and game developers to use this language as they see fit, provided that you credit me for its creation. I don't want the lack of access to an exolanguage be the reason your tabletop sci-fi game doesn't feel authentic. I don't want game developers to be discouraged by an inability to construct these languages themselves.

As a final note, to better facilitate the comprehension of this text, let me say outright that I will attempt to present every linguistic concept mentioned in this book in two ways: (1) in terms of the linguistic, scientific understanding of the phenomena and (2) in lay terms, free of jargon, to better speak to learners of the language without a linguistics background.

I hope you enjoy learning this language as much as I enjoyed creating it.

CHAPTER 1

Phonology

In spoken language, sounds are fundamental. It is important to know how sounds are pronounced both in isolation and in interaction with one another. For your speech to be considered fluent, you need to be aware of how the sounds change depending on their environment. In this chapter, we will look at the fundamental sounds of the Katalopsi constructed language, ways of combining those sounds into syllables, and the different forms sounds take while interacting in natural speech.

1.1: THE SOUNDS

1.1.1: TONES

The most striking characteristic of the phonological system of Katalopsi, especially to speakers of English, is its use of tone. You may be familiar with *intonation*, the variation of pitch throughout a sentence to get across differences in meaning. For example, speakers of English often raise the pitch of their voice at the end of a sentence to indicate a question. Tone is similar, except that it involves varying the pitch of your voice over single words to yield distinct meanings. You might have encountered this phenomenon in languages like Mandarin Chinese.

Consider the following pairs of Katalopsi words that differ only in tone, noting their English translations. For now, we will use characters from the Latin alphabet to represent these words, but in Chapter 5 you will learn the language's unique orthographical system.

jò	"lake, pond"
jó	"day"
kì	"route"
ki̱	"eye"
klã	"floor"
klā	"dirt"

These are called minimal pairs, meaning the members of the pairs differ from one another by a single feature, which in this case is tone. What these examples show is that in Katalopsi, tone is distinctive. That is, it results in different meanings.

In the above examples, we can discern five different tones, represented by diacritics on the vowels: the rising tone (ú), the falling tone (ù), the high tone (ū), the low tone (u̱), and the mordent tone (ũ). There are three additional tones we will shortly identify, but their distribution is much narrower, while the abovementioned tones are essentially ubiquitous.

It will be helpful for some to note that from this point on, we will be using symbols from the International Phonetic Alphabet (IPA), a set of characters used to exactly describe how something is pronounced. For many readers, this will probably not be useful, but if ever there is any doubt how to truly pronounce something, a study of the IPA will benefit you.

In Table 1, you will see every tone that occurs in Katalopsi, complete with examples. You will see that the tones have been divided into *basic* and *complex* tones, a distinction that will prove useful in our discussion of vowels in §1.1.3.

Type	Tone	Example	Translation
Basic	Rising	ró	"zero"
	Falling	kè	"nothing"
	High	pī	"after"
	Low	keo̱	"imagine"
	Neutral	klujĩ	"information"
Complex	Mordent	srõ	"black"
	Rising-Falling	muô	"lie"
	Falling-Rising	kfǔ	"watch"

Table 1. Tones of Katalopsi

1.1.1.1: Basic Tones

The basic tones of Katalopsi are five-fold. The rising tone, the falling tone, the high tone, and the low tone occur in every type of syllable more or less without restriction. The neutral tone can only occur in conjunction with the complex mordent tone, which we will describe more fully in the next section.

The rising tone starts at a relatively low pitch and raises to a relatively high pitch by the end of the syllable. In our Latin orthographical representations of Katalopsi, we will be using the acute accent to represent the rising tone. Where exactly the accent is placed will be discussed in embryo in our discussion of syllable types in §1.2 and more fully in the chapter 5 discussion of orthography.

ní   "year"

pió   "control"

kfú   "because"

The falling tone is the reverse of the rising tone. To perform this tone, you start the syllable with a relatively high pitch and fall to a relatively low pitch by the end of the syllable. The grave accent is used to represent this tone:

muà   "climb"

fò	"not"
cì	"she/her"

The high tone does not involve a change in pitch but rather involves flatly holding a relatively high pitch throughout the syllable. This is represented by a macron above the vowel:

clū	"five"
klā	"soil"
kriā	"attack"

The low tone is analogous to the high tone in that you realize it by maintaining a relatively low pitch throughout the syllable. This is represented by a macron *below* the vowel.

ps̱o	"building"
pe̱	"both"
kri̱	"eight"

Finally, the neutral tone, which only occurs in conjunction with the mordent tone—one of the complex tones described further in the next section—is also a stable pitch tone. Like the high and low tones, you do not vary the pitch of your voice throughout the syllable, but the pitch you aim for is relatively in the middle of the pitches of adjacent high and low tones. The neutral tone is represented by the absence of a diacritic on the vowel. Note that this is distinct from some unmarked vowels, like in the words just mentioned, e.g. *pió, muà*, etc. The exact distinction will be elucidated later in this chapter. The following words have examples of both the neutral tone and the mordent tone:

pojõ	"basis"
sisõ	"reading"
cekũ	"donator"

4

1.1.1.2: Complex Tones

The complex tones come in three varieties, the first of which is the previously mentioned mordent tone. The principle of the mordent tone is that every syllable occurring in the same word, before the syllable with the mordent tone, is realized with a neutral tone. If the word is monosyllabic, having a single syllable, this effect is not observed, but di- and trisyllabic words as well as still more lengthy words will have co-occurring neutral tones. Note how the mordent tone is marked with a perispomene, also known as a tilde:

cẽ	"night"
praklũ	"business"
crukoxũ	"impactful"

The mordent tone is realized much like the musical ornament from which it gets its name. Starting the syllable at a neutral level, or guiding, pitch, you quickly dip the pitch of your voice downward and then quickly come back up to the same level at which you started. When dipping downward, you do not necessarily go as low as the pitch of a low tone, but just enough so that the dip is discernible to a listener.

The second of the three complex tones is known as the rising-falling tone, as it involves realizing both a rising and then a falling tone in the same syllable. That is, you begin at a relatively low pitch, rise to a high pitch, and then fall back to the low pitch at which you started. This tone as well as the next and last complex tone to be discussed occur only on diphthongs, where one vowel glides into another. We will discuss this further in the section on vowels and in the section on syllables. Consider the following examples of words with the rising-falling tone, which is represented with a circumflex above the last vowel of the diphthong:

xuŷ	"worry"
kliâ	"cost"
meî	"want"

The third complex tone is known as the falling-rising tone and is the reverse of the tone just discussed. This involves starting the syllable with a relatively high pitch, falling down to a low pitch, and then rising back to the high pitch at which you started. This tone is represented with a háček, also known as a caron, above the vowel:

cuǎ	"make sense"
kliǒ	"drink"
psiě	"expect"

1.1.2: Consonants

In this section, we will discuss the fourteen consonants that occur in Katalopsi. Similar to tone, the complete set of consonants, shown in Table 2, do not necessarily occur in every environment. However, it is important that we look at the consonants in isolation before we start trying to construct syllables with them, complete with an exposition on the asymmetries of their phonological environments.

Table 2 is a simplified version of the International Phonetic Alphabet chart, containing only the consonants of Katalopsi. The letters of our shorthand Latin alphabet will appear to the left in chevrons (e.g. ⟨m⟩). The IPA symbol will appear to the right of the Latin grapheme in square brackets (e.g. [m]). Where two pairs of symbols occur, the upper pair is the voiceless variant, while the lower pair is the voiced variant.

	Bilabial	Dental	(Post) alveolar	Palatal	Velar
Plosive	⟨p⟩ – [p]	⟨c⟩ – [t]			⟨k⟩ – [k]
Nasal	⟨m⟩ – [m]	⟨n⟩ – [n]			
Fricative	⟨f⟩ – [ɸ] ⟨v⟩ – [β]		⟨s⟩ – [ʃ] ⟨z⟩ – [ʒ]		⟨x⟩ – [x] ⟨g⟩ – [ɣ]
Approximant				⟨j⟩ – [j]	
Tap			⟨r⟩ – [ɾ]		
Lateral Approximant		⟨l⟩ – [l]			

Table 2. Consonants of Katalopsi

Some of these consonants will be unfamiliar to many speakers of English, so they bear greater attention and explanation. We will first review those sounds that will be familiar to native English speakers and then consider those sounds that will be problematic.

1.1.2.1: Familiar Consonants

Each of the so-called *plosive* consonants occur in English in some form: ⟨p⟩, ⟨c⟩, and ⟨k⟩. The ⟨p⟩ is performed with a puff of air blown between closed lips and occurs in English words such as *part*, *happen*, and *sap*. The ⟨c⟩ sound is like the ⟨t⟩ occurring in words *tarnish*, *hurt*, and *treat*, except that the puff of air is pushed through the closure created by the tip of your tongue and the back of your teeth. The ⟨k⟩ sound is identical to that occurring in words like *keep*, *seek*, and *skip*.

Nasal consonants are extremely common across the natural languages of the world due to that distinctive titular quality. Katalopsi has just two nasals, ⟨m⟩ and ⟨n⟩, which in their graphic representations do not mislead. The ⟨m⟩ sound is realized just as in the English words *mother*, *ham*, and *ammo*, while the ⟨n⟩ sound is just as in words *noun*, *hand*, and *mantis*.

Two of the six fricatives of Katalopsi also occur in English, ⟨s⟩ and ⟨z⟩. The ⟨s⟩ sound is often spelled ⟨sh⟩, as in *shock* and *marsh*, but also occurs as ⟨ch⟩, as in *chic* and *cache*. The ⟨z⟩ sound has a more constrained distribution in English but is the voiced variant of ⟨s⟩, meaning you vibrate your vocal cords while performing it. It occurs as ⟨s⟩ in words like *pleasure* and *lesion*, as ⟨g⟩ in a word like *genre*, and so on.

The two abovementioned approximants will also be familiar to speakers of English, ⟨l⟩ and ⟨j⟩. The sound ⟨l⟩ refers to is as the grapheme suggests, that sound in the words *late*, *pal*, and *illusion*. Finally, the ⟨j⟩ sound is equivalent to the sound represented as ⟨y⟩ in *yes*, *yawn*, and *yard*.

The final consonant that will be familiar to speakers of English is ⟨r⟩, or the tap consonant [ɾ]. Although it does occur in English, it is not distinctive, so it does not result in different meanings. In Katalopsi, it *is* distinctive and is produced like the American English pronunciation of ⟨t⟩ in *litter* or ⟨d⟩ in *ladder*. It is a flick of the tongue, a tap or flap of the tip of the tongue against the alveolar ridge. In English, this sound only occurs in the middle of words, between vowels or between sonorants;

to pronounce it in Katalopsi, you should become used to pronouncing it at the beginning of words as well.

1.1.2.2: Unfamiliar Consonants

There are consonants in Table 2 which do not occur in English, represented in the Latin orthography as ⟨f⟩, ⟨v⟩, ⟨x⟩, and ⟨g⟩ and in IPA as [ɸ], [β], [x], and [ɣ], respectively.

The voiceless bilabial fricative, ⟨f⟩ or [ɸ], will sound a lot like an English ⟨f⟩, as in *fog, gaffe*, and *sift*. However, the English ⟨f⟩ sound is made by pressing your lower lip against your upper teeth, whereas the Katalopsi ⟨f⟩ is realized by putting your upper and lower lips together. Think of it as blowing friction through your lips. You may be familiar with the sound in languages like Japanese or some dialects of Spanish[1]. If you try to make an ⟨f⟩ sound using just your lips, you will be able to produce the Katalopsi ⟨f⟩ with ease.

A very similar sound is the voiced bilabial fricative, ⟨v⟩ or [β], the voiced variant of the fricative we just discussed. It is therefore like producing an English ⟨v⟩ sound, as in *vest, tavern*, and *have*, but with your upper and lower lips together. It is important not to let your lips be too lax when producing this sound because you may accidentally produce a bilabial trill, a sort of raspberry sound often made by infants.

Another fricative which may be an issue is the voiceless velar fricative, ⟨x⟩ or [x]. You have probably heard it before without realizing it. Occurring in languages like German and Russian, this fricative can be realized by articulating a ⟨k⟩ as previously described, but instead of creating a complete closure between your tongue and your velum, you make a slightly lax closure that allows air to pass through, making a friction sound. It will probably sound quite harsh at first, but with practice, you will find that you can give it more or less energy and soon you will be producing it as confidently as any other sound.

The final challenging sound to be discussed is the voiced velar fricative, ⟨g⟩ or [ɣ], the voiced variant of the fricative just described.

---

[1] For a description of Japanese phonology, see Itō and Mester (1995), and for Spanish phonology, see Hammond (2001).

Once you are able to produce the ⟨x⟩ sound, simply add the vibration of your vocal cords to the production of the sound, and you will be producing ⟨g⟩. In other words, if you articulate a ⟨g⟩ as in the words *gourd*, *stag*, and *haggard*, but create a slightly lax closure—as for ⟨x⟩—the voiced velar fricative will be the result.

1.1.3: VOWELS

There are six vowels in Katalopsi, and they can combine in specific ways to form eighteen diphthongs. They can also be influenced by surrounding sounds, resulting in different pronunciations. We will explore this subject of phonological interaction in §1.3. Table 3 shows the six vowels in their basic monophthong forms:

	Front	Central	Back
Close	⟨i⟩ – [i]		⟨u⟩ – [u]
Near-Mid	⟨e⟩ – [e]		
Mid		⟨y⟩ – [ə]	
Near-Open	⟨a⟩ – [æ]		
Open			⟨o⟩ – [ɑ]

Table 3. Vowels of Katalopsi (Monophthongs)

These sounds combine to create diphthongs, or sounds where one vowel glides into another. As we will see later, this distinction between monophthong and diphthong vowels is significant for the lexicology of the language.

1.1.3.1: Monophthongs

The six vowels mentioned above are all vowels that occur in English; learning their orthographical representations will likely be more difficult than learning to pronounce them for the majority of readers.

The sound we represent as ⟨i⟩, a close front unrounded vowel, occurs in English in a variety of spellings, such as ⟨ea⟩ in *read*, ⟨ee⟩ in *peek*, and ⟨i⟩ in *magazine*, among others.

The sound ⟨e⟩, a near-mid front unrounded vowel, occurs in English but only in the form of a diphthong. If you listen carefully to the sound of ⟨ay⟩ in *bay*, ⟨ai⟩ in *raid*, and ⟨a⟩ in *made*, you will hear two vowel qualities, the first gliding into the second. The sound we are representing as ⟨e⟩ is the first of these two vowel qualities. To successfully pronounce this vowel, try pronouncing the diphthongs in the words *bay*, *raid*, and *made*, but cut off the second half.

The vowel ⟨a⟩, a near-open front unrounded vowel, is identical to that in English, most often spelled as ⟨a⟩, as in *gnash*, *tack*, and *past*.

The sound ⟨y⟩, a mid central unrounded vowel, is also found in its exact form in English, but with a variety of spellings. The ⟨a⟩ in *attend*, the ⟨e⟩ in *return*, and the ⟨o⟩ in *welcome* are all good examples of this vowel in use.

The close back rounded vowel, ⟨u⟩, is similar to ⟨e⟩ mentioned above, in that it only occurs in English as part of a diphthong. This is the sound occurring as ⟨oo⟩ in *boot*, as ⟨u⟩ in *absolute*, and as ⟨eu⟩ in *neutral*. If you pronounce these words slowly, you will notice that you narrow your lips as you pronounce the diphthong. In order to pronounce this vowel in Katalopsi, you need to avoid narrowing your lips and only pronounce the first half of the diphthong.

The sound we represent as ⟨o⟩, the open back unrounded vowel, is pronounced as ⟨a⟩ in *father*, as ⟨o⟩ in *bother*, and as ⟨oa⟩ in *broad*, among other spellings. In this form, this vowel should be very familiar to speakers of English and does not bear close consideration.

Once you have a firm grasp of the pronunciation of these six vowels, you can safely move on to the next section on the combination of monophthongic vowels into diphthongs.

1.1.3.2: Diphthongs

The six vowels described in the previous section can combine into diphthongs, vowels in which one vowel quality glides into another. These are very common in English, but those of Katalopsi will probably seem across the board a little peculiar. The diphthongs of English are pairings of *vowels* with *semivowels*, a linguistic term referring to sounds like the ⟨y⟩ in *yes* or the ⟨w⟩ in *wave*. While their exact realization may vary due to factors we will shortly discuss, the diphthongs of Katalopsi are composed of a vowel with a vowel, a phenomenon you may recognize from languages like Lithuanian[2].

Eighteen diphthongs can be formed from the combination of the six monophthongs. This might come as a surprise to any of you keen on analyzing the combinatorics of the situation. That is, if the first vowel of the diphthong is one of six, and the second is one of the remaining five, would we not expect a product of thirty possible diphthongs? While this is mathematically accurate, additional constraints on the vowels that can combine limit this to only eighteen. Katalopsi diphthongs are subject to a constraint which we may call *anti-harmony*.

This term is derived from a known concept in linguistics called *vowel harmony*, a phenomenon occurring in languages like Turkish and Hungarian[3], in which words are required to contain only vowels from the same category. For example, Turkish words for the most part have vowels that are either only front or only back, either only rounded or only unrounded. That is, the vowels are *harmonious* with one another.

In Katalopsi, the phenomenal domain is the diphthong, and the vowels must *not* be in the same category. They must be *anti-harmonious*. There are three categories of relevance: category A ("high vowels"), containing ⟨i⟩ and ⟨u⟩; category B ("neutral vowels"), containing just ⟨e⟩; and category C ("low vowels"), containing ⟨a⟩, ⟨y⟩, and ⟨o⟩. This anti-harmony is applied *anticipatorily*, meaning that once the first vowel is chosen, the second vowel is compared categorically to the first to confirm the anti-harmony. E.g. if the first vowel is ⟨i⟩, then the second vowel can be any vowel other than ⟨i⟩ and ⟨u⟩. Table 4 shows all possible diphthongs and marks the impossible diphthongs for the reason they do not occur:

---

[2] Dambriunas et al. (1966) describes these diphthongs. While some Lithuanian diphthongs are analyzable as a vowel and a semivowel, at least in practice, others are more like a vowel gliding into another vowel.

[3] Kabak (2011) describes vowel harmony in Turkish, while Hayes et al. (2009) addresses the same in Hungarian.

		Second Vowel					
		i	u	e	a	y	o
First Vowel	i	✕	△	ie	ia	iy	io
	u	△	✕	ue	ua	uy	uo
	e	ei	eu	✕	☐	ey	eo
	a	ai	au	☐	✕	△	△
	y	yi	yu	☐	△	✕	△
	o	oi	ou	☐	△	△	✕

Table 4. Vowels of Katalopsi (Diphthongs)

Combinations marked with an ✕ are so marked because they do not create diphthongs but rather long vowels, which are not distinctive in Katalopsi; those marked with a △ indicate a diphthong that is impossible because it is not anti-harmonious; and finally, the ☐ indicates that the potential combination is a *simple gap*, meaning that although it is anti-harmonious, it simply doesn't occur in the language.

Practice these diphthongs as though they are always realized as one vowel quality gliding into another. In §1.3, we will describe conditions under which the pronunciation of some diphthongs is simplified. For now, we turn our attention to the syllable.

1.2: SYLLABLES

At this point, you should have a handle on the most basic sounds of the language—the tones, the consonants, and the vowels. The next step is to combine the sounds into larger structures. The next biggest structure is the syllable, the rhythmic units of language.

Many people have an intuitive idea of the syllable, but if you have any doubts about your ability to identify one in general, the best way to learn to distinguish them is to see a few examples. Consider the word *epiphany*. If you were to break this word down into smaller rhythmic parts, how would you do it? In fact, the breakdown would look like this: *e-pi-pha-ny*. Try saying each of the four parts of this word slowly, and you will be well on your way to identifying syllables.

What about the word *manliness*? There is an important difference between the syllables of this word and those of *epiphany*. Looking at the breakdown *man-li-ness*, you will notice that two syllables have consonants after their vowels, unlike the syllables in *epiphany*. This reflects a fact about the syllable, namely that it has three parts, the *onset*, the *nucleus*, and the *coda*.

In the monosyllabic word *sand*, for example, ⟨s⟩ appears in the onset, ⟨a⟩ in the nucleus, and ⟨nd⟩ in the coda. It is an important facet of the syllabic structure of Katalopsi words that the coda is always underlyingly empty. The onset will be filled by consonants—if it is filled at all—and the nucleus may be filled by either a consonant or a vowel. The exact nature of these smaller parts of the syllable delineate the syllabic type, and this distinction between types will be useful in our discussion of lexicology in chapter 2.

1.2.1: SYLLABLE TYPES

1.2.1.1: Type I Syllables

This first group of syllables are the simplest of the language. They involve what are called *syllabic consonants*, meaning the syllable is rhythmically significant while lacking a vowel. While this method of creating syllables is not pervasive in English by any means, it is not altogether absent. Consider what it means to say, "Mmm" or "Mhm." These utterances have syllabic structure even though they lack vowels. In some dialects of English, the consonant ⟨r⟩, as in *read*, can also occur as a vowel. It is common, for example, in American English to pronounce the words *herd*, *first*, and *learn* with ⟨r⟩ as the vowel. The vowels of these words—in the traditional sense of spelling—are in these cases entirely orthographic.

This sort of syllabification of consonants is much more common in Katalopsi, where eight distinct consonants may occur within the nucleus of the syllable. When this happens, no other consonant appears in the syllable—either in the onset or the coda. Table 5 lays out these eight consonants with examples:

Consonant	Example	Translation
m	ḿ	"must"
n	ń	"want to"
l	l̩	"be willing to"
r	r̃	"should"
j	j̠	"be going to"
v	ṽ	PERFECT marker
z	ź	PAST marker
g	ḡ	"would"

Table 5. Syllabic Consonants

Though this type of syllable consists of a single consonant, they are just the same able to carry tone like vowels, as you can see by the above examples. However, not all eight tones are available to Type I syllables. Instead, they occur with four of the basic tones—the rising, falling, high, and low tones—and just one of the complex tones—the mordent tone.

1.2.1.2: Type II Syllables

The second group of syllables are slightly more complex than that of the previous section. Type II syllables always have a monophthongic vowel, which means that consonants can fill the onset slot. However, only eleven of the fourteen total consonants discussed can appear in these syllables, as ⟨v⟩, ⟨z⟩, and ⟨g⟩ are exclusive to Type I syllables.

While Type II syllables differ in the distribution of sounds both in the nucleus and in the coda, they are identical to Type I syllables in the set of available tones: Type II syllables are able to use the rising, falling, high, low, and mordent tones. We have seen several Type II syllables this chapter, but for convenience, consider the following examples:

kfí	"light"
plà	"problem"
psī	"idea"
ra̱	"wind"
clĩ	"scene"

1.2.1.3: Type III Syllables

With respect to the consonants appearing in the onset slot, Type III syllables have an identical distribution to Type II syllables. However, they are the most complex class, in that they strictly use diphthongic vowels (not either syllabic consonants or monophthongs) and that they can use all eight tones.

Tone has a distinct pattern of realization when vocalized over diphthongs. While high and low vowels behave predictably, with the respective pitches carried over both vowel qualities, it may be less obvious how the other tones ought to behave.

The rising and falling tones are analogous sounds, and thus their realization over a diphthong is much the same. The rising tone begins at a relatively low pitch at the start of the first vowel of the diphthong and then rises to a relatively high pitch by the end of the second vowel. By the same token, the falling tone begins at a relatively high pitch at the start of the diphthong, falling to a relatively low pitch by the end. In short, these tones mimic their realization over monophthong vowels but are stretched over two vowel qualities instead.

The neutral and mordent tones only occur as a couplet in Type III syllables. The first vowel of the diphthong is realized as a neutral tone, and then the mordent tone begins during the articulation of the second vowel.

The most complicated of circumstances arise with the rising-falling and falling-rising tones. The rising-falling tone is realized over a diphthong by producing a rising tone on the first vowel and a falling tone on the second. Analogously, the falling-rising tone is performed by articulating a falling tone on the first vowel and a rising tone on the second. While this may seem simple enough, the status of these tones as *complex tones*—a concept you will remember from Table 1 in §1.1.1—bears significance in how tones and vowels interact. This concept we will detail in §1.3, but before that, we must say a word about consonant clusters.

1.2.2: Consonant Clusters

In the previous section, we discussed how Type I syllables have a syllabic consonant and an onset that cannot be filled, while Type II and Type III syllables have access to the same range of consonants for their onset slot. Although this is accurate, it glosses over the fact that multiple consonants may appear in the onset slot simultaneously. However, as with the combination of vowels into diphthongs, the consonants must cluster together in conformity with certain rules. This is known as *phonotactics*.

It is perhaps best to start with the consonants that cannot appear in clusters at all. We already know that three consonants, ⟨v⟩, ⟨z⟩, and ⟨g⟩, can only appear in the nucleus of Type I syllables, but the consonants ⟨m⟩, ⟨n⟩, and ⟨j⟩—while able to appear in the onset of syllables of Types II and III—are unable to cluster with other consonants in those positions.

This leaves eight consonants which may in some way cluster together: ⟨p⟩, ⟨c⟩, ⟨k⟩, ⟨f⟩, ⟨s⟩, ⟨x⟩, ⟨l⟩, and ⟨r⟩. In total, Katalopsi has eleven consonant clusters, a slim majority of which are plosives preceding the lateral approximant or the alveolar tap: ⟨pl⟩, ⟨cl⟩, ⟨kl⟩, ⟨pr⟩, ⟨cr⟩, and ⟨kr⟩. Two of the remaining five are preceded by fricatives: ⟨fr⟩ and ⟨sr⟩. And the last three are rare affricate-like clusters, combining an anterior plosive with a posterior fricative: ⟨ps⟩, ⟨cx⟩, and ⟨kf⟩.

For native speakers of English, clusters such as ⟨cl⟩, ⟨fr⟩, ⟨ps⟩, ⟨cx⟩, and ⟨kf⟩ will prove challenging and warrant practice. These are challenges you can overcome as you proceed through the next couple chapters, without concern that they will impede your progress.

With that note, we have addressed all the different ways that the basic sounds of the language—the tones, the consonants, and the vowels—can combine into larger structures. However, in the last section of this chapter, we dive into the consequences of these combinations. Sounds don't exist in vacuums, and when they occur together in language, they interact and influence one another. This topic of interactions will be the last relating to phonology, and in the next chapter, we will turn to the lexicology and morphology of the language.

1.3: INTERACTIONS

Having read to this point, you should now have a good idea how the sounds of Katalopsi are pronounced *in general*. What we have discussed so far, however, is a bit more abstract than natural speech. In speaking Katalopsi, as with any natural language, sounds interact and mutually influence one another, and as a result there are several changes to pronunciation in particular environments that will make your pronunciation sound fluent.

The sounds we previously discussed are in linguistic jargon referred to as *phonemes*, meaning they are the *idea* we have about how the sounds are pronounced in the abstract, i.e. without consideration of environmental factors. In this section we will discuss *allophones*, or the concrete pronunciations of the sounds given the environment they find themselves in.

1.3.1: VOWEL ROUNDING

Rounding is the process by which a vowel or consonant becomes rounded due to proximity with some contextually significant sound. A sound is considered *rounded* when you articulate your lips roughly into a circle when you pronounce it. It is otherwise *unrounded* when your lips are relatively relaxed.

You may recall from earlier in this chapter that one vowel is underlyingly rounded (i.e. ⟨u⟩), and the others are unrounded (i.e. ⟨i⟩, ⟨e⟩, ⟨a⟩, ⟨y⟩, and ⟨o⟩). These unrounded vowels can become rounded when preceded by a consonant with an inherently rounded articulation. These are the sounds ⟨m⟩, ⟨p⟩, and ⟨f⟩, one of which also occurs in the latter part of the consonant cluster ⟨kf⟩. An unrounded vowel preceded by this consonant cluster or any of these three consonants will instead become rounded. Table 6 compares this environment to that of a preceding *unrounded* consonant with examples for each vowel. For each of the two environments, the column on the left is the representation in Latin orthography, while the column on the right holds the pronunciation in IPA. Note that for convenience the IPA representation of tone has been omitted:

		Preceded by			
		Unrounded Consonant		Rounded Consonant	
Vowel	i	sị	[ʃi]	pī	[py]
	u	lù	[lu]	kfú	[kɸu]
	e	kré	[kɾe]	fẹ	[ɸø]
	a	ká	[kæ]	mà	[mœ]
	y	nỳ	[nə]	pȳ	[pɵ]
	o	cọ	[tɑ]	mò	[mɒ]

Table 6. Vowel Rounding

Two things should be observed here. Firstly, we can confirm that the roundedness feature of the preceding consonant has no effect on the vowel ⟨u⟩. Secondly, every other vowel has undergone a change from unrounded to rounded. This change is not indicated in spelling since we are using a phonemic representation of the pronunciation. A similar philosophy underpins the unique orthographical system we will present in chapter 5.

While it may be difficult for the unengaged to exactly explain or even recognize the rounded vowels when correctly pronounced, learning to pronounce them is actually quite simple. Going through each of the five vowels that can become rounded, try first pronouncing them as already described. Then pronounce each with your lips rounded. The sound [y], the rounded variant of ⟨i⟩, and [ø], the rounded variant of ⟨e⟩, may be familiar to those who have studied French, German, or Hungarian, among others. [œ] and [ɵ] are rarer, but because their distribution is parallel with other sounds, it should be easy enough to pick them up. Finally, [ɒ] is not altogether foreign to English, although it occurs more in British English dialects. It also known to be distinctive in languages such as Hungarian.

1.3.2: VOWEL REDUCTION

For the next set of environmentally conditioned allophones, it may be helpful to review §1.1.3.2 on diphthongs or minimally Table 4. In this section, we explore a concept known as *vowel gliding* or *vowel reduction*, a concept related to the fact that the vowels ⟨i⟩ and ⟨u⟩

are *homorganic* with the consonants [j] and [w], meaning effectively that they are articulated in very similar ways. The former consonant should be recognizable as the palatal approximant already discussed, while the latter consonant occurs only in this special context. Perhaps unsurprisingly, [w] is pronounced like the letter ⟨w⟩ in *weather*.

Vowel gliding refers to the fact that ⟨i⟩ and ⟨u⟩ are often reduced to these two approximants, also known as *glides*. This process occurs only in the diphthongs of Type III syllables, and the conditions under which it can occur implicate both the preceding consonants and the tone.

Of the eighteen diphthongs we have discussed, only fifteen undergo this change. The diphthongs ⟨eu⟩, ⟨ey⟩, and ⟨eo⟩ are always realized straightforwardly as they are represented. Otherwise, two conditions must be checked to determine whether a given diphthong will be reduced:

(1) Is the preceding consonant a trill or approximant (i.e. ⟨r⟩, ⟨l⟩, or ⟨j⟩) and the first vowel ⟨u⟩ or ⟨i⟩?
(2) Is the tone complex (i.e. mordent, rising-falling, or falling-rising)?

If the answer to either of these questions is yes, the diphthong is realized as already revealed in Table 4. If the answer to both of these questions is no, then the ⟨i⟩ or ⟨u⟩ is pronounced as a glide and the diphthong is reduced. Table 7 documents this phenomenon in full:

Diphthong	Pronunciation	
	Normal	Reduced
⟨ie⟩	[ie]	[je]
⟨ia⟩	[iæ]	[jæ]
⟨iy⟩	[iə]	[jə]
⟨io⟩	[iɑ]	[jɑ]
⟨ue⟩	[ue]	[wø]
⟨ua⟩	[uæ]	[wœ]
⟨uy⟩	[uə]	[we]
⟨uo⟩	[uɑ]	[wɒ]
⟨ei⟩	[ei]	[ej]
⟨ai⟩	[æi]	[æj]

⟨au⟩	[æu]	[æw]
⟨yi⟩	[əi]	[əj]
⟨yu⟩	[əu]	[əw]
⟨oi⟩	[ɑi]	[ɑj]
⟨ou⟩	[ɑu]	[ɑw]

Table 7. Vowel Reduction

As a final note, observe that diphthongs beginning with a reduced ⟨u⟩ will always have a rounded vowel as described in the previous section. Because [w] is an inherently rounded consonant, the vowel that follows it in the diphthong takes on this roundedness trait.

1.3.3: TONE SANDHI

We have so far in our discussion of interactions noted only changes that occur to vowels in response to conditioning by the nearby consonants and tones. In this section, we will observe how tones influence the realization of *other tones* when they are in proximity to one another. This is known as *tone sandhi*, and there are two types we should discuss: *intralexical* tone sandhi, which occurs within a word, and *interlexical* tone sandhi, which occurs between (or across) words.

1.3.3.1: Intralexical Sandhi

The best way to describe intralexical sandhi is to call back to a combinatorical point made about diphthongs. We expected more diphthongs than actually occur in the language due to the number of possible combinations of vowels. Constraints as well as accidental gaps betrayed these expectations. Something similar happens to tone when you build multi-syllabic words.

Without worrying about the potential meanings of words, consider forming a disyllabic word from the Type II syllable *po*. As a monosyllabic word, we know it could take five forms once tone is introduced: *pó*, *pò*, *pō*, *pǫ*, and *põ*. This would suggest that twenty-five possible two-syllable words could be formed simply by combining any one of these five again with any one of these five. In fact, only nine are possible:

pópō, pòpọ, pópò, pòpó, pōpò, pọpó, pōpō, pọpọ, and *popõ*. This fact is implicated in the tone sandhi process although not an example of it. What should be observed here is that the tones distribute themselves to avoid conflict from one syllable to the next. In the first example, the rising tone is followed by a high tone, as by the end of the production of the rising tone, the pitch of the speaker's voice is already in a position to pronounce the high tone—or alternatively the falling tone as in the third example, which starts with a high pitch. By the same token, if the first syllable is a low tone as in the sixth and eighth examples, the next syllable of the same word can only have a rising tone or another low tone. Table 8 illustrates this phenomenon:

First Tone	Second Tone	Example	Translation
Rising	High	súkā	"dancer"
	Falling	lísò	"design"
Falling	Low	crỳkị	"founder"
	Rising	jùsé	"examination"
High	High	pīmā	"proven"
	Falling	xūxù	"hopeful"
Low	Low	kẹmọ	"formed"
	Rising	lẹxú	"stressed"
Neutral	Neutral	japrujã	"divisible"
	Mordent	pyxũ	"long"

Table 8. Tone Distribution in Multisyllabic Words

Because this distribution of tones is maintained inside a word, when a new word is derived from another using the addition of a morpheme—a small unit of meaning—that addition can take several forms. Consider the ⟨tion⟩ added to words like *complete* and *rotate* to derive the words *completion* and *rotation*. This is an example of a morpheme in English. In Katalopsi, a morpheme can take several forms to satisfy this constraint on agreeable, non-conflicting tonality. This variation on tone in such a unit is the essence of tone sandhi intralexically. Much more will be said on the status of tone in discussions of morphology and lexical derivation in chapter 2.

1.3.3.2: Interlexical Sandhi

While patterns of non-conflicting tones are guaranteed within words, across words various underlying conflicts of tone occur. To avoid the awkward, halting, and faltering speech that would necessarily result, various processes of interlexical tone sandhi occur. The seven processes we will view in this section have been ordered from least to greatest by the relative complexity and variety of environments in which they occur.

1.3.3.2.1: Persistent Rising

In considering this first case of interlexical sandhi, it is important to understand how tone is perceived. It is not necessary that the tone be realized with specific pitches, only that the pitches from one moment to the next can be compared. The *perceived* tone is therefore determined by proximate pitches, while the *intended* or underlying tone is determined by the tonal context in general, much like how speakers of English can still use intonation—say, to communicate questions—when speaking in a relatively high- or low-pitch voice.

The phenomenon we are calling *persistent rising* happens when a syllable marked by a rising tone is followed by another such syllable. Spoken unnaturally, one could start with a low pitch and rise to a high pitch—thereby realizing the first tone—and then fall quickly down to a low pitch and start the process over. Persistent rising involves holding this rising pitch over both syllables. That is, you start at a low pitch and continue rising in pitch until both syllables have been uttered. Although the relative or *guiding* pitches have changed from syllable to syllable, it is nonetheless clear to a listener that both syllables are marked by rising tones.

This process does its part in reducing awkward and unnatural speech, but it is of course possible that three or more syllables with rising tones will occur consecutively. In these cases, it is less clear what the best strategy is. Theoretically, the persistent rising strategy could be applied in this situation as well, but as the number of consecutive such syllables rises, the slower the change in pitch is necessary in order to avoid running into natural barriers to production. The slower these changes of pitch occur, the less easy it will be to discern the intended tone.

Instead, it is better to accept that some degree of challenging, awkward speech will occasionally occur, and these processes are meant only to make that unnatural speech less common. This persistent rising process will apply then to the first two syllables in a row, but the third will lead with a new low tone, beginning the process anew.

1.3.3.2.2: Persistent Falling

The phenomenon of *persistent falling* occurs, as may be predicted given the previous section, when a syllable marked with a falling tone is followed by another falling-tone syllable. This strategy demands the same or parallel considerations as that of persistent rising. Because returning quickly to a high pitch after realizing the first falling tone constitutes a rather awkward way of speaking, especially if occurring frequently, persistent falling is induced to alleviate some of these faltering tonal transitions.

Persistent falling is achieved by beginning the first syllable with a high pitch and then falling in pitch until both syllables have been uttered. It is best to avoid doing this for more than two syllables due to natural physiological limitations on both speech and hearing. Instead, in cases where three or more falling-tone syllables occur in a row, the persistent falling strategy should begin with a new high pitch on the first, third, fifth—and so on—syllables.

1.3.3.2.3: Consecutive Mordents

As we have already seen, neutral tones occur in Type II syllables and multisyllabic Type III syllables virtually always alongside a mordent tone. In these environments, the mordent tone occurs on the last syllable of the word, while all previous syllables of the word bear a neutral tone. In chapter 2, we will look more closely at how this pattern of tones is preserved even when deriving new words, pointing to a *neutralization* effect of the mordent tone. That is, when syllables are added to a word with a mordent tone, as a result of a word derivation process, the mordent will always be on the last syllable—even if it must move to this position—and every other tone is made neutral.

This effect is inherently intralexical, but there is an analogue in interlexical tonal interactions. If two or more mordents occur in a row, all tones but the last are realized as a neutral tone. To be clear, this means that, say, four consecutive monosyllabic words marked with a mordent tone would result in only a single mordent tone when actually pronounced, each of the first three tones having been neutralized. Note how this differs from the persistent rising and persistent falling phenomena, in which no more than two syllables may be involved in any one instance of the process. As a complex tone, the mordent is more demanding of the speaker, and multiple such tones in a row are simply not realized as marked, though the markings for the tones do indeed persist in the writing.

1.3.3.2.4: Mordent Allotony

Allotony refers to the fact that a tone can take different forms, or *allotones*, in actual speech, while the abstraction (i.e., the *toneme*) to which the individual form points still remains clear to a listener. Previously, we described the mordent as relatively neutral in pitch, that is, relatively in the middle of the proximate high and low tones. But it is most distinguishable by the characteristic dip in pitch. This means that in some contexts, it is not required that you utilize a relatively neutral pitch in order to realize the tone.

One such context is between two high tones. In this context, it is most natural to pronounce the mordent at the same high pitch while still articulating the dip. This same high-pitch mordent would occur between a rising tone on the left and a falling tone on the right. If you look closely at this environment, you will see that the mordent finds itself in the same naturally high-pitch environment, where a high-pitch realization of the mordent tone is most comfortable.

In another case of mordent allotony, a mordent may occur between two low tones. Like the previously described allotone, the mordent is most naturally pronounced in this environment with the same low pitch as the surrounding tones, making sure to articulate the dip all the same. This form of the mordent tone also occurs between a falling tone on the left and a rising tone on the right, where a speaker finds the pitch of their voice in a similarly comfortable position to make such a production.

The other possible pairs of surrounding tones are numerous, and if another sandhi operation does not take precedent and apply, as with consecutive mordents, then the mordent will be realized with the relatively neutral pitch level already described. In this sense, the neutral level mordent is the default allotone.

1.3.3.2.5: Neutral Lexeme Allotony

One detail was left out of our discussion of tone and the syllabic types earlier in this chapter, namely that in a certain sense the neutral tone can occur alone in a single word. However, such words are rare and essentially functional in basis, such as *co,* meaning "and," and *li,* meaning "or." Because they tend to be functional words, they occur in a wide variety of environments and do not have lexicalized tone, meaning there is no underlying requirement of the way the tone is pronounced. Instead, the tonal environment determines pronunciation, opting for one which avoids conflict altogether.

The most obvious place to begin is with the environments implicated in the mordent allotony section. It is clear that between two high tones or between a rising and a falling tone, words with non-lexicalized tone would be comfortably pronounced with a high tone. A high tone would also be the appropriate pronunciation between a rising and a high tone or a high and a falling tone.

By the same token, words like *co* occurring between two low tones or a falling and a rising tone would be pronounced with a low tone. A low tone is also the preferred choice between a falling and a low tone or a low and a rising tone.

There are various other environments in which such a word may be found, and for the most part, simply pronouncing the word comfortably will yield the correct tone. For example, if *co* is found between a low tone on the left and a high tone on the right, then it can be pronounced with a rising tone to connect the words melodically. This rising tone would also be called for between a falling tone and a high tone or a low tone and a falling tone.

In the reverse case, a word with non-lexicalized tone between a high tone and a low tone would be pronounced with a falling tone, and just the same with a rising tone on the left and a low tone on the right or a high tone and a rising tone. Again, although there is a complicated variety of environments for a neutral lexeme to fall in, the important thing is choosing a tone contour that keeps the speech flowing as fluidly as possible. Once you have a decent understanding of how tones work in general, picking a tone for such cases should come naturally.

In the last environment of note, perhaps surprisingly given our discussion of neutral and mordent tones and their interactions so far, when a word with non-lexicalized tone comes between two mordents, it is simply pronounced with a neutral tone. That is, it does not participate or aid in the process of interlexical mordent neutralization. *But* if the environment encourages high or low mordent allotones, then mordent allotony takes precedent, and pronouncing the neutral lexeme with a high or low tone, respectively, may be justified.

There are still many other possible contexts that neutral lexemes may find themselves in, but the important point of the neutral lexeme is that pronouncing what comes naturally is the name of the game. A rigorous intellectual analysis of the possible environments is less helpful to learning the behavior of such words than simply seeing cases and practicing them, and the following chapters will offer many opportunities.

1.3.3.2.6: Flat Tone Transformations

In some cases where adjacent pitches are underlyingly incongruent, flat tones such as the high and low tones are implicated. In these environments where such a flat tone is in conflict with the subsequent tone, the flat tone may undergo a transformation in its realization to a partial rising or falling tone.

For example, when a low tone is followed by a high, falling, or even neutral tone, the low tone may be pronounced as rising toward the end of the syllable. This is a way of making the relative pitches meet in preparation for the beginning of the next syllable. Alternatively, a high tone may be followed by a low, rising, or neutral tone, and the high tone would analogously fall in pitch toward the end of the syllable.

This way of speaking will come naturally when you have become comfortable with pronouncing tones in general, and in the context of relaxed speech, this is the preferred realization. In the next and last section on interlexical tone sandhi, we will see a strategy for more careful and formal speech. This strategy applies to the flat tone conflicts described here but also to all cases of tone conflict where a lack of careful articulation may result in unnecessary ambiguity.

1.3.3.2.7: Tone Conflict Epenthesis

Linguists use the term *epenthesis* to refer generally to the process of inserting of a sound. In Katalopsi, we use this term to describe the insertion of voicelessness between words where a conflict of tone is present.

In the previous six sections on interlexical tone sandhi, we saw several strategies for dealing with tone conflict, and in most cases, these strategies serve to make speech more natural and to avoid a faltering realization of strings of tones. However, in some cases the described strategies may introduce ambiguity. For example, if a low tone is realized as a rising tone, an apt conversation partner will understand that the low tone is what is intended underlyingly, thanks in part to context. In those situations where either a low tone *or* a rising tone could have been intended, the transformation to a rising tone may not be the best way to communicate and epenthesis may be preferred.

This is a way of speaking carefully. It is realizing the low tone, cutting off your voice very briefly, and then beginning the next syllable with the high tone, falling tone, or what have you. In short, it is the halting, faltering speech that is avoided in most situations but that may be necessary to effectively communicate when ambiguity would otherwise be the result.

It is also of practical importance to acknowledge that some tonal environments may not have been described in full here, and in these cases, the use of this epenthesis is the recommended default strategy for realization.

1.3.4: TAP ARTICULATION

The alveolar tap, ⟨r⟩ or [ɾ], has multiple allophonic realizations depending on the phonological environment it finds itself in. Generally speaking, it is pronounced with the tap articulation, but in two specific environments, this articulation changes.

1.3.4.1: Homologue Approximation

The first exceptional environment involves the tap following a consonant with the same place of articulation. The tap is an alveolar consonant, so of note here is when the former consonant is ⟨s⟩ or ⟨z⟩. The ⟨s⟩ will only arise when it appears alongside the tap in an onset consonant cluster. The ⟨z⟩, on the other hand, occurs strictly in a Type I syllable and forms the relevant environment when it is followed by Type II or III syllable beginning with ⟨r⟩.

When either of these situations arise, the tap is *approximated*, meaning it is pronounced as an approximant. The voicing and place of articulation don't change, leaving the voiced alveolar approximant [ɹ] as the result. This is a sound very familiar to speakers of English, as it is the sound occurring in the words *reader*, *bar*, and *myriad*. This also means that the consonant cluster written ⟨sr⟩ will only ever be pronounced as [ʃɹ] and never as [ʃɾ].

1.3.4.2: Syllabic Trilling

When the tap manifests as a syllabic consonant, i.e. as a Type I syllable, it is lengthened to allow for the prosodic overlay of tone. In effect, this means that the tap becomes a *trill*, whereby the tongue vibrates against the alveolar ridge. This is also known colloquially as a *rolled R* and occurs in many natural languages, including Spanish, Arabic, and Gaelic. In IPA, we represent this simply as [r].

1.3.5: SYLLABIC REDUCTION

As we have seen, Type I syllables are consonants that carry tone and bear syllabic weight. In the right environments, this syllabicity can disappear, and the consonant in question can become part of another syllable.

Generally speaking, any time a Type I syllable follows either a Type II or Type III syllable, this type of syllable reduction may occur. Additional constraints on the environment, however, stipulate that matching tones are in place.

The simplest case is that of the high and low tones, where the Type I syllable is pronounced as a consonant in the coda of the previous syllable. That is, the Type I syllable loses its syllabicity and is simply pronounced as part of the previous word with a high tone if they both share a high tone and with a low tone of they both share a low.

A slightly more complex case is that of the rising and falling tones, where the respective persisting rising and persistent falling strategies take effect *in addition* to that of syllabic reduction. That is, if both the Type I syllable and the previous Type II or III syllable share a rising tone, then the Type I consonant populates the coda of the previous syllable and a single, though perhaps long, rising tone is articulated. Similarly, if a falling tone appears on both, then the Type I syllable is so reduced and a single, long falling tone is heard.

The case of a mordent on both syllables in question is similarly complex as the consecutive mordents strategy must apply. The Type I syllable is reduced and occupies the coda position of the previous syllable, and then the mordent is pronounced roughly during the coda, either starting during the vowel just before and carrying into the coda consonant or else starting and finishing on the coda.

Finally, in the most complex of the applicable cases, a Type I syllable may follow a Type III syllable that is carrying either a rising-falling or falling-rising tone, a feature which we know to be unique to this syllabic type. In these cases, a rising tone on the Type I syllable is considered to match with a falling-rising on the previous syllable. Likewise, a falling tone on the Type I syllable matches with a rising-falling tone on the preceding syllable. Therefore, in these environments, the Type I syllable is reduced, the consonant once again filling the coda position of the Type III syllable. The respective persistent rising or persistent falling strategies then take effect.

1.3.6: VOWEL LENGTHENING

We close this chapter with one final example of interactions between sounds in natural speech, specifically vowels and tones. This phenomenon will probably come naturally and not require practice, but a thorough description of Katalopsi allophony requires its mention.

This is the phenomenon of *vowel lengthening*, the process of vowels being pronounced as relatively longer, i.e. with more duration, given the appropriate environmental trigger. Before we discuss this environment, it is useful to have an anchoring point for reference. While the exact vowel quality is not important, if a vowel carries a high, neutral, or low tone, it is among the shortest of the language.

Other tones, however, will serve to make the duration of that vowel longer. The general rule is that the more a pitch must vary when articulating the tone, the longer the vowel will be. Therefore, the next longest vowels are those carrying the rising or falling tones. It is important to keep in mind, however, that this variation of length is not distinctive. That is, it does not result in a difference of meaning, so there is no need to concentrate on making certain vowels relatively longer or shorter. Instead, think of it as something that will happen naturally in the background as you learn the language.

The next longest vowels are those carrying complex tones. There are a couple important points to be made here. It is clear that the mordent tone, which varies by pitch in two directions, would be somewhat longer than the rising or falling tones, which vary in only one direction. The rising-falling and falling-rising tones, on the other hand, always appear on diphthongs. Because diphthongs are predictably longer than monophthongic vowels in and of themselves, diphthongs with rising-falling and falling-rising tones are articulated with the longest durations of the language.

CHAPTER 2
Lexicology & Morphology

In this chapter, we will describe how the phonology of Katalopsi informs the part of speech of a word, what common morphology to expect given a particular part of speech, how lexemes can be used in distinct ways, where lexical gaps exist, and what these multivariate factors mean for future expansion of the lexicon.

2.1: CATEGORIES OF TYPE I SYLLABLES

The Type I syllables described in the previous chapter—where a consonant is realized syllabically—occur with two major lexical categories, both of them largely functional in their semantic content and usage. These categories are so essential to the communicative force of the language that a Katalopsi sentence will more often contain one than not.

2.1.1: AUXILIARIES

The first of these lexical categories is the somewhat nebulously named *auxiliaries*, which includes expressions for tense, aspect, and mood, sometimes collectively referred to as TAM. Table 9 lists every such auxiliary. Note the class of the auxiliaries, each of which we will explore in more detail. You will also see some words which could theoretically exist but do not currently have a usage and are merely included for the sake of structural parallelism in the table:

Auxiliary	Class	Translation	Auxiliary	Class	Translation
ḿ	M	"must/have to"	j́	M	hypothetical marker
ṁ	M	"like to"	j̀	M	"intend to"
m̄	M	"try to"	j̄	A/M	"keep/continue to"
m	M	"love to"	j	M	"can/be able to"
m̃	T	"will/shall"	j̃	M	"hope to"
ń	M	doubt marker	v́	M	"might"
ǹ	M	"want to"	v̀	M	question marker
ñ	M	"begin/start to"	v̄	—	—
n	T/A	"used to"	v	T/A	frequentative marker
ñ	M	"look forward to"	ṽ	A	perfect marker
ĺ	M	"hate to"	ź	T	past marker
l̀	M	"manage to"	ż	M	"may/be allowed to"
l̄	M	"need to"	z̄	—	—
l	M	"be willing to"	z	M	emphatic marker
l̃	M	"be afraid to"	z̃	T	recent past marker
ŕ	T	"be about to"	ǵ	—	—
r̀	A	progressive marker	g̀	M	imperative marker
r̄	A	"tend to"	ḡ	M	conditional marker
r	M	inferential marker	g	M	"dare to"
r̃	M	"should"	g̃	M	self-doubt marker

Table 9. Auxiliaries of Katalopsi

2.1.1.1: Tense

Tense tells us when the event or state described by a sentence occurred relative to the time of speaking. Like most languages, Katalopsi distinguishes between past, present, and future tense. There are six (or arguably seven) auxiliaries to express tense, but some of these auxiliaries also communicate aspectual meaning and therefore bear further explanation in the section on aspect.

2.1.1.1.1: Past Tense

The past tense auxiliaries are *n̲*, *ź*, and *z̃*. The first of these, more or less equivalent to *used to* in English, both indicates that a described event happened in the past and also that the event was frequentative, meaning it happened multiple times. This category of aspectual meaning will be explored further shortly.

The auxiliary *ź* simply means that the described event happened in the past. In English, this meaning is marked on the verb, as on *bought* in *Alex bought a car*, or the front-most auxiliary, as on *was* in *Alex was buying a car*.

The auxiliary *z̃* also refers to an event that occurred in the past, but unlike the previous auxiliary, it can only refer to the *immediate* or *recent* past[4]. In this sense, it is easily translated into English with the word *just*. This is the difference between *Alex bought a car* and *Alex just bought a car*. While this flavor of past tense is foreign to English verb morphology, it is nonetheless a meaning frequently communicated and so will probably ring intuitively.

2.1.1.1.2: Present Tense

The present tense can be expressed in one of two ways. The simplest is with an absence of any word indicating tense. This is known as a *null morpheme*, i.e. it lacks any phonological realization, linguistic jargon meaning that it is without sound. Put simply, as long as you do not speak any word expressing tense, your sentence will be assumed to be in the present tense.

With that said, there is another auxiliary which could be said to express present tense, the word *y̲*. Like the past tense word mentioned previously, it expresses frequentative meaning. To understand the

---

[4] For a natural language which makes a grammatical distinction for the recent past, see Sharman and Meeussen (1956)'s description of the tense system of Bemba, one of several Bantu languages known for complex tense morphology.

meaning of this word, consider the present tense in English. Ostensibly, it is used to denote what is happening at the time of speaking; however, a sentence like *John takes taxis*—though in the present tense—actually suggests that John makes a *habit* of taking taxis, i.e. he does it frequently. A better way to express what is currently happening is with something like *John is taking a taxi*. The auxiliary *v* is used to express the former case, in statements about present habitual behavior. The latter sentence is better expressed with the null morpheme previously discussed.

2.1.1.1.3: Future Tense

The distribution of auxiliaries indicating the future tense resembles that of past tense auxiliaries. Katalopsi makes a distinction between expressing the future in general and the *imminent* or *near* future[5] in particular. The generic future is expressed with the word *m̃*, which is easily translated as *will* or *shall* in English.

The imminent future, on the other hand, could be translated with the English *about to*, as in *Mary is about to go to work*. To express this meaning, you use the word *r̂*.

2.1.1.2: Aspect

In this section we will discuss aspect, a way of characterizing the nature of an event. While tense contextualizes an event ceteris paribus as occurring before, during, or after something, aspect communicates two distinct dimensions of meaning: (1) whether an event occurs at a point in time, over a duration of time, or in several points or durations, and (2) whether the tense of an event should be interpreted relative to the time of speaking or the time of another event.

We have already seen that aspect can intersect with tense in the auxiliaries *ṇ* and *v*, those in which the frequentative aspect is expressed. A way of illustrating this aspectual meaning is to say that it characterizes an event as happening in several points in time or over several durations of time. Other auxiliaries express frequentative aspect, including *r̄*,

---

[5] Sharman and Meeussen (1956) also describes the presence of an analagous future tense in Bemba.

meaning *tend to*—a statement of statistics as well as aspect—and *j̄*, meaning *keep* as in *Marsha keeps forgetting her book*—an auxiliary with a shade of emotive force indicative of *perseveration*. Both of these auxiliaries can be combined with tense auxiliaries to express habitual behavior in various time frames.

Along this same dimension, the event may also occur in a single point or over a single duration. The former description should be regarded as the default, as it is expressed by omitting any aspect-implicating auxiliaries—much like the phonologically null expression of present tense. The latter description appears in many grammar texts with the label *progressive aspect*. What is common to the sentences *Eli was reading a book*, *John is painting with oils*, and *Al will be looking for volunteers* is this progressive aspect, in each case indicating that the described event occurred, occurs, or will occur over a period of time, rather than at a point. The word *r̃* is the way of expressing this in Katalopsi.

The second dimension of aspect communicates the way tense should be interpreted, either relative to the time of speaking, which is the default, or relative to another event which may or may not be mentioned. The latter is known as *perfection*, and the word *ṽ* is said to be expressing *perfective aspect*, meaning that the event described in the accompanying sentence happened relative to the time of another event and not relative to the time of speaking the sentence. This is the difference between *Mark finished the book* and *Mark had finished the book*. In the latter sentence, the assumption is that this is being said relative to some other point in time, such as that of another event.

While the meaning of perfection can be difficult to parse out at times, it is important to understand that it denotes a change in the point of reference against which tense is evaluated. Perfective tense can be described to completion with the following schema: (a) If both the described event and the reference event occurred in the past, use past tense; (b) If both the described event and the reference event occurred in the future, use future tense; (c) Otherwise, use present tense.

To be clear, these are the only three possible circumstances, as the perfective aspect already means the event being described happened before the reference event, so there is no need to worry about circumstances where the described event happens after the reference event, at least for the purposes of tense-aspect evaluation.

2.1.1.3: Modality

The last subcategory of auxiliaries express mood, and speakers of English will recognize their closest translations as many of the common English verbs. These *moods*, however, comprise more than just emotion but include several different attitudes one might have with respect to an action. The classes of modal auxiliaries we will shortly delve into are the *emotive*, the *evidential*, the *obligative*, the *functional*, and the *miscellaneous*.

2.1.1.3.1: Emotive

The largest class of modal auxiliaries are emotive in nature, i.e. they express the way someone feels about something. We can think of such modals as falling into three groups: positive, negative, and neutral, where neutral means that it could be expressing positive or negative emotion depending on the context.

Among the positive emotive modals are $\dot{m}$, meaning "like to"; $\underline{m}$, meaning "love to"; $\dot{n}$, meaning "want to"; and $\tilde{n}$, meaning "look forward to." Note that as auxiliaries, these words combine with predicates, expressing actions, states, or events. In other words, you cannot use ñ to "look forward to the party," but you can use it to "look forward to going to the party." We will discuss more how these auxiliaries can be used in sentences in chapter 3 on syntax.

The negative emotive modals include $\dot{l}$, meaning "hate to"; $\tilde{l}$, meaning "be afraid to"; and $\tilde{g}$, meaning—somewhat esoterically—to do something with self-doubt. That is, in the same sense that "hating to read" is having an attitude of hate toward reading, "$\tilde{g}$ to read" is having an attitude of self-doubt toward the same.

The neutral emotive modals all express an emotional attitude toward the predicate, but only the context can determine whether that emotion is positive or negative. For example, the meaning of *manage to* implies that some effort was made to carry out a successful action, and it can be expressed with l. The phrase *intend to*, on the other hand, means effort was made to do something, but it is ambiguous about whether the action was completed successfully; it can be expressed with j. The auxiliary $\bar{m}$ is a lot like *intend to*, except that it strongly implies that the action failed or will be a failure. It could perhaps be translated as "try to."

The final two neutral emotives have to do with acting in defiance or contrary to expectations, which again may be positive or negative. The auxiliary $\bar{j}$ means "continue to" or "keep" as in *He keeps forgetting his keys*. It's understood with this attitude that someone expects an alternative behavior, and either purely by accident or in direct defiance, you perseverate the same behavior. For g, on the other hand, it is understood that the behavior is deliberate, an act of defying expectations. It would best be translated as "dare to," as in *Miriam dared to follow her dreams*.

In the next section, we will deal with a class of modal auxiliaries which will probably be altogether foreign to speakers of English.

2.1.1.3.2: Evidential

In this category, auxiliaries engage degrees of belief and evidence, sometimes deliberately setting the matter aside and other times attaching a degree to the relevant party's credulity with respect to an action, event, or state[6].

The lowest a speaker may engage with the matter of belief and evidence is to expressly disregard it. This is known as *inferential mood* or *report stance*, and you would use it to report what another person said—without either confirming or disconfirming it[7]. To do this, you use the auxiliary r.

On the flip side, you may express the highest degree of confidence that something is the case, with an attitude of certainty or near-certainty. The auxiliary z accomplishes this with similarity to the English auxiliary

---

[6] This notion of evidential modality, which is sometimes known as *epistemic* modality and other times merely as an intersection of it, is described by de Haan (1999). He relates fragments of evidential grammar in several natural languages, such as Tarahumara and Kashaya.

[7] This phenomenon occurs morphologically in German and is known in grammar books as *Konjunktiv I*.

do, as when someone says, "I *did* go to sleep early." In this sense, z is emphatic.

You can also back off from this high degree of certainty and make a normative declaration that something is the case. Much like with tense and aspect, not explicitly referring to the dimension of evidentiality can carry semantic weight. The lack of a referring auxiliary expresses a normal degree of confidence in something—enough that you believe it, but not enough to emphasize your certainty by way of the aforementioned auxiliary z.

Another way to engage with degree of credulity is to say that you don't have strong belief at all, that in fact you doubt whether something is the case. The auxiliary *ń* communicates this. For example, if someone tells you that they need to borrow your glasses, you can respond using this auxiliary. The meaning of your response would effectively be "I doubt that you need to borrow my glasses" or better still "You say you need to borrow my glasses, but I doubt it."

The final two evidential auxiliaries will often work as a pair. The first is used to express a hypothetical situation; in other words, you have no belief in the state of affairs you describe, but you are imagining a world in which they are the case. This auxiliary, *j*, easily correlates therefore to the word *if* in English. The other member of the pair, *ḡ*, is much like *then* in the so-called *if-then statements*. That is, it expresses the *conditional*, implicated in English words like *would* and *could*. Because these types of combinations of sentences are so essential to everyday communication, you can rest assured that they will be well exemplified in chapter 3.

2.1.1.3.3: Obligative

Obligative modals express different kinds of obligation that someone has to do something. These auxiliaries are translated to many of the most recognizable modals of the English language.

With the greatest degree of obligation, *ī* can be translated as "need to." In other words, it can be used to communicate that someone is obligated to do something in order to fulfill a need. The auxiliary *ṁ* is ambiguous about the source of the obligation and in fact expresses a lesser degree of it. It is most like the English modal *must* and the periphrastic *have to*. The word *r̃* expresses the smallest non-zero degree of obligation in that it means it would benefit someone to do something. It is best translated as "should."

The final two modals that court the notion of obligation are *l̲* and *ż̲*. These words imply a lack of obligation, the former translatable as "be willing to" and the latter as "be allowed to." This implication is not a necessary component of their meaning, however, and so their essential meanings of willingness and permission, respectively, should be considered primary.

2.1.1.3.4: Functional

The auxiliaries of the functional category bear little similarity to each other in meaning. They appear together here due to the fact that they are often grammaticalized in syntax and inflectional morphology in other languages. In Katalopsi, questions are often and commands are always expressed with the morphologically simple auxiliaries *v̂*[8] and *g̊*, respectively. Due to their comparatively greater complexity in other languages, these meanings certainly demand examples to elucidate the difference; however, we will save this exercise for chapter 3, where we will see large varieties of sentences, including both questions and commands.

2.1.1.3.5: Miscellaneous

The final modal auxiliaries to be mentioned—before moving on to the second lexical category of Type I syllables—fall into the miscellaneous class. These three words prove especially difficult to categorize or perhaps deserve categories of their own.

The word *j̲* refers to ability and is best translated as "can" or "be able to." The auxiliary *n̄* refers to the start of an action, event, or state and is much like *begin to* as in *The car began to rust*. Finally, the word *v́* asserts the possibility of something being the case, much like the English word *might* in *He might build a career from this*.

---

[8] Scottish Gaelic is an example of a natural language for which there is an overt question marker. For a description of the Gaelic interrogative words, see Lamb (2003).

2.1.2: DISAMBIGUATORS

The second lexical category surfacing as Type I syllables may be referred to as *disambiguators*. While perhaps not a common name for this phenomenon, disambiguators are in a sense elaborations on the verb (or more generally, the predicate) that tell you how to interpret it and its *arguments*[9].

For example, consider the difference between the sentences *Marie is dressing her daughter* and *Her daughter is getting dressed*. They are similar in that they both involve *dressing*; however, in the former case, the person mentioned *after* the verb is the one putting clothes on, while in the latter case, the person mentioned *before* the verb is the one putting clothes on.

In Katalopsi, the verb will always look the same. The word coming after the verb, on the other hand, will differ and thereby tell you how to interpret the arguments accompanying it, e.g. as either the person dressing or the person getting dressed, among other more complicated situations. This word is the disambiguator and is perhaps the most grammatically significant lexical category of the language for unambiguous communication. In the following examples, the disambiguator is marked with a "D":

Cuě m̀ psũ.
dress D child
"The children are getting dressed."

Cuě m̀ psũ o̱kru̱.
dress D child parent
"The parents are dressing the children."

Cuě Í psũ.
dress D child
"The children are being dressed."

---

[9] A similar phenomenon occurs in Turkish, whereby a bound morpheme will change the argument structure of the verb. Both the valency—or *transitivity*—of the verb and the role assignment are affected. Montrul (2001) is a good introduction to the topic.

The disambiguator serves two grammatically interlinked functions. The first is to inform you of how many arguments the verb has, also known as its *valency*. An argument is a pronoun or noun phrase that is a necessary participant in the action, state, or event being described, one that can be assigned a specific *role*. The second function of the disambiguator is to clue you in as to what roles to assign to the arguments that follow. By considering the consonant and tone of the disambiguator, patterns can be identified both in the valency they point to and in the roles that are signed to the participating arguments. Table 10 shows the twenty-four disambiguators of the language, including one theoretical word, *j́*, which has no assigned function but is included for the sake of structural parallelism:

Word	Valency	Object I	Object II	Subject
∅	0	—	—	—
ḿ	1	—	—	AG
m̀	2	TH	—	AG
m̃	3	TH	BEN	AG
ń	1	—	—	CA/INST
ǹ	2	TH	—	CA/INST
ñ	3	TH	REC	AG
ĺ	1	—	—	TH
l̀	2	LOC	—	TH
l̃	3	TH	BEN/REC	CA/INST
ŕ	1	—	—	PA
r̀	2	PA	—	AG
r̃	3	TH/PA	STIM	AG
j́	∅	∅	∅	∅
j̀	2	LOC	—	AG
j̃	3	TH/PA	LOC	AG
v́	2	INST	—	TH
v̀	2	INST	—	AG

ṽ	3	TH/PA	INST	AG
ź	1	—	—	EXP
ẑ	2	TH	—	EXP
z̃	2	STIM	—	EXP
ǵ	2	REC	—	AG
g̀	2	BEN	—	AG
g̃	2	TH	—	BEN

Table 10. Disambiguators of Katalopsi

While we will describe these patterns in the sections that follow, we will refrain from detailing how these words can be used productively until chapter 3 on syntax. For now, focus on how the tone or consonant informs on these valency and role assignment patterns.

2.1.2.1: Valency Patterns

The first of these patterns relates to the use of the rising tone and teaches an important lesson about the distribution of these patterns: Most are not rules that apply absolutely but rather are *tendencies*, something that the phonology hints toward in most cases. The rising tone on a disambiguator is indicative of the monovalent pattern, meaning that the majority of such disambiguators require a single argument. Six of the eight such words point to this single argument, while the remaining two, *v́* and *ǵ*, point to two arguments. Notably, however, no *other* disambiguator is monovalent, so the connection between the rising tone and monovalency is quite strong.

The next pattern is one which *does* apply in every relevant case. This is the falling tone, which is indicative of divalency, or having two arguments. All eight of the falling-tone disambiguators are divalent. Despite this consistency, however, divalency occurs in other disambiguators as well, namely the two words mentioned above and additionally the *z̃*, *ǵ*, and *g̃* disambiguators. So while a divalent will not always have a falling tone, the falling tone always indicates divalency.

The pattern of mordent-tone disambiguators is another strong, but not absolute, tendency. Such words are trivalent six out eight times, meaning they most often point to three arguments. The two exceptions,

$\bar{z}$ and $\tilde{g}$, are divalent, as we have already seen. Importantly, even though the mordent tone does not always indicate trivalency, it is the case that trivalent disambiguators always have a mordent tone, as no other disambiguators point to three arguments.

2.1.2.2: Role Assignment Patterns

Several strong patterns also exist for role assignment. Looking again at Table 10, you will see several roles indicated with abbreviations. While we will elaborate on these abbreviations and the related patterns here, a proper understanding of semantic roles will be available to you only after a study of chapter 3 on syntax and especially chapter 4 on semantics.

There is first of all the *agent* role, marked "AG" in Table 10, which is strongly associated with the ⟨m⟩ and ⟨j⟩ disambiguators. For these two consonants, any given disambiguator will involve an argument marked with the agent role, the sentient *doer* of an action. Also noteworthy is that the ⟨j⟩ disambiguators always involve the *location* role, marked "LOC." This role, of course, refers to the location of an event, action, or state—perhaps the place toward, away from, or nearby which it occurs, among other specifications, the mechanic of which will be elaborated in the coming sections and chapters.

The *theme* role, marked "TH," is indicated by many disambiguators without pattern, but the ⟨l⟩ words are noteworthy in that they always point to the existence of such a role. The theme is that which undergoes the event, action, or state described by the predicate and changes thereby in some way. A close counterpart is the *patient* role, or "PA," which similarly undergoes the event, action, or state but which does not change as a result[10]. The ⟨r⟩ disambiguators could be regarded as always marking for a patient, although the word $\bar{r}$ allows for optionally a theme *or* patient, but not both. In this sense, one could say it marks

---

[10] Usage of the words *theme* and *patient* is legendarily various even in the scholarly linguistics literature. In fact, the meaning of the words is sometimes reversed, *patient* being used to refer to an argument that undergoes change and *theme* used to refer to one that undergoes no change. Despite this confusion of terms, you should simply note our usages here and proceed with clarity.

for an *undergoer*, a more general role that does not specify change in the argument.

The ⟨v⟩ disambiguators always involve the *instrument* role, abbreviated "INST," which specifies what was used in the unfolding of some action or event. The instrument role is also marked by other disambiguators but only ever in optionality relationships with the *cause* role, or "CA." The cause role could be regarded as a counterpart to that of the agent, in that the cause is also the doer of an action or event, but it does so without sentience. Therefore, agents will usually be humans or other less intelligent animals, while causes will usually be unconscious forces like the wind, an earthquake, and so on. As we will see in chapter 4, these implications and others can be exploited to express nuances of meaning.

The next pattern to be described is perhaps the strongest of all roles mentioned here. The *experiencer* role, or "EXP," only occurs with ⟨z⟩ disambiguators, and furthermore, the ⟨z⟩ consonant always points to an experiencer, meaning that this pattern reflects a one-to-one relationship. The experiencer role refers to the mental participant in an action, state, or event, often reflecting one the experiencer feels or is doing in their minds. Consider for example the sentence *Alan heard a plane nearby*. Because hearing is something that happens without choice and agency, it can only be that Alan is experiencing the sound of the plane, regardless of whether he made a conscious choice to listen.

Part and parcel to an experience is the *stimulus*, or "STIM," which in the previous example is the thing that is heard. Generally speaking, the stimulus is that which causes the experience but for which there's no reason to posit agency or even action. You may see the sidewalk, forget a memory, or think about a puzzle, among other experiences, and the sidewalk, memory, and puzzle are the respective stimuli. While it is logical therefore that the stimulus role occurs alongside the experiencer role, there is not in fact a good pattern involved in its usage.

The final two semantic roles yet to mentioned are the *beneficiary*, or "BEN," and the *recipient*, or "REC." There are many actions, states, and events for which either may optionally occur, though usually not both. The beneficiary is the person or thing for whom an action or event is done, that which stands to benefit from it. The recipient, on the other hand, is the person or thing that receives something, usually a patient. There are not strong phonological patterns for these roles, but for completion, it is important to mention them here. It is nonetheless noteworthy that a beneficiary or recipient is only marked by a disambiguator when it is di- or trivalent, never monovalent. This is a typologically common—though not absolute—pattern across natural language.

2.2: CATEGORIES OF TYPE II SYLLABLES

Katalopsi words exhibiting strictly Type II syllables fall into a much wider array of categories than Type I syllables. They manifest as determiners, pronouns, conjunctions, prepositions, complementizers, numerals, nouns, adjectives, and adverbs. They also appear in compounds with Type III syllables, which we will explore in §2.3.

2.2.1: DETERMINERS

Generally speaking, *determiners* are words which are linked to nouns to specify the referent in the real world. Compared to English and many other natural languages, the determiner system of Katalopsi is somewhat impoverished. This is due in part to the fact that Katalopsi does not distinguish definiteness, so articles like *the* and *a/an* do not exist.

Katalopsi determiners do, however, allow for *place deixis* and *quantification*. The former involves linking a noun to a location and therefore calls to mind words like *this* and *that*. Quantification, as the name suggestions, allows speakers to inform on quantities, howsoever generic. We will discuss both of these determiner types in this section.

Before we continue, it is important to note that some grammars regard possessive words like *my* and *your* to be a type of determiner as well. However, for the sake of simplicity of presentation, we cover these in §2.2.2 as pronouns.

2.2.1.1: Demonstratives

Demonstratives are determiners that specify the distance of something from the speaker. They can be used in a literal or concrete sense, as when referring to the physical distance in space, or they can be used in a figurative or abstract sense, as when speaking of something more or less relevant to context.

In English, demonstratives are distinguished by two dimensions of distance, near and not near, and by two dimensions of number, singular and plural, to produce the words *this*, *that*, *these*, and *those*. As we will see more in later chapters, Katalopsi does not distinguish number grammatically, so words like *this* and *these* are fused into one in the present language.

Katalopsi also has three dimensions of distance: near, somewhat far, and very far. Near objects are usually those that can be touched at a whim, while the somewhat far objects are those that would take a little time to get to. The very far objects, on the other hand, would take a long time to get to. The now archaic English words *yon* and *yonder* express this third distance, referring to, for example, distant mountains. Those familiar with Spanish grammar will also be aware of the word *aquel* and its gendered and numbered forms for this same kind of distance marking.

These facts of number and distance considered together, Katalopsi therefore has three demonstrative determiners:

sĩ	"this/these"
sỹ	"that/those"
srã	"that/those over there"

2.2.1.2: Quantifiers

Unlike numerals, which we will consider later in this chapter, quantifiers usually establish a vague number of some object. Semantically, they establish sets and subsets that allow you to interpret the truth of a statement under a variety of conditions.

For example, it may be the case that an entire group is implicated, and so you may use the quantifier *all*. This word establishes the set of things described, such as *all cats* or *all accountants,* and connotes that the group as a whole is in consideration. Contrast this with the words *every* and *each,* which similarly establish the entire group—*every cat* and *each accountant*—but involve a greater focus on the individual.

Sometimes you are not dealing with the entire group, but rather some subset between one and all. The words *many* and *a lot of* mean that a high number of some group are involved but imply that it is not *all.* The word *some,* on the other hand, simply means *more than one,* leaving open the possibility that it could be a lot or just a few. A quantifier also exists for the latter case, the word *few.* This also means more than one but is more specific that it's a small amount.

The word *most* establishes a majority of the given group. It is vague in that it could be just over half or it could be close to all, though it implies that not all of the group is involved. The word *half,* of course, means exactly 50 percent of the group, or less than most.

Some determiners quantify for specifically two items, the words *either* and *both.* These words can also participate in what are called *correlating conjunctions,* a topic we will discuss more fully later. For now, consider the fact that *either* may be used simply as a quantifying determiner, as in "either book," or in a conjunction phrase, e.g. "either the book or the magazine." By the same token, *both* can be a quantifier, as in "both books," or in a conjunction phrase, e.g. "both the book and the magazine."

Finally, it could be that zero of the set of objects have some trait, participate in some event, or what have you. While you can use the word *zero* in this case, it is more colloquial to use the word *no,* as in *no cats* and *no accountants.*

The complete set of Katalopsi quantifiers appears in Table 11. Note that translations of the words include several that we have not covered. This is because Katalopsi is not sensitive to *polarity* in its quantifier system. *Polarity items* are words that can only exist in a grammatically affirmative or negative environment. Consider the word *any,* which in some contexts could mean something similar to *some* or even to *every/ each.* The difference can be seen in sentences *I have some apples* and *I don't have any apples.* While a sentence like *I don't have some apples* is acceptable to many people, there is a preference for the use of the word *any.* By not considering polarity in quantification, Katalopsi dispenses with this problem.

Katalopsi	English
clà	"all"
nè	"every"
	"each"
	"any"
kfū	"most"
xã	"half"
srẹ	"many"
	"a lot of"
rỳ	"some"
	"any"
lú	"either"
	"neither"
pẹ	"both"
pé	"few"
	"a few"
sọ	"no"

Table 11. Quantifiers

As a final note before continuing to pronouns, if you know the specific number of the objects to be quantified, then numerals are encouraged over quantifiers. See §2.2.5 for the discussion of numerals.

2.2.2: PRONOUNS

The pronoun system of Katalopsi, as a functional closed category, largely resembles that of English. There are personal pronouns, possessive pronouns, reflexive and reciprocal pronouns, relative and interrogative pronouns, impersonal pronouns, and demonstrative pronouns.

2.2.2.1: Personal Pronouns

Katalopsi personal pronouns are distinguished by first, second, and third person; singular and plural number; and to a degree masculine, feminine, and neuter genders. Katalopsi does not, however, have *case*, meaning that English words like *I* and *me* are represented by the same word in the present language.

Number	Person	Gender		
		Masculine	Feminine	Neuter
Singular	First	pò		
	Second	kù		
	Third	cá	cì	lá
Plural	First	plō		
	Second	klū		
	Third	cla̱	clī	la̱

Table 12. Personal Pronouns of Katalopsi

In Table 12, you will see that gender distinguishes pronouns only in the third person and has both singular and plural varieties for each. This is in contrast to English, which distinguishes gender in the third person singular but not in the plural. I.e. English uses only the word *they* (or *them* per case rules). Therefore, you would use the word *cla̱* when talking about a group of men, *clī* for a group of women, and *la̱* for either a mix of the two or a group of objects.

Also noteworthy is that Katalopsi distinguishes number in the second person. While some English dialects do this by using words like *you all* and *y'all*, among others, some dialects will only ever use the word *you* regardless of the number of people addressed. Katalopsi does make this distinction by referring to a single person as *kù* and two or more people as *klū*.

The remaining pronouns essentially parallel English. In the first person, *pò* means "I" or "me," while *plō* means "we" or "us." In the third person singular, *cá* translates as "he" or "him," *cì* as "she" or "her," and *lá* as "it." The latter pronoun refers strictly to non-gendered animals and objects and can be used as a dummy pronoun in certain contexts. To refer to a person without reference to gender, see §2.2.2.5 on impersonal pronouns.

2.2.2.2: Possessive Pronouns

The so-called possessive pronouns, which mark some form of ownership ("my car"), role ("his mother"), or affiliation ("their state"), are derived from personal pronouns by the addition of a morpheme. So far this chapter, we have seen only monomorphemic words, meaning words that have a single part, a single meaningful unit. By adding other meaningful units to *root* words, e.g. personal pronouns, new words are derived.

Possessive pronouns are created by the addition of the morpheme ⟨ma⟩. This could be compared to the ⟨'s⟩ in English, which is added to nouns to relate the analogous meaning of possession, e.g. *Carl's house*. In Katalopsi, therefore, to say "my," I take the personal pronoun for *I* and add the possessive morpheme, ⟨pò⟩ + ⟨ma⟩, yielding the possessive pronoun *pòmá*. Table 13 lays out all possessive pronouns:

Number	Person	Gender		
		Masculine	Feminine	Neuter
Singular	First	pòmá		
	Second	kùmá		
	Third	cámà	cìmá	lámà
Plural	First	plōmà		
	Second	klūmà		
	Third	clamá	clīmà	lamá

Table 13. Possessive Pronouns of Katalopsi

Just as for personal pronouns, it is important to note how Katalopsi distinguishes between gender in the third person. While the English possessive pronoun *their* is non-gendered, Katalopsi can refer to possession by a group of men, a group of women, or a group of the two or of non-gendered animals or objects. By the same token, the English word *your* is broken into two more specific words in Katalopsi.

You may have also noticed that the ⟨ma⟩ morpheme varies in its tone, realizing as either the rising or the falling tone. To understand this, remember what was said about tone within a single word in §1.3.3.1. The constraints of intralexical sandhi require smooth transitions between syllables on the tonal level. This means that morphemes when added to a word during the derivation process will realize as one of several *allomorphs*, or variations of the same morpheme. In later sections, we will see morphemes that can vary more broadly. Because pronouns are a closed category, we will not discuss patterns of tone assignment here, but such patterns will become more and more apparent as we progress through chapter 2.

As a final point on possessive pronouns, it is worth mentioning that they can be used as more than just determiners or adjectives, as we've already seen with words such as *pòmá*, meaning "my"; *plōmà*, meaning "our"; and so on. They can also be used more like a noun. These are words such as *mine, yours, hers*, and *theirs*. Another way to look at this is that the possessive pronouns of Katalopsi can be used without an accompanying noun, an idea which will be intuitive to speakers of English and many other languages.

2.2.2.3: Reflexive and Reciprocal Pronouns

Reflexive and reciprocal pronouns refer to arguments used in the same sentence. In English, reflexives include words such as *myself, yourself, ourselves*, and *themselves*, among others. Reciprocals are pronouns like *each other* and *one another*.

Katalopsi, as it turns out, has a single reflexive pronoun that can refer back to any argument regardless of person or number. This is a characteristic common e.g. to Balto-Slavic natural languages like Russian and Lithuanian[11]. The word itself, *kfò*, could therefore simply be translated as "self." It does, however, stand in where we would see the above-listed reflexives and others, such as *himself, herself, itself*, and *yourselves*.

Reciprocal pronouns point to a mutual relationship between entities mentioned in the sentence. When there are only two entities, the phrase *each other* is used, as in *Matthew and Alan bought each other gifts*. The equivalent Katalopsi term is *kōlō*. When more than two people are involved, however, the phrase *one another* is used, as in *Matthew,*

---

[11] In Russian, the word is *себ-*, and in Lithuanian *sa(v)-*, with the exact ending dependent upon case declension rules.

Alan, and Martha bought one another gifts. In this situation, Katalopsi uses *mylí*.

In chapter 3, we will see a variety of sentences in which these reflexive and reciprocal pronouns are used.

2.2.2.4: Relative and Interrogative Pronouns

In Katalopsi, there is a union of relative and interrogative pronouns. This means that while some natural languages keep these two categories of pronouns completely separate, and others have partial overlap, Katalopsi uses them in both contexts.

In the phrase *the book which I bought yesterday,* "which I bought yesterday" is a relative clause. And the word *which* is a relative pronoun. Interrogative pronouns, on the other hand, are used in forming questions. They are words like *what, who,* and *where.* The topics of relative clauses and question formation are both heavily syntactic in nature, so we will consider them more fully in the next chapter. For now, consider the following table and each of the pronouns therein. Their interrogative translations are given, while the most likely translation of the relative pronoun usages will be elaborated in chapter 3.

Pronoun	English
fã	which
fèja	what... like
fõ	who(m)
fõmà	whose
fù	what
já	why
jỹ	how
rapse	how many
ri	where
rù	when

Table 14. Relative/Interrogative Pronouns

2.2.2.5: Impersonal Pronouns

Impersonal pronouns are for the most part derived from quantifiers and in some cases are actually homophonous with their sources. It is important for understanding the derivation process that some impersonal pronouns—even in English—could be regarded as noun phrases with a modifying quantifier. As a result, if no specific noun appears, the phrase could still be grammatical having only a quantifier present.

Consider therefore the English words *none, few, many, all, each, both,* and *either.* While *none* is an impersonal pronoun formed from the quantifier *no,* the latter six can appear as both modifying quantifiers and as pronouns on their own. Certainly these six words could be analyzed as described above, as quantifiers without an accompanying noun, but they do function as pronouns as a result. These seven have been grouped together, however, because the Katalopsi equivalents treat the quantifier and pronoun forms the same, i.e. as homophones.

For those with a superficially apparent derivation process, on the other hand, this often means a pronoun relating to one person, place, or thing.

While English impersonal pronouns pointing to people use the word *one* or *body,* as in *someone* and *everybody,* the equivalent Katalopsi terms use the word *ni,* meaning "person."

Impersonal pronouns referring to locations use *mā,* meaning "place." Compare this to English, which uses the word *where,* as in *somewhere* and *everywhere,* although words like *someplace* are not unheard of.

Finally, impersonal pronouns pointing to objects use the word *cu,* meaning "thing," much like English. There are underived exceptions, however, as the English word *nothing* is translated as the morphemically simple word *kè.* See Table 15 for these twelve principal impersonal pronouns:

	Katalopsi	English
Person	soni	"no one"
	clàni	"everyone"
	nèni	"anyone"
	rỳni	"someone"

Location	sómā	"nowhere"
	clāmā	"everywhere"
	nēmā	"anyplace"
	rȳmā	"somewhere"
Object	kè	"nothing"
	clàcu̱	"everything"
	nècu̱	"anything"
	rỳcu̱	"something"

Table 15. Impersonal Pronouns

2.2.2.6: Demonstrative Pronouns

In the previous section, we saw that some impersonal pronouns could simply be regarded as quantifying determiners used without a noun. The so-called demonstrative pronouns, by the same token, may be regarded as demonstrative determiners without the nominal complement. Therefore, they surface quite straightforwardly as homophones of the determiners. This is identical to their usage in many languages, including English, Spanish, and German.

2.2.2.7: Trace Pronoun

The final pronoun to be discussed is the so-called *trace pronoun*. The word *trace* refers to a linguistic theory that words have an underlying position in the sentence and that some undergo movement to the positions in which they appear in speech. Some theory furthermore posits that a trace is left behind in the words' original positions that prohibits further movement of one kind or another from occurring[12].

Important here is that in most cases, the trace is thought to be phonologically empty, having no pronunciation in speech. Katalopsi has a phonologically weighted trace pronoun, and when movement occurs, the trace will appear in the position at which the moving word started. This pronoun is the neutral lexeme *cu*. We will see more on this subject in chapter 3.

---

[12] The syntactic research on these subjects is broad, rich, complex, and numerous. Let it suffice that Chomsky (1975) first communicated the concept of a trace with movement.

2.2.3: LOGICAL CONNECTIVES

Logical connectives are terms that affect the logical interpretation of words, phrases, and sentences, sometimes expressing ways of connecting them into larger structures both syntactically and semantically. Generally speaking, the words are used to connect syntactically similar structures, but arguably some are multifunctional, such as the word *and*. This conjunction can connect words and phrases on the one hand and entire sentences on the other hand. This is much unlike other logical connectives we will see, which only connect sentences. We will see four strategies for logical connection: conjunction, disjunction, negation, and implication.

2.2.3.1: Conjunction

Conjunction refers to words with an *and*-like character, meaning that the two or more things connected by the word must be the case in order for the complete statement to be true. Consider the sentence *Mel bought the movie tickets and the popcorn*. What the word *and* tells us in this sentence is that in order for the complete sentence to be true, the two simpler sentences must be true: *Mel bought the movie tickets* and *Mel bought the popcorn*.

Several Katalopsi words fall into this category. The first is *co*, which is easily translated as *and*. The word *sa*, on the other hand, is used for *non-exclusive conjunction*, meaning that it creates a list that is acknowledged straightforwardly to be incomplete, either possibly or certainly so. While the word *co* is a generic word for *and*, because the alternative conjunction *sa* exists, *co* is assumed connotatively to mean a complete list. To get a sense of the usage of *sa*, simply consider the meaning of phrases like *among them* and *including* in the context of creating a list of elements. These phrases leave open the possibility that more items belong in the list but are simply not mentioned. This is the meaning of *sa*.

In our discussion of quantifiers, we mentioned the word *pe*, meaning "both," and how it may be combined into conjunction phrases. When combined with the word *co*, you get the Katalopsi equivalent of English phrases like *both the fork and the knife*. Translated into Katalopsi, this would be *pę psù co xàmǫ*. It is of course possible to use the word *pę* without using the word *co* and without giving up the logical character of conjunction, suggesting that this word is underlyingly conjunctive as well.

The next word is equivalent to the English *but*. The word *but* connects sentences together, and although they are both true, they are in some way opposed to one another. It is often the context that determines in what specific way the sentences are in opposition, indicating that this meaning is *pragmatic* in character. The Katalopsi word is *mã*. This should be contrasted with *but* used to connect phrases, often appearing as *but rather*. In a sentence like *I don't want to play guitar, but (rather) piano*, the alternative meaning of *but* is apparent. For this meaning of *but*, the Katalopsi word *fẽ* should be used.

Another word which combines two true sentences while implying some sort of pragmatic opposition is the word *though*—or equally *although* and *even though*. Interestingly, the contrary sentence headed by this word may appear either first or second, unlike with the word *but*. The Katalopsi word is *klá*.

2.2.3.2: Disjunction

Disjunction refers to words with the meaning of *or*. It allows for an optionality, meaning that if two sentences are connected by it, only one must be true in order for the entire sentence to be true. Consider the sentence *The coach or the quarterback decided the play*. In this case, if either the sentence *The coach decided the play* or *The quarterback decided the play* is true, then the complete sentence disjoined by *or* is true. Important for disjunction is that it is often ambiguous between inclusive and exclusive disjunction, the former being when both could be true, and the latter being when only one—but not both—is true.

The Katalopsi term *li* is equivalent to English *or* in that it is ambiguous along this inclusive/exclusive dimension. And like the generic conjunction term *co*, *li* may connect sentences, phrases, or words. When used alongside the word *lú*, however, the exclusive disjunction meaning is derived. The phrase *either the sword or the shield* could therefore be translated as *lú pru̱ li korĩ*, where either option is available, but not both.

The word *whether* also has disjunctive character, and like *though* or the Katalopsi *klá*, it can connect two sentences by appearing before the first or the second. The equivalent Katalopsi word is *pȳ*. This word may also be paired with *li* as in an expression like *whether or not*, i.e. *pȳ li fò*.

2.2.3.3: Negation

A logical connective involving *negation* is one which reverses the truth value of a sentence. The most obvious example is the word *not*. Let us first look at the affirmative sentence *I learned to play the piano*. We can reverse the truth value of this sentence by inserting *not*, yielding *I did not learn to play the piano*. Although English grammar also requires inserting the auxiliary *do*, this is not something we must consider for Katalopsi. Instead we must only observe that if the affirmative sentence was true, then the negative sentence must be false; and furthermore that if the affirmative sentence was false, then the negative sentence must be true. The equivalent Katalopsi term is *fò*.

Although some languages, such as Swedish, offer more than one word to perform this function[13], Katalopsi has only the one. There is one other term that is worth mentioning, however, that may in some—but not all—circumstances affect the truth value of a sentence. This is a quantifying determiner that we have already seen, *so̱*, meaning "no." In many languages, such a term does have negative character, but in Katalopsi, it is merely a way of quantifying zero of something. Consider the two following English sentences:

We purchased new chairs for the club room.
We did not purchase new chairs for the club room.

The use of the negative particle *not* does in fact reverse the truth values of the first sentence. However, if we try to insert *no* before "new chairs," we get different results depending on the sentence. When we say, "We purchased *no* new chairs for the club room," we seem to mean the

---

[13] In Swedish, these are the common *inte* versus the rare *icke* and the constrained *ej*.

same thing as the second sentence above, i.e. the truth values do indeed reverse on the affirmative sentence. However, if we say, "We did *not* purchase *no* new chairs for the club room," many English speakers would say that this is very colloquial language but that it still means no chairs were purchased. In other words, in some environments, *no* will not result in a reversal of truth values.

The Katalopsi word *so* is strictly a quantifying determiner, meaning that while truth values may be affected because the sentences describe different amounts of chairs, it is actually not a reversal of truth values across the board, which is the essence of negation. We will see a lot more examples of such sentences in chapter 3, but for now, see the following two sentences:

Ź peú Í so na.
PAST buy D no chairs
"No chairs were purchased."
OR "It is the case that no chairs were purchased."

Ź peú Í so na fò.
PAST buy D no chairs not
"No chairs were not purchased."
OR "It is not the case that no chairs were purchased."

Because *so* is, in effect, another way of saying "zero," it should not be interpreted relative to the presence or absence of the negative particle *fò*. There's no such thing as a double negative in Katalopsi unless *fò* simply appears twice. That is why the more periphrastic translations of the above sentences have been provided. In the affirmative sentence appearing first, the speaker is simply saying that zero chairs were purchased. In the negative sentence, the speaker is implying that one or more chairs were purchased, because they are denying the idea that zero were purchased. Of course the meaning would change—the way we interpret the truth or falsity of the sentences would change—if the quantifier was not present, but it would change only in the quantificational sense, and then the presence or absence of the negation particle is applied to the sentence as a whole as in any sentence.

2.2.3.4: Implication

In logic, implication is the relationship that one truth value necessitates another truth value. I.e. one sentence being true means that another must obligatorily be true, that one being true means another must be false, that one being false means another must be false, or that one being false means another must be true. It is a way of marking the logical consequence of one truth value from another. In language, the words and structures for marking such logical implication are often also used to mark cause and effect and to mark impetus or rationale. Therefore, we will in this section cover each structure that may mark implication, even should it be used with another function more frequently.

We should start with the words *j* and *akra*. Typically, the word *j* is an auxiliary used to establish a hypothetical situation. When used in combination with the auxiliary *ḡ* in another clause, the result is a *conditional* statement, i.e. something like saying that if something is the case, something else would be the case. This is not actually logical implication, but more hypothesizing on what would happen or what someone would do if some situation were reality. When used with *akra*, on the other hand, the meaning of logical or material implication is the result. In this sense, *akra* could be translated as "then." It should be noted that conditionals are also known as if-then statements on occasion, but understanding the meaning difference will be helpful. So while combination of the words *j* and *akra* will mean the logical implication, the combination of the words *j* and *ḡ* are actually ambiguous and could point to either implication or conditionality. The following examples show the implication in effect:

Ĵ roì Í mý, akra lè Í klā.
if there is D rain then wet D ground
"If it's raining, then the ground is wet."

If *akra* is used alone in a single clause, i.e. without combining with another clause, then something like "That means..." is derived. It can also be taken as conclusory in nature:

A̱kra̱ fruô ź kù fò.
then care D you not
"Then you don't care."
OR "That means you don't care."

It is also possible to link sentences and derive the meaning of implication by using the word *kfú*, or "because." As a complementizer, this word will be explored more fully in the next section, but for now, let it suffice that *kfú* begins one clause, while the connected clause is not required to use any special word to mark the connection. It is also possible to order these clauses in either of two possible ways without changing the directionality of the implication:

Rei̱ ž̃ junẽ pò kfú my̱ u sásù Í lá.
like D music I because means of creation D it
"I like music because it is a means of creation."

Kfú my̱ u sásù Í junẽ rei̱ ž̃ lá pò.
because means of creation D music like D it I
"Because music is a means of creation, I like it."

2.2.4: Prepositions and Complementizers

In this section, we will look at prepositions and complementizers. Prepositions are words that come before a noun, determiner, or pronoun phrase, allowing the phrase to be connected to another element. The specific preposition chosen tells us how to interpret that noun, determiner, or pronoun in the context of the utterance. Often they are used as a way of adding an additional participant or bit of information about an action, state, or event, or even a bit more information about an argument.

We are also looking at complementizers in this section because many languages have at least partial overlap between the preposition category and the complementizer category, with some words being used with both functions. Complementizers are like prepositions appearing before the entire sentence, often allowing sentences to be connected in ways distinct from those of logical connectives.

In Tables 16–19, you will see these words divided into three subsets: (1) those that can only be used as prepositions (Tables 16, 17), (2) those that can only be used as complementizers (Table 18), and (3) those that can be used as either (Table 19). When a word can surface with both parts of speech, it may be translated the same way in English or have two different translations. This simply means that the categories overlap differently in English than in Katalopsi.

Katalopsi	Translation
a̱	on (*vertical*)
cà	down
clý	beside/next to/by
crā	along/by
cro̱fro̱	outside of
cú	in
fèsré	inside of
fo̱céplā	toward
frō	among
frú	in front of
fú	up
kàrá	past
ke̱	above
kolũ	around
krínè	under
lùjo̱	across (from)
menẽ	over
mé	on top of/atop
mu̱	on (*horizontal*)
né	far from
pìcé	away from
ple̱	through
psí	behind
rèply̱	below
rēcōlỳ	beyond

resú	ago
sýnō	between
xi	near

Table 16. Locative/Temporal Prepositions

Looking at the subsets in Table 16 and 17, there are a few patterns you should notice. Many languages are notorious for having few dedicated temporal prepositions. Instead, many of the same prepositions used to mark locative relations are applied by analogy to discuss time. All locative prepositions, and as a result most temporal prepositions, are unable to be used as complementizers, so they surface strictly with the prepositional category.

Katalopsi	Role	Translation
fē	Cause	by/through
fîli	Instrument	with
ìna	~Concomitant	without
kápē	Perspective	to/for
kfì	Source	from/out of
klé	Comparison	as/than
lāmēklī	Claimant	according to
mē	Goal	for/toward/at
nū	Agent/Experiencer	by
ó	Recipient	to
plu	Beneficiary	for/on behalf of
prypé	Concomitant	with/alongside
sro	Patient/Theme	on/upon
u	Various/Relational	of

Table 17. Semantic Role Prepositions

A similar story can be told for the exclusively prepositional lexemes listed in Table 17. In some circumstances, it may be necessary to mark a participant with its semantic role, but because it is not an argument, its role is not made clear by the disambiguator. In this environment, the participant may be marked by the prepositions in Table 17. Note that some semantic roles mentioned in this table are not ones we have previously discussed. We will see more about these words and their unique semantic role assignment patterns in chapter 3 on syntax and chapter 4 on semantics.

Katalopsi	Translation
klá	although/(even) though
klè	that
nỳklẹ	in order that/so that
pȳ	whether
xò	unless

Table 18. Complementizers

The brief list of lexemes in Table 18 are used strictly as complementizers, meaning they are used to connect sentences. You will recognize many as logical connectives we covered in §2.2.3, such as the conjunctive *klá*, the implicational *nỳklẹ* and *xò*, and the both implicational and disjunctive *pȳ*. We have not previously seen *klè*, or "that," and its syntactic function will be made clearer in chapter 3. However, one could also argue that it is used to mark the sentence with the *proposition* semantic role, one that is not infrequently left out of semantic role inventories.

Katalopsi	Translation	
	Comp.	Prep.
fé	before/prior to	
cìrụ	despite	
clȳ	when	at the time of
fòklé	instead of/rather than	
fūlā	apart from/other than/aside	
ká	until	
kfú	because/since	because of/due to
krẽ	(ever) since	
lomã	except for	
méràplỵ	in addition to	

pī	after	
ròlú	about/regarding	
rọxọ	while	during

Table 19. Prepositions/Complementizers

The thirteen lexemes in Table 19 are those that can be used either as complementizers, heading sentences, or as prepositions, heading noun, determiner, and pronoun phrases. As mentioned previously, because English has a different overlap between these two categories lexically, the translation into English will sometimes vary by its categorical usage. There is an important point to bring up here about how some complementizers require *nonfinite* sentences and others require *finite* sentences. We will not explore this fully here, but suffice it to say that nonfinite clauses are those that require *to* before the verb or *-ing* tacked on to the end of the verb, while finite clauses are those that allow for a more varied marking of tense. A word like *despite* requires nonfinite marking, as in *Despite him leaving early*, while *when* marks for finite morphology, as in *When he left early*. This distinction is important for English syntax, but as we will see in the next chapter, it is not one that is important for Katalopsi. Native speakers of English, however, may have trouble treating these two types of complementizers identically, so it is important that we see many examples when we discuss syntax.

2.2.5: NUMERALS

Katalopsi numerals are centered around a *base-ten*, or *decimal*, number system, meaning that it has ten basic numerical concepts upon which the larger system is constructed. These basic numbers are zero through nine, after which the system starts over with a new zero in the form of the number ten. This pattern repeats with a new zero every ten numbers[14].

---

[14] If it is not clear why this is important, see Avelino (2006)'s description of the Pamean languages, which use an octal number system (i.e. based on the number 8) or Mazaudon (2007)'s description of Chepang, which uses a duodecimal system (i.e. based on the number 12).

2.2.5.1: Zero to Ten

To begin our exploration of Katalopsi numerals, we will first look at the numbers zero through ten, i.e. our ten basic numbers plus the number *ten*, which also has its own unique word. Since each of these words are monomorphemic, little needs to be explained here, but in the next section, we will see that elements of the system begin to repeat after the number *ten* is enumerated.

Numeral	English	Katalopsi
0	zero	ró
1	one	xȳ
2	two	pĩ
3	three	jẹ
4	four	clí
5	five	clū
6	six	frũ
7	seven	psị
8	eight	krị
9	nine	kfé
10	ten	plè

Table 20. Basic Numerals

2.2.5.2: Eleven to Ninety-Nine

Starting with the number *eleven*, words combine using *co*, meaning "and." In other words, the translation of *eleven* literally means "ten-and-one," i.e. *plè co xȳ*. The numbers twelve through nineteen follow this schema with "ten-and-two," or *plè co pĩ*; "ten-and-three," or *plè co jẹ*; "ten-and-four," or *plè co clí*; and so on until "ten-and-nine," or *plè co kfé*.

As you might be expecting, a new schema must be introduced with the number *twenty*. Twenty, and other multiples of ten up to and including ninety, are formed by the combination first of a number two through nine and second the morpheme ⟨pa⟩. The tone appearing on this morpheme varies by word. See Table 21 for the complete list:

Numeral	English	Katalopsi
20	twenty	pipã
30	thirty	jepa
40	forty	clípā
50	fifty	clūpā
60	sixty	frupã
70	seventy	psipa
80	eighty	kripa
90	ninety	kfépā

Table 21. Multiples of Ten

As with eleven through nineteen, numbers *between* the multiples of ten are constructed with *co* and a number between one and nine from Table 20. Here are a handful of examples:

pipã co xȳ	"twenty-one"
jepa co pĩ	"thirty-two"
clūpā co clí	"fifty-four"
psipa co psi	"seventy-seven"
kripa co kfé	"eighty-nine"

Numbers are, multiples of ten aside, constructed like this from twenty to ninety-nine. After *kfépā co kfé*, or "ninety-nine," new lexemes must be introduced.

2.2.5.3: One Hundred to One Million

At the numbers *one hundred* and up, a consistent pattern emerges. Katalopsi has a unique word for each addition of a zero. Just as ten has a unique lexeme, the numbers *one hundred, one thousand, ten thousand, one hundred thousand,* and *one million* also have unique lexemes. English does this only to an incomplete degree, with unique numbers for one, two, and three zeroes, but after this, words are combined to reach the value intended, until six zeroes or the word *million*.

To understand this, consider the word *myriad,* which in the source language of Greek actually means "ten thousand." That is, Greek has a unique word for four zeroes, unlike English. Katalopsi takes this a step further, having, as we've said, a unique word for each addition of a zero. This is shown in Table 22:

Numeral	English	Katalopsi
100	hundred	fā
1,000	thousand	clọ
10,000	ten thousand	plí
100,000	hundred thousand	sò
1,000,000	million	rũ

Table 22. Adding Zeroes

Two pieces of machinery are needed before you'll be able to construct any number. The second-to-last is how to specify multiples of the various values in Table 22. While multiples of ten involve a special morpheme, multiples of these five new numerals require the use of the word *u*, meaning "of." To be clear, a word like *hundred* or *thousand* can mean *one hundred* and *one thousand*, respectively, but you can also use this machinery to be more specific. By inserting a number from Table 20 and then the word *u* before the numbers in Table 22, multiples are derived. Consider the following examples. Note how the second column shows the possible English translations, while the third column shows transliteration of the Katalopsi to better illuminate the Katalopsi numerical combination schemes.

fā	"(one) hundred"	(hundred)
xȳ u fā	"(one) hundred"	(one-of-hundred)
pǐ u fā	"two hundred"	(two-of-hundred)
jẹ u clọ	"three thousand"	(three-of-thousand)
clí u plí	"forty thousand"	(four-of-ten-thousand)
frũ u sò	"six hundred thousand"	(six-of-hundred-thousand)
krị u rũ	"eight million"	(eight-of-million)

Once you can use this technique to create magnitudes like these, the last element to form any number is how to order the words in the more complicated numbers. Roughly speaking, they are ordered from greatest to least, with the phrases pointing to lesser values following those pointing to greater values. Look at the following complicated examples and see how the words are organized:

101	fā co xȳ	(hundred-and-one)
159	fā clūpā co kfé	(hundred-fifty-and-nine)
740	psi̱ u fā clípā	(seven-of-hundred-forty)
1,310	clo̱ je̱ u fā plè	(thousand-three-of-hundred-ten)
5,874	clū u clo̱ kri̱ u fā psi̱pa co clí	(five-of-thousand-eight-of-hundred-seventy-and-four)
20,017	pĩ u plí plè co psi̱	(two-of-ten-thousand-ten-and-seven)
4,501,268	clí u rũ clū u sò clo̱ pĩ u fā frupā co kri̱	(four-of-million-five-of-hundred-thousand-thousand-two-of-hundred-sixty-and-eight)

There are a few things to take special note of in these examples. Firstly, you will only ever see the word *co* once, if you see it at all. It occurs only as a pairing with a number between one and nine at the end of the word. If such a number does not appear at the end, then *co* will not appear either.

Secondly, you can see multiple usages of the word *u*. There will be up to as many usages of *u* as there are *magnitude* numbers that are greater than one. The magnitude numbers are those appearing in Table 22. As we have learned, and as is probably intuitive for speakers of English, a magnitude number like *hundred* can be used as plainly written or with the word *one* appearing before it, without changing the meaning, while multiples like *two hundred*, *six hundred*, etc. obligatorily have a number before them. That is, their multiplicand is greater than one and must be explicitly stated. To understand what this means, look back at the example for the number 4,501,268. While the magnitude numbers for million, hundred-thousand, and hundred all use an *u*-phrase, as is required, the word for *one thousand* appears simply as *clǫ*. In the end, then, we have four magnitude numbers but only three *u*-phrases. We could of course have four *u*-phrases by stylizing *clǫ* as *xȳ u clǫ*, but this is often not used in larger numbers to reduce complexity and therefore the chance for misunderstanding.

A corollary to this fact is that the *u*-phrases do not have to appear one after another. As long as an intervening magnitude number has a multiplicand of one, a simple statement of the magnitude can interrupt the string of *u*-phrases. However, since this behavior of the multiplicand *one* before a magnitude number also occurs in English, this will probably ring intuitively for most readers. The only difference, of course, is the use of the word *u* between the two elements.

2.2.6: Nouns

Katalopsi nouns come in a variety of forms: (a) They can be monomorphemic, or underived, meaning that they have a single part and do not stand in morphological relation to another word; (b) they can be deverbal, meaning they are derived from a verb; (c) they can be deadjectival, meaning they are derived from an adjective; (d) they can be denominal, meaning they are derived from another noun; and (e) they can be compounds—a distinct process from (d)—in which two or more words are fused into a new noun.

2.2.6.1: Monomorphemic Nouns

Monomorphemic nouns are lexically the simplest type of noun. They do not therefore bear close and careful consideration. However, it is worth noting that they come in monosyllabic, disyllabic, and trisyllabic varieties. Some examples of monosyllabic nouns include *psĩ*, meaning "bird," and *ké*, meaning "job." Underived disyllabic nouns include *rocĩ*, meaning "jewelry," and *plīklē*, meaning "recipe." Finally, some underived trisyllabic nouns are *l̩ilácī*, meaning "desert," and *sìcrǫca*, meaning "archipelago."

2.2.6.2: Deverbal Nouns

There are several processes by which nouns can be derived from verbs. When doing such derivations, considerations of *tone contour*, or the shape of tone over the word, come into play.

To begin to understand these processes, it might be helpful to first consider a few natural languages with analogous phenomena. You may be familiar with an interesting behavior of Semitic languages like Arabic and Hebrew, namely a type of nonconcatenative morphology called *transfixation*. In these languages, sets of consonants called *consonantal roots* have vowels inserted between them to derive distinct but semantically related words. Using this process, the Arabic words for "book," "write," and "writer" share the same set of consonants but have distinct intervening vowels that delineate the more specific meanings.

Katalopsi could be compared to these languages in that it also uses a transfixation process to derive new words. However, it is more aptly described as having sets of vowels—and to a lesser degree tones—between which consonants are inserted. This is a process distinct from the concatenative morphology common to English in which a cluster of sounds is tacked on at the beginning (a prefix) or the end (a suffix) of a word.

Two such derivational processes create deverbal nouns in Katalopsi. The first is the creation of an agentive noun, a way of referring to the person or thing that *does* an action. This is like the ⟨er⟩ in the English words *writer*, *attacker*, and *designer*, i.e. the person that writes, attacks, or designs something, respectively. Verbs fall into the Type III syllable category, meaning in a sense that they always have two vowels. To create the agentive noun, the sound ⟨k⟩ is inserted between these vowels:

pseў "write"	→	psèký "writer"
kriā "attack"	→	krīkā "attacker"
liô "design"	→	líkò "designer"

The insertion of this ⟨k⟩ raises two important questions of phonological realization.

In §1.3.2, we described how diphthongs in Type III syllables may be reduced, one vowel becoming an approximant. Some combinations of vowels resisted this reduction, and others would change only in certain contexts. It is logical then to wonder whether this process has any bearing on the derivation of nouns or other new words from verbs. In fact, reduction does not need to be considered, as the diphthong of a verb will always be treated as two vowels between which a consonant is being inserted. Vowel reduction is only relevant to the pronunciation of the verb.

The second question that should be raised relates to how transfixation affects the tone on the diphthong. For some tones, the result is straightforward. E.g., if the diphthong is realized with a low tone, then the derived noun will have two vowels with a low tone on each. Diphthongs with a high tone behave in a parallel fashion, as illustrated above with the words *kriā* and *krīkā*.

Also shown above are the more complicated evaluations of the complex rising-falling and falling-rising tones. The word *liô* has a rising-falling tone, and after this derivation process is applied, it is broken up into a rising tone on the first vowel and a falling tone on the second. The falling-rising tone, as on *pseў*, follows the predictable opposite path: Breaking the diphthong in two results in a falling tone on the first vowel and a rising tone on the second. While involving more complex tonal environments, the solution of breaking complex tones into the two more basic tones is likely to feel very intuitive.

The final complex tone up for discussion is that of the mordent tone. In the case of verbs with a mordent tone, the diphthong is broken into the first vowel with a neutral tone and the second vowel with the mordent.

For the five tonal environments so far described, these methods of evaluating tone contour are absolute, i.e. they are the solutions for all instances of the transfixation process. For the rising and falling tones, however, the solution is dependent upon the particular instance of transfixation. For now, we will concentrate solely on the solution for the deverbal agentive noun morphology, but later we will see morphology with a distinct solution to the tone contour for the rising and falling tones.

When deriving an agentive noun from a verb with a rising tone, the first vowel of the diphthong is realized with a rising tone, but the second vowel is realized with a high tone. The following example illustrates this:

cxiá "follow"   →   cxíkā "follower"

When deriving from a verb with a falling tone, on the other hand, the first vowel is realized with a falling tone, while the second is realized with a low tone:

nìè "send" → nìk̲e "sender"

Another process by which a noun can be derived from a verb is with the insertion of an ⟨s⟩. This process works identically with that of the agentive noun including on the level of tone contour, the ⟨s⟩ being inserted—like the ⟨k⟩—between the two vowels of the verbal diphthong. The meaning of this morphology is "the process of or an instance of doing something." In this sense, it is much like ⟨tion⟩ in the English words *starvation* and *production*, ⟨ment⟩ in *statement* and *improvement*, among several other morphemes that are used less commonly.

Note in the following examples that the tone contour in each case of derivation is identical with that of the ⟨k⟩ morpheme, including for the rising and falling tones:

ruá "invest"	→	rúsā "investment"
nìò "love (v.)"	→	nìso̲ "love (n.)"
krēō "improve"	→	krēsō "improvement"
psy̲i "recognize"	→	psy̲si "recognition"
nìõ "pray"	→	nisõ "prayer"
xuŷ "worry (v.)"	→	xúsỳ "worry (n.)"
frìă "present"	→	frìsá "presentation"

In a later section, we will see another transfixation process nearly identical to the two described here, save for the fact that the tone contours differ.

2.2.6.3: Deadjectival Nouns

One morpheme in Katalopsi allows for the derivation of a noun from an adjective. It follows a pattern of suffixation which will be very familiar to speakers of English. This is the morpheme ⟨cli⟩, which corresponds closely to English suffixes like ⟨ness⟩ and ⟨ity⟩, as in *cleverness* and *purity*, respectively. It is a way of referring to the quality or degree of the adjective from which the noun is derived.

⟨cli⟩ is a suffixing morpheme, meaning it is concatenated, or attached, to the end of the noun. In terms of tone, the ⟨cli⟩ occurs in only three varieties: with a rising tone, a falling tone, and a mordent tone. In the following examples, note how the tone on ⟨cli⟩ is assigned in order to fulfill the requirements of intralexical sandhi as laid out in §1.3.3.1:

jịfí "pure"	→	jịfíclì "purity"
psè "punctual"	→	psèclí "punctuality"
fȳ "quiet"	→	fȳclì "quietness"
cxụ "round"	→	cxụclí "roundness"
capsũ "formal"	→	capsuclĩ "formality"

The derivational morpheme first looks at the tone of the last syllable of the adjective. If it is either a rising or a high tone, ⟨cli⟩ takes a falling tone, as in *jịfíclì* and *fȳclì*. In a reflection of these facts, if the previous syllable has a falling or low tone, the morpheme takes a rising tone, as in *psèclí* and *cxụclí*.

The most complex situation occurs when the final syllable of the adjective takes a mordent tone: In this environment, the syllable changes to a neutral tone, while the deadjectival morpheme takes on the mordent tone, as in *capsuclĩ*. This evaluation of tone contour demonstrates a point on the nature of neutral and mordent tones leveled in chapter 1: Only the final syllable of a given word will carry the mordent tone, and all preceding syllables will necessarily carry the neutral tone. Suffixing morphemes therefore preserve this pattern by shifting the mordent tone to the final syllable, neutralizing the remaining tones of the word.

2.2.6.4: Denominal Nouns

Two Katalopsi morphemes allows for the derivation of nouns from other nouns. The first involves careers or roles that people take upon themselves. Like deriving *librarian* from the word *library* or *artist* from the word *art*, the morpheme ⟨pra⟩ is used to indicate a practitioner or careerist working in some way with the originating noun.

⟨pra⟩ is, like ⟨cli⟩, a suffix and is attached to the end of the root noun. In terms of the distribution of tone, ⟨pra⟩ functions identically to the deadjectival morpheme described in the previous section, where a rising or high tone on the final syllable of the noun results in a falling tone on the suffix; a falling or low tone results in a rising tone on the suffix; and a mordent tone is shifted to the final syllable of the new word, with all other tones neutralized. The following examples show all relevant tonal environments:

pèxó "linguistics"	→	pèxóprà "linguist"
cxà "law"	→	cxàprá "lawyer"
pócxā "masonry"	→	pócxāprà "mason"
kfi̱lṵ "funeral"	→	kfi̱lṵprá "funeral director"
lã "art"	→	laprã "artist"

Despite the existence of this morpheme, it is important to note that many career names in Katalopsi are derived from verbs using the agentive noun morphology described in §2.2.6.2. In other cases, they can even be monomorphemic.

The second denominal noun morpheme is more difficult to describe as it is partly a suffix and partly a *reduplication* strategy. Reduplication involves the partial or complete repetition of sounds in the source word. In English, reduplication is used to communicate various meanings, including authenticity: In response to an inquiry about *fruitcake*, one might respond, "No, it was a *cake-cake*." Partial reduplication may also be used to express denigration, as in *fancy-shmancy* or *late-shmate*. In Katalopsi, the reduplication strategy is used in just two contexts: for denominal nouns, as we will see shortly, and for denumeral adjectives, which we will see in §2.2.7.2.

The denominal noun morpheme allows for the derivation of *diminutive* nouns, or words that indicate a smaller or cuter version of the original, often used as endearments or to describe baby animals. English has several such morphemes, such as the ⟨let⟩ in *piglet*, the ⟨ling⟩ in *duckling*, and the ⟨ette⟩ in *statuette*. The equivalent Katalopsi morpheme is first and foremost a suffix, beginning with ⟨n⟩. After that, however, reduplication springs into action by repeating the vowel of the former syllable. If the originating noun is monosyllabic, the repeated vowel will of course be the only vowel in the root, but otherwise it will simply be that in the last syllable.

cre̯cú "duck"	→	cre̯cúnū "duckling"
līkù "statue"	→	līkùnu̯ "statuette"
clōrā "horse"	→	clōrānā "foal"
ru̯ "cat"	→	ru̯nu̯ "kitten"
nã "brain"	→	nanã "cerebellum"

As you can see from these examples, the distribution of tone on this reduplicated vowel follows a familiar pattern. After rising and high tones, the new syllable takes on a high tone, while after the falling and low tones, the syllable is marked with a low tone. Finally, if the root noun should carry a mordent tone, that tone is shifted to the final reduplicant vowel, and the next-to-last syllable will then have a neutral tone.

2.2.6.5: Compound Nouns

Noun compounding involves taking two or more words, usually both nouns themselves, that can stand on their own and combining them into a new word. We just saw one example in the previous section, where the words *pè*, meaning "language," and *xó*, meaning "study" or "research," were combined to create the word meaning "linguistics." This is a common example of noun compounding, considering other examples such as *clexō*, literally "life study" but in fact meaning "biology."

This example also highlights the fact that the tones on the words must sometimes change in order to have non-conflicting tone contours. Other examples along this line include *sréxō*, "number study" or "mathematics," and *sy̯xó*, "book study" or "literature." In the former case, the tone on *sré*, meaning "number," remains the same, while the tone on *xó* has changed. In the latter case, the tone on *sy̯*, meaning "book," changes, while *xó* remains the same. The effect compounding has on tone is not patterned, so you must approach them on a case-by-case basis.

There are several words that may be compounded to derive nouns, and the best way to learn them is to study the vocabulary, e.g. through a reading of the dictionaries in chapter 7. However, the following list, which is not exhaustive, is provided to give you a sense of the possibilities: (1) *Cã*, meaning "room," is used commonly in words such as *jolucã*, "bedroom," and *cumucã*, "laundry room"; (2) Some terms for tools or weapons are formed by way of compounding, as with the word *cìkrí*, meaning "hammer," in *lūcìkrí*, "sledgehammer," and *mōcìkrí*, "war hammer"; (3) *Ṇi*, meaning "person," is sometimes added to the ends of words to indicate a user or practitioner of something, such as in *pruṇi*, "swordsman," and *sròṇi*, "gunman."

2.2.7: ADJECTIVES

Katalopsi adjectives are by far the most morphologically diverse category. In addition to being monomorphemic—having just one part—they can be derived from numbers, derived from verbs, derived from nouns, derived from other adjectives, and compounded.

2.2.7.1: Monomorphemic Adjectives

Like nouns, monomorphemic Katalopsi adjectives do not require close analysis, but they do vary in their syllabic cardinality. Below are a handful of examples:

lỳ "empty"
nũ "fair"
kràci "entire"
prafí "opaque"

2.2.7.2: Denumeral Adjectives

Using the reduplication process, ordinal adjectives are derived from cardinal numbers. This process corresponds most closely to the morpheme ⟨th⟩ in words like *sixth* and *seventh*. While English has numerous processes to derive such adjectives, due in part to irregularity for numbers less than four, Katalopsi is relatively regular and uses this single reduplication process to create such words.

Consider the follow examples from Katalopsi, noting the evaluation of tone contour:

xȳ "one"	→	xȳxȳ "first"
pĩ "two"	→	pipĩ "second"
je̱ "three"	→	je̱je̱ "third"
clí "four"	→	clíclī "fourth"
plè "ten"	→	plèple̱ "tenth"

For these basic monosyllabic numbers, both high and low tones on the syllable license complete reduplication, i.e. of the consonants, vowels, *and* tones. For the other tones, only partial reduplication is possible in order to remain within the constraints of intralexical tone sandhi. While the mordent tone demands the familiar mordent-shifting strategy, the rising tone requires a high tone on the new syllable, and the falling tone requires a low tone to follow.

For other numbers—with two syllables or more—partial reduplication is a matter of course, as only the final syllable is ever repeated. They do, however, still follow the tone contour evaluations already outlined. Consider, for example:

je̱pa̱ "thirty"	→	je̱pa̱pa̱ "thirtieth"
clípā co pĩ "forty-two"	→	clípā co pipĩ "forty-second"
fā co kfé "hundred and nine"	→	fā co kfékfē "hundred-and-ninth"
frũ u sò "six hundred thousand"	→	frũ u sòso̱ "six-hundred-thousandth"
clí u rũ "four million"	→	clí u rurũ "four-millionth"

As you can see, only the last syllable is reduplicated, whether it's a basic numeral or a magnitude number. Also note that the preposition *u* and the conjunction *co* have no bearing on the reduplication process, neither to interfere with nor to contribute directly to the formation of the ordinal.

2.2.7.3: Deverbal Adjectives

Three morphological processes allow for the derivation of adjectives from verbs, each of them transfixation strategies, which we saw previously with deverbal nouns.

The first of these strategies functions identically to that of the ⟨k⟩ and ⟨s⟩ morphemes that produced nouns. The morpheme ⟨m⟩ corresponds to the ⟨ed⟩ and ⟨en⟩ in English words *beckoned* and *beaten*, respectively, and produces adjectives. In English, such words are used as past participles—as in *He was badly beaten by a mugger*—and as adjectives—as in *The beaten man went to the hospital*. We hinted in §2.1.1.2 to the fact that Katalopsi does not have past participles due to the fact that the perfect aspect is communicated strictly by an auxiliary. We will see more on this in chapter 3 on syntax, but suffice it to say that the analogously derived terms in Katalopsi are only used as adjectives.

The transfixation process is realized, as we've seen before, by inserting the ⟨m⟩ morpheme between the two vowels of the verb. This results in an adjective meaning roughly "having the quality of undergone the process" described by the verb.

In the following examples, you will see that tone contour behaves as the parallel morphologies of the deverbal nouns.

cryú "bite"	→	crýmū "bitten"
fuò "fail"	→	fùmo̱ "failed"
joū "break"	→	jōmū "broken"
pai̱ "play"	→	pa̱mi̱ "played"
xoũ "raise"	→	xomũ "raised"
psuê "beat"	→	psúmè "beaten"
niǎ "claim"	→	nìmá "claimed"

It is important to take note of the evaluation of the rising and falling tones for this and the previously described morphological processes, as the next method of adjective derivation evaluates differently.

A seemingly important morpheme for any language is that which denotes the ability of something to undergo a process. In English, this is ⟨able⟩ as in *acceptable* and *teachable*. The equivalent morphology in Katalopsi comes in two parts. One is the familiar insertion of a consonant, in this case ⟨j⟩, between the vowels of the verb, the other is effectively a prefix, a morphophonological unit attached at the beginning of the word, ⟨ja⟩.

In §2.2.6.2, we pointed out that the evaluation of tone contour upon applying the transfixation process was absolute for five verbal tones. This is therefore the logical place for examples to begin:

srai͞ "depend" → jāsrājī "dependable"
keo̬ "imagine" → ja̬ke̬jo̬ "imaginable"
cliã "obtain" → jaclijã "obtainable"
kluâ "identify" → ja̬klújà "identifiable"
fei̯ "prefer" → jāfèjí "preferable"

As expected, when transfixation of a verb occurs, a high tone will become two high tones, a low tone two low tones; a mordent tone will remain at the end while the previous syllables will be neutral; and a rising-falling tone will split into a rising tone and a falling tone, while a falling-rising tone will split into a falling and a rising. The differences in this morphology manifest in the rising and falling tones only:

puá "accept" → japujá "acceptable"
luè "believe" → jālūjè "believable"

Unlike for previous morphological processes, the ⟨ja⟩ + ⟨j⟩ derivation morphology requires that the tones of the originating verbs remain on the final syllable, with the appropriate penultimate tone selected to maintain intralexical tone sandhi. In other words, verbs with a rising tone evaluate to a rising tone on the last syllable and a low tone on the second-to-last, and verbs with a falling tone evaluate to a falling tone on the last syllable and a high tone on the second-to-last.

The last point on this morphological process is the matter of the tone that the ⟨ja⟩ prefix takes. The tone on this morpheme will always be *flat*, meaning it will be a high, low, or neutral tone. As would be expected, the neutral tone is the appropriate choice if the source verb has a mordent tone. As for the high tone, it manifests if the following syllable is either high or falling; and the low tone appears if the next syllable is low or rising. With these facts and others in place, the patterns of tone within a word are probably becoming increasingly apparent.

The final deverbal adjective morphology is similar to the previous process in that it has two parts and involves transfixation. In this process, ⟨l⟩ is inserted between the vowels of the verb, and ⟨le⟩ is suffixed to the end. This morphology relates the quality of engaging in some activity with frequency or skill. While its correspondence with English morphemes is less strong, its meaning will be apparent by example:

klaí "hate"	→	klálīlē "hateful"
jyù "repeat"	→	jỳlu̱le̱ "repetitive"
piō "forget"	→	pīlōlē "forgetful"
psyu̱ "confront"	→	psylu̱le̱ "confrontational"
kliõ "notice"	→	klilolē "observant"
cruê "preach"	→	crúlèle̱ "preachy"
ploǐ "talk"	→	plòlílē "talkative"

It is important to note that the evaluation of the rising and falling tones do not follow the pattern of the ⟨ja⟩ + ⟨j⟩ morphology. Instead, it conforms with the other transfixation processes previously described. The rising tone appears on the first vowel of the verb with a high tone on the second, while the falling tone similarly appears on the first vowel with a low tone following on the second vowel. The other tones are evaluated as seen in every case of transfixation.

As for the tone on the ⟨le⟩ morpheme, this is determined by similar constraints of intralexical sandhi for suffixes. If the second-to-last syllable carries a rising or high tone, ⟨le⟩ will take a high tone; if the penultimate syllable carries a falling or low tone, ⟨le⟩ will take a low tone; and if the source verb carries a mordent tone, that mordent is unsurprisingly shifted to the ⟨le⟩ morpheme, while the other syllables take the neutral tone.

2.2.7.4: Denominal Adjectives

Two morphemes allow for the derivation of adjectives from nouns. These morphemes delineate a difference in meaning not often made in English, with English words frequently pointing ambiguously to one or the other. The first is the prefix ⟨py⟩, which means "of or relating to" the noun. The second is the suffix ⟨xu⟩, which means "exhibiting the qualities of" the noun.

Consider the word *sècri̱*, meaning "condition" in the sense of a requirement. The derived adjective *pȳsècri̱* may be used to modify a noun to indicate that the noun relates to conditions. For example, when you say that something is a "conditional matter," you are saying that the matter relates to conditions. The adjective *sècri̱xú* refers on the other hand to something having the quality of conditions. When you talk of a "conditional agreement," you mean that the agreement is subject to conditions, and therefore *sècri̱xú* is used. The following word pairs similarly delineate this difference:

rìfro̱ "evidence" → pȳrìfro̱ "evidential"; rìfro̱xú "evidenced"

psūxī "system" → pȳpsūxī "systemic"; psūxīxù "systematic"

cẽ "night" → pycẽ "nightly"; cexũ "nocturnal"

krōpsù "disease" → pȳkrōpsù "pathological"; krōpsùxú "diseased"

The tone contour patterns of these morphemes present no surprises. The ⟨py⟩ prefix is flat and so occurs only with high, neutral, and low tones: It takes a high tone before high and falling tones, a neutral tone before neutral and mordent tones, and a low tone before low and rising tones.

The ⟨xu⟩ suffix takes rising, falling, and mordent tones. The rising tone will occur if the second-to-last syllable carries a falling or low tone, and the falling tone will occur if the second-to-last syllable has a rising or high tone. ⟨xu⟩ is realized with a mordent tone in line with the mordent-shifting rule, where the presence of a mordent tone on the last syllable means the mordent should move to the suffix, and all other tones of the word are neutralized.

2.2.7.5: Deadjectival Adjectives

By one morphological process, adjectives can be derived from other adjectives. This deadjectival morpheme ⟨i⟩, which is a prefixed to the original adjective, is like ⟨un⟩ and ⟨non⟩, among others in English standing in for the word *not*. The meaning of this morphology will in all likelihood strike as intuitive, given the prevalence of English pairs such as *lucky* and *unlucky*, *possible* and *impossible*, *linear* and *nonlinear*, etc. The most difficult aspect of this morpheme is the assignment of tone, though utilizing a pattern which we have seen before. Consider the following examples:

xá "lucky"	→	i̠xá "unlucky"
krèka̠ "popular"	→	īkrèka̠ "unpopular"
xōcà "accurate"	→	īxōcà "inaccurate"
ry̠kfa̠ "native"	→	i̠ry̠kfa̠ "non-native"
lomũ "necessary"	→	ilomũ "unnecessary"

As we've seen with several flat prefixes already, the ⟨i⟩ morpheme takes one of three tones, a high, a neutral, or a low tone. For the sake of clarity, we repeat: It takes the high tone before high or falling tones, the neutral tone before neutral or mordent tones, and the low tone before low or rising tones.

2.2.7.6: Compound Adjectives

Words can also compound to form new adjectives. Such compounds are often the result of two independent adjectives and are in line with expectations likely held by speakers of English.

For example, two colors may be fused together to indicate a color somewhere between the two: *Sā*, meaning "green," and *prī*, meaning "blue," combine into *sāprī*, "green-blue." In this semantic realm, the word *pi̠* may be used independently to mean "dark" in the sense of color, or it can be compounded with the colors themselves to create new adjectives: *piprimu*, "dark brown," *pixé*, "dark red," etc. By the same token, *ký*, meaning "light" in color, can form words such as *kýlā*, "light purple," *kýpūrī*, "light yellow," and so on.

2.2.8: ADVERBS

Adverbs come in three varieties. There are the monomorphemic adverbs, the deadjectival adverbs, and the compound adverbs. The compound adverbs we will shortly explore could be analyzed as *phrases*, a concept we will consider more fully in chapter 3, but since they often parallel adverbial usages in English, they should be considered fully here.

2.2.8.1: Monomorphemic Adverbs

The monomorphemic lexemes of the adverb part of speech, as with any part of speech, are various and not easily categorized semantically. However, they not uncommonly refer to locations, as with *pricy*, "here," and *suku*, "there"; refer to times, as with *mĩ*, "then," and *klỳ*, "now"; or mark frames, junctures, and other concepts in *discourse*, or conversational language. These discourse items may include *fròlú*, "anyway," *cxa*, "moreover," and *fiko*, "however."

Monomorphemic adverbs also surface as intensifiers and other degreed terms, like *nūjè*, "very," *jy*, "rather," and *clare*, "somewhat"; words with modal character, like *mùrý*, "already," and *psèpó*, "almost"; and words with frequentative character, including *fòfra*, "never," *plỳ*, "always," and *sājà*, "again."

2.2.8.2: Deadjectival Adverbs

Adverbs can be derived from adjectives using the morpheme ⟨ro⟩, which works similarly to the ⟨ly⟩ in English words *humbly, swiftly,* and *usefully,* among others. ⟨ro⟩ is a suffix morpheme, binding to the end of the source adjective and indicating that something does or is something in a certain way. Consider the following examples:

mú "correct"	→	múrō "correctly"
kfíxù "bright"	→	kfíxùro̱ "brightly"
kū "sleepy"	→	kūrō "sleepily"
cy̱ "good"	→	cy̱ro̱ "well"
moxũ "natural"	→	moxurõ "naturally"

As you can see from these examples, the ⟨ro⟩ morpheme has a predictable tonal pattern. If it follows a syllable with a rising or high tone, it will have a high tone; if it comes after a syllable with a falling or low tone, it will have a low tone; and if it follows a mordent tone, the mordent-shifting rule takes effect, neutralizing the tone on the final syllable of the source word and applying a mordent tone to ⟨ro⟩.

It is important to understand that English words with the ⟨ly⟩ morpheme will not always have ⟨ro⟩ in Katalopsi, and Katalopsi words that have ⟨ro⟩ will not always have ⟨ly⟩ in English. This is especially true because English allows some adjectives to be used as adverbs without the addition of a morpheme. For example, one can say, "He finished the project *quickly*" or simply "He finished the project *quick*." Katalopsi adverbs on the other hand, if derived, will always have the ⟨ro⟩ suffix.

2.2.8.3: Compound Adverbs

There are not many compound adverbs in Katalopsi to be straightforwardly translated to English, but there is a productive process of adverb compounding that will be of benefit to communication. If two adverbs that are underlyingly contradictory in nature are followed one after another, a meaning between the two is the result. For example, in English, we may say, "He walks at a moderate pace." In Katalopsi, this could be expressed with the following:

Riè m̀ cá cxārō-cryro̱.
walk D he quickly-slowly
"He walks at a moderate pace."

Note that because the words do not fully compound, i.e. they do not result in non-conflicting tonal contours, we will simply represent their union with a hyphen. Other examples of this compounding strategy follow:

Ź nuá Í plō xypra-cèro.
PAST arrive D we early-late
"We arrived right on time."

Noì Í kràre sùro-xoro.
shine D lantern brightly-dimly
"The lantern is shining lambently."

Note that in cases where a Katalopsi term already exists to express the middling meaning, as with the phrase *on time*, using this compounding strategy also communicates there was some uncertainty of whether the outcome would have been one or the other.

2.2.8.4: Prepositions Revisited

In the previous sections, we looked at various adverbs, which on the whole form a rather morphologically simple category but nonetheless have the possibility for morphological derivation. This makes adverbs much like the adjectives, nouns, and other categories that came before them. However, in this section, we will briefly reprise our discussion of Katalopsi prepositions, which exhibit essentially no derivation at all. We saw in §2.2.4 that the vast majority of Katalopsi prepositions are identical to either complementizers or adverbs, hence their reappearance here.

Consider the word *before*. In the sentence *I used to be a babysitter before*, the word may be analyzed as a preposition without a complement, or it may be thought of as an adverb. After all, the adverb really means "in the past" rather than before some unspecified time. When specifying the time, however, the prepositional nature is unmistakable: *I used to be a babysitter before my current job*. But the word can also be a complementizer, marking a whole sentence, as in *Before I started my current job, I used to be a babysitter*.

Not every preposition can do this in English, but Katalopsi is a lot more liberal about the usage of prepositions as both adverbs and complementizers. The locative and temporal prepositions of Table 16 and the dual preposition-complementizers of Table 19 are by and large also used as adverbs. This is not the case for each and every one, but when in doubt, a review of these in the dictionary of chapter 7 will benefit.

2.2.9: PREDICATIVES

We close this section with a brief discussion of predicates and turn to verbs in the next. The natural role of the verb is to serve as a predicate describing an action, state, or event, but verbs are not the only words that can serve in this way. The part of speech of a word is a good clue as to how a word is used, but it does not always tell you what can appear in the predicate position.

Because this is a heavily syntactic topic, predicates will be addressed more fully in chapter 3, but it is important to keep in mind that the pronouns, the adjectives, the nouns, and the prepositions we considered can also all be used as predicates in Katalopsi.

2.3: CATEGORIES OF TYPE III SYLLABLES

Type III syllables always occur as verbs, which also means that they are always used in the predicate position of complete sentences. We will see more on this in chapter 3. However, it will be helpful to keep in mind when learning the lexicology of the Katalopsi language that some verbs serve the role that adjectives serve in English. This phenomenon is a matter of course for natural languages, as lexicons never completely and sufficiently overlap across languages, even within a single syntactic category.

We will also see that a small handful of verbs can compound with words of other categories to yield a special kind of phrasal predicate. By some analyses this process is morphological and by others syntactic, so we shall consider them both here and in chapter 3.

2.3.1: VERBS

In this section, we will look at the various morphological forms that Katalopsi verbs take. They may be monomorphemic, which is the case for the vast majority of verbs; they may be derived from adjectives; or they may occur in compounds.

2.3.1.1: Monomorphemic Verbs

Monomorphemic verbs are immediately recognizable as being solely Type III monosyllables. No underived verbs are multisyllabic. They can have any of the eighteen diphthongs and seven diphthong tone contours. Here are several examples:

cxiă	"cause"
neú	"wonder"
plyì	"drool"
laū	"paint"
friē	"destroy"

2.3.1.2: Deadjectival Verbs

Katalopsi has one morpheme allowing for the derivation of verbs from adjectives. Much like the ⟨ify⟩ morpheme in *unify*, the ⟨ize⟩ in *neutralize*, and the ⟨ate⟩ in *activate*, the Katalopsi suffix ⟨nuo⟩ results in verbs that mean "to make something have the quality" of the source adjective. Consider the following examples:

plạmó "perfect (adj.)"	→	plạmónuō "perfect (v.)"
prò "distinct"	→	prònuọ "distinguish"
mū "equal"	→	mūnuō "equalize"
srùklụ "flat"	→	srùklụnuọ "flatten"
cryclũ "complex"	→	cryclunuõ "complicate"

In a pattern we've now seen several times before, observe that the ⟨nuo⟩ suffix takes a high tone following a rising or high tone on the previous syllable, a low tone following a falling or low tone, and mordent tone when affixing to an adjective ending with a mordent. And as per the mordent-shifting rule, in the latter case, the mordent on the root adjective is neutralized.

2.3.1.3: Compound Verbs

Katalopsi is quite different from English in that it has a productive verb-compounding strategy. By combining two verbs, a related but new meaning can be derived. For example, the word *fiē*, meaning "fell," can be combined with several other verbs to yield more specific varieties of making something fall:

keò "hit" + fiē "fell"	→	keōfiē "knock down"
fyu̠ "cut" + fiē "fell"	→	fyúfiē "cut down"
ryŭ "explode" + fiē "fell"	→	ryŭfiē "demolish"

Some verbs are certainly more productive than others in this respect, but it will be useful to get a sense of such derivations in general. This is particularly true because tone will sometimes change to ensure non-conflicting tonal contours intralexically, as is shown above. The following examples demonstrate a greater variety of lexemes and tonal interactions:

preū "sound" + joū "break"	→	preūjoū "shatter"
pie̠ "know" + xeō "test"	→	piéxeō "experiment"
ryŭ "explode" + sriò "throw"	→	ryŭsriò "launch"
xiã "help" + kraĩ "kill"	→	xiakraĩ "euthanize"
kiè "behave" + sryí "train"	→	kièsryí "tame"
kloī "pursue" + piã "follow"	→	kloipiã "stalk"
liõ "suffer" + clia̠ "die"	→	lio̠clia̠ "die a painful death"
keŏ "express" + ploĭ "talk"	→	keŏploĭ "articulate"
kià "burn" + friē "destroy"	→	kiāfriē "firebomb"

It is important at this time to reprise the various deverbal derivational morphemes mentioned in §2.2. These behave differently for compound verbs, in short because the derivational morpheme must often be duplicated, but other times the morphology behaves in perhaps unexpected ways.

Remember the agentive morpheme ⟨k⟩. Usually, this morpheme must be inserted between the two vowels of the verbal diphthong. In the case of compound verbs, the ⟨k⟩ is inserted twice, between each of the diphthongs:

piéxeō "experiment"	→	píkēxēkō "experimentalist"
kloipiã "stalk"	→	klokipikã "stalker"
keŏploĭ "articulate"	→	kèkóplòkí "articulator"

Apart from the insertion of a second instance of the morpheme, nothing is significantly different about the derivation process. The tone is still assigned to the individual vowels of the diphthong per the previously described rules, and evaluation of the tone is done independently from the other Type III syllable. The ⟨s⟩ morpheme, which also derives nouns from verbs, works identically:

ryŭfiē "demolish"	→	rỳsúfīsē "demolition"
kièsryí "tame"	→	kìsẹsrýsī "taming"
xiakraĩ "euthanize"	→	xisakrasĩ "euthanasia"
ryŭsriò "launch (v.)"	→	rỳsúsrìsọ "launch (n.)"

We also learned of a method of deriving a supine adjective from a verb using the ⟨m⟩ morpheme. Since it uses a transfixation process like the noun-deriving morphemes just described, it is distinguishable morphologically only in that it yields an adjective:

preūjoū "shatter"	→	prēmūjōmū "shattered"
keōfiē "knock down"	→	kēmōfīmē "knocked down"
ryŭsriò "launch"	→	rỳmúsrìmọ "launched"
xiakraĩ "euthanize"	→	ximakramĩ "euthanized"

Apart from nouns and adjectives, we can also derive a new verb from these compound verbs using the ⟨e⟩ prefixing morpheme. Few new words are derived in this way due to various semantic and pragmatic limitations, but for the sake of completion, see the following example:

ryŭsriò "launch"	→	ēryŭsriò "relaunch"

As you can see, because ⟨e⟩ is a prefix and not a transfixing morpheme, it does not need to be duplicated. It is simply affixed to the beginning of the source compound verb. The same will be said for any morphology involving a prefix or a suffix, even if transfixation is also necessary. For example, the ⟨le⟩ suffix is part of a morphological process for deriving an adjective from a verb, and like the ⟨e⟩ prefix, it is not duplicated, though the transfixed ⟨l⟩ is:

keŏploĭ "articulate (v.)" → kèlóplòlílē "articulate (adj.)"

In this process, the transfixation morpheme is duplicated as expected, appearing in both of the original verbs, but the suffix appears only once.

Finally, we should see an example of the ⟨ja⟩ + ⟨j⟩ morphology to derive the ability adjective. The ⟨j⟩ is transfixational, so it is duplicated, but the ⟨ja⟩ is a prefix and so appears only once. Also remember that tone contours are evaluated differently with this morphology:

kièsryí "tame" → jākījèsryjí "tameable"

2.3.2: COMPOUNDS

A small number of verbs can be compounded with either adjectives or nouns to create what we may call *compound predicates*. This topic is an important one for syntax, so in chapter 3, we will see many sentences in which they are used. For now, let us look solely at how the compounding works morphologically.

This type of compound occurs with *copular* words or *linking verbs* like *kio̱*, meaning "become" or "get," or words that serve to link the subject with a quality, state, or position described by the chosen adjective or noun. For example, if a movie suddenly "becomes interesting," then in Katalopsi it "interesting-becomes," or *sýcòxú-kio̱*. Note that for these linking verbs, we will simply use a hyphen to connect them because they do not fuse so closely as to demand non-conflicting tonal contours. Here are further examples of *kio̱*, using both adjectives and nouns:

kfýlà-kio̠	"become frequent"
sēklū-kio̠	"become a relationship"
sry̠-kio̠	"become poor"
laprã-kio̠	"become an artist"

Other such compounding words include *kreú*, meaning "seem," *roi̠*, meaning "feel," *cxiõ*, meaning "stay" or "remain," and *kiè*, meaning "act." Examples of each follow:

sỳklú-kreú	"seem relative"
kfújè-kreú	"seem noteworthy"
nékfē-kreú	"seem like/to be the maximum"
īlùle̠le̠-kreú	"seem incredulous"
kysũ-kreú	"seem like/to be a hobby"
fru̠co̠xú-roi̠	"feel active"
kre̠fílè-roi̠	"feel like a catastrophe"
kū-roi̠	"feel tired"
li̠sy-roi̠	"feel like a requirement"
sã-roi̠	"feel sick"
cxékỳ-cxiõ	"remain a teacher"
julixũ -cxiõ	"stay attentive"
jèli̠le̠-cxiõ	"stay rested"
klīkȳ-cxiõ	"remain a student"
fà-cxiõ	"remain calm"
prùni̠-kiè	"act strange"
psĩ-kiè	"act like a bird"
fe̠-kiè	"act stupid"
réklù-kiè	"act serious"
mureprã-kiè	"act like a doctor"

One linking verb that should still be mentioned for its importance in

English is the copula *par excellence*, the word *be*. Not every language has such a word overtly, and indeed many opt to simply put the adjective, noun, or preposition in the predicate position on its own. Katalopsi is one such language. While *kio̜*, *kreú*, *ro̜i*, *cxiõ*, and *kiè* also link the subject a to quality, state, or position by appearing alongside the adjective, noun, or preposition in the predicate, when the meaning of equivalence or set membership is the intension, the adjective, noun, or preposition appears alone. This is indeed an important topic for syntax, so we will see more on this in the next chapter.

2.4: GAP DISTRIBUTION AND FUTURE EXPANSION

Apart from and in addition to correcting errors, later editions of this book and language will be done almost certainly for the purpose of expanding the lexicon. As we will see in chapter 7, the dictionary accompanying this grammar has just over ten thousand entries. It is estimated that the average speaker of any language knows around forty thousand words and furthermore that English has close to two million lexemes. These facts together easily mean that the lexicon of this edition has significant gaps that may be filled by later editions.

With that said, by using computational tools, we have selected what are the most common verbs, the most common nouns, the most common words of every category as speakers of English use them, and we based the bulk of this limited ten-thousand-word lexicon on these most frequent usages. The hope therefore is that the communicative force of the language will be quite high despite its lexicon being small compared to any given natural language.

We have also worked toward the goal of preparing this language for use by role players and game developers by loading the lexicon with words from fantasy and science fiction contexts. Future expansion of the lexicon will no doubt do more to fulfill this goal, but for now we consider the lexicon quite effective for these and other uses.

CHAPTER 3

Syntax

Chapter 1 began by describing Katalopsi in the smallest possible units, the sounds, including consonants, vowels, and tones. Then it showed how those sounds combine to create larger structures: (a) vowels to create diphthongs and (b) vowels, consonants, and tones to create syllables.

Chapter 2 showed how the phonology of syllables informs the part of speech of words and described in detail how mono- or multisyllabic units of meaning called morphemes could combine to create new words.

Now, in this chapter, we will discuss how words can combine to form phrases, sentences, and other utterances. *Syntax* is the body of rules that govern how words can combine to form these larger structures. In short, they are the rules concerning *word order*.

After you have a thorough understanding of the syntax of phrases and sentences in Katalopsi, we will turn to how these utterances may be simplified in casual speech or even combined into more complex utterances. We will then look at several constructions common to any rigorous study of syntax and prominent in the grammar books of natural languages.

3.1: PHRASES

Before words can form complete sentences, they first combine into smaller constituent structures known as phrases. You should think of phrases as clusters of words that seem intuitively to belong together.

Consider the sentence *The technician repaired the broken computer.* There are several identifiable phrases in the statement, among them *the broken computer*, *the technician*, and even *repaired the broken computer*. The latter example points to the fact that phrases can also exist inside of other phrases, creating a hierarchy of constituency that at its top constitutes the entire sentence—or more broadly the utterance, as the case may be.

In this section we will explain the syntactic rules governing phrases, including the role the category of a word plays, what this means for the usage of pronouns, and how phrases can combine with one another to create larger phrases.

3.1.1: MODIFICATION

The term *modification* refers to the optional association of one word with another, usually serving to specify meaning and narrow the scope of its referent in the real world. Consider the word *cats* in the sentence *Cats are very intelligent.* This is a general statement about cats, but with modification, the group of cats to which the sentence refers is narrowed. By saying "*Siamese cats* are very intelligent," we have now referred to a much smaller group. A similar thing happens with *These cats are very intelligent.* This sentence now refers to a contextually relevant group of cats but not *all* cats.

In these sentences, phrases were formed from the standalone noun *cats*. The former example illustrated modification by an adjective, and the latter exhibited modification by a determiner. Modification is a way of constructing phrases with optional words, which we will explore more closely here. Afterward, we will see how phrases are also constructed from grammatical requirements of the language. Then we will look at some grammatical consequences of the constituency inherent to phrases.

3.1.1.1: Modification of Nouns

We begin our closer study of modification with Katalopsi noun phrases. When discussing the syntax of phrases, we are often talking about the position that elements take with respect to one another. A noun may be preceded by or followed by the modifying element depending on its part of speech. These processes can be iterated and can occur simultaneously, much as in natural languages.

Think first about how adjectives can be used to modify nouns in English. Although English sometimes allows adjectives to follow a noun in certain constructions, for the most part they appear before it. In Katalopsi, on the other hand, the modifying adjective will always follow the noun. Consider a few examples:

psȳ pīlōlē
dog forgetful
"the forgetful dog"

krụpýprà prèkịxú
soldier cowardly
"the cowardly soldier"

Although Katalopsi places less emphasis on the use of determiners than English, demonstratives and possessive markers that do occur are placed before the modified noun. Note in the following phrases the co-occurrence of modifying adjectives for further exemplification of this postpositional element:

srã pẹclú
that mountain
"that mountain"

sĩ lāfrà ịxá
this community unfortunate
"this unfortunate community"

pòmá sīmìsrụjó kụ

95

my pocket watch shiny
"my shiny pocket watch"

sỹ cámà méclō sẽ
that his clothes expensive
"those expensive clothes of his"

Observe in the last example that both a determiner and a possessive appear, but the possessive occurs after the determiner and before the noun. This is the order required by Katalopsi syntax, and we will see more examples shortly. It is important to take a moment to compare this to English, however, in which a determiner and a possessive cannot both appear before the noun, resulting in periphrastic expressions like *of his* being tacked on to the end to complete the phrase.

Nouns can also be modified by specifying number. Using cardinal numerals in modification is much like determiners and possessives in that they occur before the noun, but it is important to note that ordinal numerals like *fourth* and *fifth* are treated as adjectives and therefore appear after the noun. With that said, the question arises where cardinal numerals ought to appear relative to the determiner and the possessive, which we illustrate in the following:

je paki
three musician
"three musicians"

sĩ clí fráfỹ
this four magazine
"these four magazines"

cìmá pĩ jí
her two friend
"her two friends"

sỹ lamá clū plīklē
this their five recipe
"these five recipes of theirs"

As you can see, the cardinal numeral appears closest to the noun, always after the possessive and always after the determiner.

It is noteworthy that the more vague terms for enumeration, like English *few* and *many*, have an optionality in their realization. These quantifiers can be treated like nouns, linked to the quantified noun phrase by a preposition, or they may be treated as the cardinal numerals and appear just to the left of the noun:

srẹ u sĩ plà
many of this problem
"many of these problems"

sĩ srẹ plà
this many problem
"these many problems"

clà u pòmá rẽ rà cy̲
all of my work most good
"all of my best work"

pòmá clà rẽ rà cy̲
my all work most good
"all my best work"

The final method by which a noun can be modified is by appending a prepositional phrase to the end of the noun phrase. Adpositional elements in Katalopsi are strictly prepositions, meaning they always appear to the left of their complement. Almost all English adpositions are prepositional—words such as *before*, *from*, and *due to*—but a handful are postpositional, such as *ago*. Katalopsi prepositional phrases are formed, therefore, by having a preposition on the left and a noun phrase on the right:

clý x̲i̲rú cxèsọ
next to court building
"by the courthouse"

mu̱ srã cxẽ
on that table
"on that table (over there)"

We can now modify nouns by adjoining these prepositional phrases to the right side. Note that this happens after any adjectives modifying the same noun:

praklũ lō clý xi̱rú cxèso̱
business new next to court building
"the new business next to the courthouse"

pỳ sópū mu̱ srã cxẽ
bowl pretty on that table
"the pretty bowl on that table (over there)"

Taking into account the six modifying elements we have described here, the following schema can be generated to model the structure of the Katalopsi noun phrase:

{Demonstrative} {Possessive} {Numeral/Quantifier} {Noun} {Adjective} {Preposition}

The following examples show each of these fields of the noun phrase being used:

sỹ pòmá pĩ sȳ lu̱ u klápù
that my two book big of poetry
"those two big books of poetry of mine"

sĩ kùmá clà clỳrá fùmo̱ mē lùprí
this your all effort failed at analysis
"all these failed efforts at analysis of yours"

3.1.1.2: Modification of Adjectives

Compared to noun phrases, the modification of adjectives is relatively simple. Adjectives are modified by adverbs and prepositional phrases to narrow the exact meaning of the trait or property being described. The adverbial modifier may be an intensifier like *nūjè*, meaning "very," or more meaningful words, which may draw comparisons, indicate time constraints, or communicate various other meanings. Consider the following examples:

sipsýxùro sýcòxú
momentarily interesting
"momentarily interesting"

pijé nísāxù
somehow different
"somehow different"

cránōxùro krà
infamously strong
"infamously strong"

cròro pīmō
easily forgotten
"easily forgotten"

klỳ kòxu
now middle-aged
"now middle-aged"

frucikárō jāpsījō
thoroughly enjoyable
"thoroughly enjoyable"

As you can see, the adverbial modifier of an adjective always appears to the left of the modified. This will be familiar and intuitive for native speakers of English and many other languages.

It is also important to mention here that the so-called *comparative* and *superlative* forms of adjectives are achieved with an adverb rather than a suffixed morpheme as is often the case in English. The comparative form of an adjective allows you to identify something as having a characteristic that is greater than or less than another thing, as in the sentence *Zachary is taller than Emily*. Note here that the morpheme ⟨er⟩ has been appended to *tall*. However, depending on the word, it may be preferred to use an adverb, as in *Emily is more intelligent than Jessica*.

The superlative works similarly in English, with the morpheme ⟨est⟩ sometimes suffixed to the adjective, and other times with the adjective modified by the adverb *most*. The superlative, of course, serves to identify the best example of a trait or that which exhibits the trait to the greatest degree. So we can have sentences like *My dog's coat is the shiniest* and *This vase is the most expensive*, showing both possible formulations of the superlative in English.

Katalopsi does not have bound-morpheme morphology for adjectives, opting instead to use only modifying adverbs *pró*, meaning "more," and *rà*, meaning "most." The following examples illustrate their use:

pró sóxù
more healthy
"healthier"

pró cìpsáxù
more theoretical
"more theoretical"

rà lō
most new
"newest"

rà jācìjé
most applicable
"most applicable"

The more difficult elements of these constructions, such as accompanying prepositional phrases or predicative usages, will be addressed in §3.4.1 on comparison.

With that said, the other element which may modify an adjective is a prepositional phrase. Some adjectives may in fact require a prepositional phrase in order to make sense semantically or syntactically. As we saw in chapter 2, prepositions have a strong relationship to the semantic roles for which they mark. When adjectives are used predicatively, it's often the case that the disambiguator will do the job and a preposition is not needed, but when adjectives are used as modifiers, they fall into three groups: (1) those that cannot take a prepositional modifier, (2) those that optionally take prepositional modifiers in order to be more specific, and (3) those that obligatorily take prepositional modifiers for grammaticality. We will see examples of each in the following.

The first group of adjectives are those that cannot take a prepositional modifier. We know supine adjectives derived from verbs can almost always take such a complement, but apart from this fact, this group can be somewhat unpredictable. In many cases it depends on what is possible semantically. For example, it turns out that many *relational* adjectives, those derived from nouns using the ⟨py⟩ morpheme, are incapable of being modified by a preposition simply because they cannot be interpreted as describing a trait *to a certain degree*. Consider the word *pȳmà*, or "botanical." Something cannot truly be *more* or *less* botanical; something is either related to plants or not. This is also the case for words like:

pȳkā	"earthly"
pypá	"lingual"
py̱jýkrē	"renal"

However, it is important to keep in mind that not all words derived in this way will also fall into this category. Some can take degreed interpretations, therefore also allowing prepositional complements.

Other adjectives that cannot take a prepositional complement are sporadic but include the following:

réxī	"single"
nóxù	"winged"
pūmō	"married"

As you can see, semantics seems to be the biggest predictor as to whether the adjective can take a prepositional phrase as a complement. Because these words have a discrete *Boolean* character, meaning they're either true or false and not degreed, they are not easily modified by prepositions.

Adjectives that optionally take prepositional complements form a particularly large category in part because supine adjectives derived from verbs are usually able to specify the same semantic roles that the originating verbs can, with the exception of the role that the modified noun would theoretically fill. At the same time, these deverbal adjectives never require this level of specification. Apart from derivations, however, there are also many monomorphemic adjectives that can specify more information about the trait through the use of a preposition, even though those prepositions are not necessary. These prepositions can range from the generic, such as *u*, to the idiomatic, i.e. prepositions that are very closely linked to the trait the adjective describes, due to the semantic role it underlyingly specifies for.

Consider first the use of prepositions that mark roles that disambiguators of the source verb specify for:

plạcrạ ròmú nū pòmá prūrī
sweater made by my mother
"the sweater made by my mother"

jelõ nìmẹ ó pò
letter sent to me
"the letter sent to me"

lýxēclù frīmē fē jẽ prẹ
landscape destroyed by weather bad
"the landscape destroyed by the bad weather"

cxèso̯ cxèmo̯ mē kfòsi̯ pȳpsōfrū
building built for entertainment sports-related
"the building built for sports entertainment"

In none of these cases are the prepositions used strictly necessary. Semantically, other prepositions could have been used just as easily. And syntactically, while one might argue that the phrases shown here sound somewhat awkward *without* a preposition, the specific prepositions used are by no means required by the governing adjective.

While supine adjectives allow for a handful of optional prepositions marking semantic roles inherent to the source verb, many adjectives—both supine and underived—also allow for optional prepositions marking for roles never indicated by a disambiguator. They describe some additional information about the quality denoted by the adjective. With a locative, it may tell where specifically the quality appears—if it's not, say, ubiquitous to the modified element. A temporal element on the other hand may tell when the quality was present if it was not present the entire time. Consider the following:

ni̯ prì fé pò
person ready before me
"the person ready before me"

fy̯psa̯ xé fūlā kúkī
jacket red apart from zipper
"the red—apart from the zipper—jacket"

me̯lo̯ nūjè sópū kápē cì
violin very pretty to her
"the to-her-very-pretty violin"

cxẽ ku̯ mé lá
table shiny on top of it
"the table shiny on top"

kí nō ó crì
man rude to woman

"the man rude to women"

Finally, some adjectives *require* the use of a prepositional phrase because the adjectival modifier is simply insufficient to communicate a characteristic in full. The theory here is that some adjectives have a valency—they require an argument beyond that bearing the quality described by the adjective—and a particular semantic role must be explicitly communicated at first mention or out of context to get the full picture. When one is not mentioned, ungrammaticality is the result. For later mentions, it is likely that context will justify the omission of the prepositional phrase, though we may analyze that omission as *elision*, a phenomenon of omitting repeated material which we will discuss in more depth later. Several examples of such adjectives follow:

Marí fē jē cȳlòxú Í Basil.
fond by weather cloudy D Basil
"Basil is fond of cloudy weather."

rỳni̱ ma̱rí fē cu̱ prànú
anyone fond by thing simple
"anyone fond of simple things"

Psocrē klé my̱lí Í rỳ pè.
similar to one another D some language
"Some languages are similar to one another."

sy̱ psocrē klé mìku̱
house similar to mansion
"the house similar to a mansion"

Adjectives that optionally take a preposition often display idiomaticity: *full, afraid, angry, addicted, worthy*, inter alia. For words like these, Katalopsi allows a failsafe usage of the preposition *u* to establish the related argument, relying on context to clear up the meaning. But the most effective communication will use semantic-role-assigning prepositions, as in the following examples:

pỳ xe̱ prypé/u xō
bowl full with/of water
"a bowl full of water"

Nēlūlē fē/u xō Í ru̱ cūpā.
afraid by/of water D cat often
"Cats are often afraid of water."

Makfuxũ fē/u cxyco-mã cxysũ Í cá.
angry by/of government's decision D he
"He's angry at the government's decision."

pu̱ke̱ klùxú sro̱/u psy̱si̱
beginner worthy on/of recognition
"the beginner worthy of recognition"

While it will be easy enough to apply the failsafe preposition of *u*, it will make your speech sound more mature to select a more descriptive word. To do this for any adjective capable of taking such a prepositional phrase, just think about the role of the prepositional complement takes on a semantic level. Consider reviewing §2.2.4, which describes prepositions and the roles they assign, but also keep in mind that we will raise the subject of semantic roles later in this chapter and again in chapter 4.

3.1.1.3: Modification of Adverbs

Adverbs are similar to adjectives in that they are also modified solely by adverbs and prepositions. While some theory suggests that adjectives and adverbs are part of the same overarching category, under the analysis that they should be separate, adverbs are unique in that they constitute the only category that can be modified by itself. Just like adverbs modifying adjectives, adverbs modifying adverbs appear to the left of the modified element:

psèpó kfúmèro̱ īnàpu̱
almost completely irrelevant
"almost completely irrelevant"

In this example, notice that *psèpó* does not modify *īnàpu̱*. Rather, it modifies *kfúmèro̱*, meaning one adverb is modifying another. Several more examples follow:

cla̱re̱ prùni̱ro̱
somewhat strangely
"somewhat strangely"

múlòle̱ro̱ cryro̱
deceptively slowly
"deceptively slowly"

xyklo̱ xi̱ro̱
particularly closely
"particularly closely"

Adverbs can also be modified by prepositional phrases, and when this occurs, it is in line with expectations from our discussion of adjectival modification. In other words, if the preposition is possible—or required—as a complement of the source adjective, then generally speaking the complement is possible for the derived adverb as well. A frequent exception to this, however, is the vast majority of supine adjectives, which strongly resist the derivation process necessary to create an adverb. Here are a few examples where it does work:

xy̱pra̱ ro̱xo̱ fī
early during morning
"early in the morning"

nōrō ó crì
rudely to woman
"rudely to women"

múlòle̱ro̱ frú lēkū
deceitfully in front of investigator
"deceitfully in front of the investigators"

krulolerõ klé psȳ
obediently as dog
"obediently as a dog"

3.1.1.4: Modification of Verbs

When it comes to the modification of verbs, the modifying elements take two strikingly different forms. They may be required by the grammar, as with disambiguators and arguments, or they may be *adjunctive*—or optional—as with auxiliaries, adverbs, and prepositional phrases. The matter of grammatical and adjunctive modification of verbs is a topic best left for the syntax of sentences, because when one speaks of the complete verb phrase, either with or without modifiers, it is possible one is speaking of the entire sentence. As a result, we'll leave the bulk of the matter for §3.2 shortly to follow. For now we must focus on as small of chunks of the sentence as we can.

3.1.2: GRAMMATICAL PHRASES

In some cases, verbs may combine with a disambiguator and one or more arguments without forming the complete sentence. In these cases, we will call this collection a *grammatical phrase*, as disambiguators and arguments are the only complements of the verb ever required by the grammar. It's possible to argue that underlyingly the verb selects for a disambiguator, and the disambiguator selects for the arguments, but since they are so closely linked, almost syllogistically, we will consider them as a single phrasal unit.

It is important to note here that a small set of verbs, specifically weather and natural event verbs, will often require no disambiguator because there are no semantically required roles to be realized as arguments. Consider a sentence like *It is raining*. While the word *it* is syntactically a subject in this sentence, it does not actually stand for anything in the meaning. Katalopsi represents this fact with the absence of arguments for this and other similar verbs denoting natural events, like snow, thunder, and earthquakes. The lack of arguments means there is nothing to disambiguate, and so the verb will be the only item in the entire grammatical phrase.

In the vast majority of cases, however, the verb will have a disambiguator, which appears to its right. The disambiguator then selects for one or more arguments, which subsequently appear to its respective right. The specific order of those arguments is something we introduced in embryo in §2.1.2, but we will see further elaboration on this difficult topic in §3.2.3. For now, understanding this ordering of categories within the grammatical phrase will suffice.

3.1.3: PRONOMINALIZATION

Pronominalization is the replacement of a word or phrase with a pronoun. We have so far in this chapter attempted to endow you with a sense of the phrase as a syntactic construct, and how words and phrases combine with other words and phrases to form larger phrases still. This an important subject for pronominalization because, as we will see, pronouns may sometimes replace only portions of a phrase, but what is replaced must in a sense be complete on its own. That is, there are limitations on what can or cannot undergo pronominalization, and often the concept of a phrase is necessary for understanding those limitations.

In this section, we will introduce the concepts of pronominalization of nouns, determiners, and adjuncts. The more difficult cases will see greater analysis in sections still to come.

3.1.3.1: Noun Phrase Pronominalization

The pronominalization of noun phrases is a ripe area for the discussion of pronouns and how their usage relates to phrasal structure. Let us start with personal pronouns, words like *she, you, they*, and so on. For a review of these pronouns, turn to §2.2.2.1.

Let us first assume for the sake of example that we are discussing a man. There are many ways we may refer to this person, e.g. by their first name, by their relationship, by a description of their appearance, and so on. See in the following how the length of a phrase may vary even when referring to the same individual:

David

pòmá mịrá "my father"

sỹ kí júnì "that tall man"

If we were to refer to this person with a pronoun, we'd most likely use *cá*, or "he." In a sentence using the name *David*, therefore, a pronominal rewording would simply see *cá* in the position that *David* used to be. This is unsurprising, but a point of interest arises when trying to rephrase the second or third examples above. The word *mịrá*, or "father," is a noun, and if we attempt to replace it with a pronoun, we would end up with the ungrammatical phrase *pòmá cá*, "my he." That is, it seems that not only is a pronoun *able* to replace more than one word, but also it is sometimes *necessary* for grammaticality. We can confirm this by attempting to pronominalize the third example above, where we have a determiner, a noun, and an adjective. In this example, we can neither replace any single word with the pronoun nor either pair of words. In fact, it is the entire phrase that must be replaced.

This is the essential nature of prominalization that must be understood. That is, pronouns may be able to replace single words, but the larger phrases show us that it is the phrase that is targeted by pronominal replacement. Among linguists, this point leads to the argument that even single words must be interpreted as belonging to a hierarchically dominant if homophonous phrase. For the purposes of learning Katalopsi, however, it is only important to understand that this behavior lends credence to the idea that a phrasal structure exists in language and that sometimes, a grasp of the syntax of phrases is necessary to speak grammatically. This is, of course, to say nothing of the syntax of complete sentences.

Before moving forward to other types of phrases that may be targeted for pronominalization, it should be made clear that these facts do not apply only to personal pronouns. Although this is the only class of pronouns we have so far mentioned in this context, other classes exhibit this behavior as well, including interrogative and relative pronouns. We will see examples of each in §3.2.6.1 on questions and §3.3.2.2.3 on relative clauses.

3.1.3.2: Determiner Pronominalization

In another type of pronominalization, the prenominal material may be replaced by a pronoun. We will call this *determiner pronominalization*, although in fact, we argue that determiners, possessive pronouns, and quantifiers are all potential targets of the operation. Consider for example the following complex noun phrase which we saw earlier, simplified by removing the postnominal material:

> sỹ pòmá pĩ sȳ
> that my two book
> "those two books of mine"

The word *fã*, or "which," is one word which is capable of replacing prenominal material. It also approaches the noun from the left, and so three possible phrases may be formed following the determiner pronominalization process:

> fã pòmá pĩ sȳ
> which my two book
> "which of my two books"

> fã pĩ sȳ
> which two book
> "which two books"

> fã sȳ
> which book
> "which books"

Make note that context is important for understanding this syntactic process, as no doubt other similar-looking phrases are possible and perhaps even spring to mind. The assumption of the previous three formulations of the pronominalized material is that the original complex noun phrase had already been uttered, and so pronominalization is applying to a phrase in the minds of the interlocutors. Other similar-looking formulations may be possible, especially provided that a different set of books, and a phrase referring thereto, are in mind. In these cases, therefore, it is possible to have both the interrogative pronoun and the determiner, both the determiner and the quantifier but not the intervening possessive pronoun, and other such combinations in which the interrogative is not conceived of as replacing material. In these cases and even when referring to a set of books from context, the following formulations using *u* may be seen, but pronominalization—or the replacement of material with a pronoun—cannot be said necessarily to have occurred:

fã u sȳ pòmá pĩ sȳ
which of that my two book
"which of those two books of mine"

fã u sȳ pĩ sȳ
which of that two book
"which of those two books"

fã u pòmá sȳ
which of my book
"which of my books"

It is also worthwhile to consider other pronouns capable of replacing prenominal material. The distribution of the words *fōmà* and *rapsę* differ from *fã* due to their semantic content. The word *fōmà*, or "whose," is both interrogative and possessive in nature, and because determiner pronominalization approaches from the left, it must obligatorily replace any determiner in order to replace a possessive pronoun that may follow. If a determiner is necessary, the use of an *u*-phrase may be used:

fōmà pĩ sȳ
whose two book
"whose two books"

fōmà u sȳ sȳ
whose of that book
"whose of those books"

The word *rapse̲*, or "how many/much," on the other hand, has both interrogative and quantificational properties, and so it must replace not only the determiner and the possessive pronoun but the entirety of the prenominal material in order for pronominalization to be carried out. Otherwise, pronominalization is not possible, and the *u*-phrase is again used:

rapse̲ sȳ
how many book
"how many books"

rapse̲ u sỹ sȳ
how many of that book
"how many of those books"

rapse̲ u pòmá sȳ
how many of my book
"how many of my books"

rapse̲ u pĩ sȳ
how many of two book
"how many of the two books"

It is important to keep these facts in mind of which of the prenominal material the pronoun can replace, *fã* being the most versatile, *fõmà* replacing a more narrow range, and *rapse̲* being the most narrow. If any material that must obligatorily be replaced by the pronominalization is better off expressed, then the process need not apply and *u* should be used.

3.1.3.3: Adjunct Pronominalization

In §3.2, we will explore the syntax of sentences. One item you should expect to see again is sentential adjunction, or the attachment to the sentence of words or phrases that are not required by the grammar. Without going into too much detail prematurely, what you should know now is that such adjuncts tend to be adverbs or prepositions, adverbial phrases or prepositional phrases. They might describe participants in an event, the time of an event, the location of an event, or what have you. In these three named scenarios, however, pronominalization is likely to occur.

To start with, underlying adverbs and adverbial phrases are not able to be pronominalized, although they may themselves have replaced a more complex structure. It is unclear from current theory whether the usage of, say, a deictic adverb like *then* or *there* in place of a more lexically weighty prepositional phrase should be considered pronominalization, but you should be aware of the existence of this process. That is, the word *sų̄kų*, meaning "there," can stand in for a phrase like *mų cxẽ psyxũ*, "on the wood table," but it may be merely deixis rather than pronominalization that has taken place.

In the more versatile of cases, a prepositional adjunct, whether a single word or a phrase, may be replaced by interrogative and demonstrative pronouns, among other deictics including and in addition to those we have just seen. Importantly, it is oftentimes either the internal noun phrase or the entire prepositional phrase that can be targeted for pronominalization, so we'll see examples of both, though the former case may be considered another variety of noun phrase pronominalization. First, let us see more cases of deixis involving prepositional phrases:

Ř pliè ḿ clōrā xi̱ cy̱ u su̱.
PROG eat D horse near field of bean
"The horses are eating near the bean field."

Ř pliè ḿ clōrā lāsùcy̱.
PROG eat D horse over there
"The horses are eating over there."

R̃ prìnųo m̀ kfò plō fé pi̱jó-mà pa̱fri̱.
should ready D self we before tomorrow's event
"We should ready ourselves before tomorrow's event."

R̃ prìnųo m̀ kfò plō fé mĩ.
should ready D self we before then
"We should ready ourselves before then."

As you can see in these examples, just as with the examples of pronominalization in previous sections, a phrase of multiple words in an adjunct position may still be replaced with a single word given the right conditions. Syntactically, this process of deixis is identical to pronominalization, with seemingly only a semantic difference. This will be made more obvious by the examples of pronominalization in the following sentences, where another type of deixis takes place, the use of a demonstrative pronoun:

R̃ prìnuo m̀ kfò plō fé sỹ.
should ready D self we before that
"We should ready ourselves before that."

Ròlú kenỹ ījōmū, g̀ peú m̀ lō plō prànúrō.
regarding plate broken IMP buy D new we simply
"Regarding the broken plate, let's just buy a new one."

Ròlú sĩ, g̀ peú m̀ lō plō prànúrō.
regarding this IMP buy D new we simply
"Regarding this, let's just buy a new one."

The replacement of such an adjunct with an interrogative pronoun requires other facts of syntax which we will ignore for now and return to in §3.2.6.1. Instead, pay attention here only to the way the interrogative pronoun can replace either the complete adjunct or just the noun phrase appearing alongside the preposition:

Ź luo m̀ peprĩ pò cú kracã.
PAST leave D wallet I at classroom
"I left my wallet in the classroom."

V̀ ź luo m̀ peprĩ pò ri?
Q PAST leave D wallet I where
"Where did I leave my wallet?"

V̀ ź luo m̀ peprĩ pò cú ri?
Q PAST leave D wallet I at where

"Where did I leave my wallet at?"

Loũ ž cxù lō pò fé xesỹ pysá.
need D schedule new I before performance final
"I need the new schedule before the final performance."

V̀ loũ ž cxù lō kù rù?
Q need D schedule new you when
"When do you need the new schedule?"

V̀ loũ ž cxù lō kù fé rù?
Q need D schedule new you before when
"When do you need the new schedule by?"

3.1.4: Logical Connection of Phrases

Recall the logical connectives we described in §2.2.3, some of which could link only sentences—or clauses—and others which could link words, phrases, and clauses, i.e. every level of syntactic constituency. In this section, we will see examples of the logical connection of words and phrases to better understand the nature of phrasal constituency.

There are six logical connectives which can connect phrases below the sentential level. For each, we will see first its use in connecting words, and then in connecting phrases of various sizes. Where possible, we will try to vary the syntactic categories of the connected elements, i.e. whether they are nouns, adjectives, verbs, adverbs, or what have you.

The first logical connective to be discussed is the word *co*, or "and," which communicates connotatively exclusive conjunction in Katalopsi. Let us first see the conjunction of single words:

xé co prī
red and blue
"red and blue"

pro co pacxa
hill and valley
"hills and valleys"

siõ co pseў
read and write
"read and write"

cxārō co fȳrō
quickly and quietly
"quickly and quietly"

sĩ co sỹ lȳrū
this and that sheep
"these and those sheep"

The *conjuncts*, or connected units, can of course be larger than a single word, however. The following examples show this in effect. We have tried to use modified varieties of the examples we've just seen, but note that it will not be possible to discuss verb phrases here since they are often implicated in the sentence at large.

srūrō xé co cḷaṛe prī
slightly red and somewhat blue
"slightly red and somewhat blue"

pṛo jè co pạcxạ crũ
hill small and valley enormous
"small hills and enormous valleys"

nūjè cxārō co lụṛo fȳrō
very quickly and mostly quietly
"very quickly and, for the most part, quietly"

sĩ pĩ co sỹ clí lȳrū
this two and that four sheep
"these two and those four sheep"

In the linguistics literature, phrases connected by a conjunction are not uncommonly said to form a *conjunction phrase*, and if this is correct, then we should expect to see these conjunction phrases conjoined into still larger conjunction phrases. In fact, we do:

pro jè co srūrō xé co pacxa crũ co clare prī
hill small and slightly red and valley enormous and somewhat blue
"the small and slightly red hills and the enormous and somewhat blue valleys"

As you can see, quite large phrases can be joined together by the *co* conjunction. Of course, the same can be said for *sa*, the denotatively non-exclusive conjunction which could also be translated as "and." Since this word functions identically to *co*, we will see just a few brief examples of its use:

xō sa cxõ
water and rock
"the water and rocks"

nūjè sryxũ sa klāxù
very salty and dirty
"very salty and dirty"

xō nūjè sryxũ sa cxõ froplí
water very salty and rock jagged
"the very salty water and jagged rocks"

The word *mã*, or "but," has conjunctive character but also the connotation of contrast. It does, however, connect words and phrases the same way as *co* and *sa* do:

īlō mã fò naro
old but not boring
"old but not boring"

rȳfrà psyǐ mã plāpỳro piō
sometimes remember but usually forget
"sometimes remember but usually forget"

lȳrū mã nùca rupi
sheep but also cow
"the sheep but also the cows"

Next, we should consider examples of the word pe, or "both," which as we saw has conjunctive character on the logical level but is a determiner on the syntactic level. It is important that we think about it closely in this context, even though we cannot say that it connects phrases, since it will often be used alongside co, which does. We will see just a few examples below:

pe mé co kò
both top and bottom
"both the top and the bottom"

pe pòmá kfũ krỹ co frà clā
both my hand left and arm right
"both my left hand and right arm"

pe xé sa prī
both red and blue
"both red and blue (and other colors)"

The last two logical connectives to be mentioned work, syntactically speaking, along lines we have already seen. The disjunction li, or "or," works the same as the words co and sa, in that it can connect multiple syntactic categories, be them adjectives, nouns, verbs, or phrasal varieties of the same:

pru li xàmo
sword or knife
"a sword or knife"

kĩ psyxũ li cxóxù
tool wooden or metal
"a wooden or metal tool"

frucoxúrō li psèpó frucoxúrō
actively or almost actively
"actively or almost actively"

The word may also be used alongside *lú*, or "either," and works identically to the combination of *pe* with a conjunction *co* or *sa*:

lú rā li xā
either hot or cold
"either hot or cold"

lú fráki li krakríprà
either mechanic or technician
"either the mechanic or the technician"

xi lú kùclu frúxù li plucla
near either door front or exit
"near either the front door or the exit"

3.2: SENTENCES

After combining phrases into larger and larger structures, we arrive at what traditional grammarians would call a sentence. Linguistically, we might equate the sentence to a complementizer phrase. But considering only the appearances of language as they are presented to us, a Katalopsi sentence is often complete as a mere grammatical phrase, though it may indeed be embedded in a complementizer phrase and be a sentence. We will see several examples of each as well as still other varieties of sentences in the coming sections.

3.2.1: GENERAL STRUCTURE

In describing the syntax of Katalopsi sentences, a good place to begin is with the *general structure*, or what might be called the *canonical* structure, of the sentence. This is in a sense the underlying word order of Katalopsi sentences, the common order against which variations are evaluated. Later in the chapter, we will see how various processes alter the word order to express nuances of meaning. After that, we will consider ways sentences combine into larger utterances.

The canonical structure of the sentence could be characterized in the following way:

{Auxiliaries} {Predicate} {Disambiguator} {Arguments}

That is, generally speaking, auxiliaries occur at the beginning of the sentence, followed by the predicate, then the disambiguator, and finally the arguments. The following sentences show each of these sections in action:

Ḡ m̀ pai̱ m̃ rỳ junẽ plō liniprã.
would like play D some music we pianist
"The pianist would like to play us some music."

Ź ñ r̀ e̱kuó z̃ cámà cxysũ plíkà.
PAST begin PROG rethink D his decision manager
"The manager was beginning to rethink his decision.

With the exception of the predicate, each of these four subsections of the sentence could be empty, depending on the meaning you are communicating.

Recall from §2.1.1 that the absence of one type of auxiliary can also communicate meaning. For example, by neglecting to speak an overt tense auxiliary, you are communicating the present tense; by not speaking an overt aspect auxiliary, you are saying that something happened at a single point in time; and so on. It is possible therefore to have a sentence that begins with a predicate simply because you are using these phonologically empty words in the auxiliary position:

Meî z̃ cxẽ lō plōmà ràki̱.
want D table new our waiter
"Our waiter wants a new table."

Kliȳ m̀ sréxō pòmá fòny̱.

study D math my son
"My son studies math."

Alternatively, you may be using multiple auxiliaries, and if so, these words take on a particular internal order. Remember the acronym TAM from chapter 2, standing for "tense, aspect, and mood." Katalopsi auxiliaries follow this order when they organize internally, meaning auxiliaries marking the tense are spoken before those marking the aspect, and the latter are in turn spoken before those marking the mood:

Ź r̀ m̄ nuȳ m̀ rỳ rísē pò.
PAST PROG try find D some work I
"I was trying to find some work."

See how in this example, the past auxiliary ź precedes the marker for progressive aspect r̀, which is itself followed by m̄, the modal auxiliary meaning "try."

Now that we have a handle on the auxiliary position of the canonical sentence, we should move on to the next position over. The situation of the predicate is more complex and bears further analysis in §3.2.2. In §3.2.3, we will examine the problem of disambiguators and arguments in tandem, as the complexities of these sentential subsections are closely linked.

3.2.2: MORE ON PREDICATES

In order to understand the predicate, it is first and foremost important to understand that it can be a verb, an adjective, a noun, or a preposition. The most familiar situation to speakers of English is likely the verbal predicate, of which we have already seen several examples. The other situations are more conceptually difficult because, in the syntax of Katalopsi, there is no copular *be*. Consider the following English sentences, paying special attention to what appears to the right of the *be*-wordform:

Your food is on the table.
Maria was a good friend.
Her book will be very interesting.

In these sentences, the various forms of *be* are really ways of linking the subject to a quality on the right as well as a place to mark the tense. Some languages, including natural languages like Arabic and Hungarian, do not always require such a wordform to be present. Katalopsi is in this respect much the same, as instead of a copula appearing in the predicate position, the adjective, noun, or preposition appears:

Mu̧ cxẽ Í kùmá psá.
on table D your food
"Your food is on the table."

Ź jí cy̱ Í Maria.
PAST friend good D Maria
"Maria was a good friend."

M̃ nūjè sýcòxú Í cìmá sȳ.
will very interesting D her book
"Her book will be very interesting."

As you can see, whether it's a prepositional phrase, a noun phrase, or an adjectival phrase, the predicate appears between the auxiliaries and the disambiguator, with a copular *be* entirely absent.

Of course we know from §3.1 that each of these predicate types—whether prepositions, nouns, or adjectives—can form large phrases. Theoretically speaking, there is no limit on the size of the phrase, but pragmatically, we know the longer the phrase, the less likely it is to occur, simply because it becomes difficult to say and difficult to comprehend. It will be useful therefore to see some examples of such larger phrases appearing in the predicate position.

Mu̧ cxẽ co krínè xénȳ Í ru̧.
on table and under sofa D cat
"The cats are on the table and under the sofa."

Sákù prō co nūjè klyxũ Í Maria.
creator smart and very skilled D Maria
"Maria is a smart and very skilled creator."

M̃ nūjè sýcòxú kápē sikŏ kfýlà Í cìmá sȳ.
will very interesting to reader frequent D her book
"Her book will be very interesting to frequent readers."

3.2.3: MORE ON DISAMBIGUATORS AND ARGUMENTS

After the predicate position is the slot for the disambiguator. Like with auxiliaries, this slot is not always filled, but in the vast majority of cases, it will be. The disambiguator could be regarded as part of the predicate as its first function is to elaborate on the event or state described by the predicate. Its second function, however, is to enumerate and identify the participants in the event or state that the speaker intends to name, so in this way, it could be regarded as a syntactic entity in its own right. Since the disambiguator also speaks to the interpretation of the associated participants, or arguments, it is usually necessary as a semantic unit as well.

We will in this section look first at disambiguators as syntactic units and specifically how they establish predicative *valency*. After that, we will preview disambiguators as a semantic topic. This will be fully fleshed out in chapter 4, as the nuance of disambiguator selection and usage is essential to a thorough understanding of meaning in Katalopsi.

3.2.3.1: Valency and Number of Arguments

Recall from §2.1.2 the first function of the disambiguator, namely to specify the number of arguments—or grammatically required participants in an action, state, or event—that will be mentioned in the sentence. In a subsection thereof, §2.1.2.1, we discussed patterns of valency in the disambiguators. Some verbs are able to vary in this respect, which means that selection of the correct disambiguators will be obligatory for forming grammatical sentences.

With respect to valency specification, disambiguators present four possible circumstances: nonvalency (or zero arguments), monovalency (or one argument), divalency (or two arguments), and trivalency (or three arguments). Nonvalency is possible with a small handful of verbs, typically those related to weather, for which no argument is possible on the semantic level. This is represented by a lack of a disambiguator, as in the following examples:

Ř niỳ.
PROG storm
"It's storming."

Ź ruē fecẽ.
PAST thunder last night
"It thundered last night."

Note how adjunctive material may directly follow the verb due to the lack of either disambiguators or arguments. One way to think of this is that there is no grammatical phrase but rather just a verb phrase.

In the following sentences, we see examples of monovalency, i.e. where the disambiguator points to a single argument to follow:

M̀ siõ m̀ cì.
like to read D she
"She likes to read."

Ẑ pia̱ Í kru̱.
RECENT sink D boat
"The boat just sunk."

The next couple sentences illustrate divalency, the presence of a divalent disambiguator and two arguments:

Ź prenuõ ǹ cìmá nàmó sȳ.
PAST broaden D her imagination book
"The book broadened her imagination."

Ź nuȳ v́ my̱ ipamũ lisỹ.
PAST find D means unknown object
"The object was found by unknown means."

And finally, the following examples demonstrate trivalency, where three arguments follow a disambiguator which has in the antecedent material enumerated them:

M̃ kaĩ j̃ līmī clōrā pò.
will fasten D saddle horse I
"I'll fasten the saddle to the horse."

Ř praí m̃ kòcǫ clạ plō.
PROG solve D puzzle they we
"We're solving a puzzle for them."

We should next talk about a few situations where valency may vary on the same predicate. The set of possible circumstances is in this respect much more plentiful than for verbs that only ever have one valency. Some verbs exhibit both mono- and divalency; others di- and trivalency; and still others mono-, di-, *and* trivalency. In fact, as we will see in the next section, many verbs that are able to vary in valency may also use multiple disambiguators that have the same valency but distinct interpretation of arguments. For now, let us see examples of verbs that vary in their valency.

To start with, we will look at verbs that can be both monovalent or divalent. Consider the verb *siõ*, or "read" in English, which works much the same in both languages in terms of their possible arguments. One could talk about habitually engaging in the behavior, speaking generically and not about what the agent may be reading:

R̄ siõ m̀ Sean nūjè.
tend to read D Sean very
"Sean tends to read a lot."

You can also specify the object of the reading, however, and this requires a change of disambiguator reflecting the divalency of the verb:

R̄ siõ m̀ fráfȳ Sean nūjè.
tend to read D magazine Sean very
"Sean tends to read magazines a lot."

With this change, we know to expect two arguments to follow rather than just one. The following examples show the use of different disambiguators while still exhibiting a change in valency from one to two:

Ź xuè Í pòmá saclĩ.
PAST cure D my illness
"My illness was cured."

Ź xuè ǹ pòmá saclĩ srẹ jèsi.
PAST cure D my illness a lot of rest
"A lot of rest cured my illness."

Ṽ fànuọ ź srỹsè.
have calm D audience
"The audience has calmed down."

Ṽ fànuọ z̃ xesỹ srỹsè.
have calm D performance audience
"The performance has calmed the audience down."

Next, let us consider a few verbs that can be both divalent and trivalent, having either two or three arguments. The word *niè*, or "send," is a good example. It is typical in English to mention the person who did the sending and the thing that was sent, which in Katalopsi is a divalent construction:

Ź niè m̀ cámà xōsī cámà cõ pòsrẹ.
PAST send D his belonging his boss previous
"His old boss sent his belongings."

When you want to mention the recipient of the thing that is sent, a trivalent construction is an option:

Ź niè ñ cámà xōsī plō cámà cõ pòsrẹ.
PAST send D his belonging we his boss previous
"His old boss sent us his belongings."

The following sentences include other verbs and disambiguators marking the di-/trivalent variation:

M̃ kliâ ǹ srẹ fè sĩ sy̱.
will cost D a lot of money this house
"This house will cost a lot of money."

M̃ kliâ Ĩ srẹ fè lạ sĩ sy̱.
will cost D a lot of money they this house
"This house will cost them a lot of money."

Ř miâ ř klạ u nàjọcạ Noam.
PROG count D box of wine Noam
"Noam is counting the boxes of wine."

Ř miâ ĵ klạ u nàjọcạ kōlà Noam.
PROG count D box of wine cellar Noam
"Noam is in the cellar counting the boxes of wine."

Some verbs are able to have one, two, *or* three arguments, and their disambiguators vary along this dimension. In fact, some of the verbs we have already seen fall into this category. The word *siõ* has the option of including a beneficiary or recipient argument and becoming trivalent, as in the following:

Siõ m̃ fráfȳ mịrá ju̱ Sean.
read D magazine father old Sean
"Sean reads magazines to his elderly father."

The word *paị*, or "play," is used strictly to describe the activity of playing musical instruments. It is capable of being used alongside one-, two-, and three-argument grammatical phrases. Here are examples of each:

Ź paị ń linĩ sópūrō.
PAST play D piano beautifully
"The piano was played beautifully."

Ź pai̯ v̀ linĩ Sarah sópūrō.
PAST play D piano Sarah beautifully
"Sarah played the piano beautifully."

Ź pai̯ ṽ plèso̜ linĩ Sarah.
PAST play D song piano Sarah
"Sarah played the song on piano."

3.2.3.2: Interpretation of Arguments

In the previous section, we discussed how the disambiguator specifies the number of arguments, and how various verbs fall into classes based on the number of arguments, and therefore which disambiguators, that they may use. In this section, we will be concentrating on the second function of the disambiguator, which is to establish the semantic roles of the arguments that saturate the grammatical phrase.

The first important lesson in this respect relates to how flexible or inflexible the disambiguators are in their duties. When it comes to establishing the number of arguments to be expected, there is no room for misunderstanding: Disambiguators are divided with hard lines as to how many arguments they mark for. With respect to their contribution to meaning, however, they are more loose.

When it comes to the interpretation of arguments and its interaction with syntax, however, an important classification of predicates must be established. When the predicate is a verb, any number of different disambiguators may be used, and the exact set ultimately depends on the verb itself. However, when the predicate is a noun, adjective, or prepositional phrase, only two disambiguators are possible: í and ź. Refer to §3.2.2 for an example of a noun, adjective, and prepositional phrase in the predicate position.

This latter category implies a copular construction, where a single argument is said to have a quality or qualities or belong to a group of entities with a quality or qualities. For this reason, this classification of predicate is always monovalent. You may recall from §2.1.2 that í is monovalent, and the single associated argument bears the *theme* semantic role. However, in one of these copular constructions, usually translated with the word *be*, it is really only used to say that the argument *has a state*, not that it is undergoing a *change of state*. This is a notable difference in the usage of *í*, which with a verb always implies a change of state.

The reason *ź* is possible for copular expressions is that some entities that have a quality or are in a particular state are entities that are capable of experiencing. While *í* can basically be used for any copular construction with any argument, *ź* can only be used when the argument is experiencing the state or quality on a psychological level. This will mean the argument is at least animate but possibly even rational, depending on the context.

With that out of the way, we can turn to the more complex class of predicates, the verbs. While nominal, adjectival, and prepositional predicates can only have a one of the two aforementioned disambiguators, verbal predicates run the gamut and are highly dependent on the underlying meaning of the verb. Much of what could be said in this respect would be repeating facts about the patterns of role assignment from §2.1.2.2, so we encourage a review of this section before proceeding.

The role assignment that disambiguators facilitate becomes a particularly syntactic phenomenon when discussing the distribution of those roles in di- and trivalent constructions. To understand what this means, you should be familiar with the concept of subject-verb-object positioning in English and language typology in general. Researchers in language typology seek, among other things, to compare languages on the basis of the order of these three elements. It has been found that the most common order is SOV, or subject first, object second, and verb third, with 45% of languages surveyed presenting this canonical order. English has SVO order, making it one of 42% of languages in this second-most common category. Katalopsi could be said to have VOS order, with the verb first, the object second, and the subject third, like 3% of the natural languages included in this research.

In a certain sense, this somewhat outdated analysis of word order requires an understanding of the terms *subject* and *object* on the basis of role assignment. The subject is that which tends to be assigned the agent, cause, or experiencer roles; the direct object is that which is assigned theme, patient, or stimulus roles; and the indirect object is that which is assigned the recipient or beneficiary roles. Clearly the order of such arguments cannot be determined from monovalent constructions, so we will work our way up from non- and monovalent verbs to trivalent verbs and see what conclusions we can draw about the distribution of role assignment. Katalopsi also allows for unmarked locative and instrumental arguments, which impairs the efficacy of this approach, but we will set this aside temporarily.

We know first of all that some verbs do not require a disambiguator because no argument is necessary or possible. Such nonvalent verbs do not have an overt disambiguator, so we can move on to monovalency. Only five disambiguators are monovalent, one of which assigns one of two possible semantic roles depending on context, for a total of six semantic roles. Three of these six are the agent, cause, and experiencer roles, hinting at the position of the subject, but the other three are the theme, patient, and instrument, so it's difficult to come to any conclusions here. However, we will use these six semantic roles as the basis of our consideration of the divalent and subsequently trivalent constructions.

With the introduction of divalency, it becomes possible to start making inferences about the canonical order of Katalopsi arguments, as it is then possible to have both a subject and an object in the same construction. There are twelve divalent disambiguators, and six of those assign an agent role. More importantly, each of those six have the agent role on the right, i.e. in the second argument position, while the left—or first—argument may variably be assigned the theme, patient, location, instrument, recipient, or beneficiary role. The location and instrument roles are treated somewhat extraordinarily in Katalopsi syntax, but the other four roles correspond to our expectations about direct and indirect objects. These six role assignment distributions therefore support a tentative VOS analysis of Katalopsi.

The remaining six divalent disambiguators provide their support, although not as strongly. One assigns either the cause or instrument role to the right argument and theme role to the left argument. Two other disambiguators assign the experiencer role to the right argument and the theme or stimulus role, respectively, to the left. These three distributions seem to weakly support the VOS analysis, but for the three disambiguators that remain, it is unclear whether a conclusion can be drawn.

The three remaining divalent disambiguators each assign a theme role, but not in a consistent way. Two assign theme to the right argument, and the third assigns theme to the left. The paired arguments are variably assigned locative, instrument, and beneficiary roles. With respect to these three disambiguators, what we're left with at best is an image of constructions containing a direct and indirect object but no subject. In this sense, however, it is worthwhile to mention English passive constructions, which permit speakers of English the option of leaving the canonical subject out and instead mentioning only the direct object, the indirect object, or both, from the original or underlying active sentence. Such passive constructions do not change our understanding of English as an SVO language, and so it may be justified to disregard this handful of disambiguators which do not contain an argument we'd typically call the subject.

Six disambiguators are trivalent and are to a great degree homogeneous with respect to their assignment of roles. Five assign the agent role to the right argument, while the sixth assigns either the cause or the instrument role to the same. This means that every trivalent grammatical phrase has what we would typically call a subject. What's more is that the left argument is always assigned either the theme or the patient role, in other words roles typical of the direct object. Three assign strictly the theme role to this left argument, while the remaining three may assign either the theme or the patient role depending on context. Finally, the middle argument is highly variable, in the case of three disambiguators assigning common indirect object roles, i.e. the beneficiary, the recipient, or optionally the beneficiary or recipient. For the other three, the middle argument is assigned the stimulus, locative, or instrument roles.

At this point, we can say with certainty that Katalopsi has a VOS order to its syntax. Furthermore, the indirect object will come between the direct object and the subject when possible. The argument to which the stimulus, locative, and instrument roles are assigned is in most cases treated the same as the indirect object, although expectations about the behavior of the indirect object do sometimes fail for these roles.

In chapter 7, you will see that verb entries include a list of the disambiguators most likely to be used with the verb or that may be used in a somewhat eccentric way with that verb. It should be assumed that other disambiguators are possible, but using them will in any case require a confident understanding of semantic roles and the way disambiguators are used to communicate them. Therefore, for a more in-depth analysis of the meaning of disambiguators, see §4.1.

3.2.4: SENTENTIAL VS. PHRASAL NEGATION

The position of the negation particle can sometimes be a difficult topic for syntax. In some languages, negation is incorporated into morphology on the verb; in others, it is a free morpheme with a strict position in the syntax. Katalopsi leans toward the latter phenomenon with respect to the negation of the entire sentence but is more loose with respect to the negation of individual phrases.

When it is the complete sentence which is the target of negation, i.e. the difference between the sentences *I saw a swan today* and *I didn't see a swan today*, the Katalopsi negation particle *fò* appears at the end of the sentence, after the grammatical phrase. In this sense, it is treated much like other sentence-modifying adverbs, which follow the grammatical phrase or appear at the beginning of the sentence. However, the negation particle appears after any and all adjuncts, or to put it another way, adjuncts intervene between the grammatical phrase and the negation particle:

Ź niè m̀ srìsá pò ó lāfràfra fò.
PAST send D application I to university not
"I didn't send the application to the university."

Ź piō ž̃ nècu cì clȳjō fò.
PAST forget D something she today not
"She didn't forget anything today."

As you can see, whether the adjunct is a prepositional phrase or an adverb, the negation particle will still come after them.

It is also possible for negation to apply to individual phrases, rather than the complete sentence. Under these circumstances, the particle appears before the negated element. Often this syntax is indicative of *metalinguistic* phenomena, i.e. phenomena in which the acceptability of some word or phrase is evaluated rather than the truth of the same.

Therefore, comparison structures not infrequently co-occur with the metalinguistic negation particle as the words or phrases are compared to one another. The compared elements may be arguments or adjuncts and one of a variety of syntactic categories:

Ź riǒ z̃ fò m̤il̤u fẽ fāsā pò.
PAST see D not lizard but snake I
"I saw not a lizard but a snake."

Ź meȳ j̃ kàrá c̤if̤u fóxỳ fò c̤ixú.
PAST run D past tree animal not furry
"A non-furry animal ran past the trees."

Fò m̤u fẽ mé sȳkrēpī Í sȳ.
not on but on top of bookshelf D book
"The book isn't on but rather on top of the bookshelf."

Ź kfuê m̀ mìklá cá fò féjō.
PAST finish D task he not yesterday
"It's not yesterday that he finished the ask."

Ź fò pluê fẽ sriò m̀ lȳ psũ.
PAST not drop but throw D ball child
"The child didn't drop the ball but threw it."

These examples show how when the negation particle targets a single word or phrase, the category of the target is more or less irrelevant. We also know from these examples that when this particular type of negation is used, *fò* may appear in a large variety of places in the sentence. It is only when the complete sentence is negated is the particle sure to be found at the end.

In the coming sections, we will see more complex sentences which will reveal more facts about the position of the sentential negation particle. In considering the examples in this section, we can conclude superficially that the particle occurs at the end of the sentence, but more complex sentences will illuminate the simplicity of this description and point to more nuanced syntactic facts.

3.2.5: SENTENTIAL ADJUNCTION

In §3.1.3.3, we introduced the concept of sentential adjunction, in which an element—usually an adverbial or prepositional phrase—is linked to the sentence as a whole to further modify it. In that section, we looked primarily at how such elements may be pronominalized or otherwise replaced by another word, essentially a reflection of the syntactic facts of phrases. Here, however, we are concerned with the implications of the syntax of the complete sentence when such adjunction occurs. For this reason, it is important to keep fresh in mind the lessons of the previous section on sentential negation, in which we learned, generally speaking, that negation of the complete sentence is possible with the use of the negation particle at the end of the sentence.

As we have said, sentential adjuncts often surface between the grammatical phrase and the negation particle if they are used in the sentence at all. However, as we will see in the coming sections, various elements are able to occur elsewhere in the sentence, even in such a way that they seem to *move* from their original positions. This is also true for the adjuncts provided a few distinct syntactic facts. For now, see the following sentences which demonstrate the possible positions of such adjuncts, starting with single-word cases:

Kliõ z̃ lisỹ jýmù rókū plāpỳrǫ fò.
notice D object hidden player usually not
"The players don't notice hidden objects usually."

Sýcòxúrō kliõ z̃ lisỹ jýmù rókū fò.
interestingly notice D object hidden player not
"Interestingly, the players don't notice hidden objects."

These sentences show adverbial adjuncts in their two most common positions: (1) the typical, post–grammatical phrase, pre–negation particle position and (2) the discourse position at the front of the sentence.

Prepositional phrases are an interesting topic for adjuncts as they present the possibility of mentioning event participants in a form other than an argument in the grammatical phrase. These may be roles that cannot be assigned by a disambiguator, like the concomitant and its inverse, or ones that can be assigned by a disambiguator but that the speaker chooses to express with adjuncts:

Xoũ m̀ klujũ rò pò plu̧ pòmá crì.
lift D furniture heavy I for my wife
"I lift the heavy furniture for my wife."

Ź siõ m̀ sȳ Carl prypé̱ Alice.
PAST read D book Carl with Alice
"Carl read the book with Alice."

Such prepositional adjuncts can also appear at the front of the sentence for reasons we will explore in the coming sections on methods of varying the general structure of the sentence:

Plu̧ pòmá crì xoũ m̀ klujũ rò pò.
for my wife lift D furniture heavy I
"For my wife, I lift the heavy furniture."

Prypé̱ Alice ź siõ m̀ sȳ Carl.
with Alice PAST read D book Carl
"With Alice, Carl read the book."

3.2.6: VARIATION ON THE GENERAL STRUCTURE

In this section, we will look at several challenging syntactic phenomena frequently raised in grammar books. Some of these have a noteworthy effect on Katalopsi's canonical word order. Others are a problem for many natural languages but are in Katalopsi quite simple.

3.2.6.1: Questioning

In English, question formation often results in a variation of word order. The declaratory statement *You are looking for a house* undergoes such a change when a yes-or-no question is formed from it:

Are you looking for a house?

Specifically, the subject and auxiliary change places. Similarly, various interrogative pronouns—or question words—can be introduced at the beginning of the sentence, standing in for former arguments and requiring further changes to word order:

What are you looking for?
Who is looking for a house?
Why are you looking for a house?
Where are you looking for a house?

Depending on the type of question and the information that is sought, changes to the word order in Katalopsi may be necessary. In the case of the yes-or-no question, remember that in §2.1.1.3.4, we introduced the idea that a question could be expressed using an auxiliary. This is the word *v̀*, and if used without any interrogative pronouns, a yes-or-no question is the result. In the examples that follow, note the use of "Q" to mark the question auxiliary:

V̀ fiè m̀ sy̱ kù?
Q look for D house you
"Are you looking for a house?"

V̀ paũ z̃ pòmá fòlo̱ kù mùrý?
Q know D my brother you already
"Do you already know my brother?"

Notice that these questions do not require a change of word order. They only involve usage of the question auxiliary.

For the open-ended questions using interrogative pronouns, the situation is rather different. For the pronouns *fō* ("who"), *fù* ("what"), *fã* ("which"), and *fōmà* ("whose"), which always replace either an argument or a portion of an argument, there is an optionality that may or may not affect the structure of the sentence. The first option is to use the question auxiliary, *v̀*, in which case the question word remains *in situ*, or in the location of the word or set of words it is replacing:

V̀ fiè m̀ sy fō?
Q look for D house who
"Who is looking for a house?"

V̀ fiè m̀ fù kù?
Q look for D what you
"What are you looking for?"

V̀ rei z̃ fã sy kù?
Q like D which house you
"Which house do you like?"

V̀ feǐ z̃ fōmà sy kù?
Q prefer D whose house you
"Whose house do you prefer?"

The second option is to omit the auxiliary and simply move the interrogative pronoun to the beginning of the sentence, ahead of all potential auxiliaries. While the question auxiliary is not necessary for this option, you do need to insert the trace pronoun where the question word originates. We will mark the trace in the gloss with "TR."

Fō fiè m̀ sy cu?
who look for D house TR
"Who is looking for a house?"

Fù fiè m̀ cu kù?
what look for D TR you
"What are you looking for?"

Fã sy rei z̃ cu kù?
which house like D TR you
"Which house do you like?"

Fōmà sy feǐ z̃ cu kù?
whose house prefer D TR you
"Whose house do you prefer?"

Whether you use the first or the second option, it is important that you use both respective elements necessary for each form in order for the sentence to be grammatical. This also aids in unambiguous communication.

As a final point on these four interrogatives, you should notice how words like *fã*, or "which," and *fōmà*, or "whose," bring the entire noun phrase with them when they move to the front. That is, they bring along the modified word *sy*. This is because *fã* and *fōmà* may act as interrogative determiners, as they do in the above examples, or as interrogative pronouns, replacing the entire noun phrase. In the following sentences—variations of the two we just saw—the entire noun phrase has been replaced by the interrogative pronoun.

V̀ reị ž̌ fã kù?
Q like D which you
"Which do you like?"

Fã reị ž̌ cu kù?
which like D TR you
"Which do you like?"

V̀ feǐ ž̌ fōmà kù?
Q prefer D whose you
"Whose do you prefer?"

Fōmà feǐ ž̌ cu kù?
whose prefer D TR you
"Whose do you prefer?"

The pronoun *rạpsẹ*, meaning "how many," is similar to *fã* and *fōmà* in that it can stand in for a whole argument or as the determiner portion of an argument. Though it acts the same, it is useful to see several examples. First we will show a contextualizing sentence, then a pair of sentences replacing all or part of an argument, and then a second pair using the alternative question structure.

L̄ peú m̀ rỳ lákà cxóxù sẹpé.

need buy D some stool metal church
"The church needs to buy some metal stools."

V̀ Ī peú m̀ ra̠pse̠ lákà la̠?
Q need buy D how many stool they
"How many stools do they need to buy?"

V̀ Ī peú m̀ ra̠pse̠ la̠?
Q need buy D how many they
"How many do they need to buy?"

Note in these sentences how *ra̠pse̠* may occur as an interrogative determiner, replacing only part of the original argument, "rỳ lákà cxóxù," or as an interrogative pronoun, replacing the entire noun phrase. The following pair shows the same two questions but with the movement strategy for question formation:

Ra̠pse̠ lákà Ī peú m̀ cu la̠?
how many stool need buy D TR they
"How many stools do they need to buy?"

Ra̠pse̠ Ī peú m̀ cu la̠?
how many need buy D TR they
"How many do they need to buy?"

The interrogative pronouns *jȳ* ("how"), *já* ("why"), and *rù* ("when") never stand in for an argument, and as a result, the respective questions can only be expressed by placing them at the beginning of the sentence, ahead of any and all auxiliaries. Because they are not replacing an argument later in the sentence, the trace pronoun is not required:

Jȳ ż nuȳ m̀ sy̠ nỳ pla̠mó cá?
how PAST find D house so perfect he
"How did he find so perfect a house?"

Já fiè m̀ sy̠ lō kù?
why look for D house new you

"Why are you looking for a new house?"

Rù ź peú m̀ kùmá sy̱ kù?
when PAST buy D your house you
"When did you buy your house?"

The pronoun *fèja* also never stands in for an argument, but it is useful to discuss it separately to distinguish its meaning from *fû*, or "what," which may be a point of confusion for native English speakers. In English, *fèja* translates as "what... like," as in the sentence *What was the music like*? It's a way of generically asking for a description of something, of its characteristics. And although English uses the word *what* in both of them, the pronouns are distinct in Katalopsi. Several examples of the pronoun in use follow. Note that the *v̀*-form question is not possible here because an argument is not being pronominalized, just like the three previously discussed adjunctive pronouns.

Fèja̱ Í junẽ?
what like D music
"What is the music like?"

Ź fèja̱ Í jẽ ro̱xo̱ xesỹ?
PAST what like D weather during performance
"What was the weather like during the performance?"

M̃ fèja̱ Í psá?
will what like D food
"What will the food be like?"

As you can see in these examples, the word *fèja* effectively takes the place of the predicate in the sentence, as it appears between the auxiliary and the disambiguator when both are present. It only resembles other interrogatives, which may or necessarily do appear at the beginning of the sentence, when no auxiliary is used.

Finally, the interrogative pronoun *ri̱* ("where") may stand in for an argument or may be added later. How to deal with this grammatically depends partially on context as you may have to actually alter the disambiguator in order to make the question work. Recall from §3.2.3 how some disambiguators can be used to mark the presence of locative arguments. If you reformulate such a sentence using the same disambiguator, then *ri* behaves essentially the same as *fõ, fû,* and *fã* above, where you may optionally (a) leave the question word *in situ* and put the *v̂* auxiliary at the beginning or (b) move the question word to the beginning, leaving a trace pronoun in its place, and omit *v̂*:

Ź luǫ j̃ pòmá mạsrá cìcxụ pò.
PAST leave D my backpack library I
"I left my backpack in the library."

V̀ ź luǫ j̃ kùmá mạsrá rị kù?
Q PAST leave D your backpack where you
"Where did you leave your backpack?"

Rị ź luǫ j̃ kùmá mạsrá cu kù?
where PAST leave D your backpack TR you
"Where did you leave your backpack?"

On the other hand, if your conversation partner does not use such a disambiguator to specify location, you may need to introduce a new disambiguator to create a grammatical sentence that requests this information:

Ĺ juý m̀ sỹ klẹ pò.
need return D that movie I
"I need to return that movie."

V̀ ĺ juý j̃ lá rị kù?
Q need return D it where you
"Where do you need to return it?"

Rị ĺ juý j̃ lá cu kù?
where need to return D it TR you
"Where do you need to return it?"

Notice that in the contextualizing sentence, the speaker uses the disambiguator m̀, which marks for two arguments, the first a theme and the second an agent. The rejoining question seeks to find *where* the movie should be returned, calling for a locative disambiguator, j̃, changing both the valency and role assignment pattern of the verb.

This is not a necessary grammatical step, however, but rather one that is available due to the presence of locative disambiguators in the language. Locative expressions can also be joined to the sentence as adjuncts, i.e. in practice as an adverb or prepositional phrase. This possibility is generally reserved for prepositional phrases that serve to clarify the exact locative relationship. In the following examples you will see r̠i being used in prepositional phrases with both the *in situ* and the movement strategies applied:

Ź nuȳ m̀ lāsū sópū pò mē sy̠.
PAST find D painting beautiful I for house
"I found a beautiful painting for the house."

V̀ ź nuȳ m̀ lāsū kù cú r̠i?
Q PAST find D painting you at where
"Where'd you find the painting at?"

Cú r̠i ź nuȳ m̀ lāsū kù?
at where PAST find D painting you
"Where'd you find the painting at?"

It is important to note that in this formulation of the response, the locative expression is not found within the grammatical phrase, making it an adjunct. The consequence of this is that when the interrogative is fronted, the entire prepositional phrase comes along, and no trace pronoun is left behind. However, as we've already seen, it is possible to use a preposition to further clarify a locative argument when a locative disambiguator is used. In this specific context, in which the locative expression appears within the grammatical phrase, the entire prepositional phrase may move or may remain in place, but in both cases, the trace pronoun must be used. Observe both the disambiguator and the change in the order of the participants in the following two examples:

Ri̱ ź nuȳ ȷ̃ lāsū cú cu kù?
where PAST find D painting at TR you
"Where'd you find the painting at?"

Cú ri̱ ź nuȳ ȷ̃ lāsū cu kù?
at where D find D painting TR you
"Where'd you find the painting at?"

As the final topic for this section, we should discuss *multiple questioning*, or the use of multiple interrogatives in the same sentence. This is reflected in English sentences such as *Who bought what?* Both strategies for question formation are still available for multiple questioning, except that for the movement strategy, only one interrogative moves to the beginning of the sentence. And because Katalopsi uses disambiguators and phonologically heavy trace pronouns, an additional layer of optionality is introduced in that you may move any interrogative pronoun to the front while expressing the same underlying meaning. In the following three examples, you will see all three methods of forming a question from a sentence with two interrogative pronouns:

V̇ peú m̀ fù fō?
Q buy D what who
"Who's buying what?"

Fō peú m̀ fù cu?
who buy D what TR
"Who's buying what?"

Fù peú m̀ cu fō?
what buy D TR who
"Who's buying what?"

Of course, it is also possible to have three or more pronouns, but as you add more interrogatives, the necessary complexity of the response and therefore the impairment of your interlocutor's ability to respond becomes greater. Even still, see the following four examples which exemplify the four methods of forming a question from a sentence with three interrogatives:

V̀ caũ j̃ fù ri̱ fõ?
Q bring D what where who
"Who's bringing what where?"

Fõ caũ j̃ fù ri̱ cu?
who bring D what where TR
"Who's bringing what where?"

Ri̱ caũ j̃ fù cu fõ?
where bring D what TR who
"Who's bringing what where?"

Fù caũ j̃ cu ri̱ fõ?
what bring D TR where who
"Who's bringing what where?"

3.2.6.2: Focusing

One syntactic phenomenon that is relatively uncommon in English—but does occur frequently in languages like German or Mandarin—is that of *focusing*. It is a way of emphasizing some element of a sentence by moving it to the beginning before the locus of auxiliaries. Adverbs and various prepositional phrases can often be voiced in this position to no consequence, but when the relocated element is an argument, this has notable syntactic effects.

Recall that moving an interrogative pronoun to the beginning of the sentence requires leaving the trace pronoun in the original position. Focusing of arguments works the same way. This movement indicates to your conversation partner(s) that special attention should be paid to the focused element. Consider the following example in which the focused element is emphasized:

Cy̱ méclō r̃ caũ ĵ cu xi̱ra̱ kù plý.
good clothing should bring D TR beach you always
"You should always bring good clothing to the beach."

Just like with the movement of interrogative pronouns, the trace pronoun *cu* is left behind, and the disambiguator remains the same to allow for unambiguous interpretation.

This construction is also usefully applied in correcting incorrect information, a sort of metalinguistic usage. Consider the following example complete with context:

Luè ż lá jò klè li̱y n̄ mēplù plīklē.
believe D it I that require D lemon recipe
"I believe the recipe requires lemons."

Là, *rōsì* li̱y n̄ cu lá.
no lime require D TR it
"No, it requires *limes*."

Here, the focused element has been moved to the front of the sentence to demarcate the correct information from the incorrect.

Optionality in other sentence restructuring processes also imports the notion of focusing, one might say, "for free." Consider the previously described multiple questioning syntax, in which multiple interrogatives appear in the same sentence. While the auxiliary strategy for question formation does not involve movement to the front of the sentence, the movement strategy, of course, does. In multiple questioning, this strategy of question formation necessarily communicates in the same dimension of meaning as focusing. That is, because you have the ability to choose which pronoun moves, the chosen pronoun has pragmatic significance, a way of slightly emphasizing that piece of information— or more aptly the request for that piece of information—over the others.

The topic of focusing also arises with respect to the use of auxiliaries when no other element precedes this section of the sentence. Typically, multiple auxiliaries will appear in the TAM order: tense words first, aspect words second, and mood words third. However, you may flout this rule, to emphasize it, for example, again, to correct incorrect information.

Ź m̀ siõ m̀ cì, né?
PAST like read D she yes
"She liked to read, didn't she?"

Là, Í ź siõ m̀ cì.
no hate PAST read D she
"No, she *hated* to read."

3.2.6.3: Commanding

Much like the question marker auxiliary, the command marker offers a lexical solution to a sometimes difficult syntactic problem in natural language. Although English is relatively simple when it comes to forming commands—or *imperatives*—many languages, such as German, have special imperative forms of verbs that are not otherwise used in the language.

In Katalopsi, the verb is proceeded by the command auxiliary, g̀, and then the specific variety of command will simply depend on the disambiguator and subsequent arguments. In English, imperative sentences lack tense or agreement marking and any subject usually appears before the verb, thereby indicating the second person. *Cohortative* or *inclusive* commands will be marked by use of *Let's* or *Let us*. Other command types are not common to English but could be said to exist in Katalopsi. Consider the following English examples:

Be quiet!
Remember my name!
Speak loudly!
Let's eat!
Let's be friends!
Let's go to the store!

Taking the second-person commands first, consider the following Katalopsi translations:

Ġ fȳ!
IMP quiet
"Be quiet!"

Ġ psyǐ ž pòmá kfĩ!
IMP remember D my name
"Remember my name!"

Ġ ploǐ cxirõ.
IMP speak loudly
"Speak loudly!"

Notice that in the first and third examples, no disambiguator is present, as no arguments are mentioned overtly. This state of affairs can only mean that the person to whom you are speaking is the person who should be quiet, speak loudly, or what have you. In the second example, an argument is mentioned, so a disambiguator appears as well. But note that the disambiguator implies there should be two arguments to follow despite the fact that only one occurs. This is because we know the second argument to be the unmentioned object of the command, though like in English it can indeed be spoken overtly:

Ġ psyǐ ž pòmá kfĩ kù!
IMP remember D my name you
"(You) remember my name!"

The important lesson here is that second-person commands like these always have an underlying target, even if it goes unmentioned. So if arguments are mentioned at all, the disambiguator that marks for the object of the command should be used, even if you decide to leave off that argument in realizing the sentence.

The first-person English commands have a more consistent form in Katalopsi in that the object of the command is always overt. Because of this, the cohortative commands will always have a disambiguator. In all other ways, however, these commands are structurally identical to the second-person variety:

Ġ plìè m̄ plō!
IMP eat D we
"Let's eat!"

Ġ jí Í plō!
IMP friend D we
"Let's be friends!"

Ġ mio m̀ klẹ plō!
IMP go D store we
"Let's go to the store!"

In addition to the cohortative (first-person) and imperative (second-person) commands, Katalopsi could be said to have *jussive*, or third-person, commands. It is difficult to satisfactorily translate such sentences—as might occur in Arabic, for example—into English, but in effect, they mean that a third person *should* or *must* do something, and the person voicing the command has the authority to make them do it. Similar to the cohortative, this type of command is realized by always overtly mentioning the third person:

Ġ plụkfá Í cì!
IMP honest D she
"She should be honest!"

Ġ ruǎ m̀ srōfì cá clȳjō.
IMP deliver D message he today
"He must deliver the message today."

In the end, the first-, second-, and third-person commands do not end up looking significantly different in practice. Each use the command auxiliary followed by the verb. Only the second-person commands are distinct in that they have the option of leaving off the disambiguator and therefore any arguments, or alternatively leaving off the object of the command alone.

AUTHORITATIVE GUIDE TO THE KATALOPSI CONSTRUCTED LANGUAGE

3.2.6.4: Topicalization

The notion of *topicalization* is syntactically related to focusing in that it involves the placement of an element at the beginning of the sentence before the auxiliaries. However, it is distinct in that the element placed at the beginning does not replace an element later in the sentence. It is a way of announcing the topic of the sentence, much like the English words *as for* and *regarding*, as in the sentences *As for fruit, my favorite is honeydew* and *Regarding the letter, I think it's time to send a new one.*

Through syntax alone, Katalopsi topicalization is realized, and the use of prepositions is not necessary. Imagine that all you know about a Katalopsi sentence is that a non-auxiliary appears before any and all auxiliaries. There are three possibilities to explain this. If the word is an interrogative pronoun, then you know it is a question or relative clause. If it is something else, then you know to look for the trace pronoun later in the sentence. If the trace pronoun appears, then the purpose of the word at the vanguard is focusing. If the trace pronoun is absent, i.e. no arguments are missing, then topicalization is the intended meaning. Here are a few examples:

Psũ ḡ ǹ saí ż fòny co ūcò pò.
child would like have D son and daughter I
"As far as children are concerned, I'd like to have a son and a daughter."

Féprỳ kuó ż lá pò klè m̃ pliō m̃ pò.
contest think D it I that will win D I
"As for the contest, I think I'm going to win."

Cxù Ī cxié m̃ pǫ u plòkí pipĩ plō.
schedule need change D time of speaker second we
"Regarding the schedule, we need to change the time of the second speaker."

3.2.6.5: Exclamation

An exclamation is an expression of great emotion at some quality or thing. It is often one of elation, surprise, frustration, or anger. In

English, these are expressions like *How exciting!* or *What a surprise!* Syntactically, we may taxonomize two types of exclamation in Katalopsi: those involving an adjective and those involving a noun. See first an example with an adjective:

Jy rỳlilẹ Í!
so exciting D
"How exciting!"

There are a couple important items to digest here. Firstly, the word *jy* is used. Normally, this adverb would simply mean "so" or "very" in English, but in this context, it is much like the word *how*. And even though it is translated a little differently here, it is still an adverb modifying the adjective from the left. The next important item is the use of the disambiguator Í. We know by now that this disambiguator is used alongside predicates to express qualities or states, but we also know that it is monovalent, so it is surprising not to see an argument follow it. In this way, it is not much different from the lack of overt target in second-person commands. That is, the thing which is exciting in this example is obvious from context, like with any such exclamation, and need not be mentioned overtly.

In the example we just saw, the speaker exclaimed at the quality in a way that was, in a manner of speaking, disembodied. That is, the adjective was not modifying anything. It is, however, still possible to react to such a quality even when a noun is modified by the adjectival target, as in the following example:

Klú jy rỳlilẹ Í!
news so exciting D
"Such exciting news!"

It is also possible to translate such a sentence as "How exciting a news story!" This shows that the exclamation is at the adjectival quality and not necessarily the complete noun phrase. In Katalopsi, this is made clear by the consistent use of the word *jy*.

When one *is* reacting to a noun, the word *rỳ* is instead used.

Typically, this word corresponds to the quantifier *some*, but here, the word preceding the noun is perhaps more accurately translated as "what," as in the equivalent English exclamations:

Rỳ rīsā Í!
some answer D
"What an answer!"

Notably, this sentence could also be translated into English as "That's *some* answer!" That is, English also allows the use of the quantifier *some*, albeit with a prominent inflection, to make such exclamations. Also important to observe here is the continued use of the disambiguator *Í*. While the modifier will vary categorically according to the target of exclamation, either an adjectival quality or a nominal thing, the common thread between these two classes of exclamation is that the both seem to be elided sentences, where some information you typically expect is missing. They are predicates followed by a disambiguator but with no argument to complete the grammatical phrase.

It is important for the sake of completion to also show how the modification of such a noun by an adjective may or may not affect the structure of the exclamation. Previously, we saw that reaction to an adjectival quality is not phased even should that adjective be modifying a noun. It is similarly true that a noun need not be affected by the presence of an adjectival modifier in exclamation expressions:

Rỳ jypla cryclũ Í!
some situation complex D
"What a complex situation!"

In this example, the word *rỳ* tells us that the speaker is reacting to the entire noun phrase, the *complex situation*. If the speaker *did* want to react to the complexity, rather than to the situation, we should instead see the following formulation:

Jypla jy cryclũ Í!
situation so complex D
"How complex a situation!"

In other words, it is solely the use of either the adjective-modifying adverb *jy* or the noun-modifying quantifier *rỳ* that tells us the target of exclamation in these more complex noun phrases.

So far, we've seen only present-tense exclamations. While these expressions do share similarities with second-person commands, imperatives seem to have an inherent present-tense nature. This shouldn't be the case for exclamations, which we would predict to be directed toward past or imagined future events at discretion. This is, in fact, the case. Exclamations may be formulated essentially the same as we have seen but with tense auxiliaries in the front:

Ź jy̱ kōxù Í!
PAST so colorful D
"How colorful it was!"

M̃ jy̱ psēpròxú Í!
will so profitable D
"How profitable it will be!"

Ź rỳ crūrȳ rì Í!
PAST some process long D
"What a long process it was!"

M̃ rỳ ri̱nu̱ký Í!
will some miracle D
"What a miracle it will be!"

3.3: OTHER UTTERANCES

Now that we have a concept of phrases and the sentences formed from them, it is important that we discuss the great variety of other utterances that are available to speakers of language.

For one, it doesn't in practice always make sense to respond with a complete sentence. People generally respect what is known as the *maxim of brevity*, which means that if they can express something in fewer words without sacrificing the communicative force of their speech, they should do so. When such utterances are smaller than a sentence, we will call them *simple utterances.*

Complex utterances, on the other hand, are larger than a sentence and often require some sort of connecting element, whether a conjunction or a complementizer. These sentences are often formed in service to the *maxim of quantity,* that one should provide as much information as necessary. Both the simple utterances and complex utterances have syntactic rules that describe the flow of speech.

3.3.1: SIMPLE UTTERANCES

Utterances smaller than the sentence are often so for one of two reasons: (1) They are formalized expressions that communicate a high degree of meaning in few words, or (2) They are shortened versions of longer utterances that are nonetheless comprehensible due to context. We will view both cases in this section.

3.3.1.1: Interjections

Interjections are words which on their very face serve to allow brevity in responses, e.g. to requests for information. There are some which will be quite familiar to speakers of virtually any language, while others are more the stuff of languages like Katalopsi.

Suppose you are asked a yes-or-no question, for example the sentence *Are you leaving soon?* It would not generally be respectful to the maxim of brevity to respond with "I am leaving soon" or "I am not leaving soon" because English has interjections such as *yes* and *no,* standing of course for affirmation of the originating declarative statement or negation of the same, respectively. The Katalopsi words are *né,* for "yes," and *là,* for "no." Other common responses to the question are, arguably, either adverbs or interjections depending on the context. These include words like *maybe,* which in Katalopsi is the word *frá,* and *probably,* or in Katalopsi the word *claklurõ.*

When engaging politeness or respect, phrases like *thank you* ("Clõ ó kù") and *you're welcome* come up, which are also interjectory in nature. There are additionally the various greetings, such as *cyjó,* meaning "hello," *cýfī*, meaning "good morning," *cymẹrí*, meaning "good evening," and so on.

Some interjections are unique to Katalopsi and other languages with evidentiality grammar. We hinted at this in §2.1.1.3.2 on evidential auxiliaries. For example, the auxiliary *z* normally expresses a high degree of confidence in something being the case, but in response to a yes-or-no question, it means something like "Definitely" or "Yes, definitely." This should be contrasted with *né*, which simply expresses a normative degree of confidence in the affirmation of something. The auxiliary *ń*, on the other hand, expresses a low degree of confidence, meaning something like "I doubt it" or "Probably not."

Evidentiality, however, is not the only area where auxiliaries may be used as interjections. A handful of others also play this role, such as *g̣*, the command auxiliary. After a particular command has already been established in context, the auxiliary may be repeated and means something like "Do it." In English, such an expression stated out of the blue would be difficult to comprehend, as it is not clear what should be done, but with the right context, *g̣* could do the job of emphasizing the command that should be followed.

3.3.1.2: Elided Sentences

Interjections tend to be very useful for answering yes-or-no questions briefly, often because affirmation, negation, or degree of belief is all that is necessary to satisfy the interrogator. But if the question is more complex, as in *open* questions, working respectfully within the bounds of the maxim of brevity allows for what is called *elision*. Elision is the process of intentionally deleting part of a sentence because it is understood by the context to be there underlyingly. For example, one may ask the yes-or-no question *Did you go to the store?* And in response, one may say, "I did." Because this is an abbreviation, the full sentence *I did (go to the store)* is only implied. The parenthetical information has been elided because it is obvious to anyone listening to the conversation what the speaker did.

In the English example just described, the verb phrase had been elided, but the subject and auxiliary remained. The elision process may apply to any number of different syntactic features, however, resulting in phrasal responses and incomplete sentences, depending on the target of the process. Open questions, for example, often allow for phrasal responses, as in answering the question *What did you find at the garage sale?* One may respond with a full sentence, e.g. "I found an old guitar at the garage sale," but an elided phrasal response is better. This means responding with just the direct object, "An old guitar."

Katalopsi syntax does have an effect on what is or is not possible in elision, and the results will thereby sometimes differ from English. It is generally possible to respond to open questions, those with an interrogative pronoun, with just the requested information. In the following examples, we will show the elided information in parentheses and gloss the resulting abbreviated response.

> Fù ź piō ž cu kù?
> what PAST forget D TR you
> "What did you forget?"

> (Ź piō ž) pòmá rofrĩ (pò).
> PAST forget D my lunch I
> "My lunch."

> Ri Í lāfràfra?
> where D university
> "Where's the university located?"

> Cú Stockholm (Í lāfràfra).
> in Stockholm D university
> "In Stockholm."

> Fō v luo ĵ lámà nì lèkfu cu?
> who HABIT leave D their key kitchen TR
> "Who's leaving their keys in the kitchen?"

> (V luo ĵ pòmá nì lèkfu) pò.
> HABIT leave D my key kitchen I
> "I am."

In these examples, we see a variety of different parts of the sentence being elided. It is especially important to note in the last example that only the personal pronoun *pò* is required, which is distinct from English for a couple reasons. While one could respond to the English question with just a pronoun, the response must, for reasons of grammatical case, be "Me" and not "I." If you do choose to say "I," it must be followed with "am," as we have glossed above.

In this section, we looked at simple utterances which were the result of applying elision to basic sentences. In §3.3.2.3, we will revisit the topic of elision to understand utterances which are the result of applying elision to *complex* utterances. First, we will need an understanding of the variety of complex utterances available.

3.3.2: MORE COMPLEX UTTERANCES

Sometimes communication requires the use of multiple complete sentences that are connected in some way. These complex utterances may be connected by conjunctions or by complementizers, such as the many logical connectives we saw in chapter 2, or they may be embedded within one another in various ways.

3.3.2.1: Coordinated Clauses

When two sentences are able to stand on their own syntactically, their connection is known as *coordination*. In §2.2.3, we saw several examples of logical connectives which allow for the connection of two independent phrases or sentences. Some of them had *conjunctive* character, like *co*, "and," and *mã*, "but." Others had *disjunctive* character, such as *lú*, "either," and *li*, "or." In this section, we will concentrate on their ability to coordinate complete, independent sentences.

Some of these words also work in tandem with complementizers, which were introduced in §2.2.4. Note that both conjunctions and complementizers are frontmost in the sentence, ahead of both focused and topicalized elements. Other than this fact, however, little new syntax need be introduced here, so instead we will concentrate on exemplifying the words in their possible combinations.

We will start first with examples where only a single word is needed, a conjunction connecting two sentences:

Sópū Í rų, co ǹ xoī ż plè co pĩ pò.
beautiful D cat and want own D ten and two I
"Cats are beautiful, and I want to own twelve."

Niò z̃ nį pò, mã klaí z̃ lą pòmá rýnì.
love D people I but hate D they my sister
"I love people, but my sister hates them."

M̃ Ī juy̌ Í srāsū li nuě m̀ nų lùsǫxú plō.
will need reduce D spending or collect D tax additional we
"Spending will need to be reduced or we'll need to collect more taxes."

M̃ nánuō Í lá, sa m̃ pró-kã-kio̧ Í lá.
will harden D it and will more-resilient-become D it
"It will harden, and it will become more resilient."

Next, we will see where two conjunctions are used:

Pę psey̌ m̀ klápù cì co paį m̀ junẽ (cì).
both write D poetry she and play D music she
"She both writes poetry and plays music."

Lú ṽ y̨ psuà ḿ cá pró cūpā kfȳrō, li kfoí ż méclō cá nūjè cyrǫ.
either have HABIT exercise D he more often lately or fit D clothes he very well
"Either he's been exercising more lately, or his clothes fit him really well."

It's also possible to connect two sentences using just a complementizer. In the case of the words *klá*, "although," and *kfú*, "because," the complementizer may appear in front of either of the two sentences to be connected:

Klá meî z̃ rỳ rafi pò fò, z̨ meî z̃ rỳ naprą.

although want D some cake I not EMPH want D some fruit
"Although I don't want any cake, I do want some fruit."

Meî z̃ rỳ ra̱fi̱ pò fò, kfú kfý ź pò mùrý.
want D some cake I not because full D I already
"I don't want any cake because I'm already full."

Now we should see how a complementizer may be paired with a conjunction, the use of the complementizer *pȳ* and the conjunction *li*:

Pȳ Ī cliã m̀ ké lō pò li (Ī) cxuě m̀ ké so̱ji̱ (pò)...
whether need get D job new I or need keep D job current I
"Whether I need to get a new job or keep my current job..."

Up to this point, we have seen how clauses may be coordinated using words with conjunctive or disjunctive character. Although their syntactic category varies—sometimes conjunctions and sometimes complementizers—they all fit into one of these two types of logical connection with shades of implication otherwise. However, it may also be argued that clauses may be linked using the logical connective of negation. By negating the first clause, heading it like a complementizer with the particle *fò*, and then starting the second clause with the affirmative *fẽ*, negation seems to be capable of coordinating two clauses:

Fò klè feǐ z̃ fy̱clá pò, fẽ klè cxiǎ ǹ lá kfūlỳ klè sã Í pò.
not that prefer D potato I but that cause D it cauliflower that sick D I
"It's not that I prefer potato, but that cauliflower makes me sick."

Also note in this example how the complementizer *klè* must appear alongside the words *fò* and *fẽ*. While this complementizer typically makes the related clause incapable of standing as a sentence on its own, bringing the validity of a coordination analysis into question, the word is actually working with the negation and affirmation particles to achieve coordination between the independent clauses.

In a final example of coordination, we will reprise a topic from §2.2.3.4 on the use of an auxiliary with a complementizer to form an implication relation. Earlier in this section, we illustrated the use of the complementizers *klá* and *kfú*. Although they have conjunctive character, they also have shades of implication, particularly in the case of *kfú*, which is versatile in describing cause and effect, if-then conditionals, and logical implication. The words *j* and *akra* are also capable of creating a logical implication, and on the syntactic level, these words allow independent clauses to be coordinated into a more complex utterance much like the other cases we've seen here. Similar to *kfú*, the exact clause on which the word appears is variable, so the larger utterance is expressible in at least two ways:

Ĵ joū Í kùmá klǫlạ, ạkrạ r̃ pyŭ m̀ krāprà kù.
if break D your sole then should visit D cobbler you
"If your sole breaks, then you should visit a cobbler."

Ạkrạ r̃ pyŭ m̀ krāprà kù ĵ joū Í kùmá klǫlạ.
then should visit D cobbler you if break D your sole
"Then you should visit a cobbler, if your sole breaks."

3.3.2.2: Embedded Clauses

When a sentence or clause cannot stand on its own but rather must be part of another sentence, this is popularly known in grammar books as *subordination*. From a syntactic point of view, such clauses are in some way embedded in another sentence, and so we will refer to this variety collectively as *embedded clauses*. In this section, we will look more closely at the three varieties of embedding that occur in Katalopsi: (1) embedded subject clauses, in which a full, but dependent, sentence appears in the subject position; (2) subordinated object clauses—the classical example of subordination—in which dependent sentences appear in an object position; and (3) relative clauses, in which a dependent sentence is attached to a noun or pronoun phrase to modify it.

3.3.2.2.1: Embedded Subject Clauses

In the following two English sentences, you will see how a subordinated clause may appear embedded in the subject position.

It really surprised me that she translated the poem in its entirety.

That she translated the poem in its entirety really surprised me.

In the first example, you can see the subject position of the sentence is filled by the pronoun *it*, while a dependent clause is linked to the independent—or *matrix*—clause by way of the complementizer *that*. In this example, we could argue that the word *it* does not actually refer to anything and that the complete meaning is only ascertained by the fixation of the dependent clause. Another way to look at it, however, is that the word *it* and the clause *that she translated the poem in its entirety* are coindexed, meaning they refer to the same thing. Under this analysis, the semantics could be considered redundant, but it may also be syntactically necessary.

Regardless of the appropriate semantic and syntactic analysis, we can see in the second example that the dependent clause can simply be embedded in the subject position, dispensing with the need for the pronoun *it*. It is this sort of embedding and communication of meaning, in which a proposition is the subject of the sentence, which is the task of this section.

Differences in the syntax of such embedded subject clause constructions create difficulty in Katalopsi specifically because the language has what is known as *VOS order*, meaning that the verb is followed by what is typically called the object, which is then subsequently followed by what is typically called the subject. If Katalopsi allows dependent clauses to be connected to a matrix sentence on its right side, then this means that such a dependent clause will be adjacent to the position the subject occupies. How, then, does this affect subject clause embedding?

Although these syntactic elements are adjacent in Katalopsi, the situation of subject clause embedding is actually much the same as in English. The personal pronoun *lá* may appear in the subject position or it may be omitted, and in the latter case, the dependent clause will automatically be in position to fulfill the need of a subject. See the following examples:

Xá plu̱ plō Í lá klè cyr̠o psumõ Í pé fò.
lucky for us D it that well understood D language not
"It is lucky for us that the language is not well understood."

Xá plu̱ plō Í klè cyr̠o psumõ Í pé fò.
lucky for us D that well understood D language not
"That the language is not well understood is lucky for us."

As you can see, the removal of *lá* serves to place the dependent clause exactly in a position where we may now say that it is embedded in the matrix clause as a subject, rather than just connected and dependent on it. There is no particular reason to prefer one formulation of the sentence to the other from a linguistic point of view. Consider this merely an acknowledgement of the optionality of the Katalopsi syntactic system.

The situation does change, however, when the matrix clause is negated. Because the negation particle surfaces, much like adverbs, at the end of the sentence, i.e. after the arguments, it comes between the subject position and the adjoined dependent clause. In the above two examples, this would mean coming between *lá* and *klè*. When this happens, the removal of the pronoun no longer means that the dependent clause in a position to be embedded; but directly embedding the clause before the negation particle is not an available strategy, due to the distance it puts between the negation particle and the bulk of the matrix clause. This would also mean that negation in the dependent clause could be adjacent to the negation of the matrix clause, which is easily confusing. Instead, the strategy of embedding dependent clauses in the subject position is cut off from possibility when the matrix clause is negated or adverbially modified after the arguments. The only available strategy then is the use of the pronoun and its coindexation with the extrapositional dependent clause. The following examples show this in effect:

Xá plu̱ plō Í lá fò klè cyr̠o psumõ Í pé fò.
lucky for us D it not that well understood D language not
"It isn't lucky for us that the language is not well understood."

Ź srųsę̣ kápē la̧ Í lá fò klè ź pró-pre̱-kio̧ Í rolų.
PAST obvious to they D it not that PAST worse-become D plague
"It wasn't obvious to them that the plague was getting worse."

An interesting thing happens to the embedded subject clause in interaction with the focusing syntax we previously discussed. In this situation, the dependent clause is focused—moved to the front of the sentence—and a trace pronoun is left behind in the starting position. But importantly, fronting of such a clause does not allow the use of the *lá* pronoun. Only the trace pronoun need appear to allow such dependent clause focusing to occur:

Klè ź nỳ lo̧xú Í nò ź ríxū Í cu kápē pò.
that PAST so fatty D meat PAST disgusting D TR to I
"That the meat was so fatty was disgusting to me."

Klè nai̧ ž rálìclí cá xuŷ ž cu pò
that used to D violence he worry D TR I
"That he's used to the violence worries me."

3.3.2.2.2: Subordinated Object Clauses

Typically, the word *subordination* is used to refer to the appearance of dependent clauses in an object position, as in the sentence *The board thinks that the staff should offer ideas during meetings*. Generally speaking, some verbal predicates require a subordinate clause more often than not, and *think* is one strong example. Syntactically, however, we must observe that such verbs do not allow the adjacency of the *lá* pronoun and the coindexed, dependent clause due to the intervening subject. Because of this, Katalopsi syntax does not in fact allow the embedding of the clause in the object position, so the only option is the use of the pronoun:

Kuó ž lá srịkry klè r̃ psyû m̀ psī psùpre̱ ro̧xo̧ krosų.
think D it board that should offer D idea staff during meeting
"The board thinks that the staff should offer ideas during meetings."

As you can see here, two items refer to the same thing, the pronoun *lá* in the direct object position and the dependent clause after the subject. This coindexation allows the disambiguator to confer the stimulus role on the dependent clause, as it is directly assigning it to the coindexed pronoun in the grammatical phrase.

Note that because of this, the notion of intervening modifiers or negation particles is no longer relevant. The rule is effectively this: The dependent clause may be embedded in the position of the replaced argument, with no pronoun, so long it is the rightmost argument of the matrix sentence and no information intervenes between the position and the connected clause. In the following example you will see that negation does not affect the syntax of subordinated object clauses, because the subject, here *sri̱kry̱*, already intervenes:

Kuó ż lá sri̱kry̱ fò klè r̃ psyû m̀ psī psùpre̱ ro̱xo̱ kro̱su̱.
think D it board not that should offer D idea staff during meeting
"The board doesn't think that the staff should offer ideas during meetings."

And in the next few sentences, you will see a variety of argument positions bearing the semantic weight of the dependent clause. The position typically called the subject generally always allows such embedding given its position consistently on the right, but we focused on embedding dependent clauses in the subject position in the previous section, so here you should observe how the direct and indirect objects mutually interact with verb valency and the dependent clause:

Ź cuỹ m̃ lá cá pò klè r̀ fiè m̀ cxi̱plý lō pò.
PAST mention D it he I that PROG seek D model new I
"I mentioned to him that I was looking for a new model."

Ź cuỹ g̃ lá cá klè r̀ fiè m̀ cxi̱plý lō pò.
PAST mention D it he that PROG seek D model new I
"It was mentioned to him that I was looking for a new model."

Ź cuỹ Í klè r̀ fiè m̀ cxi̱plý lō pò.
PAST mention D that PROG seek D model new I

"It was mentioned that I was looking for a new model."

The first important observation about the object positions is that the dependent clause may only be associated with the direct object and not the indirect object, not just for the verb *cuỹ* but for any verbal predicate permitting a proposition. This is due more to semantics than syntax, but it does have its effect on the structure of possible descriptions of an event. In the first example, with a trivalent grammatical phrase, the indirect object and subject intervene between the direct object position and the dependent clause, so *lá* is used. The second example, which has a divalent construction and no subject, still has intervening material in the form of the indirect object, so again *lá* appears. In the third example, however, a monovalent construction is used, and because no material intervenes between the direct object position and the dependent clause, the clause can fill the position with ease.

Returning to the topic of interaction between embedded clauses and focusing phenomena, subordinated object clauses can also become focuses of the sentence. What's more, under these circumstances, the pronoun *lá* cannot be used, just like for embedded subject clauses. What this means is that the subordinated object clause is moved to the front of the sentence, and then the trace pronoun *cu* appears where *lá* would normally appear. This is surprising because normally we expect *cu* to appear where the moved argument originated, but of course we know that subordinated object clauses can only appear in this position if they are the rightmost argument. This fact of the underlying position makes no difference for the syntax of such focused clauses, which requires only the trace pronoun and not the third-person singular pronoun:

Klè ż srau m̀ srò cá fé frisa ż moî ź cu plō nūjè.
that PAST shoot D gun he before order PAST surprise D TR we very
"That he fired the gun before the order really surprised us."

Klè ploï m̀ cì ròlú kfò plý klaí ź cu cá.
that talk D she about self always hate D TR he
"That she always talks about herself, he hates."

Klè r̃ cxoì m̀ kùmá rýnì kù pró cy̱ luè ź cu plō.
that should treat D your sister you more good believe D TR we
"That you should treat your sister better, we believe."

3.3.2.2.3: Relative Clauses

Relative clauses are a way of modifying a noun or pronoun phrase with a complete sentence. Generally they serve to narrow scope, as when one says "the tree we planted in the yard." We know thanks to the modifying relative clause that we are not discussing just any tree, but rather the specific one planted in the yard.

In §2.2.2.4, when we introduced relative and interrogative pronouns, we pointed out the union that exists between these two categories in Katalopsi. In effect, this means that if a particular pronoun is used to form a question, it is that same pronoun which is used to connect a relative clause to the modified noun or pronoun. In a reformulation of the example we just described, we might perhaps ask the question, "What did we plant in the yard?" The relative clause may have the word *that*, as in "the tree that we planted"; the word *which*, as in "the tree which we planted"; or nothing at all, as we've already seen in "the tree we planted." The Katalopsi question would use the interrogative pronoun *fù*, and so this is the same pronoun we see appear in the relative clause:

ci̱fu̱ fù ź freý j̃ cú cxi̱ cu plō
tree what PAST put D in yard TR we
"the tree we planted in the yard"

You can see in this example that, just like for question formation, a trace pronoun is placed in the position in which the relative pronoun originates. This will be the case for any argument specified in the relative clause by the pronoun, while adjuncts, as ever, do not require the trace.

The disparity between the Katalopsi word and the variety of English translations is a predictable point of confusion, so to fully understand the union of these categories in the present language, we must exemplify each pronoun individually, as we did in §3.2.6.1 on question formation.

For each pronoun, where possible, we will give an example of a relative clause modifying a noun or pronoun in isolation and then a second example of a noun or pronoun phrase so modified used in a complete sentence. First, see the following complete sentence using the word *fù*:

Ź késīxù Í srōfènú fù ź pliè m̀ cu pò.
PAST tasty D blackberry what PAST eat D TR I
"The blackberries that I ate were tasty."

The word *fã*, though translatable as "which," is only possible as an interrogative, and so we won't see examples using it as a relative pronoun. This may be confusing, since the word *which* so commonly appears in English relative clauses.

The word *fō*, or "who," does appear in relative clauses. Katalopsi grammar errs on the side of consistency, so if the modified item refers to a person, then *fō* is used, but if to an object, abstract or otherwise, *fù* is used. Here we see examples with a person:

kí fō ź siě m̀ cámà crý cu
man who PAST lose D his hat TR
"the man who lost his hat"

Loũ ž cesũ fȳnū fō pliâ m̀ sepé cu.
need D donation priest who manage D church TR
"The priest who manages the church needs donations."

Occurring in similar environments to *fō*, is the word *fōmà*, or "whose":

cxékỳ fōmà cxú rié m̀ cu cú cìmá clējī
teacher whose student work D TR in her office
"the teacher whose student works in her office"

Cxeì j prìcy nāsù fōmà sȳ xoī ž cu pò pijó.
come D here author whose book own D TR I tomorrow
"An author whose book I own is coming here tomorrow."

Although *fōmà* is capable as a relative pronoun, other pre-nominal pronouns will not occur on their own, but rather in *u*-phrases.

In a more restricted environment, the word *já*, or "why," may appear. Typically it will be used to modify words like *reason* or *explanation*, words that indicate abstract thought and rationale. Notably, such expressions do not necessarily require the word *why* in English, but in Katalopsi, the pronoun must appear:

plỹ já m̀ ryŭfiē Í cxèso̱
reason why must demolish D building
"the reason (why) the building must be demolished"

R̀ fiè m̀ nīsō já loũ z̃ crópsà lùso̱xú klūmà psùpre̱ plō.
PROG look for D explanation why need D resource additional your staff we
"We're looking for an explanation why your staff needs additional resources."

The pronoun *ri̱* is another case where its usage in a relative clause is heavily dependent on the lexical semantics of the modified item. Easily translated as "where," *ri̱* attaches to items interpretable as a location. Like for *why*, the word *where* may not always be necessary in English, but Katalopsi will be sure to use the pronoun. To best avoid the confusion caused by English translations of relative clauses, it is also important that you consider the use of a locative preposition with a relative pronoun in both languages. In English, this will require the pronoun *which*, as in "at which" or "by which," but Katalopsi uses *ri̱* whether it is internal to a prepositional phrase or not. This furthermore relates to a syntactic fact about Katalopsi, the treatment of movement when the pronoun originates in the grammatical phrase as an argument or when it is adjunctive, which of course has an effect on syntax in the form of the respective presence or absence of the trace pronoun. Here are examples of locative relative clauses in isolation and in a sentence:

rȳmā ri̱ j niè j̃ pūsē cu pò
somewhere where can send D complaint TR I

"somewhere (where) I can send a complaint"

Ř pyǔ j nikfé cú ri īcxàxú Í lá cá.
PROG visit D country in where illegal D it he
"He's visiting a country where it's illegal."

These facts about *ri* raise the question about prepositional adjuncts and how they interact with relative clauses in general. Of course if the preposition is specifying information about location, you use *ri*, as we have already learned, but there are many possible roles that the objects of prepositions may hold. Ultimately, such pronouns work along lines we've already seen. If they are interpretable as a person, you use *fō*. Otherwise, *fù* is used, as the pronoun must refer to some abstract or concrete object, something to which we do not ascribe personhood. In other words, while the prepositions help guide us to the correct interpretation of the entity to which the pronoun refers, the reference has already decided the pronoun we use. E.g. if the entity bears the instrument role and originates in the grammatical phrase of the relative clause, merely *fù* is used; but if it originates in a prepositional adjunct with the word *fili*, then the only difference in the relative clause construction is the appearance of the preposition:

cìkrí fù ź nuē ṽ lí cu cla
hammer what PAST damage D wall TR they
"the hammer (which) they damaged the wall with"

cìkrí fìli fù ź nuē ṁ lí cla
hammer with what PAST damage D wall they
"the hammer with which they damaged the wall"

It is also worthwhile to see other relative pronouns which are the object of prepositions so that we may get a sense to what extent prepositions choose the pronoun to be used. Where possible, we will also include a version without embedding the relative pronoun inside a prepositional phrase, as we did with the previous example:

mureprã ó fō ź cuỹ ṁ plà cì

physician to who PAST mention D problem she
"the physician to whom she mentioned the problem"

mureprã fõ ź cuỹ ñ plà cu cì
physician who PAST mention D problem TR she
"the physician who she mentioned the problem to"

prifo̱ clý ri̱ ź pia̱ Í kru̱
island next to where PAST sink D boat
"the island next to which the boat sank"

prifo̱ ri̱ ź pia̱ Ì cu kru̱
island where PAST sink D TR boat
"the island where the boat sank"

lìkfi̱ ròlú fù r̀ ploĭ m̀ lēkū
crime about what PROG talk D investigator
"the crime the investigators are talking about"

The last interrogative pronoun which is capable of being used in relative clauses is *rù*, or "when." Like with many of the pronouns we've just considered, the use of *rù* is determined by the meaning of the modified element. If it is meant as a period or duration of time, then *rù* is the word which will be used to link the relative clause to it. This word is also another example where the English pronoun may sometimes be omitted but where Katalopsi requires it:

si̱psý rù ź kfiò ź cì
moment when PAST break down D she
"the moment (when) she broke down"

G̀ psyĭ ž̃ lúmā fé nimũ rù ź psumõ Í sra̱ fò.
IMP remember D era before science when PAST understood D body not
"Remember the era before science when the body was not understood."

It is of course also possible to embed *rù* in a prepositional phrase, notably because temporal roles are never assigned within the grammatical phrase. If the general framing of the time is understood, simply *rù* may be used, but otherwise, increased specificity may be yield by way of a prepositional phrase:

cẽ pī rù ź nuȳ Í xǫjǫ
night after when PAST find D corpse
"the night after which the corpse was found"

pafri rǫxǫ rù ź nuē m̀ cìmá lȳ plèkǫ
event during when PAST damage D her voice singer
"the event during which the singer damaged her voice"

Despite similarities with the word *ri*, this temporal pronoun *rù* will only ever relate to an adjunct, as time expressions are not expressible as arguments within the grammatical phrase. As a result, the trace pronoun will never appear in clauses of this type.

Three interrogative pronouns remain which have so far not been mentioned. Those replacing the predicate or replacing adjuncts which describe methods are not capable of being used as relative pronouns. This means that the words *fèja*, or "what... like," and *jȳ*, or "how," do not occur as relative pronouns. Similar can be said for *rapse*, or "how many," and *fã*, or "which," which we mentioned earlier. Ultimately, while the equivalent English phrases may look like relative clauses, in fact they are embedded object clauses of the kind we saw in the previous section with the only difference being that they have an interrogative character. An example of each follows. Note how the clause does not link to a noun or pronoun as though it is modifying it, as relative clauses do, but rather exhibits the embedded object clause syntax we've come to recognize:

Piɇ ż lá pò fò m̀ fèja Í klēmèfa.
know D it I not will what like D professor
"I don't know what the professor will be like."

Psuõ ż lá pò jȳ ź praí m̀ plà cá jy fȳrō.
understand D it I how PAST solve D problem he so quickly
"I understand how he solved the problem so quickly."

Neú ż lá pò rapse so loũ z̃ cu pò.
wonder D it I how much rope need D TR I
"I wonder how much rope I need."

Ř suo m̀ lá cì fã sȳ m̀ peú m̀ cu cì.
PROG ask D it she which book must buy D TR she
"She's asking which book she has to buy."

3.3.2.3: Elision in Complex Utterances

Now that you have a sense of the variety of complex utterances that are possible, it is important that we reprise a topic from §3.3.1 on simple utterances, the process of elision. While elision can be used to create simple utterances from the canonical sentence, it can also be applied to complex utterances to create unique structures.

Large and complex chunks may remain after elision. While these chunks can still be smaller than the sentence, they may be as big as a disambiguator phrase or grammatical phrase.

V̀ r̀ peú m̀ fù fõ?
Q PROG buy D what who
"Who's buying what?"

Ř peú m̀ rafi John co (r̀ peú) m̀ méklā Stephanie.
PROG buy D cake John and PROG buy D pork Stephanie
"John's buying the cake and Stephanie the pork."

In this example, the first half of the sentence is complete, while the second half is just a grammatical phrase. In a sense, the first complete sentence has licensed the elision going on in the second sentence, and then they've been conjoined by *co*. Note that we have indeed used the complete grammatical phrase here and not simply a string of arguments. Though elision has occurred, in order for the elided sentence to be grammatical, the disambiguator must be included, completing the grammatical phrase. This is necessary even when one of the arguments is understood to be repeated:

Ceũ ñ rỳ nāsū lēkū John co (ceũ) ñ sūklā
donate D some equipment investigator John and donate D additional
crópsà srịkry pȳlēsū (John).
resource board investigative John
"John is donating some equipment to the investigator and other
resources to the investigative board."

As you can see, the two sentences joined here have the same subject,
John. Therefore, it does not need to be repeated and is instead elided
from the second sentence just like the repeated verb *ceũ*. Despite one
of the arguments missing from the grammatical phrase and despite the
repetition of the lexeme, however, the disambiguator ñ still appears in the
second sentence.

Questions may also be elided. When this occurs, a relatively
complex utterance may be derived from otherwise simple sentences.
You should also observe in these examples how targeting a single
argument does not necessarily mean you are targeting the grammatical
phrase. Consequently, when it is just a single argument targeted, the
disambiguator can be omitted, but it is grammatical in either case. It
is only when multiple arguments survive elision, as in the previous
examples, that the disambiguator is mandatory:

V́ roì Í mý, li v́ (roì Í) rākē?
Q there is D rain or Q there is D snow
"Is it raining or (is it) snowing?"

A good rule of thumb is that if the disambiguator indicates
monovalency in the grammatical phrase, then it is not necessary in
similarly elided sentences. However, if the valency of the disambiguator
is greater than one, omission of the disambiguator in such sentences is
only possible when a single argument survives elision. This omission
is not obligatory, however.

Fù ź peú m̀ cu kù co (fù ź) ciȳ (m̀ cu kù)?
what PAST buy D TR you and what D sell D TR you
"What did you buy and (what did you) sell?"

3.4: COMMON CONSTRUCTIONS

In §3.2.6, we discussed several processes which either affect Katalopsi's canonical word order or are known to do so in many languages and therefore receive special emphasis in grammar books. The topics in this section also bear emphasis, but not because the word order is expected necessarily to be different from what we have so far seen. Instead, they are special because the constructions are very common, and this description of Katalopsi would not be complete and useful without spending some time on them.

Syntactically, many of these topics will not be especially startling, including comparison, anaphora, and conditionals. However, in the case of so-called *small clauses* and linking verbs, there are notable differences between Katalopsi and English.

3.4.1: COMPARISON

In grammar, *comparison* is the sizing up of one object with an object of comparison along some degreed dimension. Canonically— and perhaps most often—the attribute being compared is indicated by an adjective, as with *tall* in the sentence *Martin is as tall as Robert*. However, it is also possible that the attribute is represented with a noun, as in *Molly is as much a mathematician as Paul*, or a combination of the two, as in *Mark is as good a player as Alyssa*.

These structures point to one of three types of comparison, known as *equivalence*. We will also look at the *comparative*, where something has more or less of an attribute, and the *superlative*, where something exhibits the attribute to the greatest or least observed degree.

3.4.1.1: Equivalence

When you want to comment on whether something exhibits a trait to the same degree as a given object of comparison, you use the equivalent comparison morphosyntax. The trait or attribute indicated with an adjective is marked by the adverb *si*, or "as" in English, while the object of comparison is marked by the preposition *klé*, which is also translated as "as." That is, although English uses homophones to mark these two very different functions, Katalopsi has a distinct word for each.

When the equivalence comparison is made as a statement, the attribute appears in the predicate position, adverb and adjective both. The object of comparison, as a prepositional phrase, is modifying the grammatical phrase and so appears after the arguments. Consider the following examples:

Si̱ cra̱ Í si̱ kỹmì klé sỹ.
as cheap D this apple as that
"These apples are as cheap as those."

Si̱ sāprà Í si̱ xṳrú klé nè fõnì fù ṽ keí z̃ cu pò
as strong D this vodka as any whiskey what have taste D TR I
"This vodka is as strong as any whiskey that I've tasted."

Ź si̱ īsròxú Í Maria-mã cxysũ klé cámà fò.
PAST as illogical D Maria's decision as his not.
"Maria's decision wasn't as illogical as his."

Notice in the last example that the statement of equivalence can be negated, but this does not affect the syntax. The negative particle still appears after the sentential modifiers, which themselves appear after the arguments.

Something new must be introduced to deal with attributes expressed with a noun or noun phrase. Instead of the word *si̱*, as with adjectival attributes, *rékā* marks for nominal attributes. In other contexts, *rékā* is simply used to communicate similarity, as the English word *like*. The following examples show the word being used in various positions with the less complicated sense and construction. As you will see, it may behave the same as any preposition, modifying nouns and adjectives or acting as the predicate:

Rékā mỳcxí Í pòmá ru̱.
like lion D my cat
"My cat is like a lion."

kí rékā psũ
man like child
"the man like a child"

lu̧ rékā pȩclú
big like mountain
"big like a mountain"

When the word is used in an equivalence construction, however, it precedes a noun or noun phrase being used as the attribute expression, and it is translated as "as much." The following examples show it in use:

Rékā cxokũ Í cámà jí klé nèni̧.
as much supporter D his friend as anyone
"His friend is as much (of) a supporter as anyone."

Rékā mỳcxí Í pòmá ru̧ klé kùmá.
as much lion D my cat as yours
"My cat is as much (of) a lion as yours (is)."

Ź rékā psèký Í kù klé Kerouac.
PAST as much writer D you as Kerouac
"You were as much (of) a writer as Kerouac (was)."

In these examples, note that the parenthetical information is merely included as optional information in English. These parenthetical words actually correspond to no information in Katalopsi but are not necessary in English anyway. You should also note that the word marking the object of comparison is still *klé*. This does not change when the attribute of comparison is a noun or noun phrase.

The next important syntactic topic for equivalence comparison arises when the equivalence is expressed as a modifier of a noun phrase. As before, such modifiers begin with *si* when the attribute of comparison is an adjective. *Si* is itself a modification of the adjective, making the equivalence structure in this instance an adjective phrase. As we've already seen when discussing modification, adjective phrases come after the nouns they modify, resulting in noun phrases like the following:

kí si̱ klyxũ klé cá
man as talented as him
"a man as talented as him"

mò si̱ fro̱xú klé sỹ
war as bloody as that
"a war as bloody as that one"

cxù si̱ cyro̱ kúmō klé pòmá
plan as well thought out as mine
"a plan as well thought out as mine"

In another case of modification, equivalence structures can also surface as adverbs. Just as *si* can modify an adjective, it can also modify another adverb, which in turn is typically modifying a sentence in some way.

Ź meȳ m̀ nōplā cá si̱ cxārō klé lìcxa̱.
PAST run D trail he as quickly as rabbit
"He ran the trail as quickly as a rabbit."

Ploĭ m̀ cì si̱ moxurõ klé kràsrúprà.
speak D she as naturally as politician
"She speaks as naturally as a politician."

Pseẏ m̀ pò si̱ psỳro̱ klé klēmèfa̱ fò.
write D I as neatly as professor not
"I don't write as neatly as the professor."

In these examples, of course, the equivalence structures modify the respective grammatical phrases and so appear after the arguments rather than beginning in the predicate position. You should also observe in the third example how the complete equivalence phrase appears between the arguments on the left and the negation particle on the right.

When the equivalence construction is modifying a noun, but the attribute of comparison is not an adjective or adverb but rather also a noun, the word *rékā* again surfaces. The following examples show *rékā*-constructions modifying noun phrases:

mìklá u lã rékā līkù klé lāsū
piece of art as much statue as painting
"the artwork as much (of) a statue as a painting"

jelõ rékā klúsē klé krasũ
letter as much warning as invitation
"the letter as much (of) a warning as an invitation"

Unlike for *si*, we cannot show *rékā*-constructions modifying grammatical phrases because *rékā* cannot mark adverbial attributes.

The final topic to be discussed vis-à-vis equivalence comparison harkens back to the topic of elision. Elision can apply in the equivalence structures to remove the object of comparison when the context allows interlocutors to understand the role without overt specification. For completeness, several examples with predicative and modificatory usages follow:

Si fasuxú Í sĩ mà fò.
as poisonous D this plant not
"This plant is not as poisonous."

Rékā paki Í pò.
as much musician D I
"I am as much (of) a musician."

rolu si frīlēlē
plague as destructive
"a plague as destructive"

Ź pai ḿ paki lō si sópūrō.
PAST play D musician new as beautifully
"The new musician played as beautifully."

While the elided variants of the equivalence structure may demand more context to be fully comprehensible, they will come up as naturally in speech as they do in English, so it is important to be familiar with them.

3.4.1.2: Comparative

When commenting on something having an attribute to a greater or lesser degree than something else, the comparative morphosyntax is used. As we have already seen in §3.1.1.2 on the modification of adjectives, the comparative is expressed not through a suffixing morpheme as is often the case in English but rather through an adverb modifying the adjective. In the sense of "more than," it is the adverb *pró*, but in the sense of "less than," it is the adverb *nù*.

When forming a comparative construction, as with equivalence, there is optionality as to whether the object of comparison is mentioned explicitly. When it is, we again use the preposition *klé*. This is contrary to expectations from English, which has the object of comparison marked with *as* in equivalence constructions and with *than* in comparative constructions.

The following examples show comparative constructions using *pró*, with the attribute realized as an adjective in the predicate position:

R̲ pró cýjỳxú Í sófī klé l̲y̲.
REPORT more powerful D king than god
"It is said that the king is more powerful than a god."

Pró rēcrōxù Í s̲o̲n̲i̲ klé cì.
more superficial D no one than her
"No one is more superficial than her."

Pró psyxũ Í késī u sĩ fõnì klé plāpỳ.
more woody D flavor of this whiskey than usual
"The flavor of this whiskey is woodier than the usual."

The following show the same but with *nù*:

Nù lùxú Í kl̲a̲ klé fù ź psiě z̃ cu pò.
less heavy D box than what PAST expect D TR I
"The box is less heavy than what I expected."

Nù jìfí Í sĩ xō klé lìsy pȳcxà.
less pure D this water than requirement legal
"This water is less pure than the legal requirement."

Nù móplò Í mureprã lō klé pòmá pòsre̖.
less rough D doctor new than my previous
"The new doctor is less rough than my previous."

We should next turn to the use of comparative constructions to modify noun phrases. As you will see, the construction is again, like equivalence, regarded as an adjectival modifier of the noun, while the adverb *pró* or *nù* only comes first after the noun because it is modifying the adjectival attribute from its left side.

re̖se̖ pró jìcrì klé fāsā-mà
venom more dangerous than snake's
"venom more dangerous than a snake's"

frỳ nù sóxù klè plōmà
marriage less healthy than ours
"a marriage less healthy than ours"

lākū xȳxȳ pró sálùle̖ klé cá
painter first more creative than him
"the first painter more creative than him"

pra̖ nù rē klé pòmá mi̖rá-mà
beard less thin than my father's
"a beard less thin than my father's"

We should also see a few cases where comparative constructions, like with equivalence, act on adverbs modifying the grammatical phrase.

Ź r̀ juê m̀ la̖xé pró fȳrō klé pùsry̖.
PAST PROG move D tiger more quietly than mouse
"The tiger was moving more quietly than a mouse."

M̃ riā m̀ cá nù plu̱kfárō klé cámà fòlo̱.
will answer D he less honestly than his brother
"He will answer less honestly than his brother."

Ź crió m̀ srīkō kfìká pró kúlōlērō klé cxàprá.
PAST look D claimant judge more pensively than lawyer
"The judge looked more pensively at the claimant than the lawyer."

Comparative constructions are also possible with a noun phrase surfacing as the compared attribute. In these cases, we still use the words *pró* and *nù*, but the preposition *u* is inserted between the adverb and the noun or noun phrase. We will see both predicative and noun-modificatory examples.

Pró u xóprà Í cá klé cxékỳ.
more of researcher D he than teacher
"He's more of a researcher than a teacher."

Nù u na̱pra̱ Í nērù klé jỳple̱.
less of fruit D pumpkin than tomato
"A pumpkin's less of a fruit than a tomato (is)."

kí pró u fóxỳ klé kínì
man more of animal than human
"the man more of an animal than a human"

cxèso̱ nù sy̱ klé pso̱
building less house than hut
"the building less of a house than a hut (is)"

And as a last topic for this section, we should see where comparative constructions and elision co-occur. Remember that the object of comparison can often be left off a comparison structure, whether it is an equivalence expression or a comparative expression as we've been exploring here. The following examples show predicative, noun-modificatory, and grammatical phrase–modificatory comparative constructions with both adjectival and nominal attributes where possible.

Pró rú Í jẽ klỳ.
more clear D weather now
"The weather's clearer now."

Nù u psī cy̱ Í kùmá lāmēklī pò.
less of idea good D your according to I
"Yours is less of a good idea in my opinion."

ni̱ pró plīkrè
person more lonely
"a more lonely person"

psī nù ījỳklú
idea less impossible
"a less impossible idea"

Cxeò m̀ sy̱ plu̱ psī̃ pò pró cre̱ro̱.
build D house for bird I more loosely
"I build bird houses more loosely."

R̄ piō z̃ nìxý kéxù pò nù cròro̱.
tend to forget D responsibility professional I less easily
"I tend to forget my professional responsibilities less easily."

3.4.1.3: Superlative

A *superlative* construction is a method of saying how something, upon comparison with all members of a given group, exhibits a trait to the greatest degree. For example, you may say that a book is "the rarest book in the collection." Like with the comparative morphosyntax we have already seen, the superlative in Katalopsi is not marked by a bound morpheme suffixed to the adjective but rather by a modifying adverb—specifically *rà* in the sense of "most" and *ónō* in the sense of "least."

One notable difference between the comparative and the superlative is that the latter does not involve an object of comparison but rather the specification of a class of objects, which may or may not be explicitly stated. Interestingly, when this class is mentioned, it is not separated from the attribute either, as is often the case with objects of comparison in equivalence and comparative constructions. If the superlative construction is predicative, both the attribute and the class appear—in that order—in the predicate position. When the construction is instead modificatory, they will, as expected, appear together and again in the mentioned order. Let us first see some predicative examples using both *rà* and *ónō*:

> Rà rálìlẹ u clȳjō-mà sréxōprà Í Ian.
> most successful of today's mathematician D Ian
> "Ian is the most successful of today's mathematicians."

> Ónō julaxũ u cxō u crūrȳ Í lá.
> least essential of part of process D it
> "It's the least essential part of the process."

> Rà sópū u lāsū fù ṽ riǒ z̃ cu pò Í sȳ.
> most beautiful of painting what have see D TR I D that
> "That's the most beautiful painting I've ever seen."

> Z̃ ónō jālūjè u cámà srīsō Í sȳ kfụrụrọ.
> PAST least believable of his assertion D that definitely
> "That was definitely the least believable of his assertions."

Notice how in each of these examples the preposition *u* is used to establish the class of objects in which the described entity is superlative. In the first example, the class is *clȳjō-mà sréxōprà*, "today's mathematicians," while in the fourth, it is *cámà srīsō*, "his assertions." It is of course also possible to elide the class if it is clear from context, in which case only the attribute is present in the predicate position:

> Rà krà Í cá.
> most strong D he
> "He is the strongest."

> M̃ ónō srụsẹ Í sĩ kòcọ claklurõ.
> will least obvious D this puzzle probably
> "This puzzle will probably be the least obvious."

If the superlative construction is not in the predicate position, i.e. if it is instead modificatory, then the attribute will instead appear after the noun like any adjectival phrase. In this environment, it is often the modified element which makes the object class obvious, but if an object class does appear, it will often serve to make it more specific than the modified element managed to. The following examples show modificatory superlative phrases with and without an established object class expression:

Jỳ Í kòco̱ rà fri̱.
next D puzzle most difficult
"The most difficult puzzle is next."

psȳ ónō krulolẽ u lì
dog least obedient of group
"the least obedient dog of the group"

rìpsa̱ rà fẽclỳxú
nightmare most horrific
"the most horrific nightmare"

Ź pseí j fo̱céplā plō fāsā ónō re̱se̱ u lámà sý.
PAST jump D toward us snake least venomous of its kind
"The least venomous snake of its kind jumped toward us."

3.4.2: SMALL CLAUSES AND LINKING VERBS

In English, several constructions including *small clauses* and *linking verbs* have resulted in the proposed theory of *control*, the idea that syntactic arrangement can predetermine the interpretation of the underlying subject of a dependent clause as one of a couple of the same entities mentioned in the matrix clause. While these constructions provoke enormously complex theoretical discussion of the syntax of English, we will see in this section that the corresponding structures in Katalopsi are far less complex due to the fact that control structures are not possible. When it comes to the Katalopsi analogue of small clauses, for example, the constructed language is more similar to Spanish, in that the clause in question will be a complete sentence that could theoretically—albeit with a complementizer removed—stand on its own. The same cannot be said for English small clauses which would be ungrammatical in isolation regardless of complementizer.

There are two varieties of clause that we should first consider. These are, under standard English syntactic analyses, *subject-control* clauses and *object-control* clauses. The first is when the subject of the dependent clause must obligatorily be interpreted as the same entity that is the subject of the matrix clause. In the following English sentence, the second verb *buy* has an underlying subject, and we are forced to understand it as the same subject appearing earlier in the sentence, "Jean". In other words, it is impossible for this sentence to mean that "his wife" will be buying some vegetables:

Jean promises his wife to buy some vegetables.

Pseī ñ lá cámà crì Jean klè m̃ peú m̀ rỳ sa̲pru̲ cá.
promise D it his wife Jean that will buy D some vegetable he.
"Jean promises his wife he will buy some vegetables."

In the Katalopsi equivalent, on the other hand, you can see that no corresponding control structure appears. Instead, a full but dependent clause appears, headed by the complementizer *klè*. The alternative translation we have provided also reveals an optionality to English communication that is not ultimately the subject of this book.

Next, we should see an example of *object control*, which is much more common and so more likely to cause confusion. In the following sentence, the object of the verb *order* must obligatorily be interpreted of the subject of the dependent clause, the person who does the leaving. That is, it is unable to be Jean:

Jean ordered me to leave.

Ź fria̲ m̀ lá Jean klè cloí ḿ pò.
PAST order D it Jean that leave D I
"Jean ordered that I leave."

The Katalopsi equivalent requires a complete, dependent clause, and the alternative English translation again shows that structures other than those of control are available to English. This is not true in every case, however. The following object-control verb only allows for a control structure, while a complementizer-headed dependent clause is blocked:

Jean forced me to leave.

Ź kfiê m̀ lá Jean klè cloí m̀ pò.
PAST force D it Jean that leave D I
"Jean forced me to leave."

Ultimately the lesson here is that while English has some verbs that require control structures, some verbs that can use control or an alternative structure, and some verbs that cannot use control structures, Katalopsi is not able to use them at all and defaults to complete dependent clauses.

We should also reprise the earlier topic of linking verbs here. In Katalopsi, the appropriate, semantically parallel sentences, do not use small clauses and linking. Where English uses such structures, Katalopsi uses a compounding strategy. In §2.3.2, we showed how nouns and adjectives may compound with copular verbs to create more complex predicates. It is important to see how these predicates appear in complete sentences:

Ź krupýprà-kio Í plōmà fòlo kfȳrō.
PAST soldier-become D our brother recently
"Our brother recently became a soldier."

R̀ prùni̠-kiè m̀ cxékỳ clȳjō.
PROG strange-act D teacher today
"The teacher is acting strange today."

As you can see, after compounding, they appear in the canonical predicate position as usual—i.e. after the auxiliaries and before the disambiguator. Do note in these and the examples that follow that the disambiguator depends on the particular verb and not on the adjective or noun it is compounded with.

185

Finally, we should address the use of *modified* nouns or adjectives used with linking verbs. Rather than a single word compounding with the verb, these circumstances permit the compounding of a phrase with the verb to create at times rather large new phrasal predicates. Internally to the compound, normal rules of phrasal syntax apply, while little on the sentential level changes:

M̃ klīkȳ-pū-cxiõ Í cá pli̱rí.
will student-lazy-stay D he forever
"He will stay a lazy student forever."

R̀ pró-kfýlà-kio̱ Í kre̱fílè pypléfrō.
PROG more-frequent-become D disaster environmental
"Environmental disasters are becoming more frequent."

Cla̱re̱-kū-ro̱i ź pò mùrý.
somewhat-tired-feel D I already
"I feel somewhat tired already."

3.4.3: ANAPHORA

Anaphora is the process by which a word or phrase, especially a pronoun, is interpretable only as referring to another entity mentioned in context. Sometimes, the context may be as narrow as the same clause or as broad as the same sentence—in the case of conjoined or coordinated clauses—or a former sentence in conversation.

In the simplest case, *anaphors* may be personal pronouns. When a pronoun like *he*, *she*, *they*, and so on refers to someone obvious from context, then we are talking about a more distant form of anaphora. In other words, these personal pronouns would never be used in the same clause as the entity to which the pronoun refers. They may be in separate but connected clauses or separate sentences altogether. The following show examples of each:

V̀ pie̱ ż lá kù pȳ pa̱i m̀ rỳ pa̱si Matthew?
Q know D it you whether play D any instrument Matthew
"Do you know whether Matthew plays any instruments?"

Là, kuó ż lá pò fò klè pai m̀ rỳ cá.
no, think D it I not that play D any he
"No, I don't think he plays any."

Nixú Í Maria, mã nūjè prō Í cì fò.
good people D Maria but very smart D she not
"Maria's a good person, but she's not very smart."

In the first pair of sentences, we see how a personal pronoun may be used to refer to the same entity mentioned in a previous sentence, even when the earlier sentence is voiced by another person. The third sentence shows that a personal pronoun may refer to an entity mentioned in the same sentence as long as they are in separate clauses.

It is also possible to have anaphora in a single clause, like when reflexive and reciprocal pronouns refer to another entity also mentioned therein. In this narrow context, more complicated and elaborate syntactic facts emerge. Because Katalopsi has a canonical verb-object-subject order, all clause-internal anaphora in the grammatical phrase is *cataphoric*, meaning the reflexive or reciprocal pronoun in question is said before the entity to which it refers. This also means that such *cataphors* only occur in minimally divalent grammatical phrases, if indeed the anaphora is in the grammatical phrase at all. Let us see some examples of this:

Ź keò ṽ kfò cìkrí Jason īlēlōrō.
PAST hit D self hammer Jason unintentionally
"Jason accidentally hit himself with a hammer."

Ř roú m̀ kré kōlō Katie co Arthur.
PROG play D game each other Katie and Arthur
"Katie and Arthur are playing games with eachother."

In these and the examples to follow, it's also important to remember that Katalopsi has a single reflexive pronoun *kfò*, so there's no need to think about personalizing it like the English reflexives *myself, himself,* and so on.

Such reflexive and reciprocal pronouns may also occur as anaphors outside the grammatical phrase, but obligatorily as adjuncts, which will usually follow the grammatical phrase unless focusing has occurred.

When anaphors surface as adjuncts, it is no longer important the valency of the grammatical phrase as, theoretically, the adjunctive anaphor could refer to any of the arguments within it:

Ź niè m̀ fasũ cla̱ ó kfò.
PAST send D gift they to self
"They sent gifts to themselves."

R̄ ploǐ ḿ Maria ròlú kfò lèpe̱.
tend to talk D Maria about self too much
"Maria tends to talk about herself too much."

R̀ cliā Í la̱ frú mylí.
PROG cry D they in front of one another
"They're crying in front of one another."

While anaphors within the grammatical phrase are strictly cataphoric, adjunctive anaphors can theoretically occur both before and after the mutually linked entity. In the examples just shown, they occurred afterward in adjunctive prepositional phrases. However, these expressions may be fronted in focusing processes, placing them in front of the expression by which they are interpreted. We will see several examples of this:

Pry̱pé kfò ź cxuě m̀ jelõ cá.
with self PAST keep D letter he
"He kept the letter with him."

Ó kōlō ploǐ ḿ la̱ fȳrō.
to each other talk D they quietly
"They are talking to each other quietly."

Plu̱ kfò saù Í macaxuclĩ prāmē.
for self exist D villainy only
"Villainy exists for itself alone."

3.4.4: Conditionals

When it comes to the syntax of Katalopsi, conditional statements are to a degree a nonissue. However, because some natural languages undergo alteration of the canonical word order to express them, it is necessary to see the full case of the Katalopsi conditional laid out here. Syntactically, there are two notable types of conditional statement: (1) one expressing a consequence, and (2) one expressing both the condition and the consequence.

In the first—and simplest—case, one may simply voice a consequence with the assumption that the condition is understood. In English, this often involves the word *would*, though others may be used instead, sometimes in the subjunctive mood. In Katalopsi, the auxiliary *ḡ* is used, also known as the conditional marker, and we don't need more than one clause:

Ḡ sã-kio̱ Í pò kfu̱ru̱ro̱.
would sick-become D I definitely
"I'd definitely get sick."

Ḡ ṽ luo̱ m̀ sȳ pò.
would have leave D book I
"I would have left my books."

In the second and more complex case, both a condition and the consequence is voiced, requiring at least two clauses. The condition is set up by the evidential auxiliary *j́*, also known as the hypothetical marker. Equivalent clauses in English usually begin with the word *if*, and the subjunctive mood may appear on the verb. As you will see in the following examples, the condition and consequence can appear in either order:

J́ saí z̀ sre̱ fè pò, ḡ prou̱ m̀ clẽ u sófī pò.
if have D a lot money I would live D life of king I
"If I had a lot of money, I would live the life of a king."

Ḡ kfy̱nuo̱ Í méclō, j́ freý j̃ la̱ xō plō.
would soften D clothes if put D they water we
"The clothes would soften up if we put them in water."

Importantly, even though we translate the word *j* as "if" here, it is actually an auxiliary, rather than a complementizer, which means that anything fronted would appear ahead of it:

có u mīmā j kreō m̀ cu plō
source of energy if improve D TR we
"if we were to improve the power source"

We will see more about these auxiliaries and their interactions in the next chapter on semantics. For now, simply note these minor syntactic facts of if-then statements.

C H A P T E R 4
Semantics & Pragmatics

In this chapter, we will be discussing dimensions of meaning and how they are communicated in Katalopsi. Sometimes, they may be semantically encoded, i.e. found in the denotation of words. Other times, meaning is determined through connotation, or it is pragmatically encoded. What this means is that while some elements of meaning can be encoded directly in speech, other elements of meaning are communicated by some combination of context and world knowledge. We will see that several dimensions of meaning common to the morphology of other languages are not expressed in Katalopsi morphology and must be communicated in a different way.

4.1: SEMANTIC ROLES

We have at various times in the last two chapters looked at the disambiguators of Katalopsi from lexical, morphological, and syntactic points of view, and in each case we had to provide a brief discussion of semantic roles in order for the various points to be at all cognizable. In this section, we will finally give a full-fledged description of the distinctively marked semantic roles of Katalopsi, making sure to point out where the language is not quite as specific.

4.1.1: AGENCY—CA VS. AG

The first way in which Katalopsi uses disambiguators to communicate layers of meaning is in its distinction of *agency*. The prototypical role which supersedes here could simply be called the *cause*, the thing which causes some event or state. This is quite ambiguous, as it does not elaborate on whether the cause is a thinking agent or merely some natural force. Indeed, many languages stop here and do not make this further distinction. Katalopsi, on the other hand, does so.

If the cause of some event or state is construed as one capable of making the decision to do so, then we would say it is an agent. The disambiguators that mark for this semantic role are numerous and in all include *ḿ, ṁ, m̃, ñ, ř, r̃, j, j̃, v́, ṽ, ǵ*, and *g̣*. The following are a few examples of this. We will use some of disambiguators that have appeared less often in previous examples for the sake of also demonstrating their usage:

Kfaû ř junẽ fè pò prāmē.
produce D music money I only
"I only produce music for the money."

Ź piò ṽ psōsrē cámà frāsrò krụpýprà cxārō
PAST aim D target his rifle soldier quickly
"The soldier quickly aimed at the target with his rifle."

M̃ riè j lạmá nōplā plīkrè lỵ plịrí.
will walk D their path lonely god forever
"The gods will walk their lonely paths forever."

If, on the other hand, the cause is incapable of such decisions, whether it is an unintelligent organism or a natural force like a storm, an earthquake, or the wind, we will simply refer to it as the cause.

Despite this dimension of meaning being important enough to be marked in Katalopsi, however, it is necessary to understand that the unthinking cause semantic role is not uniquely and individually marked by disambiguators in the language. Rather, the same words which mark for this role—*ń, ǹ*, and *ĺ*—may for other words or other contexts mark the instrument role. There is a typological basis for this behavior, as various languages, Russian among them, will use the *instrumental case*, case being a morphosyntactic phenomenon irrelevant to Katalopsi, to mark the non-agentive cause just as they use it to mark instruments. Here are some examples of the cause role in action:

Ź friē ǹ krṵ jě fé ź j̣ pluô v̀ lá plō.
PAST destroy D boat weather before PAST can use D it we
"The weather destroyed the boat before we were able to use it."

Sruô ń pòmá psȳ.
act up D my dog
"My dog is acting up."

M̃ cxiǎ Î sṛe plà clṵ nìsy̱.
will cause D a lot problem they storm
"The storm will cause a lot of problems for them."

As we go through these few sections on the dimensions of meaning within semantic role marking, we will see again and again that the distinctions may be exploited to communicate somewhat unique or idiosyncratic things within the language. This agency distinction is not an exception.

Take first any obvious case of agency. For example, if a mugger attacks someone, we would generally say they chose to do so as a sentient and self-determining human being. However, by using a disambiguator marking the cause role, you imply the mugger is not in full possession of their faculties, attacking much like an animal, as a human may frenzy in anger or one mentally ill may aggress without control:

R̀ kriā m̀ pòmá srý nūnō!
PROG attack D my family thief
"A thief is attacking my family!"

R̀ kriā ǹ pòmá srý nūnō!
PROG attack D my family thief
"A thief is (wildly) attacking my family!"

As you can see, this distinction in meaning can express an absence of control. Speakers may thereby use this strategy to distance the agent from the choice or the outcome, much like the so-called *se inocente* of Spanish, in which a non-agent may be blamed or credited for some event in place of the agentive cause. Several examples follow:

Ź joū ṽ crìja̱ lỹ pò.
PAST break D window ball I
"I broke the window with a ball."

Ź joū ǹ crìja̱ pòmá lỹ.
PAST break D window my ball
"My ball broke the window."

Ź pluê j̃ kenỹ lèkfu̱ cì.
PAST drop D plate kitchen she
"She dropped the plate in the kitchen."

Ź pluê Ĩ kenỹ lèkfu̱ cìmá kfũ kálỳ.
PAST drop D plate kitchen her hand tired
"Her tired hands dropped the plate in the kitchen."

Ź pliō m̀ kré clī (fìli̱ klỹ).
PAST win D game they with skill
"They won the game (with skill)."

Ź pliō ǹ kré klỹ (plu̱ clī).
PAST win D game skill for they
"Skill won the game (for them)."

4.1.2: INTENTIONALITY—EXP VS. AG

Intentionality involves making a semantic distinction between whether the experience of an agent was done with intension on the part of the agent. Note that this is a different dimension of meaning from agency, which as we saw serves to highlight whether the cause of something was a thinking agent. In this case, we take it for granted that the entity in question is sentient, but we are not yet sure whether the action experienced was one the entity engaged in with intention.

Think first of something that we know to be the act of a thinking agent, like swinging one's fist or pulling a trigger. We know such actions are intentional of the agent specified because interlocutors assume them to be done willfully unless, say, an adverb like *accidentally* or *unintentionally* is included as a modifier. We would say that the agent experienced the event of swinging their fist or of pulling a trigger, but we know this to be the case because they did it intentionally. The fact that intention was present in their mind leads us to focus more closely on their choice as an agent and less so on their experience.

If, however, an event experienced by an agent does not involve intention on the part of that agent, then we focus more on that experience on a psychological level. This implication is present in words like *think*, *feel*, *enjoy*, *taste*, and *hear*. While it may be possible to construe such things with intentionality in some instances, very often we regard them instead as experiences that happen in a given agent's brain without their choice.

Katalopsi recognizes this distinction in semantic role with the use of the disambiguators ź, ż, and z̃, which each mark for an experiencer. To exemplify this class of disambiguators, let us first view several verbs which cannot be construed with intention:

Moī ź clīmà o̯kru̯.
agree D her parents
"Her parents agree."

M̄ liý ż lá pò klè m̃ frã-kiè m̀ cì.
want trust D it I that will right-act D she
"I want to trust her to act right."

Neú z̃ línò u sỹ núkfō plō cūpā.
wonder D purpose of that arch we often
"We often wonder about the purpose of that arch."

Because this division in disambiguators is available in Katalopsi, the indicated dimension of meaning can be exploited to use verbs in more specific ways. For those verbs that can have an experiential character, it is also possible to use agentive disambiguators to bring in a notion of intentionality. Note in the following examples that the English translation is rarely different since English does not as easily mark the different semantic roles. In other words, while English may require the difference be determined through context, Katalopsi can mark the distinction overtly.

Kuó z̃ l̰amá rīsā klīkȳ.
think D their answer student
"The students are thinking about their answers."

Kuó m̊ l̰amá rīsā klīkȳ.
think D their answer student
"The students are thinking of their answers."

In the former case above, the answers are a stimulus provoking thought out of the students. In context, this will usually mean that the answers have already been created, and the students are considering them. This type of thought could be translated instead as "pondering." The latter case, on the other hand, is an intentional kind of thought, meaning they are actively applying their thought for the purpose of creating their answers. Another way to put this is that the experiential thought is reactionary in nature, while the agentive thought is intentional.

Several more examples where this distinction comes in handy follow:

J̰ ruê z̃ xō pò.
can feel D water I
"I can feel the water."

J̰ ruê m̊ xō pò.
can feel D water I
"I can feel the water."

In the former example here, the experiential usage of *ruê* means that the subject is experiencing the sensation of the water touching them.

In the second example, the agentive usage means that the subject has reached out and touched the water, e.g. to see what the sensation was like.

In the previous two pairs of examples, the semantic distinction is not one that is easily detected in English by the superficial appearance of the sentence. The context really is necessary in that sense. For some verbs that allow for this intentionality distinction, however, a difference is observed in English, while the difference in Katalopsi is again only the disambiguator. The following examples show this well:

R̄ ryù z̃ pòmá fòlo̱ pò.
tend to confuse D my brother I
"My brother tends to confuse me."

R̄ ryù m̀ pòmá fòlo̱ pò.
tend to confuse D my brother I
"I tend to confuse my brother."

This pair is interesting in that it shows English will sometimes simply move around arguments when Katalopsi requires a change of disambiguator. Note that each of the two English translations here, however, are still ambiguous about intentionality; the change of arguments just makes it clearer *who* may be either the agent or the stimulus, *who* may be either the experiencer or the theme. In Katalopsi, the confusion happens not to be possible in this case.

To wrap up this section, two final pairs of examples will follow. With these, it should now be clear how to use disambiguators to distinguish intentionality. In these examples, the predicate usages are monovalent, allowing a single argument to be distinguished along the single dimension of intentionality:

Ḿ klau̱ z̀ plō.
have to dream D we
"We have to dream."

Ḿ klau̱ m̀ plō.
have to dream D we
"We have to dream."

Here the subject of the sentence is the only argument and is distinguished as either an experiencer, as in the former case, or an agent, as in the latter case. When the subject is an experiencer, the speaker is commenting on the inevitability of dreaming as a cognitive experience, perhaps because we are humans, because we are animals, because we have brains, or what have you. When the subject is instead an agent, it is easier to take the metaphorical interpretation of dreaming, where we are now discussing the act of imagining goals and aspirations, an intentional consideration of those experiences. The following pair permit a similar analysis:

Ř mię ź cxékỳ.
PROG laugh D teacher
"The teacher is laughing."

Ř mię ḿ cxékỳ.
PROG laugh D teacher
"The teacher is laughing."

In the first of this pair of examples, the experiential usage of *mię* means that the teacher is laughing uncontrollably, i.e. they are reacting to something, and they couldn't help but laugh. In the second example, however, the teacher has chosen to laugh intentionally, as indicated by the selection of the agentive disambiguator.

4.1.3: ALTERATION—PA vs. TH

In our initial presentation of disambiguators, we explained that on some occasions, either the patient or the theme semantic role could be intended for a coincident argument. This is due, of course, to the fact that both patients and themes are part of a more basic role called an undergoer. The disambiguators which are indecisive on this point are *r̃, j̃,* and *ṽ.*

In some cases, however, a distinction is important, and it happens along the semantic dimension of *alteration*. In other words, did the action which the undergoer underwent cause a change from one state to another in the undergoer? When a change of state is observed in the undergoer, we call it a theme. When no change of state occurs, it is instead a patient. We see many disambiguators solely assigning the theme role and never the patient role, and the complete list includes ṁ, m̃, í, ì, ĩ, v́, ż, and g̃. On the other hand, a small number of disambiguators assign the patient role and never the theme role, specifically ŕ and r̀.

The following examples show the patient in use. Note how the actions described do not result in a change of state to the undergoer:

Ź xyí r̀ cámà ūcò mịrá srerõ.
PAST glare D his daughter father sternly
"The father glared sternly at his daughter."

Ź kuè r̀ kùclụ cīkȳ mīmāxùrọ.
PAST knock D door salesman energetically
"The salesman knocked energetically on the door."

The next few examples show the theme role being used. In this case, the actions clearly result in a change to the undergoer:

M̃ ryŭfiē Í lá pịjó.
will demolish D it tomorrow
"It will be demolished tomorrow."

R̀ sraû ṁ plȳcrò xisaprã.
PROG organize D file assistant
"The assistant is organizing the files."

Because Katalopsi is capable of making this distinction of alteration, this dimension of meaning can for some verbs be played with to indicate more specific information about the impact of some event. A study of Table 10 in chapter 2 will make identifying these verbs easier, especially when combined with the knowledge in the dictionary entries of chapter 7. But with that said, it will no doubt be helpful to see the minimal pairs where this dimension of meaning makes the difference.

In each of the following pairs, you should note how the expression of alteration, or lack thereof, on the undergoer changes the description of the event and any listener's understanding of it. We will go through each pair one by one:

Ź keò m̀ cxõ cá psōxùrǫ.
PAST hit D rock he forcefully
"He hit the rock forcefully."

Ź keò r̀ cxõ cá psōxùrǫ.
PAST hit D rock he forcefully
"He hit the rock forcefully."

The implication of the latter formulation, using the disambiguator r̀, is that the rock was not moved, was not damaged, and in short underwent no change. The situation in which this formulation is appropriate may be very special, like that it was a large, solid boulder that would not be easily moved or damaged. The former formulation, on the other hand, does imply a change, like that the rock was knocked away or that it broke apart. For this to be possible, of course, it's more likely the situation is one of a small rock, a pebble. Therefore, the selection between these disambiguators may depend highly on context and on the meaning you would like to connote.

R̀ sau̧ m̀ kèkra̧ pòmá prūrī.
PROG press D orange my mother
"My mother is pressing the oranges."

R̀ sau̧ r̀ kèkra̧ pòmá prūrī.
PROG press D orange my mother
"My mother is pressing the oranges."

In these sentences, the word *press* should be understood as applying force to a small area. The latter example denoting a patient object implies, again, that no change is effectuated by the action, and one might say this when checking that the oranges are ripe and healthy. On the other hand, in the former example, change is taking place, which we know because the disambiguator indicates a theme object. This would be appropriate to say when squeezing oranges or other fruits for their juice.

As you can see, it can sometimes be important to bear in mind whether the event described results in a change of state, and it may sometimes reveal a great deal of contextual information that is not otherwise stated. This small amount of information is compared to our knowledge of the world, and we come to conclusions based on the usage of either the theme-object or patient-object disambiguator.

4.1.4: Proposition—STIM vs. TH

In our discussion of intentionality, we listed several verbs with such a strong psychological component that a semantic role known as an experiencer was justified over any other. Verbs like *think, hear, believe, prefer, imagine*, and *feel* are experiential in nature, and something is the stimulus for that experience. When the stimulus is an entity, like when hearing a *noise*, we will simply say the noise is a stimulus. But when that stimulus has a cognitive character, like a complete idea, a story, or what have you, we instead call it a proposition. Often this will require context to justify it, so we will look at several examples and provide explanations for what is going on:

Ź si̧e ž càxi̧ kfì clējī pò.
PAST hear D click from office I
"I heard a click sound from the office."

Ź si̧e ż lá pò klè ź mi̧e ž klȩ kù.
PAST hear D it I that PAST laugh D movie you
"I heard you laughing at the movie."

Feǐ ž pàpru̧ cá fòklé rìpru̧.
prefer D shortsword he to longsword
"He prefers a shortsword to a longsword."

Feǐ ż lá cá klé pluô v̀ pàpru̧ kù.
prefer D it he that use D shortsword you
"He prefers that you use a shortsword."

It is noteworthy that this particular phenomenon is semantic and not syntactic, so although it is easy to imagine propositions as complete, if subordinate, clauses, of course words like *idea, concept, suggestion,* and *story* may in context refer to a proposition in fewer words. In these cases, shorter and less complex sentences are derived while still drawing a line between a stimulating entity and a stimulating proposition.

Rei̯ ż psī pò nūjè.
like D idea I really
"I really like the idea."

Ź moî ż cámà krisỹ plō.
PAST surprise D his suggestion we
"His suggestion surprised us."

Luè ż cámà ka̠sa̠ pò fò.
believe D his story I not
"I don't believe his story."

4.1.5: Benefit—REC vs. BEN

In some semantic theories, it is suggested that the recipient and beneficiary semantic roles should be collapsed into a single category, sometimes labeled BEN/REC. Certainly many languages do not make a grammatical distinction between the two, either in morphology or in syntax. In Katalopsi, however, this distinction is sometimes necessary for grammaticality, specifically in the choice of disambiguator. For example, the verb *xiã*, or "help" in English, inherently involves a beneficiary, someone who benefits from your actions. While we can say that the beneficiary "receives help," it is nonetheless grammatically incorrect to use a disambiguator that assigns the recipient role. It must obligatorily assign the beneficiary role.

This is a distinction much like agency or intentionality, where one role that we typically assign is actually a superset, while the other is a more specific variety. The relevant dimension of meaning is what we will call *benefit*. If an entity receives anything, the recipient role is assigned, but if it also benefits from the action, or if the purpose of the event or action is to benefit the entity, then it is a beneficiary. In other words, the beneficiary role is a more specific variety of recipient, and for some words, like *xiã*, no other interpretation of the recipient is possible.

Only two disambiguators assign the recipient role, *ñ* and *g̀*. Three, however, assign the beneficiary role: *m̃*, *g̣*, and *g̃*. Along this dimension of meaning, only one disambiguator remains, the word *Ĩ*. Rather than assigning strictly either the recipient or the beneficiary role, it is ambiguous in much the same way as the undergoer disambiguators. In other words, it is a BEN/REC disambiguator, able to assign either role, which is decided pragmatically.

Several words are able to use disambiguators which vary along this dimension of meaning. A few examples follow which show this variation in action:

R̀ niè ñ jelõ cámà srý Matthew.
PROG send D letter his family Matthew
"Matthew is sending a letter to his family."

R̀ niè m̃ jelõ cámà srý Matthew.
PROG send D letter his family Matthew
"Matthew is sending a letter for his family."

In the first sentence here, the disambiguator *ñ* is used. From this we know that the second, or middle, argument is the recipient of the *send* event, the entity which received the letter. The second sentence is the same as the first save for the disambiguator *m̃*. This word tells us that the family is instead the beneficiary, the entity for whom the *send* event was carried out. If this distinction is not clear, imagine that your family has asked you to send a letter. When you do so, you are benefitting them by fulfilling their request, but that does not mean the letter is going to them. If it were, they would instead be the recipient. The fact that English can be ambiguous along this dimension of meaning is obvious in the fact that both of these sentences could be translated as "Matthew is sending his family a letter." Only context allows a listener to be sure whether the family is the recipient or the beneficiary in this instance, though one interpretation and usage may be more common than another.

M̃ niõ ǵ ly f̄ȳnū.
will pray D god priest
"The priest will pray to god."

M̃ niõ g̀ fỳkú càlu̠ f̄ȳnū.
will pray D miner dead priest
"The priest will pray for the dead miners."

In this pair, we see a variation of the disambiguators ǵ and g̀, which mark respectively for the recipient and beneficiary roles. In this case, the verb is divalent, so the argument of interest is the first. Unlike for the English verb *send*, the verb *pray* cannot take unmarked internal arguments, so we're forced to use the prepositions *to* and *for* to communicate the intended meanings in translation. This also raises an interesting point about the distribution of semantic roles in Katalopsi disambiguators, namely that no disambiguator will mark for both the recipient and the beneficiary roles in the same grammatical phrase, so we're forced to use at least one preposition to get both. There are a several ways to do this:

M̃ niõ ǵ ly f̄ȳnū plu̠ fỳkú càlu̠.
will pray D god priest for miner dead
"The priest will pray to god for the dead miners."

See in this case that the recipient is an argument within the grammatical phrase, while the beneficiary must be marked with a preposition *plu̠*.

M̃ niõ g̀ fỳkú càlu̠ f̄ȳnū ó ly.
will pray D miner dead priest to god
"The priest will pray for the dead miners to god."

In this variation, the direct object is a beneficiary, while the recipient is marked with a preposition *ó*.

M̃ niõ ḿ f̄ȳnū ó ly plu̠ fỳkú càlu̠.
will pray D priest to god for miner dead
"The priest will pray to god for the dead miners."

M̃ niõ ḿ fȳnū plu̱ fỳkú càlu̱ ó ly̱.

will pray D priest for miner dead to god

"The priest will pray for the dead miners to god."

And finally, in this pair of examples, the disambiguator allows for a monovalent usage of the verb *niõ*, meaning that to mention both the recipient and beneficiary of the *pray* event, two prepositional phrases are required, which may surface in one of the two above orders.

As a final note, remember that the disambiguators which assign the beneficiary role are also analogized to the expression of *detriment*. As a contrastive counterpart to benefit, the meaning of detriment also calls for an equivalent to the beneficiary, which we could call the *detrimentary*. Some verbs actually imply a detriment rather than a benefit, and in these cases, the beneficiary-marking disambiguators are nonetheless used but interpreted slightly differently.

4.1.6: TRANSIENCE—EXP VS. TH

In §3.2.3, we described how nominal, adjectival, and prepositional predicates demand a different understanding of disambiguators than verbal predicates. While the disambiguator *í*, for example, typically marks for the theme role when paired with a verb, when it occurs to the right of a noun, adjective, or preposition in the predicate position, it is said generally to refer to the state of the argument mentioned later in the grammatical phrase. To put this another way, the argument has a quality or belongs to a group of similar entities that have that characteristic. We also learned that inanimate objects, or arguments that are incapable of experience, are forced to use this disambiguator, while humans and other experiencers may use the *ź* disambiguator to mark the state they find themselves in.

This latter category of entities is unique in that Katalopsi permits speakers to mark the transience of the described state by selecting between either *í* or *ź*. For example, a human being may be *sick*, but this state could be relatively permanent or relatively transitory. When it is considered to be a temporary state, then *ź* is used, as it is a condition the speaker is currently experiencing. When the illness is instead thought to be permanent, then *í* will be used. This is of course another instance of disambiguator selection which reflects a nuance of meaning not easily translated into English.

This meaning can sometimes come into conflict with the lexical meaning of nouns, adjectives, and adverbs. For example, the word *sojirọ*, or "currently," implies transience, and so to use *í* with it given a non-verbal predicate and an animate entity is semantically contradictory. So such a sentence would look like the following, obligatorily using *ź*:

> Fụ ź pò sọjirọ.
> weak D I currently
> "I'm weak at the moment."

On the other hand, using an adverb like *plý*, or "always," implies a lack of transience, and so the use of *ź* would be inappropriate. Instead, *í* would be used to suggest that it's an inherent characteristic of the argument, which is consistent with the meaning of *plý*:

> Fụ Í pò plý.
> weak D I always
> "I am always weak."

Naturally, if the argument is an entity incapable of experiencing something psychologically, then transience is no longer a factor, and *í* is always used:

> Fụ Í fý sọjirọ.
> weak D bridge currently
> "The bridge is weak currently."

> Fụ Í fý plý.
> weak D bridge always
> "The bridge is always weak."

4.2: NUMBER

Grammatical number refers to the impact the quantity of something may have on the grammatical rules of a given language. There are several ways to discuss this topic in English, though fewer than in other languages more complex in this respect.

Although there are occasional morphological exceptions, English distinguishes a group of some entity from a solitary instance of the same entity by use of the suffixing morpheme ⟨s⟩. The fact that this group may have two or more members is what leads linguists to call English a *plural* language, and these respective representations are known by laypeople and experts with the names *plural* and *singular*.

While this numerical information may be represented by morphology on the noun or by lexeme when it comes to pronouns, the same information is marked on the verb or front-most auxiliary in what is known as *agreement*. That is, the number information marked on a given noun must also be marked on the verb. This is the difference between the incomplete sentences *The dog is* and *The dogs are*. Spanish and many other languages have agreement between nouns and adjectives, not only on number but also gender, while Arabic and others have agreement on gender between nouns and verbs.

Agreement is a large topic in the study of language, and number frequently comes up, but when it comes to Katalopsi, it must be emphasized that number is not a grammatical factor. There is no morphology on nouns or verbs which indicate the number of participants, and only pronouns can be said to have inherent number. For their part, pronouns show that Katalopsi is a plural language because it only distinguishes the singular and the plural. This is in contrast to, say, Lithuanian, which has a *dual* system, meaning it has a three-way grammatical distinction in number: the singular, or one entity; the dual, or two entities; and the plural, or more than two entities. However, because this numerical marking is not present for any other part of speech, it is by no means a productive characteristic of the Katalopsi language.

The one area where number is embedded and essential to acceptable speech is in the use of pronouns. As we saw in §2.2.2.1, Katalopsi distinguishes the singular and plural in this category not only for first and third person—like in the English words *I* and *we*, *she* and *they*—but also in the second person. This may be confusing depending on the dialect of English you speak. In standard American English, you may use the word *you* to refer to a single person or a group of people. In other dialects, you might say "you all," "y'all," or even "youse" for a group. Katalopsi uses *kù* and *klū* for the respective singular and plural varieties. With that said, the number inherent to a pronoun is still not used to distinguish morphology on the verb.

We have so far discussed number in the grammatical sense, which does communicate some color of meaning but is highly enveloped in the morphosyntax of the given language. This is irrelevant to Katalopsi, but it is also important to reiterate how number is communicated when speaking the language. Remember that Katalopsi also has quantifiers and numerals. The latter category of words allows for very specific communication of quantity, while the perhaps confusingly named quantifiers give somewhat more general information about number. Using these expressions, we can communicate the meaning that English does with morphology and with analogous lexemes.

It is not essential to elaborate on the meaning of numerals in Katalopsi because they work essentially the same way as in English. They deal with specific, literal enumeration of quantities, so the specifics of the language do not come into play. It *is* worthwhile to mention how quantifiers carve out a dimension of meaning for themselves, however.

When quantifying a number of items in a generic way in English, we use words like *some*, *many*, *most*, and *all*. Regardless of exactly how many items there are in the designated group, quantifiers like these can be used to share information about the quantity of relevance, which may be the whole group or a subset of the group.

In §2.2.1.2, we introduced the various quantifiers Katalopsi offers, and as it turns out, they divide the quantification dimension of meaning in a way that is distinct from English. Let us first look at the quantifiers that speak to a specific amount and then second look at the quantifiers that express ranges.

There are five quantifiers in Katalopsi which can be said to point unambiguously or specifically to a quantity. A further division could be made in whether the quantifier is equivalent to enumeration, but this point is perhaps not important here. The words are *sǫ*, or "no," *pe*, or "both," *xã*, or "half," *nè*, or "each/every," and *clà*, or "all." Only *pǫ* tells you the relevant group of items has a particular enumeration—that is, two—while the other quantifiers identify a subset without telling you the size of the set. The word *sǫ*, we know, always identifies a subset with zero members. The word *xã* identifies a subset exactly fifty percent the size of the set. And finally, the words *nè* and *clà* identify a subset which includes one hundred percent of the identified set.

Already, with this category of quantifiers, we can see differences from English. English does make the divisions in meaning that the abovementioned quantifiers do, but it also has the word *a*. This article has other functions besides quantification, but it also points to a set of size one, as unambiguously as *both* points to two.

The second category of quantifiers are those which establish a range of possible values. These we can surely say do not enumerate either like numerals or even like some of the more specific quantifiers. The words are *lú*, or "either," *pé*, or "few," *rỳ*, or "some/any," *srǫ*, or "many/a lot," and *kfū*, or "most." The word *lú* comes closest to enumeration since, by usage, we know it refers to one or two. The words *rỳ* and *srǫ* probably have the largest ranges of possible values. The former seems to establish a subset between two and all. The latter is highly contextual, i.e. what may be considered a lot will vary by context, but it also seems to identify a range from at least two all the way to the complete set, however large that may be. Generally speaking, we just know that *srǫ* is used when the actual value is greater than the value tending to be referred to by *rỳ*, a fact of implicational meaning. The word *pé* also relates both contextual and implicational meaning in that it tends to be small and most likely smaller than any value that *rỳ* might usually refer to. That said, it still seems to indicate a minimum of two. Finally, *kfū* uses percentages to identify a range greater than fifty percent but typically less than one hundred percent.

4.3: COUNTABILITY

A popular topic in semantic inquiry, related to but distinct from number, is *countability*, or the grammatical distinction between a word like *rice* and a word like *bean*. The former is known as a *mass noun* in English, meaning it is not something we tend conceptually to count or distinguish as individual units. One manifestation of this is the fact that it is not grammatical to say "one rice," "two rice(s)," etc. You must instead use some more specific, measured quantity, like a *cup* of rice. The individual units, on the other hand, have their own word, i.e. you have a *grain* of rice. Other such mass nouns include *water*, *air*, and *blood*.

The word *bean* is a *count noun*, something we do indeed tend to count. When we say "one bean," "two beans," etc., this is grammatically correct. If we tried to treat this as a mass noun and say something like "a cup of bean," this would sound very strange. Grammar dictates that the word be marked with the plural morpheme, as in "a cup of beans." Other such count nouns include *cat*, *cloud*, and *key*. It is important to understand, however, that given the right context, it is possible to use count nouns as mass nouns or vice versa.

Countability is not a marked dimension of meaning in Katalopsi, so nouns will look the same regardless of whether you mean them in the count sense or the mass sense. This does lend one more freedom in using nouns as either count or mass to one's preference. For example, in using the word *cuku*, or "rice," one may say "clū cuku" and mean either "five grains of rice" or "five kinds of rice," the former being the count sense and the latter being the mass sense. Likewise, to say "rỳ cuku," or "some rice," would mean just a few grains of rice in the count sense or a generic amount of rice in the mass sense.

Although the lack of distinction in countability gives license to use the nouns more creatively, it is of course also the case that ambiguity may arise from it. In cases where specificity is necessary, longer, more descriptive phrases may be justified. Often the phrases will be constructed from use of the word *u*, or "of," as in the following:

mìklá u cuku
piece of rice
"a grain of rice"

clū sý u cuku
five kind of rice
"five kinds of rice"

xalã u cụkụ
cup of rice
"a cup of rice"

mìklá u sụ
piece of bean
"a bean"

clū sý u sụ
five kind of bean
"five kinds of bean"

xalã u sụ
cup of bean
"a cup of beans"

4.4: DEFINITENESS

In our discussion of determiners in chapter 2, we introduced the concept of definiteness, which is not a dimension of meaning so straightforwardly expressed in Katalopsi. In English, we have the definite article *the* and the indefinite articles *a* and *an*. Katalopsi, on the other hand, does not have such words, although the expression of definiteness is not altogether impossible.

Consider what it means for a noun to be definite. In effect, using a word like *the* tells your conversation partner that you're talking about a relevant entity from the context, from the discussion, or from the surrounding environment. In this sense, its meaning is quite generic, and it is the pragmatics of the situation that allow you to discern the object. It is also the fact that you did not use the word *a* or *an*, which tells you that the modified noun may be present or may not be, but it is one of such a thing that is being discussed generically.

With this explanation, the meaning of definiteness and indefiniteness is probably much clearer. Knowing this, it should also be clearer that Katalopsi demonstratives, whether used as determiners or as pronouns, have an inherent definiteness to them. We also know that such demonstratives may be used to refer to physical entities or abstract, conceptual entities, which means that they can and often do play the roles that *the* does.

That said, we have seen many examples so far of translations in which the use of the word *the* was appropriate. In a subsection of those cases, we cannot simply replace the definite article with a demonstrative determiner without some awkward phrasing as a result. Therefore, it is important that we see still more examples that try to delineate how definiteness is understood from the absence of a determiner. This will often require the description of context and the use of world knowledge, much as speakers of English do all the time to determine the exact entity referred to when that entity is modified by *the*.

Ź siě m̀ pòmá nì.
PAST lose D my key
"I lost my keys."

M̀ prìcy Í nì.
must here D key
"The keys must be here."

In this pair of sentences, we see an object—a set of keys—be established. Specifically, the speaker refers to "pòmá nì," or "my keys," using a possessive pronoun. In response, the second speaker simply refers to "nì" without a modifier. That is, it has already been established by the first speaker which set of keys are being discussed, subsequent to which the other speaker may simply refer generically to keys. In English, we mark this understanding with the definite article *the*, but since Katalopsi does not make such a distinction overtly, one simply uses the unmodified noun.

Fiã m̀ lá pò klè saí ż rỳ léfī (pò).
wish D it I that have D some pie I
"I wish I had some pie."

Saí ż léfī pò cú lèkfụ.
have D pie I in kitchen
"I have a pie in the kitchen."

In this exchange, the first speaker establishes a generic object, not necessarily a known object in the vicinity, "rỳ léfĩ," or "some pie." To this, the second speaker responds by grounding that object in the immediate environment, referring to it, like in the previous example, with the unmodified noun, "léfĩ." In this case, based on the context, the appropriate translation uses the indefinite article and not the definite article, since there was no specific pie to which the initial speaker was referring. Katalopsi, again not having this distinction of definiteness, however, simply presents an unmodified noun.

Indefiniteness is quite a different beast from definiteness in part because it brings into play the meaning of quantification, as we saw in §4.2. When *the* is used, a singular or a plural noun may follow. The English indefinite articles *a* and *an* require a single item, which can of course also be done with the word *one*. The notion of an indefinite entity—not necessarily one in the context or out of it, one that may be present in the discussion or the environment or not—is also expressed by the quantifier and impersonal pronoun *some*. Therefore, parsing the appropriate time to use words like *xỹ*, "one," and *rỳ*, "some," versus the time to omit a determiner altogether, can be a difficult problem in Katalopsi. Keep in mind the lessons about countability and number from this chapter, and you will have no problem determining when the specific enumeration of *xỹ* may be more preferable to a generic mass quantification like *rỳ*.

4.5: TEMPORAL DISTANCE

Recall from our discussion in chapter 2 of auxiliaries that may differentiate the recent past from the distant past, the imminent future from the remote future. Not every language has such parallel and grammaticalized methods of expressing tense in this way. In English, the past and future tenses are generic, the former being expressed by bound morphology, the latter by the auxiliaries *will* and *shall*. The recent past is also expressible but works in conjunction with the generic past tense morphology with the addition of the adverb *just* to the sentence. The imminent future is expressed with the phrase *about to* appearing before the verb.

This idea of the *temporal distance* of an event allows us to make decisions about how to use Katalopsi auxiliaries, and depending on how an event is being discussed, the exact tense used may vary. There is thereby a pragmatic element to the communication of tense. But this fact is also due to the interactions of lexical meaning and the choice to use one term over another. This is the notion of *implicature,* or a meaning which is communicated by other than the direct denotative meaning of the word or words used.

Semantically, Katalopsi tense auxiliaries are first divided into the present and the non-present. Only the non-present tenses are capable of distinguishing temporal distance. An interesting thing happens when the past and future tense auxiliaries are evaluated along this dimension of meaning. Those that are *near* to the present, i.e. the recent past and the imminent future, are specific tenses, while the remaining two are generic in nature, the past and the future. Because they are generic, it is possible to use them to refer to something that, respectively, happened recently or will happen soon. That is what it means for them to be generic, that they do indeed overlap with the more specific terms. The following pair shows how the two past tenses may refer to the same event. It is instead the context that determines which is more appropriate:

Ź siě m̀ cìmá ru pòmá prūrī.
PAST lose D her cat my mother
"My mother lost her cat."

Ẑ siě m̀ cìmá ru pòmá prūrī.
RECENT lose D her cat my mother
"My mother just lost her cat."

And the following pair shows how the generic future and the imminent future tenses may also apply to the same event:

M̃ nūjè fri̱ Í klè ēcxeò m̀ plō pī sĩ krefílè.
will very difficult D that rebuild D we after this catastrophe
"Rebuilding after this catastrophe will be very difficult."

Ŕ nūjè fr̩ Í klè ēcxeò m̀ plō pī sĩ kr̩fílè.
about to very difficult D that rebuild D we after this catastrophe
"Rebuilding after this catastrophe is about to be very difficult."

However, because Katalopsi does have these terms for the specific, near tenses, use of the generic terms *strongly implies* the distant past and remote future. This is due to your conversation partner's assumptions about the information you are giving them; they believe that if the fact that the event happened recently or will happen shortly is important, you would use the specific near-tense terms. Since you didn't, you must therefore mean the distant past or the remote future.

4.6: EVIDENTIALITY

An interesting dimension of meaning in Katalopsi is the communication of evidentiality, which is more robustly grammaticalized in the constructed language than in English. With evidential auxiliaries, the speaker need never make a statement without expressing their degree of belief in it or even whether their belief is a factor at all.

4.6.1: REPORTATIVITY

Reportativity refers to a subset of evidential meaning wherein you distinguish what another has claimed from what you yourself claim. When reporting what another person has said, you may take the *report stance*. The report stance allows speakers of Katalopsi to repeat what another person has said without also saying whether or not they believe it. The report stance in many languages is grammaticalized in conjugation, as with the German *Konjunktiv I*, a type of subjunctive mood. Katalopsi speakers take the report stance by using the auxiliary r̩. Several examples follow:

R̩ kraĩ Í kí lùjo̩ jõ.
REPORT kill D man across street
"Reportedly, a man was killed across the street."

Ploī m̀ lá cá klè ź r̝ riǒ z̃ rìsr̲e cá rēcōlỳ p̲eclú.
say D it he that PAST REPORT see D monster he beyond mountain
"He says he saw a monster beyond the mountains."

R̲ xyklo̲ j̲icr̲i Í kry ro̲xo̲ cẽ.
REPORT especially dangerous D cave during night
"It's said the cave is particularly dangerous at night."

M̃ sriō m̀ lá cxycõ klè ź r̝ roì Í so̲ srúsò.
will claim D it government that PAST REPORT there be D no
wrong-doing
"The government will claim that there was no wrong-doing."

Importantly, because such an auxiliary exists, the omission of the
term implies a degree of belief in what is reported. You may choose to
omit the reportative auxiliary when the person who made the claim is
someone you trust to a reasonable degree, but of course other evidential
auxiliaries allow you to be still more specific about your degree of belief.

4.6.2: DEGREE OF CONFIDENCE

When you do have a degree of belief in something that you would like
to communicate, Katalopsi makes a three-waẏ distinction. For reasons
of normativity, the absence of an evidential auxiliary is semantically
weighty. It means that you have a reasonable degree of belief in your
statement, neither a very low amount nor an uncharacteristically high
amount. When expressing a low degree of belief in something—or to
put it another way, when you *doubt* something—you use the auxiliary
ń. On the other hand, a high degree of belief in something is related
with the auxiliary z̲, which also takes on an emphatic character. This is
a way of expressing certainty or near-certainty. See the following three
sentences which make this three-way distinction in belief clear:

Pró cy̲ Í cá klé pò mē lāsū.
more good D he than I at painting
"He is better than me at painting."

Z̲ pró cy̲ Í cá klé pò mē lāsū.
EMPH more good D he than I at painting
"He is definitely better than me at painting."
OR "He *is* better than me at painting."

Ń pró cy̲ Í cá klé pò mē lāsū.
DOUBT more good D he than I at painting
"I'm not sure he's better than me at painting."
OR "I doubt he's better than me at painting."

As you can see, because English does not have a highly grammaticalized system of evidentiality, it's usually possible to translate these evidential Katalopsi words in more than one way. We have done that here to make the underlying evidential meaning clear.

An interesting thing happens when combining the report stance with an evidential auxiliary. Because the report stance involves stating what another has said without confirming or disconfirming it, the mention of degree of belief is taken to be something that the original, reported speaker communicated. In other words, if one speaker uses ń to indicate their doubt in something, a second speaker could report what the original speaker said using both the reportative auxiliary and the doubt auxiliary and the result is a statement more about their doubt and less about the judged proposition. Several examples follow:

Kuó z̲ lá pòmá mureprã klè r̲ z̲ r̃ meȳ ḿ pò pró cūpā.
think D it my doctor that REPORT EMPH should run D I more often
"My doctor thinks that I should *definitely* run more often."

In this sentence, the speaker is not saying they believe the doctor, despite the word z̲ marking confidence. Rather, by combining the inferential auxiliary with the emphatic auxiliary, they are leaving open whether they believe them and drawing attention instead to the fact that the doctor said they are *certain*. This is why a falling intonation will appear on the word *definitely* in translation, as the speaker would like listeners to notice the doctor expressed the certainty, rather than the speaker themselves.

Ź psyi m̀ lá pòmá mı̠rá klè r̠ ń saí ż ké pòmá fòlo̠.
PAST acknowledge D it my father that REPORT DOUBT have D job my brother
"My dad acknowledged his doubt that my brother has a job."

The same could be said for this example, though it instead involves the speaker drawing attention to the doubt marker. That is, they would like listeners to know that the father is the one who expressed doubt and not the speaker themselves. Without the inclusion of the report auxiliary in either of these examples, listeners would instead understand the speaker as expressing the degree of belief in any such auxiliary, as in the following rephrases:

Kuó ż lá pòmá mureprã klè z̠ r̃ meȳ m̀ pò pró cūpā.
think D it my doctor that EMPH should run D I more often
"My doctor thinks that I should run more, and I definitely agree."

Ź psyi m̀ lá pòmá mı̠rá klè ń saí ż ké pòmá fòlo̠.
PAST acknowledge D it my father that DOUBT have D job my brother
"My dad acknowledged that my brother has a job, but I (still) doubt it."

These facts are similarly reflected in the absence of an evidential auxiliary, a fact which we've already discussed with other words. Put another way, when reporting what another person has said, if that person did not use an evidential auxiliary, then we know them to be expressing a normal degree of belief, but if you don't take the report stance, then that normal degree of belief is transferred to you. That is, you are reporting what someone said and also implying that you believe them. If this is not intended, this can be easily corrected by simply including r.

4.6.3: HYPOTHETICALS

The so-called *hypothetical* auxiliary allows you to pose a situation you know not to exist, simply for the sake of argument. Semantically, this auxiliary overlaps with the English complementizer *if*. The word *if* also sets up hypothetical situations, but it is traditionally described as setting up the condition in if-then statements, also known as conditionals. In light of this fact, the Katalopsi auxiliary has a broader meaning which includes that of the conditional.

When this auxiliary is used in the sense of conditional statements, the resulting sentences parallel English sentences in unsurprising ways. We already saw several examples of this in §3.4.4 in demonstration of the syntactic facts, e.g. that the two clauses may be in either order and that the word appears in the auxiliary position. However, for completeness, several more examples follow:

Ĵ ǹ plíkà Í kù rỳ jó, Ī lejã Í kù.
if want manager D you some day need hard-working D you
"If you want to be a manager some day, you need to work hard."

Ĵ peú m̀ xȳ cá, ḡ joū m̀ lá cá klȳkàro̱.
if buy D one he would break D it he immediately
"If he were to buy one, he would break it immediately."

Ź ṽ ĵ siě m̀ kùmá krō kù, ḡ nūjè xā Í kù mēklì.
PAST PERFECT if lose D your coat you would really cold D you right now
"If you had lost your coat, you'd be freezing right now."

The significance of this broader meaning reveals itself in the combined use of the hypothetical and a handful of syntactic constructions previously introduced in chapter 3. With these combinations, meanings equivalent to the English expressions *what if* and *what about* are obtained. For example, by using the interrogative auxiliary and the hypothetical auxiliary—in that order, canonically—you may pose a hypothetical situation and at the same time request the addressee's (or addressees') thoughts or reactions. The following examples show this construction in action:

V̀ ĵ pliō m̀ plōmà lì?
Q if win D our group
"What if our group were to win?"

V̀ ĵ nuȳ m̀ có lō u cxa̱jý pò fé nõ jỳ?

Q if find D source new of income I before month next
"What if I find a new source of income before next month?"

Ź v̀ ȷ́ nuá Í kru̱ xy̱pra̱?
PAST Q if arrive D boat early
"What if the boat had arrived early?"

It is also possible to use the hypothetical auxiliary in an elided topicalization construction to suggest entities in the same sense as the English phrase *what about*. Note that this type of utterance is not easily said to be part of a conceptually complete sentence. The following communicate this meaning in the specific:

Rỳ junẽ ȷ́?
some music if
"How about some music?"

Kfè rì ȷ́?
scarf long if
"What about a long scarf?"

Pùkra̱ ȷ́?
riddle if
"How about a riddle?"

In some contexts, either of these constructions may be used with more or less the same meaning. The question that may be raised is the appropriateness of the relatively shorter or longer constructions. The following examples give contextualizing sentences followed by the two possible hypothetical constructions with which a respondent may continue the conversation. Observe how in these contexts, the constructions are able to make the same suggestion, to pose the same hypothetical situation.

Ḿ pseў m̀ rỳcu̱ pò mē pòmá krá.
must write D something I for my class
"I have to write something for my class."

Rỳ klápù j̈?
some poetry if
"What about some poetry?"

V̀ j̈ pseў m̀ sȳ kràci̠ kù?
Q if write D book entire you
"What if you wrote a whole book?"

Ľ pliè m̀ psá pró sóxù pò.
need to eat D food more healthy I
"I need to eat healthier food."

Sēkā sa fy̠clá j̈?
broccoli and potato if
"What about broccoli and potatoes?"

V̀ j̈ neu̠ j̃ rỳ sa̠pru̠ kùmá syl̠o kù prànúrō?
Q if include D some vegetable your breakfast you simply
"What if you simply include some vegetables in your breakfast?"

4.7: GENDER

An important dimension of meaning and grammar in language is that of *gender*, which gets its name from the correlation of noun and pronoun categories with sex and gender in human beings. This is by no means an injective relationship, meaning the correlation is not one to one with the human trait, and so in many respects the linguistic phenomenon is rightfully called *grammatical* gender. When it does relate to the grammar, the discussion is then one of agreement, where the gender on the noun or pronoun must also be marked on the modifying determiner or adjective, as in e.g. Spanish, or on the verb, as in e.g. Arabic.

For the purposes of Katalopsi, we will make a distinction between grammatical gender and lexical gender, specifically because the former does not exist in the language. Lexical gender refers to the fact that some nouns and pronouns have an underlying gender coloring. It could be as straightforward as Katalopsi pronouns, for which a three-way distinction exists, or more complicated as in the distribution of semantic fields in the noun system.

Katalopsi pronouns are distinguished by being masculine, feminine, or neuter, where *neuter* simply means non-gendered. All first- and second-person pronouns in the language are non-gendered, while the third-person pronouns are gendered regardless of number. This is unlike English which only genders the singular third-person pronouns. How exactly these gendered and non-gendered third-person pronouns are chosen is a matter of some importance because languages that have even identical lexical paradigms do not necessarily use them the same way.

When discussing a masculine-gendered human or animal, the masculine pronoun *cá* is used. The same goes for feminine-gendered humans and animals and the feminine pronoun *cì*. Importantly, some humans do not identify with the masculine or feminine genders, in which case the non-gendered pronoun *lá* is used. Because *lá* is also used for objects, we translate it as "it," but you should not allow the dehumanizing connotation of English *it* to affect your understanding of the usage of *lá*. In short, it can be used to refer to (a) any human that does not identify with the binary gender system, (b) any animal that you do not feel the need to relate the gender of, and (c) any object or organism incapable of having a gender.

It is also necessary that we discuss the plural third-person pronouns of Katalopsi, which have a similar three-way distinction in gender as the singulars do. A group of masculine humans or animals use *clạ*; a group of feminine humans or animals use *clī*; and a group of nonbinary humans, a group of non-gendered animals, a mixture of gendered and/ or non-gendered humans or animals, or a group of objects will each use *lạ*. In English, all three pronouns are simply translated as "they."

The final point of interest along this dimension is the distribution of gender among noun lexemes. To get a sense of what this means, consider words like *congressman*, *congresswoman*, and *congressperson*. While the third is a relatively recent invention, the first and second indicate the ability of the language to add the words *man* and *woman* to other words to communicate the gender of the person referenced. Katalopsi is unlike English in this respect as the person who does a job or fills a role is only ever indicated in a gender-neutral way. In other words, when a compound is formed, it is only ever *ni*, or "person," which is added to the root word. Other nouns referring to people may be derived from verbs with the agentive noun morphology or from other nouns using the morpheme ⟨pra⟩.

4.8: MATHEMATICS

Various conjunctions, prepositions, and verbs may be used to communicate mathematical concepts. While quantifiers and other determiners point to more generic, more abstract enumerations, numerals, when used with these words, communicate specific quantities and their potential relationships to one another.

4.8.1: ADDITION AND SUBTRACTION

When it comes to the communication of addition and subtraction, there are several words and phrases worth seeing exemplified.

Addition may be communicated in one of two ways. In the sense of a mathematical formula or algebraic equation, the word *pró*, or "more," is used where in English we would say "plus." This means that an expression such as *kri pró clū* would be translated as "eight plus five." On the other hand, you may speak in a less specialized way about adding quantities to other quantities, in which case you may use the verb *luò*, or "add." When adding just two quantities, this will take one of two forms, shown below:

Ġ luò m̀ ję co psi.
IMP add D three and seven
"Add three and seven (together)."

Ġ luò ṽ ję psi.
IMP add D three seven
"Add three to seven."

In the first example, you can see we have just one object, a conjunction phrase of the two quantities to be summed. In the second example, we have two objects, this time each of them numeral phrases but still the same two quantities to be added together. This is accomplished with the use of the instrumental disambiguator v̄. When adding three or more quantities, the previous form is much more common, but the second form is still possible with the use of another conjunction phrase:

Ġ luò m̀ jẹ, psị, co kfé.
IMP add D three seven and nine
"Add three, seven, and nine (together)."

Ġ luò v̄ jẹ co psị kfé.
IMP add D three and seven nine
"Add three and seven to nine."

Subtraction works similarly to addition in that a statement of mathematical operation, i.e. what in English would involve the word *minus*, will again borrow a term from comparison morphosyntax. We use the word *nù*, or "less," to represent this, as in *plè nù clí*, or "ten minus four."

When speaking more informally, however, a verbal predicate may be used. In this case, it is the word *kleọ*, which in other contexts means "remove." Note that in this case, we do not have access to multiple possible structures or disambiguation strategies. This is because addition involves *summands*, or numbers to be added together, and summands may appear in any order without changing the answer. This is in contrast to subtraction, where order is important. The disambiguator then is necessary to define the *minuend* and *subtrahend*, the former being the quantity *from which* a value is subtracted and the latter being *the value* that is subtracted:

Ġ kleọ j̃ frũ jẹpạ.
IMP remove D six thirty
"Subtract six from thirty."

Ġ kleọ j̃ clū plè co pĩ.
IMP remove D five ten and two
"Subtract five from twelve."

As you can see, the disambiguator *j̃* defines the first number as the subtrahend and the second number as the minuend. Typically this disambiguator is locative in character, the second argument being the location, so you can think of it as defining second argument as the source away from which another number is being taken.

4.8.2: MULTIPLICATION AND DIVISION

Multiplication and division are worth separating into their own category, not only for their distinct conceptual character in mathematics, but because the formal language in Katalopsi uses prepositions for the both of them, rather than the comparison adverbs used for addition and subtraction.

In the statement of formulas and equations, the word *lùjo̱*, which typically means "across," is used to mean "multiplied by" or simply "by." That is, an expression like *plè lùjo̱ kri̱* would mean "ten multiplied by eight" or simply "ten by eight." In less formal language, however, you would use the verb *freý*, or "put." In using this word, it is possible to include *lùjo̱* or to omit it like for any locative argument:

Ġ freý j̃ plè co clū clí.
IMP put D ten and five four
"Multiply fifteen by four."

Ġ freý j̃ plè co clū lùjo̱ clí.
IMP put D ten and five across four
"Multiply fifteen by four."

Note that the elements of a multiplication operation are like summands, in that the *multiplicands* may occur in any order without affecting the answer.

In expressing division, the formal or formulaic language is closely related to the everyday, colloquial language. The words *pruã*, "divide," and *fili̱*, "with," make multiple appearances. The supine adjective *prumã* is combined with the preposition to create expressions such as *fã prumã fili̱ plè*, or "one hundred divided by ten." The colloquial language uses the source verb and optionally the preposition in the adjunctive instrument construction:

Ġ pruã ṽ fã plè.
IMP divide D hundred ten
"Divide one hundred by ten."

Ġ pruã m̀ fã kù fìli̱ plè.
IMP divide D hundred you with ten
"Divide one hundred by ten."

4.8.3: EQUALITY AND INEQUALITY

Whether doing addition, subtraction, multiplication, or division, it will sooner or later be necessary to specify the value to which the operation resolves. In English, the words *equal*, *make*, and *come to* are used. Katalopsi uses the respective sum, difference, product, or quotient as the predicate with the intervening disambiguator *Í*. An example of each follows:

Fã Í plè pró kfépã
hundred D ten plus ninety
"Ten plus ninety equals one hundred."

Fã Í fã co plè nù plè.
hundred D hundred and ten minus ten
"One hundred and ten minus ten equals one hundred."

Je̱ u fã Í fã lùjo̱ je̱.
three of hundred D hundred times three
"Three times one hundred makes three hundred."

Pipã co clū Í clūpã prumã fìli̱ pĩ.
twenty and five D fifty divided by two
"Fifty divided by two comes to twenty-five."

Alternatively, you may want to specify an inequal relationship, *greater than* or *less than*. Here, the comparative constructions from chapter 3 make a return, including the use of the preposition *klé*, which marks the object of comparison as expected. Rather than the words *greater* and *less*, however, the phrases *pró lu* and *pró jè* are used, or "bigger" and "smaller," respectively.

Pró lu Í kripa prumã fìli clí klé plè co kfé.
more big D eighty divided by four than ten and nine
"Eighty divided by four is greater than nineteen."

Pró jè Í psi pró plè klé frũ lùjo je.
more small D seven plus ten than six times three
"Seven plus ten is less than six times three."

CHAPTER 5
Orthography

Until now, we have been representing the Katalopsi language with an orthography based on the Latin alphabet and a handful of diacritics. While not necessary for a constructed language, a unique writing system is a delight to create, and one exists for this language.

Where possible, the Katalopsi writing system mirrors the mechanics of the Roman text used in chapters 1 through 4. In this chapter we will explore this unique writing system in all its finer details. We will begin with the basics of writing, then we will discuss how the smaller parts come together to represent the spoken word. After this, we will show how potential ambiguities arise and how the intended meaning can be discerned.

5.1: THE BASICS

The Katalopsi writing system—hereon called *KWS*—is alphabetic, meaning that it is a system for combining symbols which represent the individual sounds of the language. This is as opposed to writing systems like that of Japanese, which employ syllabaries, systems of symbols representing syllables. These alphabetic symbols, known comfortably as *letters*, represent the consonants, vowels, and tones of Katalopsi.

In terms of the directionality of the script, KWS is a vertical system, meaning it is written from the top of the page to the bottom. It is also sinistrodextral, or written from the left to the right. Critically, KWS characters are written relative to a vertical guiding line, so for practice or creative writing, it is easy enough to turn a horizontally ruled paper on its side if vertically ruled paper is not available. KWS might be compared to Devanagari—the writing system of Hindi, among many other languages—which displays a prominent, albeit broken, horizontal guiding line. Here are a few sentences on specialized paper, demonstrating the basics of the writing system:

Illustration 1. The Katalopsi Writing System

As we go through the following sections, we will break down the elements of the system to the finer points and see how the letters representing consonants, vowels, and tones are combined to create larger orthographic structures.

5.2: COMPOSITIONALITY

In terms of writing systems and orthography, *compositionality* means that, to some degree, independently meaningful symbols combine to create larger representations. Generally speaking, KWS consonants are written to the left of the guiding line, while the vowel and tone appear to the right of the guiding line. The guiding line itself is written and represented as part of the vowel, and the tone symbol appears above or below the relevant vowel symbol depending on its contour.

We will first look at these consonant, vowel, and tone symbols individually, and then we will see how they can be combined into syllables. Finally, we will see how larger structures like Type III syllables and multisyllabic words are formed from these parts.

5.2.1: CONSONANTS

KWS has eleven letters representing consonant sounds. Recall from §1.1.2 that Katalopsi has fourteen consonantal phonemes. Three of these eleven letters are performing double duty, which accounts for this incongruity. As already described in the previous section, three pairs of phonemes—all fricatives—differ within their respective pairs solely by the voicing feature, i.e. whether the sound is voiced or voiceless. KWS recognizes this fact by using the same letter for both sounds, though, as we will see shortly, this is disambiguated by other elements of the orthography.

Table 23 shows the eleven consonants of KWS alongside the Latin representations you are by now well familiar with. Also note the third column, which shows the names Katalopsi has for the individual letters. Each of these words uses the sound to which the accompanying letter refers, so they can be useful mnemonic devices for learning the character.

Latin	KWS	Name
p	⊥	pícū, "edge"
c	Ꮒ	còpi̧, "belt"
k	ᑭ	kf̃ē, "flag"
m	ẟ	mòri̧, "bauble"
n	∀	nẽ, "horn"
f / v	⊊	fãsā, "snake"
s / z	↓	sàpy, "rake"
x / g	⊔	xalā, "cup"
l	∧	lò, "shock"
r	○	ré, "orb"
j	ɸ	jófē, "skewer"

Table 23. KWS Consonants

Note that while the tables of this chapter will represent the symbols as relatively the same size, the consonants are actually smaller than the vowels. In later writing samples combining these elements, this will become more apparent.

5.2.2: VOWELS

KWS has seven vowel symbols, six of which correspond to the six vowel phonemes described in chapter 1. The seventh is a way of representing syllabic consonants—or Type I syllables. In effect, this special character is a way of saying that no vowel is present. Used in combination with the three fricatives mentioned in the previous section, the addition of voicing to the normally voiceless consonants is therefore also indicated by the character. Table 24 shows these seven vowel characters:

Latin	KWS
i	
e	
a	
y	
u	
o	
ø	

Table 24. KWS Vowels

There are two things to observe in Table 24. First of all, as previously stated, we are representing KWS's vertical guiding line as part of the vowels. Because this is merely the line against which consonant and vowel positions are determined and evaluated, it could just as easily be left out. However, it is included here to show that each of the vowel symbols obligatorily touch the guiding line in their realization.

The second thing to observe is the absence of any characters marking tone. In the next section we will see how all tones are marked, whether basic or complex, but in Table 24, the neutral tone is in a sense already apparent. The neutral tone is, like in our Latin representations,

231

represented by the absence of a diacritic, so it will be useful to keep this in mind as you proceed through the following sections.

5.2.3: TONES

KWS has five tone symbols, some of which bear close similarity to the Latin diacritics. The letters for the rising and falling tones will be very familiar, while those for the high, low, and mordent tones are distinct. Because tone letters must be interpreted relative to the position of the vowel, the following table shows each of the thirty-five tone-vowel combinations, including the five representing a tone-carrying consonant. Note that the absolute position of the tone diacritic varies by vowel, but it does appear in the same relative area:

		Tone Diacritic				
		x́	x̀	x̄	x̠	x̃
V	i	ʃ̌	ʃ̌	ʃ̄	ʃ̠	ʃ̃
o	e					
w	a					
e	y					
l	u					
	o					
	ø					

Table 25. KWS Tone-Vowel Pairs

As you can see from Table 25, the rising and falling tones are essentially the same as the Latin diacritics, an acute or grave accent above the vowel. The high and low tones again appear above and below the vowel, respectively, but rather than a macron, a circle is used. Finally, the mordent tone, usually represented by the perispomene, is instead marked with an *x* above the vowel.

It is important to observe that no symbol for the rising-falling or falling-rising tones is present in this table. This is because KWS marks the individual vowels of diphthongs with the appropriate acute and grave diacritics rather than using a unique pair of symbols. That is, the rising-falling tone is marked with an acute accent on the first vowel and a grave accent on the second, while the falling-rising tone is marked with the opposite, a grave accent on the first and an acute accent on the second. We will see many examples of these and all syllable types in the next section.

5.2.4: SYLLABLES

Now that we've seen the symbols for the consonants, vowels, and tones of the language, let us now try putting them together to form syllables. In this pursuit, two problems arise that we must deal with. While Type I syllables only ever have one consonant, Type II and III syllables can take consonant clusters. We know so far that consonants appear to the left of the guiding line, but we do not yet have a mechanism for a cluster. We also have the problem of diphthongs in Type III syllables. How do we represent multiple vowels?

To start with, let's look at what we previously described as the phonologically simplest type of syllable. Type I syllables are syllabic consonants, so the vowel symbol we use will always be the same. We also know that only five tones are possible, so in the following examples, we'll use the full range.

Illustration 2. Type I Syllables in KWS

As you can see, Type I syllables always use the syllabic consonant symbol to the right of the guiding line, and the tone diacritic is positioned depending on the tone intended, as we've already learned. As for the consonants, they appear to the left and are centered relative to the guiding line. Note that this rule will not always be the case for consonants across KWS, but it is one that consistently applies to Type I syllables, as they are only ever monosyllabic words.

Type II syllables herald several of the complicating factors described above. We can now use multiple vowel symbols, and multisyllabic words can occur. Importantly, it is also now possible to have consonant clusters.

The following examples demonstrate mono- and multisyllabicity and also show how to cluster onset consonants together.

ki   nē   sa   cry   rũ   kfò

fèke   nọsụ   mȳsrỳclí

Illustration 3. Type II Syllables in KWS

When two consonants belong to the same syllable, clustered together in the onset, they appear sequentially left to right and horizontally across from the vowel appearing in the nucleus of the same syllable. Consonants—and of course also vowels—appearing vertically relative to one another must by extension belong to distinct syllables.

The creation of Type III syllables, which always have two vowels marked even if they are pronounced as a diphthong, introduces its own complications. They can be mistaken for disyllabic Type II syllables if other facts of graphical representation are not known. Therefore, we will explore these more closely in §5.3 on graphical disambiguation.

5.2.5: WORDS

While the previous section purported to present the construction of syllables, of course many of the examples given were in fact complete words. As we know, all Type I syllables are also words in themselves. Other monosyllabic words are either Type II or Type III syllables. The words left after excising these categories must necessarily be constructed morphologically by combining Type II syllables, Type III syllables, or both Type II and Type III.

In terms of the orthography, words are understood for the most part as combinations of syllables—vowels following one after the other on the right side of the line according to the syllable to which they belong, and consonants (and consonant clusters) doing the same on the left side. The line continues until the word is complete, and then there is a break in the line to indicate a given word has ended and the next word is, with its own line, soon to begin. Another way to look at KWS is that words are combinations of vowels, some of which do not have accompanying consonants, some of which do. With this understanding, we can parse words either that are or that include Type III syllables.

5.3: GRAPHICAL DISAMBIGUATION

Several orthographical rules in KWS serve to distinguish otherwise ambiguous representations. In this section, we will discuss how rules relating to consonant and tone placement can disambiguate some of the more difficult issues of syllabicity we've previously mentioned and otherwise how rules relating to word separation and punctuation disambiguate on the sentential level.

5.3.1: MULTISYLLABIC WORDS VS. DIPHTHONGIC SYLLABLES

As we have already seen, the vowels of words with two or more syllables are strung along the right side of an unbroken guiding line. If you compare this to the representation of Type III syllables, in which two vowels appear but may be diphthongized, you will see the first potential ambiguity. That is, how do you tell whether two vowels in the same word are part of a Type II disyllabic word or a Type III monosyllabic word?

Additionally, the succession of vowels in the same word present challenges for tone interpretation, which depends for some tones, as we have seen, on their placement either above or below the vowel. How is a tone written between the vowels therefore interpreted? We will answer both of these questions in this section.

5.3.1.1: Consonant Placement

We saw previously that for Type I and II monosyllabic words, onset consonants—whether clusters or singleton—are positioned on the same horizontal level across from the vowel, over the vertical guiding line. This rule is tweaked somewhat by a superseding rule which serves to disambiguate Type III monosyllables from Type II disyllables. When the word is a Type III monosyllable, the onset consonant or consonant cluster is *shared* between the vowels, i.e. it is placed in the middle of the imaginary horizontal lines representing the respective centers of the first and second vowels.

Compare this to the placement of consonants in Type II words. When they are monosyllabic and have an identical cluster, they will simply appear directly across from the vowel. When the word is disyllabic and the consonants are instead separated, the first belonging to the onset of the first syllable and the second to the onset of the second syllable, they appear across from their respective vowels.

In other words, while the information on the right side of the guiding line may look the same for a Type II disyllable and a Type III monosyllable, the information on the left side completely disambiguates pronunciation. Several examples follow.

cleĭ   celĭ   psiŏ   pìsó   kroŭ   korŭ

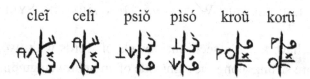

Illustration 4. Type II vs. Type III Words

While we show only consonant clusters here, it is important to keep in mind that for Type III syllables, even singleton consonants in the onset position will be shared between the vowels.

5.3.1.2: Tone Diacritics

Tone diacritics can be confusing in multisyllabic words because it is sometimes unclear to which syllable (or vowel) the tone belongs. This is because position above or below the vowel symbol is important for interpretation of the diacritic. For example, the symbol for the high and low tones is identical—a circle—save for the fact that it appears above or below the vowel, respectively. Therefore, one might suspect that in a disyllabic word, a low tone on the first vowel could be interpreted as a high tone on the second vowel simply due to its position in the graphical architecture. In practice, this does not happen, due in part to the expectation of an understanding of Katalopsi phonology but due also to an awareness of another tone diacritic later in the word.

Remember how tone distribution patterns work intralexically. If the first vowel has a low tone, it can only be followed by a rising tone or another low tone. If it is followed by a rising tone, then what you will find in a given disyllabic word is two tone diacritics between the two vowels: the low tone diacritic just above the rising tone diacritic. Effectively, then, because the low tone diacritic is blocked by the rising tone diacritic, there's no opportunity to believe the circle of the low tone actually belongs to the second vowel.

If the low tone is followed by another low tone, on the other hand, it is certainly possible to carelessly read the circle symbol as a high tone on the second vowel. This requires a certain degree of myopia because, of course, there is a second tone diacritic in the word: the second circle below the second vowel. So if the second diacritic *must* belong to the second vowel, it is impossible that the first circle could be a high tone and must therefore be a low tone on the first vowel.

Similar reasoning applies for the high tone. If the first syllable of a disyllabic word has a high tone, it may be followed by a high tone or a falling tone. The latter set of circumstances is easy to grasp: You see the circle above the first vowel and are forced to interpret it as a high tone diacritic, and so the second diacritic is obviously a falling tone on the second vowel. When both tones are high, you may observe that the high tone diacritic above the second vowel could be interpreted as a low tone diacritic below the first vowel. This again requires a degree of tunnel vision because a complete consideration of the word will also observe a definite high tone on the first vowel, making the assignment of the second tone diacritic to the first vowel impossible, whatever the tone or vowel combinations may be.

There is another important point about the usage of tones that we briefly skirmished in §5.2.3, in which we introduced the tone diacritics. In our Latin script representations of Katalopsi up to this point, we have been using the circumflex for rising-falling tones and the háček for falling-rising tones. This was useful, since by regarding the average verb as a Type III syllable on its own would benefit our eventual understanding of KWS. But now that we are here, it is important to understand that there are not unique symbols for these complex tones, and they are instead written with rising and falling tones on the respective vowels: one rising followed by one falling in the case of the rising-falling tone and one falling followed by one rising in the case of the falling-rising tone. We know vowels marked this way, even in Type III syllables, are impossible to pronounce as diphthongs and are pronounceable only as two distinct vowel qualities, each with their own tone. An example of the falling-rising tone graphemics appears in Illustration 4, and the rising-falling tone is analogous in the predictable way.

This is in contrast, however, with Type III syllables with just a single rising or a single falling tone. In these cases, we piece together some familiarity in that only the second vowel will have a tone diacritic, and regardless of whether the vowels are pronounceable as a diphthong, the rising or falling tone is pronounced over the complete syllable. Therefore, although the rising-falling and falling-rising tones use the same symbols in KWS as the rising tone and falling tone, they never serve to confuse as to which is intended. Only in Type III syllables is this confusion theoretically possible, but the presence of either one or two tones on the Type III syllable settles the question of pronunciation.

5.3.2: SEPARATION OF WORDS

Unlike English, some writing systems do not separate words from one another with either spaces or symbols, a style known as *scriptio continua*, or "continuous script." While KWS could employ such a system, it is more like English in that it uses spaces to separate words from one another. More specifically, spaces are breaks in the vertical guiding line. On unruled paper, it is obvious that one would need to draw the guiding line to make its absence, and therefore the separation of words, clear. On ruled paper, on the other hand, drawing the guiding line is particularly important to distinguish it from the inked ruling itself.

Look back at Illustration 1 in §5.1 and note how the breaks in the vertical guiding line make the separation of words very clear. As long as the vertical guiding line is continuous, readers will assume that the attached series of vowels and consonants are indeed part of the same word.

A few other symbols appear in this illustration that we have yet to discuss. These are the subject of the next section.

5.3.3: SENTENTIAL PUNCTUATION

In this section, we will go over a few symbols of punctuation and their associated rules of use. A complete system of punctuation would necessitate the creation of a style guide much like *The Chicago Manual of Style* or the *New Oxford Style Manual* for English writing, but to do this would be well beyond the scope of this book. Instead, we will focus here on how to use punctuation in the most common of situations: ending sentences, conjoining sentences, making lists, marking questions and exclamations, and indicating dialogue.

The first symbol is analogous to the *period* or *full stop* and ends declarative sentences. It is a horizontal line placed below the last word of the sentence, connected neither to the vertical guiding line of the text before it nor to the guiding line of the text which follows it, if any. Essentially, running text in KWS follows the verticle line, but that line is firmly broken at this horizontal strikethrough before the text continues. Several examples of this appear in Illustration 1.

Two other symbols work in tandem and function much like the double quotation marks used in English. These punctuation symbols also break the vertical guiding line and may be used to mark dialogue or to mark words used as terms. These symbols are half-circles, the first opening upward away from the text to be enclosed and the second opening downward away from the same, fully enclosing it. They are both written symmetrical to the guiding line, although without connecting them to the running text.

The symbol used to connect elements of a list, whether those elements are words, phrases, or complete sentences, is similar to the perispomene or the tilde. It connects elements much like a comma, although it should be made clear that a list is three items or more in this sense. So while English may in some circumstances encourage the use of a comma between *two* complete sentences connected by a conjunction, Katalopsi would only do this if *three* sentences were conjoined.

Parenthetical information or any material of an interjectory or elucidatory nature is introduced by a segment of the vertical guiding line without consonant, vowel, or tone information. In this way, it could be described as an em dash rotated ninety degrees. If this information ends the sentence, then the normal end-of-sentence punctuation follows, but if the interjection is followed by the completion of the interrupted text, then a second line segment is used, again like an em dash.

Some non-declarative sentences would under normal circumstances demand unique punctuation. In the case of Katalopsi interrogatives, this is not the case. Questions are frequently marked at the beginning of the sentence with the question auxiliary or alternatively with an interrogative pronoun, and for this reason, KWS takes the interrogative nature of a sentence to be straightforward enough not to require a question symbol.

On the other hand, exclamatory statements—or any declarative sentences said with emphasis, excitement, or high volume—permit the use of the KWS equivalent of an exclamation point. This involves a horizontal line segment, like the KWS period, with two shorter, parallel line segments crossing the horizontal line segment perpendicularly.

In the next section, we will discuss production using Katalopsi, including KWS, and various sample writings will demonstrate this system of symbols at length.

CHAPTER 6

Production

Up to this point, we have been teaching you the basics of the Katalopsi language, from the pronunciation in chapter 1 to the nature of words in chapter 2, from the ordering of words and phrases in chapter 3 to the nuances of meaning in chapter 4. Chapter 5 gave you the ability to take these things together and write in the language with an original writing system. Now, in this chapter, we will attempt to prepare you for production, the free use of the language either in speech or in writing.

There are several strategies we will employ in an attempt to prepare you. First, we will provide you with several vocabulary groups, which will allow you to learn and sort through a subset of the complete lexicon in natural semantic categories. Second, we will provide tips for speaking and writing creatively, picking up where the dictionary in chapter 7 and this guide as a whole is insufficient. These tips will help you create new words and personal names and apply rhetorical devices in your use of Katalopsi. Finally, we will give several writing samples, including a poem and two translations. By way of these tools, we hope to greatly increase your ability to produce not only conversational language but artful, creative language as well.

6.1: VOCABULARY GROUPS

In this section, we provide thirteen groups—and thirty subgroups—of vocabulary terms which should prove useful any time you are using Katalopsi to write, speak, or create. These vocabulary terms are conveniently organized whether you are looking for terms relating to: (a) everyday interactions, (b) human biology, (c) various animals and their products, (d) plants, (e) careers, (f) geoscience, (g) clothing, (h) food and food groups, (i) tools and weapons, (j) society and government, (k) family, (l) colors, and (m) home life.

6.1.1: EVERYDAY EXPRESSIONS—*KÈSÓ PYJÓ*

In this section, you will find everyday expressions like greetings, interjections, common questions and responses, and other standard statements of emotion and interest.

Hello/Hi.	Cyjó.	How are you (s.)?	Fèja Í kù?
Goodbye.	Ġ julolẽ.	How are you (pl.)?	Fèja Í klū?
I am well.	Cy ź pò.	See you soon.	Riǒ ní.
Yes.	Né.	What's your name?	Fù siê m̀ cu kù?
No.	Là.	My name is …	Siê m̀ … pò.
Maybe.	Frá.	I understand.	Psuǒ ź pò.
Welcome.	Núsā fru.	I don't understand.	Psuǒ ź pò fò.
Good morning.	Cýfī.	I know.	Pie ź pò.
Good afternoon.	Cyjó.	I don't know.	Pie ź pò fò.
Good evening.	Cymerí.	I love you.	Niò ž kù pò.
Good night.	Cycẽ.	Help!	Ġ xiã!
Please.	Jo.	Good luck.	Xáclì cy.
Thanks.	Clõ.	You're welcome.	Kè Í lá.
Many thanks.	Sre clõ.	You're very welcome.	Kè Í lá múrō.
Thank you (s.).	Clõ ó kù.	I like …	Rei ž … pò.
Thank you (pl.).	Clõ ó klū.	I don't like …	Rei ž … pò fò.
Do you speak English (s.)?	V̀ ploǐ m̀ inyklisǐ kù?		

Do you speak English (pl.)?	V̇ ploǐ m̀ inyklisǐ klū?
Do you speak Katalopsi (s.)?	V̇ ploǐ m̀ kacalopsǐ kù?
Do you speak Katalopsi (pl.)?	V̇ ploǐ m̀ kacalopsǐ klū?

6.1.2: HUMAN BIOLOGY—*CLEXÕ U KÍNÌ*

In this section, you will learn terminology for the ins and outs of human biology. We will separate the vocabulary into three groups: (1) external anatomy, (2) internal anatomy, and (3) bodily functions.

Exterior—*Crǫfrǫ*

head	kó	ear	plò	wrist	jā
hair	crṳ	lip	kfṳ	elbow	sòcló
eye	ki̱	moustache	nékrī	forearm	fanõ
nose	mì	beard	pra̱	skin	sró
mouth	clỳ	neck	kỳ	navel	lòra̱
forehead	mūprè	shoulder	palỹ	back	krȳ
scalp	sé	chest	py̱	waist	plú
brow	xī	breast	nàprú	abdomen	lacrã
eyebrow	kíxī	nipple	xùfi̱	torso	jūpsò
eyelash	psā	arm	frà	thigh	cxỹ
cheek	cópsȳ	hand	kfũ	leg	nē
kneecap	ra̱krǫ	buttocks	xṳpla̱	thumb	plé
shin	pý	scrotum	xe̱plṳ	labia	crýpè
ankle	srūfā	nostril	necũ	palm	na̱kí
finger	pócì	earlobe	lápsā	clitoris	nõplì
foot	sri̱	temple	srùfú	testicle	fōclù
toe	kfā	penis	rēnù	heel	ce̱
nail	cò	vagina	lāfū	toenail	kfãcò
fingernail	pócīcò	body	sra̱		

Interior—*Fèsré*

brain	nã	brainstem	nacrõ	pancreas	se̱mú
cerebral	pynã	lung	xỹ	pancreatic	pyse̱mú
milk	kly̱	pulmonary	pyxỹ	bladder	srālè

palate	fólū	heart	rỹ	bile	pó
spine	crýjò	stomach	rèci̱	windpipe	lyjé
tooth	rū	anus	srū	egg	kfó
dental	pȳrū	anal	pysrū	blood	fro̱
tongue	pá	intestines	prākfē	uterus	lȳprù
lingual	pyₚá	intestinal	pȳprākfē	uterine	pȳlȳprù
uvula	klelõ	throat	clūrū	ovary	pluklã
nasal cavity	mákrȳ pȳmì	semen	kli̱	ovarian	pypluklã
ear (internal)	fràfe̱	vocal cords	pācē	rib cage	cóklù
vein	mỹ	bone	pù	fat	lo̱
liver	psu̱rá	kidney	jýkrē	feces	sru̱có
muscle	kòply̱	urethra	fùpi̱	urine	clīsē
muscular	kòply̱xú	rectum	ji̱ní	cartilage	klýsē
gall bladder	làsró	sinew	sȳkfò	glottis	pācē
pelvis	psēcrỳ	trachea	lyjé	glottal	pȳpācē
skull	jū	tracheal	py̱lyjé		

Functions—*Kūjì*

yawn	jié	pass out	syi̱	cry	cliã
snore	kleū	scratch	sraǐ	laugh	mie̱
sleep	xeý	smile	cleú	exercise	psuà
eat	pliè	frown	psyì	stretch	cliě
bite	cryú	digest	kloĩ	give birth	uà
chew	caǔ	ejaculate	cxaú	sweat	nia̱
sneeze	suỳ	glare	xyí	burp	xoû
breathe	laǐ	hiccough	nue̱	groan	sreî
sigh	juȳ	suffocate	xyū	defecate	sruò
vomit	feù	urinate	cliē	cough	cuǒ
menstruate	myǔ	shrug	piǒ	nod	cuó
drool	plyì	salivate	criȳ	kiss	miò
swallow	poú	fornicate	kfyī		

6.1.3: ANIMALS—*FÓXỲ*

In this section, we will look at animals, their products, and their anatomy. The information of the latter will be narrower than that of human biology simply for the infrequency of many such terms.

Animals—*Fóxỳ*

chicken	pì	cat	ru̱	dog	psȳ
chick	pìni̱	kitten	ru̱nu̱	puppy	psȳnȳ
cow	ru̱pi̱	pig	plūjē	deer	kre̱na̱
calf	ru̱pi̱ni̱	piglet	plūjēnē	bird	psĭ
goat	rácxā	horse	clōrā	sheep	lȳrū
bee	ce̱ni̱	foal	clōrānā	turkey	sýnī
duck	cre̱cú	goose	ji̱pé	buffalo	mūpsā
duckling	cre̱cúnū	gosling	ji̱pénē	llama	xōlè
rabbit	lìcxa̱	crab	pàjé	fish	frĩ
bunny	lìcxa̱na̱	lobster	kfíklù	lion	mỳcxí
tiger	la̱xé	camel	plēnà	mouse	pùsry̱
rat	clésē	alligator	cxu̱lú	spider	nācxì
ant	co̱fé	scorpion	fèle̱	beetle	frākè
butterfly	frēcè	moth	prūrī	shark	ne̱fé
turtle	ki̱fo̱	lizard	mi̱lu̱	bear	ke̱no̱
worm	sà				

Animal Products—*Cīsȳ u Fóxỳ*

egg	kfó	milk	kly̱	mohair	jècla̱
leather	plu̱fé	poultry	frùry̱	pork	méklā
feather	jēxè	beef	ly̱fy̱	venison	kry̱cu̱
wool	monõ	chevon	kly̱kfi̱	honey	rākfè
mutton	sykro̱	wax	kōcò	hide	kípsō

Animal Biology—*Clexõ u Fóxỳ*

tail	crī	fur	ci̱	scale	prỹ
whisker	kècá	furry	ci̱xú	scaly	pryxũ
fang	prũ	stripe	clinũ	maw	nyfũ
venom	re̱se̱	fin	me̱	tentacle	kfūrỳ

venomous	r̀esèxú	tailfin	ạmé	stinger	kúký̄
claw	rã	feather	jēxè	shell	klí
paw	frē	wing	nó	beak	plē
sheath	psì	winged	nóxù	eyestalk	fẹprẹ
mandible	xỳfry̱	thorax	xójī	spot	kràmy̱
sucker	pralõ	tendril	jilĩ	spotted	kràmy̱xú
plume	raclã	mane	pló	hoof	pō
snout	mị				

6.1.4: PLANTS—*CLEXÕ U MÀ*

petal	kfùfý	bark	cẹklí	flower	kfụcọ
stem	crõ	root	fí	sap	rísrī
leaf	xì	seed	kfạ	grain	cxōpī
bean	sụ	amber	cléjū	fruit	nạprạ
grass	cụjọ	moss	kẹcré	cactus	sàklé
succulent	lỳprụ	tree	cịfụ	apple tree	ký̄mìcịfụ
orange tree	kèkrạcịfụ				

6.1.5: CAREERS—*KÉ*

This section is devoted to careers and other roles that one may hold. You will see how several of these terms are derived from other words using one of a couple morphological strategies, while others are monomorphemic.

blacksmith	lékī	librarian	cìcxụprá	professor	klēmèfạ
musician	pạkị	actor	kìkẹ	alchemist	psènóprà
miner	fỹkú	nurse	nunẽ	physician	mureprã
bartender	fòrúprà	cook	fíkò	innkeeper	crȳnȳprà
builder	cxèkọ	artist	laprã	weatherperson	jeprã
mason	pócxāprà	teacher	cxéký̀	custodian	cápā
hunter	sròkị	priest	fỹnū	mortician	fēkrùprá
mechanic	frákì	welder	klukõ	author	nāsù
engineer	rùkó	writer	psèký	shopkeeper	klẹprá

chef	fíkò	prostitute	rāclīprà	soldier	krupýprà
technician	krakríprà	lawyer	cxàprá	accountant	luploprã
judge	kfìká	editor	crékỳ	sailor	psókū
economist	krexóprà	physicist	psòxóprà	funeral director	kfiluprá
linguist	pèxóprà	chemist	xèpsexóprà	biologist	clexoprã

6.1.6: GEOSCIENCE—*Kaxó*

When referring to characteristics of the earth, whether geological formations, biomes, or other elemental traits, the following geoscience terms will be helpful.

desert	lilácī	cave	kry	swamp	ne
forest	majẽ	dale	nōfò	lava	cèle
tundra	xuklu	glen	plù	lavaflow	cèlecuclú
taiga	lōrū	valley	pacxa	wetland	lèlý
river	mēplỹ	hill	pro	land	lý
lake	jò	hilly	proxú	grassland	cujolý
stream	cuclú	ocean	krumú	coral reef	rìkla kliprũ
rapids	fikrá	oceanic	krumúxù	rainforest	mymajẽ
plain	no	ice cave	krikry	bog	jòfá
mountain	peclú	highland	klylý	estuary	srēlù
mountainous	peclúxù	volcano	crokfó	marsh	kófī
plateau	xylỹ	volcanic	pycrokfó	peninsula	cxūnī
island	prifo	isle	mūmà	peninsular	pỹcxūnī
prairie	xìpla	paddy field	sukry	terrace	lōkrē
freshwater	jāxō	saltwater	srỹxō	abyss	cèfy
geyser	srōnù	waterfall	xìnoma	beach	xira
sand	psỹlỹ	tide	crīfū	archipelago	sìcroca
sandy	psỹlỹxù	jungle	fràklo	badland	clinulý
air	sũ	cloud	cỹlò	klā	soil

6.1.7: CLOTHING—*MÉCLŌ*

This section is devoted to terms referring to the various things one may wear. These have been divided into garments (cloth- and leather-related clothing), jewelry, and armor.

Garments—*Méclō*

boot	jyplĩ	cape	psý	coat	krō
glove	sí	cap	prā	brassiere	nalý
bracer	srārè	cowl	pròko	robe	kēprè
hat	crý	sock	cré	underwear	māpè
scarf	kfè	vest	pã	shirt	cxé
shawl	nùcá	jacket	fypsa	sweater	placra
blouse	nỹ	overcoat	mỳcrisa	pants	clō
trousers	clō	shoe	krā	shoestring	kràcari
zipper	kúkī	thread	jīlè	seam	cró
sole	klola	dress	cxũ	skirt	pȳfù
belt	còpi	suspenders	salĩ	suit	lúplȳ
jumpsuit	plikro	gown	sū	nightgown	kūsū
button	cino	needle	sìni	dye	nū
fly	sīrè	waistband	pokfe	apron	fèke
coif	jorá	glasses	clánì	purse	klùjo
wallet	peprĩ	sash	kekú	cassock	klìplu
stole	frāfè	cloak	jocry	buckle	rōprè
ribbon	melỹ	collar	fiká	cuff	lura
tie	klicé	pocket	sīmì	sleeve	frò
wig	klȳfù	backpack	masrá	briefcase	cxūcà
satchel	prepo	strap	jusá	lingerie	clòmo
veil	krācà	sunglasses	juclánì		

Jewelry—*Rocĩ*

necklace	nāklì	wristwatch	srujó	medal	kýclō
ring	prù	bracelet	sìný	earring	plōprù
pendant	kénà	amulet	clōrù	cuff link	luracxó
pocket watch	sīmìsrujó	talisman	mōrū	charm	mōrū

Armor—*Crè*

gauntlet	plóklā	helmet	mòkró	legplates	nēcrè
chainmail	klùpsu̠	chestplate	jūpsōcrè	sallet	mòkró
shield	korī̃	cuirass	me̠srḭ		

6.1.8: Food—*Psá*

The terms referring to food are various, and so they have been divided into meals, fruits, vegetables, beverages, and other miscellaneous items.

Meals—*Lāpì*

breakfast	sylo̠	lunch	rofrī̃	dinner	kripsā
snack	òre̠	soup	mù	dessert	ru̠sḭ
roast	kōsūfìso̠	cake	ra̠fḭ	pie	léfī̃

Fruits—*Na̠pra̠*

grape	ējī̃	melon	láxā	pumpkin	nērù
apple	kȳmì	orange	kèkra̠	lemon	mēplù
banana	pa̠prú	tomato	jẏple̠	lime	rōsì
olive	nḭclé	berry	fènú	blueberry	prīfènú
blackberry	srōfènú	raspberry	xéfènú		

Vegetables—*Sa̠pru̠*

lettuce	kyrḭ	broccoli	sēkā	cauliflower	kfūlẏ
cabbage	le̠pá	spinach	cxa̠lú	carrot	sírù
potato	fyclá	onion	nykā	brussels sprout	lūfē

Beverages—*Klìsó*

milk	kly̠	juice	sòlá	wine	nàjo̠ca̠
beer	jòca̠	water	xō	whiskey	fōnì
vodka	xu̠rú	mead	na̠crḭ	coffee	lòno̠
tea	kìrḭ				

Other Foods—*Psá Lùso̠xú*

bread	fró	noodle	sa̠pó	rice	cu̠ku̠
oil	krẏ	grain	cxōpī̃	fish	frī̃

beef	ly̱fy̱	chicken	pì

6.1.9: INSTRUMENTS—*Kĩ*

In this section, you will find various instruments, including hand tools and small machines, weapons, and musical instruments.

Tools—*Kĩ*

pliers	klācū	hammer	cìkrí	screwdriver	sùni̱múkȳ
wire	jùplí	bolt	pse̱	nut	clūsū
nail	xí	washer	rācrū	wrench	srokě
caliper	lìkrý	screw	sùní	wire cutter	jùpli̱fyku̱
axe	pūxà	mallet	krulũ	hatchet	pūxà
knife	xàmo̱	wheel	klīpē	sledgehammer	lūcìkrí
pulley	còju̱	rope	so̱	scythe	mýxā
sickle	sypé	rivet	kòfro̱	trowel	nícà
shovel	ri̱fe̱	saw	kȳ	ruler	krīfō
scissors	làkla̱	corkscrew	psīlè	loom	clū
backpack	ma̱srá	fork	psù	spinning wheel	psỳni̱
spoon	lē	satchel	pre̱po̱		

Weapons—*Rècé*

halberd	crèja̱	quarterstaff	cle̱	bow	klà
sword	pru̱	crossbow	klýklà	arrow	sē
staff	cle̱	spear	cóklȳ	gun	srò
mace	pēfà	cannon	lȳxò	bayonet	rénā
pike	cóklȳ	handgun	kfūsrò	rifle	frāsrò
battleaxe	mōpūxà	war hammer	mōcìkrí	flail	fo̱cró
maul	mōcìkrí				

Musical Instruments—*Pa̱si̱*

guitar	kre̱lí	harp	ècé	piano	linĩ
violin	me̱lo̱	drum	sru̱cí	flute	lȳlù
lute	ryme̱	gong	yrá	bell	sélī

6.1.10: CIVILIZATION—*RŪNÀ*

The terms relating to civilization and society have been divided into five categories: (1) buildings, (2) infrastructure, (3) economy, (4) government, and (5) transportation.

Buildings—*Cxèso̱*

library	cìcxu̱	city hall	clu̱ni̱	courthouse	xi̱rú cxèso̱
restaurant	fro̱so̱	café	pso̱cí	church	se̱pé
funeral home	kfi̱lu̱ cxèso̱	cemetery	cxo̱fó	mausoleum	clùná
temple	srùfú	fort	kilẽ	range	pri̱cxé
hospital	cíxùpli̱	school	fra̱	university	lāfràfra̱
castle	fu̱cú	bank	clófō		
community center	lāfrà cxèso̱	training grounds	srýsī klā		

Infrastructure—*Pōjōkfàpo̱*

building	cxèso̱	trail	nōplā	farm	kfỹ
bridge	fý	tunnel	nu̱ci̱	dam	kfẽ
road	jõ	sewer	fe̱sí	electricity	ra̱pímīmā
energy	mīmā	park	krì	lighthouse	kfísỳ
port	psu̱	railroad	rakajõ		

Economy—*Kre̱*

currency	kfi̱pre̱	money	fè	market	kre̱
cash	srāsū	commerce	pìpó	trade	cxē
bartering	plisã	good(s)	rý	service(s)	krāklē
production	kfásù	distribution	klìkró	demand	mēsū
management	plísà	resource(s)	crópsà	business	praklũ
work	rísē	industry	kukfẽ	supply	fēsō

Government—*Cxycõ*

town	prápē	colony	kliprũ	empire	x<u>u</u>j<u>e</u>
city	k<u>o</u>	colonial	pykliprũ	imperial	x<u>u</u>j<u>e</u>xú
metropolis	kárā	state	kl<u>u</u>p<u>a</u>	village	prápē
district	psỳps<u>u</u>	capital	kárā	representative	fràkí
voter	crúkȳ	judge	kfìká	court	x<u>i</u>rú
monarchy	cxūràr<u>i</u>	king	sófī	queen	j<u>u</u>psí
royality	krēnàs<u>a</u>	territory	kl<u>u</u>s<u>i</u>krí	border	mùklú

Transportation—*J<u>e</u>sy*

vessel	klūkù	car	psỳpl<u>u</u>	train	r<u>a</u>k<u>a</u>
boat	kr<u>u</u>	airplane	suklukũ	railroad	rakajõ
port	ps<u>u</u>	bus	sulõ	spacecraft	júklūkù

6.1.11: FAMILY—*SRÝ*

The following includes a modest range of familial relationships.

mother	prūrī	aunt	níprỳ	parent	<u>o</u>kr<u>u</u>
father	m<u>i</u>rá	uncle	jāfū	cousin	ỳf<u>o</u>
sibling	kl<u>i</u>j<u>a</u>	son	fòn<u>y</u>	boy	fòn<u>y</u>
brother	fòl<u>o</u>	daughter	ūcò	girl	ap<u>i</u>
sister	rýnì	child	psũ	wife	crì
husband	kí	girlfriend	néfrõ	boyfriend	kýnȳ

6.1.12: COLORS—*Kō*

The following terms allow for the discussion of colors. Note that the colors listed here are in their adjectival forms. The nominal forms will require compounding with the word *kō*, or a tonally adjusted equivalent.

red	xé	blue	prī	green	sā
yellow	pūrī	white	plū	black	srõ
purple	lā	grey	lȳnò	orange	n<u>u</u>jú
brown	pr<u>i</u>m<u>u</u>	light	ký	dark	p<u>i</u>

6.1.13: HOME—*SRŌ*

In this final collection, you will find terms referring to the home, either the furniture in it, or the rooms throughout the household.

Furniture—*Klujũ*

chair	nạ	desk	kӯclù	cradle	kùkrụ
stool	lákà	cabinet	clụplú	wardrobe	kōrè
bed	jolũ	chest	mólō	larder	plẹmá
table	cxē	couch	xénӯ	lamp	frè
shelf	krēpī	curtain	klipī̃	lantern	kràrẹ
bookcase	sӯkrēpī	sofa	xénӯ	toilet	crècrọ
crib	kùkrụ	rug	kàlụ	mattress	pōkrò
sink	nèklụ	throne	frӯpò	bench	xùplị

Rooms—*Cã*

bedroom	jolucã	bathroom	clūlū	office	kfàcá
throne room	frypocã	library	cìcxụ	attic	cājē
study	kfàná	living room	kròpí	dining room	kripsacã
closet	cōnē	crawlspace	pīklī	basement	kōlà
nook	sylocã	laundry room cumucã	pantry	fàcá	

6.2: TIPS FOR CREATION

Various topics relating to using a given language creatively and productively were unfit for inclusion in previous chapters. They are, however, faculties that are engaged on a daily or near-daily basis and mustn't be left out in any complete description of the language. These are neologism, onomastics, and rhetoric.

6.2.1: NEOLOGISM

Neologism is the process—and product thereof—whereby a new word is created. This could be the linking of a new collection of phonemes to a meaning that existed previously, the linking of a collection of phonemes that existed previously to a new meaning, or the linking of a new collection of phonemes to a new meaning.

New words are created all the time because language is an inherently productive system of communication. Creating words in Katalopsi may be difficult for a beginner, however, and so we would encourage you to attempt this only after you have a thorough understanding of the system of phonemes and phonological rules explained in chapter 1.

Depending on what you are using Katalopsi for, you may be wishing that you had access to a word that is not listed in the dictionary in chapter 7. This is understandable, as English is thought to have at least a couple hundred thousand words but possibly over a million, depending on how they are counted. In these situations, you should be comfortable to neologize on the fly and use the new word among your group of Katalopsi speakers—even though it may not be considered an official or canonical word.

Though a thorough understanding of the material in chapter 1 is requisite, it may be additionally helpful to keep the following rules in mind when constructing a new word: (1) Only use consonants and consonant clusters that you see in other words; (2) use diphthong vowels strictly for verbs; (3) use syllabic consonants for auxiliaries and disambiguators; and (4) preserve non-conflicting tonal contours intralexically.

6.2.2: Onomastics

Onomastics, or the study of proper names, is a subject that could quite easily have appeared earlier in this book. However, because names are deeply rooted in culture, the topic has been left for here. This language and its lexicon have been designed as much as possible to be independent of culture, save for one or two contentious tolerances for the sake of utility. This will, we believe, allow learners of Katalopsi to embed the language in worlds of their own creation. That said, it would be difficult to create those worlds without having names to use, and so it may be worthwhile to consider a few common strategies for name creation that will fit neatly in the framework of the Katalopsi language.

To begin with, first and last names are often synonymous with animals, plants, or other natural features such as geological formations.

This is reflected in names encountered in the English-speaking world like *Wolf, Daisy*, and *River*. The vocabulary groups in §6.1.3, §6.1.4, and §6.1.6 are therefore helpful sources for possible names.

Other first names will be derived from positive traits expressed in adjectives. While not common in the English-speaking world, words like *beautiful, loyal*, and *friendly* surface as personal names in various cultures in the world. In Katalopsi, the names *Sópū, Òlu̧, Jíxù*, and others like them, could therefore be used.

A common strategy for last names is to base them on kinship to one's father or mother. Languages like Icelandic and Arabic offer interesting patronymic strategies whereby the words for *son* and *daughter* are incorporated into the name. E.g. an Icelandic father called *Jón* would give his son the last name *Jónsson* and his daughter the last name *Jónsdóttir*, meaning "Jón's son" and "Jón's daughter," respectively. Katalopsi permits the creation of such names using the equivalent terms *fòny̧* and *ūcò*. A man called *Òlu̧* might pass on the last name *Òlu̧máfòny̧* to his son, applying the possessive morphology. A mother called *Sópū* might name her daughter with *Ūcò u Sópū*, utilizing a periphrastic, prepositional alternative.

People are also across the world named after locations, for example their place of birth, that of their parents, or an ancestral home, among others. In this way, the prepositions *kfì*, or "from," and *u*, or "of," are potentially useful for name creation. A person called *Rékfī*, born in the fictional town of *Maçacá*, could be named in full *Rékfī kfì Maçacá*. Another called *My̧cxí*, with an ancestral home in *Srēlù*, may simply be called *My̧cxí Srēlù*.

Any of these strategies could be used, or you could create your own. For those who understand the phonology of chapter 1 well, the neologism strategies of the previous sections could also be applied to the creation of names, leaving little outside the realm of possibility.

6.2.3: RHETORIC

There are some rules of rhetoric that are common to any language, natural or constructed. For example, the repeated use of a particular consonant or consonant cluster engages what is called *alliteration*. The repeated use of a vowel is known as *assonance*, and assonance used at the end of nearby lines is the essence of *rhyming*.

However, some rules are peculiar to a particular language or set of languages, simply due to the fact that languages use different sounds in structurally different ways. For example, Latin distinguishes between long and short vowels on the phonemic level, and as a result, the counting of meter and metrical feet in classical poetry depends on patterns of long and short. English does not have distinctive long and short vowels, so its meter is analyzed as patterns of stressed and unstressed syllables.

The meaning of this is that while Katalopsi has features that many or all languages have—allowing common rhetorical devices like alliteration, assonance, and rhyming—it also has features that make it unique, and creative and productive speakers and writers of Katalopsi ought to be able to exploit these features to create a uniquely Katalopsian artform out of their speech or writing.

A fine example of this is the way Katalopsi engages tonal contours. Within the word, this is a morphophonological necessity, but from word to word, conflicts of tone should occur in natural speech all the time. However, just as a poem or speech which uses meter may be considered more beautiful or more engaging than one which does not, a poem or speech which avoids conflicts of tone interlexically will be considered more beautiful or engaging than one which does not. This rhetorical device serves to allow Katalopsi speech to flow musically and could easily be incorporated into good writing or speaking with some preparation.

6.3: WRITING SAMPLES

In this section, we will provide several examples of writing in Katalopsi to permit you to study the grammar that is necessary, the rhetoric that is optional but laudable, and the writing system with its many symbolic rules. As samples, we have included a translation of a short story, a few verses of original poetry, and a translation of the opening to Charles Dickens's *Great Expectations*. For each sample, we will provide the writing in Katalopsi, using both the Latin orthographical conventions and the Katalopsi writing system, followed by an English translation where appropriate.

6.3.1: Short Story

In this section, you will be reading a translation of the fairy tale "Frau Trude" (often translated as "Mother Trudy") from Jakob and Wilhelm Grimm's *Kinder- und Hausmärchen*.

6.3.1.1: Latin

First, let us see the story in the Latin shorthand.

Lùny Cru̱cy

Ź roì Í a̱pi̱ jè fō ź lìmi̱ co su̱lo̱le̱ Í cu, co clȳ ź meū m̀ lá cìmá o̱kru̱ klè caì m̀ rỳcu̱ cì, ź pruǎ m̀ cì. V̀ jỳklú Í lá klè m̀ niô Í cu̱ cy plu̱ cì? Xȳ jó ź ploī ñ lá cìmá o̱kru̱, "Ź si̱e̱ z̃ sre̱ ròlú Lùny Cru̱cy pò. Ḡ m̀ pyŭ m̀ cì pò. R̲ jy prùni̱ Í cìmá sy̱ co r̲ niô ì su̱ku̱ cu̱ prùni̱. Sýcòxú-kreú Í cì kápē pò."

O̱kru̱ ź cué m̀ lá cu klè mi̱o̱ j̲ xi̱ sy̱ cì fò, co ź ploī ñ lá cì la̱, "Lùny Cru̱cy crì ma̱ju̱ Í cu, co caì m̀ cu̱ ma̱ju̱. Cì j̲ mi̱o̱ co riǒ m̀ cu kù, a̱kra̱ plōmà psū Í kù cxáfò fò."

Mã ̇ź faū ñ julĩ lá psū fù ź ploī m̀ cu cìmá o̱kru̱, co Lùny Cru̱cy ź cloí j̲ cu cì fròlú. Clȳ ź nuá ì sy̱ cì, ź su̱o̱ ñ lá cì Lùny Cru̱cy: "Já jy plū Í kù?"

"Ò." Ź psyĩ Í cìmá sra̱ co ź ploī m̀ lá cì, "Ź riǒ z̃ rỳcu̱ fù ź neū z̃ cu pò pò."

"Fù ź riǒ z̃ cu kù?"

"Ź riǒ z̃ kí srõ pò."

"Ź lékī Í sȳ prànúrō."

"Jỳ ź riǒ z̃ kí sā pò."

"Ź sròki̱ Í sȳ prànúrō."

"Pī sȳ ź riǒ z̃ kí xé ūsū fro̱ pò."

"Ź kípsōprà Í sȳ prànúrō."

"Ò. Lùny Cru̱cy, ź jy nēlūlē ź pò. Ź crió m̀ pò ple̱ crìja̱ co riǒ z̃ kù pò fò, mã z̲ ź riǒ z̃ rìsre̱ prypé kó jixú."

"À! A̱kra̱ ź riǒ z̃ fuprã prypé cìmá clà rocĩ kuklĩ. V̄ saí z̀ xū pò klè j̲ cxeì j̲ prìcy̱ kù, co ṽ piè m̀ pò plĩ. J̲ cleĩ m̀ rỳ kfí pò kù."

Prypé kè sūklā ź piŏ ṽ a̱pi̱ mìklá u psỹ cì co sriò j̃ lá ji̱. Ro̱xo̱
ź r̃ kià Í lá cxirõ, ź cxaì m̀ cì clý ji̱, púnuō Í cì, co ploī m̀ lá cì,
"Nūjè ẕ noì Í sỹ sùro̱."

6.3.1.2: KWS

Now we will see the same text in the KWS.

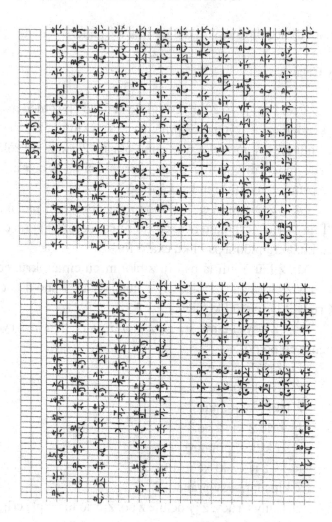

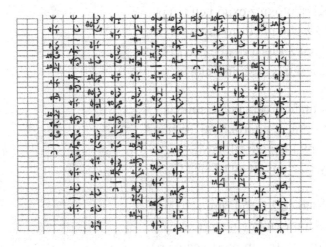

6.3.2: POETRY

In this section, you will be reading a few verses of original poetry. This is an opportunity to think about applying both traditional and language-specific rhetorical devices in your writing.

6.3.2.1: Latin

Larósī

Mē fasũ u plèso cruô m̄ pò sro ly:
Fē junẽ m̄ ploï Í pòmá māsū pà ó klũ
prypé xū klè kuó ż lá clī ūsū rỳcu cy,
klè clóprìxúrō cxeì ń nȳ kfì pòmá fólū.

Cú prápē co krínè xànu júnì
ź uà ź pò co nuȳ m̄ pòmá kì:
Ź lá Í klè cýjỳ Í pasū cūpā,
co nỳ pò m̄ fiè j plo cu mē sūklā.

Ź cloí j srō u pòmá pēclì pò
co pseī m̄ lá pò klè z nuý m̄ pò fò
nỳkle j piȩ m̄ pò sro ipime,
nỳkle j siȩ m̄ pò sro isime.

Kí rēlōfòxú ź cxuó Í cu frú pò
fō ź ploĭ m̀ cu sro̜ my̨ u fũ.
Ź saí ż kíprù rà nĩ cá cú kfũ:
la̜rósī u lȳnōkō ūsū clò.

Ź maū m̀ cámà nùlé sìmé lá:
mòprá, fȳnū, rōkràxú, sa fuprã,
clípȳ ìna̜ pojõ fìli̜ co̜si̜,
lý fù ź nuȳ m̀ cu cá sa̜jà fò.

Ro̜xo̜ cẽ ź freó Í rùni̜ si̜ cxārō
co luo̜ j̃ cú kùclu̜ cu̜ fuxũ cá.
Fìli̜ lá ź frai̜ m̀ pò sro̜ cámà pè,
sỹ rēlōfò, pá kacalopsixũ.

Fȳrō ź siõ ñ xōpȳ fuxũ kfò pò.
Ź reȳ Ì pòmá rỹ mésì rò
klè ź nuȳ m̀ nùlé léfrōxù pò
co klè ź pruò m̀ kfò pò ó psìky̨.

"Xȳ fō j̀ pi̜e ź cu fē klū prāmē:
Ź cloí j̀ pòmá nùlé mē klūmà.
Klūmà fràkí sìmé ź peȳ m̀ cu pò,
kí fō j̃ fiè m̀ plo̜ frélōlē cu ūsū pò.
Frá ź meî ż lá cá klè nuȳ m̀ klū pò
kfú ź ṽ siě m̀ klỹ cá cìru̜ kfò.
Nỳ g̀ maū m̀ cámà ka̜sa̜ pò ó klū.
Fē junẽ g̀ cxeì j̀ cxàlú sĩ ka̜sa̜."

6.3.2.2: KWS

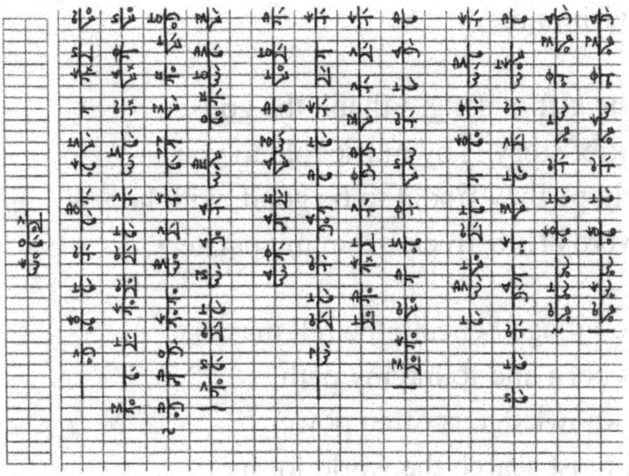

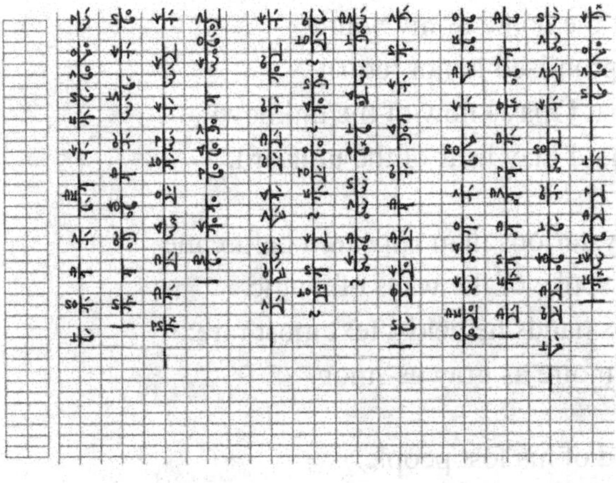

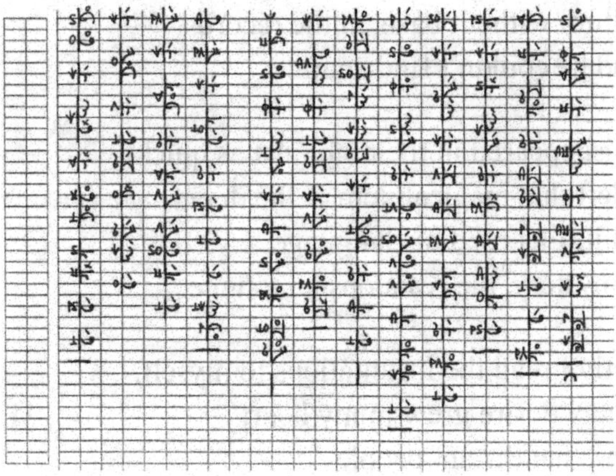

6.3.2.3: English

The Grimoire

For the gift of song, I thank the gods:
My brief story is by music told to you
with hope they find it to be good, with hope
the words flow freely from my palate.

In the village beneath the tall massif,
I was born and found my path:
That knowledge is often power,
and I must search the world for more.

I left the home of my youth
and promised to not return
so that I may know of the unknown,
so that I may hear of the unheard.

A mysterious man appeared before me
who spoke of the ways of magic.
In his hands he held a text most rare:
a grimoire as gray as smog.

It told of his lost people:
warriors, priests, wisemen, and magicians,
a culture without basis in the records,
a land he couldn't find again.

He disappeared in the night just as quickly
and left that magical item at the door.
With it, I learned his language,
that mystery, the Katalopsian tongue.

Quietly I read the incantations to myself.
A heavy desire grew in my heart
to find that distant people

and to introduce myself to the leader.

"I am only one who means to know you:
I left my people for yours.
I met your lost representative,
a man who like me seeks a vanishing world.
Perhaps he wanted me to find you
as he'd lost the ability despite himself.
Therefore, let me tell his story to you.
Let these stories by music come together."

6.3.3: NOVEL

In this section, you will be reading a translation of the opening paragraphs of Charles Dickens's *Great Expectations*. While the details of translation theory are beyond the scope of this book, consider this section a demonstration of the ability of Katalopsi to tell a story that was originally told in English.

6.3.3.1: Latin

Kfú ź Pìripy Í pòmá mirá-mà srykfĩ co Fìlipy Í pòmá kfĩ xȳxȳ, kè pró rì li pró sruse klé Pìpy ź j roŭ m̀ cu pòmá pá pypsũ kfî pe kfĩ. Nỳ ź siê m̀ Pìpy pò co ź Pìpy-kio Í pòmá kfĩ.

Ūsū pòmá mirá-mà srykfĩ ź faũ m̀ Pìripy pò fìli fifũ u cámà sakí co pòmá rýnì, fō ź puō m̀ lékī Só Kàrykyri cu. Kfú ź riŏ ž̃ pòmá mirá li pòmá prūrī pò fòfra co ź riŏ ž̃ rỳ plācxȳ u lú u la pò fòfra (kfú ź nūjè fé jó u kfesé Í lamá jó), ź īsròxúrō climã kfî lamá sakí Í pòmá nàmó xȳxȳ ròlú lá ź fèja Í la. Psy u pliclý a pòmá mirá-mà ź faũ ñ psī prùni pò cu klè ź kí cxójē, klinĩ, pi prypé cru ráxù srŏ. Kfú mŏ co nèsy u kíprù, "Nùca Sòrysínà, Crì u Cá Ke," ź nuá Ì kfìsá psuxũ klè ź kràmyxú co fu Í pòmá prūrī. Sro clū lýklū cxoxũ jè—fù ź pucí Í cu mē psỳsí u pòmá clū fòlo pró pē—crúlòle Í pò mē lùse, fù ź kuó ž̃ cu pò macricixúrō, klè ź ṽ uà ź cla prypé lá klè ź mu klā Í clamá krȳ co lá klè ź fèsré sīmì u clamá clō Í clamá kfũ co ź ṽ kleo m̀ la cla roxo sĩ luxã u

sàsu̱ fòfra̱. Ź saí ż xi̱ro̱ xȳ co xã àkle̱ u pỹ nè lýklū co ź sraû Í la̱
ūsū kyfi̱ psỳ clý cla̱má ka̱psi̱. Ź ṽ kuõ m̀ lá cla̱ nũjè xypra̱ ro̱xo̱
sỹ krúsò pymulukfĩ klè ḡ m̀ cliã m̀ krīsè cla̱.

6.3.3.2: KWS

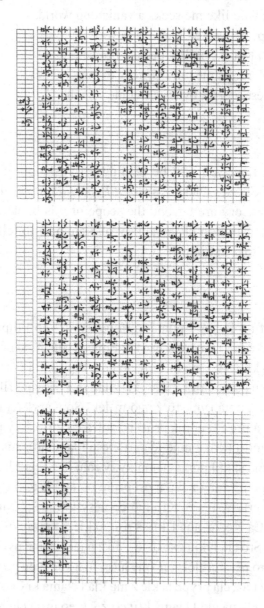

6.3.3.3: English

Great Expectations

My father's family name being Pirrip, and my Christian name Philip, my infant tongue could make of both names nothing longer or more explicit than Pip. So, I called myself Pip, and came to be called Pip.

I gave Pirrip as my father's family name, on the authority of his tombstone and my sister - Mrs. Joe Gargery, who married the blacksmith. As I never saw my father or my mother, and never saw any likeness of either of them (for their days were long before the days of photographs), my first fancies regarding what they were like, were unreasonably derived from their tombstones. The shape of the letters on my father's, gave me an odd idea that he was a square, stout, dark man, with curly black hair. From the character and turn of the inscription, 'Also Georgina Wife of the Above,' I drew a childish conclusion that my mother was freckled and sickly. To five little stone lozenges, each about a foot and a half long, which were arranged in a neat row beside their grave, and were sacred to the memory of five little brothers of mine - who gave up trying to get a living, exceedingly early in that universal struggle - I am indebted for a belief I religiously entertained that they had all been born on their backs with their hands in their trouser-pockets, and had never taken them out in this state of existence.

Ours was the marsh country, down by the river, within, as the river wound, twenty miles of the sea. My first most vivid and broad impression of the identity of things seems to me to have been gained on a memorable raw afternoon towards evening. At such a time I found out for certain that this bleak place overgrown with nettles was the churchyard; and that Philip Pirrip, late of this parish, and also Georgiana wife of the above, were dead and buried; and that Alexander, Bartholomew, Abraham, Tobias, and Roger, infant children of the aforesaid, were also dead and buried; and that the dark flat wilderness beyond the churchyard, intersected with dikes and mounds and gates, with scattered cattle feeding on it, was the marshes; and that the low leaden line beyond was the river; and that the distant savage lair from which the wind was rushing was the sea; and that the small bundle of shivers growing afraid of it all and beginning to cry, was Pip.

CHAPTER 7
Dictionary

In this final chapter, you will find the English–Katalopsi and Katalopsi–English dictionaries. The former contains approximately 5,100 translations, and the latter around 5,200. Before jumping in with the first entry, we will briefly describe the elements of the entries to facilitate the understanding of the information contained therein.

7.1: GUIDE TO ENTRIES

The translation dictionaries that follow are divided first and foremost into *entries*. Entries are a way of organizing translations and especially groups of translations in such a way as to aid the user in their search for information. For some dictionaries, there is a union between the two concepts, where one entry is equal to one translation and vice versa. For approximately 80 percent of the entries in this book, this union holds true, but for the remaining 20 percent, two or more translations appear under the single entry.

There are several reasons why this may occur. If, for example, an English word is translatable to multiple Katalopsi words, as with synonyms, then multiple translations appear to reflect this fact. Alternatively, the English word may out of context be ambiguous between more than one meaning, as with homographs, and in this case the multiple Katalopsi translations serve to distinguish these meanings.

It is also possible that the word in the entry heading is a participant in phrases or is otherwise used in a way that may be confusing, and in these cases, additional translations are elucidatory and may even include the aforementioned phrases as subheadings.

The most basic entry—with just a single translation—will have four or five parts, depending on factors shortly to be discussed. The more complex entries with more than one translation will frequently have repetitions of these same parts and no more. It is possible, however, that a translation is justified by a phrase the word is used in, and in this case the complex entry will also include a special part called a subheading, i.e. the phrase itself. The four ubiqitous features of an entry are: (1) the heading, which is also the word or phrase to be translated; (2) the number of the translation, starting at one with each entry and incrementing with each additional set of translation facts; (3) the part of speech of the translation at hand; and (4) the translation itself, which will be a Katalopsi word or phrase in the case of the English–Katalopsi dictionary and an English word or phrase in the case of the Katalopsi–English Dictionary.

We will go through each of these entry features one by one and consider the implications and demand for additional information in some circumstances. After describing the internal structure of the translations, we will move on to the external structure of the dictionaries.

7.1.1: OBLIGATORY ENTRY FEATURES

7.1.1.1: Heading

Each entry begins with a heading. This heading will be a word or phrase in the source language and will be formatted with bold text. Most typically, the heading will be just a single word, but in some cases, phrases present a meaning collectively which their respective parts do not and thereby justify an entry of their own. As we will see, the likelihood of confusion along these lines will mean that some phrases appear not only as a heading for an entry of their own but also as a subheading within an entry headed by a word used in that phrase. Besides dissolving this potential confusion, this also serves to increase the utility of the dictionary as a tool for translation and for learning vocabulary.

7.1.1.2: Translation Number

Each possible translation of the word or phrase in the heading begins with a number to better distinguish the details of the translations. Each entry contains at least one translation number, but when more than one is present, you should also note the division of the translations by semicolons. In other words, all translations but the last will be followed by a semicolon, while the last will be followed by a period, ending the entry. This numbering starts with 1 and sometimes gets as high as 9, as in the entry for the word *put*, for example.

7.1.1.3: Part of Speech

Each translation within an entry includes a part of speech, the syntactic category of the translation. We should make very clear that, because we have assumed readers to be familiar with the functions of English words, the part of speech listed for each translation corresponds specifically to the Katalopsi word or phrase, whether it is the translation, as in the English–Katalopsi dictionary, or the heading, as in the Katalopsi–English dictionary. Sometimes the syntactic category of the word or phrase in Katalopsi is simply not the same as the English equivalent, and so this feature seeks to illuminate facts about Katalopsi syntax and lexicology that could otherwise only be guessed at.

Translations are divided into thirteen parts of speech, a slight simplification of linguistic facts for the purpose of presenting the lexicographical information in a more immediately accessible way. This feature is formatted in italics and includes the following designations:

adj.	adjectives
adv.	adverbs
aux.	auxiliaries
comp.	complementizers
conj.	conjunctions
det.	determiners
dis.	disambiguators
intj.	interjections

n.	nouns
num.	numbers
prep.	prepositions
pn.	pronouns
v.	verbs

Notably, in some cases multiple translations will be provided solely to demonstrate the fact that the word or phrase may be used with multiple parts of speech, which may not be immediately obvious with other notations.

7.1.1.4: Translation

After the part of speech comes the translation. Like the heading, the translation could be a word or a phrase. The English–Katalopsi dictionary will have Katalopsi translations in this position, while the Katalopsi–English dictionary will have English translations in the same.

7.1.2: Optional Entry Features

Some features appear within an entry only when certain other conditions are met. Under these circumstances, more than four features are present, including the possible repetition of some features due to the appearance of more than one translation.

7.1.2.1: Disambiguator Set for Verbs

In the first case of additional entry features, translations marked with the verb part of speech will also include a list of disambiguators in curly brackets before the translation. Typically, the list won't be exhaustive but will include the disambiguators most likely to be used with the verb. To expand beyond the list provided for a given verb will require a thorough understanding of grammatical phrase syntax and the information on predicates in §3.2.2 as well as the semantics of role assignment in §4.1.

Disambiguators are, of course, used with predicates and not simply verbs; however, the circumstances of disambiguator usage with non-verbal predicates are highly simplified, and so adjectives, nouns, and prepositions do not include a disambiguator list. A review of §3.2.3.2 may be called for should doubt arise about the selection of a disambiguator for adjectival, nominal, and prepositional predicates.

Note that even though the disambiguator list is specific to Katalopsi verbs, it will appear in both the English–Katalopsi and the Katalopsi–English dictionaries to demarcate disambiguator usage for the verb, much as how the part of speech reflects a fact about Katalopsi categorization, regardless of the directionality of translation.

7.1.2.2: Meaningful Elaboration of Translations

In some cases, it is necessary to elaborate on the intended meaning of a translation. There are many reasons this may occur. In the case of homographs, for example, an elaboration would serve to remove ambiguity. Words and phrases with highly idiomatic usages may also benefit from such elaboration. Some words may have closely related but nonetheless distinct meanings which are represented the same in one language but distinctly in the other. Whenever this elaboration is deemed necessary, it will follow the translation in parentheses. When only a single translation appears, this means the parenthetical elaboration appears just before the period closing the entry; but when multiple translations appear, the elaboration might appear before a semicolon separating the translation information sets. In any case, a present elaboration is always the last bit of information provided for a translation.

The strategy of elaboration varies on a case-by-case basis. To distinguish nuance of meaning, it is sometimes simple enough to provide a synonym. This provision may also be rooted in the relatively simple Katalopsi lexicon, where multiple words in English are translated to the same word in Katalopsi. Of course, the opposite also occurs, where multiple Katalopsi words are translatable to the same English word, though it is more rare. Another strategy involves providing the text that typically follows the given translation, as when an English verb is paired with a prepositional phrase. When this strategy is employed, it is not infrequently because Katalopsi does not require such a prepositional phrase, due to the nature of semantic role disambiguation.

One particularly complex strategy of elaboration seeks to explain how a particular word is used, establishing arguments or even laying out the basic structure of a statement when that structure is predicted to be difficult or out of the ordinary for English. It could be as brief as using abbreviations such as *s.o.* (someone), *s.th.* (something), or *s.w.* (somewhere) to establish the syntactic or semantic nature of related arguments, or a combination of such impersonal pronouns with a meaningful elaboration strategy mentioned above.

In the final elaboration strategy, grammatical terminology or explanation may be used to specify meaning or usage. When the words used are strictly grammatical terminology or elaborating on grammar, they will appear in italics. In some cases, grammatical elaboration will appear alongside another elaboration strategy, and the two are usually separated by a comma or semicolon as necessary. As we will see more on shortly, when multiple translations are present, this may be because usage varies in a significant way in English that is explained in Katalopsi simply by a disambiguator. In these and other nuanced grammatical cases, the translation may be the same for each information set, though the disambiguator list varies, and the elaborations serve only to explain the separation of the translation into two or more sets along these grammatical lines.

7.1.2.3: Subheading

As previously stated, subheadings will sometimes appear at the forefront of a translation information set, prior to the part-of-speech feature, when multiple translations are contained within the entry. The subheading is often a way of making the dictionary more useful by providing a common phrase within which the word heading the entry is used. This sometimes means duplication of a subheading as a heading elsewhere in the dictionary, underscoring its appearance for the sake of utility and ease of access. Other times, the heading may present a homograph which is likely to confuse, and so the subheading is a way of elaborating on intended meanings while also indicating the subheading is translatable in the way shortly to follow it.

Some words have many usages, not just because the word itself is polysemic but because it is used in idiomatic expressions. This is another area where subheadings may be used, listing the idiomatic expression as the source of the translation operation, the translation to follow being the target.

7.1.2.4: Semantic Roles for Disambiguators

For disambiguator entries, it is not possible to provide an English translation, so in lieu of the translation in these cases, an enumeration of the assigned semantic roles is instead provided. These will appear within curly brackets in the same order that the roles are assigned.

7.1.3: ORGANIZATION OF ENTRIES

Features of entries aside, there are additional elements of structure to the dictionaries which aim to make the dictionaries useful and accessible. These relate to the order of translations within entries and to the order of the entries themselves.

7.1.3.1: Internal Order of Translations

Some thought was put into the internal order of translations for those entries that have more than one, though a consistent system has not been established. Instead, the translations are ordered roughly by their estimated utility. If one among a pair of translations is thought to be used more often than the alternative, then it will be listed under number 1, with the other listed under number 2. However, if no translation is thought to be more frequently used, then the translations will generally appear in alphabetical order by the part of speech—not by the translation itself. This way, if you are looking for a particular translation with a particular syntactic categorization, this information will be more immediately available.

7.1.3.2: External Order of Entries

The most familiar aspect of structure to a dictionary is the order of its entries, almost invariably alphabetical. This is the case for the dictionaries to follow, and the English–Katalopsi dictionary presents no surprises. However, the order of the Katalopsi–English dictionary engages a peculiarity of orthography that is little familiar to speakers of English. Katalopsi has tone diacritics, and so it is necessary to establish a rule for ordering words which use them against one another if the Katalopsi–English dictionary is going to be useful.

First and foremost, the dictionary is ordered alphabetically, as in English. The Latin orthography used to represent Katalopsi contains only twenty of the twenty-six letters common to English, so the Katalopsi–English dictionary is divided into twenty subsections corresponding to these twenty letters. Spaces in the word or phrase are also ordered before hyphens, and hyphens before the letter *a*, at which point the normal alphabetical order takes effect. Capitalization is ignored.

In addition to ordering the entries by the alphabetics of their headings, the dictionary is ordered by the diacritics on the letters. What this means is exemplified in the words *frià*, *friạ*, and *friă*. They contain the same letters in the same order, and so alphabetical ordering guarantees that they will be next to eachother in the dictionary. However, an additional layer of ordering has been applied on the basis of their diacritics. This is the order that has been applied, from first to last: (1) no diacritic/neutral tone; (2) acute accent/rising tone; (3) grave accent/ falling tone; (4) macron above/high tone; (5) macron below/low tone; (6) tilde/mordent tone; (7) circumflex/rising-falling tone; and (8) háček/ falling-rising tone.

7.2: ENGLISH TO KATALOPSI

A

a lot, 1. *pn.* srẹ.
a lot of, 1. *det.* srẹ.
abdomen, 1. *n.* lacrã.

ability, 1. *n.* klỹ.

able to, 1. *aux.* j̣.

able-bodied, 1. *adj.* nìcxị.

about, 1. *prep.* ròlú (*topic*).

about to, 1. *aux.* ŕ (be about to).

above, 1. *prep.* kẹ.

abysmal, 1. *adj.* cèfy̱xú.

abyss, 1. *n.* cèfy̱.

accept, 1. *v.* {m̀, m̃} puá.

acceptability, 1. *n.* ja̱pu̱jáclì.

acceptable, 1. *adj.* ja̱pu̱já.

acceptance, 1. *n.* púsā.

accepted, 1. *adj.* púmā.

access, 1. *n.* lèsy̱; 2. *v.* {m̀} leỳ.

according to, 1. *prep.* lāmēklī (in s.o.'s opinion).

account, 1. *n.* nīsō (explanation); 2. *v.* {m̀, ǹ} niō (for s.th.).

accountant, 1. *n.* luploprã.

accounted for, 1. *adj.* nīmō (explained).

accounting, 1. *n.* luplõ.

accuracy, 1. *n.* xōcàclí.

accurate, 1. *adj.* xōcà.

achievable, 1. *adj.* ja̱rijá.

achieve, 1. *v.* {ḿ, m̀, Í} riá.

achievement, 1. *n.* rísā.

achiever, 1. *n.* ríkā.

acid, 1. *n.* plìcị.

acidic, 1. *adj.* plìcịxú.

acidity, 1. *n.* plìcịxúclì.

acknowledge, 1. *v.* {m̀} psyị.

acknowledgement, 1. *n.* psy̱sị (recognition).

across, 1. *prep.* lùjọ.

act, 1. *n.* kìsẹ; 2. *n.* pạlẹ; 3. *v.* {ḿ, m̀} kiè (behave, take action; *compounds*); 4. *v.* {ḿ, ń} sruô (up, misbehave).

action, 1. *n.* kìsẹ.

active, 1. *adj.* fru̱cọxú.

actively, 1. *adv.* fru̱cọxúrō.

activity, 1. *n.* fru̱co̱.

actor, 1. *n.* kìke̱.

actress, 1. *n.* kìke̱.

actual, 1. *adj.* xýmà.

actually, 1. *adv.* xýmàro̱.

add, 1. *v.* {j̃, ṽ} luò (include, arithmetic); 2. *v.* {Í, ż} cuă (up, make sense).

added, 1. *adj.* lùmo̱.

addition, 1. *n.* lùso̱; 2. **in addition to** *prep.* méràply.

additional, 1. *adj.* lùso̱xú; 2. *adj.* sūklā (another).

additionally, 1. *adv.* lùso̱xúrō.

address, 1. *n.* párò.

admissibility, 1. *n.* jākējūclì.

admissible, 1. *adj.* jākējū.

admission, 1. *n.* kēsū (entry); 2. *n.* kfúsō (confession).

admit, 1. *v.* {m̀, ñ} kfuó (confess); 2. *v.* {m̀, m̃} keū (permit entry).

admittance, 1. *n.* kēsū (entry).

admitted, 1. *adj.* kēmū (allowed to enter); 2. *adj.* kfúmō (confessed).

advantage, 1. *n.* prékfȳ.

advantageous, 1. *adj.* prékfȳxù.

aerial, 1. *adj.* pysū.

affect, 1. *v.* {ż} xiō.

affected, 1. *adj.* xīmō.

affection, 1. *n.* fi̱.

afford, 1. *v.* {m̀} fié (able to pay for s.th.).

affordable, 1. *adj.* ja̱fi̱jé.

afraid, 1. *aux.* Ī̀ (be afraid to do s.th.); 2. *adj.* nēlūlē.

after, 1. *comp.* pī; 2. *prep.* pī.

again, 1. *adv.* sājà.

age, 1. *n.* krè.

aged, 1. *adj.* krèxú (e.g. wine).

aggressive, 1. *adj.* krīlālē.

ago, 1. *prep.* re̱sú.

agree, 1. *v.* {ź, ż} moī (with s.th./s.o.); 2. *v.* {m̃, m̀} cxyí (to s.th.).

agreeable, 1. *adj.* cxýlūlē (amenable); 2. *adj.* ja̱cxyjú (acceptable).

agreed, 1. *adj.* cxýmū (to).

agreement, 1. *n.* cxýsū.

aim, 1. *n.* pìso̲ (objective); 2. *v.* {m̀, m̄, v̀, ṽ} piò (take aim at s.th.).

air, 1. *n.* sũ.

airplane, 1. *n.* suklukũ.

alchemist, 1. *n.* psènóprà.

alchemy, 1. *n.* psènó.

alive, 1. *v.* {Í} puỹ (be alive).

all, 1. *det.* clà; 2. *pn.* clà.

alligator, 1. *n.* cxu̲lú.

allow, 1. *v.* {m̀, m̃} muō.

allowable, 1. *adj.* jāmūjō.

allowed, 1. *adj.* mūmō (permitted); 2. **be allowed to** *aux.* z̀.

almost, 1. *adv.* psèpó; 2. *adv.* xi̲ro̲ (nearly).

along, 1. *prep.* crā.

already, 1. *adv.* mùrý.

also, 1. *adv.* nùca̲.

alter, 1. *v.* {Í, m̀, m̃} cxié.

alteration, 1. *n.* cxísē (change).

altered, 1. *adj.* cxímē (changed).

although, 1. *comp.* klá.

always, 1. *adv.* plý.

amatory, 1. *adj.* pyfi̲.

amber, 1. *n.* cléjū.

ambergris, 1. *n.* lìli̲xámà.

ameliorate, 1. *v.* {m̀, m̃, Í} kreō.

among, 1. *prep.* frō.

amount, 1. *n.* cli̲ (quantity).

amulet, 1. *n.* clōrù.

amusing, 1. *adj.* kfòli̲le̲.

anal, 1. *adj.* pysrũ.

analysis, 1. *n.* lùprí.

analytical, 1. *adj.* pȳlùprí (relating to analysis); 2. *adj.* lùpríxù (meticulous).

and, 1. *conj.* co; 2. *conj.* sa (non-exclusive).

anger, 1. *n.* makfũ.

angle, 1. *n.* pylã.

angry, 1. *adj.* makfuxũ.

angular, 1. *adj.* pypylã.

animal, 1. *n.* fóxỳ; 2. *n.* rìsrẹ (monster).

animalistic, 1. *adj.* fóxỳxú.

ankle, 1. *n.* srūfā.

annual, 1. *adj.* pȳnī.

another, 1. *det.* sūklā; 2. *pn.* sūklā.

answer, 1. *n.* rīsā; 2. *v.* {ḿ, m̀} riā.

answerable, 1. *adj.* jārījā.

ant, 1. *n.* cọfé.

anus, 1. *n.* srũ.

any, 1. *det.* nè (every) 2. *det.* rỳ (some).

anybody, 1. *pn.* nènị (each person); 2. *pn.* rỳnị (some person).

anymore, 1. *adv.* cxáfò.

anyone, 1. *pn.* nènị (each person); 2. *pn.* rỳnị (some person).

anyplace, 1. *adv.* nēmā; 2. *pn.* nēmā.

anything, 1. *pn.* nècụ.

anyway, 1. *adv.* fròlú.

anywhere, 1. *adv.* rȳmā; 2. *pn.* rȳmā.

apart from, 1. *comp.* fūlā; 2. *prep.* fūlā.

apartment, 1. *n.* clemã.

apocalypse, 1. *n.* kọklímà.

apocalyptic, 1. *adj.* kọklímàxú.

apparent, 1. *adj.* srụsẹ (obvious).

appear, 1. *v.* {Í, ż} cxuó; 2. *v.* {Í} kreú (seem).

appearance, 1. *n.* cxúsō.

apple, 1. *n.* kȳmì.

applicable, 1. *adj.* jācìjé.

applicant, 1. *n.* srìká.

applicated, 1. *adj.* cìmé.

application, 1. *n.* cìsé (e.g. of a tool); 2. *n.* srìsá (e.g. to a job).

applied, 1. *adj.* cìmé (applicated).

apply, 1. *v.* {v̀, ṽ} cìě (use s.th. on s.th.); 2. *v.* {v̀} sriǎ (for e.g. recompense); 3. *v.* {m̀} sriǎ (to e.g. a job).

approximately, 1. *adv.* ácē.

apron, 1. *n.* fèkẹ.

arch, 1. *n.* núkfō.

archer, 1. *n.* klànị.

archery, 1. *n.* klàxó.

archipelago, 1. *n.* sìcroca̲.

area, 1. *n.* ma̲sra̲.

arguable, 1. *adj.* jājūjè.

argue, 1. *n.* {m̄, m̀} juè (about s.th.).

argued, 1. *adj.* jùme̲.

argument, 1. *n.* jùse̲ (charged discussion).

argumentative, 1. *adj.* jùle̲le̲.

arm, 1. *n.* frà.

armor, 1. *n.* crè.

army, 1. *n.* lēmỳ.

around, 1. *prep.* kolũ; 2. *adv.* ácē (approximately).

arrange, 1. *v.* {m̀, m̃} kruó (prepare or plan).

arranged, 1. *adj.* krúmō (prepared).

arrangement, 1. *n.* krúsō (preparation or plan).

arrival, 1. *n.* núsā.

arrive, 1. *v.* {Í, Ì} nuá (at a location).

arrow, 1. *n.* sē.

art, 1. *n.* lã.

article, 1. *n.* klelỹ.

articulate, 1. *adj.* kèlóplòlílē; 2. *v.* {m̀, ñ} keǒploǐ.

articulated, 1. *adj.* kèmóplòmí.

articulately, 1. *adv.* kèlóplòlílērō.

articulation, 1. *n.* kèsóplòsí.

articulator, 1. *n.* kèkóplòkí.

artist, 1. *n.* laprã.

as, 1. *prep.* si̲ (*as* interesting as s.th.); 2. *prep.* klé (as interesting *as* s.th.); 3. *prep.* ūsū (function or character).

as long as, 1. *comp.* ro̲xo̲.

as much, 1. *prep.* rékā (*as much* ... as s.th.); 2. *prep.* like.

aside, 1. *prep.* fūlā.

aside from, 1. *comp.* fūlā; 2. *prep.* fūlā.

ask, 1. *v.* {m̀, ñ} suo̲.

asked, 1. *adj.* su̲mo̲.

asker, 1. *n.* su̲ko̲.

asleep, 1. *n.* xésȳxù.

asocial, 1. *adj.* īrūnàxú.

assailant, 1. *n.* krīkā.

assist, 1. *v.* {g̲} xiã (s.o.); 2. *v.* {m̀} xiã (with doing s.th.).

assistance, 1. *n.* xisã.

assistant, 1. *n.* xisaprã.

assisted, 1. *adj.* ximã.

assume, 1. *v.* {m̀} riŷ.

assumption, 1. *n.* lùsé.

asymmetrical, 1. *adj.* ip̲sa̲cíxù.

at, 1. *prep.* cú (*location*); 2. *prep.* clý (next to); 3. **at least** *adv.* py̲si̲ciṟo̲;
4. **at most** *adv.* py̲nékfēṟō.

at first, 1. *adv.* pyp̲u̲se̲ṟo̲.

at most, 1. *adv.* py̲nékfēṟō.

at times, 1. *adv.* rȳfrà.

atheoretical, 1. *adj.* īcìpsáxù.

attack, 1. *n.* krīsā; 2. *v.* {ḿ, m̀} kriā; 3. **attack preemptively** *v.* {ḿ, m̀}
psiěkriã; 4. **preemptive attack** *n.* psìsékrīsā.

attacked, 1. *adj.* krīmā.

attacker, 1. *n.* krīkā.

attention, 1. *n.* julĩ.

attentive, 1. *adj.* julixũ.

attic, 1. *n.* cājē.

atypical, 1. *adj.* i̲sýxù.

audible, 1. *adj.* ja̲si̲je̲.

audience, 1. *n.* srȳsè.

aunt, 1. *n.* níprỳ.

aural, 1. *adj.* pȳfràfe̲.

author, 1. *n.* nāsù.

authoritative, 1. *n.* pyfifũ.

authority, 1. *n.* fifũ.

automatic, 1. *adj.* prāsòma̲.

automatically, 1. *adv.* prāsòma̲ṟo̲.

autumn, 1. *n.* còclu̲.

autumnal, 1. *adj.* pȳcòclu̲.

availability, 1. *n.* clyxaclĩ.

available, 1. *adj.* clyxã.

average, 1. *n.* lȳclà (mean); 2. *adj.* lȳclàxú.
avian, 1. *adj.* pypsĩ.
avoid, 1. *v.* {m̀} kfuâ.
avoidable, 1. *adj.* jakfújà.
avoidance, 1. *n.* kfúsà.
await, 1. *v.* {m̀, m̃} piè.
away, 1. *adv.* pìcé.
away from, 1. *prep.* pìcé.
axe, 1. *n.* pūxà.
axiomatic, 1. *adj.* kfoxũ.

B

back, 1. *n.* krȳ (anatomy); 2. *n.* psí (side).
backpack, 1. *n.* masrá.
backward, 1. *adv.* áklò.
bad, 1. *adj.* prę.
badland, 1. *n.* clinulý.
badly, 1. *adv.* pręro.
bailiwick, 1. *n.* cxĩ (field).
balance, 1. *n.* solȳ.
balanced, 1. *adj.* solyxũ.
ball, 1. *n.* lȳ.
banana, 1. *n.* paprú.
bank, 1. *n.* clófō (financial); 2. *n.* núcē (e.g. on a river, embankment).
bar, 1. *n.* fòrú.
barely, 1. *adv.* mũ.
bark, 1. *n.* cęklí.
barmaid, 1. *n.* fòrúprà.
barman, 1. *n.* fòrúprà.
barrel, 1. *n.* mȳpsĩ.
barren, 1. *adj.* fęró.
barricade, 1. *n.* sōkỳ.
barrier, 1. *n.* prìjú.
bartender, 1. *n.* fòrúprà.
barter, 1. *n.* plisã; 2. *v.* {ḿ, m̀, v̀, ṽ} pliã.

bartered, 1. *adj.* plimã.

barterer, 1. *n.* plikã.

base, 1. *v.* {n̄, ṽ} kruè (s.th. on s.th.).

basement, 1. *n.* kōlà.

basic, 1. *adj.* clỹ.

basically, 1. *adv.* clyrõ.

basis, 1. *n.* pojõ.

bathroom, 1. *n.* clūlū.

batter, 1. *v.* {m̄, Í} psuê (beat).

battleaxe, 1. *n.* mōpūxà.

bauble, 1. *n.* mòri̠.

bayonet, 1. *n.* rénā.

beach, 1. *n.* xi̠ra̠.

beak, 1. *n.* plē.

beam, 1. *n.* psẽ.

bean, 1. *n.* su̠.

bear, 1. *n.* ke̠no̠; 2. **bear cub** *n.* ke̠no̠no̠; 3. **be born** *v.* {ź} uà.

beard, 1. *n.* pra̠.

bearded, 1. *adj.* pra̠xú.

beat, 1. *v.* {m̄, Í} psuê (batter).

beaten, 1. *adj.* psúmè (battered).

because, 1. *comp.* kfú; 2. *conj.* kfú.

because of, 1. *prep.* kfú.

become, 1. *v.* {Í} ki̠o̠ (*compounds*).

beckon, 1. *v.* {m̄} liē; 2. {m̄} liē (for s.o.)

beckoned, 1. *adj.* līmē.

beckoner, 1. *n.* līkē.

bed, 1. *n.* jolũ.

bedroom, 1. *n.* jolucã.

bee, 1. *n.* ce̠ni̠.

beef, 1. *n.* lyfy̠.

beer, 1. *n.* jòca̠.

beetle, 1. *n.* frākè.

before, 1. *comp.* fé; 2. *prep.* fé (prior to); 3. *prep.* frú (in front of).

beg, 1. *v.* {m̄, ṽ} lué.

beggar, 1. *n.* lúkē.

begin, 1. *v.* {m̀} puẹ (s.o./s.th.); 2. **begin to** *aux.* ñ.

beginner, 1. *n.* pu̠kẹ.

beginning, 1. *n.* pusẹ.

begun, 1. *adj.* pu̠mẹ (started).

behind, 1. *prep.* psí.

belief, 1. *n.* lùsẹ.

believable, 1. *adj.* jālūjè.

believe, 1. *v.* {ź, z̃} luè (s.o./s.th.); 2. *v.* {z̀} luè (*propositions*).

believed, 1. *adj.* lùmẹ.

believer, 1. *n.* lùkẹ.

bell, 1. *n.* sélī.

belly button, 1. *n.* lòra̠.

belong, 1. *v.* {z̀} xoī.

belonging, 1. *n.* xōsī (possession).

below, 1. *prep.* rèply̠.

belt, 1. *n.* còpi̠; 2. **belt buckle** *n.* rōprè.

bench, 1. *n.* xùpli̠.

bend, 1. *n.* fèsi̠; 2. *v.* {m̀, Í} feì; 3. *v.* {ṽ} feì (into s.th.).

bendy, 1. *adj.* fèli̠lẹ.

beneath, 1. *prep.* krínè.

benefit, 1. *n.* pi̠ka̠.

beneficial, 1. *adj.* pi̠ka̠xú.

bent, 1. *adj.* fèmi̠.

berry, 1. *n.* fènú.

beside, 1. *prep.* clý.

besides, 1. *comp.* fūlā; 2. *prep.* fūlā.

best, 1. *adj.* rà cy̠.

better, 1. *adj.* pró cy̠.

between, 1. *prep.* sýnō.

beyond, 1. *prep.* rēcōlỳ.

big, 1. *adj.* lu̠.

bile, 1. *n.* pó.

biliary, 1. *adj.* pypó.

bilious, 1. *adj.* póxù.

bill, 1. *v.* {m̀, m̃} liǎ (in business).

biological, 1. *adj.* pyclexõ.

biologist, 1. *n.* clexoprã.

biology, 1. *n.* clexõ.

bird, 1. *n.* psĩ.

birth, 1. *n.* cé; 2. **give birth to** *v.* {m̀} uà (s.o.).

bite, 1. *n.* crýsū; 2. *v.* {ḿ, m̀, Í} cryú.

biter, 1. *n.* crýkū.

bitten, 1. *adj.* crýmū.

black, 1. *adj.* srõ; 2. *n.* srōkō.

blackberry, 1. *n.* srōfènú.

blacken, 1. *v.* {m̀, Í} sronuõ.

blackened, 1. *adj.* sronumõ.

blackness, 1. *n.* sroclĩ.

blacksmith, 1. *n.* lékī.

bladder, 1. *n.* srālè; 2. **gall bladder** *n.* làsró.

blanket, 1. *n.* pọfó.

blaspheme, 1. *v.* {ḿ, m̀} leû.

blasphemer, 1. *n.* lékù.

blasphemous, 1. *adj.* lésùxú.

blasphemy, 1. *n.* lésù.

blight, 1. *n.* fonũ.

blind, 1. *adj.* nómī; 2. *v.* {m̀, Í} noí.

blinded, 1. *adj.* nómī.

blindness, 1. *n.* nómīclì.

blood, 1. *n.* frọ.

bloody, 1. *adj.* frọxó.

blouse, 1. *n.* nỹ.

bludgeon, 1. *n.* cùrụ.

blue, 1. *adj.* prī; 2. *n.* prīkō.

blueberry, 1. *n.* prīfènú.

blueness, 1. *n.* prīclì.

blush, 1. *n.* sèsy̱; 2. *v.* {ź, ž} seỳ (at s.th.).

board, 1. *n.* plȳ (wood); 2. *n.* sṟikry̱ (administrative).

boat, 1. *n.* krụ.

bodily, 1. *adj.* pysṟạ (related to the body).

body, 1. *n.* srạ.

bog, 1. *n.* jòfá.

bolt, 1. *n.* pse̱ (building material, crossbow ammunition).

bomb, 1. *n.* krèra̱.

bombardier, 1. *n.* rỳkúsrìko̱.

bone, 1. *n.* pù.

bony, 1. *adj.* pùxú.

book, 1. *n.* sȳ.

book-related, 1. *adj.* pȳsȳ.

bookcase, 1. *n.* sȳkrēpī.

bookish, 1. *adj.* sȳxù.

bookshelf, 1. *n.* sȳkrēpī.

boot, 1. *n.* jyplĩ.

border, 1. *n.* mùklú (of a territory, etc.).

boredom, 1. *n.* na̱ro̱clí.

boring, 1. *adj.* na̱ro̱.

born, 1. *adj.* ùma̱ (given birth to).

boss, 1. *n.* cõ.

bossy, 1. *adj.* coxũ.

botanical, 1. *adj.* pȳmà.

both, 1. *det.* pe̱; 2. *pn.* pe̱.

bottom, 1. *n.* kò.

bought, 1. *adj.* pémū.

bow, 1. *n.* klà (arrow weapon).

bowl, 1. *n.* pỳ.

bowman, 1. *n.* klàni̱.

bowmanship, 1. *n.* klàxó.

bowtie, 1. *n.* kli̱cé.

box, 1. *n.* kla̱.

boy, 1. *n.* fòny̱.

boyfriend, 1. *n.* kýnȳ.

bra, 1. *n.* na̱lý (brassiere).

bracelet, 1. *n.* sìný.

bracer, 1. *n.* srārè.

brag, 1. *v.* {ḿ} kliè.

braggart, 1. *n.* klìke̱.

brain, 1. *n.* nã.

brainstem, 1. *n.* nacrõ.

branch, 1. *n*. klõ.

brassiere, 1. *n*. nalý.

brave, 1. *adj*. krǫ.

bravely, 1. *adv*. krǫrǫ.

bravery, 1. *n*. krǫclí.

bread, 1. *n*. fró.

break, 1. *v*. {ṁ, Í, ṽ} joū.

break down, 1. *v*. {ź} kfiò (mentally).

breakable, 1. *adj*. jājōjū.

breakdown, 1. *n*. kfìsǫ (nervous).

breakfast, 1. *n*. sylǫ.

breakfast nook, 1. *n*. sylocã.

breast, 1. *n*. nàprú.

breath, 1. *n*. làsí.

breathe, 1. *v*. {ź} laǐ.

brevity, 1. *n*. pàclí.

brick, 1. *n*. lýklū.

bridge, 1. *n*. fý.

brief, 1. *adj*. pà.

briefcase, 1. *n*. cxūcà.

briefly, 1. *adv*. pàrǫ.

bright, 1. *adj*. sù; 2. *adj*. kfíxù (luminous); 3. *adj*. ký (color).

brighten, 1. *v*. {ṁ, ṅ, Í, ṽ} sùnuǫ.

brightened, 1. *adj*. sùnumǫ.

brightly, 1. *adv*. sùrǫ; 2. *adv*. kfíxùrǫ (luminously).

bring, 1. *v*. {ṁ, m̃, j̃} caũ.

broad, 1. *adj*. prẽ (wide).

broaden, 1. *v*. {ṁ, Í, v́, ṽ} prenuõ.

broadly, 1. *adv*. prerõ.

broccoli, 1. *n*. sēkā.

broken, 1. *adj*. jōmū (an object).

bronze, 1. *n*. mōpsò; 2. *adj*. mōpsòxú (made of bronze).

brother, 1. *n*. fòlǫ.

brotherly, 1. *adj*. fòlǫxú.

brought, 1. *adj*. camũ (along).

brow, 1. *n*. xī.

brown, 1. *adj.* prịmụ; 2. *n.* prịmúkō.

brush, 1. *n.* kīsrà (bushes, etc); 2. *n.* ríjà (for hair).

brussels sprout, 1. *n.* lūfē.

buckle, 1. *n.* rōprè (belt).

budget, 1. *n.* fȳpȳ.

buffalo, 1. *n.* mūpsā.

build, 1. *v.* {ḿ, m̀, m̃} cxeò.

builder, 1. *n.* cxèkọ.

building, 1. *n.* cxèsọ.

built, 1. *adj.* cxèmọ.

bump, 1. *n.* jèfọ.

bumpiness, 1. *n.* jèfọxúclì.

bumpy, 1. *adj.* jèfọxú.

bunny, 1. *n.* lìcxạnạ.

burn, 1. *n.* kìsạ; 2. *v.* {m̀, m̃, Í} kià.

burned, 1. *adj.* kìmạ.

burnt, 1. *adj.* kìmạ.

burp, 1. *n.* xósù; 2. *v.* {ź} xoû.

bus, 1. *n.* sulõ.

business, 1. *n.* pìpó (commerce); 2. *n.* praklũ (company).

business-related, 1. *adj.* pȳpìpó.

busy, 1. *adj.* kȳ.

but, 1. *conj.* mã; 2. *conj.* fẽ (but rather).

butt, 1. *n.* xụplạ (buttocks).

butterfly, 1. *n.* frēcè.

buttocks, 1. *n.* xụplạ.

button, 1. *n.* cịnọ (clothing); 2. *n.* rājì (technology); 3. **belly button** *n.* lòrạ.

buy, 1. *v.* {m̀, m̃} peú (purchase); 2. *v.* {ḿ} kleȳ (pay).

buyer, 1. *n.* pékū.

by, 1. *prep.* clý (next to); 2. *prep.* crā (along); 3. *prep.* nū (*agent, experiencer*); 4. *prep.* fẽ (*cause, stimulus*).

C

cabinet, 1. *n.* clụplú.

cabbage, 1. *n.* lẹpá.

cactus, 1. *n.* sàklé.

café, 1. *n.* psọcí.

cake, 1. *n.* rạfị.

calf, 1. *n.* rụpịnị.

caliper, 1. *n.* lìkrý.

call, 1. *v.* {m̀} siê (s.o. is called s.th.); 2. {m̀} psaī (telephone); 3. **call for** *v.* {m̀} liē (beckon).

called, 1. *adj.* psāmī (by telephone); 2. *adj.* līmē (beckoned).

caller, 1. *n.* psākī (by telephone).

calm, 1. *adj.* fà; 2. *n.* fàclí; 3. *v.* {m̀, ǹ, Í, ź, ẑ} fànuọ.

calmly, 1. *adv.* fàrọ.

calmness, 1. *n.* fàclí.

camel, 1. *n.* plēnà.

camera, 1. *n.* fráfrī.

campaign, 1. *n.* cákù (mission).

can, 1. *v.* {ḿ, m̀, m̃} peị (put by); 2. *aux.* j (be able to).

cancer, 1. *n.* ōpī.

cancerous, 1. *adj.* ōpīxù.

canine, 1. *adj.* pȳpsȳ.

canned, 1. *adj.* pẹmị.

canner, 1. *n.* pẹkị.

cannon, 1. *n.* lȳxò.

cap, 1. *n.* prā.

cape, 1. *n.* psý.

capital, 1. *n.* crápsà (financial); 2. *n.* kárā (city).

car, 1. *n.* psỳplụ.

caravan, 1. *n.* sạlásā.

card, 1. *n.* frẹ.

cardiac, 1. *adj.* pyrỹ.

care, 1. *n.* frúsò (mindfulness); 2. *n.* kịsạ (caretaking); 3. *v.* {ź, ẑ} fruô (have feelings for, about); 4. *v.* {m̀} kiạ (take care of s.o./s.th. e.g. as hospice).

career, 1. *n.* ké (job).

careful, 1. *adj.* julolẽ.

caretaker, 1. *n.* kịkạ.

caring, 1. *adj.* frúsòxú (kindhearted).

carrot, 1. *n.* sírù.

carry, 1. *v.* {m̀, m̃, Ì, j̃} jey̱; 2. *v.* {m̀} moí (support, e.g. a team).

cartilage, 1. *n.* klýsē.

cartilaginous, 1. *adj.* klýsēxù.

case, 1. *n.* kú (instance).

cash, 1. *n.* srāsū; 2. *n.* kfi̱pre̱ (currency).

cashier, 1. *n.* ca̱púprà (teller, clerk).

cassock, 1. *n.* klìplu̱.

castle, 1. *n.* fu̱cú.

cat, 1. *n.* ru̱.

catastrophe, 1. *n.* kre̱fílè.

catastrophic, 1. *adj.* kre̱fílèxú.

catastrophically, 1. *adv.* kre̱fílèxúrō.

catch, 1. *n.* cxýsū (a fish, etc); 2. *v.* {m̀, ǹ, ṽ} cxyú; 3. *v.* {ḿ, Í, g̀} fruõ (up to s.o./s.th.).

catcher, 1. *n.* cxýkū.

categorical, 1. *adj.* cocroxũ.

category, 1. *n.* cocrõ.

caught, 1. *adj.* cxýmū (fish, etc).

cauldron, 1. *n.* mènu̱ká.

cauliflower, 1. *n.* kfūlỳ.

causal, 1. *adj.* p̄ycxìká.

causation, 1. *n.* cxìsá.

cause, 1. *n.* cxìká; 2. *v.* {m̀, ǹ, Ĩ} cxiă.

caused, 1. *adj.* cxìmá.

cave, 1. *n.* kry̱; 2. **ice cave** *n.* kri̱kry̱.

cavity, 1. *n.* mákrȳ.

cell, 1. *n.* jecõ (organism); 2. *n.* pòro̱ (prison).

cellar, 1. *n.* kōlà.

cellular, 1. *adj.* pyjecõ.

cemetery, 1. *n.* cxo̱fó.

cerebellum, 1. *n.* nanã.

cerebral, 1. *adj.* pynã.

certain, 1. *adj.* kfu̱ru̱.

certainly, 1. *adv.* kfu̱ru̱ro̱.

certainty, 1. *n.* kfu̠ru̠clí.

cessation, 1. *n.* fòsú.

chainmail, 1. *n.* klùpsu̠.

chair, 1. *n.* na̠.

challenge, 1. *n.* mȳkfū.

challenging, 1. *adj.* mȳkfūxù; 2. *adj.* mēsūxù (demanding).

chance, 1. *n.* krỳpló (opportunity); 2. *n.* xáclì (luck).

change, 1. *n.* cxísē (alteration); 2. *v.* {m̀, m̃, Í} cxié (alter); 3. *v.* {ḿ, m̀} kiŷ (clothes).

changed, 1. *adj.* cxímē (altered); 2. *adj.* kímỳ (clothes).

character, 1. *n.* klȳfrè (literary); 2. *n.* crēxà (moral); 3. *n.* pli̠clý (orthografic).

characteristic, 1. *n.* sìfá.

charge, 1. *v.* {m̀} sriō (claim); 2. *v.* {m̀, m̃} liă (in business).

charm, 1. *n.* mōrū (talisman).

cheap, 1. *adj.* cra̠ (inexpensive); 2. *adj.* i̠xúnāxù (bad quality).

check, 1. *n.* psìsó; 2. *v.* {m̀, m̃} psiǒ.

cheek, 1. *n.* cópsȳ.

chef, 1. *n.* fíkò.

chemical, 1. *n.* xèpsé.

chemist, 1. *n.* xèpse̠xóprà.

chemistry, 1. *n.* xèpse̠xó.

chest, 1. *n.* py̠ (anatomy); 2. *n.* mólō (container).

chestplate, 1. *n.* jūpsōcrè.

chevon, 1. *n.* kly̠kfi̠.

chew, 1. *v.* {ḿ, m̀} caŭ.

chewed up, 1. *adj.* kàmú.

chewiness, 1. *n.* lòle̠clí.

chewy, 1. *adj.* lòle̠ (tough).

chick, 1. *n.* pìni̠.

chicken, 1. *n.* pì.

chief, 1. *n.* crū.

chieftain, 1. *n.* crū.

child, 1. *n.* psũ.

childhood, 1. *n.* psu̠pro̠su̠.

childish, 1. *adj.* psuxũ.

chin, 1. *n.* clýrȳ.

choice, 1. *n.* pȳsū; 2. *n.* xósū (pick).

choose, 1. *v.* {m̀, m̃} pyū.

chosen, 1. *adj.* pȳmū.

chubby, 1. *adj.* klinĭ.

chuckle, 1. *n.* psìsá; 2. *v.* {ḿ, ž, ǵ} psiă.

church, 1. *n.* sępé.

cigar, 1. *n.* clāfò.

cigarette, 1. *n.* clāfò.

cinematic, 1. *adj.* klęxú.

circa, 1. *adv.* ácē (approximately).

circle, 1. *n.* jùfrị.

circular, 1. *adj.* jùfrịxú.

circumstances, 1. *n.* jyplạ.

circumstantial, 1. *adj.* pyjyplạ.

city, 1. *n.* kọ; 2. *n.* kárā (capital).

city hall, 1. *n.* clụnị.

civilization, 1. *n.* rūnà (society).

claim, 1. *n.* srīsō (assertion); 2. *n.* nìsá (e.g. of property); 3. *v.* {m̀} sriō (assert); 4. *v.* {m̀} niǎ (e.g. as property).

claimant, 1. *n.* srīkō.

claimed, 1. *adj.* nìmá (e.g. as property).

clarity, 1. *n.* préclì.

class, 1. *n.* krá.

claw, 1. *n.* rã.

clay, 1. *adj.* rujęxú; 2. *n.* rụję.

clean, 1. *adj.* psò; 2. *adj.* xìmạ (cleaned); 3. *v.* {ḿ, m̀, m̃} xià.

clear, 1. *adj.* pré (translucent); 2. *adj.* srụsę (obvious); 3. *adj.* rú (weather); 4. *v.* {m̀} jué (empty s.th.); 5. *v.* {ṽ} jué (clear s.th. of s.th.).

cleared, 1. *adj.* júmē.

clearly, 1. *adv.* srụsęrọ (obviously).

clerk, 1. *n.* cạpúprà (teller, cashier).

clever, 1. *adj.* klèlạ.

cleverness, 1. *n.* klèlạclí.

click, 1. *n.* càxị (sound).

climb, 1. *v.* {ḿ, m̀, j̃} muà.

climber, 1. *n.* mùka̱.

clitoral, 1. *adj.* pȳnōplì.

clitoris, 1. *n.* nōplì.

cloak, 1. *n.* jo̱cry̱.

close, 1. *adj.* xi̱ (nearby); 2. *v.* {m̀, m̃} muā (shut).

closed, 1. *adj.* mūmā.

closely, 1. *adv.* xi̱ro̱.

closeness, 1. *n.* xi̱clí (nearness).

closet, 1. *n.* cōnē.

closure, 1. *n.* mūsā (closing).

clothes, 1. *n.* méclō.

clothing, 1. *n.* méclō.

cloud, 1. *n.* cȳlò.

cloudy, 1. *adj.* cȳlòxú.

club, 1. *n.* cùru̱ (bludgeon).

coast, 1. *n.* júkā.

coastal, 1. *adj.* py̱júkā.

coat, 1. *n.* krō.

cobbler, 1. *n.* krāprà.

code, 1. *n.* mālī.

coerce, 1. *v.* {m̀} kfiê.

coerced, 1. *adj.* kfímè.

coercion, 1. *n.* kfísè.

coercive, 1. *adj.* kfílèle̱.

coffee, 1. *n.* lòno̱.

coffin, 1. *n.* nu̱pry̱.

coif, 1. *n.* jo̱rá.

coin purse, 1. *n.* fēklùjo̱.

cold, 1. *adj.* xā; 2. *adj.* srĩ (cool); 3. *n.* xāclì.

collar, 1. *n.* fi̱ká (e.g. on a shirt).

collect, 1. *v.* {m̀, m̃} nuĕ.

collected, 1. *adj.* nùmé.

collectibility, 1. *n.* jānùjéclì.

collectible, 1. *adj.* jānùjé.

collection, 1. *n.* nùsé.

collective, 1. *adj.* nùséxù.

collector, 1. *n.* nùké.

colonial, 1. *adj.* pyklirū.

colony, 1. *n.* kliprū.

color, 1. *n.* kō.

column, 1. *n.* nýrȳ.

come, 1. *v.* {ḿ, j} cxeì.

command, 1. *n.* frisa̱; 2. *v.* {m̀, Í, g̃} fria̱.

commander, 1. *n.* frika̱.

commerce, 1. *n.* pìpó; 2. *n.* cxē (trade).

commercial, 1. *adj.* pȳpìpó.

commit, 1. *v.* {m̀, r̃} kfiè (s.th. to s.th.).

commit suicide, 1. *v.* {ḿ} friý.

common, 1. *adj.* lùjú.

commonality, 1. *n.* lùjúclì.

communal, 1. *adj.* pȳlāfrà.

communicate, 1. *v.* {ḿ, m̀, ñ, g̍} nyĩ.

communication, 1. *n.* nysĩ.

communicative, 1. *adj.* pynysĩ.

communicator, 1. *n.* nykĩ.

community, 1. *n.* lāfrà.

community center, 1. *n.* lāfrà cxèso̱.

companion, 1. *n.* cèsy̱ly̱.

company, 1. *n.* klēkè (people); 2. *n.* praklū (business).

comparable, 1. *adj.* jākrījà.

compare, 1. *v.* {m̀, ṽ} krià (contrast); 2. *v.* {ǹ} cliǒ (be similar to s.th.).

comparison, 1. *n.* krìsa̱.

competition, 1. *n.* féprỳ.

competitive, 1. *adj.* féprỳxú.

complain, 1. *v.* {ḿ, m̀, ñ} puē (about s.th.).

complaint, 1. *n.* pūsē.

complete, 1. *adj.* kfúmè; 2. *v.* {m̀, m̃, ṽ} kfuê.

completed, 1. *adj.* kfúmè.

completely, 1. *adv.* kfúmèro̱.

completion, 1. *n.* kfúsè.

complex, 1. *adj.* cryclū.

complexity, 1. *n.* crycluclĩ.

compliant, 1. *adj.* frúlōlē.

complicate, 1. *v.* {m̀, ǹ, Í, v́, ṽ} cryclunuõ.

complicated, 1. *adj.* cryclunumõ; 2. *adj.* cryclũ (complex).

comply, 1. *v.* {m̋, m̀} fruó (with s.th.).

comprehensible, 1. *adj.* japsujõ.

computer, 1. *n.* plùjȩ.

con, 1. *n.* plùsé (scam); 2. *v.* {m̀, Í} pluě (swindle).

concept, 1. *n.* psī (idea); 2. *n.* kúsō (thought).

conceptual, 1. *adj.* psīxù.

concern, 1. *n.* xúsỳ (worry); 2. *v.* {Í, ǹ} mué (involve); 3. *v.* {ź, ż, z̃} xuŷ (worry).

concerned, 1. *adj.* xúmỳ (worried); 2. *adj.* múmē (involved).

condition, 1. *n.* sècrị (requirement); 2. *n.* luxã (status).

conditional, 1. *adj.* pȳsècrị (relating to a condition); 2. *adj.* sècrịxú (subject to conditions).

conditionality, 1. *n.* sècrịxúclì.

cone, 1. *n.* naxẽ.

confess, 1. *v.* {m̀, ñ} kfuó (admit).

confessed, 1. *adj.* kfúmō.

confession, 1. *n.* kfúsō.

confirm, 1. *v.* {m̀, Í} luē.

confirmation, 1. *n.* lūsē.

confirmed, 1. *adj.* lūmē.

confront, 1. *v.* {m̀, m̃} psyụ.

confrontation, 1. *n.* psysụ.

confrontational, 1. *adj.* psylụlȩ.

confuse, 1. *v.* {m̀, Í, z̃} ryù; 2. *v.* {ż} ryù (*propositions*).

confused, 1. *adj.* rỳmụ.

confusing, 1. *adj.* rỳlụlȩ.

confusion, 1. *n.* rỳsụ.

conic, 1. *adj.* naxexũ.

conman, 1. *n.* plùké.

connect, 1. *v.* {m̀, ǹ} cluǎ; 2. *v.* {m̀, Í, v́, ṽ} liâ (link).

connected, 1. *adj.* clùmá; 2. *adj.* límà (linked).

connection, 1. *n.* clùsá.

consent, 1. *v.* {m̋, m̀} cxyí (agree to s.th.).

considerate, 1. *adj.* crēmē.

consist, 1. *v.* {v́} muě (of s.th.).

consistency, 1. *n.* jàcu̬clí.

consistent, 1. *adj.* jàcu̬.

constant, 1. *adj.* sòpo̬.

constantly, 1. *adv.* sòpo̬ro̬.

contact, 1. *n.* pseje̬ (touching); 2. *v.* {m̀, m̃, ṽ} fuo̬.

contain, 1. *v.* {ǹ} fruō.

contained, 1. *adj.* frūmō.

containment, 1. *n.* frūsō.

contemplative, 1. *adj.* kúlōlē; 2. *adj.* kúsōxù.

contemplatively, 1. *adv.* kúlōlērō; 2. *adv.* kúsōxùro̬.

contentious, 1. *adj.* krýkōxù.

contest, 1. *n.* féprỳ.

context, 1. *n.* ci̬ké.

contextual, 1. *adj.* pyci̬ké.

continue, 1. *v.* {Í, m̀} cley; 2. **continue to** *aux.* j̄.

continued, 1 *adj.* cle̬my.

continuity, 1. *n.* recyclī̬.

continuous, 1. *adj.* recỹ.

contribute, 1. *v.* {m̀, ñ, ǵ} cxei̬.

contribution, 1. *n.* cxe̬si̬.

contributor, 1. *n.* cxe̬ki̬.

control, 1. *n.* písō; 2. *v.* {m̀, m̃} pió; 3. **in control** *adj.* fifuxũ (have authority).

controllable, 1. *adj.* japi̬jó.

controlled, 1. *adj.* pímō.

controller, 1. *n.* píkō.

controlling, 1. *n.* písōxù.

cook, 1. *n.* fíkò (chef); 2. *v.* {ḿ, m̀, m̃} fiô.

cooked, 1. *adj.* fímò.

cool, 1. *adj.* crã (neat); 2. *adj.* srĩ (cold).

copied, 1. *adj.* sèmu̬ (facsimile).

copy, 1. *n.* sèsu̬ (facsimile); 2. *v.* {m̀, m̃} seù.

coral, 1. *n.* rìkla̬.

coral reef, 1. *n.* rìkla̬ kliprũ.

corkscrew, 1. *n.* psīlè.

corporeal, 1. *adj.* pysrạ.

corps, 1. *n.* srạ (military, etc.).

corpse, 1. *n.* xọjọ.

correct, 1. *adj.* mú (true); 2. *v.* {m̀, m̃} sruā.

correctable, 1. *adj.* jāsrūjā.

corrected, 1. *adj.* srūmā.

correction, 1. *n.* srūsā.

correctly, 1. *adv.* múrō.

cosmic, 1. *adj.* pymulukfĩ.

cosmopolitan, 1. *adj.* plọxú.

cosmos, 1. *n.* mulukfĩ.

cost, 1. *n.* fĩ; 2. *v.* {ǹ, Ĩ} kliâ.

costly, 1. *adj.* fixũ; 2. *adj.* sẽ (expensive).

couch, 1. *n.* xénȳ.

cough, 1. *n.* cùsó; 2. *v.* {j̣, ź} cuŏ.

count, 1. *v.* {ḿ, m̃, ǹ, ñ, r̀} miâ; 2. *v.* {ǹ, Ĺ} pluó.

countable, 1. *adj.* jạmíjà.

countdown, 1. *n.* plúsō.

countless, 1. *adj.* ịjạmíjà (uncountable).

country, 1. *n.* crōnù (rural area); 2. *n.* nịkfé (nation).

county, 1. *n.* psỳpsụ (district).

couple, 1. *n.* pujĩ (group of two).

course, 1. *n.* xụká (route).

court, 1. *n.* xịrú.

courthouse, 1. *n.* xịrú cxèsọ.

courtyard, 1. *n.* krírē.

cousin, 1. *n.* ỳfọ.

cover, 1. *n.* krúsà (e.g. a sheet); 2. *v.* {m̀, ṽ} kruâ; 3. *v.* {r̃} kleȳ (pay for s.th.).

covered, 1. *adj.* krúmà.

cow, 1. *n.* rụpị.

coward, 1. *n.* prèkị.

cowardly, 1. *adj.* prèkịxú; 2. *adj.* ịkrọ (not brave).

cower, 1. *v.* {ḿ} preì.

cowl, 1. *n.* pròkọ.

crab, 1. *n.* pàjé.

cradle, 1. *n.* násrē.

craft, 1. *n.* cu̱kré (skill); 2. *n.* klūkù (vessel).

crawlspace, 1. *n.* pīklī.

craziness, 1. *n.* kfáclì.

crazy, 1. *adj.* kfá; 2. *adj.* i̱psú (insane); 3. **drive crazy** *v.* {m̀, Í, v́, ṽ} kfánuō.

create, 1. *v.* {m̋, m̀, m̃, Í} saû; 2. *v.* {m̋, m̀, m̃} roŭ (make).

created, 1. *adj.* sámù.

creation, 1. *n.* sásù.

creative, 1. *adj.* sálùle̱.

creatively, 1. *adv.* sálùle̱ro̱.

creativity, 1. *n.* sálùle̱clí.

creator, 1. *n.* sákù. 2. *n.* ròkú (maker).

credible, 1. *adj.* jālūjè.

credit, 1. *n.* līklē (financial); 2. *n.* fìmi̱ (acknowledgement).

credulity, 1. *n.* lùle̱le̱clí.

credulous, 1. *adj.* lùle̱le̱.

credulously, 1. *adv.* lùle̱le̱ro̱.

credulousness, 1. *n.* lùle̱le̱clí.

crib, 1. *n.* kùkru̱.

crime, 1. *n.* lìkfi̱.

criminal, 1. *adj.* lìkfi̱xú; 2. *n.* lìkfi̱prá.

criminally, 1. *adv.* lìkfi̱xúrō.

critic, 1. *n.* cékì.

critical, 1. *adj.* cékìxú.

criticism, 1. *n.* césì.

criticize, 1. *v.* {m̀} ceî.

criticized, 1. *adj.* cémì.

critique, 1. *n.* césì.

crop, 1. *n.* rēsȳ.

cross, 1. *v.* {m̀, j̱, ṽ} puy̌ (traverse).

crossbow, 1. *n.* klýklà.

cruel, 1. *adj.* korũ.

cruelty, 1. *n.* koruclī.

cry, 1. *v.* {ǹ, Í} cliā (tears); 2. *v.* {m̀} keŷ (scream).

crybaby, 1. *n.* clīlālē.

crystal, 1. *adj.* mi̱xyxú; 2. *n.* mi̱xy.

crystalline, 1. *adj.* mi̱xyxú.

crystallization, 1. *n.* mi̱xy̱xúnūsō.
crystallize, 1. *v.* {m̀, ǹ, Í} mi̱xy̱xúnuō.
crystallized, 1. *adj.* mi̱xy̱xúnūmō.
cube, 1. *n.* srú.
cubic, 1. *adj.* srúxù.
cuff, 1. *n.* lu̱ra̱.
cuirass, 1. *n.* me̱sri̱.
cultural, 1. *adj.* py̱clípȳ.
culture, 1. *n.* clípȳ.
cup, 1. *n.* xalã.
curable, 1. *adj.* jāxùje̱.
cure, 1. *n.* xùse̱; 2. *v.* {m̀, ǹ, v́, ṽ} xuè.
cured, 1. *adj.* xùme̱.
curl, 1. *n.* rá.
curly, 1. *adj.* ráxù.
currency, 1. *n.* kfi̱pre̱.
current, 1. *adj.* so̱ji̱.
currently, 1. *adv.* so̱ji̱ro̱.
curse, 1. *n.* lùsa̱; 2. *v.* {m̀, Í} luà.
cursed, 1. *adj.* lùma̱.
curtain, 1. *n.* klipĩ.
custodian, 1. *n.* cápā.
customer, 1. *n.* ce̱ku̱.
cut, 1. *adj.* fy̱mu̱ (lacerated); 2. *v.* {m̀, m̃} fyu̱ (lacerate); 3. *v.* {m̀, m̃, ṽ} fyúfīē (down).
cut down, 1. *adj.* fy̱múfīmē.
cycle, 1. *n.* pòke̱.
cyclical, 1. *adj.* pòke̱xú.
cylinder, 1. *n.* sa̱ca̱.
cylindrical, 1. *adj.* sa̱ca̱xú.

D

daily, 1. *adj.* py̱jó.
dale, 1. *n.* nōfò.
dam, 1. *n.* kfẽ.

damage, 1. *n.* nūsē; 2. *v.* {m̀, ǹ} nuē.

damaged, 1. *adj.* nūmē.

damaging, 1. *adj.* prỳcóxù (deleterious).

dance, 1. *n.* súsā; 2. *v.* {ḿ, ń} suá.

dancer, 1. *n.* súkā.

danger, 1. *n.* jicriclí.

dangerous, 1. *adj.* jicri.

dangerously, 1. *adv.* jicriro.

dare to, 1. *aux.* g.

dark, 1. *adj.* xo (absence of light); 2. *adv.* pi (color).

darken, 1. *v.* {m̀, ǹ, Í, ṽ} xonuo (in light); 2. *v.* {m̀, ǹ, Í, ṽ} pinuo (in color).

darkened, 1. *adj.* xonumo (in light); 2. *adj.* pinumo (in color).

darkness, 1. *n.* xoclí.

data, 1. *n.* lacó.

data-related, 1. *adj.* pylacó.

data-rich, 1. *adj.* lacóxù.

date, 1. *n.* cxí (day).

daughter, 1. *n.* ūcò.

day, 1. *n.* jó.

daytime, 1. *n.* jó.

dead, 1. *adj.* càlu; 2. *n.* càlu.

deal, 1. *v.* {m̀, Í, ṽ} koî (with s.th.).

dealt with, 1. *adj.* kómì (handled).

death, 1. *n.* clémō.

debate, 1. *n.* krýkō.

decagon, 1. *n.* plēkrùprý.

decagonal, 1. *adj.* plēkrùprýxù.

deceitful, 1. *adj.* múlòle.

deceitfully, 1. *adv.* múlòlero.

decide, 1. *v.* {m̀, Í} cxyũ.

decided, 1. *adj.* cxymũ.

decision, 1. *n.* cxysũ.

decisive, 1. *adj.* cxysuxũ.

declaration, 1. *adj.* xìsó (statement).

declare, 1. *v.* {m̀, ñ} xið.

declared, 1. *adj.* xìmó (stated).

deep, 1. *adj.* srē; 2. *adj.* m̤oxú.

deepen, 1. *v.* {m̀, Í} srēnuō.

deeply, 1. *adv.* srērō.

deer, 1. *n.* kr̤ena̤.

defecate, 1. *v.* {j̤, ź} sruò.

defecation, 1. *n.* srùs̤o.

defend, 1. *v.* {m̀, Í} naí.

defended, 1. *adj.* námī.

defender, 1. *n.* nákī.

defense, 1. *n.* násī.

defensible, 1. *adj.* j̤ana̤jí.

defensive, 1. *adj.* nálīlē.

defensively, 1. *adv.* nálīlērō.

definite, 1. *adj.* kfṳrṳ.

definitely, 1. *adv.* kfṳrṳr̤o (certainly).

definition, 1. *n.* lēklȳ (detail); 2. *n.* frépȳ (of a word, etc).

definitional, 1. *adj.* py̤frépȳ.

deity, 1. *n.* ly̤.

deleterious, 1. *adj.* prỳcóxù.

deliberate, 1. *adj.* lēlō.

deliberately, 1. *adv.* lēlōrō.

delicacy, 1. *n.* meclĩ (fineness).

delicate, 1. *adj.* mẽ (fine).

deliver, 1. *v.* {m̀, ñ, ǵ} ruǎ.

delivered, 1. *adj.* rùmá.

delivery, 1. *n.* rùsá.

demand, 1. *n.* mēsū; 2. *v.* {m̀} meū.

demanded, 1. *adj.* mēmū.

demanding, 1. *adj.* mēsūxù (challenging); 2. *adj.* mēlūlē (nagging).

demolish, 1. *v.* {m̀, Í} ryǔfiē.

demolished, 1. *adj.* rỳmúfĩmē.

demolition, 1. *n.* rỳsúfĩsē.

demonstrator, 1. *n.* kfakũ (presenter).

denial, 1. *n.* clísè.

denier, 1. *n.* clíkè.

deny, 1. *v.* {m̀} cliê (s.th.); 2. *v.* {m̃} cliê (s.o. s.th.).
department, 1. *n.* mùcxe̱.
departmental, 1. *adj.* pȳmùcxe̱.
depend, 1. *v.* {v́} kfuō (be dependent on s.th.); 2. *v.* {m̀, ż} sraī (rely on s.o./s.th.).
dependable, 1. *adj.* jāsrājī.
dependence, 1. *n.* kfūsō (contingence); 2. *n.* srāsī (reliance).
dependent, 1. *n.* srākī; 2. *adj.* srākīxù.
depiction, 1. *n.* plācxȳ.
depressed, 1. *adj.* clyroxū.
depression, 1. *n.* clyrõ.
depressive, 1. *adj.* clyroxū.
depth, 1. *n.* mo̱.
dermal, 1. *adj.* py̱sró.
describe, 1. *v.* {m̀, ñ} sruě.
described, 1. *adj.* srùmé.
description, 1. *n.* srùsé.
desert, 1. *n.* li̱lácī.
design, 1. *n.* lísò; 2. *v.* {m̀, m̃} liô.
designed, 1. *adj.* límò.
designer, 1. *n.* líkò.
desirable, 1. *adj.* ja̱méjì.
desire, 1. *n.* mésì.
desired, 1. *adj.* mémì (wanted).
desirous, 1. *adj.* mékìxú.
desk, 1. *n.* kȳclù.
despair, 1. *n.* úprā.
despise, 1. *v.* {z̃} klaí (s.o./s.th.); 2. *v.* {ż} klaí (*propositions*).
despite, 1. *comp.* cìru̱; 2. *prep.* cìru̱.
dessert, 1. *n.* ru̱si̱.
destination, 1. *n.* núsā.
destroy, 1. *v.* {m̀, m̃, ǹ, ñ} friē.
destroyed, 1. *adj.* frīmē.
destroyer, 1. *n.* frīkē.
destruction, 1. *n.* frīsē.
destructive, 1. *adj.* frīlēlē.

detail, 1. *n.* lēklȳ.

detriment, 1. *n.* prỳcó.

detrimental, 1. *adj.* prỳcóxù.

develop, 1. *v.* {m̀, m̃} krié; 2. *v.* {Í} kfeɣ̌ (grow up).

developed, 1. *adj.* krímē; 2. *adj.* krísēxù.

developer, 1. *n.* kríkē.

development, 1. *n.* krísē.

developmental, 1. *adj.* pykrísē.

device, 1. *n.* ràkfi̱.

diamond, 1. *n.* cla̱kfí; 2. *adj.* cla̱kfíxù.

die, 1. *v.* {Í} cli̱a̱; 2. **die a painful death** *v.* {Í} li̱o̱cli̱a̱.

differ, 1. *v.* {Í} niá; 2. *v.* {v́} niá (from s.th.).

difference, 1. *n.* nísā.

different, 1. *adj.* nísāxù; 2. *adj.* prò (distinct).

differentiate, 1. *v.* {m̀, Í} prònu̱o̱.

differentiated, 1. *adj.* prònu̱mo̱.

differentiation, 1. *n.* prònu̱so̱.

difficult, 1. *adj.* fri̱.

difficulty, 1. *n.* fri̱clí.

digest, 1. *v.* {ḿ, m̀, Í} kloĩ.

digested, 1. *adj.* klomĩ.

digestion, 1. *n.* klosĩ.

digestive, 1. *adj.* pyklosĩ.

dilute, 1. *v.* {m̀, ǹ, Í} kyì.

diluted, 1. *adj.* kỳmi̱.

dim, 1. *adj.* xo̱; 2. *v.* {m̀, Í} xo̱nu̱o̱.

dimension, 1. *n.* klarikõ.

dimensional, 1. *adj.* pyklarikõ; 2. **one-dimensional** *adj.* xyklarikoxũ; 3. **two-dimensional** *adj.* piklarikoxũ; 4. **three-dimensional** *adj.* jeklarikoxũ; 5. **four-dimensional** *adj.* cliklarikoxũ.

dimly, 1. *adv.* xo̱ro̱.

dimmed, 1. *adj.* xo̱nu̱mo̱.

dining room, 1. *n.* kripsacã.

dinner, 1. *n.* kripsã.

direction, 1. *n.* crēcò.

dirt, 1. *n.* klā.

dirtiness, 1. *n.* cxẹclí.
dirty, 1. *adj.* klāxù; 2. *adj.* cxẹ (not clean).
disabled, 1. *adj.* īnìcxi̱ (not able-bodied).
disadvantageous, 1. *adj.* i̱prékfȳxù.
disagreeable, 1. *adj.* i̱cxýlūlē.
disappear, 1. *v.* {í} freó.
disappearance, 1. *n.* frésō.
disaster, 1. *n.* krẹfílè.
disastrous, 1. *adj.* krẹfílèxú.
disastrously, 1. *adv.* krẹfílèxúrō.
disc, 1. *n.* frāmà.
disciplinary, 1. *adj.* pȳfācỳ.
discipline, 1. *n.* fācỳ.
disciplined, 1. *adj.* fācỳxú.
discontinuous, 1. *adj.* irecȳ.
discount, 1. *n.* klȳpó.
discouraging, 1. *adj.* ipselilē.
discover, 1. *v.* {m̀} xuě.
discoverable, 1. *adj.* jāxùjé.
discovered, 1. *adj.* xùmé.
discoverer, 1. *n.* xùké.
discovery, 1. *n.* xùsé.
discreet, 1. *adj.* nākī̱.
discrete, 1. *adj.* xọprọ.
discreteness, 1. *n.* xọprọclí.
discretion, 1. *n.* nākīclì.
discuss, 1. *v.* {m̀} sroũ; 2. *v.* {ñ} sroũ (with s.o.).
discussion, 1. *n.* srosũ.
disease, 1. *n.* krōpsù.
diseased, 1. *adj.* krōpsùxú.
disgusting, 1. *adj.* ríxū.
disgustingly, 1. *adv.* ríxūrō.
dishonest, 1. *adj.* iplu̱kfá.
dishonestly, 1. *adv.* iplu̱kfárō.
dishonesty, 1. *n.* iplu̱kfáclì.
disk, 1. *n.* frāmà.

disobedient, 1. *adj.* ikrulolḛ.

disorderly, 1. *adj.* īmèxú.

disorganized, 1. *adj.* i̱srásùxú.

dissimilar, 1. *adj.* ipsocrḛ.

dissimilarity, 1. *n.* ipsocreclī̃.

distance, 1. *n.* léfrō.

distant, 1. *adj.* léfrōxù.

distinct, 1. *adj.* prò (different).

distinguish, 1. *v.* {m̀, Í} prònuo̱.

distinguished, 1. *adj.* prònu̱mo̱ (differentiated).

distribution, 1. *n.* klìkró.

distributional, 1. *adj.* pȳklìkró.

distributive, 1. *adj.* klìkróxù.

district, 1. *n.* psỳpsu̱.

divide, 1. *v.* {m̀, ṽ} pruã.

divided, 1. *adj.* prumã.

divider, 1. *n.* prukã.

divine, 1. *adj.* ly̱xú.

divinity, 1. *n.* ly̱xúclì.

divisibility, 1. *n.* japrujaclī̃.

divisible, 1. *adj.* japrujã.

division, 1. *n.* prusã.

divisor, 1. *n.* prukã.

do, 1. *aux.* ẕ (*emphasis marker*); 2. *v.* {m̀} caì (s.th.).

doctor, 1. *n.* mureprã (physician); 2. *n.* klēmèfa̱ (professor).

dog, 1. *n.* psȳ.

doggy, 1. *n.* psȳnȳ.

donate, 1. *v.* {ḿ, m̀, ñ} ceũ.

donated, 1. *adj.* cemũ.

donation, 1. *n.* cesũ.

donor, 1. *n.* cekũ.

door, 1. *n.* kùclu̱.

doorman, 1. *n.* kēkū.

down, 1. *adv.* cà; 2. *n.* cà; 3. *prep.* cà.

draw, 1. *v.* {ḿ, m̀, m̃, ṽ} reǒ.

drawer, 1. *n.* rèkó (artist).

drawing, 1. *n.* rèsó (sketch).

drawn, 1. *adj.* rèmó (sketched).

dream, 1. *n.* kl̯as̯u; 2. *v.* {ź, ž} klau̯ (about s.o./s.th.); 3. *v.* {ž} klau̯ (*propositions*).

dreamer, 1. *n.* kl̯ak̯u.

dreamscape, 1. *n.* kl̯asúxēclù.

dress, 1. *n.* cxũ (article of clothing); 2. *v.* {ḿ, m̀} cuě.

dressed, 1. *adj.* cùmé.

dried, 1. *adj.* fánūmō.

drink, 1. *v.* {ḿ, m̀} klið.

drinker, 1. *n.* klìkó.

drive, 1. *v.* {j̇, j̃} plið (a vehicle); 2. *v.* {m̀, ṽ} muý (in a nail, a screw, etc); 3. **drive insane** *v.* {m̀, Í, v́, ṽ} kfánuō.

driver, 1. *n.* plikð.

drool, 1. *n.* plỳs̯i̯; 2. *v.* {Í} plyì.

drooly, 1. *adj.* plỳl̯il̯e.

drop, 1. *v.* {m̀, Í, Ì} pluê.

drought, 1. *n.* ps̯upá.

drum, 1. *n.* sr̯ucí.

drummer, 1. *n.* sr̯ucíprà.

drunken, 1. *adj.* klìlólē.

drunkenly, 1. *adv.* klìlólērō.

dry, 1. *adj.* fá; 2. *v.* {m̀, ǹ, Í, v́, ṽ} fánuō.

dryness, 1. *n.* fáclì.

duck, 1. *n.* cr̯ecú.

duckling, 1. *n.* cr̯ecúnū.

due to, 1. *prep.* kfú (because of).

dull, 1. *adj.* fícā (not sharp); 2. *adj.* n̯ar̯o (boring).

dullness, 1. *n.* fícāclì (not sharp); 2. *n.* n̯ar̯oclí (boring).

dumb, 1. *adj.* f̯e.

durability, 1. *n.* krīlòclí.

durable, 1. *adj.* krīlò.

during, 1. *prep.* r̯ox̯o.

dye, 1. *n.* nū.

E

each, 1. *det.* nè; 2. *pn.* nè.

each other, 1. *pn.* kōlō.

ear, 1. *n.* plò (external); 2. *n.* fràfẹ (internal).

earlobe, 1. *n.* lápsā.

early, 1. *adj.* xy̱prạ; 2. *adv.* xy̱prạ.

earring, 1. *n.* plōprù.

earthly, 1. *adj.* pȳkā.

earwax, 1. *n.* pạklú.

ease, 1. *n.* cròclí.

easily, 1. *adv.* cròrọ.

east, 1. *adj.* cly̱; 2. *adv.* cly̱; 3. *n.* cly̱.

eastern, 1. *adj.* cly̱xú.

eastward, 1. *adv.* cly̱.

easy, 1. *adj.* crò.

eat, 1. *v.* {ḿ, m̀, m̃} pliè.

eaten, 1. *adj.* plìmẹ.

eater, 1. *n.* plìkẹ.

eclipse, 1. *n.* jycókō.

economic, 1. *adj.* py̱krẹ.

economics, 1. *n.* krẹxó.

economist, 1. *n.* krẹxóprà.

economy, 1. *n.* krẹ.

edge, 1. *n.* pícū.

edibility, 1. *n.* jāplījèclí.

edible, 1. *adj.* jāplījè.

edit, 1. *v.* {m̀, Í} creŷ.

edited, 1. *adj.* crémỳ.

editing, 1. *n.* crésỳ.

editor, 1. *n.* crékỳ.

editorial, 1. *adj.* py̱crésỳ.

education, 1. *n.* rỳsú.

educational, 1. *adj.* pȳrỳsú (relating to education); 2. *adj.* rỳsúxù (informative).

effect, 1. *n.* pláplỳ.

effective, 1. *adj.* pláplỳxú.

effectively, 1. *adv.* pláplỳxúrō.

effort, 1. *n.* clỳrá.

effortful, 1. *adj.* clỳráxù.

egg, 1. *n.* kfó.

eight, 1. *num.* kri̱.

eighth, 1. *adj.* kri̱kri̱.

eightieth, 1. *adj.* kri̱pa̱pa̱.

eighty, 1. *num.* kri̱pa̱.

either, 1. *det.* lú; 2. *pn.* lú.

ejaculate, 1. *n.* cxásū; 2. *v.* {ź} cxaú.

ejaculation, 1. *n.* cxásū.

ejaculatory, 1. *adj.* py̱cxásū.

elbow, 1. *n.* sòcló.

electricity, 1. *n.* ra̱pímīmā.

ellipse, 1. *n.* mu̱li̱.

elliptical, 1. *adj.* mu̱li̱xú.

elsewhere, 1. *adv.* rȳmā prò (somewhere else).

embankment, 1. *n.* núcē.

embarrassed, 1. *adj.* nēclū.

embarrassment, 1. *n.* nēclūclì.

emerald, 1. *n.* crénù; 2. *adj.* crénùxú.

empire, 1. *n.* xu̱je̱.

emptied, 1. *adj.* lỳnu̱mo̱.

emptiness, 1. *n.* lỳclí.

empty, 1. *adj.* lỳ; 2. *v.* {m̀, Í} lỳnu̱o̱.

enable, 1. *v.* {m̀, ǹ} kliô.

enabler, 1. *n.* klíkò.

enclose, 1. *v.* {m̀, Í, Ì, j̃} faú.

enclosed, 1. *adj.* fámū.

enclosure, 1. *n.* fásū.

encourage, 1. *v.* {m̀, Í} pseĩ.

encouraged, 1. *adj.* psemĩ.

encouragement, 1. *n.* psesĩ.

encouraging, 1. *adj.* pselilẽ.

end, 1. *n.* sá (of a race, game, etc); 2. *v.* {m̀, m̃, Í} pluē.

energetic, 1. *adj.* mīmāxù.

energetically, 1. *adv.* mīmāxùrọ.

energy, 1. *n.* mīmā.

engineer, 1. *n.* rùkó; 2. *v.* {m̀, Í} ruǒ.

engineered, 1. *adj.* rùmó.

engineering, 1. *n.* rùsó.

English, 1. *n.* inyklisĩ (language).

enjoy, 1. *v.* {z̃} psiō (s.o./s.th.); 2. *v.* {ż} psiō (*propositions*).

enjoyable, 1. *adj.* jāpsījō.

enjoyment, 1. *n.* psīsō.

enlarge, 1. *v.* {m̀, Í} lụnuọ.

enlarged, 1. *adj.* lụnụmọ.

enormity, 1. *n.* cruclĩ.

enormous, 1. *adj.* crũ.

enrich, 1. *v.* {m̀} kfõnuō.

enriched, 1. *adj.* kfõnūmō.

entertain, 1. *v.* {m̀, ǹ, Í} kfoì.

entertainer, 1. *n.* kfòkị.

entertaining, 1. *adj.* kfòsịxú.

entertainment, 1. *n.* kfòsị.

enthusiast, 1. *n.* nōfā.

enthusiastic, 1. *n.* nōfāxù.

entire, 1. *adj.* kràcị.

environment, 1. *n.* pléfrō.

environmental, 1. *adj.* pyplēfrō.

epistle, 1. *n.* jelõ (letter).

epistolary, 1. *adj.* pyjelõ.

equal, 1. *adj.* mū.

equality, 1. *n.* mūclì.

equalization, 1. *n.* mūnūsō.

equalize, 1. *v.* {Í} mūnuō.

equalized, 1. *adj.* mūnūmō.

equally, 1. *adv.* mūrō.

equinox, 1. *n.* plémē.

equip, 1. *v.* {m̀, Í, v́, ṽ} naū.

equipment, 1. *n.* nāsū.

equipped, 1. *adj.* nāmū.

equivalence, 1. *n.* mūclì.
equivalent, 1. *adj.* mū.
era, 1. *n.* lúmā.
esophageal, 1. *n.* pȳclūrū.
esophagus, 1. *n.* clūrū.
especially, 1. *adv.* xyklǫ.
essence, 1. *n.* julã.
essential, 1. *adj.* julaxũ.
essentially, 1. *adv.* julaxurõ.
established, 1. *adj.* crỳmị.
establishment, 1. *n.* crỳsị.
estate, 1. *n.* plìkrị (property).
estival, 1. *adj.* pȳfrùmí.
estuary, 1. *n.* srēlù.
eulogy, 1. *n.* nìpǫ.
euthanasia, 1. *n.* xisakrasĩ.
euthanize, 1. *v.* {m̀, m̃, Í} xiakraĩ.
euthanized, 1. *adj.* ximakramĩ.
even, 1. *adj.* sónī (numerically); 2. *adj.* cūplī (deals settled); 3. *adv.* úclū.
even though, 1. *comp.* klá.
evening, 1. *n.* mẹrí.
evenly, 1. *adv.* mūrō (in distribution).
event, 1. *n.* pạfrị.
eventual, 1. *adj.* jịfị.
eventually, 1. *adv.* jịfịrǫ.
every, 1. *det.* nè.
everybody, 1. *pn.* clànị (all people); 2. *pn.* nènị (each person).
everyone, 1. *pn.* clànị (all people); 2. *pn.* nènị (each person).
everything, 1. *pn.* clàcụ.
everywhere, 1. *adv.* clāmā; 2. *pn.* clāmā.
evidence, 1. *n.* rìfrǫ.
evidenced, 1. *adj.* rìfrǫxú (well).
evidential, 1. *adj.* pȳrìfrǫ.
evil, 1. *adj.* mạjụ; 2. *n.* mạjụclí.
evitable, 1. *adj.* jạkfújà.
exact, 1. *adj.* ky̌kfõ.

exactly, 1. *adv.* kýkfōrō.

exam, 1. *n.* sú (test).

examination, 1. *n.* jùsé.

examine, 1. *v.* {m̀, m̃} juě.

examined, 1. *adj.* jùmé.

examiner, 1. *n.* jùké.

example, 1. *n.* rycrĩ.

except for, 1. *comp.* lomã; 2. *prep.* lomã.

exchange, 1. *n.* cxē (a trade).

excite, 1. *v.* {z̃} ryì; 2. *v.* {z̀} ryì (*propositions*).

excited, 1. *adj.* rỳmi̱.

excitement, 1. *n.* rỳsi̱.

exciting, 1. *adj.* rỳli̱le̱.

exemplary, 1. *adj.* rycrixũ.

exercise, 1. *n.* psùsa̱; 2. *v.* {ḿ, m̀} psuà.

exist, 1. *v.* {Í} saù.

existence, 1. *n.* sàsu̱.

exit, 1. *n.* plu̱cla̱.

expectable, 1. *adj.* jāpsìjé.

expectation, 1. *n.* psìsé.

expect, 1. *v.* {z̃} psiě (s.o./s.th.); 2. *v.* {z̀} psiě (*propositions*).

expected, 1. *adj.* psìmé.

expensive, 1. *adj.* sẽ.

experience, 1. *n.* jīlì (effectual event); 2. *n.* pro̱su̱; 3. *v.* {z̃} prou̱ (s.th.).

experienced, 1. *adj.* jīlìxú.

experiencer, 1. *n.* pro̱ku̱.

experiential, 1. *adj.* pȳjīlì.

experiment, 1. *n.* písēxēsō; 2. *v.* {ḿ, m̀, r̃} piéxeō (on s.th. with s.th.).

experimental, 1. *adj.* py̱písēxēsō (relating to experiment); 2. *adj.* písēxēsōxù (for the purpose of experiment).

experimentalist, 1. *n.* píkēxēkō.

explain, 1. *v.* {m̀} kreỳ.

explainable, 1. *adj.* jākrējỳ.

explanation, 1. *n.* krèsy̱.

explained, 1. *adj.* krèmy̱.

explode, 1. *v.* {Í} ryǔ.

explosion, 1. *n.* rỳsú.

explosive, 1. *adj.* rỳsúxù.

express, 1. *v.* {m̀, ñ} keǒ.

expressed, 1. *adj.* kèmó.

expression, 1. *n.* kèsó (of opinion, etc); 2. *n.* xōpȳ (saying).

expressive, 1. *adj.* kèsóxù; 2. *adj.* kèlólē.

extend, 1. *v.* {m̀, ṽ} feû.

extended, 1. *adj.* fémù.

extensible, 1. *adj.* ja̱féjù.

extension, 1. *n.* fésù.

exterior, 1. *n.* cro̱fro̱.

extinguish, 1. *v.* {m̀, ǹ, Í, v́, ṽ} ra̱u̱ (e.g. a fire).

extinguished, 1. *adj.* ra̱mu̱.

eye, 1. *n.* ki̱.

eyebrow, 1. *n.* kíxī.

eyeglasses, 1. *n.* ki̱clánì.

eyelash, 1. *n.* psā.

eyelid, 1. *n.* rēklà.

eyestalk, 1. *n.* fe̱pre̱.

F

face, 1. *n.* ry̱; 2. *v.* {m̀, m̃} psyu̱ (confront); 3. *v.* {m̀} crió (look at s.th.).

facial, 1. *adj.* py̱ry̱.

facility, 1. *n.* mākìprý.

fact, 1. *n.* clù.

factory, 1. *n.* pro̱sy̱.

factual, 1. *adj.* clùxú.

fail, 1. *v.* {m̀, m̃, ǹ, Ĩ } fuò.

failed, 1. *adj.* fùmo̱.

failure, 1. *n.* fùso̱.

fair, 1. *adj.* nũ (just).

fairly, 1. *adv.* nurõ.

fairness, 1. *n.* nuclĩ.

fall, 1. *n.* còclu̱ (season); 2. *v.* {Í, Ì} neũ.

false, 1. *adj.* sī.

falsity, 1. *n.* sīclì.

fame, 1. *n.* pòjo̱.

familial, 1. *adj.* py̱srý.

familiar, 1. *adj.* pi̱me̱; 2. *v.* {ż, ž} nai̱ (be used to s.th.).

familiarity, 1. *n.* kli̱sy̱.

family, 1. *n.* srý; 2. **family name** *n.* srykfĩ.

famine, 1. *n.* kécā.

famous, 1. *adj.* pòjo̱xú.

famously, 1. *adv.* pòjo̱xúrō.

fan, 1. *n.* nōfā (enthusiast).

fang, 1. *n.* prũ.

far, 1. *adj.* né; 2. *adj.* léfrōxù (distant); 3. *prep.* né (from s.th.).

far away, 1. *adj.* né; 2. *adj.* léfrōxù (distant); 3. *adj.* né (from s.th.).

farm, 1. *n.* kfỹ (also garden).

farmer, 1. *n.* kfyprã.

fast, 1. *adj.* cxā; 2. *adj.* meprexũ (speedy).

fasten, 1. *v.* {m̀, Í} kaĩ (s.th.); 2. *v.* {Ì, ɉ̃} kaĩ (s.th. to s.th.).

fastenable, 1. *adj.* jakajĩ.

fastened, 1. *adj.* kamĩ.

fat, 1. *n.* lo̱; 2. *adj.* klinĩ (chubby); 3. *adj.* frīrā (obese).

father, 1. *n.* mi̱rá.

fatherhood, 1. *n.* mi̱ra̱pro̱su̱.

fatherly, 1. *adj.* mi̱ráxù (behaving as father).

fatigue, 1. *n.* kálỳclí.

fatigued, 1. *adj.* kálỳ.

fatten, 1. *v.* {m̀, Í} klininuõ (up).

fatty, 1. *adj.* lo̱xú (not lean).

favorite, 1. *adj.* núxē; 2. *n.* núxē.

fawn, 1. *n.* kre̱na̱na̱.

fear, 1. *n.* nēsū; 2. *v.* {ž} neū (s.th.); 3. *v.* {ż} neū (*propositions*).

fearful, 1. *adj.* nēlūlē.

feather, 1. *n.* jēxè.

featural, 1. *adj.* pȳsìfá.

feature, 1. *n.* sìfá (characteristic).

fecal, 1. *adj.* pysru̱có.

feces, 1. *n.* sru̱có.

fed, 1. *adj.* srímē (given food).

feeble, 1. *adj.* fu̱.

feed, 1. *v.* {m̃, g̲̀} srié.

feel, 1. *v.* {m̀} ruê (touch); 2. *v.* {z̃} ruê (sense); 3. *v.* {ź̲} roi̲ (*compounds*).

feeling, 1. *n.* rúsè (sensation).

fell, 1. *v.* {m̀, ṽ} fīē (e.g. a tree).

fellatiate, 1. *v.* {ḿ, m̀} fyì.

fellatio, 1. *n.* fẙsi̲.

felled, 1. *adj.* fīmē (e.g. a tree).

felt, 1. *adj.* rúmè (touched).

feminine, 1. *adj.* crìxú.

femininity, 1. *n.* crìxúclì.

few, 1. *det.* pé; 2. *pn.* pé.

field, 1. *n.* cỳ̲ (of crops, etc); 2. *n.* cxĩ (bailiwick).

fiery, 1. *adj.* ji̲xú.

fifth, 1. *adj.* clūclū.

fiftieth, 1. *adj.* clūpāpā.

fifty, 1. *num.* clūpā.

fight, 1. *n.* krúsò; 2. *v.* {ḿ, r̃} kruô.

fighter, 1. *n.* krúkò.

figure, 1. *n.* sré (number); 2. *n.* klȳfrè (character); 3. *n.* psy̲ (shape).

filament, 1. *n.* pro̲kélò.

filamentary, 1. *adj.* py̲pro̲kélò.

file, 1. *n.* plȳcrò.

fill, 1. *v.* {m̀, ṽ} kreí.

filled, 1. *adj.* krémī.

film, 1. *n.* klō (thin layer); 2. *n.* kle̲ (movie).

fin, 1. *n.* me̲; 2. **tail fin** *n.* a̲mé.

final, 1. *adj.* py̲sá.

finally, 1. *adv.* py̲sárō.

find, 1. *v.* {m̀, m̃} nuȳ.

finder, 1. *n.* nūkȳ.

finding, 1. *n.* xùsé (discovery).

fine, 1. *adj.* mẽ (delicate).

fineness, 1. *n.* meclĩ (delicacy).

finger, 1. *n.* pócì.

fingernail, 1. *n.* pócīcò.

finish, 1. *v.* {m̀, m̃, ṽ} kfuê (complete); 2. *v.* {m̀, m̃, Í} pluē (end).

finished, 1. *adj.* plūmē.

fire, 1. *n.* jị̄; 2. *v.* ryǔsriò (e.g. a cannon, artillery).

firebomb, 1. *v.* {m̀, m̃, ǹ, ñ} kiāfriē.

firebombed, 1. *adj.* kīmāfrīmē.

firebomber, 1. *n.* kīkāfrīkē.

firebombing, 1. *n.* kīsāfrīsē.

fired, 1. *adj.* rỳmúsrìmọ (e.g. a rocket, a missile).

firm, 1. *adj.* ná (hard).

firmness, 1. *n.* náclì (hardness).

first, 1. *adj.* xȳxȳ; 2. **at first** *adv.* pypụsẹrọ.

firstly, 1. *adv.* xȳxȳrō.

fish, 1. *n.* frĩ.

fishy, 1. *adj.* frixũ.

fit, 1. *v.* {Í, ż} kfoí (clothing).

five, 1. *num.* clū.

flag, 1. *n.* kfē.

flail, 1. *n.* fọcró.

flammable, 1. *adj.* jākījà.

flat, 1. *adj.* srùklụ.

flatten, 1. *v.* {m̀, ǹ, v́, ṽ} srùklụnuọ.

flattened, 1. *adj.* srùklụnụmọ.

flautist, 1. *n.* lȳlùprá.

flavor, 1. *n.* késī.

flavorful, 1. *adj.* késīxù.

flesh, 1. *n.* rý.

flight, 1. *n.* srīsē.

flip, 1. *v.* {m̀} koū (s.th. over).

floor, 1. *n.* klã.

flower, 1. *n.* kfụcọ.

flute, 1. *n.* lȳlù.

fly, 1. *n.* sīrè (on clothing); 2. *v.* {m̀, j̀, j̃} sriē.

foal, 1. *n.* clōrānā.

focus, 1. *n.* plýsē.

focused, 1. *adj.* plýsēxù.

fog, 1. *n.* lùjo̱.

foggy, 1. *adj.* lùjo̱xú.

fold, 1. *v.* {m̀, ṽ} plyù.

folded, 1. *adj.* plỳmy̱.

follow, 1. *v.* {m̀, Í} cxiá; 2. *v.* {m̀} piã (come after, succeed).

follower, 1. *n.* cxíkā.

fond, 1. *adj.* ma̱rí (of s.th./s.o.).

food, 1. *n.* psá.

foot, 1. *n.* sri̱ (anatomy); 2. *n.* àkle̱ (measurement).

footstep, 1. *n.* psõ.

for, 1. *prep.* mē (*reason, goal*); 2. *prep.* ply̱ (*beneficiary*); 3. *prep.* kápē (s.o.'s perspective); 4. *comp.* nỳkle̱ (so that).

forbid, 1. *v.* {m̀, Í} cué.

forbidden, 1. *adj.* cúmē.

force, 1. *n.* kfísè (coercion); 2. *n.* psō (physical); 3. *v.* {m̀} kfiê (coerce).

forced, 1. *adj.* kfímè (coerced).

forceful, 1. *adj.* psōxù.

forcefully, 1. *adv.* psōxùro̱.

forearm, 1. *n.* fanõ.

forehead, 1. *n.* mūprè.

foreign, 1. *adj.* cxã.

forest, 1. *n.* majẽ.

forever, 1. *adv.* pli̱rí.

forget, 1. *v.* {z̃} piō (s.o./s.th.); 2. *v.* {z̀} piō (*propositions*).

forgetful, 1. *adj.* pīlōlē.

forgetfulness, 1. *n.* pīlōlēclì.

forgettable, 1. *adj.* jāpījō.

forgivable, 1. *adj.* jānījà.

forgive, 1. *v.* {m̀, r̃} nià.

forgiven, 1. *adj.* nìma̱.

forgiveness, 1. *n.* nìsa̱.

forgiving, 1. *adj.* nìla̱le̱.

forgotten, 1. *adj.* pīmō.

fork, 1. *n.* psù.

form, 1. *n.* cý; 2. *v.* {Í} kreo̱ (come into shape); 3. *v.* {v́} kreo̱ (into s.th.); 4. *v.* {m̀, m̃} roǔ (create).

formal, 1. *adj.* capsũ.

formality, 1. *n.* capsuclĩ.

formation, 1. *n.* kreso.

formed, 1. *adj.* kremo.

fornicate, 1. *v.* {ḿ} kfyī.

fornication, 1. *n.* kfȳsī.

fornicator, 1. *n.* kfȳkī.

fort, 1. *n.* kilẽ.

fortunate, 1. *adj.* xá.

fortunately, 1. *adv.* xárō.

fortune, 1. *n.* xáclì.

fortieth, 1. *adj.* clípāpā.

forty, 1. *num.* clípā.

forward, 1. *adv.* focéplā.

found, 1. *adj.* nūmȳ; 2. *v.* {m̀, m̃, Í, j̃} cryì (establish e.g. a business).

found object, 1. *n.* nūsȳ.

foundation, 1. *n.* rēcrỳ.

foundational, 1. *adj.* pȳrēcrỳ.

founded, 1. *adj.* crỳmi̱.

founder, 1. *n.* crỳki̱.

founding, 1. *n.* crỳsi̱.

four, 1. *num.* clí.

fourth, 1. *adj.* clíclī.

frame, 1. *n.* ka̱pé (e.g. of a painting).

fraud, 1. *n.* plùsé (scam).

fraudulent, 1. *adj.* plùséxù.

free, 1. *adj.* clóprìxú (unrestrained).

freedom, 1. *n.* clóprì.

freely, 1. *adv.* clóprìxúrō.

freeze, 1. *v.* {m̀, Í} kruy.

freezing, 1. *adj.* kru̱lyle̱.

frequency, 1. *n.* kfýlàclí.

frequent, 1. *adj.* kfýlà.

frequently, 1. *adv.* kfýlàro̱.

freshwater, 1. *n.* jāxō.

friend, 1. *n.* jí.

friendliness, 1. *n.* jíxùclí.

friendly, 1. *adj.* jíxù.

from, 1. *prep.* kfî (*source, origin*).

front, 1. *adj.* frúxù; 2. *n.* frú.

frown, 1. *n.* psỳsi̱; 2. *v.* {m̀, r̀} psyì (at s.o./s.th.).

frozen, 1. *adj.* kru̱my̱.

fruit, 1. *n.* na̱pra̱.

full, 1. *adj.* xe̱ (filled); 2. *adj.* kfý (satiated).

fullness, 1. *n.* xe̱clí (filled); 2. *n.* kfýclì (satiation).

fully, 1. *adv.* xe̱ro̱.

fun, 1. *adj.* cēxù; 2. *n.* cē.

function, 1. *n.* kūjì.

functional, 1. *adj.* pȳkūjì.

fundament, 1. *n.* rēcrỳ.

fundamental, 1. *adj.* rēcrỳxú.

fundamentally, 1. *adv.* rēcrỳxúrō.

funeral, 1. *n.* kfi̱lu̱.

funeral director, 1. *n.* kfi̱lu̱prá.

funeral home, 1. *n.* kfi̱lu̱ cxèso̱.

funerary, 1. *adj.* pykfi̱lu̱.

funny, 1. *adj.* mékrè (humorous).

fur, 1. *n.* ci̱.

furious, 1. *adj.* makfuxũ.

furnished, 1. *n.* klujuxũ.

furniture, 1. *n.* klujũ.

furry, 1. *adj.* ci̱xú.

fury, 1. *n.* makfũ.

future, 1. *adj.* py̱fri̱ry̱; 2. *n.* fri̱ry̱.

futurescape, 1. *n.* fri̱rýxēclù.

futuristic, 1. *adj.* fri̱ry̱xú.

G

gadget, 1. *n.* ràkfi̱.

gadgeteer, 1. *n.* ràkfi̱prá.

gain, 1. *n.* xōsū; 2. *v.* {m̀, z̀} xoū (earn); 3. *v.* {m̀, Í, g̀} fruõ (on s.o./s.th.).

galactic, 1. *adj.* pyséplālō.

galaxy, 1. *n.* séplālō.

gall bladder, 1. *n.* làsró.

game, 1. *n.* kré.

garden, 1. *n.* kfỹ (also farm); 2. *n.* cxi̱ (yard).

gas, 1. *n.* clo̱ró (petrol).

gauntlet, 1. *n.* plóklā.

generosity, 1. *n.* celuleclĩ.

generous, 1. *adj.* celulẽ.

generously, 1. *adv.* celulerõ.

gentle, 1. *adj.* ne̱pó.

gentleman, 1. *n.* rùni̱ (respectable man).

gentleness, 1. *n.* ne̱póclì.

gently, 1. *adv.* ne̱pórō.

get, 1. *v.* {m̀, m̃} cliã (obtain); 2. *v.* {g̃} ceỳ (receive); 3. *v.* {ź, ż, z̃} psuõ (understand).

geyser, 1. *n.* srōnù.

giant, 1. *adj.* kúfū.

gift, 1. *n.* fasũ.

girder, 1. *n.* lókfē.

girl, 1. *n.* a̱pi̱.

girlfriend, 1. *n.* néfrō.

give, 1. *v.* {ñ} faũ (transfer); 2. *v.* {ḿ, m̀, ñ} ceũ (donate); 3. **give birth to** *v.* {m̀} uà (s.o.).

give up, 1. *v.* {ḿ, m̀, ź} kuõ (surrender).

given, 1. *adj.* famũ.

giver, 1. *n.* fakũ.

glare, 1. *n.* xýsī; 2. *v.* {ḿ, ŕ, r̀} xyí (at s.o./s.th.).

glasses, 1. *n.* clánì.

glen, 1. *n.* plù.

glimmer, 1. *n.* kfùsy̱; 2. *v.* {ĺ} kfuỳ.

global, 1. *adj.* pyplo̱.

glottal, 1. *adj.* pȳpācē.

glottis, 1. *n.* pācē.

glove, 1. *n.* sí.

go, 1. *v.* {m̃, j} mio̱; 2. **go back** *v.* {m̃, j, Í, Ì} nuý (return); 3. **go home** *v.* {j} mio̱ srō; 4. **go unconscious** *v.* {ź} syi̱.

goal, 1. *n.* pìso̱ (aim); 2. *n.* plī (objective).

goal-oriented, 1. *adj.* plīxù.

goat, 1. *n.* rácxā.

god, 1. *n.* ly̱ (deity).

goddess, 1. *n.* ly̱ (deity).

godliness, 1. *n.* ly̱xúclì.

godly, 1. *adj.* ly̱xú.

gold, 1. *n.* ri̱kry̱; 2. *adj.* ri̱kry̱xú (made of gold).

golden, 1. *adj.* ri̱kry̱xú.

gong, 1. *n.* y̱rá.

good, 1. *adj.* cy̱; 2. *adv.* cy̱ro̱ (well).

good people, 1. *adj.* ni̱xú.

goods, 1. *n.* rȳ (in a store).

goose, 1. *n.* ji̱pé.

gosling, 1. *n.* ji̱pénē.

government, 1. *n.* cxycõ.

governmental, 1. *adj.* pycxycõ.

gown, 1. *n.* sū.

grain, 1. *n.* cxōpī.

grape, 1. *n.* ējī.

grapevine, 1. *n.* ējīnà.

grass, 1. *n.* cu̱jo̱.

grassland, 1. *n.* cu̱jo̱lý.

gratitude, 1. *n.* crúsò; 2. *n.* clõ (thanks).

grave, 1. *n.* ka̱psi̱.

gravestone, 1. *n.* sa̱kí.

gray, 1. *adj.* lȳnò; 2. *n.* lȳnōkō.

great, 1. *adj.* lu̱.

greatly, 1. *adv.* lu̱ro̱.

green, 1. *adj.* sā; 2. *n.* sākō.

grimoire, 1. *n.* la̱rósī.

groan, 1. *n.* srésì; 2. *v.* {m̃} sreî.

groceries, 1. *n.* cru̱já.

ground, 1. *n.* klā (dirt); 2. *n.* klã (floor).

group, 1. *n.* lì.

grow, 1. *n.* rēsȳ; 2. *v.* {m̀, m̃, Í, Ì} reȳ; 3. *v.* {Í} kfeў (up).

growable, 1. *adj.* jārējȳ.

grower, 1. *n.* rēkȳ (e.g. of plants).

growl, 1. *n.* klỳsú; 2. *v.* {ḿ, ģ} klyǔ (at s.th.).

grown, 1. *adj.* rēmȳ.

grown-up, 1. *adj.* kfèmý.

guide, 1. *n.* srīpȳ.

guilt, 1. *n.* fìro̩clí.

guiltily, 1. *adv.* fìro̩ro̩.

guilty, 1. *adj.* fìro̩.

guitar, 1. *n.* kre̩lí.

guitarist, 1. *n.* kre̩líprà.

gun, 1. *n.* srò.

gunman, 1. *n.* sròni̩.

gunner, 1. *n.* sròni̩.

gust, 1. *n.* ra̩na̩.

H

hair, 1. *n.* cru̩.

hairbrush, 1. *n.* ríjà.

hairy, 1. *adj.* cru̩xú.

halberd, 1. *n.* crèja̩.

half, 1. *n.* xã.

halt, 1. *v.* {ḿ, m̀} foǔ (stop).

halted, 1. *adj.* fòmú.

hammer, 1. *n.* cìkrí.

hand, 1. *n.* kfũ; 2. **on the one hand** *adv.* xý; 3. **on the other hand** *adv.* xỳ.

handgun, 1. *n.* kfūsrò.

handle, 1. *v.* {m̀, Í, ṽ} koî (deal with s.th.).

handsome, 1. *adj.* sópū.

happen, 1. *v.* {Í, Ì} niô (occur).

happiness, 1. *n.* si̩pi̩clí.

happy, 1. *adj.* si̩pi̩.

hard, 1. *adj.* fri̱ (difficult); 2. *adj.* ná (firm).

hard-working, 1. *adj.* lejã.

harden, 1. *v.* {m̀, Í, v́, ṽ} nánuō.

hardened, 1. *adj.* nánūmō.

hardly, 1. *adv.* mũ (barely).

hardness, 1. *n.* náclì (firmness).

harp, 1. *n.* ècé.

harpist, 1. *n.* ècéprà.

hat, 1. *n.* crý.

hatchet, 1. *n.* pūxà.

hate, 1. *n.* klásī; 2. *v.* {ž} klaí (s.o./s.th.); 3. *v.* {ż} klaí (*propositions*); 4.
hate to *aux.* Í.

hated, 1. *adj.* klámī.

hateful, 1. *adj.* klálīlē.

hatefully, 1. *adv.* klálīlērō.

hater, 1. *n.* klákī.

hatred, 1. *n.* klásī.

have, 1. *v.* {ż} saí (possess); 2. *aux.* ṽ (*perfect aspect*); 3. **have to** *aux.* m̀
(must).

he, 1. *pn.* cá.

head, 1. *n.* kó.

health, 1. *n.* só.

health-related, 1. *adj.* pysó.

healthily, 1. *adv.* sóxùro̱.

healthy, 1. *adj.* sóxù.

hear, 1. *v.* {ž} si̱e̱ (s.o./s.th.); 2. *v.* {ż} si̱e̱ (*propositions*).

heard, 1. *adj.* si̱me̱.

hearer, 1. *n.* si̱ke̱.

hearing, 1. *n.* si̱se̱ (sense).

heart, 1. *n.* rỹ.

heat, 1. *n.* plũ; 2. *n.* rāclì; 3. *v.* {m̀, ǹ, Í} rānuō (up).

heavy, 1. *adj.* rò; 2. *adj.* lùxú (weighty).

heel, 1. *n.* ce̱.

height, 1. *n.* klýclì.

heighten, 1. *v.* {m̀, Í} klýnuō.

heightened, 1. *adj.* klýnūmō.

hello, 1. *intj.* cyjó.

hellscape, 1. *n.* jíxēclù.

helmet, 1. *n.* mòkró.

help, 1. *n.* xisã; 2. *v.* {g̀} xiã (s.o.); 3. *v.* {m̀} xiã (*propositions*).

helped, 1. *adj.* ximã.

helper, 1. *n.* xikã.

helpful, 1. *adj.* xilalã.

helpfulness, 1. *n.* xilalaclĩ.

heptagon, 1. *n.* psíkrùprý.

heptagonal, 1. *adj.* psíkrùprýxù.

her, 1. *pn.* cì; 2. *adj.* cìmá.

here, 1. *adv.* prìcy; 2. *n.* prìcy.

hero, 1. *n.* fàjá.

heroic, 1. *adj.* fàjáxù.

heroine, 1. *n.* fàjá.

heroism, 1. *n.* fàjáxùclí.

hers, 1. *n.* cìmá.

herself, 1. *pn.* kfò.

hexagon, 1. *n.* frūkrùprý.

hexagonal, 1. *adj.* frūkrùprýxù.

hey, 1. *intj.* cyjó.

hi, 1. *intj.* cyjó.

hibernal, 1. *adj.* pynępó.

hiccough, 1. *n.* nusę; 2. *v.* {ź} nuę.

hiccup, 1. *n.* nusę; 2. *v.* {ź} nuę.

hidden, 1. *adj.* jýmù.

hide, 1. *n.* kípsō (animal skin); 2. *v.* {ḿ, m̀, ǹ, Í, v́, ṽ} jyû.

high, 1. *adj.* klý.

highland, 1. *n.* klylý.

hill, 1. *n.* prǫ.

hilly, 1. *adj.* prǫxú.

him, 1. *pn.* cá.

himself, 1. *pn.* kfò.

his, 1. *adj.* cámà; 2. *n.* cámà.

hit, 1. *adj.* kèmǫ; 2. *v.* {m̀, m̃, ǹ, ṽ} keò.

hitter, 1. *n.* kèkǫ.

hobby, 1. *n.* kysŭ.

hold, 1. *v.* {m̀, m̃} pleŏ (carry); 2. *v.* {ḿ, m̀, j} piè (wait).

hold-up, 1. *n.* pìse̱ (wait).

holiness, 1. *n.* pu̱cíclì.

hollow, 1. *adj.* ro̱ko̱; 2. *v.* {m̀, ǹ, Í, ṽ} ro̱ko̱nuo̱ (out).

hollow out, 1. *v.* {m̀, ǹ, Í, ṽ} ro̱ko̱nuo̱.

hollowed, 1. *adj.* ro̱ko̱nu̱mo̱ (out).

holy, 1. *adj.* pu̱cí.

home, 1. *adv.* srō; 2. *n.* srō; 3. **go home** *v.* {j} mio̱ srō.

honest, 1. *adj.* plu̱kfá.

honestly, 1. *adv.* plu̱kfárō.

honesty, 1. *n.* plu̱kfáclì.

honey, 1. *n.* rākfè.

honeywine, 1. *n.* na̱cri̱ (mead).

hoof, 1. *n.* pō.

hope, 1. *n.* xū; 2. **hope to** *aux.* j̃.

hopeful, 1. *adj.* xūxù.

hopefully, 1. *adv.* xūxùro̱.

hopeless, 1. *adj.* úprāxù.

hopelessness, 1. *n.* úprāxùclí.

horn, 1. *n.* nẽ.

horrific, 1. *adj.* fēclỳxú.

horror, 1. *n.* fēclỳ.

horse, 1. *n.* clōrā.

hospital, 1. *n.* cíxùpli̱.

hot, 1. *adj.* rā; 2. *adj.* pluxŭ (heated).

house, 1. *n.* sy̱.

housing, 1. *n.* cȳprȳ.

how, 1. *adv.* jȳ (in what way); 2. *adv.* fèja̱ (what... like).

how many, 1. *det.* ra̱pse̱; 2. *pn.* ra̱pse̱.

however, 1. *adv.* fi̱ko̱; 2. *conj.* mã.

human, 1. *n.* kínì.

humorous, 1. *adj.* mékrè.

hundred, 1. *num.* fā; 2. **hundred thousand** *num.* sò.

hundredth, 1. *adj.* fāfā; 2. **hundred thousandth** *adj.* sòso̱.

hunger, 1. *n.* kluclĩ.

hungrily, 1. *adv.* klurõ.
hungry, 1. *adj.* klũ.
hunt, 1. *n.* sròs<u>i</u>; 2. *v.* {ḿ, m̀, Í, r̃} sroì.
hunted, 1. *adj.* sròm<u>i</u>.
hunter, 1. *n.* sròk<u>i</u>.
hurt, 1. *adj.* prìmó (injured); 2. *v.* {z̃} prið (s.o./s.th.); 3. *v.* {z̀} prið (*propositions*).
hurtful, 1. *adj.* prìlólē.
hut, 1. *n.* ps<u>o</u>.
hyperbola, 1. *n.* f<u>y</u>rí.
hyperbolic, 1. *adj.* f<u>y</u>ríxù.

I

I, 1. *pn.* pò.
ice, 1. *n.* krí.
icy, 1. *adj.* kríxù.
idea, 1. *n.* psī.
ideal, 1. *adj.* cx<u>i</u>plýxù.
ideation, 1. *n.* k<u>e</u>s<u>o</u>.
identifiable, 1. *adj.* j<u>a</u>klújà.
identification, 1. *n.* klúsà.
identified, 1. *adj.* klúmà.
identify, 1. *v.* {m̀, m̃, Í} kluâ.
if, 1. *aux.* j́ (*hypothetical marker*).
ignorance, 1. *adj.* cxóplȳ.
ignorant, 1. *n.* cxóplȳclì.
ill, 1. *adj.* sã (sick).
illegal, 1. *adj.* īcxàxú (not allowed by law).
illegality, 1. *n.* īcxàxúclì.
illegible, 1. *adj.* ijasijõ.
illness, 1. *n.* saclĩ (sickness).
illogical, 1. *adj.* īsròxú.
image, 1. *n.* s<u>y</u> (picture); 2. *n.* psī (idea).
imaginable, 1. *adj.* j<u>a</u>k<u>e</u>j<u>o</u>.
imagination, 1. *n.* nàmó.

imaginative, 1. *adj.* nàmóxù.
imagine, 1. *v.* {z̃} keo̱ (s.o./s.th.); 2. *v.* {z̀} keo̱ (*propositions*).
immaterial, 1. *adj.* i̱no̱lu̱le̱.
immeasurable, 1. *adj.* i̱ja̱xíjà.
immediacy, 1. *n.* klȳkàclí.
immediate, 1. *adj.* klȳkà.
immediately, 1. *adv.* klȳkàro̱.
immortal, 1. *adj.* īfrècí.
immortality, 1. *n.* īfrècíclì.
immortalization, 1. *n.* īfrècínūsō.
immortalize, 1. *v.* {m̀, ǹ, Í, ṽ} īfrècínuō.
immortalized, 1. *adj.* īfrècínūmō.
immovable, 1. *adj.* i̱ja̱jújè.
impact, 1. *n.* crukõ.
impactful, 1. *adj.* crukoxũ.
impatience, 1. *n.* i̱me̱róclì.
impatient, 1. *adj.* i̱me̱ró.
impatiently, 1. *adv.* i̱me̱rórō.
imperfect, 1. *adj.* i̱pla̱mó.
imperfection, 1. *n.* i̱pla̱móclì.
imperfectly, 1. *adv.* i̱pla̱mórō.
imperial, 1. *adj.* xu̱je̱xú.
impersonal, 1. *adj.* i̱py̱ni̱.
implication, 1. *n.* kfésī.
implied, 1. *adj.* kfémī.
imply, 1. *v.* {m̀, ñ} kfeí.
importance, 1. *n.* no̱su̱.
important, 1. *adj.* no̱su̱xú.
importantly, 1. *adv.* no̱su̱xúrō.
impossibility, 1. *n.* ījỳklúclì.
impossible, 1. *adj.* ījỳklú.
impossibly, 1. *adv.* ījỳklúrō.
impoverish, 1. *v.* {m̀} sry̱nuo̱.
impoverished, 1. *adj.* sry̱nu̱mo̱; 2. *adj.* sry̱ (poor).
imprecise, 1. *adj.* i̱ký̱kfō.
impregnate, 1. *v.* {m̀, Í} nókènuo̱.

impregnated, 1. *adj.* nókènumo̠.

impress, 1. *v.* {m̀, z̃} mua̠; 2. *v.* {z̀} mua̠ (*propositions*).

impressed, 1. *adj.* mu̠ma̠.

impression, 1. *n.* mu̠sa̠.

impressive, 1. *adj.* mu̠la̠le̠.

impressively, 1. *adv.* mu̠la̠le̠ro̠.

improbable, 1. *adj.* iclaklũ.

improbably, 1. *adv.* iclaklurõ.

improve, 1. *v.* {m̀, m̃, í} kreō.

improved, 1. *adj.* krēmō.

improvement, 1. *n.* krēsō.

impure, 1. *adj.* i̠ji̠fí.

impurity, 1. *n.* i̠ji̠fíclì.

in, 1. *prep.* cú (*location*); 2. *prep.* fèsré (inside of); 3. in s.o.'s opinion *prep.* lāmēklī; 4. in addition to *prep.* méràply̠.

in fact, 1. *adv.* xýmàro̠.

in front, 1. *adj.* frúxù.

in front of, 1. *prep.* frú.

in order that, 1. *comp.* nỳkle̠.

inaccuracy, 1. *n.* īxōcàclí.

inaccurate, 1. *adj.* īxōcà.

inactive, 1. *adj.* i̠fru̠co̠xú; 2. *adj.* cily̠ (passive).

inactively, 1. *adv.* i̠fru̠co̠xúrō; 2. *adv.* cilyrõ (passively).

inadmissible, 1. *adj.* ījākējū.

inapplicable, 1. *adj.* ījācìjé.

inaudible, 1. *adj.* i̠ja̠si̠je̠.

include, 1. *v.* {m̀, m̃, ŕ, j̃} neu̠.

included, 1. *adj.* ne̠mu̠.

inclusion, 1. *n.* ne̠su̠.

income, 1. *n.* cxa̠jý.

incomparable, 1. *adj.* ījākrījà.

incomplete, 1. *adj.* i̠kfúmè.

incomprehensible, 1. *adj.* ijapsujõ.

inconsiderate, 1. *adj.* īcrēmē.

inconsistency, 1. *n.* ījàcu̠clí.

inconsistent, 1. *adj.* ījàcu̠.

incorrect, 1. *adj.* sī (false).

increase, 1. *n.* sésō; 2. *v.* {m̀, Í} seó.

incredible, 1. *adj.* ījālūjè.

incredulity, 1. *n.* īlùlẹlẹclí.

incredulous, 1. *adj.* īlùlẹlẹ.

incredulousness, 1. *n.* īlùlẹlẹclí.

incurable, 1. *adj.* ījāxùjẹ.

indefensible, 1. *adj.* ịjạnạjí.

independent, 1. *adj.* īsrākīxù.

independently, 1. *adj.* īsrākīxùrọ.

indicate, 1. *v.* {m̀} foũ.

indicated, 1. *adj.* fomũ.

indication, 1. *n.* fosũ.

indivisible, 1. *adj.* ijaprujã.

industrial, 1. *adj.* pykukfẽ.

industrious, 1. *adj.* kukfexũ.

industriousness, 1. *n.* kukfexuclĩ.

industry, 1. *n.* kukfẽ.

inedible, 1. *adj.* ījāplījè.

ineffective, 1. *adj.* ịpláplỳxú.

inevitable, 1. *adj.* ịjạkfújà.

inevitably, 1. *adj.* ịjạkfújàrọ.

inexpensive, 1. *adj.* isẽ.

inexperienced, 1. *adj.* ījīlìxú.

infamous, 1. *adj.* cránōxù.

infamously, 1. *adv.* cránōxùrọ.

infamy, 1. *n.* cránō.

inflammable, 1. *adj.* jākījà.

influence, 1. *n.* psusẽ; 2. *v.* {m̀, ǹ, Í} psuẽ.

influencer, 1. *n.* psukẽ.

influential, 1. *adj.* psusexũ; 2. *adj.* psulelẽ.

inform, 1. *v.* {m̃, g̀} fryù.

informal, 1. *adj.* icapsũ.

informality, 1. *n.* icapsuclĩ.

informant, 1. *n.* frỳkụ.

information, 1. *n.* klujĩ.

informational, 1. *adj.* pyklujĩ.

informative, 1. *adj.* klujixũ.

informed, 1. *adj.* frỳmṵ.

infrastructure, 1. *n.* pōjōkfàpo̱.

infrequency, 1. *n.* i̱kfýlàclí.

infrequent, 1. *adj.* i̱kfýlà.

infrequently, 1. *adv.* i̱kfýlàro̱.

initial, 1. *adj.* py̱pṵse̱.

initially, 1. *adv.* py̱pṵse̱ro̱.

injured, 1. *adj.* prìmó (hurt).

injustice, 1. *n.* inuclĩ.

inn, 1. *n.* crȳnȳ.

innkeeper, 1. *n.* crȳnȳprà.

innocence, 1. *n.* xècléclì.

innocent, 1. *adj.* xèclé.

innocently, 1. *adv.* xèclérō.

inquisitve, 1. *adj.* sṵlo̱le̱.

insane, 1. *adj.* i̱psú; 2. *adj.* kfá (crazy); 3. **drive insane** *v.* {m̀, Í, v́, ṽ} kfánuō.

insanity, 1. *n.* i̱psúclì.

insecure, 1. *adj.* īkàcṵxú.

insensitive, 1. *adj.* īcrēmē (inconsiderate).

insensitivity, 1. *n.* īcrēmēclì (lack of consideration).

inside, 1. *adj.* fèsré; 2. *adv.* fèsré; 3. *n.* fèsré; 4. **inside of** *prep.* fèsré.

insignificance, 1. *n.* īxūlēlēclì.

insignificant, 1. *adj.* īxūlēlē.

instance, 1. *n.* srākrà (moment).

instant, 1. *adj.* srākràxú.

instantaneous, 1. *adj.* srākràxú.

instead, 1. *adv.* fòklé.

instead of, 1. *prep.* fòklé.

institution, 1. *n.* cxe̱psṵ (organization).

instrument, 1. *n.* pa̱si̱ (musical).

insufficient, 1. *adj.* i̱sópū.

intangible, 1. *adj.* ījākūjà.

intelligence, 1. *n.* prōclì.

intelligent, 1. *adj.* prō.

intelligible, 1. *adj.* cùlálē.
intelligibly, 1. *adv.* cùlálērō.
intend to, 1. *aux.* j̀.
intentional, 1. *adj.* lēlō.
intentionally, 1. *adv.* lēlōrō.
interest, 1. *n.* sýcò (intrigue); 2. *n.* leclã (fiduciary).
interesting, 1. *adj.* sýcòxú.
interestingly, 1. *adv.* sýcòxúrō.
interior, 1. *n.* fèsré.
intermediary, 1. *adj.* cléfỳxú.
intestinal, 1. *n.* pȳprākfē.
intestines, 1. *n.* prākfē; 2. **large intestines** *n.* prākfē lu̱; 3. **small intestines** *n.* prākfē jè.
intrigue, 1. *n.* sýcò.
intriguing, 1. *adj.* sýcòxú.
introduce, 1. *v.* {m̀, ñ} pruò.
introduction, 1. *n.* prùso̱.
introductory, 1. *adj.* prùso̱xú.
invade, 1. *v.* {ḿ, m̀, m̃, Í} lyú.
invaded, 1. *adj.* lýmū.
invader, 1. *n.* lýkū.
invasion, 1. *n.* lýsū.
invasive, 1. *adj.* lýlūlē.
invest, 1. *v.* {ḿ, m̀} ruá (e.g. money); 2. *v.* {g̀} ruá (in s.th.).
invested, 1. *adj.* rúmā.
investigate, 1. *v.* {ḿ, m̀, m̃, Í} leū.
investigated, 1. *adj.* lēmū.
investigation, 1. *n.* lēsū.
investigator, 1. *n.* lēkū.
investigatory, 1. *adj.* pȳlēsū.
investment, 1. *n.* rúsā.
investor, 1. *n.* rúkā.
invisibility, 1. *n.* ījārìjóclì.
invisible, 1. *adj.* ījārìjó.
invitation, 1. *n.* krasũ.
invite, 1. *v.* {m̀, Í, j̃} kraũ.

involve, 1. *v.* {n̂, Í} mué (concern, have to do with); 2. *v.* {m̂, r̃} siȳ.
involved, 1. *adj.* múmē.
involvement, 1. *n.* sīsȳ.
invulnerability, 1. *n.* īsīlēklūclì.
invulnerable, 1. *adj.* īsīlēklū.
iron, 1. *n.* klùnú; 2. *adj.* klùnúxù (made of iron).
irreducible, 1. *adj.* ījājùjý.
irreducibly, 1. *adj.* ījājùjýrō.
irrelevance, 1. *n.* īnàpu̲clí.
irrelevant, 1. *adj.* īnàpu̲.
irreplaceable, 1. *adj.* i̲jakre̲jó.
irresponsible, 1. *adj.* īnìxýxù.
island, 1. *n.* pri̲fo̲.
isle, 1. *n.* mūmà (small island).
islet, 1. *n.* mūmà (small island).
issuance, 1. *n.* clúsū.
issue, 1. *n.* clúsū (issuance).
it, 1. *pn.* lá.
item, 1. *n.* cu̲ (thing).
its, 1. *adj.* lámà; 2. *n.* lámà.

J

jacket, 1. *n.* fypsa̲.
jade, 1. *adj.* ripri̲xú; 2. *n.* ripri̲.
jagged, 1. *adj.* fro̲plí.
janitor, 1. *n.* cápā.
jaw, 1. *n.* ro̲.
jewelry, 1. *n.* rocĩ.
job, 1. *n.* ké.
join, 1. *v.* {m̂, m̀} kleī.
judge, 1. *n.* kfìká; 2. *v.* {m̂, ṽ} kfiă.
judged, 1. *adj.* kfìmá.
judgement, 1. *n.* kfìsá.
judgemental, 1. *adj.* kfìsáxù.
juice, 1. *n.* sòlá.

jump, 1. *v.* {m̂, ĵ} pseí.
jumpsuit, 1. *n.* pli̱kro̱.
jungle, 1. *n.* fràklo̱.
just, 1. *adj.* nũ (fair); 2. *aux.* z̃ (*recent past*).
justice, 1. *n.* nuclĩ.
justly, 1. *adv.* nurõ.

K

Katalopsi, 1. *n.* kacalopsĩ (language).
keep, 1. *v.* {m̀, m̃} cxuě (s.th.); 2. *aux.* ȷ̄ (continually).
keepsake, 1. *n.* cxùsé.
kept, 1. *adj.* cxùmé.
key, 1. *n.* nì (for a door, etc); 2. *n.* cusrũ (of a map, chart, etc).
kick, 1. *v.* {m̀, Î} kriò.
kid, 1. *n.* rácxānā (infant goat); 2. *n.* psũ (child).
kidney, 1. *n.* jýkrē.
kill, 1. *v.* {m̀, m̃, Î} kraĩ; 2. *v.* {z̃} xiỹ (s.th. hurts).
killed, 1. *adj.* kramĩ.
killer, 1. *n.* krakĩ.
kind, 1. *adj.* fru̱ (nice); 2. *n.* sý (type).
kindhearted, 1. *adj.* frúsòxú (caring).
kindness, 1. *n.* fru̱clí.
king, 1. *n.* sófī.
kiss, 1. *n.* mìso̱; 2. *v.* {m̂, m̀, Î} miò.
kissed, 1. *n.* mìmo̱.
kisser, 1. *n.* mìko̱.
kitchen, 1. *n.* lèkfu̱.
kitten, 1. *n.* ru̱nu̱.
knee, 1. *n.* ra̱kro̱.
kneecap, 1. *n.* ra̱kro̱.
knife, 1. *n.* xàmo̱.
knock, 1. *v.* {r̀} kuè (on s.th.); 2. *v.* {m̀, Î} liě (out s.o.).
knock down, 1. *v.* {m̀, m̃, ṽ} keōfiē.
knocked down, 1. *adj.* kēmōfĩmē.
know, 1. *v.* {ź, ż} pie̱ (be familiar with); 2. *v.* {z̃} paũ (facts).

knowable, 1. *adj.* japajũ.
knowledge, 1. *n.* pasũ.
knowledgeable, 1. *adj.* pi̱le̱le̱.
knowledgeably, 1. *adv.* pi̱le̱le̱ro̱.
known, 1. *adj.* pi̱me̱ (familiar); 2. *adj.* pamũ (facts).

L

labia, 1. *n.* crýpè (anatomy).
labial, 1. *adj.* py̱kfu̱ (relating to lip).
labyrinth, 1. *n.* melafrã.
labyrinthine, 1. *adj.* melafraxũ.
lack, 1. *n.* pséplō.
lacustrine, 1. *adj.* pȳjò.
ladder, 1. *n.* cúpsā.
lady, 1. *n.* lùny̱ (respectable woman); 2. *det.* Lùny̱ (respectful title).
lake, 1. *n.* jò (pond).
lamb, 1. *n.* lȳrūnū.
lamp, 1. *n.* frè.
land, 1. *n.* lý.
landscape, 1. *n.* lýxēclù.
language, 1. *n.* pè.
lantern, 1. *n.* kràre̱.
larder, 1. *n.* ple̱má.
large, 1. *adj.* lu̱.
largely, 1. *adv.* lu̱ro̱ (mostly).
last, 1. *v.* {ḿ, m̀, ń, ǹ} cru̱e̱ (persist); 2. *v.* {ḿ, m̀, ń, ǹ} xaū (survive); 3.
last night *adv.* fecẽ.
late, 1. *adj.* cè (tardy); 2. *adj.* pȳcrū (dead); 3. *adv.* cèro̱ (tardy).
lately, 1. *adv.* kfȳrō (recently).
laugh, 1. *v.* {ḿ, ź} mie̱; 2. *v.* {m̀, z̃} mie̱ (at s.th.).
laughable, 1. *adj.* ja̱mi̱je̱.
laughter, 1. *n.* mi̱se̱.
launch, 1. *n.* rỳsúsrìso̱ (of e.g. a rocket, a missile); 2. *v.* {m̀, Í} ryŭsriò (e.g. a rocket, a missile).
launched, 1. *adj.* rỳmúsrìmo̱ (e.g. a rocket, a missile).

laundry, 1. *n.* cumũ.

laundry room, 1. *n.* cumucã.

lava, 1. *n.* cèl̯e̯.

lavaflow, 1. *n.* cèl̯e̯cu̯clú.

law, 1. *n.* cxà.

lawyer, 1. *n.* cxàprá.

lax, 1. *adj.* krī (not strict); 2. *adj.* cre̯ (loose).

lay, 1. *v.* {m̀, Í, Ì, j} jeì (down, rest).

lazily, 1. *adv.* pūrō.

laziness, 1. *n.* pūclì.

lazy, 1. *adj.* pū.

lead, 1. *v.* {m̀, m̃} psiỳ.

leader, 1. *n.* psìky̲.

leaf, 1. *n.* xì.

learn, 1. *v.* {m̀, m̀} fra̯i̯.

learnable, 1. *adj.* j̯afra̯j̯i̯.

learned, 1. *adj.* fra̯mi̯.

learner, 1. *n.* fra̯ki̯.

least, 1. *adv.* ónō (*superlative*); 2. **at least** *adv.* py̲s̲i̲c̲i̲r̲o̲.

leather, 1. *adj.* plu̯féxù; 2. *n.* plu̯fé.

leave, 1. *v.* {m̀, j} cloí (exit); 2. *v.* {m̀, j̃} lu̯o̯ (s.th. s.w.).

left, 1. *adj.* lu̯mo̯ (behind); 2. *adj.* krỹ (side or direction); 3. *adv.* krỹ (to the left); 4. *n.* krỹ.

leg, 1. *n.* nē.

legal, 1. *adj.* p̄ycxà (relating to law); 2. *adj.* cxàxú (allowed by law).

legality, 1. *n.* cxàxúclì.

legibility, 1. *n.* jasijoclĩ.

legible, 1. *adj.* jasijõ.

legplates, 1. *n.* nēcrè.

lemon, 1. *n.* mēplù.

lend, 1. *v.* {m̀, m̀, m̃, g̲} kliě.

lender, 1. *n.* klìké.

length, 1. *n.* pỹ.

lengthen, 1. *v.* {m̀, Í, v́, ṽ} rìnu̯o̯.

lengthened, 1. *adj.* rìnu̯mo̯.

lengthy, 1. *adj.* pyxũ.

lent, 1. *adj.* klìmé (loaned).

less, 1. *adv.* nù.

let, 1. *v.* {m̀} keū (*propositions*); 2. *v.* {m̀, m̃} keū (allow); 3. *v.* {m̀, m̃} kliě (lend).

letter, 1. *n.* jelõ (epistle); 2. *n.* plic̲lý (orthographic).

lettuce, 1. *n.* kyr̲i̲.

level, 1. *n.* frȳ.

liar, 1. *n.* múkò.

librarian, 1. *n.* cìcxu̲prá.

library, 1. *n.* cìcxu̲.

lie, 1. *v.* {ḿ, m̀, ñ, ģ} muô.

life, 1. *n.* clẽ.

lift, 1. *v.* {m̀} xoũ (s.th. up).

lifted, 1. *adj.* xomũ (up).

light, 1. *n.* kfí; 2. *adj.* sù (bright); 3. *adj.* prú (weight); 4. *adj.* ký (color); 5. *adv.* ký (color); 6. *v.* {m̀, m̃, ǹ, Í, v́, ṽ} niý (e.g. a fire).

lighthouse, 1. *n.* kfísỳ.

likable, 1. *adj.* ja̲re̲ji̲.

like, 1. *v.* {z̀, z̃} rei̲ (s.th. pleases s.o.); 2. **like to** *aux.* m̀; 3. **what... like** *adv.* fèja̲; 4. *prep.* ūsū (function or character, as).

likely, 1. *adj.* claklũ.

lime, 1. *n.* rōsì.

limit, 1. *n.* josũ; 2. *v.* {m̀} joũ (s.th.); 3. *v.* {ĵ} joũ (s.o./s.th. to s.th).

limitation, 1. *n.* josũ.

limited, 1. *adj.* jomũ.

line, 1. *n.* kyf̲i̲.

linear, 1. *adj.* kyf̲i̲xú.

linearity, 1. *n.* kyf̲i̲xúclì.

lingerie, 1. *n.* clòmo̲.

lingual, 1. *adj.* pyp̲á.

linguist, 1. *n.* pèxóprà.

linguistics, 1. *n.* pèxó.

link, 1. *n.* frèru̲ (e.g. in a chain); 2. *n.* lísà (connection); 3. *v.* {m̀, Í, v́, ṽ} liâ (connect).

linked, 1. *adj.* límà (connected).

linguistic, 1. *adj.* pȳpè (relating to language); 2. *adj.* pȳpèxó (relating to linguistics).

lion, 1. *n.* mỳcxí.

lip, 1. *n.* kfu̠.

list, 1. *n.* ki̠pró.

listen, 1. *v.* {ḿ, m̀, m̃} jiè (to s.th. audibly); 2. *v.* {ḿ, m̀} fruó (comply with).

listenable, 1. *adj.* jājījè.

listener, 1. *n.* jìke̠.

literal, 1. *adj.* cralē.

literally, 1. *adv.* cralerõ.

literary, 1. *adj.* py̠sy̠xó.

literature, 1. *n.* sy̠xó.

little, 1. *adj.* jè.

live, 1. *v.* {Ì} cley̌ (reside); 2. *v.* {Í} puy̌ (be alive); 3. *v.* {z̃} prou̠ (experience).

livelihood, 1. *n.* krīsè (living).

liveliness, 1. *n.* clexuclĩ.

lively, 1. *adj.* clexũ.

liver, 1. *n.* psu̠rá.

living, 1. *n.* krīsè (livelihood).

living room, 1. *n.* kròpí.

lizard, 1. *n.* mi̠lu̠.

llama, 1. *n.* xōlè.

loan, 1. *n.* klìsé.

lobster, 1. *n.* kfíklù.

local, 1. *adj.* frȳjò.

locally, 1. *adv.* frȳjòro̠.

location, 1. *n.* nòclý.

locative, 1. *adj.* pȳnòclý.

lock, 1. *n.* lé.

logic, 1. *n.* srò (reason).

logical, 1. *adj.* sròxú.

loneliness, 1. *n.* plīkrèclí.

lonely, 1. *adj.* plīkrè.

long, 1. *adj.* rì; 2. *adj.* pyxũ (lengthy).

longbow, 1. *n.* rīklà.

longbowman, 1. *n.* rīklàni̠.

longstaff, 1. *n.* rìcle̯.

longsword, 1. *n.* rìpru̯.

longswordsman, 1. *n.* rìpruni̯.

look, 1. *v.* {ḿ, m̀} crió (at s.th.); 2. *v.* {ḿ, m̀} fiè (search for s.th.); 3. *v.* {r̃} fiè (s.w. for s.th.); 4. **look forward to** *aux.* ñ.

loom, 1. *n.* clũ.

loose, 1. *adj.* cre̯ (not taut).

loosely, 1. *adv.* cre̯ro̯.

loosen, 1. *v.* {m̀, Í} cre̯nuo̯.

loosened, 1. *adj.* cre̯numo̯.

looseness, 1. *n.* cre̯clí.

lord, 1. *det.* rùni̯ (respectful title).

lose, 1. *v.* {Í, ż} jeỹ (a game, etc); 2. *v.* {m̀} siě (misplace).

loser, 1. *n.* jekỹ (sports, games).

loss, 1. *n.* sìsé.

lost, 1. *adj.* jemỹ (sports, games); 2. *adj.* sìmé (misplaced).

loud, 1. *adj.* cxĩ.

loudly, 1. *adv.* cxirõ.

loudness, 1. *n.* cxiclĩ.

love, 1. *n.* nìso̯; 2. *n.* fi̯ (affection); 3. *v.* {z̃} niò (s.o./s.th.); 4. *v.* {ż} niò (*propositions*); 5. **love to** *aux.* m̱.

lover, 1. *n.* nìko̯.

low, 1. *adj.* cri̯ (not high); 2. *adj.* sru̯ (requiring stock).

lower, 1. *adj.* càxú; 2. *v.* {m̀, Í} cri̯nuo̯.

lowered, 1. *adj.* cri̯numo̯.

loyal, 1. *adj.* òlu̯.

loyalty, 1. *adj.* òlu̯clí.

luck, 1. *n.* xáclì.

luckily, 1. *adv.* xárõ.

lucky, 1. *adj.* xá.

luggage, 1. *n.* casũ.

lukewarm, 1. *adj.* má.

luminous, 1. *adj.* kfíxù (bright).

luminously, 1. *adv.* kfíxùro̯.

lunar, 1. *adj.* pȳlū.

lunch, 1. *n.* rofrĩ.

lung, 1. *n.* xỹ.

lute, 1. *n.* rymę.

lutist, 1. *n.* rymęprá.

M

mace, 1. *n.* pēfà (bludgeon weapon).

machine, 1. *n.* klolĩ.

made, 1. *adj.* ròmú (created).

magazine, 1. *n.* fráfỹ.

mage, 1. *n.* fuprã

magic, 1. *n.* fũ.

magical, 1. *adj.* fuxũ.

magician, 1. *n.* fuprã.

magnet, 1. *n.* rapí.

magnetic, 1. *adj.* rapíxù.

magnetization, 1. *n.* rapíxùnuso.

magnetize, 1. *v.* {m̀, ǹ, Ĩ, v́} rapíxùnuo.

magnetized, 1. *adj.* rapíxùnumo.

mail, 1. *n.* kà.

main, 1. *adj.* crá (primary).

mainly, 1. *adv.* crárō.

make, 1. *v.* {ḿ, m̀, m̃} roǔ (create); 2. make sense *v.* {Í, ż} cuǎ.

maker, 1. *n.* ròkú.

mallet, 1. *n.* krulũ.

man, 1. *n.* kí.

manage, 1. *v.* {m̀, m̃, Í} pliâ (e.g. a business); 2. manage to *aux.* Ì.

manageable, 1. *adj.* japlíjà.

managed, 1. *adj.* plímà (business, etc).

management, 1. *n.* plísà (of a business, etc).

manager, 1. *n.* plíkà.

managerial, 1. *adj.* pyplísà.

mandible, 1. *n.* xỳfry.

mane, 1. *n.* pló.

manifest, 1. *v.* {Í, ż} cxuó (appear).

manliness, 1. *n.* kíxùclí.

manly, 1. *adj.* kíxù.

mansion, 1. *n.* mìku̱.

manual, 1. *adj.* pykfũ (hand-related).

many, 1. *det.* sre̱; 2. *pn.* sre̱.

map, 1. *n.* ky̱.

march, 1. *n.* klýsù (military); 2. *v.* {ḿ, j̱} klyû (militarily).

marital, 1. *adj.* pȳfrỳ.

mark, 1. *v.* {m̀, Í, ṽ} pruá.

marked, 1. *adj.* prúmā.

market, 1. *n.* kre̱.

marriage, 1. *n.* frỳ (relationship); 2. *n.* pūsō (ceremony).

married, 1. *adj.* pūmō.

marry, 1. *v.* {ḿ, m̀, Í̱} puō.

marsh, 1. *n.* kófī.

masculine, 1. *adj.* kíxù.

masculinity, 1. *n.* kíxùclí.

mason, 1. *n.* pócxāprà.

masonry, 1. *n.* pócxā.

massif, 1. *n.* xànu̱; 2. *n.* pe̱clú (mountain).

material, 1. *n.* sràplu̱; 2. *adj.* no̱lu̱le̱ (important).

maternal, 1. *adj.* prūrīxù (behaving as mother); 2. *adj.* pȳprūrī (relating to mother, mother's side, etc).

maternity, 1. *n.* prūrìpro̱su̱.

math, 1. *n.* sréxō.

mathematical, 1. *adj.* py̱sréxō.

mathematician, 1. *adj.* sréxōprà.

mathematics, 1. *n.* sréxō.

matte, 1. *adj.* clè.

matter, 1. *n.* rajã (physical); 2. *v.* {Í̱} nou̱ (be important); 3. *v.* {ż} nou̱ (to s.o.).

mattress, 1. *n.* pōkrò.

maul, 1. *n.* mōcìkrí (war hammer).

mausoleum, 1. *n.* clùná.

maw, 1. *n.* nyfũ.

maximal, 1. *adj.* py̱nékfē.

maximally, 1. *adv.* py̱nékfērō.

maximum, 1. *n.* nékfẽ.

may, 1. *aux.* ż (be allowed to); 2. *aux.* v́ (might).

maybe, 1. *adv.* frá; 2. *intj.* frá.

maze, 1. *n.* melafrã.

me, 1. *pn.* pò.

mead, 1. *n.* nạcrị.

meal, 1. *n.* lãpì.

mean, 1. *v.* {m̀} xuē (signify); 2. *n.* lȳclà (average).

meaning, 1. *n.* xūsē.

meaningful, 1. *adj.* xūsēxù.

means, 1. *n.* mỵ (method).

measurable, 1. *adj.* jạxíjà.

measure, 1. *v.* {m̀, Í, ṽ} xiâ.

measured, 1. *adj.* xímà (on a scale).

measurement, 1. *n.* xísà.

meat, 1. *n.* nò.

meaty, 1. *adj.* nòxú.

mechanic, 1. *n.* frákì.

medal, 1. *n.* kýclõ.

media, 1. *n.* ràpsẹ (news, entertainment); 2. *n.* cléfỳ (means).

medicinal, 1. *adj.* murexũ.

medicine, 1. *n.* murẽ.

medium, 1. *n.* cléfỳ.

meet, 1. *v.* {m̀} peỳ (encounter); 2. *v.* {m̀, r̃} kroụ (on schedule).

meeting, 1. *n.* krọsụ (business, etc); 2. *n.* pēsȳ (encounter).

melon, 1. *n.* láxā.

member, 1. *n.* rákfẽ (of a group, etc).

memorable, 1. *adj.* jãpsỳjí.

memorialize, 1. *v.* {m̀, Í} miě.

memory, 1. *n.* psỳsí.

menstrual, 1. *adj.* pȳmỳsú.

menstruate, 1. *v.* {ź} myǔ.

menstruation, 1. *n.* mỳsú.

mental, 1. *adj.* pynã.

mention, 1. *n.* cusỹ; 2. *v.* {m̀, ñ, Í} cuỹ.

mentionable, 1. *adj.* jacujỹ.

mentioned, 1. *adj.* cumỹ.

meow, 1. *v.* {m̀} moù.

mere, 1. *adj.* cȳ.

merely, 1. *adv.* cȳrō; 2. *adv.* prāmē (only).

message, 1. *n.* srōfì; 2. *n.* māsū.

metal, 1. *n.* cxó.

metallic, 1. *adj.* cxóxù.

method, 1. *n.* my̱.

methodical, 1. *adj.* py̱my̱.

metropolis, 1. *n.* kárā (capital city).

middle-aged, 1. *adj.* kòxu̱.

might, 1. *n.* cýjỳ (power); 2. *aux.* v́.

military, 1. *n.* kru̱pý.

milk, 1. *n.* kly̱.

million, 1. *num.* rũ.

millionth, 1. *adj.* rurũ.

mindful, 1. *adj.* julolẽ.

mindfulness, 1. *n.* jusõ.

mind, 1. *n.* nã; 2. *v.* {m̀, ź} juõ (be mindful); 3. *v.* {m̀, ž} juõ (be mindful of s.th.); 4. **of sound mind** *adj.* psú.

mine, 1. *n.* pòmá (*possessive*); 2. *n.* fỹsú (excavation); 3. *v.* {m̀} fyǔ (for s.th.).

mined, 1. *adj.* fỹmú.

miner, 1. *n.* fỳkú.

minimal, 1. *adj.* py̱si̱ci̱.

minimally, 1. *adv.* py̱si̱ci̱ro̱.

minimum, 1. *n.* si̱ci̱.

minute, 1. *n.* kfìrí (time).

miracle, 1. *n.* ri̱nu̱ký.

miraculous, 1. *adj.* ri̱nu̱kýxù.

misbehave, 1. *v.* {m̀, ń} sruô.

misbehavior, 1. *n.* srúsò.

miscreant, 1. *n.* srúkò.

miserliness, 1. *n.* mỹsrỳclí.

miserly, 1. *adj.* mỹsrỳ.

misfortune, 1. *n.* i̱xáclì.

misplace, 1. *v.* {m̀} siě (lose).

miss, 1. *v.* {m̀, Í} kleǐ (a target, etc); 2. *v.* {ż, z̃} fuê (emotionally).

mission, 1. *n.* cákù (campaign).

mist, 1. *n.* ropró.

model, 1. *adj.* cxiplýxù; 2. *n.* cxiplý.

mohair, 1. *n.* jècla̱.

moment, 1. *n.* sipsý.

momentarily, 1. *adv.* sipsýxùro̱.

momentary, 1. *adj.* sipsýxù.

monarch, 1. *n.* cxūràriprá.

monarchy, 1. *n.* cxūràri.

monetary, 1. *adj.* pȳfè.

money, 1. *n.* fè; 2. *n.* srāsū (cash); 3. *n.* kfipre̱ (currency).

monogamous, 1. *adj.* frỳxú.

monolith, 1. *n.* srūkūkù.

monolithic, 1. *adj.* srūkūkùxú.

monster, 1. *n.* rìsre̱.

monstrous, 1. *adj.* rìsre̱xú.

month, 1. *n.* nõ.

monthly, 1. *adj.* pynõ.

mood, 1. *n.* xè.

moody, 1. *adj.* xèxú.

moon, 1. *n.* lū.

morbid, 1. *adj.* clémōxù.

morbidity, 1. *n.* clémōxùclí.

more, 1. *adv.* pró (*comparative*); 2. *det.* sūklā; 3. *pn.* sūklā.

moreover, 1. *adv.* cxa̱.

morgue, 1. *n.* fēkrù.

morning, 1. *n.* fī; 2. **good morning** *intj.* cýfī.

mortal, 1. *adj.* frècí.

mortality, 1. *n.* frèciclì.

mortar, 1. *n.* pròcó.

mortician, 1. *n.* fēkrùprá.

mortuary, 1. *n.* fēkrù (morgue); 2. *n.* kfilu̱ cxèso̱ (funeral home).

moss, 1. *n.* ke̱cré.

most, 1. *adv.* rà (*superlative*); 2. *det.* kfũ (majority); 3. *pn.* kfũ (majority); 4. **at most** *adv.* pynékfērō.

mostly, 1. *adv.* lu̲ro̲.

moth, 1. *n.* prūrī.

mother, 1. *n.* prūrī.

motherhood, 1. *n.* prūrìpro̲su̲.

motherly, 1. *adj.* prūrīxù (behaving as mother).

motionless, 1. *adj.* ìmy̲.

motionlessly, 1. *adv.* ìmy̲ro̲.

mountain, 1. *n.* pe̲clú.

mountainous, 1. *n.* pe̲clúxù.

mouse, 1. *n.* pùsry.

moustache, 1. *n.* nékrī.

mouth, 1. *n.* clỳ; 2. **roof of mouth** *n.* fólū.

movable, 1. *adj.* ja̲jújè.

move, 1. *v.* {ḿ, m̀, m̃, Í} juê.

moved, 1. *adj.* júmè (shifted).

movement, 1. *n.* júsè (motion).

mover, 1. *n.* júkè (of furniture, etc).

movie, 1. *n.* kle̲ (film).

mug, 1. *n.* xalã.

murmur, 1. *n.* pso̲si̲; 2. *v.* {ḿ, m̀, ñ} pso̲i̲.

murmurer, 1. *n.* pso̲ki̲.

murmuring, 1. *n.* pso̲si̲.

muscle, 1. *n.* kòply.

muscular, 1. *adj.* kòply̲xú (strong); 2. *adj.* pȳkòply̲.

music, 1. *n.* junẽ.

musical, 1. *adj.* pyjunẽ (relating to music); 2. *adj.* junexũ (having the quality of music).

musician, 1. *n.* pa̲ki̲.

must, 1. *aux.* ḿ.

muster, 1. *v.* {m̀, ż} preu̲.

mutton, 1. *n.* sykro̲.

my, 1. *adj.* pòmá.

myriad, 1. *num.* plí.

myself, 1. *pn.* kfò.

mysterious, 1. *adj.* rēlōfòxú.
mysteriously, 1. *adv.* rēlōfòxúrō.
mystery, 1. *n.* rēlōfò.

N

nail, 1. *n.* cò (organic); 2. *n.* xí (used with hammer).
name, 1. *n.* kfĩ; 2. **family name** *n.* srykfĩ.
narrative, 1. *adj.* pȳkò.
narrow, 1. *adj.* jì.
narrowness, 1. *n.* jìclí.
nasal, 1. *n.* pȳmì.
nasal cavity, 1. *n.* mákrȳ pȳmì.
natal, 1. *adj.* pycé.
nation, 1. *n.* nikfé.
national, 1. *adj.* pynikfé.
native, 1. *adj.* rykfa.
natural, 1. *adj.* moxũ.
naturally, 1. *adv.* moxurõ.
nature, 1. *n.* mõ.
navel, 1. *n.* lòra.
near, 1. *adj.* xi; 2. *prep.* xi.
nearby, 1. *adj.* xi.
nearly, 1. *adv.* xiro.
nearness, 1. *n.* xiclí.
neatly, 1. *adv.* psỳro (tidily).
necessarily, 1. *adv.* lomurõ.
necessary, 1. *adj.* lomũ.
neck, 1. *n.* kỳ.
necklace, 1. *n.* nāklì.
Necronomicon, 1. *n.* Larósī u càlu.
need, 1. *v.* {ž} loũ (s.o./s.th.); 2. *v.* {ž} loũ (*propositions*); 3. *n.* losũ; 4.
need to *aux.* Ī.
needed, 1. *adj.* lomũ (necessary).
needily, 1. *adv.* lolulerõ.
needle, 1. *n.* sìni.

needy, 1. *adj.* lolulẽ.

neither, 1. *det.* lú.

neophyte, 1. *n.* pu̲ke̲.

nervous, 1. *adj.* kfìko̲xú.

nervous breakdown, 1. *n.* kfìso̲.

nervous wreck, 1. *n.* kfìko̲.

network, 1. *n.* plíclī.

never, 1. *adv.* fòfra̲.

new, 1. *adj.* lō.

news, 1. *n.* klú.

newspaper, 1. *n.* projũ.

next, 1. *adj.* jỳ; 2. *adv.* jỳ.

next to, 1. *prep.* clý.

nice, 1. *adj.* fru̲ (kind); 2. *adj.* srù (pleasant).

night, 1. *n.* cẽ; 2. **good night** *intj.* cycẽ; 3. **last night** *adv.* fecẽ.

nightgown, 1. *n.* kūsū.

nightly, 1. *adj.* pycẽ.

nightmare, 1. *n.* rìpsa̲.

nightmarish, 1. *adj.* rìpsa̲xú.

nine, 1. *num.* kfé.

ninetieth, 1. *adj.* kfépāpā.

ninety, 1. *num.* kfépā.

ninth, 1. *adj.* kfékfē.

nipple, 1. *n.* xùfi̲.

no, 1. *intj.* là; 2. *det.* so̲.

no one, 1. *pn.* so̲ni̲.

nobody, 1. *pn.* so̲ni̲.

nocturnal, 1. *adj.* cexũ.

nod, 1. *n.* cúsō (of the head); 2. *v.* {ḿ, m̀} cuó.

non-native, 1. *adj.* i̲rykfa̲.

nonagon, 1. *n.* kfékrùprý.

nonagonal, 1. *adj.* kfékrùprýxù.

none, 1. *pn.* so̲.

nonlinear, 1. *adj.* i̲kyfi̲xú.

nonlinearity, 1. *n.* i̲kyfi̲xúclì.

nonviolence, 1. *n.* i̲rálìclí.

noodle, 1. *n.* sapó.

nook, 1. *n.* sylocã (breakfast).

nor, 1. *conj.* li.

north, 1. *adj.* ka; 2. *adv.* ka; 3. *n.* ka.

northern, 1. *adj.* kaxú.

northward, 1. *adv.* ka.

nose, 1. *n.* mì.

nostril, 1. *n.* necũ.

not, 1. *adv.* fò.

note, 1. *n.* jiclĩ (message); 2. *n.* lumĩ (musical).

noteworthiness, 1. *n.* kfújèclí.

noteworthy, 1. *adj.* kfújè.

nothing, 1. *n.* kè.

notice, 1. *v.* {z̃} kliõ (s.o./s.th.); 2. *v.* {ż} kliõ (*propositions*).

noticeable, 1. *adj.* jaklijõ.

notoriety, 1. *n.* cránō.

notorious, 1. *adj.* cránōxù.

notoriously, 1. *adv.* cránōxùro.

novel, 1. *n.* kanu (book).

now, 1. *adv.* klỳ; 2. **right now** *adv.* mēklì.

nowhere, 1. *adv.* sómā; 2. *pn.* sómā.

number, 1. *n.* sré.

numerical, 1. *adj.* pysré.

nurse, 1. *n.* nunẽ.

nut, 1. *n.* clūsū (building material).

nutrition, 1. *n.* sumerĩ.

nutritional, 1. *adj.* pysumerĩ.

nutritious, 1. *adj.* sumerixũ.

O

obedience, 1. *n.* frúsō.

obedient, 1. *adj.* krulolẽ.

obediently, 1. *adv.* krulolerõ.

obelisk, 1. *n.* fùcipa.

obese, 1. *adj.* frīrā.

obesity, 1. *n.* frīrāclì.

obey, 1. *v.* {m̂, m̀} fruó (comply with s.th.).

obeyed, 1. *adj.* krumõ.

object, 1. *n.* lisỹ.

object of desire, 1. *n.* mésì.

objective, 1. *n.* plī.

observant, 1. *adj.* klilolẽ.

obstacle, 1. *n.* lárì.

obstinate, 1. *adj.* lìmị.

obtain, 1. *v.* {m̀, m̃} cliã.

obtainable, 1. *adj.* jaclijã.

obtained, 1. *adj.* climã.

obvious, 1. *adj.* srụsẹ.

obviously, 1. *adv.* srụsẹrọ.

obviousness, 1. *n.* srụsẹclí.

occasion, 1. *n.* mufũ.

occasional, 1. *adj.* mufuxũ.

occasionally, 1. *adv.* mufuxurõ.

occur, 1. *v.* {í, ì} niô (happen).

occurrence, 1. *n.* nísò.

ocean, 1. *n.* krụmú.

oceanic, 1. *adj.* krụmúxù.

octagon, 1. *n.* kríkrùprý.

octagonal, 1. *adj.* kríkrùprýxù.

octahedral, 1. *adj.* krírēcrōxù.

octahedron, 1. *n.* krírēcrō.

ocular, 1. *n.* pykị.

odd, 1. *adj.* fylĩ (numerically); 2. *adj.* prùnị (strange).

oddly, 1. *adv.* prùnịrọ (strangely).

of, 1. *prep.* u.

offer, 1. *v.* {m̂, m̀, m̃} psyû.

offered, 1. *adj.* psýmù.

offering, 1. *n.* psýsù.

office, 1. *n.* clējī (bureau); 2. *n.* *n.* kfàná (study).

official, 1. *adj.* clējīxù.

often, 1. *adv.* cūpā.

oil, 1. *n.* krỳ.

oily, 1. *adj.* krỳxú.

old, 1. *adj.* ju̱ (in age); 2. *adj.* īlō (not new).

olive, 1. *n.* ni̱clé.

on, 1. *prep.* sro̱ (*patient, theme*); 2. *prep.* a̱ (*vertical*); 3. *prep.* mu̱ (*horizontal*).

on purpose, 1. *adv.* lēlōrō.

on time, 1. *adj.* psè; 2. *adv.* psèro̱.

on top of, 1. *prep.* mé.

one, 1. *num.* xȳ; 2. **one hundred** *num.* fā; 3. **one thousand** *num.* clo̱; 4.

one hundred thousand *num.* sò; 5. **one million** *num.* rũ.

one another, 1. *pn.* mylí.

onion, 1. *n.* nykã.

only, 1. *adv.* prāmē.

opal, 1. *n.* xõ; 2. *adj.* xoxũ.

opalescent, 1. *adj.* xoxũ.

opaline, 1. *adj.* xoxũ.

opaque, 1. *adj.* pra̱fí.

open, 1. *adj.* cūmā (e.g. a door); 2. *adj.* nemỹ (e.g. a business); 3. *v.* {ḿ, m̀, m̃, Í} cuā; 4. *v.* {Í} neỹ (a business, etc).

opened, 1. *adj.* cūmā; 2. *adj.* nemỹ (e.g. a business).

operate, 1. *v.* {j̱, j̃} pliõ (a machine, e.g. a vehicle).

operation, 1. *n.* plisõ (e.g. of a machine).

operator, 1. *n.* plikõ.

opinion, 1. *n.* jārē; 2. **in s.o.'s opinion** *prep.* lāmēklī.

opinionated, 1. *adj.* jārēxù.

opportunity, 1. *n.* krỳpló.

optical, 1. *adj.* pyḵi̱.

option, 1. *n.* rúfrè.

optional, 1. *adj.* rúfrèxú.

optionality, 1. *n.* rúfrèxúclì.

or, 1. *conj.* li.

orange, 1. *adj.* nu̱jú (color); 2. *n.* nu̱júkō (color); 3. *n.* kèkra̱.

orb, 1. *n.* ré.

order, 1. *n.* mè (as opposed to chaos); 2. *n.* mèsy̱ (sequence, sorting); 3. *n.* fri̱sa̱ (command); 4. *v.* {m̀, Í, g̃} fri̱a̱ (command); 5. *v.* {m̀, Í, ṽ} meỳ (sort).

orderly, 1. *adj.* mèxú.

organization, 1. *n.* srásù (order or orderliness); 2. *n.* cxɛpsu̱ (institution).

organizational, 1. *adj.* py̱cxɛpsu̱.

organize, 1. *v.* {m̀, Í} sraû.

organized, 1. *adj.* srásùxú; 2. *adj.* srámù.

orgasm, 1. *n.* risỹ; 2. *v.* {ź} riỹ.

orgasmic, 1. *adj.* risyxũ.

origin, 1. *n.* có (source).

original, 1. *adj.* sŕnì (unique).

other than, 1. *comp.* fūlā; 2. *prep.* fūlā.

otherwise, 1. *adv.* nélī.

our, 1. *adj.* plōmà.

ours, 1. *n.* plōmà.

ourselves, 1. *pn.* kfò.

outcome, 1. *n.* másū.

outside, 1. *adj.* cro̱fro̱; 2. *adv.* cro̱fro̱; 3. *n.* cro̱fro̱; 4. **outside of** *prep.* cro̱fro̱.

oval, 1. *n.* mu̱li̱; 2. *adj.* mu̱li̱xú.

ovarian, 1. *adj.* pyplu̱klã.

ovary, 1. *n.* pluklã.

oven, 1. *n.* ló (range).

over, 1. *prep.* menẽ.

over there, 1. *adv.* lāsùcy̱; 2. *n.* lāsùcy̱.

overcoat, 1. *n.* mỳcri̱sa̱.

own, 1. *v.* {ż} xoī (belong to); 2. *v.* {ż} saí (have).

owned, 1. *adj.* xōmī (as property).

owner, 1. *n.* xōkī.

ownership, 1. *n.* xōsī.

P

pack, 1. *n.* cxì (packet).

packet, 1. *n.* cxì.

paddy field, 1. *n.* su̱kry̱.

page, 1. *n.* srì.

paginal, 1. *adj.* pȳsrì.

pagoda, 1. *n.* kla̱psó.

paid, 1. *adj.* klēmȳ.

pain, 1. *n.* prìsó.

paint, 1. *v.* {ḿ, m̀, Í, v́, ṽ} laū.

painted, 1. *adj.* lāmū.

painter, 1. *n.* lākū.

painting, 1. *n.* lāsū.

pair, 1. *n.* psó.

palatal, 1. *adj.* py̆fólū.

palate, 1. *n.* fólū.

palm, 1. *n.* na̱kí (of hand).

pancreas, 1. *n.* se̱mú.

pancreatic, 1. *adj.* pyse̱mú.

pantry, 1. *n.* fàcá.

pants, 1. *n.* clō.

paper, 1. *n.* lìné.

parabola, 1. *n.* pàkle̱.

parabolic, 1. *adj.* pàkle̱xú.

paralysis, 1. *n.* kýnì.

paralytic, 1. *adj.* pykýnì.

paralyzed, 1. *adj.* kýnìxú.

parasite, 1. *n.* no̱klú.

parasitic, 1. *adj.* no̱klúxù.

parched, 1. *adj.* crỳ (thirsty).

parent, 1. *n.* o̱kru̱.

parental, 1. *adj.* o̱kru̱xú.

park, 1. *n.* krì (public garden).

part, 1. *n.* cxō (section); 2. **for the most part** *adv.* lu̱ro̱.

particularly, 1. *adv.* xyklo̱.

pass, 1. *v.* {ḿ} jou̱ (not participate); 2. *v.* {m̀, m̃} jaī (a ball, etc); 3. *n.* jāsī (of a ball, etc).

pass out, 1. *v.* {ź} syi̱.

passed out, 1. *adj.* symi̱.

passion, 1. *n.* sy̆plá.

passionate, 1. *adj.* sy̆pláxù.

passive, 1. *adj.* cilỹ.

passively, 1. *adv.* cilyrõ.

past, 1. *adv.* kàrá; 2. *prep.* kàrá.

pastime, 1. *n.* kysũ.

paternal, 1. *adj.* mi̱ráxù (behaving as father); 2. *adj.* py̱mi̱rá (relating to father, father's side, etc).

paternity, 1. *n.* mi̱ra̱pro̱su̱.

path, 1. *n.* nōplā (trail); 2. *n.* kì (route).

pathological, 1. *adj.* pȳkrōpsù (relating to disease); 2. *adj.* krōpsùxú (diseased).

patience, 1. *n.* me̱róclì.

patient, 1. *adj.* me̱ró.

patiently, 1. *adv.* me̱rórō.

paw, 1. *n.* frē.

pay, 1. *v.* {m̀, m̀} kleȳ; 2. *v.* {r̃} kleȳ (for s.th.).

payable, 1. *adj.* jāklējȳ.

payment, 1. *n.* klēsȳ.

pelvic, 1. *adj.* pȳpsēcrỳ.

pelvis, 1. *n.* psēcrỳ.

pendant, 1. *n.* kénà.

penile, 1. *adj.* pȳrēnù.

peninsula, 1. *n.* cxūnī.

peninsular, 1. *adj.* pȳcxūnī.

penis, 1. *n.* rēnù.

pensive, 1. *adj.* kúsōxù; 2. *adj.* kúlōlē.

pensively, 1. *adv.* kúsōxùro̱; 2. *adv.* kúlōlērō.

pentagon, 1. *n.* clūkrùprý.

pentagonal, 1. *adj.* clūkrùprýxù.

people, 1. *n.* ni̱ (general); 2. *n.* nùlé (ethnicity).

percentage, 1. *n.* laclẽ.

perfect, 1. *adj.* pla̱mó; 2. *v.* {m̀, Í} pla̱mónuō.

perfected, 1. *adj.* pla̱mónūmō.

perfection, 1. *n.* pla̱móclì.

perfectly, 1. *adv.* pla̱mórō.

perform, 1. *v.* {m̀, m̀, m̃} xeȳ.

performance, 1. *n.* xesȳ.

performer, 1. *n.* xekȳ.

period, 1. *n.* pròprí (of time); 2. *n.* crēlà (punctuation); 3. *n.* lúmā (era).

periodic, 1. *adj.* pròpríxù.

periodicity, 1. *n.* pròpríxùclí.

permissible, 1. *adj.* jāmūjō.

permission, 1. *n.* mūsō.

permit, 1. *v.* {m̀, m̃} muō.

permitted, 1. *adj.* mūmō (allowed).

persist, 1. *v.* {ḿ, m̀, ń, ǹ} cruę (last).

person, 1. *n.* nị.

personable, 1. *adj.* nịxú.

personal, 1. *adj.* pyṇị.

personally, 1. *adv.* pyṇịrǫ.

perspective, 1. *n.* fòxạ.

perspiration, 1. *n.* nịsạ.

perspire, 1. *v.* {Í} niạ.

pestle, 1. *n.* kròkỵ.

petal, 1. *n.* kfùfý.

petrol, 1. *n.* clǫró.

phase, 1. *n.* rèclý (stage).

philosophical, 1. *adj.* pyplikfã (relating to philosophy); 2. *adj.* plikfaxũ (thought-provoking).

philosophy, 1. *n.* plikfã.

phone, 1. *n.* xȳkrā (telephone).

photo, 1. *n.* kfęsé.

photograph, 1. *n.* kfęsé.

physical, 1. *adj.* clęfǫ.

physically, 1. *adv.* clęfǫrǫ.

physician, 1. *n.* mureprã.

physicist, 1. *n.* psòxóprà.

physics, 1. *n.* psòxó.

pianist, 1. *n.* liniprã.

piano, 1. *n.* linĩ.

pick, 1. *n.* xósū (choice); 2. *v.* {m̀, m̃, Í} xoú (choose).

pickpocket, 1. *n.* ǫlíkì.

picture, 1. *n.* plācxȳ (depiction).

picturesque, 1. *adj.* plācxȳxù.

pie, 1. *n.* léfī.

351

piece, 1. *n.* mìklá.

pig, 1. *n.* plūjē.

piglet, 1. *n.* plūjēnē.

pike, 1. *n.* cóklȳ.

pillow, 1. *n.* jùmu̱.

piscine, 1. *adj.* pyfrĩ.

place, 1. *n.* mā (location); 2. *v.* {ĵ} freý (put on s.th.); 3. *v.* {m̀} freý (put s.th. down).

plague, 1. *n.* ro̱lu̱.

plain, 1. *n.* no̱ (prairie).

plan, 1. *n.* cxù (schedule); 2. *n.* pusõ; 3. *v.* {m̀, m̃} puõ.

plane, 1. *n.* suklukũ (airplane).

planet, 1. *n.* kā.

planned, 1. *adj.* cxùxú (well); 2. *adj.* pumõ (in general).

planner, 1. *n.* pukõ.

plant, 1. *n.* mà (organism); 2. *n.* pro̱sy̱ (industrial).

plantation, 1. *n.* klócrījè.

plastic, 1. *adj.* cxo̱cry̱xú; 2. *n.* cxo̱cry̱.

plate, 1. *n.* kenỹ.

plateau, 1. *n.* xylỹ.

platinum, 1. *n.* kèkrá; 2. *adj.* kèkráxù (made of platinum).

play, 1. *v.* {ḿ} roú (have fun); 2. *v.* {g̀} roú (with s.o.); 3. *v.* {m̀, m̃, v̀, ṽ} pai̱ (music).

playable, 1. *adj.* ja̱pa̱ji̱ (music).

played, 1. *adj.* pa̱mi̱ (performed, music).

player, 1. *n.* rókū (sports, games); 2. *n.* pa̱ki̱ (musician).

playful, 1. *adj.* rólūlē.

playfully, 1. *adv.* rólūlērō.

pleasant, 1. *adj.* srù.

please, 1. *adv.* jo̱; 2. *intj.* jo̱; 3. *v.* {ż, ž} rei̱.

pliers, 1. *n.* klācū.

plinth, 1. *n.* kópī.

plume, 1. *n.* raclã.

pocket, 1. *n.* sīmì.

pocket watch, 1. *n.* sīmìsru̱jó.

poem, 1. *n.* klápù.

poet, 1. *n.* klápùprá.

poetic, 1. *adj.* klápùxú.

poetry, 1. *n.* klápù.

point, 1. *n.* klẽ; 2. *v.* {j} psyí (at s.o./s.th.).

pointy, 1. *n.* klexũ.

poison, 1. *n.* fa̱su̱; 2. *v.* {m̀, Í} fau̱.

poisoned, 1. *adj.* fa̱mu̱.

poisonous, 1. *adj.* fa̱su̱xú.

policy, 1. *n.* malẽ.

political, 1. *adj.* pȳkràsrú.

politician, 1. *n.* kràsrúprà.

politics, 1. *n.* kràsrú.

pond, 1. *n.* jò (lake).

poor, 1. *adj.* sry̱ (impoverished).

poorly, 1. *adv.* pre̱ro̱.

popular, 1. *adj.* krèka̱.

popularity, 1. *n.* krèka̱clí.

popularize, 1. *v.* {m̀, Í} krèka̱nuo̱.

popularized, 1. *adj.* krèka̱nu̱mo̱.

popularizer, 1. *n.* krèka̱nu̱ko̱.

popularly, 1. *adv.* krèka̱ro̱.

pork, 1. *n.* méklā.

port, 1. *n.* psu̱.

position, 1. *n.* mūfrè (location); 2. *n.* jārē (opinion).

positional, 1. *adj.* pȳmūfrè.

possession, 1. *n.* xōsī.

possibility, 1. *n.* jỳklúclì.

possible, 1. *adj.* jỳklú.

possibly, 1. *adv.* jỳklúrō.

post, 1. *n.* kà.

postal, 1. *adj.* pȳkà.

pot, 1. *n.* fré.

potability, 1. *n.* jāklìjóclì.

potable, 1. *adj.* jāklìjó.

potato, 1. *n.* fy̱clá.

potion, 1. *n.* mo̱kló.

poultry, 1. *n.* frùry.

pounce, 1. *n.* xusỹ; 2. *v.* {m̂, ĵ, j̃} xuỹ.

pouncer, 1. *n.* xukỹ.

poverty, 1. *n.* sryclí.

power, 1. *n.* cýjỳ.

powerful, 1. *adj.* cýjỳxú.

practice, 1. *n.* srómỳ (e.g. rehearsal).

practiced, 1. *adj.* srómỳxú.

prairie, 1. *n.* xìpla; 2. *n.* no (plain).

pray, 1. *v.* {ġ} niõ (to s.o.); 2. *v.* {ġ} niõ (for s.o.); 3. *v.* {m̂, ñ} niõ (*propositions*).

prayer, 1. *n.* nisõ.

preach, 1. *v.* {m̂, ǹ, ġ} cruê.

preacher, 1. *n.* crúkè.

preachy, 1. *adj.* crúlèle.

precipice, 1. *n.* plukulã.

precipitous, 1. *adj.* plukulaxũ.

precise, 1. *adj.* kýkfõ.

precisely, 1. *adv.* kýkfõrõ.

precision, 1. *n.* kýkfõclì.

prefer, 1. *v.* {z̃} feǐ (s.o./s.th.); 2. *v.* {z̀} feǐ (*propositions*).

preferable, 1. *adj.* jāfèjí.

preference, 1. *n.* fèsí.

preferred, 1. *adj.* fèmí.

pregnancy, 1. *n.* nókèclí.

pregnant, 1. *adj.* nókè.

preparation, 1. *adj.* clusẽ.

prepare, 1. *v.* {m̂} cluẽ (make s.th. ready).

prepared, 1. *adj.* clumẽ.

present, 1. *v.* {m̂, ñ} friă.

presentable, 1. *adj.* jāfrìjá.

presentation, 1. *n.* frìsá.

presenter, 1. *n.* kfakũ.

press, 1. *v.* {m̂, m̃} croī (push e.g. a button); 2. *v.* {m̂} jau (urge s.o./s. th.); 3. *v.* {m̂, m̃, r̀} sau (crush e.g. grapes).

pressure, 1. *n.* sòkly.

presume, 1. *v.* {m̀} riŷ.

presumed, 1. *adj.* rímỳ.

pretty, 1. *adj.* sópū.

prevent, 1. *v.* {m̀} sriô.

preventable, 1. *adj.* ja̱sríjò.

prevention, 1. *n.* srísò.

previous, 1. *adj.* pòsre̱.

previously, 1. *adv.* pòsre̱ro̱.

price, 1. *n.* fĩ.

pricy, 1. *adj.* fixũ.

priest, 1. *n.* fȳnū.

primarily, 1. *adv.* xȳxȳrō (firstly); 2. *adv.* cráró (mainly).

primary, 1. *adj.* crá (main).

prince, 1. *n.* mo̱ci̱.

princess, 1. *n.* ky̱ci̱.

printer, 1. *n.* sȳprà (of books).

prior to, 1. *prep.* fé.

probable, 1. *adj.* claklũ (likely).

probably, 1. *adv.* claklurõ.

problem, 1. *n.* plà.

problematic, 1. *adj.* plàxú.

process, 1. *n.* crūrȳ.

produce, 1. *v.* {ḿ, m̀, m̃} kfaû (movies, music, etc); 2. *v.* {ḿ, m̀, m̃, Í} saû (create).

produced, 1. *adj.* kfámù (movies, music, etc).

producer, 1. *n.* kfákù (of movies, music, etc).

product, 1. *n.* cīsȳ (of labor, etc.); 2. *n.* rȳ (in a store).

production, 1. *n.* kfásù.

professor, 1. *n.* klēmèfa̱.

profit, 1. *n.* psēprò.

profitability, 1. *n.* psēpròxúclì.

profitable, 1. *adj.* psēpròxú.

program, 1. *n.* ju̱cú (social or political); 2. *n.* plokrõ (computational).

programmatic, 1. *adj.* plokroxũ.

prohibit, 1. *v.* {m̀, Í} cué.

prohibited, 1. *adj.* cúmē.

prohibition, 1. *n.* cúsē.
promise, 1. *n.* psēsī; 2. *v.* {m̀, ñ} pseī.
promised, 1. *adj.* psēmī.
proof, 1. *n.* pīsā.
prop, 1. *v.* {m̀, j̃} fruē (s.th. up).
proper, 1. *adj.* plàlo̠.
properly, 1. *adv.* plàlo̠ro̠.
property, 1. *n.* clòxú.
propose, 1. *v.* {m̀, ñ} kriỹ (suggest).
prostitute, 1. *n.* rāclīprà.
prostitution, 1. *n.* rāclī.
protect, 1. *v.* {m̀, r̃} jaù.
protection, 1. *n.* jàsu̠.
protective, 1. *adj.* jàlu̠le̠.
protector, 1. *n.* jàku̠.
provable, 1. *adj.* jāpījā.
prove, 1. *v.* {m̀, m̃} piā.
proven, 1. *adj.* pīmā.
proverb, 1. *n.* xōpỹ (saying).
provide, 1. *v.* {m̀, m̃, ñ} cleī.
provided, 1. *adj.* clemī.
provider, 1. *n.* clekī.
provision, 1. *n.* clesī.
pub, 1. *n.* fòrú.
publication, 1. *n.* psúsà.
publish, 1. *v.* {m̀, Í} psuâ.
publishable, 1. *adj.* ja̠psújà.
published, 1. *adj.* psúmà.
publisher, 1. *n.* psúkà.
pull, 1. *v.* {m̀, Í, Ì, j̃} frià.
pulley, 1. *n.* còju̠.
pulmonary, 1. *n.* pyxỹ.
pumpkin, 1. *n.* nērù.
punch, 1. *n.* kùsy̠; 2. *v.* {m̀, Í} kuỳ.
punched, 1. *adj.* kùmy̠.
punctual, 1. *adj.* psè.

punctuality, 1. *n.* psèclí.

punctually, 1. *adv.* psèrǫ.

pupil, 1. *n.* cxú.

puppy, 1. *n.* psȳnȳ.

purchase, 1. *n.* pésū; 2. *v.* {m̀, m̃} peú.

purchased, 1. *adj.* pémū.

pure, 1. *adj.* ji̧fí.

purely, 1. *adv.* ji̧fírō.

purification, 1. *n.* ji̧fínūsō.

purified, 1. *adj.* ji̧fínūmō.

purifier, 1. *n.* ji̧fínūkō.

purify, 1. *v.* {m̀, ǹ, í, ṽ} ji̧fínuō.

purity, 1. *n.* ji̧fíclì.

purple, 1. *adj.* lā; 2. *n.* lākō.

purpose, 1. *n.* línò; 2. **on purpose** *adv.* lēlōrō.

purse, 1. *n.* klùjǫ.

pursue, 1. *v.* {m̀, í} kloī.

pursued, 1. *adj.* klōmī.

pursuer, 1. *n.* klōkī.

pursuit, 1. *n.* klōsī.

push, 1. *v.* {m̀, j̃} kluò; 2. *v.* {m̀, m̃} croī (press e.g. a button); 3. **push down/over** *v.* {m̀, í} kluōfiē.

pushed down, 1. *adj.* klūmōfīmē.

pushed over, 1. *adj.* klūmōfīmē.

put, 1. *v.* {j̃} freý (set); 2. **put down** *v.* {m̀} freý; 3. **put down** *adj.* frémȳ; 4. **put away** *v.* {m̀} psaū; 5. **put away** *adj.* psāmū; 6. **put by** *v.* {ḿ, m̀, m̃} pei̧ (can foodstuffs); 7. **put by** *adj.* pȩmi̧ (canned); 8. **put out** *v.* {m̀, ǹ, í, v́, ṽ} rau̧ (e.g. a fire); 9. **put out** *adj.* ra̧mu̧.

puzzle, 1. *n.* kòcǫ.

Q

quality, 1. *adj.* xúnāxù; 2. *n.* xúnā.

quantity, 1. *n.* cli̧.

quarter, 1. *n.* mupī̧ (one-fourth).

quarterstaff, 1. *n.* clȩ (wielded stick).

queen, 1. *n.* jupsí.

question, 1. *n.* suso; 2. *n.* plamõ.

quick, 1. *adj.* cxā (fast).

quickly, 1. *adv.* cxārō.

quickness, 1. *n.* cxāclì.

quiet, 1. *adj.* fȳ.

quietly, 1. *adv.* fȳrō.

quietness, 1. *n.* fȳclì.

quietude, 1. *n.* fȳclì.

quite, 1. *adv.* jy.

R

rabbit, 1. *n.* lìcxa.

radio, 1. *n.* clèplo.

rage, 1. *n.* makfũ.

rageful, 1. *adj.* makfuxũ.

railroad, 1. *n.* rakajõ.

rain, 1. *n.* mý.

rainforest, 1. *n.* mymajẽ.

rainy, 1. *adj.* mýxù.

raise, 1. *v.* {m̀} xoũ (lift up); 2. *v.* {m̀} muỳ (children, etc); 3. *v.*{m̀} cuỹ (mention s.th.).

raised, 1. *adj.* xomũ (lifted up); 2. *adj.* mùmy (reared).

rake, 1. *n.* sàpy.

range, 1. *n.* ló (oven); 2. *n.* mō (of numbers, options, etc); 3. **shooting range** *n.* pricxé.

rapids, 1. *n.* fikrá.

rare, 1. *adj.* nĩ.

rarely, 1. *adv.* nirõ.

rarity, 1. *n.* niclĩ.

raspberry, 1. *n.* xéfènú.

rat, 1. *n.* clésē.

rate, 1. *n.* nynũ.

rather, 1. *adv.* jy (quite); 2. **rather than** *comp.* fòklé; 3. *prep.* fòklé; 4. **but rather** *conj.* fẽ.

raw, 1. *adj.* prí.

re-experience, 1. *v.* {z̃} ẹprou̯.

reach, 1. *v.* {m̀} suó (for s.th.); 2. *v.* {j} nuá (arrive at).

reachable, 1. *adj.* ja̱su̱jó.

read, 1. *adj.* simõ; 2. *v.* {ḿ, m̀, m̃, ñ} siõ.

reader, 1. *n.* sikõ.

readied, 1. *adj.* prìnu̱mo̱.

readily, 1. *adv.* prìro̱.

readiness, 1. *n.* prìclí.

reading, 1. *n.* sisõ.

ready, 1. *adj.* prì; 2. *v.* {m̀, Í} prìnuo̱.

real, 1. *adj.* cíxù.

reality, 1. *n.* cí; 2. **in reality** *adv.* múrō (in truth).

realization, 1. *n.* cxòsí.

realize, 1. *v.* {m̀, Í} cxoï̆ (effectuate).

really, 1. *adv.* nūjè (very).

reappear, 1. *v.* {Í} ẹcxuó.

reappearance, 1. *n.* ẹcxúsō.

reapply, 1. *v.* {v̀} ēsriă (for e.g. recompense); 2. *v.* {m̀} ēsriă (to e.g. a job).

reared, 1. *adj.* mùmy̱ (raised).

rearrange, 1. *v.* {m̀, m̃} ẹkruó.

rearranged, 1. *adj.* ẹkrúmō.

reason, 1. *n.* srò (logic); 2. *n.* plỹ (impetus).

reasonable, 1. *adj.* sròxú.

rebuild, 1. *v.* {ḿ, m̀, m̃} ēcxeò.

rebuilt, 1. *adj.* ēcxèmo̱.

recall, 1. *v.* {ź, ż, z̃} psyĭ.

receipt, 1. *n.* cèsy̱ (receiving).

receive, 1. *v.* {g̃} cey̆.

receiver, 1. *n.* cèky̱.

received, 1. *adj.* cèmy̱; 2. *adj.* psumõ (understood).

recency, 1. *adj.* kfỹclì.

recent, 1. *adj.* kfỹ.

recently, 1. *adv.* kfỹrō.

recipe, 1. *n.* plīklē.

reclaim, 1. *v.* {m̀} ēniǎ (e.g. as property).

reclaimed, 1. *adj.* ēnìmá.

reclamation, 1. *n.* ēnìsá.

recognition, 1. *n.* psy̲si̲ (acknowledgement).

recognizable, 1. *adj.* ja̲kli̲jy̲.

recognize, 1. *v.* {m̀} psy̲i̲ (acknowledge); 2. *v.* {ž} kliy̲ (s.o./s.th. is familiar to s.o.); 3. *v.* {ž̀} kliy̲ (*propositions*).

recognized, 1. *adj.* psy̲mi̲.

recollect, 1. *v.* {ź, ż, ž̃} psy̌ (remember).

recollected, 1. *adj.* psỳmí (remembered).

reconnect, 1. *v.* {m̀, ǹ} ēcluǎ.

reconsider, 1. *v.* {ż, ž̃} e̲kuó.

record, 1. *n.* co̲si̲; 2. *v.* {m̀, m̃} coi̲.

recorder, 1. *n.* co̲ki̲.

recording, 1. *n.* co̲si̲.

recount, 1. *v.* {m̀, m̀, m̃, ǹ, ñ} e̲miâ (count again).

recreate, 1. *v.* {m̀, m̃} e̲saû.

recreation, 1. *n.* e̲sásù.

rectal, 1. *adj.* pyji̲ní.

rectangle, 1. *n.* krìkfi̲.

rectangular, 1. *adj.* krìkfi̲xú.

rectum, 1. *n.* ji̲ní.

red, 1. *adj.* xé; 2. *n.* xékō.

redden, 1. *v.* {m̀, Í} xénuō.

redesign, 1. *v.* {m̀, m̃} e̲liô.

rediscover, 1. *v.* {m̀} ēxuě.

rediscovered, 1. *adj.* ēxùmé.

redness, 1. *n.* xéclì.

redraw, 1. *v.* {m̀, m̃, ṽ} ēreǒ.

reduce, 1. *v.* {m̀, Í} juy̌; 2. *v.* {v́, ṽ} juy̌ (by s.th.).

reducible, 1. *adj.* jājùjý.

reduction, 1. *n.* jùsý.

reef, 1. *n.* rìkla̲ kliprũ (coral).

reexamination, 1. *n.* ējùsé.

reexamine, 1. *v.* {m̀, m̃} ējuě.

refer, 1. *v.* {m̀, ǹ, ṽ} kfua̲.

reference, 1. *n.* kf<u>u</u>s<u>a</u>.

refire, 1. *v.* {m̀, Í} ēryŭsriò (e.g. a cannon, artillery).

reflect, 1. *v.* {ḿ, m̀} clió; 2. *v.* {j̃} clió (at s.th.).

reflected, 1. *adj.* clímō.

reflection, 1. *n.* clísō.

reform, 1. *v.* {Í} <u>e</u>kre<u>o</u> (come into shape); 3. *v.* {v́} <u>e</u>kre<u>o</u> (into s.th.).

refusal, 1. *n.* prùsá.

refuse, 1. *v.* {m̀, m̃, g̀} pruă.

regard, 1. *v.* {m̀} mué (have to do with s.th.); 2. *v.* {ṽ} pseĭ (consider s.o./s.th. as s.th.).

regarding, 1. *prep.* ròlú (*topic*).

register, 1. *n.* c<u>a</u>pú (till).

reimagine, 1. *v.* {ž} <u>e</u>ke<u>o</u> (s.o./s.th.); 2. *v.* {ż} <u>e</u>ke<u>o</u> (*propositions*).

relate, 1. *v.* {v́} jiỳ (to s.th. abstractly); 2. *v.* {v́} kfuā (familial).

relationship, 1. *n.* sēklū.

relative, 1. *adj.* sỳklú.

relatively, 1. *adv.* sỳklúrō.

relaunch, 1. *v.* {m̀, Í} ēryŭsriò (e.g. a rocket, a missile).

release, 1. *n.* kf<u>i</u>s<u>o</u>; 2. *v.* {m̀, Í, Ì, j̃} kfi<u>o</u>.

relevance, 1. *n.* nàp<u>u</u>clí.

relevant, 1. *adj.* nàp<u>u</u>.

religion, 1. *n.* m<u>a</u>cr<u>i</u>c<u>i</u>.

religious, 1. *adj.* m<u>a</u>cr<u>i</u>cixú (pious) ; 2. *adj.* pym<u>a</u>cr<u>i</u>c<u>i</u> (relating to religion).

religiously, 1. *adv.* m<u>a</u>cr<u>i</u>cixúrō.

relive, 1. *v.* {ž} <u>e</u>pro<u>u</u>.

rely, 1. *v.* {m̀, ż} sraī (depend on s.o./s.th.).

remain, 1. *v.* {Í, Ì} cxiõ (stay; *compounds*); 2. *v.* {Í, Ì} cuê (be left).

remainder, 1. *n.* cúsè.

remake, 1. *v.* {m̀, m̃} ēroŭ; 2. *n.* ēròsú.

remarkable, 1. *adj.* kfújè.

remeasure, 1. *v.* {m̀, Í, ṽ} <u>e</u>xiâ.

remedy, 1. *n.* pūnìx<u>u</u>.

remember, 1. *v.* {ź, ż, z̃} psyĭ.

remembered, 1. *adj.* psỳmí (recollected).

remembrance, 1. *n.* psỳsí.

removal, 1. *n.* klęsǫ.

remove, 1. *v.* {m̀, m̃, j̃} kleǫ (displace).

renal, 1. *adj.* py̆jýkrē.

rent, 1. *n.* ký.

rental, 1. *adj.* py̆ký.

repair, 1. *n.* frási; 2. *v.* {m̀, Í, v́, ṽ} fraî.

repaired, 1. *adj.* frámì.

repeat, 1. *v.* {m̀, ñ} jyù.

repeatable, 1. *adj.* jāj̄ȳjù.

repeated, 1. *adj.* jỳmų.

repetition, 1. *n.* jỳsų.

repetitive, 1. *adj.* jỳlųlę.

replace, 1. *v.* {m̀, Í, ṽ} kreó.

replaceable, 1. *adj.* jąkręjó.

replacement, 1. *n.* krésō.

replay, 1. *v.* {ḿ} ęroú (a game, etc); 2. *v.* {m̀, m̃} ępaį (music).

reply, 1. *n.* cxǫsų; 2. *v.* {m̀, ñ, ǵ} cxoų.

report, 1. *n.* cxisē̃ (formal complaint); 2. *n.* nįsǫ (e.g. in journalism, business, etc); 3. *v.* {m̀} cxiē̃ (formal complaint); 4. *v.* {m̀} niǫ (on s.th. as in journalism, business, etc).

represent, 1. *v.* {m̀, g̀} fraǐ (officially); 2. *v.* {ǹ} klyũ (symbolize).

representation, 1. *n.* klysũ (depiction, symbol); 2. *n.* fràsí (e.g. in government).

representative, 1. *n.* fràkí.

require, 1. *v.* {m̀, ǹ} liy̨.

requirement, 1. *n.* lįsy̨; 2. *n.* sècrį (condition).

reread, 1. *v.* {m̀, m̃, ñ} esiõ̃.

rescue, 1. *n.* cýsū; 2. *v.* {m̀, m̃} cyú (save s.o./s.th.); 2. *v.* {r̃} cyú (from s.th.).

research, 1. *n.* xó (scholarly).

researcher, 1. *n.* xóprà.

resell, 1. *v.* {m̀, m̃} ēciȳ.

resend, 1. *v.* {m̀, ñ} ēniè (s.th. to s.o.); 2. *v.* {j̃} ēniè (s.th. s.w.).

reside, 1. *v.* {ì} cley̌ (s.w.).

resilience, 1. *n.* kaclĩ.

resilient, 1. *adj.* kã.

resource, 1. *n.* crópsà.

resourceful, 1. *adj*. crópsàxú.

resources, 1. *n*. crópsà.

respect, 1. *n*. kfùsǫ; 2. *v*. {m̀, z̃} kfuò (s.o./s.th.); 3. *v*. {z̀} kfuò (*propositions*).

respectable, 1. *adj*. jākfūjò.

respected, 1. *adj*. kfùmǫ.

respectful, 1. *adj*. kfùlǫlę.

respiration, 1. *n*. làsí.

respiratory, 1. *adj*. pȳlàsí.

respond, 1. *v*. {m̀, ñ, ǵ} cxoų.

response, 1. *n*. cxǫsų.

responsibility, 1. *n*. nìxý.

responsible, 1. *adj*. nìxýxù.

rest, 1. *n*. jèsị (relaxation); 2. *v*. {m̀, Í, Ì, j} jeì.

restate, 1. *v*. {m̀, ñ} ēxiǒ (declare);

restaurant, 1. *n*. frǫsǫ.

restauranteur, 1. *n*. frǫsǫprá.

rested, 1. *adj*. jèlịlę.

result, 1. *n*. kryrǫ; 2. *n*. másū (outcome); 3. *v*. {Í} maú; 4. *v*. {m̀} maú (in s.th.).

resultant, 1. *adj*. kryrǫxú.

resultative, 1. *adj*. pykryrǫ.

resurrect, 1. *v*. {m̀, Í, ṽ} kriá.

resurrected, 1. *adj*. krímā.

resurrection, 1. *n*. krísā.

retard, 1. *v*. {m̀, m̀, Í, ṽ} crynuǫ.

retardation, 1. *n*. crynụsǫ (slowing down).

retarded, 1. *adj*. crynụmǫ (slowed down).

retell, 1. *v*. {m̀} ēmaū.

rethink, 1. *v*. {z̀, z̃} ękuó.

retrain, 1. *v*. {m̀, m̀} ęsryí.

retrained, 1. *adj*. ęsrýmī.

return, 1. *n*. júsȳ (e.g. to a store); 2. *v*. {m̀, Í, Ì} nuý (oneself s.w.); 3. *v*. {m̀, j̃} juý (s.th.).

returnable, 1. *adj*. jajụjý.

returned, 1. *adj*. júmȳ (an object).

reusable, 1. *adj*. ęjąplújò.

reuse, 1. *v*. {ṽ} ępluô; 2. *n*. ęplúsò.

reused, 1. *adj.* e̠plúmò.

reveal, 1. *v.* {m̀, ǹ, Í} pryũ.

revealed, 1. *adj.* prymũ.

revelation, 1. *n.* prysũ.

revisit, 1. *v.* {m̀} ēpyǔ (people); 2. *v.* {j} ēpyǔ (locations).

rewatch, 1. *v.* {m̀, m̃} ēkfuy̌.

rewatchable, 1. *n.* ējākfùjý.

rewrite, 1. *v.* {m̀, m̃, ñ} ēpsey̌; 2. *n.* ēpsèsý.

rewritten, 1. *adj.* ēpsèmý.

rib cage, 1. *n.* cóklù.

ribbon, 1. *n.* melỹ.

rice, 1. *n.* cu̠ku̠.

rich, 1. *adj.* kfō (wealthy).

riddle, 1. *n.* pùkra̠.

rifle, 1. *n.* frāsrò.

right, 1. *adj.* frã (morally); 2. *adj.* mú (true); 3. *adj.* clā (side or direction); 4. *adv.* clā (to the right); 5. *n.* clā (side).

rightly, 1. *adv.* frarō (morally); 2. *adv.* múrō (truly, correctly).

ring, 1. *n.* prù (jewelry); 2. *v.* {m̀, ǹ, Í} cxaí (produce sound).

rise, 1. *n.* plùso̠; 2. *v.* {Í, v́} pluò.

risk, 1. *n.* srí.

risky, 1. *adj.* síxù.

rival, 1. *n.* fryc̠o̠.

river, 1. *n.* mē̠plỹ.

rivet, 1. *n.* kòfro̠.

road, 1. *n.* jõ.

roast, 1. *n.* kōsūfìso̠; 2. *v.* {ḿ, m̀, m̃} koūfiò.

roasted, 1. *adj.* kōmūfìmo̠.

robe, 1. *n.* kēprè.

rock, 1. *n.* cxõ.

rocky, 1. *adj.* cxoxũ.

role, 1. *n.* murã.

roll, 1. *n.* sra̠si̠; 2. *v.* {m̀, Í, Ì, j̃} sra̠i̠.

roof, 1. *n.* fē̠crì; 2. **roof of mouth** *n.* fólū.

room, 1. *n.* cã.

root, 1. *n.* fí.

rope, 1. *n.* sǫ.

rotate, 1. *v.* {ḿ, m̀, Í} neỳ.

rotated, 1. *adj.* nèmy̱.

rotation, 1. *n.* nèsy̱.

rough, 1. *adj.* clá (surface); 2. *adj.* móplò (not gentle).

roughly, 1. *adv.* móplòrǫ (not gently); 2. *adv.* ácē (approximately).

roughness, 1. *n.* cláclì (surface).

round, 1. *adj.* cxy̱; 2. *adj.* jùfri̱xú (circular); 3. *adj.* jìkúxù (spherical).

roundness, 1. *n.* cxy̱clí.

route, 1. *n.* kì; 2. *n.* xy̱ká (course).

royalty, 1. *n.* krēnàsa̱.

ruby, 1. *n.* frū; 2. *adj.* frūxù.

rude, 1. *adj.* nō (unkind).

rudely, 1. *adv.* nōrō (unkindly).

rudeness, 1. *n.* nōclì.

rug, 1. *n.* kàly̱.

rule, 1. *n.* cxà (law).

ruler, 1. *n.* krīfō (for measurement).

run, 1. *v.* {ḿ, r̀} meȳ (jog); 2. *v.* {m̀} pliâ (manage); 3. *n.* mēsȳ (athletic); 4. *adj.* plímà (managed).

runner, 1. *n.* mēkȳ (athletic).

rural, 1. *adj.* crōnùxú.

S

sacred, 1. *adj.* py̱cí.

sacredness, 1. *n.* py̱cíclì.

saddle, 1. *n.* līmī.

safe, 1. *adj.* ca̱; 2. *adj.* nūklèxú.

safely, 1. *adv.* ca̱rǫ.

safety, 1. *n.* nūklè.

said, 1. *adj.* plōmī (mentioned).

sail, 1. *n.* psósū; 2. *v.* {m̀, Í} psoú.

sailed, 1. *adj.* psómū.

sailor, 1. *n.* psókū.

salesman, 1. *n.* cīkȳ.

salesperson, 1. *n.* cīkȳ.

saleswoman, 1. *n.* cīkȳ.

saliva, 1. *n.* crīsȳ.

salivate, 1. *v.* {ź} criȳ.

salivation, 1. *n.* crīsȳ.

sallet, 1. *n.* mòkró.

salt, 1. *n.* srỹ.

saltwater, 1. *n.* srȳxō.

salty, 1. *adj.* sryxũ.

sand, 1. *n.* psȳlȳ.

sandy, 1. *adj.* psȳlȳxù.

sane, 1. *adj.* psú.

sanity, 1. *n.* psúclì.

sap, 1. *n.* rísrī.

sapphire, 1. *n.* òcxé; 2. *adj.* òcxéxù (made of sapphire).

sash, 1. *n.* kẹkú.

satchel, 1. *n.* prẹpọ.

satellite, 1. *n.* mạplíjē.

satiated, 1. *adj.* kfý.

satiation, 1. *n.* kfýclì.

save, 1. *v.* {m̀, m̃} cyú (rescue s.o./s.th.); 2. *v.* {r̃} cyú (from s.th.).

savings, 1. *n.* rẹ.

savory, 1. *adj.* plúclì.

saw, 1. *n.* kȳ.

say, 1. *v.* {m̀, ñ} ploī.

saying, 1. *n.* xōpȳ (proverb).

scalar, 1. *adj.* pysọjụ.

scale, 1. *n.* sọjụ (for measurement); 2. *n.* prỹ (organic).

scalp, 1. *n.* sé.

scaly, 1. *adj.* pryxũ.

scam, 1. *n.* plùsé; 2. *v.* {m̀, Í} pluě.

scammer, 1. *n.* plùké.

scarce, 1. *adj.* pséplōxù.

scarcity, 1. *n.* pséplō.

scared, 1. *adj.* nēlūlē.

scarf, 1. *n.* kfè.

scene, 1. *n.* clĩ (drama).

scenery, 1. *n.* xēclù.

scenic, 1. *adj.* clixũ.

schedule, 1. *n.* cxù.

scholarly, 1. *adj.* xóxù.

scholastic, 1. *adj.* py̆fra̰.

school, 1. *n.* fra̰.

science, 1. *n.* nimũ.

scientific, 1. *adj.* pynimũ.

scientist, 1. *n.* nimuprã.

scissors, 1. *n.* làkla̰.

scorpion, 1. *n.* fèlḛ.

scratch, 1. *n.* sràsí; 2. *v.* {m̀, Í} sraĭ.

scratched, 1. *adj.* sràmí.

scratchy, 1. *adj.* sràlílē.

scream, 1. *n.* késỳ; 2. *v.* {m̀} keŷ.

screen, 1. *n.* cràpro̰ (display).

screw, 1. *n.* sùní (building material).

screwdriver, 1. *n.* sùnḭmúkȳ.

scrotum, 1. *n.* xḛplṵ.

scythe, 1. *n.* mýxā.

seascape, 1. *n.* krṵmúxēclù.

seam, 1. *n.* cró.

search, 1. *n.* fìsḛ; 2. *v.* {ḿ} fiè; 3. *v.* {j} fiè (a location or thing); 4. *v.* {r̃} fiè (s.w. for s.th.).

season, 1. *n.* ālèrḭ.

seasonal, 1. *adj.* ālèrḭxú.

second, 1. *adj.* pipĩ.

secondhand, 1. *adj.* srà.

secret, 1. *adj.* xḛklixú; 2. *n.* xḛklḭ.

secretive, 1. *adj.* xḛklixú.

section, 1. *n.* cxō.

sectional, 1. *adj.* pȳcxō.

sectioned, 1. *adj.* cxōxù (segregated).

secure, 1. *adj.* kàcṵxú.

security, 1. *n.* kàcṵ.

see, 1. *v.* {ȥ} riǒ (s.o./s.th.); 2. *v.* {ż} riǒ (*propositions*).

seed, 1. *n.* kfa̱.

seek, 1. *v.* {m̀} fiè (s.th.).

seeker, 1. *n.* fìke̱.

seem, 1. *v.* {Í} kreú (*propositions, compounds*).

seen, 1. *adj.* rìmó (observed).

segregated, 1. *adj.* cxōxù (sectioned).

seldom, 1. *adv.* nirõ (rarely).

self-evident, 1. *adj.* kfoxũ.

sell, 1. *v.* {ḿ, m̀, m̃} ciȳ.

seller, 1. *n.* cīkȳ (salesperson).

semen, 1. *n.* kli̱.

send, 1. *v.* {m̀, ñ} niè (s.th. to s.o.); 2. *v.* {ĵ} niè (s.th. s.w.).

sender, 1. *n.* nìke̱.

sensation, 1. *n.* rúsè.

sense, 1. *n.* crē (possible meaning).

sensitive, 1. *adj.* crēmē (considerate).

sensitivity, 1. *n.* crēmēclì (consideration).

sent, 1. *adj.* nìme̱.

separable, 1. *adj.* jācrējù.

separate, 1. *v.* {m̀, Í} creù; 2. *v.* {v́, ṽ} creù (from s.th.).

separated, 1. *adj.* crèmu̱.

separation, 1. *n.* crèsu̱.

series, 1. *n.* psárì (items in sequence).

serious, 1. *adj.* réklù.

seriously, 1. *adv.* réklùro̱.

seriousness, 1. *n.* réklùclí.

sermon, 1. *n.* crúsè.

servant, 1. *n.* krukõ.

serve, 1. *v.* {ḿ, m̀, ñ} raì (food, etc); 2. *v.* {m̀} kruõ (obey).

served, 1. *adj.* ràmi̱ (food, drinks, etc); 2. *adj.* krumõ (obeyed).

server, 1. *n.* ràki̱ (waiter, waitress).

service, 1. *n.* krāklē (military, etc).

set, 1. *v.* {ĵ} freý (put); 2. **set down** *v.* {m̀} freý.

setting, 1. *n.* pléfrō (environs).

settle, 1. *v.* {m̀, Í} kroũ (resolve agreeably); 2. *v.* {Í, Ì} xiè (as powder, sediment, etc).
settled, 1. *adj.* kromũ.
settlement, 1. *n.* krosũ.
seven, 1. *num.* psi̱.
seventh, 1. *adj.* psi̱psi̱.
seventieth, 1. *adj.* psi̱pa̱pa̱.
seventy, 1. *num.* psi̱pa̱.
sewer, 1. *n.* fe̱sí.
sex, 1. *n.* psà.
sexy, 1. *adj.* psàxú.
shadow, 1. *n.* celĩ.
shadowy, 1. *adj.* celixũ.
shake, 1. *v.* {m̀, ń, Í} psyĩ.
shaken, 1. *adj.* psymĩ.
shaking, 1. *n.* psysĩ.
shaky, 1. *adj.* psylilẽ.
shall, 1. *aux.* m̃.
shallow, 1. *adj.* plã (not deep); 2. *adj.* rēcrõxù (superficial).
shallowly, 1. *adv.* plarõ.
shallowness, 1. *n.* placlĩ.
shape, 1. *n.* psy̱.
share, 1. *v.* {m̀, Í} kreĩ; 2. *v.* {m̃, g̱, g̃} kreĩ (with s.o.).
shark, 1. *n.* ne̱fé.
sharp, 1. *adj.* xĩ; 2. *adj.* klèla̱ (clever).
sharpen, 1. *v.* {m̀, Í, v́, ṽ} xinuõ.
sharpened, 1. *adj.* xinumõ.
sharpener, 1. *n.* xinukõ.
sharpness, 1. *n.* xiclĩ; 2. *n.* klèla̱clí (cleverness).
shatter, 1. *v.* {m̀, ǹ, Í} preũjoũ.
shattered, 1. *adj.* prēmũjõmū.
shawl, 1. *n.* nùcá.
she, 1. *pn.* cì.
sheath, 1. *n.* psì.
sheep, 1. *n.* lȳrū.
shelf, 1. *n.* krēpĩ.

shell, 1. *n.* klí.

shield, 1. *n.* korĩ.

shimmer, 1. *n.* kfùsy̱; 2. *v.* {Í} kfuỳ.

shimmery, 1. *adj.* kfùly̱le̱.

shin, 1. *n.* pý.

shine, 1. *v.* {m̀, Í, v́, ṽ} ku̱nuo̱ (make shiny); 2. *v.* {Í} noì (make light); 3. *n.* nòsi̱ (e.g. of the sun).

shined, 1. *adj.* ku̱nu̱mo̱.

shining, 1. *n.* nòsi̱ (e.g. of the sun).

shiny, 1. *adj.* ku̱.

shirt, 1. *n.* cxé.

shock, 1. *n.* lò (of hay).

shoe, 1. *n.* krā.

shoestring, 1. *n.* kràca̱ri̱.

shoot, 1. *v.* {m̀, ṽ} srau̱; 2. *v.* {ñ} srau̱ (s.th. at s.o.).

shooter, 1. *n.* sra̱ku̱.

shopkeeper, 1. *n.* kle̱prá.

shopping, 1. *n.* cru̱já (groceries).

short, 1. *adj.* pà (not long); 2. *adj.* cxójē (stout).

shortbow, 1. *n.* pāklà.

shortbowman, 1. *n.* pāklàni̱.

shorten, 1. *v.* {m̀, Í, v́, ṽ} pànuo̱.

shortened, 1. *adj.* pànu̱mo̱.

shortness, 1. *n.* pàclí.

shortstaff, 1. *n.* pàcle̱.

shortsword, 1. *n.* pàpru̱.

shortswordsman, 1. *n.* pàpru̱ni̱.

shot, 1. *n.* sra̱su̱ (of a gun, etc.).

should, 1. *aux.* r̃.

shoulder, 1. *n.* palỹ.

shout, 1. *v.* {ḿ, m̀, ñ} peí; 2. *v.* {ġ} peí (at s.th.).

shovel, 1. *n.* ri̱fe̱.

show, 1. *v.* {m̀, ġ, ñ} kfaũ; 2. *v.* {m̀, ñ} kfaũ (*propositions*) 3. **show off** *v.* {m̀, ñ} kfaũ (present); 4. **show off** *v.* {ḿ} kliè (brag); 5. **show-off** *n.* klìke̱ (braggart).

shown, 1. *adj.* kfamũ (demonstrated).

shrug, 1. *n.* pìsó; 2. *v.* {ḿ, ǵ} piǒ (at s.o./s.th.).

shut, 1. *adj.* clāmī; 2. *v.* {m̀, m̃} muā (close s.th. vertically planar, e.g. a door); 3. *v.* {m̀, m̃, ǹ, ĺ} claī (close s.th. horizontally planar, e.g. a chest).

sibling, 1. *n.* klį̀ja.

sick, 1. *adj.* sā̃ (ill); 2. *adj.* ríxū (disgusting).

sicken, 1. *v.* {ż, ẓ} sanuõ.

sickened, 1. *adj.* sanumõ.

sickle, 1. *n.* sypé.

sickness, 1. *n.* saclī̃ (illness).

side, 1. *n.* krùprý.

sigh, 1. *n.* jūsȳ; 2. *v.* {ḿ, r̀, ź, ẓ} juȳ (at s.th.).

sight, 1. *n.* sę.

sign, 1. *n.* jé.

significance, 1. *n.* xūlēlēclì.

significant, 1. *adj.* xūlēlē.

significantly, 1. *adv.* xūlēlērō.

signify, 1. *v.* {m̀} xuē.

silver, 1. *n.* cife; 2. *adj.* cifexú (made of silver).

silvertongued, 1. *adj.* mèpu.

similar, 1. *adj.* psocrē̃; 2. **be similar to...** *v.* {ǹ} cliǒ.

similarity, 1. *n.* psocreclī̃.

similarly, 1. *adv.* psocrerõ.

simple, 1. *adj.* prànú.

simplicity, 1. *n.* prànúclì.

simplify, 1. *v.* {m̀, ǹ, ĺ, v́, ṽ} prànúnuō.

simplified, 1. *adj.* prànúnūmō.

simply, 1. *adv.* prànúrō.

since, 1. *comp.* krē̃ (temporal); 2. *prep.* krē̃ (temporal); 3. *comp.* kfú (because).

sinew, 1. *n.* sȳkfò.

sinewy, 1. *adj.* sȳkfòxú.

sing, 1. *v.* {ḿ, m̀, m̃} pleò.

singer, 1. *n.* plèko.

single, 1. *adj.* clē (relationship status); 2. *adj.* réxī (one).

sink, 1. *n.* nèklu (basin); 2. **bathroom sink** *n.* clūlū nèklu; 3. **kitchen sink** *n.* lèkfu nèklu; 4. *v.* {m̀, ǹ, ĺ, v́, ṽ} pia (e.g. a boat).

sister, 1. *n.* rýnì.

sit, 1. *v.* {ḿ} cxaì (down); 2. *v.* {j} cxaì (s.w.).

site, 1. *n.* mā (place).

situation, 1. *n.* jypla̱ (circumstances).

situational, 1. *adj.* py̱jypla̱ (circumstantial).

six, 1. *num.* frũ.

sixth, 1. *adj.* frufrũ.

sixtieth, 1. *adj.* frupapã.

sixty, 1. *num.* frupã.

sizable, 1. *adj.* fy̱xú.

size, 1. *n.* fy̱.

skeletal, 1. *adj.* pȳrūklò.

skeleton, 1. *n.* rūklò.

skewer, 1. *n.* jófē.

skill, 1. *n.* klỹ.

skilled, 1. *adj.* klyxũ.

skillful, 1. *adj.* klyxũ.

skin, 1. *n.* sró; 2. *n.* kípsō (hide).

skinny, 1. *adj.* nȳlò.

skirt, 1. *n.* pȳfù.

skull, 1. *n.* jū.

sky, 1. *n.* xẽ.

slab, 1. *n.* lýklū.

sledgehammer, 1. *n.* lūcìkrí.

sleep, 1. *n.* xésȳ; 2. *v.* {Í} xeý (be asleep); 3. *v.* {ḿ} xeý (go to sleep); 4. *v.* {ḿ, ń} leî (turn in).

sleeper, 1. *n.* xékȳ.

sleepily, 1. *adv.* kūrō.

sleepy, 1. *adj.* kū.

sleeve, 1. *n.* frò.

slight, 1. *adj.* srū.

slightly, 1. *adv.* srūrō.

slow, 1. *adj.* cry̱; 2. **slow down** *v.* {ḿ, m̀, Í, ṽ} cry̱nuo̱.

slowed down, 1. *adj.* cry̱nu̱mo̱.

slowly, 1. *adv.* cry̱ro̱.

slug, 1. *n.* cu̱sru̱ (animal).

small, 1. *adj.* jè.

smart, 1. *adj.* prō; 2. *adj.* klèl̠a (clever).

smile, 1. *n.* clésū; 2. *v.* {m̄} cleú; 3. *v.* {r̄} cleú (at s.o./s.th.).

smiley, 1. *adj.* clélūlē.

smith, 1. *v.* {m̄, m̀, v̀, ṽ} leí.

smithing, 1. *n.* lésī.

smoke, 1. *n.* clò.

smoky, 1. *adj.* clòxú.

smooth, 1. *adj.* srỳ (surface); 2. *adj.* mèpu̠ (silvertongued).

smoothness, 1. *n.* srỳclí (surface).

snack, 1. *n.* òre̠.

snail, 1. *n.* àcri̠.

snake, 1. *n.* fāsā.

sneeze, 1. *n.* sùsy̠; 2. *v.* {j̠, ź} suỳ (on s.th.).

sneezy, 1. *adj.* sùlyle̠.

snore, 1. *n.* klēsū; 2. *v.* {Í} kleū.

snout, 1. *n.* mi̠.

snow, 1. *n.* rākē.

snowy, 1. *adj.* rākēxù.

so, 1. *adv.* jy̠ (quite); 2. *adv.* nỳ (thus); 3. *conj.* nỳ; 4. **so that** *comp.* nỳkle̠.

sociable, 1. *adj.* rūnàxú.

social, 1. *adj.* rūnàxú.

societal, 1. *adj.* pȳrūnà.

society, 1. *n.* rūnà.

sock, 1. *n.* cré.

sofa, 1. *n.* xénȳ.

soft, 1. *adj.* kfy̠ (to touch).

soften, 1. *v.* {m̀, Í, v́, ṽ} kfy̠nuo̠.

softened, 1. *adj.* kfy̠nu̠mo̠.

softness, 1. *n.* kfy̠clí (to touch).

soil, 1. *n.* klā (dirt).

solar, 1. *adj.* pyjú.

solar system, 1. *n.* júpsūxī.

sold, 1. *adj.* cīmȳ.

soldier, 1. *n.* kru̠pýprà.

sole, 1. *n.* klo̠la̠.

solstice, 1. *n.* moklỹ.

solution, 1. *n.* prásī (e.g. to a problem).

solve, 1. *v.* {m̀, m̃, Í, ṽ} praí.

solved, 1. *adj.* prámī.

some, 1. *det.* rỳ; 2. *pn.* rỳ.

somebody, 1. *pn.* rỳni̱.

somehow, 1. *adv.* pi̱jé.

someone, 1. *pn.* rỳni̱.

something, 1. *pn.* rỳcṵ.

sometimes, 1. *adv.* rȳfrà.

somewhat, 1. *adv.* cla̱rẹ.

somewhere, 1. *adv.* rȳmā; 2. *pn.* rȳmā; 3. **somewhere else** *adv.* rȳmā prò.

son, 1. *n.* fòny.

song, 1. *n.* plèso̱.

soon, 1. *adv.* ní.

sorrow, 1. *n.* nāpā.

sorrowful, 1. *adj.* nāpāxù.

sort, 1. *v.* {m̀, Í, ṽ} meỳ (order); 2. *v.* {m̀, Í} sraû (organize).

sorting, 1. *n.* mèsy̱ (order).

sought, 1. *adj.* fìmẹ (after, for).

sound, 1. *n.* mó; 2. *v.* {m̀, Í} preū.

soup, 1. *n.* mù.

soupy, 1. *adj.* mùxú.

source, 1. *n.* có (origin).

south, 1. *adj.* jī; 2. *adv.* jī; 3. *n.* jī.

southern, 1. *adj.* jīxù.

southward, 1. *adv.* jī.

space, 1. *n.* jo̱kry̱ (area).

spacecraft, 1. *n.* júklūkù.

spatial, 1. *adj.* py̱jo̱kry̱.

speak, 1. *v.* {ḿ, m̀, ǵ} ploǐ.

speakable, 1. *adj.* jāplòjí.

speaker, 1. *n.* plòkí.

spear, 1. *n.* cóklȳ.

specific, 1. *adj.* càry̱.

specifically, 1. *adv.* càryro̱.

speech, 1. *n.* plòsí.
speed, 1. *n.* meprẽ.
spend, 1. *v.* {m̀} sraū.
spender, 1. *n.* srākū (of money).
spent, 1. *adj.* srāmū.
sphere, 1. *n.* jìkú.
spherical, 1. *adj.* jìkúxù.
spider, 1. *n.* nācxì.
spiderweb, 1. *n.* clã.
spinach, 1. *n.* cxa̱lú.
spine, 1. *n.* crýjò.
spinning wheel, 1. *n.* psỳni̱.
spire, 1. *n.* mȳ.
spit, 1. *n.* crēsī; 2. *v.* {ḿ, m̀} creī.
splash, 1. *n.* ce̱si̱; 2. *v.* {ñ, Ì, Ĩ, j} cei̱.
spoken, 1. *adj.* plòmí.
spoon, 1. *n.* lē.
sport, 1. *n.* psōfrū.
sports, 1. *n.* psōfrū.
sporty, 1. *adj.* psōfrūxù.
spot, 1. *n.* kràmy̱ (mark).
spotted, 1. *adj.* kràmy̱xú.
spotty, 1. *adj.* kràmy̱xú.
spring, 1. *n.* rùlo̱ (season).
square, 1. *n.* frí; 2. *adj.* fríxù; 3. *adj.* cūplī (deals settled).
staff, 1. *n.* psùpre̱ (personnel); 2. *n.* cle̱ (wielded stick).
stage, 1. *n.* krīkè (theater); 2. *n.* rèclý (phase).
stalk, 1. *v.* {m̀, Í} kloipiã.
stalker, 1. *n.* klokipikã.
stalking, 1. *n.* klosipisã.
stand, 1. *v.* {ḿ} fruē (up); 2. *v.* {j} fruē (s.w.); 3. *v.* {m̀, j̃} fruē (prop s.th. up).
standard, 1. *n.* psýplō; 2. *adj.* psýplōxù.
star, 1. *n.* jú.
star system, 1. *n.* júpsūxī.
start, 1. *n.* pu̱se̱ (beginning); 2. *v.* {m̀, m̃} pue̱ (s.o./s.th.); 3. **start to** *aux.* ñ.

started, 1f. *adj.* p̲u̲m̲e̲ (begun).

starvation, 1. *n.* klìsy̲.

starve, 1. *v.* {m̀, Í, ź} kliỳ.

starved, 1. *adj.* klìmy̲.

state, 1. *n.* kl̲u̲p̲a̲ (sovereignty); 2. *n.* luxã (status); 3. *v.* {m̀, ñ} xiǒ (declare); 4. *v.* {m̀} sriō (assert, claim); 5. *v.* {m̀, ñ} ploī (say).

stated, 1. *adj.* xìmó (declared).

statement, 1. *adj.* xìsó (declaration).

statue, 1. *n.* līkù.

statuesque, 1. *adj.* līkùxú.

statuette, 1. *n.* līkùn̲u̲.

status, 1. *n.* luxã.

stay, 1. *v.* {Í, Ì} cxiõ (*compounds*); 2. *v.* {ḿ, m̀} foǔ (stop).

steel, 1. *n.* mỳ; 2. *adj.* mỳxú.

stellar, 1. *adj.* pyjú.

stem, 1. *n.* crõ.

step, 1. *n.* psõ (footstep).

stern, 1. *adj.* srẽ.

sternly, 1. *adv.* srerõ.

steward, 1. *n.* rēkī; 2. *v.* {m̀, m̃, Í} reī.

stewardess, 1. *n.* rēkī.

stewardship, 1. *n.* rēsī.

stick, 1. *n.* klõ (branch).

still, 1. *adj.* ìmy̲ (motionless); 2. *adv.* ìmy̲r̲o̲ (motionlessly); 3. *adv.* òcr̲i̲ (yet).

sting, 1. *n.* kúsȳ; 2. *v.* {m̀, Í} kuý.

stinger, 1. *n.* kúkȳ.

stock, 1. *n.* kf̲o̲fr̲u̲ (inventory).

stole, 1. *n.* frāfè.

stomach, 1. *n.* rèc̲i̲; 2. **stomach acid** *n.* pó (bile).

stone, 1. *adj.* cxoxũ (made of stone); 2. *n.* cxõ.

stool, 1. *n.* lákà (chair).

stop, 1. *v.* {ḿ, m̀} foǔ (halt).

stopped, 1. *adj.* fòmú.

store, 1. *n.* kl̲e̲.

storied, 1. *adj.* kò.

storm, 1. *n.* nìsy; 2. *v.* {Ø} niỳ.

story, 1. *n.* ka̠sa̠.

stout, 1. *adj.* cxójē (short).

straight, 1. *adj.* kùpe̠.

straighten, 1. *v.* {m̀, Í} kùpe̠nuo̠.

straightened, 1. *adj.* kùpe̠nu̠mo̠.

strange, 1. *adj.* prùni̠.

strangely, 1. *adv.* prùniro̠.

strangeness, 1. *n.* prùni̠clí.

strap, 1. *n.* ju̠sá.

strategic, 1. *adj.* pyplo̠cló (relating to strategy); 2. *adj.* plo̠clóxù (calculated).

strategist, 1. *n.* plo̠clóprà.

strategy, 1. *n.* plo̠cló.

stream, 1. *n.* cu̠clú.

strength, 1. *n.* kràclí (physical).

strengthen, 1. *v.* {m̀, Í, ṽ} ktrànuo̠.

stress, 1. *n.* le̠.

stressed, 1. *adj.* le̠xú.

stretch, 1. *n.* clìsé; 2. *v.* {ḿ, m̀, ń, ǹ} cliě.

stretched, 1. *adj.* clìmé.

stretchy, 1. *adj.* clìlélē.

strict, 1. *adj.* srẽ (in behavior).

strictly, 1. *adv.* prāmē; 2. *adv.* srerõ (in behavior).

strictness, 1. *n.* sreclĩ (in behavior).

string, 1. *n.* ca̠ri̠.

stripe, 1. *n.* clinũ.

striped, 1. *adj.* clinuxũ.

strong, 1. *adj.* krà (physically); 2. *adj.* sāprà (in flavor, etc).

strongly, 1. *adv.* kràro̠ (physical); 2. *adv.* sāpràro̠ (flavor, etc).

structural, 1. *adj.* pȳkfàpo̠.

structure, 1. *n.* kfàpo̠.

structured, 1. *adj.* kfàpo̠xú.

stubborn, 1. *adj.* lìmi̠.

student, 1. *n.* klīkȳ; 2. *n.* cxú (pupil).

studio, 1. *n.* frújỳ.

studious, 1. *adj.* klīlȳlē.

studiously, 1. *adv.* klīlȳlērō.

studiousness, 1. *n.* klīlȳlēclì.

study, 1. *n.* klīsȳ (i.e. as a student); 2. *n.* xó (scholarly research); 3. *n.* kfàná (office); 4. *v.* {ḿ, m̀} kliȳ.

stung, 1. *n.* kúmȳ.

stupid, 1. *adj.* fẹ.

stupidity, 1. *n.* fẹclí.

stupidly, 1. *adv.* fẹrọ.

style, 1. *n.* núrù.

stylistic, 1. *adj.* pynúrù.

subject, 1. *n.* júprà (*topic*).

succeed, 1. *v.* {ḿ, v̀} raî (be successful); 2. *v.* {m̀} piã (come after).

success, 1. *n.* rásì.

successful, 1. *adj.* rálìlẹ.

successfully, 1. *adv.* rálìlẹrọ.

succession, 1. *n.* pisã.

successor, 1. *n.* pikã.

succulent, 1. *n.* lỳprụ.

sucker, 1. *n.* pralõ (organic).

sudden, 1. *adj.* lẽ.

suddenly, 1. *adv.* lerõ.

suffer, 1. *v.* {ź} liõ; 2. *v.* {ž} liõ (from s.th.).

sufferer, 1. *n.* likõ.

suffering, 1. *n.* lisõ.

sufficiency, 1. *n.* sópūclì.

sufficient, 1. *adj.* sópū.

sufficiently, 1. *adv.* sópūrō.

suffocate, 1. *v.* {ź} xyū.

suffocation, 1. *n.* xȳsū.

sugar, 1. *n.* jē.

sugary, 1. *adj.* jēxù.

suggest, 1. *v.* {m̀, ñ} kriȳ (propose); 2. *v.* {m̀, ñ} kfeí (imply); 3. *v.* {m̀} foũ (indicate).

suggested, 1. *adj.* krimȳ.

suggestion, 1. *n.* krisȳ.

suicidal, 1. *adj.* frísȳxù.

suicide, 1. *n.* frísȳ; 2. **commit suicide** *v.* {m̀} friý.

suit, 1. *n.* lúplȳ (formal clothing).

summer, 1. *n.* frùmí.

sun, 1. *n.* jú.

sundown, 1. *n.* jūcà.

sung, 1. *adj.* plèmo̱.

sunglasses, 1. *n.* ju̱clánì.

sunk, 1. *adj.* pi̱ma̱.

sunny, 1. *adj.* júxù.

sunrise, 1. *n.* ju̱fú.

sunset, 1. *n.* jūcà.

sunup, 1. *n.* ju̱fú.

superficial, 1. *adj.* pȳrēcrō (relating to surface); 2. *adj.* rēcrōxù (shallow).

supplied, 1. *adj.* fēmō.

supplier, 1. *n.* fēkō.

supply, 1. *n.* fēsō; 2. *v.* {m̀, m̃, g̱, g̃} feō.

support, 1. *n.* mu̱se̱ (of policy, etc); 2. *n.* cxosū (emotional, foundation, etc); 3. *v.* {m̀} mue̱ (be in favor of); 4. *v.* {g̱} cxoū (hold up, as e.g. scaffolding).

supported, 1. *adj.* mu̱me̱ (position, legislation); 2. *adj.* rìfro̱xú (i.e. by evidence); 3.*adj.* cxomū (of a foundation, financially, etc).

supporter, 1. *n.* mu̱ke̱ (of policy, etc); 2. *n.* cxokū (emotional, foundation, etc).

supportive, 1. *adj.* cxolulē̱.

suppose, 1. *v.* {m̀} lue̱; 2. **be supposed to** *aux.* m̀.

supposition, 1. *n.* lùsé (assumption).

surface, 1. *n.* rēcrō.

surgeon, 1. *n.* sipijoprã.

surgery, 1. *n.* sipijõ.

surgical, 1. *adj.* sipijoxū; 2. *adj.* pysipijõ (relating to surgery).

surprise, 1. *n.* mósì; 2. *v.* {m̀, z̃} moî (s.o.); 3. *v.* {z̀} moî (*propositions*).

surprised, 1. *adj.* mómì.

surprising, 1. *adj.* mólìle̱.

surprisingly, 1. *adv.* mólìle̱ro̱.

surrender, 1. *n.* kusõ; 2. *v.* {m̀, m̀, ź} kuõ.

surrendered, 1. *adj.* kumõ.

survival, 1. *n.* xāsū.

survive, 1. *v.* {m̋, m̀, ń, ǹ} xaū.

survivor, 1. *n.* xākū.

suspenders, 1. *n.* salĩ.

suspicious, 1. *adj.* plòl̲a̲.

suspiciously, 1. *adv.* plòl̲a̲r̲o̲.

swallow, 1. *v.* {m̋, m̀} poú.

swallowed, 1. *adj.* pómū.

swamp, 1. *n.* n̲e̲.

swear, 1. *n.* jásū (vow); 2. *v.* {m̋, m̀, ñ} jaú.

sweat, 1. *n.* n̲i̲s̲a̲; 2. *v.* {Í} ni̲a̲.

sweater, 1. *n.* pl̲a̲cr̲a̲.

sweaty, 1. *adj.* n̲i̲l̲a̲l̲e̲.

sweet, 1. *adj.* jà; 2. *adj.* jēxù (sugary).

sweeten, 1. *v.* {m̀, Í, v́, ṽ} jànu̲o̲.

sweetened, 1. *adj.* jànu̲mo̲.

sweetness, 1. *n.* jàclí.

swindle, 1. *n.* plùsé; 2. *v.* {m̀, Í} plu̯ě.

swindler, 1. *n.* plùké.

sword, 1. *n.* pr̲u̲.

swordsman, 1. *n.* pr̲u̲n̲i̲.

swordsmanship, 1. *n.* pr̲u̲xó.

sworn, 1. *adj.* jámū.

symbolize, 1. *v.* {ǹ} klyũ (represent).

symmetrical, 1. *adj.* ps̲a̲cíxù.

symmetrically, 1. *adv.* ps̲a̲cíxùr̲o̲.

symmetry, 1. *n.* ps̲a̲cí.

syringe, 1. *n.* mófĩnè.

system, 1. *n.* psūxī.

systematic, 1. *adj.* psūxīxù.

systematicity, 1. *n.* psūxīxùclí.

systemic, 1. *adj.* pȳpsūxī.

T

table, 1. *n.* cxẽ.

taiga, 1. *n.* lōrū.

tail, 1. *n.* crī; 2. **tail fin** *n.* ạmé.

take, 1. *v.* {m̀, m̃} cloĭ (remove, steal); 2. **take it (that...)** *v.* {m̀} riŷ (presume); 3. **take aim** *v.* {ḿ, m̀, v̀, ṽ} piò (at s.th.).

taken, 1. *adj.* clòmí (removed); 2. *adj.* prỳ (not single).

taker, 1. *n.* clòkí.

talisman, 1. *n.* mōrū.

talk, 1. *v.* {ḿ, ǵ̣} ploĭ.

talkative, 1. *adj.* plòlílē.

tall, 1. *adj.* júnì.

tame, 1. *adj.* kìmẹsrýmī; 2. *v.* {ḿ, m̀, Í} kièsryí.

tameable, 1. *adj.* jākījèsryjí.

tamed, 1. *adj.* kìmẹsrýmī.

tameness, 1. *n.* kìmẹsrýmīclì.

taming, 1. *n.* kìsẹsrýsī.

tangible, 1. *adj.* jākūjà.

tar, 1. *n.* ụnẹ.

tar pit, 1. *n.* ụnécèfỵ.

tardiness, 1. *n.* cèclí.

tardy, 1. *adj.* cè.

target, 1. *n.* psōsrē.

task, 1. *n.* mìklá.

taste, 1. *n.* késī; 2. *v.* {ǹ, z̃} keí.

taste-tester, 1. *n.* kékī.

tastiness, 1. *n.* késīxùclí.

tasty, 1. *adj.* késīxù.

taught, 1. *adj.* cxémỳ.

tax, 1. *n.* nụ.

tea, 1. *n.* kìrị.

teach, 1. *v.* {ḿ, m̀, m̃, g̣̀} cxeŷ.

teachable, 1. *adj.* jạcxéjỳ.

teacher, 1. *n.* cxékỳ.

tearful, 1. *adj.* clīlālē.

tearfully, 1. *adv.* clīlālērō.

technician, 1. *n.* krạkríprà.

technological, 1. *adj.* pỵkrạkrí.

technology, 1. *n.* krạkrí.

telephone, 1. *n.* xȳkrā.

tell, 1. *v.* {m̀, m̃} maū; 2. *v.* {m̀, m̀} kuê (discern).

teller, 1. *n.* cạpúprà (clerk, cashier).

temperature, 1. *n.* lȳcȳ.

temple, 1. *n.* srùfú.

temporal, 1. *adj.* pypọ.

ten, 1. *num.* plè; 2. **ten thousand** *num.* plí; 3. **ten thousandth** *adj.* plíplī.

tend to, 1. *aux.* r̄.

tendril, 1. *n.* jilī.

tentacle, 1. *n.* kfūrỳ.

tenth, 1. *adj.* plèplẹ.

tepid, 1. *adj.* má.

term, 1. *n.* klē (formal period); 2. *n.* nȳ (word).

terminal, 1. *adj.* pysá (final).

terrace, 1. *n.* lōkrē (farming).

terraced, 1. *adj.* lōkrēxù (farming).

territory, 1. *n.* klụsịkrí.

terror, 1. *n.* fēclỳ.

test, 1. *n.* xēsō (trial); 2. *n.* sú (academic); 3. *v.* {m̀, m̃} xeō.

testicle, 1. *n.* fōclù.

testicular, 1. *adj.* pȳfōclù.

tetrahedral, 1. *adj.* jérēcrōxù.

tetrahedron, 1. *n.* jérēcrō.

text, 1. *n.* kíprù.

text-based, 1. *adj.* kíprùxú.

textual, 1. *adj.* pykíprù.

than, 1. *prep.* klé (*comparison marker*).

thank, 1. *v.* {m̀, r̃} cruô.

thankful, 1. *adj.* crúlòlẹ.

thanks, 1. *intj.* clō̃; 2. *n.* clō̃.

that, 1. *det.* sỹ; 2. *det.* srã (distant); 3. *comp.* klè; 4. *pn.* sỹ; 5. *pn.* srã (distant).

their, 1. *adj.* clạmá (*masculine*); 2. *adj.* clīmà (*feminine*); 3. *adj.* lạmá (*neuter*).

theirs, 1. *n.* clạmá (*masculine*); 2. *n.* clīmà (*feminine*); 3. *n.* lạmá (*neuter*).

them, 1. *pn.* clạ (*masculine*); 2. *pn.* clī (*feminine*); 3. *pn.* lạ (*neuter*).

thematic, 1. *adj.* pȳpsūlò.

theme, 1. *n.* psūlò.

themselves, 1. *pn.* kfò.

then, 1. *adv.* ạkrạ (in that case); 2. *adv.* mĩ (at that time); 3. *comp.* ạkrạ (conclusory).

theoretical, 1. *adj.* cìpsáxù.

theory, 1. *n.* cìpsá.

there, 1. *adv.* sụkụ; 2. *n.* sụkụ; 3. **there is/are** *v.* {Í} roì (*existential quantification*).

therefore, 1. *adv.* nỳ; 3. *conj.* nỳ.

thermal, 1. *adj.* pyplũ.

these, 1. *det.* sĩ; 2. *pn.* sĩ.

they, 1. *pn.* clạ (*masculine*); 2. *pn.* clī (*feminine*); 3. *pn.* lạ (*neuter*).

thick, 1. *adj.* sè.

thicken, 1. *v.* {ṁ, Í, v́, ṽ} sènuọ.

thickened, 1. *adj.* sènụmọ.

thickness, 1. *n.* sèclí.

thief, 1. *n.* nūnō.

thigh, 1. *n.* cxỹ.

thin, 1. *adj.* rē; 2. *v.* {ṁ, Í, v́, ṽ} rēnuō.

thing, 1. *n.* cụ.

think, 1. *v.* {ź} kuó (ponder); 2. *v.* {z̃} kuó (about s.th.); 3. *v.* {ż} kuó (*propositions*).

thinker, 1. *n.* kúkō.

thinned, 1. *adj.* rēnūmō.

thinner, 1. *n.* rēnūkō.

third, 1. *adj.* jẹjẹ.

thirst, 1. *n.* crỳclí.

thirstily, 1. *adv.* crỳrọ.

thirsty, 1. *adj.* crỳ.

thirtieth, 1. *adj.* jẹpapạ.

thirty, 1. *num.* jẹpạ.

this, 1. *det.* sĩ; 2. *pn.* sĩ.

thorax, 1. *n.* xójī.

thorough, 1. *adj.* frụcịká.

thoroughly, 1. *adv.* frụcịkárō.

thoroughness, 1. *n.* frucikáclì.

those, 1. *det.* sỹ; 2. *det.* srã (distant); 3. *pn.* sỹ; 4. *pn.* srã (distant).

though, 1. *comp.* klá.

thought, 1. *n.* kúsō; 2. **thought out** *adj.* kúmō.

thousand, 1. *num.* clo; 2. **ten thousand** *num.* plí; 3. **hundred thousand** *num.* sò.

thousandth, 1. *adj.* cloclo; 2. **ten thousandth** *adj.* plíplī; 3. **hundred thousandth,** 1. *adj.* sòso.

thread, 1. *n.* jīlè.

three, 1. *num.* je.

throat, 1. *n.* clūrū.

throne, 1. *n.* frýpò.

through, 1. *prep.* ple.

throw, 1. *v.* {m̀, Í, Ì, j̃} srió.

thumb, 1. *n.* plé.

thunder, 1. *n.* rūsē; 2. *v.* {Ø} ruē.

thus, 1. *adv.* nỳ; 3. *conj.* nỳ.

tide, 1. *n.* crīfū.

tidily, 1. *adv.* psỳro.

tidiness, 1. *n.* psỳclí.

tidy, 1. *adj.* psỳ.

tie, 1. *n.* klicé.

tiger, 1. *n.* laxé.

tight, 1. *adj.* krū.

tighten, 1. *v.* {m̀, Í, v́, ṽ} krūnuō.

tightened, 1. *adj.* krūnūmō.

tightly, 1. *adv.* krūrō.

tightness, 1. *n.* krūclì.

till, 1. *n.* capú (register).

time, 1. *n.* po (in abstract); 2. *n.* sipsý (moment); 3. *n.* lúmā (era); 4. *n.* pròprí (period); 5. *n.* cùkfo (duration); 6. **on time** *adj.* psè; 7. **on time** *adv.* psèro; 8. **at the time of** *prep.* clȳ.

tincture, 1. *n.* klòcú.

tiny, 1. *adj.* frice.

tired, 1. *adj.* kū (sleepy); 2. *adj.* kálỳ (fatigued).

tithe, 1. *n.* crisa; 2. *v.* {ḿ, m̃, g̀} cria.

tither, 1. *n.* cri̱ka̱.

title, 1. *n.* pípà.

titular, 1. *adj.* py̱pípà.

to, 1. *prep.* ó (*destination, recipient*); 2. *prep.* kápē (s.o.'s perspective).

today, 1. *adv.* clȳjō.

toe, 1. *n.* kfā.

toenail, 1. *n.* kfācò.

together, 1. *adv.* cxàlú.

toilet, 1. *n.* crècro̱.

tomato, 1. *n.* jy̱ple̱.

tombstone, 1. *n.* sa̱kí.

tomorrow, 1. *adv.* pi̱jó.

tongue, 1. *n.* pá.

too, 1. *adv.* nùca̱ (also); 2. *adv.* lèpe̱ (overly); 3. **too much** *n.* lèpe̱.

tool, 1. *n.* kĩ.

toolbox, 1. *n.* kìkla̱.

tooth, 1. *n.* rū.

top, 1. *n.* mé; 2. **on top of** *prep.* mé.

topic, 1. *n.* júprà.

torso, 1. *n.* jūpsò.

total, 1. *adj.* kfúmè (complete); 2. *adj.* kràci̱ (whole); 3. *adj.*

touch, 1. *v.* {m̀, ǹ} kuà.

touchable, 1. *adj.* jākūjà.

tough, 1. *adj.* kã (resilient); 2. *adj.* lòle̱ (chewy).

toughness, 1. *n.* kaclĩ; 2. *n.* lòle̱clí (chewiness).

toupée, 1. *n.* klȳfù.

toward, 1. *prep.* fo̱céplā.

tower, 1. *n.* jòcxe̱.

town, 1. *n.* prápē.

toy, 1. *n.* mí.

trachea, 1. *n.* ly̱jé.

tracheal, 1. *adj.* py̱ly̱jé.

trade, 1. *n.* cxē (an exchange).

trail, 1. *n.* nōplā (path).

train, 1. *v.* {ḿ, m̀} sryí; 2. *n.* ra̱ka̱ (locomotive).

trained, 1. *adj.* srýsīxù.

trainer, 1. *n.* srýkī.

training, 1. *n.* srýsī.

training grounds, 1. *n.* srýsīklā.

transform, 1. *v.* {Í} piǒ; 2. *v.* {v́, ṽ} piǒ (into s.th.).

transformation, 1. *n.* pìsó.

transformative, 1. *adj.* pìsóxù.

transformed, 1. *adj.* pìmó.

translucent, 1. *adj.* pré.

trap, 1. *n.* jã.

trapped, 1. *adj.* jaxũ.

travel, 1. *n.* plīsȳ; 2. *v.* {ḿ, Ì, ṽ} pliȳ.

traveler, 1. *n.* plīkȳ.

traveling, 1. *n.* plīsȳ.

traverse, 1. *v.* {ṁ, j̀, ṽ} puy̌.

treat, 1. *v.* {m̃} sroī (s.o. to s.th.); 2. *v.* {ṁ} cxoì (s.o. a certain way).

tree, 1. *n.* cif̱u̱; 2. **apple tree** *n.* kȳmìcif̱u̱; 3. **orange tree** *n.* kèkṟac̱if̱u̱.

triangle, 1. *n.* noklĩ.

triangular, 1. *adj.* noklixũ.

tried, 1. *adj.* sìmá (taste-tested, etc).

trigger, 1. *n.* ma̱fá (e.g. of a gun).

trouble, 1. *n.* pi̱pro̱.

trousers, 1. *n.* clō.

trowel, 1. *n.* nícà.

true, 1. *adj.* mú.

truly, 1. *adv.* múrō.

trunk, 1. *n.* mólō (chest).

truss, 1. *n.* nirẽ.

trust, 1. *n.* lísȳ; 2. *v.* {z̃} liý (s.o./s.th.); 3. *v.* {z̀} liý (*propositions*).

trusted, 1. *adj.* límȳ.

trusting, 1. *adj.* lílȳlē.

truth, 1. *n.* kfõ; 2. *n.* múclì.

truthful, 1. *adj.* plu̱kfá (honest).

truthfully, 1. *adv.* plu̱kfárō.

try, 1. *v.* {ṁ} siǎ (test); 2. **try to** *aux.* m̄.

tundra, 1. *n.* xu̱klu̱.

tunnel, 1. *n.* nu̱c̱i̱.

turkey, 1. *n.* sýnī.

turn, 1. *v.* {m̂} koū (s.th. over, flip); 2. *v.* {m̂, ń} leî (in, go to sleep); 3. *v.* {m̂, m̂, l̂} neỳ (rotate); 4. **turn in** *v.* {m̂, ń} leî (go to sleep); 5. **turn off** *v.* {m̂, n̂, Í, v́, ṽ} rau̱ (e.g. a light); 6. **turn on** *v.* {m̂, m̃, n̂, Í, v́, ṽ} niý (e.g. a light).

turned off, 1. *adj.* ra̱mu̱.

turtle, 1. *n.* ki̱fo̱.

tusk, 1. *n.* sūrù.

twentieth, 1. *adj.* pipapã.

twenty, 1. *num.* pipã.

two, 1. *num.* pĩ.

type, 1. *n.* sý (kind).

typical, 1. *adj.* sýxù.

U

ugliness, 1. *n.* plu̱mýclì.

ugly, 1. *adj.* plu̱mý.

ultimately, 1. *adv.* i̱ja̱kfújàro̱ (finally); 2. *adv.* py̱sáro̱ (inevitably).

unacceptable, 1. *adj.* i̱japu̱já.

unaffected, 1. *adj.* īxīmō.

unaffordable, 1. *adj.* i̱jafi̱jé.

unaltered, 1. *adj.* i̱cxímē (unchanged).

unavailable, 1. *adj.* iclyxã.

unavoidable, 1. *adj.* i̱ja̱kfújà.

unbelievable, 1. *adj.* ījālūjè.

unbreakable, 1. *adj.* ījājōjū.

unbroken, 1. *adj.* ījōmū (an object).

uncertain, 1. *adj.* i̱kfu̱ru̱.

uncertainly, 1. *adv.* i̱kfu̱ru̱ro̱.

uncertainty, 1. *n.* i̱kfu̱ruclí.

unchanged, 1. *adj.* i̱cxímē.

uncle, 1. *n.* jāfū.

unclear, 1. *adj.* i̱sru̱se̱ (not obvious).

uncommon, 1. *adj.* īlùjú.

unconfirmed, 1. *adj.* īlūmē.

unconscious, 1. *adj.* sym̲i̲ (passed out).
uncontrollable, 1. *adj.* i̲j̲ap̲ijó.
uncountable, 1. *adj.* i̲j̲am̲íjà.
uncovered, 1. *adj.* i̲krúmà (not covered).
uncreative, 1. *adj.* i̲sálùl̲e̲.
undecided, 1. *adj.* icxymũ.
under, 1. *prep.* krínè.
understand, 1. *v.* {ź, ż, z̃} psuõ.
understandable, 1. *adj.* japsujõ.
understood, 1. *adj.* psumõ.
undertaker, 1. *n.* fēkrùprá.
underwear, 1. *n.* māpè.
undeveloped, 1. *adj.* i̲krímē.
undiscovered, 1. *adj.* īxùmé.
unentertaining, 1. *adj.* īkfòs̲i̲xú.
unequal, 1. *adj.* īmū.
unexamined, 1. *adj.* ījùmé.
unexcited, 1. *adj.* īrỳm̲i̲.
unexciting, 1. *adj.* īrỳl̲i̲l̲e̲.
unexplained, 1. *adj.* īkrèm̲y̲.
unexpressive, 1. *adj.* īkèlólē.
unfair, 1. *adj.* inũ.
unfairly, 1. *adv.* inurõ.
unfairness, 1. *n.* inuclĩ.
unforgettable, 1. *adj.* īj̲āpījō.
unforgivable, 1. *adj.* īj̲ānījà.
unforgiving, 1. *adj.* īnìl̲a̲l̲e̲.
unfortunate, 1. *adj.* i̲xá.
unfortunately, 1. *adv.* i̲xárō.
unfunny, 1. *adj.* i̲mékrè.
unhealthy, 1. *adj.* i̲sóxù.
unheard, 1. *adj.* i̲s̲i̲m̲e̲.
unhelpful, 1. *adj.* ixilalã.
unholy, 1. *adj.* i̲pu̲cí.
unidentifiable, 1. *adj.* i̲j̲aklújà.
unimaginable, 1. *adj.* i̲j̲ak̲ej̲o̲.

unimaginative, 1. *adj.* īnàmóxù.

unimportant, 1. *adj.* i̯nos̲u̲xú.

unimpressed, 1. *adj.* i̯mu̲ma̲.

unimpressive, 1. *adj.* i̯mu̲la̲le̲.

unintentional, 1. *adj.* īlēlō.

unintentionally, 1. *adv.* īlēlōrō.

uninteresting, 1. *adj.* i̯sýcòxú.

unique, 1. *adj.* srínì.

uniquely, 1. *adv.* srínìro̲.

unit, 1. *n.* cēsī.

university, 1. *n.* lāfràfra̲.

unjust, 1. *adj.* inũ (unfair).

unjustly, 1. *adv.* inurõ.

unkind, 1. *adj.* i̯fru̲; 2. *adj.* nō (rude).

unknowable, 1. *adj.* ijapajũ.

unknown, 1. *adj.* i̯pi̲me̲ (unfamiliar); 2. *adj.* ipamũ (facts).

unless, 1. *comp.* xò.

unlikable, 1. *adj.* i̯jare̲ji̲.

unlikely, 1. *adj.* iclaklũ.

unlimited, 1. *adj.* ijomũ.

unlistenable, 1. *adj.* ījājījè.

unluckily, 1. *adv.* i̯xárō.

unlucky, 1. *adj.* i̯xá.

unmarked, 1. *adj.* i̯prúmā.

unmentionable, 1. *adj.* ijacujỹ.

unmentioned, 1. *adj.* icumỹ.

unmoved, 1. *adj.* i̯júmè (unshifted).

unnatural, 1. *adj.* imoxũ.

unnecessarily, 1. *adv.* ilomurõ.

unnecessary, 1. *adj.* ilomũ.

unobservant, 1. *adj.* iklilolẽ.

unobtainable, 1. *adj.* ijaclijã.

unofficial, 1. *adj.* īclējīxù.

unpaid, 1. *adj.* īklēmỹ.

unplayable, 1. *adj.* i̯ja̲pa̲ji̲ (music).

unpopular, 1. *adj.* īkrèka̲.

unprepared, 1. *adj.* iclumẽ.
unpreventable, 1. *adj.* i̠a̠sríjò.
unprovable, 1. *adj.* ījāpījā.
unproven, 1. *adj.* īpīmā.
unreadable, 1. *adj.* ijasijõ.
unreal, 1. *adj.* i̠cíxù.
unreasonable, 1. *adj.* īsròxú.
unrecognizable, 1. *adj.* i̠a̠kli̠jy.
unremarkable, 1. *adj.* i̠kfújè.
unsafe, 1. *adj.* i̠ca̠.
unsaid, 1. *adj.* īplōmī (unmentioned).
unscientific, 1. *adj.* ipynimũ.
unseen, 1. *adj.* īrìmó (unobserved).
unsent, 1. *adj.* īnìme̠.
unskilled, 1. *adj.* iklyxũ.
unspeakable, 1. *adj.* ījāplòjí.
unspoken, 1. *adj.* īplòmí.
unsuccessful, 1. *adj.* i̠rálìle̠.
unsweet, 1. *adj.* ījà.
untalkative, 1. *adj.* īplòlílē.
untidy, 1. *adj.* īpsỳ.
until, 1. *comp.* ká; 2. *prep.* ká.
untouchable, 1. *adj.* ījākūjà.
untrue, 1. *adj.* i̠mú.
untruthful, 1. *adj.* i̠plu̠kfá (dishonest).
unusable, 1. *adj.* i̠a̠plújò.
unused, 1. *adj.* i̠plúmò.
unusual, 1. *adj.* īplāpỳ.
unusually, 1. *adv.* īplāpỳro̠.
up, 1. *adv.* fú; 2. *n.* fú; 3. *prep.* fú.
upper, 1. *adj.* fúxù.
urchin, 1. *n.* mòfre̠.
urethra, 1. *n.* fùpi̠.
urge, 1. *v.* {m̀} jau̠ (press s.o./s.th.).
urinate, 1. *v.* {ź} cliē.
urination, 1. *n.* clīsē.

urine, 1. *n.* clīsē.

us, 1. *pn.* plō.

usable, 1. *adj.* jạplújò.

use, 1. *v.* {v̀} pluô; 2. **used to** *aux.* ņ.

used, 1. *adj.* plúmò; 2. *adj.* srà (secondhand); 3. *v.* {ż, ž} naị (be used to s.th.); 4. **used to** *aux.* ņ.

user, 1. *n.* plúkò.

usual, 1. *adj.* plāpỳ.

usually, 1. *adv.* plāpỳrọ.

usure, 1. *v.* {ṁ, Í} proí.

usurer, 1. *n.* prókī.

usury, 1. *n.* prósī.

uterine, 1. *adj.* pȳlȳprù.

uterus, 1. *n.* lȳprù.

utterance, 1. *n.* plōsī.

uvula, 1. *n.* klelõ.

uvular, 1. *adj.* pyklelõ.

V

vagina, 1. *n.* lāfū.

vaginal, 1. *adj.* pȳlāfū.

valley, 1. *n.* pạcxạ.

valuable, 1. *adj.* kuklĩ.

value, 1. *n.* kukliclĩ.

vanish, 1. *v.* {Í} freó (disappear).

vanishing, 1. *adj.* frélōlē.

variegated, 1. *adj.* clūpīxù.

variety, 1. *n.* clūpī (diversity); 2. *n.* sý (type, kind).

varietal, 1. *adj.* pysý.

various, 1. *adj.* clūpīxù.

vegetable, 1. *n.* sạprụ.

veil, 1. *n.* krācà.

vein, 1. *n.* mỹ.

venison, 1. *n.* krycụ.

venom, 1. *n.* rẹsẹ.

venomous, 1. *adj.* rẹsẹxú.

veranda, 1. *n.* moclā̈.

verdure, 1. *n.* sāclì.

vernal, 1. *adj.* pȳrùlọ.

very, 1. *adv.* nūjè.

vessel, 1. *n.* klūkù.

vest, 1. *n.* pā̈.

vial, 1. *n.* klòcú.

victory, 1. *n.* plīsō.

village, 1. *n.* prápē.

villain, 1. *n.* macā̈.

villainous, 1. *adj.* macaxṻ.

villainy, 1. *n.* macaxuclī̈.

vine, 1. *n.* nà.

violence, 1. *n.* rálìclí.

violent, 1. *adj.* rálì.

violently, 1. *adv.* rálìrọ.

violin, 1. *n.* mẹlọ.

violinist, 1. *n.* mẹlọprá.

visibility, 1. *n.* jārìjóclì.

visible, 1. *adj.* jārìjó.

vision, 1. *n.* sẹ.

visit, 1. *n.* pỳsú; 2. *v.* {m̀} pyŭ (people); 3. *v.* {j} pyŭ (locations).

visitor, 1. *n.* pỳkú.

vocal, 1. *adj.* pylỹ (relating to voice); 2. *adj.* lyxṻ (speaking frequently or loudly); 3. **vocal cords** *n.* pācē.

vodka, 1. *n.* xụrú.

voice, 1. *n.* lỹ.

volcanic, 1. *adj.* pycrọkfó.

volcano, 1. *n.* crọkfó.

vomit, 1. *n.* fèsụ; 2. *v.* {ź} feù.

vomitous, 1. *n.* fèsụxú.

vote, 1. *v.* {ḿ} cruý; 2. *v.* {v̀} cruý (for s.o./s.th.).

voter, 1. *n.* crúkȳ.

vow, 1. *n.* jásū.

vulnerability, 1. *n.* sīlēklūclì.

vulnerable, 1. *adj.* sīlēklū.

W

waist, 1. *n.* plú.

waistband, 1. *n.* pọkfẹ.

wait, 1. *n.* pìsẹ (hold-up); 2. *v.* {ḿ, j} piè; 3. *v.* {m̀} piè (for s.o./s.th.).

waiter, 1. *n.* ràki̱ (server).

waitress, 1. *n.* ràki̱.

walk, 1. *v.* {ḿ, j̱, j̃} riè.

walker, 1. *n.* rìkẹ.

wall, 1. *n.* lí.

wallet, 1. *n.* peprĩ.

want, 1. *v.* {z̃} meî (s.o./s.th.); 2. *v.* {z̀} meî (*propositions*); 3. **want to** *aux.* ǹ.

wanted, 1. *adj.* mémì (desired).

war, 1. *n.* mò.

war hammer, 1. *n.* mōcìkrí.

wardrobe, 1. *n.* kōrè.

warlike, 1. *adj.* mòxú.

warm, 1. *adj.* pú; 2. *v.* {m̀, ǹ, Í} púnuō (up).

warmth, 1. *n.* púclì.

warn, 1. *v.* {g̀} klué (s.o.); 2. *v.* {m̀, m̃} klué (*propositions*).

warning, 1. *n.* klúsē.

warrior, 1. *n.* mòprá.

wash, 1. *v.* {m̀, m̃} muŷ.

washer, 1. *n.* rācrū (building material).

wasteland, 1. *n.* càlu̱lý.

watch, 1. *v.* {ḿ, m̀, m̃} kfuy̌; 2. *n.* sru̱jó (wristwatch).

watchable, 1. *adj.* jākfùjý.

watched, 1. *adj.* kfùmý.

watchful, 1. *adj.* kfùlýlē.

water, 1. *n.* xō (general); 2. *n.* jò (small body, e.g. lake).

waterfall, 1. *n.* xìnọma̱.

watery, 1. *adj.* xōxù.

wax, 1. *n.* kōcò.

way, 1. *n.* my̱.

we, 1. *pn.* plō.

weak, 1. *adj.* fu̱ (physically); 2. *adj.* pōprù (in flavor, etc).

weaken, 1. *v.* {m̄, Í, ṽ} fu̱nuo̱.

weakened, 1. *adj.* fu̱nu̱mo̱.

weakly, 1. *adv.* fu̱ro̱ (physical); 2. *adv.* pōprùro̱ (flavor, etc).

weakness, 1. *n.* fu̱clí (physical).

wealth, 1. *n.* sõ.

wealthy, 1. *adj.* soxũ.

weapon, 1. *n.* rècé.

wear, 1. *v.* {m̄} pleŭ (clothes, etc).

weather, 1. *n.* jẽ.

weatherman, 1. *n.* jeprã.

weatherperson, 1. *n.* jeprã.

weatherwoman, 1. *n.* jeprã.

web, 1. *n.* clã (spider).

week, 1. *n.* psa̱.

weekly, 1. *adj.* py̱psa̱.

weight, 1. *n.* lù.

weighty, 1. *adj.* lùxú (heavy).

weird, 1. *adj.* prùni̱.

weld, 1. *n.* klusõ; 2. *v.* {m̄, Í, v́, ṽ} kluõ.

welded, 1. *adj.* klumõ.

welder, 1. *n.* klukõ.

welding, 1. *n.* klusõ.

well, 1. *adv.* cy̱ro̱.

west, 1. *adj.* srè; 2. *adv.* srè; 3. *n.* srè.

western, 1. *adj.* srèxú.

westward, 1. *adv.* srè.

wet, 1. *adj.* lè.

wetland, 1. *n.* lèlý.

wetness, 1. *n.* lèclí.

what, 1. *pn.* fù; 2. **what... like** *adv.* fèja̱.

wheel, 1. *n.* klīpē.

when, 1. *adv.* rù; 2. *comp.* clȳ.

where, 1. *adv.* ri̱.

whether, 1. *comp.* pȳ.

which, 1. *det.* fã; 2. *pn.* fã.

while, 1. *n.* plĩ (period of time); 2. *comp.* ro̲xo̲.

whiny, 1. *adj.* pūlēlē.

whisker, 1. *n.* kècá.

whiskey, 1. *n.* fõnì.

white, 1. *adj.* plū; 2. *n.* plūkō.

whiten, 1. *v.* {m̀, Í} plūnuō.

whiteness, 1. *n.* plūclì.

who, 1. *pn.* fõ.

whole, 1. *adj.* kràc i̲.

wholeness, 1. *n.* kràc i̲clí.

whom, 1. *pn.* fõ.

whose, 1. *det.* fõmà; 2. *pn.* fõmà.

why, 1. *adv.* já.

wide, 1. *adj.* prẽ.

widely, 1. *adv.* prerõ.

widen, 1. *v.* {m̀, Í, v́, ṽ} prenuõ.

width, 1. *n.* preclĩ.

wife, 1. *n.* crì.

wig, 1. *n.* klȳfù.

will, 1. *aux.* m̃; 2. **be willing to** *aux.* l̲.

wilt, 1. *v.* {Í} lià.

wilted, 1. *adj.* lìm a̲.

win, 1. *v.* {ḿ, m̀, ń, ǹ} pliō.

wind, 1. *n.* ra̲.

window, 1. *n.* crìj a̲.

windpipe, 1. *n.* lyjé.

windy, 1. *adj.* ra̲xú.

wine, 1. *n.* nàjo̲c a̲.

wing, 1. *n.* nó.

winged, 1. *adj.* nóxù (having wings).

winnable, 1. *adj.* jāplĩjō.

winner, 1. *n.* plĩkō.

winter, 1. *n.* ne̲pó.

wire, 1. *n.* jùplí.

wire cutter, 1. *n.* jùpl̲i̲f̲y̲ku̲.

wisdom, 1. *n.* rōkrà.

wise, 1. *adj.* rōkràxú; 2. *adj.* p̲i̲l̲e̲l̲e̲ (knowledgeable).

wisely, 1. *adv.* rōkràxúrō; 2. *adv.* p̲i̲l̲e̲l̲e̲r̲o̲ (knowledgeably).

wish, 1. *n.* físã; 2. *v.* {m̀} fiã (for s.th., *propositions*).

with, 1. *prep.* pry̲pé (*concomitant*); 2. *prep.* fìl̲i̲ (*instrument*).

without, 1. *prep.* ìna̲.

witness, 1. *n.* súkȳ ; 2. *v.* {ż, z̃} suý.

witnessed, 1. *adj.* súmȳ.

wolf, 1. *n.* rékfī.

woman, 1. *n.* crì.

womanliness, 1. *n.* crìxúclì.

womanly, 1. *adj.* crìxú.

womb, 1. *n.* lȳprù.

won, 1. *adj.* plīmō.

wonder, 1. *v.* {z̃} neú (about s.th.); 2. *v.* {ż} neú (*propositions*).

wood, 1. *n.* psȳ̃; 2. *adj.* psyxũ (made of wood).

wooden, 1. *adj.* psyxũ.

wool, 1. *n.* monõ.

word, 1. *n.* nȳ.

work, 1. *v.* {ḿ, m̀} rié; 2. *n.* rísē; 3. *n.* rẽ (instance of, an opus).

work-related, 1. *adj.* pyrẽ.

workable, 1. *adj.* ja̲r̲i̲jé.

workaholic, 1. *adj.* rílēlē.

worker, 1. *n.* ríkē.

world, 1. *n.* plo̲.

worldly, 1. *adj.* plo̲xú.

worm, 1. *n.* sà.

worried, 1. *adj.* xúmỳ (concerned).

worry, 1. *n.* xúsỳ (concern); 2. *v.* {ź, z̃} xuŷ (about s.th.); 3. *v.* xuŷ (*propositions*).

worse, 1. *adj.* pró pre̲.

worst, 1. *adj.* rà pre̲.

worth, 1. *n.* klù.

worthiness, 1. *n.* klùxúclì.

worthless, 1. *prep.* ìna̲ klù.

worthy, 1. *adj.* klùxú.
would, 1. *aux.* ḡ (*conditional marker*).
wrench, 1. *n.* srokẽ.
wrist, 1. *n.* jā.
wristwatch, 1. *n.* sru̲jó.
write, 1. *v.* {m̄, m̀, m̃, ñ, g̀} psey̆.
writer, 1. *n.* psèký.
written, 1. *adj.* psèmý.
writing, 1. *n.* psèsý.
wrong, 1. *adj.* cro̲ (morally); 2. *adj.* sī (false, incorrect).
wrongdoing, 1. *n.* srúsò.
wrongly, 1. *adv.* cro̲ro̲ (morally); 2. *adv.* sīrō (falsely, incorrectly).

Y

yard, 1. *n.* cxi̲.
yawn, 1. *n.* jísē; 2. *v.* {ź} jié; 3. *v.* {z̃} jié (at s.th.).
year, 1. *n.* nī.
yearly, 1. *adj.* pȳnī.
yell, 1. *n.* pésī (shout).
yellow, 1. *adj.* pūrī; 2. *n.* pūrīkō.
yes, 1. *intj.* né.
yesterday, 1. *adv.* féjō; 2. *adv.* fecẽ (last night).
yet, 1. *adv.* òcri̲ (still).
yonder, 1. *det.* srã (that/those over there); 2. *pn.* srã (that/those over there).
you, 1. *pn.* kù (*singular*); 2. *pn.* klū (*plural*).
young, 1. *adj.* pē.
your, 1. *adj.* kùmá (*singular*); 2. *adj.* klūmà (*plural*).
yours, 1. *n.* kùmá (*singular*); 2. *n.* klūmà (*plural*).
yourself, 1. *pn.* kfò.
yourselves, 1. *pn.* kfò.
youth, 1. *n.* pēclì.

Z

zero, 1. *num.* ró.
zipper, 1. *n.* kúkī.

7.3: KATALOPSI TO ENGLISH

A

ácē, 1. *adv.* approximately; 2. *adv.* circa; 3. *adv.* around; 4. *adv.* roughly.
áklò, 1. *adv.* backward.
àcri̱, 1. *n.* snail.
àkle̱, 1. *n.* foot (measurement).
ālèri̱, 1. *n.* season.
ālèri̱xú, 1. *adj.* seasonal.
a̱, 1. *prep.* on (*vertical*).
a̱kra̱, 1. *adv.* then (in that case); 2. *comp.* then (conclusory).
a̱mé, 1. *n.* tail fin.
a̱pi̱, 1. *n.* girl.

C

caì, 1. *v.* {m̀} do (s.th.).
camū̃, 1. *adj.* brought (along).
capsuclī, 1. *n.* formality.
capsū̃, 1. *adj.* formal.
casū̃, 1. *n.* luggage.
caū̃, 1. *v.* {m̀, m̃, j̃} bring.
caŭ, 1. *v.* {ḿ, m̀} chew.
cá, 1. *pn.* he; 2. *pn.* him.
cákù, 1. *n.* mission; 2. *n.* campaign.
cámà, 1. *adj.* his; 2. *n.* his.
cápā, 1. *n.* janitor; 2. *n.* custodian.
cà, 1. *adv.* down; 2. *n.* down; 3. *prep.* down.
càlu̱, 1. *adj.* dead; 2. *adj.* dead.
càlu̱lý, 1. *n.* wasteland.

càry, 1. *adj.* specific.

càryrǫ, 1. *adv.* specifically.

càxi̱, 1. *n.* click (sound).

càxú, 1. *adj.* lower.

cājē̱, 1. *n.* attic.

ca̱, 1. *adj.* safe.

ca̱pú, 1. *n.* till; 2. *n.* register.

ca̱púprà, 1. *n.* teller; 2. *n.* clerk; 3. *n.* cashier.

ca̱ri̱, 1. *n.* string.

ca̱rǫ, 1. *adv.* safely.

cã, 1. *n.* room.

cei̱, 1. *v.* {ñ, Ì, Ĩ, j} splash.

ceî, 1. *v.* {m̀} criticize.

cekū, 1. *n.* donor.

celixū, 1. *adj.* shadowy.

celī̱, 1. *n.* shadow.

celuleclī, 1. *n.* generosity.

celulerõ, 1. *adv.* generously.

celulē̱, 1. *adj.* generous.

cemū, 1. *adj.* donated.

cesū, 1. *n.* donation.

ceū, 1. *v.* {ḿ, m̀, ñ} donate.

cexū, 1. *adj.* nocturnal.

ceỳ, 1. *v.* {g̃} receive; 2. *v.* {g̃} get.

cé, 1. *n.* birth.

cékì, 1. *n.* critic.

cékìxú, 1. *adj.* critical.

cémì, 1. *adj.* criticized.

césì, 1. *n.* criticism; 2. *n.* critique.

cè, 1. *adj.* tardy; 2. *adj.* late.

cèclí, 1. *n.* tardiness.

cèfy̱, 1. *n.* abyss.

cèfy̱xú, 1. *adj.* abysmal.

cèky̱, 1. *n.* receiver.

cèle̱, 1. *n.* lava.

cèle̱cu̱clú, 1. *n.* lavaflow.

cèmy̲, 1. *adj.* received.

cèro̲, 1. *adv.* late; 2. *adv.* tardy.

cèsy̲, 1. *n.* receipt (receiving).

cèsyly̲, 1. *n.* companion.

cē, 1. *n.* fun.

cēsī, 1. *n.* unit.

cēxù, 1. *adj.* fun.

ce̲, 1. *n.* heel.

ce̲klí, 1. *n.* bark.

ce̲ku̲, 1. *n.* customer.

ce̲ni̲, 1. *n.* bee.

ce̲si̲, 1. *n.* splash.

cẽ, 1. *n.* night.

ciě, 1. *v.* {v̀, ṽ} apply (use s.th. on s.th.).

cilyrõ, 1. *adv.* passively.

cilỹ, 1. *adj.* passive.

ciȳ, 1. *v.* {ḿ, m̀, m̃} sell.

cí, 1. *n.* reality.

cíxù, 1. *adj.* real.

cíxùpli̲, 1. *n.* hospital.

cì, 1. *pn.* she; 2. *pn.* her.

cìcxu̲, 1. *n.* library.

cìcxu̲prá, 1. *n.* librarian.

cìkrí, 1. *n.* hammer.

cìmá, 1. *adj.* her; 2. *n.* hers.

cìmé, 1. *adj.* applicated; 2. *adj.* applied.

cìpsá, 1. *n.* theory.

cìpsáxù, 1. *adj.* theoretical.

cìru̲, 1. *comp.* despite; 2. *prep.* despite.

cìsé, 1. *n.* application (e.g. of a tool).

cīkȳ, 1. *n.* salesman; 2. *n.* salesperson; 3. *n.* saleswoman; 4. *n.* seller.

cīmȳ, 1. *adj.* sold.

cīsȳ, 1. *n.* product.

ci̲, 1. *n.* fur.

ci̲fe̲, 1. *n.* silver.

ci̲fe̲xú, 1. *adj.* silver; 2. *adj.* made of silver.

cifu, 1. *n.* tree.

ciké, 1. *n.* context.

cino, 1. *n.* button (clothing).

cixú, 1. *adj.* furry.

claī, 1. *v.* {m̀, m̃, ǹ, Í} shut (close s.th. horizontally planar, e.g. a chest).

claklurõ, 1. *adv.* probably.

claklũ, 1. *adj.* probable; 2. *adj.* likely.

clá, 1. *adj.* rough (surface).

cláclì, 1. *n.* roughness (surface).

cláni, 1. *n.* glasses.

clà, 1. *det.* all; 2. *pn.* all.

clàcu, 1. *pn.* everything.

clàni, 1. *pn.* everyone; 2. *pn.* everybody.

clā, 1. *adj.* right (side or direction); 2. *adv.* right (to the right); 3. *n.* right.

clāfò, 1. *n.* cigar; 2. *n.* cigarette.

clāmā, 1. *adv.* everywhere; 2. *pn.* everywhere.

clāmī, 1. *adj.* shut; 2. *adj.* closed.

cla, 1. *pn.* they (*masculine*); 2. *pn.* them (*masculine*).

clakfí, 1. *n.* diamond.

clakfíxù, 1. *adj.* diamond; 2. *adj.* made of diamond.

clamá, 1. *adj.* their (*masculine*); 2. *n.* theirs (*masculine*).

clare, 1. *adv.* somewhat.

clã, 1. *n.* web; 2. *n.* spiderweb.

cleĩ, 1. *v.* {m̀, m̃, ñ} provide.

clekī, 1. *n.* provider.

clemã, 1. *n.* apartment.

clemĩ, 1. *adj.* provided.

clesĩ, 1. *n.* provision.

cleú, 1. *v.* {ḿ} smile; 2. *v.* {r̀} smile (at s.o./s.th.).

clexoprã, 1. *n.* biologist.

clexõ, 1. *n.* biology.

clexuclĩ, 1. *n.* liveliness.

clexũ, 1. *adj.* lively.

cley, 1. *v.* {Í, m̀} continue.

cleў, 1. *v.* {ì} reside (s.w.); 2. *v.* {ì} live (s.w.).

cléfỳ, 1. *n.* medium; 2. *n.* media; 3. *n.* means.

cléfỳxú, 1. *adj.* intermediary.

cléjū, 1. *n.* amber.

clélūlē, 1. *adj.* smiley.

clémō, 1. *n.* death.

clémōxù, 1. *adj.* morbid.

clémōxùclí, 1. *n.* morbidity.

clésē, 1. *n.* rat.

clésū, 1. *n.* smile.

clè, 1. *adj.* matte.

clèplọ, 1. *n.* radio.

clē, 1. *adj.* single (relationship status).

clējī, 1. *n.* office; 1. *n.* bureau.

clējīxù, 1. *adj.* official.

clẹ, 1. *n.* staff (wielded stick); 2. *n.* quarterstaff.

clẹfọ, 1. *adj.* physical.

clẹfọrọ, 1. *adv.* physically.

clẹmy, 1 *adj.* continued.

clẽ, 1. *n.* life.

cliā, 1. *v.* {ǹ, Í} cry (tears).

cliạ, 1. *v.* {Í} die.

cliã, 1. *v.* {ṁ, m̃} obtain; 2. *v.* {ṁ, m̃} get.

cliē, 1. *v.* {ź} urinate.

cliê, 1. *v.* {ṁ} deny (s.th.); 2. *v.* {m̃} deny (s.o. s.th.).

cliě, 1. *v.* {ḿ, ṁ, ń, ǹ} stretch.

cliklarikoxū, 1. *adj.* four-dimensional.

climã, 1. *adj.* obtained.

clinuxū, 1. *adj.* striped.

clinū, 1. *n.* stripe.

clió, 1. *v.* {ḿ, ṁ} reflect; 2. *v.* {j̃} reflect (at s.th.).

cliŏ, 1. *v.* {ǹ} be similar to (s.th.).

clixū, 1. *adj.* scenic.

clí, 1. *num.* four.

clíclī, 1. *adj.* fourth.

clíkè, 1. *n.* denier.

clímō, 1. *adj.* reflected.

clípā, 1. *num.* forty.

clípāpā, 1. *adj.* fortieth.

clípȳ, 1. *n.* culture.

clísè, 1. *n.* denial.

clísō, 1. *n.* reflection.

clìlélē, 1. *adj.* stretchy.

clìmé, 1. *adj.* stretched.

clìsé, 1. *n.* stretch.

clī, 1. *pn.* they (*feminine*); 2. *pn.* them (*feminine*).

clīlālē, 1. *adj.* tearful; 2. *n.* crybaby.

clīlālērō, 1. *adv.* tearfully.

clīmà, 1. *adj.* their (*feminine*); 2. *n.* theirs (*feminine*).

clīsē, 1. *n.* urine; 2. *n.* urination.

cli̠, 1. *n.* quantity; 2. *n.* amount.

cli̠nu̠lý, 1. *n.* badland.

clī̃, 1. *n.* scene (drama).

cloí, 1. *v.* { m̀, j̀} leave; 2. *v.* {m̀, j̀} exit.

cloǐ, 1. *v.* {m̀, m̃} take; 2. *v.* {m̀, m̃} remove; 3. *v.* {m̀, m̃} steal.

clófō, 1. *n.* bank (financial).

clóprì, 1. *n.* freedom.

clóprìxú, 1. *adj.* free (unrestrained).

clóprìxúrō, 1. *adv.* freely.

clò, 1. *n.* smoke.

clòkí, 1. *n.* taker.

clòmí, 1. *adj.* taken; 2. *adj.* removed.

clòmo̠, 1. *n.* lingerie.

clòxú, 1. *adj.* clòxú; 2. *n.* property.

clō, 1. *n.* pants; 2. *n.* trousers.

clōrā, 1. *n.* horse.

clōrānā, 1. *n.* foal.

clōrù, 1. *n.* amulet.

clo̠, 1. *num.* thousand; 2. *num.* one thousand.

clo̠clo̠, 1. *adj.* thousandth.

clo̠ró, 1. *n.* gas; 2. *n.* petrol.

clõ, 1. *intj.* thanks; 2. *n.* thanks; 3. *n.* gratitude.

cluǎ, 1. *v.* {m̀, ǹ} connect.

cluē̃, 1. *v.* {m̀} prepare (make s.th. ready).

clumē, 1. *adj.* prepared.

clusē, 1. *adj.* preparation.

clúsū, 1. *n.* issue; 2. *n.* issuance.

clù, 1. *n.* fact.

clùmá, 1. *adj.* connected.

clùná, 1. *n.* mausoleum.

clùsá, 1. *n.* connection.

clùxú, 1. *adj.* factual.

clū, 1. *num.* five.

clūclū, 1. *adj.* fifth.

clūkrùprý, 1. *n.* pentagon.

clūkrùprýxù, 1. *adj.* pentagonal.

clūlū, 1. *n.* bathroom; 2. **clūlū nèklu** *n.* bathroom sink.

clūpā, 1. *num.* fifty.

clūpāpā, 1. *adj.* fiftieth.

clūpī, 1. *n.* variety (diversity).

clūpīxù, 1. *adj.* various; 2. *adj.* variegated.

clūrū, 1. *n.* throat; 2. *n.* esophagus.

clūsū, 1. *n.* nut (building material).

clu, 1. *adj.* east; 2. *adv.* east; 3. *adv.* eastward; 4. *n.* east.

cluni, 1. *n.* city hall.

cluplú, 1. *n.* cabinet.

cluxú, 1. *adj.* eastern.

clũ, 1. *n.* loom.

clyroxũ, 1. *adj.* depressed; 2. *adj.* depressive.

clyrõ, 1. *n.* depression; 2. *adv.* basically.

clyxaclī, 1. *n.* availability.

clyxã, 1. *adj.* available.

clý, 1. *prep.* beside; 2. *prep.* next to; 3. *prep.* by.

clýrȳ, 1. *n.* chin.

clỳ, 1. *n.* mouth.

clỳrá, 1. *n.* effort.

clỳráxù, 1. *adj.* effortful.

clỹ, 1. *comp.* when; 2. *prep.* at the time of.

clỹjō, 1. *adv.* today.

clỹ, 1. *adj.* basic.

co, 1. *conj.* and.

cocroxū, 1. *adj.* categorical.

cocrō, 1. *n.* category.

coi̱, 1. *v.* {m̀, m̃} record.

coxū, 1. *adj.* bossy.

có, 1. *n.* source; 2. *n.* origin.

cóklù, 1. *n.* rib cage.

cóklȳ, 1. *n.* spear; 2. *n.* pike.

cópsȳ, 1. *n.* cheek.

cò, 1. *n.* nail (organic).

còclu̱, 1. *n.* autumn; 2. *n.* fall.

còju̱, 1. *n.* pulley.

còpi̱, 1. *n.* belt.

cōnē, 1. *n.* closet.

co̱fé, 1. *n.* ant.

co̱ki̱, 1. *n.* recorder.

co̱si̱, 1. *n.* recording; 2. *n.* record.

cō, 1. *n.* boss.

cralerō, 1. *adv.* literally.

cralē, 1. *adj.* literal.

crá, 1. *adj.* primary; 2. *adj.* main.

cránō, 1. *n.* infamy; 2. *n.* notoriety.

cránōxù, 1. *adj.* infamous; 2. *adj.* notorious.

cránōxùro̱, 1. *adv.* infamously; 2. *adv.* notoriously.

crápsà, 1. *n.* capital (financial).

crárō, 1. *adv.* mainly; 2. *adv.* primarily.

cràpro̱, 1. *n.* screen; 2. *n.* display.

crā, 1. *prep.* along; 2. *prep.* by.

cra̱, 1. *adj.* inexpensive; 2. *adj.* cheap.

crã, 1. *adj.* cool; 2. *adj.* neat.

creī, 1. *v.* {ḿ, m̀} spit.

creù, 1. *v.* {m̀, Í} separate; 2. *v.* {v́, ṽ} separate (from s.th.).

creŷ, 1. *v.* {m̀, Í} edit.

cré, 1. *n.* sock.

crékỳ, 1. *n.* editor.

crémỳ, 1. *adj.* edited.

crénù, 1. *n.* emerald.

crénùxú, 1. *adj.* emerald; 2. *adj.* made of emerald.

crésỳ, 1. *n.* editing.

crè, 1. *n.* armor.

crècro̱, 1. *n.* toilet.

crèja̱, 1. *n.* halberd.

crèmu̱, 1. *adj.* separated.

crèsu̱, 1. *n.* separation.

crē, 1. *n.* sense (possible meaning).

crēcò, 1. *n.* direction.

crēlà, 1. *n.* period (punctuation).

crēmē, 1. *adj.* sensitive; 2. *adj.* considerate.

crēmēclì, 1. *n.* sensitivity; 2. *n.* consideration.

crēsī, 1. *n.* spit.

crēxà, 1. *n.* character (moral).

cre̱, 1. *adj.* loose (not taut); 2. *adj.* lax.

cre̱clí, 1. *n.* looseness.

cre̱cú, 1. *n.* duck.

cre̱cúnū, 1. *n.* duckling.

cre̱nuo̱, 1. *v.* {m̀, Í} loosen.

cre̱numo̱, 1. *adj.* loosened.

cre̱ro̱, 1. *adv.* loosely.

cria̱, 1. *v.* {ḿ, m̃, g̀} tithe.

crió, 1. *v.* {ḿ, m̀} look (at s.th.); 2. *v.* {m̀} face (s.o./s.th.).

criỹ, 1. *v.* {ź} salivate.

crì, 1. *n.* wife; 2. *n.* woman.

crìja̱, 1. *n.* window.

crìxú, 1. *adj.* womanly; 2. *adj.* feminine.

crìxúclì, 1. *n.* womanliness; 2. *n.* femininity.

crī, 1. *n.* tail.

crīfū, 1. *n.* tide.

crīsỹ, 1. *n.* saliva; 2. *n.* salivation.

cri̱, 1. *adj.* low (not high).

cri̱ka̱, 1. *n.* tither.

cri̱nuo̱, 1. *v.* {m̀, Í} lower.

cri̱numo̱, 1. *adj.* lowered.

crisa, 1. *n.* tithe.
croī, 1. *v.* {m̀, m̃} push (a button, etc.); 2. *v.* {m̀, m̃} press (e.g. a button).
cró, 1. *n.* seam.
crópsà, 1. *n.* resource; 2. *n.* resources.
crópsàxú, 1. *adj.* resourceful.
crò, 1. *adj.* easy.
cròclí, 1. *n.* ease.
cròrọ, 1. *adv.* easily.
crōnù, 1. *n.* country (rural area).
crōnùxú, 1. *adj.* rural.
crọ, 1. *adj.* wrong; 2. *adj.* immoral.
crọfrọ, 1. *adj.* outside; 2. *adv.* outside; 3. *n.* outside; 4. *prep.* outside of.
crọkfó, 1. *n.* volcano.
crọrọ, 1. *adv.* wrongly; 2. *adv.* immorally.
crõ, 1. *n.* stem.
cruclī, 1. *n.* enormity.
cruẹ, 1. *v.* {ḿ, m̀, ń, ǹ} persist; 2. *v.* {ḿ, m̀, ń, ǹ} last.
cruê, 1. *v.* {ḿ, ǹ, ǵ} preach.
crukoxũ, 1. *adj.* impactful.
crukō, 1. *n.* impact.
cruô, 1. *v.* {m̀, r̃} thank.
cruý, 1. *v.* {ḿ} vote; 2. *v.* {v̀} vote (for s.o./s.th.).
crúkè, 1. *n.* preacher.
crúkȳ, 1. *n.* voter.
crúlèlẹ, 1. *adj.* preachy.
crúlòlẹ, 1. *adj.* thankful.
crúsè, 1. *n.* sermon.
crúsò, 1. *n.* gratitude.
crū, 1. *n.* chief; 2. *n.* chieftain.
crūrȳ, 1. *n.* process.
crụ, 1. *n.* hair.
crụjá, 1. *n.* groceries; 2. *n.* shopping.
crụxú, 1. *adj.* hairy.
crũ, 1. *adj.* enormous.
crycluclī, 1. *n.* complexity.
cryclunumõ, 1. *adj.* complicated.

cryclunuõ, 1. *v.* {m̃, ǹ, Í, v́, ṽ} complicate.

cryclũ, 1. *adj.* complex; 2. *adj.* complicated.

cryì, 1. *v.* {m̃, m̃, Í, j̃} found (e.g. a business); 2. *v.* {m̃, m̃, Í, j̃} establish.

cryú, 1. *v.* {ḿ, m̃, Í} bite.

crý, 1. *n.* hat.

crýjò, 1. *n.* spine.

crýkū, 1. *n.* biter.

crýmū, 1. *adj.* bitten.

crýpè, 1. *n.* labia (anatomy).

crýsū, 1. *n.* bite.

crỳ, 1. *adj.* thirsty; 2. *adj.* thirsty.

crỳclí, 1. *n.* thirst.

crỳki̱, 1. *n.* founder.

crỳmi̱, 1. *adj.* founded; 2. *adj.* established.

crỳro̱, 1. *adv.* thirstily.

crỳsi̱, 1. *n.* establishment; 2. *n.* founding.

crȳnȳ, 1. *n.* inn.

crȳnȳprà, 1. *n.* innkeeper.

cry̱, 1. *adj.* slow.

cry̱nuo̱, 1. *v.* {ḿ, m̃, Í, ṽ} slow down; 2. *v.* {ḿ, m̃, Í, ṽ} retard.

cry̱numo̱, 1. *adj.* slowed down; 2. *adj.* retarded.

cry̱nuso̱, 1. *n.* slowing down; 2. *n.* retardation.

cry̱ro̱, 1. *adv.* slowly.

cu, 1. *pn.* it (*trace pronoun*).

cuā, 1. *v.* {ḿ, m̃, m̃, Í} open.

cuǎ, 1. *v.* {Í, ż} make sense; 2. *v.* {Í, ż} add up.

cué, 1. *v.* {m̃, Í} prohibit; 2. *v.* {m̃, Í} forbid.

cuê, 1. *v.* {Í, Ì} remain; 2. *v.* {Í, Ì} be left.

cuě, 1. *v.* {ḿ, m̃} dress; 2. *v.* {ḿ} get dressed.

cumucā, 1. *n.* laundry room.

cumũ, 1. *n.* laundry.

cumỹ, 1. *adj.* mentioned.

cuó, 1. *v.* {ḿ, m̃} nod.

cuǒ, 1. *v.* {j̱, ź} cough.

cusrū, 1. *n.* key (of a map, chart, etc.).

cusỹ, 1. *n.* mention.

cuỹ, 1. *v.* {m̀, ñ, Í} mention; 2. *v.* {m̀} raise (s.th.); 3. *v.* {m̀} bring up (s.th.).

cú, 1. *prep.* in.

cúmē, 1. *adj.* prohibited; 2. *adj.* forbidden.

cúpsā, 1. *n.* ladder.

cúsè, 1. *n.* remainder.

cúsē, 1. *n.* prohibition.

cúsō, 1. *n.* nod (of the head).

cùkfo̲, 1. *n.* time; 2. *n.* duration.

cùlálē, 1. *adj.* intelligible.

cùlálērō, 1. *adv.* intelligibly.

cùmé, 1. *adj.* dressed.

cùru̲, 1. *n.* bludgeon; 2. *n.* club.

cùsó, 1. *n.* cough.

cūmā, 1. *adj.* opened; 2. *adj.* open.

cūpā, 1. *adv.* often.

cūplī, 1. *adj.* square (deals settled); 2. *adj.* even.

cu̲, 1. *n.* thing; 2. *n.* item.

cu̲clú, 1. *n.* stream.

cu̲jo̲, 1. *n.* grass.

cu̲jo̲lý, 1. *n.* grassland.

cu̲kré, 1. *n.* craft.

cu̲ku̲, 1. *n.* rice.

cu̲sru̲, 1. *n.* slug (animal).

cxaí, 1. *v.* {m̀, ǹ, Í} ring (produce sound).

cxaì, 1. *v.* {ḿ} sit (down); 2. *v.* {j} sit (s.w.).

cxaú, 1. *v.* {ź} ejaculate.

cxáfò, 1. *adv.* anymore; 2. *adv.* no longer.

cxásū, 1. *n.* ejaculation; 2. *n.* ejaculate.

cxà, 1. *n.* law; 2. *n.* rule.

cxàlú, 1. *adv.* together.

cxàprá, 1. *n.* lawyer.

cxàxú, 1. *adj.* legal (allowed by law).

cxàxúclì, 1. *n.* legality.

cxā, 1. *adj.* fast; 2. *adj.* quick.

cxāclì, 1. *n.* quickness.

cxārō, 1. *adv.* quickly; 2. *adv.* fast.

cxa̱, 1. *adv.* moreover.

cxa̱jý, 1. *n.* income.

cxa̱lú, 1. *n.* spinach.

cxã, 1. *adj.* foreign.

cxeì, 1. *v.* {ḿ, j̇} come.

cxei̱, 1. *v.* {m̀, ñ, ġ} contribute.

cxeò, 1. *v.* {ḿ, m̀, m̃} build.

cxeŷ, 1. *v.* {ḿ, m̀, m̃, g̀} teach.

cxé, 1. *n.* shirt.

cxékỳ, 1. *n.* teacher.

cxémỳ, 1. *adj.* taught.

cxèko̱, 1. *n.* builder.

cxèmo̱, 1. *adj.* built.

cxèso̱, 1. *n.* building.

cxē, 1. *n.* trade; 2. *n.* exchange.

cxe̱, 1. *adj.* dirty (not clean).

cxe̱clí, 1. *n.* dirtiness.

cxe̱ki̱, 1. *n.* contributor.

cxe̱psu̱, 1. *n.* institution; 2. *n.* organization.

cxe̱si̱, 1. *n.* contribution.

cxẽ, 1. *n.* table.

cxiá, 1. *v.* {m̀, Í} follow.

cxiă, 1. *v.* {m̀, ǹ, Ĩ} cause.

cxiclī, 1. *n.* loudness.

cxié, 1. *v.* {Í, m̀, m̃} change; 2. *v.* {Í, m̀, m̃} alter.

cxiẽ, 1. *v.* {m̀} report (formal complaint).

cxiõ, 1. *v.* {Í, Ì} stay (*compounds*); 2. *v.* {Í, Ì} remain (*compounds*).

cxirõ, 1. *adv.* loudly.

cxisẽ, 1. *n.* report (formal complaint).

cxí, 1. *n.* day; 2. *n.* date.

cxíkā, 1. *n.* follower.

cxímē, 1. *adj.* changed; 2. *adj.* altered.

cxísē, 1. *n.* change; 2. *n.* alteration.

cxì, 1. *n.* pack; 2. *n.* packet.

cxìká, 1. *n.* cause.

cxìmá, 1. *adj.* caused.

cxìsá, 1. *n.* causation.

cxi̱, 1. *n.* yard; 2. *n.* garden.

cxi̱plý, 1. *n.* model.

cxi̱plýxù, 1. *adj.* ideal; 2. *adj.* model.

cxī, 1. *adj.* loud; 2. *n.* bailiwick; 3. *n.* field.

cxoì, 1. *v.* {m̀} treat (s.o. a certain way).

cxoǐ, 1. *v.* {m̀, ĺ} realize (effectuate).

cxokũ, 1. *n.* supporter (emotional, financial, etc.).

cxolulē, 1. *adj.* supportive.

cxomũ, 1. *adj.* supported (of a foundation, financially, etc.).

cxosũ, 1. *n.* support (emotional, foundation, etc.).

cxoxũ, 1. *adj.* rocky; 2. *adj.* stone (made of stone).

cxou̱, 1. *v.* {m̀, ñ, ǵ} respond; 2. *v.* {m̀, ñ, ǵ} reply.

cxoũ, 1. *v.* {g̀} support; 2. *v.* {g̀} hold up (as e.g. scaffolding).

cxó, 1. *n.* metal.

cxójē, 1. *adj.* short; 2. *adj.* stout.

cxóplȳ, 1. *adj.* ignorance.

cxóplȳclì, 1. *n.* ignorant.

cxóxù, 1. *adj.* metallic.

cxòsí, 1. *n.* realization.

cxō, 1. *n.* section; 2. *n.* part.

cxōpī, 1. *n.* grain.

cxōxù, 1. *adj.* segregated; 2. *adj.* sectioned.

cxo̱cry, 1. *n.* plastic.

cxo̱cryxú, 1. *adj.* plastic; 2. *adj.* made of plastic.

cxo̱fó, 1. *n.* cemetery.

cxo̱su̱, 1. *n.* response; 2. *n.* reply.

cxõ, 1. *n.* rock; 2. *n.* stone.

cxuě, 1. *v.* {m̀, m̃} keep (s.th.).

cxuó, 1. *v.* {ĺ, ż} appear; 2. *v.* {ĺ, ż} manifest.

cxú, 1. *n.* pupil; 2. *n.* student.

cxúsō, 1. *n.* appearance.

cxù, 1. *n.* schedule; 2. *n.* plan.

cxùmé, 1. *adj.* kept.

cxùsé, 1. *n.* keepsake.

cxùxú, 1. *adj.* planned (well).

cxūcà, 1. *n.* briefcase.

cxūnī, 1. *n.* peninsula.

cxūràri̱, 1. *n.* monarchy.

cxūràri̱prá, 1. *n.* monarch.

cxu̱, 1. *adj.* round.

cxu̱clí, 1. *n.* roundness.

cxu̱lú, 1. *n.* alligator.

cxū, 1. *n.* dress (article of clothing).

cxycõ, 1. *n.* government.

cxyí, 1. *v.* {ḿ, m̀} consent (to s.th.); 2. *v.* {ḿ, m̀} agree (to s.th.).

cxymũ, 1. *adj.* decided.

cxysuxũ, 1. *adj.* decisive.

cxysũ, 1. *n.* decision.

cxyú, 1. *v.* {m̀, ǹ, ṽ} catch (e.g. a fish).

cxyũ, 1. *v.* {m̀, Í} decide.

cxýkū, 1. *n.* catcher.

cxýlūlē, 1. *adj.* agreeable; 2. *adj.* amenable.

cxýmū, 1. *adj.* caught (fish, etc.); 2. *adj.* agreed (to).

cxýsū, 1. *n.* agreement; 2. *n.* catch (a fish, etc.).

cxỹ, 1. *n.* thigh.

cycē, 1. *intj.* good night.

cyú, 1. *v.* {m̀, m̃} save (s.o./s.th.); 2. *v.* {r̃} save (from s.th.); 3. *v.* {m̀, m̃} rescue (s.o./s.th.); 4. *v.* {r̃} rescue (from s.th.).

cý, 1. *n.* form; 2. *n.* shape.

cýfī, 1. *intj.* good morning.

cýjỳ, 1. *n.* power; 2. *n.* might.

cýjỳxú, 1. *adj.* powerful; 2. *adj.* mighty.

cýsū, 1. *n.* rescue.

cỳ, 1. *n.* field (of crops, etc.).

cȳ, 1. *adj.* mere.

cȳlò, 1. *n.* cloud.

cȳlòxú, 1. *adj.* cloudy.

cȳprȳ, 1. *n.* housing.

cȳrō, 1. *adv.* merely.

cy̱, 1. *adj.* good; 2. **pró cy̱** *adj.* better; 3. **rà cy̱** *adj.* best.

cy̱jó, 1. *intj.* hello; 2. *intj.* hi; 3. *intj.* hey.

c̱y̱ṟo̱, 1. *adv.* well; 2. *adv.* good.

E

esiõ, 1. *v.* {m̀, m̃, ñ} reread.

ècé, 1. *n.* harp.

ècéprà, 1. *n.* harpist.

ēciȳ, 1. *v.* {m̀, m̃} resell.

ēcluǎ, 1. *v.* {m̀, ǹ} reconnect.

ēcxeò, 1. *v.* {ḿ, m̀, m̃} rebuild.

ēcxèmo̱, 1. *adj.* rebuilt.

ējākfùjý, 1. *n.* rewatchable.

ējī, 1. *n.* grape.

ējuě, 1. *v.* {m̀, m̃} reexamine.

ējùsé, 1. *n.* reexamination.

ēkfuy̌, 1. *v.* {m̀, m̃} rewatch.

ēmaū, 1. *v.* {m̀} retell.

ēniǎ, 1. *v.* {m̀} reclaim (e.g. as property).

ēniè, 1. *v.* {m̀, ñ} resend (s.th. to s.o.); 2. *v.* {ĵ} resend (s.th. s.w.).

ēnìmá, 1. *adj.* reclaimed.

ēnìsá, 1. *n.* reclamation.

ēpsey̌, 1. *v.* {m̀, m̃, ñ} rewrite.

ēpsèmý, 1. *adj.* rewritten.

ēpsèsý, 1. *n.* rewrite.

ēpyǔ, 1. *v.* {m̀} revisit (people); 2. *v.* {j} revisit (locations).

ēreǒ, 1. *v.* {m̀, m̃, ṽ} redraw.

ēroǔ, 1. *v.* {m̀, m̃} remake.

ēròsú, 1. *n.* remake.

ēryǔsriò, 1. *v.* {m̀, Í} relaunch (e.g. a rocket, a missile); 2. *v.* {m̀, Í} refire (e.g. a cannon, artillery).

ēsriǎ, 1. *v.* {v̀} reapply (for e.g. recompense); 2. *v.* {m̀} reapply (to e.g. a job).

ēxiõ, 1. *v.* {m̀, ñ} restate (declare).

ēxuě, 1. *v.* {m̀} rediscover.

ēxùmé, 1. *adj.* rediscovered.

e̱cxuó, 1. *v.* {Í} reappear.

ẹcxúsō, 1. *n.* reappearance.

ẹjạplújò, 1. *adj.* reusable.

ẹkeọ, 1. *v.* {z̃} reimagine (s.o./s.th.); 2. *v.* {ż} reimagine (*propositions*).

ẹkreọ, 1. *v.* {Í} reform (come into shape); 3. *v.* {v́} reform (into s.th.).

ẹkruó, 1. *v.* {ṁ, m̃} rearrange.

ẹkrúmō, 1. *adj.* rearranged.

ẹkuó, 1. *v.* {ż, z̃} reconsider; 2. *v.* {ż, z̃} rethink.

ẹliô, 1. *v.* {ṁ, m̃} redesign.

ẹmiâ, 1. *v.* {ḿ, ṁ, m̃, ṅ, ñ} recount (count again).

ẹpaị, 1. *v.* {ṁ, m̃} replay (music, play again).

ẹpluô, 1. *v.* {v̀} reuse.

ẹplúmò, 1. *adj.* reused.

ẹplúsò, 1. *n.* reuse.

ẹprou̯, 1. *v.* {z̃} relive; 2. *v.* {z̃} re-experience.

ẹroú, 1. *v.* {ḿ} replay (a game, etc.).

ẹsaû, 1. *v.* {ṁ, m̃} recreate.

ẹsásù, 1. *n.* recreation.

ẹsryí, 1. *v.* {ḿ, ṁ} retrain.

ẹsrýmī, 1. *adj.* retrained.

ẹxiâ, 1. *v.* {ṁ, Í, ṽ} remeasure.

F

fakũ, 1. *n.* giver.

famũ, 1. *adj.* given.

fanõ, 1. *n.* forearm.

fasũ, 1. *n.* gift.

faú, 1. *v.* {ṁ, Í, Ì, j̃} enclose.

fau̯, 1. *v.* {ṁ, Í} poison.

faũ, 1. *v.* {ñ} give (transfer).

fá, 1. *adj.* dry.

fáclì, 1. *n.* dryness.

fámū, 1. *adj.* enclosed.

fánuō, 1. *v.* {ṁ, ṅ, Í, v́, ṽ} dry.

fánūmō, 1. *adj.* dried.

fásū, 1. *n.* enclosure.

fà, 1. *adj.* calm.

fàcá, 1. *n.* pantry.

fàclí, 1. *n.* calmness; 2. *n.* calm.

fàjá, 1. *n.* hero; 2. *n.* heroine.

fàjáxù, 1. *adj.* heroic.

fàjáxùclí, 1. *n.* heroism.

fànuọ, 1. *v.* {m̀, ǹ, Í, ź, z̃} calm.

fàrọ, 1. *adv.* calmly.

fā, 1. *num.* hundred; 2. *num.* one hundred.

fācỳ, 1. *n.* discipline.

fācỳxú, 1. *adj.* disciplined.

fāfā, 1. *adj.* hundredth.

fāsā, 1. *n.* snake.

famụ, 1. *adj.* poisoned.

fasụ, 1. *n.* poison.

fasụxú, 1. *adj.* poisonous.

fã, 1. *det.* which; 2. *pn.* which.

fecẽ, 1. *adv.* last night; 2. *adv.* yesterday evening.

feì, 1. *v.* {m̀, Í} bend; 2. *v.* {ṽ} bend (s.th. into s.th.).

feǐ, 1. *v.* {z̃} prefer (s.o./s.th.); 2. *v.* {ż} prefer (*propositions*).

feō, 1. *v.* {m̀, m̃, g̀, g̃} supply.

feù, 1. *v.* {ź} vomit.

feû, 1. *v.* {m̀, ṽ} extend.

fé, 1. *comp.* before; 2. *prep.* before; 3. *prep.* prior to.

féjō, 1. *adv.* yesterday.

fémù, 1. *adj.* extended.

féprỳ, 1. *n.* competition; 2. *n.* contest.

féprỳxú, 1. *adj.* competitive.

fésù, 1. *n.* extension.

fè, 1. *n.* money.

fèja, 1. *adv.* what... like.

fèkẹ, 1. *n.* apron.

fèlẹ, 1. *n.* scorpion.

fèlịlẹ, 1. *adj.* bendy.

fèmí, 1. *adj.* preferred.

fèmị, 1. *adj.* bent.

fènú, 1. *n.* berry.

fèsí, 1. *n.* preference.

fèsi̠, 1. *n.* bend.

fèsré, 1. *adj.* inside; 2. *adv.* inside; 3. *n.* inside; 4. *prep.* inside of.

fèsu̠, 1. *n.* vomit.

fèsu̠xú, 1. *n.* vomitous.

fē, 1. *prep.* by (*cause, stimulus*).

fēclỳ, 1. *n.* horror; 2. *n.* terror.

fēclỳxú, 1. *adj.* horrific.

fēcrì, 1. *n.* roof.

fēklùjo̠, 1. *n.* coin purse.

fēkō, 1. *n.* supplier.

fēkrù, 1. *n.* morgue; 2. *n.* mortuary.

fēkrùprá, 1. *n.* mortician; 2. *n.* undertaker.

fēmō, 1. *adj.* supplied.

fēsō, 1. *n.* supply.

fe̠, 1. *adj.* stupid; 2. *adj.* dumb.

fe̠clí, 1. *n.* stupidity.

fe̠pre̠, 1. *n.* eyestalk.

fe̠ró, 1. *adj.* barren.

fe̠ro̠, 1. *adv.* stupidly.

fe̠sí, 1. *n.* sewer.

fĕ, 1. *conj.* but; 2. *conj.* but rather.

fiã, 1. *v.* {m̀} wish (for s.th., *propositions*).

fié, 1. *v.* {m̀} afford; 2. *v.* {m̀} able to pay for (s.th.).

fiè, 1. *v.* {m̀} seek (s.th.); 2. *v.* {ḿ, m̀} search (for s.th.); 3. *v.* {ḿ, m̀} look (for s.th.); 4. *v.* {r̃} look (s.w. for s.th.).

fiē, 1. *v.* {m̀, ṽ} fell (e.g. a tree).

fifuxũ, 1. *adj.* in control (have authority).

fifũ, 1. *n.* authority.

fiô, 1. *v.* {ḿ, m̀, m̃} cook.

fisã, 1. *n.* wish.

fixũ, 1. *adj.* pricy; 2. *adj.* costly; 3. *adj.* expensive.

fí, 1. *n.* root.

fícā, 1. *adj.* dull (not sharp).

fícāclì, 1. *n.* dullness (not sharp).

fíkò, 1. *n.* chef; 2. *n.* cook.

fímò, 1. *adj.* cooked.

fìke̲, 1. *n.* seeker.

fìli̲, 1. *prep.* with (*instrument*).

fìme̲, 1. *adj.* sought (after, for).

fìmi̲, 1. *n.* credit; 2. *n.* acknowledgement.

fìro̲, 1. *adj.* guilty.

fìro̲clí, 1. *n.* guilt.

fìro̲ro̲, 1. *adv.* guiltily.

fìse̲, 1. *n.* search.

fī, 1. *n.* morning.

fīmē, 1. *adj.* felled (e.g. a tree).

fi̲, 1. *n.* affection; 2. *n.* love.

fi̲ká, 1. *n.* collar (e.g. on a shirt).

fi̲ko̲, 1. *adv.* however.

fi̲krá, 1. *n.* rapids.

fĩ, 1. *n.* price; 2. *n.* cost.

fomũ, 1. *adj.* indicated.

fonũ, 1. *n.* blight.

fosũ, 1. *n.* indication.

foũ, 1. *v.* {m̀} suggest; 2. *v.* {m̀} indicate.

foŭ, 1. *v.* {ḿ, m̀} stop; 2. *v.* {ḿ, m̀} halt; 3. *v.* {ḿ, m̀} stay.

fólū, 1. *n.* palate; 2. *n.* roof of mouth.

fóxỳ, 1. *n.* animal.

fóxỳxú, 1. *adj.* animalistic.

fò, 1. *adv.* not.

fòfra̲, 1. *adv.* never.

fòklé, 1. *adv.* instead; 2. *comp.* instead of; 3. *comp.* rather than; 4. *prep.* instead of; 5. *prep.* rather than.

fòlo̲, 1. *n.* brother.

fòlo̲xú, 1. *adj.* brotherly.

fòmú, 1. *adj.* stopped; 2. *adj.* halted.

fòny̲, 1. *n.* son; 2. *n.* boy.

fòrú, 1. *n.* bar; 2. *n.* pub.

fòrúprà, 1. *n.* bartender; 2. *n.* barman; 3. *n.* barmaid.

fòsú, 1. *n.* cessation.

fòxa̱, 1. *n.* perspective.

fō, 1. *pn.* who; 2. *pn.* whom.

fōclù, 1. *n.* testicle.

fōmà, 1. *det.* whose; 2. *pn.* whose.

fōnì, 1. *n.* whiskey.

fo̱céplā, 1. *adv.* forward; 2. *prep.* toward.

fo̱cró, 1. *n.* flail (weapon).

frai̱, 1. *v.* {ḿ, m̀} learn.

fraî, 1. *v.* {m̀, Í, v́, ṽ} repair.

fraĭ, 1. *v.* {m̀, g̱̀} represent (officially).

frarõ, 1. *adv.* morally; 2. *adv.* rightly.

frá, 1. *adv.* maybe; 2. *intj.* maybe.

fráfrī, 1. *n.* camera.

fráfȳ, 1. *n.* magazine.

frákì, 1. *n.* mechanic.

frámì, 1. *adj.* repaired.

frásì, 1. *n.* repair.

frà, 1. *n.* arm.

fràfe̱, 1. *n.* inner ear.

fràkí, 1. *n.* representative.

fràklo̱, 1. *n.* jungle.

fràsí, 1. *n.* representation (e.g. in government).

frāfè, 1. *n.* stole.

frākè, 1. *n.* beetle.

frāmà, 1. *n.* disc; 2. *n.* disk.

frāsrò, 1. *n.* rifle.

fra̱, 1. *n.* school.

fra̱ki̱, 1. *n.* learner.

fra̱mi̱, 1. *adj.* learned.

frã, 1. *adj.* moral; 2. *adj.* right.

freó, 1. *v.* {Í} disappear; 2. *v.* {Í} vanish.

freý, 1. *v.* {j̃} set (s.th. s.w.); 2. *v.* {m̀} set down; 3. *v.* {j̃} put (s.th. s.w.); 4. *v.* {m̀} put down.

fré, 1. *n.* pot.

frémȳ, 1. *adj.* put down.

frépȳ, 1. *n.* definition (of a word, etc.).

frésō, 1. *n.* disappearance.

frè, 1. *n.* lamp.

frècí, 1. *adj.* mortal.

frècíclì, 1. *n.* mortality.

frèru̱, 1. *n.* link.

frē, 1. *n.* paw.

frēcè, 1. *n.* butterfly.

fre̱, 1. *n.* card.

frià, 1. *v.* {m̀, Í, Ì, j̃} pull.

fria̱, 1. *v.* {m̀, Í, g̃} command; 2. *v.* {m̀, Í, g̃} order.

friă, 1. *v.* {m̀, ñ} present.

friē, 1. *v.* {m̀, m̃, ǹ, ñ} destroy.

frixū, 1. *adj.* fishy.

friý, 1. *v.* {ḿ} commit suicide.

frí, 1. *n.* square.

fríxù, 1. *adj.* square.

frísȳ, 1. *n.* suicide.

frísȳxù, 1. *adj.* suicidal.

frìsá, 1. *n.* presentation.

frīkē, 1. *n.* destroyer.

frīlēlē, 1. *adj.* destructive.

frīmē, 1. *adj.* destroyed.

frīrā, 1. *adj.* obese; 2. *adj.* fat.

frīrāclì, 1. *n.* obesity.

frīsē, 1. *n.* destruction.

fri̱, 1. *adj.* difficult; 2. *adj.* hard.

frice̱, 1. *adj.* tiny.

friclí, 1. *n.* difficulty.

frika̱, 1. *n.* commander.

frirýxēclù, 1. *n.* futurescape.

friry̱, 1. *n.* future.

friryxú, 1. *adj.* futuristic.

frisa̱, 1. *n.* command; 2. *n.* order.

frī, 1. *n.* fish.

fró, 1. *n.* bread.

frò, 1. *n.* sleeve.

fròlú, 1. *adv.* anyway.

frō, 1. *prep.* among.

fro̱, 1. *n.* blood.

fro̱plí, 1. *adj.* jagged.

fro̱so̱, 1. *n.* restaurant.

fro̱so̱prá, 1. *n.* restauranteur.

fro̱xú, 1. *adj.* bloody.

fruē, 1. *v.* {ḿ} stand (up); 2. *v.* {j̀} stand (s.w.); 3. *v.* {m̀, j̃} prop (s.th. up); 4. *v.* {m̀, j̃} stand (s.th. up).

frufrū, 1. *adj.* sixth.

fruó, 1. *v.* {ḿ, m̀} comply (with s.th.); 2. *v.* {ḿ, m̀} obey (a rule, a law, etc..); 3. *v.* {ḿ, m̀} listen (to s.o.).

fruō, 1. *v.* {ǹ} contain.

fruõ, 1. *v.* {ḿ, Í, g̀} gain (on s.o./s.th.); 2. *v.* {ḿ, Í, g̀} catch up (to s.o./s.th.).

fruô, 1. *v.* {ź, z̃} care (about, have feelings for).

frupapã, 1. *adj.* sixtieth.

frupã, 1. *num.* sixty.

frú, 1. *n.* front; 2. *prep.* in front of.

frújỳ, 1. *n.* studio.

frúlōlē, 1. *adj.* compliant.

frúsò, 1. *n.* mindfulness; 2. *n.* care.

frúsòxú, 1. *adj.* caring; 2. *adj.* kindhearted.

frúsō, 1. *n.* obedience.

frúxù, 1. *adj.* in front; 2. *adj.* front.

frùmí, 1. *n.* summer.

frùry, 1. *n.* poultry.

frū, 1. *n.* ruby.

frūkrùprý, 1. *n.* hexagon.

frūkrùprýxù, 1. *adj.* hexagonal.

frūmō, 1. *adj.* contained.

frūsō, 1. *n.* containment.

frūxù, 1. *adj.* ruby.

fru̱, 1. *adj.* kind; 2. *adj.* nice.

fru̱ciká, 1. *adj.* thorough.

fru̱cikáclì, 1. *n.* thoroughness.

fru̱cikárō, 1. *adv.* thoroughly.

fruclí, 1. *n.* kindness.

fruco, 1. *n.* activity.

frucoxú, 1. *adj.* active.

frucoxúrō, 1. *adv.* actively.

frū, 1. *num.* six.

fryù, 1. *v.* {m̃, g̀} inform.

frýpò, 1. *n.* throne.

frỳ, 1. *n.* marriage (relationship).

frỳku, 1. *n.* informant.

frỳmu, 1. *adj.* informed.

frỳxú, 1. *adj.* monogamous.

frȳ, 1. *n.* level.

frȳjò, 1. *adj.* local.

frȳjòro, 1. *adv.* locally.

fryco, 1. *n.* rival.

fuê, 1. *v.* {ż, z̃} miss (emotionally).

fuò, 1. *v.* {m̀, m̃, ǹ, Ĩ} fail.

fuo, 1. *v.* {m̀, m̃, ṽ} contact.

fuprā, 1. *n.* mage; 2. *n.* magician.

fuxū, 1. *adj.* magical.

fú, 1. *adv.* up; 2. *n.* up; 3. *prep.* up.

fúxù, 1. *adj.* upper.

fù, 1. *pn.* what.

fùcipa, 1. *n.* obelisk.

fùmo, 1. *adj.* failed.

fùpi, 1. *n.* urethra.

fùso, 1. *n.* failure.

fūlā, 1. *comp.* besides; 2. *comp.* apart from; 3. *comp.* other than; 4. *comp.* aside from; 5. *prep.* besides; 6. *prep.* apart from; 7. *prep.* aside; 8. *prep.* aside from; 9. *prep.* other than.

fu, 1. *adj.* weak (physically); 2. *adj.* feeble.

fuclí, 1. *n.* weakness (physical).

fucú, 1. *n.* castle.

funumo, 1. *adj.* weakened.

funuo, 1. *v.* {m̀, Í, ṽ} weaken.

furo, 1. *adv.* weakly (physical).

fṹ, 1. *n.* magic.

fyì, 1. *v.* {ḿ, m̀} fellatiate.

fylĩ, 1. *adj.* odd (numerically).

fyúfīē, 1. *v.* {m̀, m̃, ṽ} cut down.

fyṳ, 1. *v.* {m̀, m̃} cut (lacerate).

fyǔ, 1. *v.* {m̀} mine (for s.th.).

fý̇, 1. *n.* bridge.

fẏkú, 1. *n.* miner.

fẏmú, 1. *adj.* mined.

fẏsị, 1. *n.* fellatio.

fẏsú, 1. *n.* mine (excavation).

fȳ̈, 1. *adj.* quiet.

fȳ̈clì, 1. *n.* quietness; 2. *n.* quietude.

fȳ̈nū, 1. *n.* priest.

fȳ̈pȳ̈, 1. *n.* budget.

fȳ̈rō, 1. *adv.* quietly.

fy̱, 1. *n.* size.

fy̱clá, 1. *n.* potato.

fy̱múfīmē, 1. *adj.* cut down.

fy̱mṵ, 1. *adj.* cut (lacerated).

fy̱psạ, 1. *n.* jacket.

fy̱rí, 1. *n.* hyperbola.

fy̱ríxù, 1. *adj.* hyperbolic.

fy̱xú, 1. *adj.* sizable.

G

ǵ, 1. *dis.* {2: *Recipient, Agent*}.

g̀, 1. *aux.* (*imperative marker*); 2. *dis.* {2: *Beneficiary, Agent*}.

ḡ, 1. *aux.* would (*conditional marker*).

g̱, 1. *aux.* dare to.

g̃, 1. *aux.* (*self-doubt marker*); 2. *dis.* {2: *Theme, Beneficiary*}.

I

icapsuclī, 1. *n.* informality.

icapsū, 1. *adj.* informal.

iclaklurõ, 1. *adv.* improbably.

iclaklū, 1. *adj.* improbable; 2. *adj.* unlikely.

iclumē, 1. *adj.* unprepared.

iclyxã, 1. *adj.* unavailable.

icumỹ, 1. *adj.* unmentioned.

icxymū, 1. *adj.* undecided.

ijaclijã, 1. *adj.* unobtainable.

ijacujỹ, 1. *adj.* unmentionable.

ijapajū, 1. *adj.* unknowable.

ijaprujã, 1. *adj.* indivisible.

ijapsujõ, 1. *adj.* incomprehensible.

ijasijõ, 1. *adj.* unreadable; 2. *adj.* illegible.

ijomū, 1. *adj.* unlimited.

iklilolē, 1. *adj.* unobservant.

iklyxū, 1. *adj.* unskilled.

ikrulolē, 1. *adj.* disobedient.

ilomurõ, 1. *adv.* unnecessarily.

ilomū, 1. *adj.* unnecessary.

imoxū, 1. *adj.* unnatural.

inuclī, 1. *n.* injustice; 2. *n.* unfairness.

inurõ, 1. *adv.* unjustly; 2. *adv.* unfairly.

inū, 1. *adj.* unjust; 2. *adj.* unfair.

inyklisī, 1. *n.* English (language).

ipamū, 1. *adj.* unknown (facts).

ipselilē, 1. *adj.* discouraging.

ipsocreclī, 1. *n.* dissimilarity.

ipsocrē, 1. *adj.* dissimilar.

ipynimū, 1. *adj.* unscientific.

irecỹ, 1. *adj.* discontinuous.

isē, 1. *adj.* inexpensive.

ixilalã, 1. *adj.* unhelpful.

ìmy, 1. *adj.* still; 2. *adj.* motionless.

ìmyrọ, 1. *adv.* still; 2. *adv.* motionlessly.

inạ, 1. *prep.* without.

īcìpsáxù, 1. *adj.* atheoretical.

īclējīxù, 1. *adj.* unofficial.

īcrēmē, 1. *adj.* insensitive; 2. *adj.* inconsiderate.

īcrēmēclì, 1. *n.* insensitivity (lack of consideration).

īcxàxú, 1. *adj.* illegal (not allowed by law).

īcxàxúclì, 1. *n.* illegality.

īfrècí, 1. *adj.* immortal.

īfrècíclì, 1. *n.* immortality.

īfrècínuō, 1. *v.* {m̀, ǹ, Í, ṽ} immortalize.

īfrècínūmō, 1. *adj.* immortalized.

īfrècínūsō, 1. *n.* immortalization.

ījà, 1. *adj.* unsweet.

ījàcu̱, 1. *adj.* inconsistent.

ījàcu̱clí, 1. *n.* inconsistency.

ījācìjé, 1. *adj.* inapplicable.

ījājījè, 1. *adj.* unlistenable.

ījājōjū, 1. *adj.* unbreakable.

ījājùjý, 1. *adj.* irreducible.

ījājùjýrō, 1. *adj.* irreducibly.

ījākējū, 1. *adj.* inadmissible.

ījākrījà, 1. *adj.* incomparable.

ījākūjà, 1. *adj.* untouchable; 2. *adj.* intangible.

ījālūjè, 1. *adj.* unbelievable; 2. *adj.* incredible.

ījānījà, 1. *adj.* unforgivable.

ījāpījā, 1. *adj.* unprovable.

ījāpījō, 1. *adj.* unforgettable.

ījāplījè, 1. *adj.* inedible.

ījāplòjí, 1. *adj.* unspeakable.

ījārìjó, 1. *adj.* invisible.

ījārìjóclì, 1. *n.* invisibility.

ījāxùje̱, 1. *adj.* incurable.

ījīlìxú, 1. *adj.* inexperienced.

ījōmū, 1. *adj.* unbroken (an object).

ījùmé, 1. *adj.* unexamined.

ījỳklú, 1. *adj.* impossible.

ījỳklúclì, 1. *n.* impossibility.

ījỳklúrō, 1. *adv.* impossibly.

īkàcuxú, 1. *adj.* insecure.

īkèlólē, 1. *adj.* unexpressive.

īkfòsixú, 1. *adj.* unentertaining.

īklēmȳ, 1. *adj.* unpaid.

īkrèka, 1. *adj.* unpopular.

īkrèmy, 1. *adj.* unexplained.

īlēlō, 1. *adj.* unintentional.

īlēlōrō, 1. *adv.* unintentionally.

īlō, 1. *adj.* old (not new).

īlùjú, 1. *adj.* uncommon.

īlùlele, 1. *adj.* incredulous.

īlùleleclí, 1. *n.* incredulity; 2. *n.* incredulousness.

īlūmē, 1. *adj.* unconfirmed.

īmèxú, 1. *adj.* disorderly.

īmū, 1. *adj.* unequal.

īnàmóxù, 1. *adj.* unimaginative.

īnàpu, 1. *adj.* irrelevant.

īnàpuclí, 1. *n.* irrelevance.

īnìcxi, 1. *adj.* disabled (not able-bodied).

īnìlale, 1. *adj.* unforgiving.

īnìme, 1. *adj.* unsent.

īnìxýxù, 1. *adj.* irresponsible.

īpīmā, 1. *adj.* unproven.

īplāpỳ, 1. *adj.* unusual.

īplāpỳro, 1. *adv.* unusually.

īplòlílē, 1. *adj.* untalkative.

īplòmí, 1. *adj.* unspoken.

īplōmī, 1. *adj.* unsaid; 2. *adj.* unmentioned.

īpsỳ, 1. *adj.* untidy.

īrìmó, 1. *adj.* unobserved; 2. *adj.* unseen.

īrūnàxú, 1. *adj.* asocial.

īrỳlile, 1. *adj.* unexciting.

īrỳmi, 1. *adj.* unexcited.

īsīlēklū, 1. *adj.* invulnerable.

īsīlēklūclì, 1. *n.* invulnerability.

īsrākīxù, 1. *adj.* independent.

īsrākīxùrọ, 1. *adj.* independently.

īsròxú, 1. *adj.* unreasonable; 2. *adj.* illogical.

īxīmō, 1. *adj.* unaffected.

īxōcà, 1. *adj.* inaccurate.

īxōcàclí, 1. *n.* inaccuracy.

īxùmé, 1. *adj.* undiscovered.

īxūlēlē, 1. *adj.* insignificant.

īxūlēlēclì, 1. *n.* insignificance.

ịcạ, 1. *adj.* unsafe.

ịcíxù, 1. *adj.* unreal.

ịcxímē, 1. *adj.* unaltered; 2. *adj.* unchanged.

ịcxýlūlē, 1. *adj.* disagreeable.

ịfrụ, 1. *adj.* unkind.

ịfrụcọxú, 1. *adj.* inactive.

ịfrụcọxúrō, 1. *adv.* inactively.

ịjafịjé, 1. *adj.* unaffordable.

ịjajújè, 1. *adj.* immovable.

ịjakẹjọ, 1. *adj.* unimaginable.

ịjakfújà, 1. *adj.* unavoidable; 2. *adj.* inevitable.

ịjakfújàrọ, 1. *adv.* unavoidably; 2. *adv.* inevitably.

ịjaklịjy, 1. *adj.* unrecognizable.

ịjaklújà, 1. *adj.* unidentifiable.

ịjakrẹjó, 1. *adj.* irreplaceable.

ịjamíjà, 1. *adj.* uncountable; 2. *adj.* countless.

ịjanají, 1. *adj.* indefensible.

ịjapajị, 1. *adj.* unplayable (music).

ịjapịjó, 1. *adj.* uncontrollable.

ịjaplújò, 1. *adj.* unusable.

ịjapụjá, 1. *adj.* unacceptable.

ịjarẹjị, 1. *adj.* unlikable.

ịjasịjẹ, 1. *adj.* inaudible.

ịjasríjò, 1. *adj.* unpreventable.

ịjaxíjà, 1. *adj.* immeasurable.

ịjịfí, 1. *adj.* impure.

ịjịfíclì, 1. *n.* impurity.

ịjúmè, 1. *adj.* unmoved; 2. *adj.* unshifted.

i̱kfújè, 1. *adj.* unremarkable.

i̱kfúmè, 1. *adj.* incomplete.

i̱kfu̱ru̱, 1. *adj.* uncertain.

i̱kfu̱ru̱clí, 1. *n.* uncertainty.

i̱kfu̱ru̱ro̱, 1. *adv.* uncertainly.

i̱kfýlà, 1. *adj.* infrequent.

i̱kfýlàclí, 1. *n.* infrequency.

i̱kfýlàro̱, 1. *adv.* infrequently.

i̱krímē, 1. *adj.* undeveloped.

i̱kro̱, 1. *adj.* cowardly (not brave).

i̱krúmà, 1. *adj.* uncovered (not covered).

i̱kýkfō, 1. *adj.* imprecise.

i̱kyfi̱xú, 1. *adj.* nonlinear.

i̱kyfi̱xúclì, 1. *n.* nonlinearity.

i̱mékrè, 1. *adj.* unfunny.

i̱me̱ró, 1. *adj.* impatient.

i̱me̱róclì, 1. *n.* impatience.

i̱me̱rórō, 1. *adv.* impatiently.

i̱mú, 1. *adj.* untrue.

i̱mu̱la̱le̱, 1. *adj.* unimpressive.

i̱mu̱ma̱, 1. *adj.* unimpressed.

i̱no̱lu̱le̱, 1. *adj.* immaterial.

i̱no̱su̱xú, 1. *adj.* unimportant.

i̱pi̱me̱, 1. *adj.* unknown; 2. *adj.* unfamiliar.

i̱pláplỳxú, 1. *adj.* ineffective.

i̱pla̱mó, 1. *adj.* imperfect.

i̱pla̱móclì, 1. *n.* imperfection.

i̱pla̱mórō, 1. *adv.* imperfectly.

i̱plúmò, 1. *adj.* unused.

i̱plu̱kfá, 1. *adj.* untruthful; 2. *adj.* dishonest.

i̱plu̱kfáclì, 1. *n.* dishonesty.

i̱plu̱kfárō, 1. *adv.* dishonestly.

i̱prékfȳxù, 1. *adj.* disadvantageous.

i̱prúmā, 1. *adj.* unmarked.

i̱psa̱cíxù, 1. *adj.* asymmetrical.

i̱psú, 1. *adj.* insane; 2. *adj.* crazy.

ipsúclì, 1. *n.* insanity.

ipụcí, 1. *adj.* unholy.

ipyni̲, 1. *adj.* impersonal.

irálìclí, 1. *n.* nonviolence.

irálìle̲, 1. *adj.* unsuccessful.

irykfa̲, 1. *adj.* non-native.

isálùle̲, 1. *adj.* uncreative.

isime̲, 1. *adj.* unheard.

isópū, 1. *adj.* insufficient.

isóxù, 1. *adj.* unhealthy.

israsùxú, 1. *adj.* disorganized.

isrụse̲, 1. *adj.* unclear; 2. *adj.* not obvious.

isýcòxú, 1. *adj.* uninteresting.

isýxù, 1. *adj.* atypical.

ixá, 1. *adj.* unlucky; 2. *adj.* unfortunate.

ixáclì, 1. *n.* misfortune.

ixárō, 1. *adv.* unluckily; 2. *adv.* unfortunately.

ixúnāxù, 1. *adj.* cheap (bad quality).

J

jaclijã, 1. *adj.* obtainable.

jacujỹ, 1. *adj.* mentionable.

jaī, 1. *v.* {m̀, m̃} pass (a ball, etc.).

jakajĩ, 1. *adj.* fastenable.

jaklijõ, 1. *adj.* noticeable.

japajū, 1. *adj.* knowable.

japrujaclĩ, 1. *n.* divisibility.

japrujã, 1. *adj.* divisible.

japsujõ, 1. *adj.* understandable; 2. *adj.* comprehensible.

jasijoclĩ, 1. *n.* legibility.

jasijõ, 1. *adj.* legible.

jaú, 1. *v.* {ḿ, m̀, ñ} swear; 2. *v.* {ḿ, m̀, ñ} vow.

jaù, 1. *v.* {m̀, r̃} protect.

jaụ, 1. *v.* {m̀} urge (press s.o./s.th.).

jaxū, 1. *adj.* trapped.

já, 1. *adv.* why.

jámū, 1. *adj.* sworn.

jásū, 1. *n.* vow.

jà, 1. *adj.* sweet.

jàclí, 1. *n.* sweetness.

jàcu̲, 1. *adj.* consistent.

jàcu̲clí, 1. *n.* consistency.

jàku̲, 1. *n.* protector.

jàlu̲le̲, 1. *adj.* protective.

jànuo̲, 1. *v.* {m̀, Í, v́, ṽ} sweeten.

jànu̲mo̲, 1. *adj.* sweetened.

jàsu̲, 1. *n.* protection.

jā, 1. *n.* wrist.

jācìjé, 1. *adj.* applicable.

jācrējù, 1. *adj.* separable.

jāfèjí, 1. *adj.* preferable.

jāfrìjá, 1. *adj.* presentable.

jāfū, 1. *n.* uncle.

jājījè, 1. *adj.* listenable.

jājōjū, 1. *adj.* breakable.

jājùjý, 1. *adj.* reducible.

jājūjè, 1. *adj.* arguable.

jājỹjù, 1. *adj.* repeatable.

jākējū, 1. *adj.* admissible.

jākējūclì, 1. *n.* admissibility.

jākfùjý, 1. *adj.* watchable.

jākfūjò, 1. *adj.* respectable.

jākījà, 1. *adj.* flammable; 2. *adj.* inflammable.

jākījèsryjí, 1. *adj.* tameable.

jāklējỹ, 1. *adj.* payable.

jāklìjó, 1. *adj.* potable.

jāklìjóclì, 1. *n.* potability.

jākrējỳ, 1. *adj.* explainable.

jākrījà, 1. *adj.* comparable.

jākūjà, 1. *adj.* tangible; 2. *adj.* touchable.

jālūjè, 1. *adj.* credible; 2. *adj.* believable.

jāmūjō, 1. *adj.* permissible; 2. *adj.* allowable; 3. *adj.* allowed.

jānījà, 1. *adj.* forgivable.

jānùjé, 1. *adj.* collectible.

jānùjéclì, 1. *n.* collectibility.

jāpījā, 1. *adj.* provable.

jāpījō, 1. *adj.* forgettable.

jāplījè, 1. *adj.* edible.

jāplījèclí, 1. *n.* edibility.

jāplījō, 1. *adj.* winnable.

jāplòjí, 1. *adj.* speakable.

jāpsìjé, 1. *adj.* expectable.

jāpsījō, 1. *adj.* enjoyable.

jāpsỳjí, 1. *adj.* memorable.

jārē, 1. *n.* opinion; 2. *n.* position.

jārējȳ, 1. *adj.* growable.

jārēxù, 1. *adj.* opinionated.

jārìjó, 1. *adj.* visible.

jārìjóclì, 1. *n.* visibility.

jārījā, 1. *adj.* answerable.

jāsī, 1. *n.* pass (of a ball, etc.).

jāsrājī, 1. *adj.* dependable.

jāsrūjā, 1. *adj.* correctable.

jāxō, 1. *n.* freshwater.

jāxùjé, 1. *adj.* discoverable.

jāxùje, 1. *adj.* curable.

jacxéjỳ, 1. *adj.* teachable.

jacxyjú, 1. *adj.* acceptable; 2. *adj.* agreeable.

jaféjù, 1. *adj.* extensible.

jafijé, 1. *adj.* affordable.

jafraji, 1. *adj.* learnable.

jajújè, 1. *adj.* movable.

jajujý, 1. *adj.* returnable.

jakejo, 1. *adj.* imaginable.

jakfújà, 1. *adj.* avoidable; 2. *adj.* evitable.

jaklijy, 1. *adj.* recognizable.

jaklújà, 1. *adj.* identifiable.

jakrejó, 1. *adj.* replaceable.

jaméjì, 1. *adj.* desirable.

jamíjà, 1. *adj.* countable.

jamije, 1. *adj.* laughable.

janají, 1. *adj.* defensible.

japaji, 1. *adj.* playable (music).

japijó, 1. *adj.* controllable.

japlíjà, 1. *adj.* manageable.

japlújò, 1. *adj.* usable.

japsújà, 1. *adj.* publishable.

japujá, 1. *adj.* acceptable.

japujáclì, 1. *n.* acceptability.

jareji, 1. *adj.* likable.

jarijá, 1. *adj.* achievable.

jarijé, 1. *adj.* workable.

jasije, 1. *adj.* audible.

jasríjò, 1. *adj.* preventable.

jasujó, 1. *adj.* reachable.

jaxíjà, 1. *adj.* measurable.

jã, 1. *n.* trap.

jecõ, 1. *n.* cell (organism).

jeì, 1. *v.* {ḿ, Í, Ì, j̀} lay (down); 2. *v.* {ḿ, Í, Ì, j̀} rest.

jeklarikoxũ, 1. *adj.* three-dimensional.

jekỹ, 1. *n.* loser (sports, games).

jelõ, 1. *n.* letter; 2. *n.* epistle.

jemỹ, 1. *adj.* lost (sports, games).

jeprã, 1. *n.* weatherman; 2. *n.* weatherperson; 3. *n.* weatherwoman.

jeỹ, 1. *v.* {Í, z̀} lose (a game, etc.).

jé, 1. *n.* sign.

jérēcrō, 1. *n.* tetrahedron.

jérēcrōxù, 1. *adj.* tetrahedral.

jè, 1. *adj.* small; 2. *adj.* little; 3. **prākfē jè** *n.* small intestines.

jècla, 1. *n.* mohair.

jèfo, 1. *n.* bump.

jèfoxú, 1. *adj.* bumpy.

jèfoxúclì, 1. *n.* bumpiness.

jèlịlẹ, 1. *adj.* rested.

jèsị, 1. *n.* rest; 2. *n.* relaxation.

jē, 1. *n.* sugar.

jēxè, 1. *n.* feather.

jēxù, 1. *adj.* sugary; 2. *adj.* sweet.

jẹ, 1. *num.* three.

jẹjẹ, 1. *adj.* third.

jẹpạ, 1. *num.* thirty.

jẹpạpạ, 1. *adj.* thirtieth.

jey̱, 1. *v.* {m̀, m̃, Ì, j̃} carry.

jẽ, 1. *n.* weather.

jiclĩ, 1. *n.* note (message).

jié, 1. *v.* {ź} yawn; 2. *v.* {z̃} yawn (at s.th.).

jiè, 1. *v.* {ḿ, m̀, m̃} listen (to s.th. audibly).

jilĩ, 1. *n.* tendril.

jiỳ, 1. *v.* {v́} relate (to s.th. abstractly).

jí, 1. *n.* friend.

jísē, 1. *n.* yawn.

jíxēclù, 1. *n.* hellscape.

jíxù, 1. *adj.* friendly.

jíxùclí, 1. *n.* friendliness.

jì, 1. *adj.* narrow.

jìclí, 1. *n.* narrowness.

jìkẹ, 1. *n.* listener.

jìkú, 1. *n.* sphere.

jìkúxù, 1. *adj.* spherical.

jī, 1. *adj.* south; 2. *adv.* south; 3. *adv.* southward; 4. *n.* south.

jīlè, 1. *n.* thread.

jīlì, 1. *n.* experience (effectual event).

jīlìxú, 1. *adj.* experienced.

jīxù, 1. *adj.* southern.

jị, 1. *n.* fire.

jịcrị, 1. *adj.* dangerous.

jịcrịclí, 1. *n.* danger.

jịcrịrọ, 1. *adv.* dangerously.

jịfí, 1. *adj.* pure.

jifíclì, 1. *n.* purity.

jifínuō, 1. *v.* {m̀, ǹ, Í, ṽ} purify.

jifínūkō, 1. *n.* purifier.

jifínūmō, 1. *adj.* purified.

jifínūsō, 1. *n.* purification.

jifírō, 1. *adv.* purely.

jifi, 1. *adj.* eventual.

jifiro, 1. *adv.* eventually.

jiní, 1. *n.* rectum.

jipé, 1. *n.* goose.

jipénē, 1. *n.* gosling.

jixú, 1. *adj.* fiery.

jolucã, 1. *n.* bedroom.

jolũ, 1. *n.* bed.

jomũ, 1. *adj.* limited.

josũ, 1. *n.* limitation; 2. *n.* limit.

joū, 1. *v.* {m̀, Í, ṽ} break.

jou, 1. *v.* {ḿ} pass (not participate).

joũ, 1. *v.* {m̀} limit (s.th.); 2. *v.* {ĵ} limit (s.o./s.th. to s.th.).

jó, 1. *n.* day; 2. *n.* daytime.

jófē, 1. *n.* skewer.

jò, 1. *n.* lake; 2. *n.* pond; 3. *n.* water (body).

jòca, 1. *n.* beer.

jòcxe, 1. *n.* tower.

jòfá, 1. *n.* bog.

jōmū, 1. *adj.* broken (an object).

jo, 1. *adv.* please; 2. *intj.* please.

jocry, 1. *n.* cloak.

jokry, 1. *n.* space; 2. *n.* area.

jorá, 1. *n.* coif.

jõ, 1. *n.* road.

jué, 1. *v.* {m̀} clear (empty s.th.); 2. *v.* {ṽ} clear (s.th. of s.th.).

juè, 1. *n.* {ḿ, m̀} argue (about s.th.).

juê, 1. *v.* {ḿ, m̀, m̃, Í} move; 2. *v.* {ḿ, m̀, m̃, Í} shift.

juě, 1. *v.* {m̀, m̃} examine.

julaxurō, 1. *adv.* essentially.

julaxũ, 1. *adj.* essential.

julã, 1. *n.* essence.

julixũ, 1. *adj.* attentive.

julĩ, 1. *n.* attention.

julolẽ, 1. *adj.* careful; 2. *adj.* mindful.

junexũ, 1. *adj.* musical (having the quality of music).

junẽ, 1. *n.* music.

juõ, 1. *v.* {ḿ, ź} be mindful; 2. *v.* {m̀, z̃} mind (be mindful of s.th.).

jusõ, 1. *n.* mindfulness.

juý, 1. *v.* {m̀, ȷ̃} return (s.th.).

juỹ, 1. *v.* {ḿ, r̀, ź, z̃} sigh (at s.th.).

juy̌, 1. *v.* {m̀, ĺ} reduce; 2. *v.* {v́, ṽ} reduce (by s.th.).

jú, 1. *n.* sun; 2. *n.* star.

júkā, 1. *n.* coast.

júkè, 1. *n.* mover (of furniture, etc.).

júklūkù, 1. *n.* spacecraft.

júmè, 1. *adj.* moved; 2. *adj.* shifted.

júmē, 1. *adj.* cleared.

júmȳ, 1. *adj.* returned (an object).

júnì, 1. *adj.* tall.

júprà, 1. *n.* topic; 2. *n.* subject.

júpsūxī, 1. *n.* solar system; 2. *n.* star system.

júsè, 1. *n.* movement; 2. *n.* motion.

júxù, 1. *adj.* sunny.

jùfri̱, 1. *n.* circle.

jùfri̱xú, 1. *adj.* circular; 2. *adj.* round.

jùké, 1. *n.* examiner.

jùle̱le̱, 1. *adj.* argumentative.

jùmé, 1. *adj.* examined.

jùme̱, 1. *adj.* argued.

jùmu̱, 1. *n.* pillow.

jùplí, 1. *n.* wire.

jùpli̱fyku̱, 1. *n.* wirecutter.

jùsé, 1. *n.* examination.

jùse̱, 1. *n.* argument (charged discussion).

jùsý, 1. *n.* reduction.

jū, 1. *n.* skull.

jūcà, 1. *n.* sunset; 2. *n.* sundown.

jūpsò, 1. *n.* torso.

jūpsōcrè, 1. *n.* chestplate; 2. *n.* chest armor.

jūsȳ, 1. *n.* sigh.

ju̱, 1. *adj.* old (in age).

ju̱clánì, 1. *n.* sunglasses.

ju̱cú, 1. *n.* program (social or political).

ju̱fú, 1. *n.* sunrise; 2. *n.* sunup.

ju̱psí, 1. *n.* queen.

ju̱sá, 1. *n.* strap.

jyplī, 1. *n.* boot.

jyù, 1. *v.* {m̀, ñ} repeat.

jyû, 1. *v.* {ḿ, m̀, Í} hide.

jýkrē, 1. *n.* kidney.

jýmù, 1. *adj.* hidden.

jỳ, 1. *adj.* next.

jỳklú, 1. *adj.* possible.

jỳklúclì, 1. *n.* possibility.

jỳklúrō, 1. *adv.* possibly.

jỳlu̱le̱, 1. *adj.* repetitive.

jỳmu̱, 1. *adj.* repeated.

jỳple̱, 1. *n.* tomato.

jỳsu̱, 1. *n.* repetition.

jȳ, 1. *adv.* how.

jy̱, 1. *adv.* so; 2. *adv.* quite; 3. *adv.* rather.

jy̱cókō, 1. *n.* eclipse.

jy̱pla̱, 1. *n.* situation; 2. *n.* circumstances.

j́, 1. *aux.* if (*hypothetical marker*).

j̀, 1. *aux.* intend to; 2. *dis.* {2: *Location, Agent*}.

j̄, 1. *aux.* continue to; 2. *aux.* keep (doing s.th.).

j̱, 1. *aux.* be able to; 2. *aux.* can.

j̰, 1. *aux.* hope to; 2. *dis.* {3: *Theme/Patient, Location, Agent*}.

K

kacalopsĭ, 1. *n.* Katalopsi (language).

kaclĭ, 1. *n.* toughness; 2. *n.* resilience.

kaĭ, 1. *v.* {m̀, ĺ} fasten (s.th.); 2. *v.* {l̀, j̃} fasten (s.th. to s.th.).

kamĭ, 1. *adj.* fastened.

ká, 1. *comp.* until; 2. *prep.* until.

kálỳ, 1. *adj.* fatigued; 2. *adj.* tired.

kálỳclí, 1. *n.* fatigue.

kárā, 1. *n.* capital (city); 2. *n.* metropolis.

kà, 1. *n.* mail; 2. *n.* post.

kàcu̠, 1. *n.* security.

kàcu̠xú, 1. *adj.* secure.

kàlu̠, 1. *n.* rug.

kàmú, 1. *adj.* chewed up.

kàrá, 1. *adv.* past; 2. *prep.* past.

kā, 1. *n.* planet.

ka̠, 1. *adj.* north; 2. *adv.* north; 2. *adv.* northward; 3. *n.* north.

ka̠nu̠, 1. *n.* novel (book).

ka̠pé, 1. *n.* frame (e.g. of a painting).

ka̠psi̠, 1. *n.* grave.

ka̠sa̠, 1. *n.* story.

ka̠xú, 1. *adj.* northern.

kã, 1. *adj.* tough; 2. *adj.* resilient.

keí, 1. *v.* {ǹ, z̃} taste.

kenỹ, 1. *n.* plate.

keò, 1. *v.* {m̀, m̃, ǹ, ṽ} hit.

keōfiē, 1. *v.* {m̀, m̃, ṽ} knock down.

keo̠, 1. *v.* {z̃} imagine (s.o./s.th.); 2. *v.* {z̀} imagine (*propositions*).

keŏ, 1. *v.* {m̀, ñ} express.

keŏploĭ, 1. *v.* {m̀, ñ} articulate.

keū, 1. *v.* {m̀, m̃} admit (permit entry); 2. *v.* {m̀} let (*propositions*).

keŷ, 1. *v.* {m̀} scream; 2. *v.* {m̀} cry.

ké, 1. *n.* job; 2. *n.* career.

kécā, 1. *n.* famine.

kékĭ, 1. *n.* taste-tester.

kénà, 1. *n.* pendant.

késī, 1. *n.* taste; 2. *n.* flavor.

késīxù, 1. *adj.* tasty; 2. *adj.* flavorful.

késīxùclí, 1. *n.* tastiness.

késỳ, 1. *n.* scream.

kè, 1. *pn.* nothing.

kècá, 1. *n.* whisker.

kèkóplòkí, 1. *n.* articulator.

kèko̠, 1. *n.* hitter.

kèkrá, 1. *n.* platinum.

kèkráxù, 1. *adj.* platinum; 2. *adj.* made of platinum.

kèkra̠, 1. *n.* orange (fruit).

kèkra̠cifu̠, 1. *n.* orange tree.

kèlólē, 1. *adj.* expressive.

kèlóplòlílē, 1. *adj.* articulate.

kèlóplòlílērō, 1. *adv.* articulately.

kèmó, 1. *adj.* expressed.

kèmóplòmí, 1. *adj.* articulated.

kèmo̠, 1. *adj.* hit.

kèsó, 1. *n.* expression (of opinion, etc.).

kèsóplòsí, 1. *n.* articulation.

kèsóxù, 1. *adj.* expressive.

kēkū, 1. *n.* doorman.

kēmōfīmē, 1. *adj.* knocked down.

kēmū, 1. *adj.* admitted (allowed to enter).

kēprè, 1. *n.* robe.

kēsū, 1. *n.* admittance; 2. *n.* entry; 3. *n.* admission.

ke̠, 1. *prep.* above.

ke̠cré, 1. *n.* moss.

ke̠kú, 1. *n.* sash.

ke̠no̠, 1. *n.* bear.

ke̠no̠no̠, 1. *n.* bear cub.

ke̠so̠, 1. *n.* ideation.

kfakū, 1. *n.* presenter; 2. *n.* demonstrator.

kfamū, 1. *adj.* shown; 2. *adj.* demonstrated.

kfaū, 1. *v.* {m̀, ǵ, ñ} show; 2. *v.* {m̀, ñ} show (*propositions*) 3. *v.* {m̀, ñ} show off (present).

kfaû, 1. *v.* {m̀, m̄, m̃} produce (movies, music, etc.).

kfá, 1. *adj.* crazy; 2. *adj.* insane.

kfáclì, 1. *n.* craziness.

kfákù, 1. *n.* producer (of movies, music, etc.).

kfámù, 1. *adj.* produced (movies, music, etc.).

kfánuō, 1. *v.* {m̀, Í, v́, ṽ} drive crazy; 2. *v.* {m̀, Í, v́, ṽ} drive insane.

kfásù, 1. *n.* production.

kfàná, 1. *n.* study; 2. *n.* office.

kfàpo̱, 1. *n.* structure.

kfàpo̱xú, 1. *adj.* structured.

kfā, 1. *n.* toe.

kfācò, 1. *n.* toenail.

kfa̱, 1. *n.* seed.

kfeí, 1. *v.* {m̀, ñ} suggest; 2. *v.* {m̀, ñ} imply.

kfey̌, 1. *v.* {Í} grow up; 2. *v.* {Í} develop.

kfé, 1. *num.* nine.

kfékfē, 1. *adj.* ninth.

kfékrùprý, 1. *n.* nonagon.

kfékrùprýxù, 1. *adj.* nonagonal.

kfémī, 1. *adj.* implied.

kfépā, 1. *num.* ninety.

kfépāpā, 1. *adj.* ninetieth.

kfésī, 1. *n.* implication.

kfè, 1. *n.* scarf.

kfèmý, 1. *adj.* grown-up.

kfē, 1. *n.* flag.

kfe̱sé, 1. *n.* photo; 2. *n.* photograph.

kfẽ, 1. *n.* dam.

kfiǎ, 1. *v.* {m̀, ṽ} judge.

kfiè, 1. *v.* {m̀, r̃} commit (s.th. to s.th.); 2. *v.* {m̀, r̃} devote (s.th. to s.th.).

kfiê, 1. *v.* {m̀} coerce; 2. *v.* {m̀} force.

kfiò, 1. *v.* {ź} break down (mentally).

kfio̱, 1. *v.* {m̀, Í, Ì, j̃} release.

kfí, 1. *n.* light.

kfíklù, 1. *n.* lobster.

kfílèle̱, 1. *adj.* coercive.

kfímè, 1. *adj.* forced; 2. *adj.* coerced.

kfísè, 1. *n.* coercion; 2. *n.* force.

kfísỳ, 1. *n.* lighthouse.

kfíxù, 1. *adj.* luminous; 2. *adj.* bright.

kfíxùrọ, 1. *adv.* luminously; 2. *adv.* brightly.

kfì, 1. *prep.* from (*source, origin*).

kfìká, 1. *n.* judge.

kfìkọ, 1. *n.* nervous wreck.

kfìkọxú, 1. *adj.* nervous.

kfìmá, 1. *adj.* judged.

kfìrí, 1. *n.* minute (time).

kfìsá, 1. *n.* judgement.

kfìsáxù, 1. *adj.* judgemental.

kfìsọ, 1. *n.* nervous breakdown.

kfịlụ, 1. *n.* funeral; 2. **kfịlụ cxèsọ** *n.* funeral home.

kfịlụprá, 1. *n.* funeral director.

kfịprẹ, 1. *n.* currency; 2. *n.* money.

kfịsọ, 1. *n.* release.

kfī̀, 1. *n.* name.

kfoí, 1. *v.* {Í, ż} fit (clothing).

kfoì, 1. *v.* {ṁ, ǹ, Í} entertain.

kfoxū̃, 1. *adj.* self-evident; 2. *adj.* axiomatic.

kfó, 1. *n.* egg.

kfò, 1. *pn.* herself; 2. *pn.* himself; 3. *pn.* myself; 4. *pn.* ourselves; 5. *pn.* themselves; 6. *pn.* yourself; 7. *pn.* yourselves.

kfòkị, 1. *n.* entertainer.

kfòlịlẹ, 1. *adj.* amusing; 2. *adj.* entertaining.

kfòsị, 1. *n.* entertainment.

kfòsịxú, 1. *adj.* entertaining.

kfō, 1. *adj.* rich; 2. *adj.* wealthy.

kfōnuō, 1. *v.* {ṁ} enrich.

kfōnūmō, 1. *adj.* enriched.

kfọfrụ, 1. *n.* stock; 2. *n.* inventory.

kfõ, 1. *n.* truth.

kfuā, 1. *v.* {v́} relate (familial); 2. *v.* be related (to s.o.).

kfuạ, 1. *v.* {ṁ, ǹ, ṽ} refer.

kfuâ, 1. *v.* {m̀} avoid.

kfuê, 1. *v.* {m̀, m̃, ṽ} finish; 2. *v.* {m̀, m̃, ṽ} complete.

kfuó, 1. *v.* {m̀, ñ} confess; 2. *v.* {m̀, ñ} admit.

kfuò, 1. *v.* {m̀, z̃} respect (s.o./s.th.); 2. *v.* {z̀} respect (*propositions*).

kfuō, 1. *v.* {v́} depend (on s.th.); 2. *v.* {v́} be dependent (on s.th.).

kfuỳ, 1. *v.* {Í} glimmer; 2. *v.* {Í} shimmer.

kfuy̌, 1. *v.* {ḿ, m̀, m̃} watch.

kfú, 1. *comp.* because; 2. *conj.* because; 3. *prep.* because of; 4. *prep.* due to; 5. *comp.* since.

kfújè, 1. *adj.* remarkable; 2. *adj.* noteworthy.

kfújèclí, 1. *n.* noteworthiness.

kfúmè, 1. *adj.* completed; 2. *adj.* complete.

kfúmèro̱, 1. *adv.* completely.

kfúmō, 1. *adj.* confessed; 2. *adj.* admitted.

kfúsà, 1. *n.* avoidance.

kfúsè, 1. *n.* completion.

kfúsō, 1. *n.* confession; 2. *n.* admission.

kfùfý, 1. *n.* petal.

kfùlo̱le̱, 1. *adj.* respectful.

kfùlýlē, 1. *adj.* watchful.

kfùlyle̱, 1. *adj.* shimmery.

kfùmo̱, 1. *adj.* respected.

kfùmý, 1. *adj.* watched.

kfùso̱, 1. *n.* respect.

kfùsy, 1. *n.* glimmer; 2. *n.* shimmer.

kfū, 1. *det.* most (majority); 2. *pn.* most (majority).

kfūlỳ, 1. *n.* cauliflower.

kfūrỳ, 1. *n.* tentacle.

kfūsō, 1. *n.* dependence; 2. *n.* contingence.

kfūsrò, 1. *n.* handgun.

kfu̱, 1. *n.* lip.

kfu̱co̱, 1. *n.* flower.

kfu̱ru̱, 1. *adj.* definite; 2. *adj.* certain.

kfu̱ru̱clí, 1. *n.* certainty.

kfu̱ru̱ro̱, 1. *adv.* certainly; 2. *adv.* definitely.

kfu̱sa̱, 1. *n.* reference.

kfũ, 1. *n.* hand.

kfyī, 1. *v.* {m̀} fornicate.

kfyprã, 1. *n.* farmer.

kfý, 1. *adj.* satiated; 2. *adj.* full.

kfýclì, 1. *n.* satiation; 2. *n.* fullness.

kfýlà, 1. *adj.* frequent.

kfýlàclí, 1. *n.* frequency.

kfýlàro̱, 1. *adv.* frequently.

kfỹ, 1. *adj.* recent.

kfỹclì, 1. *adj.* recency.

kfỹkī, 1. *n.* fornicator.

kfỹrō, 1. *adv.* lately; 2. *adv.* recently.

kfỹsī, 1. *n.* fornication.

kfy̱, 1. *adj.* soft (to touch).

kfy̱clí, 1. *n.* softness (to touch).

kfy̱nuo̱, 1. *v.* {m̀, Í, v́, ṽ} soften.

kfy̱nu̱mo̱, 1. *adj.* softened.

kfỹ, 1. *n.* farm; 2. *n.* garden.

kià, 1. *v.* {m̀, m̃, Í} burn.

kiāfriē, 1. *v.* {m̀, m̃, ǹ, ñ} firebomb.

kia̱, 1. *v.* {m̀} take care (of s.o./s.th. e.g. as hospice); 1. *v.* {m̀} care (for s.o./s.th.).

kiè, 1. *v.* {ḿ, m̀} act (behave, take action).

kièsryí, 1. *v.* {ḿ, m̀, Í} tame.

kilē, 1. *n.* fort.

kio̱, 1. *v.* {Í} become (*compounds*).

kiŷ, 1. *v.* {ḿ, m̀} change (clothes).

kí, 1. *n.* man; 2. *n.* husband.

kímỳ, 1. *adj.* changed (clothes).

kínì, 1. *n.* human.

kíprù, 1. *n.* text.

kíprùxú, 1. *adj.* text-based.

kípsō, 1. *n.* hide; 2. *n.* skin.

kíxī, 1. *n.* eyebrow.

kíxù, 1. *adj.* manly; 2. *adj.* masculine.

kíxùclí, 1. *n.* manliness; 2. *n.* masculinity.

kì, 1. *n.* route; 2. *n.* path.

kìkẹ, 1. *n.* actor; 2. *n.* actress.

kìklạ, 1. *n.* toolbox.

kìmạ, 1. *adj.* burnt; 2. *adj.* burned.

kìmẹsrýmī, 1. *adj.* tame; 2. *adj.* tamed.

kìmẹsrýmīclì, 1. *n.* tameness.

kìrị, 1. *n.* tea.

kìsạ, 1. *n.* burn.

kìsẹ, 1. *n.* action; 2. *n.* act.

kìsẹsrýsī, 1. *n.* taming.

kīkāfrīkē, 1. *n.* firebomber.

kīmāfrīmē, 1. *adj.* firebombed.

kīsāfrīsē, 1. *n.* firebombing.

kīsrà, 1. *n.* brush (bushes, etc.).

kị, 1. *n.* eye.

kịclánì, 1. *n.* eyeglasses.

kịfọ, 1. *n.* turtle.

kịkạ, 1. *n.* caretaker.

kịpró, 1. *n.* list.

kịsạ, 1. *n.* care; 2. *n.* caretaking.

kī, 1. *n.* tool.

klaí, 1. *v.* {z̃} despise (s.o./s.th.); 2. *v.* {ż} despise (*propositions*); 3. *v.* {z̃} hate (s.o./s.th.); 4. {z̃} *v.* hate (*propositions*).

klarikõ, 1. *n.* dimension.

klau, 1. *v.* {ź, z̃} dream (about s.o./s.th.); 2. *v.* {ż} dream (*propositions*).

klá, 1. *comp.* though; 2. *comp.* although; 3. *comp.* even though.

klákī, 1. *n.* hater.

klálīlē, 1. *adj.* hateful.

klálīlērō, 1. *adv.* hatefully.

klámī, 1. *adj.* hated.

klápù, 1. *n.* poem; 2. *n.* poetry.

klápùprá, 1. *n.* poet.

klápùxú, 1. *adj.* poetic.

klásī, 1. *n.* hate; 2. *n.* hatred.

klà, 1. *n.* bow (arrow weapon).

klànị, 1. *n.* bowman; 2. *n.* archer.

klàxó, 1. *n.* bowmanship; 2. *n.* archery.

klā, 1. *n.* dirt; 2. *n.* soil; 3. *n.* ground.

klācū, 1. *n.* pliers.

klāxù, 1. *adj.* dirty.

kla̱, 1. *n.* box.

kla̱ku̱, 1. *n.* dreamer.

kla̱psó, 1. *n.* pagoda.

kla̱súxēclù, 1. *n.* dreamscape.

kla̱su̱, 1. *n.* dream.

klā, 1. *n.* floor; 2. *n.* ground.

kleī, 1. *v.* {ḿ, m̀} join.

kleǐ, 1. *v.* {m̀, Í} miss (a target, etc.).

klelõ, 1. *n.* uvula.

klelȳ, 1. *n.* article.

kleo̱, 1. *v.* {m̀, m̃, j̃} remove (displace).

kleū, 1. *v.* {Í} snore.

klexū, 1. *n.* pointy.

kleȳ, 1. *v.* {ḿ, m̀} pay; 2. *v.* {ḿ} buy; 3. *v.* {r̃} pay (for s.th.).

klé, 1. *prep.* than (*comparison marker*); 2. *prep.* as (as interesting *as* s.th.).

klè, 1. *comp.* that.

klèla̱, 1. *adj.* clever; 2. *adj.* sharp; 3. *adj.* witty.

klèla̱clí, 1. *n.* cleverness; 2. *n.* sharpness.

klē, 1. *n.* term (formal period).

klēkè, 1. *n.* company (people).

klēmèfa̱, 1. *n.* professor; 2. *n.* doctor (academic).

klēmȳ, 1. *adj.* paid.

klēsū, 1. *n.* snore.

klēsȳ, 1. *n.* payment.

kle̱, 1. *n.* store; 2. *n.* movie; 3. *n.* film.

kle̱prá, 1. *n.* shopkeeper.

kle̱so̱, 1. *n.* removal.

kle̱xú, 1. *adj.* cinematic.

klẽ, 1. *n.* point.

kliâ, 1. *v.* {ǹ, Ĩ} cost.

kliè, 1. *v.* {ḿ} brag; 2. *v.* {ḿ} show off.

kliĕ, 1. *v.* {ḿ, m̀, m̃, g̀} lend.

klilolē, 1. *adj.* observant.

klininuõ, 1. *v.* {m̀, Í} fatten (up).

klinî, 1. *adj.* chubby; 2. *adj.* fat.

kliõ, 1. *v.* {z̃} notice (s.o./s.th.); 2. *v.* {ż} notice (*propositions*).

kliô, 1. *v.* {m̀, ǹ} enable.

kliŏ, 1. *v.* {ḿ, m̀} drink.

klipĩ, 1. *n.* curtain.

kliprũ, 1. *n.* colony.

kliỳ, 1. *v.* {m̀, Í, ż} starve.

kliȳ, 1. *v.* {ḿ, m̀} study.

kliy̱, 1. *v.* {z̃} recognize (s.o./s.th. is familiar to s.o.); 2. *v.* {ż} recognize (*propositions*).

klí, 1. *n.* shell.

klíkò, 1. *n.* enabler.

klìké, 1. *n.* lender.

klìke̱, 1. *n.* braggart; 2. *n.* show-off.

klìkó, 1. *n.* drinker.

klìkró, 1. *n.* distribution.

klìkróxù, 1. *adj.* distributive.

klìlólē, 1. *adj.* drunken.

klìlólērō, 1. *adv.* drunkenly.

klìmé, 1. *adj.* lent; 2. *adj.* loaned.

klìmy̱, 1. *adj.* starved.

klìplu̱, 1. *n.* cassock.

klìsé, 1. *n.* loan.

klìsy̱, 1. *n.* starvation.

klīkȳ, 1. *n.* student.

klīlȳlē, 1. *adj.* studious.

klīlȳlēclì, 1. *n.* studiousness.

klīlȳlērō, 1. *adv.* studiously.

klīpē, 1. *n.* wheel.

klīsȳ, 1. *n.* study (i.e. as a student).

kli̱, 1. *n.* semen.

kli̱cé, 1. *n.* tie; 2. *n.* bowtie.

kli̱ja̱, 1. *n.* sibling.

klisy, 1. *n.* familiarity.

kloipiã, 1. *v.* {m̀, Í} stalk.

kloī, 1. *v.* {m̀, Í} pursue.

kloĩ, 1. *v.* {ḿ, m̀, Í} digest.

klokipikã, 1. *n.* stalker.

klolĩ, 1. *n.* machine.

klomĩ, 1. *adj.* digested.

klosipisã, 1. *n.* stalking.

klosĩ, 1. *n.* digestion.

klócrĩjè, 1. *n.* plantation.

klòcú, 1. *n.* tincture; 2. *n.* vial.

klō, 1. *n.* film (thin layer).

klōkī, 1. *n.* pursuer.

klōmī, 1. *adj.* pursued.

klōsī, 1. *n.* pursuit.

klola, 1. *n.* sole.

klõ, 1. *n.* stick; 2. *n.* branch.

kluâ, 1. *v.* {m̀, m̃, Í} identify.

kluclĩ, 1. *n.* hunger.

klué, 1. *v.* {g̀} warn (s.o.); 2. *v.* {m̀, m̃} warn (*propositions*).

klujixũ, 1. *adj.* informative.

klujĩ, 1. *n.* information.

klujuxũ, 1. *n.* furnished.

klujũ, 1. *n.* furniture.

klukõ, 1. *n.* welder.

klumõ, 1. *adj.* welded.

kluò, 1. *v.* {m̀, j̃} push.

kluōfiē, 1. *v.* {m̀, Í} push down; 2. *v.* {m̀, Í, j̃} push over.

kluõ, 1. *v.* {m̀, Í, v́, ṽ} weld.

klurõ, 1. *adv.* hungrily.

klusõ, 1. *n.* weld; 2. *n.* welding.

klú, 1. *n.* news.

klúmà, 1. *adj.* identified.

klúsà, 1. *n.* identification.

klúsē, 1. *n.* warning.

klù, 1. *n.* worth; 2. **inạ klù** *prep.* worthless.

klùjo̱, 1. *n.* purse.

klùnú, 1. *n.* iron.

klùnúxù, 1. *adj.* iron; 2. *adj.* made of iron.

klùpsu̱, 1. *n.* chainmail.

klùxú, 1. *adj.* worthy.

klùxúclì, 1. *n.* worthiness.

klū, 1. *pn.* you (*plural*).

klūkù, 1. *n.* vessel; 2. *n.* craft.

klūmà, 1. *adj.* your (*plural*); 2. *n.* yours (*plural*).

klūmōfīmē, 1. *adj.* pushed down; 2. *adj.* pushed over.

klu̱pa̱, 1. *n.* state; 2. *n.* sovereignty.

klu̱si̱krí, 1. *n.* territory.

klū, 1. *adj.* hungry.

klysū̱, 1. *n.* representation (depiction, symbol).

klyū̱, 1. *v.* {ǹ} symbolize; 2. *v.* {ǹ} represent.

klyû, 1. *v.* {ḿ, j} march (militarily).

klyǔ, 1. *v.* {ḿ, ġ} growl (at s.th.).

klyxū̱, 1. *adj.* skilled; 2. *adj.* skillful.

klý, 1. *adj.* high.

klýclì, 1. *n.* height.

klýklà, 1. *n.* crossbow.

klýnuō, 1. *v.* {m̀, Í} heighten.

klýnūmō, 1. *adj.* heightened.

klýsē, 1. *n.* cartilage.

klýsēxù, 1. *adj.* cartilaginous.

klýsù, 1. *n.* march (military).

klỳ, 1. *adv.* now.

klỳpó, 1. *n.* discount.

klỳsú, 1. *n.* growl.

klȳfrè, 1. *n.* character (literary).

klȳfù, 1. *n.* wig; 2. *n.* toupée.

klȳkà, 1. *adj.* immediate.

klȳkàclí, 1. *n.* immediacy.

klȳkàro̱, 1. *adv.* immediately.

kly̱, 1. *n.* milk.

kly̱kfi̱, 1. *n.* chevon.

klylý, 1. *n.* highland.

klȳ̃, 1. *n.* skill; 2. *n.* ability.

koî, 1. *v.* {m̀, Í, ṽ} handle; 2. *v.* {m̀, Í, ṽ} deal (with s.th.).

kolū̃, 1. *prep.* around.

korī̃, 1. *n.* shield.

koruclī̃, 1. *n.* cruelty.

korū̃, 1. *adj.* cruel.

koū̃, 1. *v.* {m̀} flip (s.th. over); 2. *v.* {m̀} turn (s.th. over).

koūfiò, 1. *v.* {ḿ, m̀, m̃} roast.

kó, 1. *n.* head.

kófī̃, 1. *n.* marsh.

kómì, 1. *adj.* dealt with; 2. *adj.* handled.

kópī̃, 1. *n.* plinth.

kò, 1. *adj.* storied; 2. *n.* bottom.

kòcǫ, 1. *n.* puzzle.

kòfrǫ, 1. *n.* rivet.

kòply, 1. *n.* muscle.

kòplyxú, 1. *adj.* muscular; 2. *adj.* strong.

kòxu, 1. *adj.* middle-aged.

kō, 1. *n.* color.

kōcò, 1. *n.* wax.

kōlà, 1. *n.* basement; 2. *n.* cellar.

kōlō, 1. *pn.* each other.

kōmū̃fìmǫ, 1. *adj.* roasted.

kōrè, 1. *n.* wardrobe.

kōsū̃fìsǫ, 1. *n.* roast.

kǫ, 1. *n.* city.

kǫklímà, 1. *n.* apocalypse.

kǫklímàxú, 1. *adj.* apocalyptic.

kraî, 1. *v.* {m̀, m̃, Í} kill.

krakī̃, 1. *n.* killer.

kramī̃, 1. *adj.* killed.

krasū̃, 1. *n.* invitation.

kraū̃, 1. *v.* {m̀, Í, j̃} invite.

krá, 1. *n.* class.

krà, 1. *adj.* strong (physically).

kràcạrị, 1. *n.* shoestring.

kràcị, 1. *adj.* whole; 2. *adj.* entire.

kràcịclí, 1. *n.* wholeness; 2. *n.* entirety.

kràclí, 1. *n.* strength (physical).

kràmy, 1. *n.* spot; 2. *n.* mark.

kràmyxú, 1. *adj.* spotted; 2. *adj.* spotty; 3. *adj.* marked.

krànuọ, 1. *v.* {m̀, Í, ṽ} strengthen.

kràrẹ, 1. *n.* lantern.

kràrọ, 1. *adv.* strongly (physical).

kràsrú, 1. *n.* politics.

kràsrúprà, 1. *n.* politician.

krā, 1. *n.* shoe.

krācà, 1. *n.* veil.

krāklē, 1. *n.* service (military, etc.).

krāprà, 1. *n.* cobbler.

krạkrí, 1. *n.* technology.

krạkríprà, 1. *n.* technician.

kreí, 1. *v.* {m̀, ṽ} fill.

kreĩ, 1. *v.* {m̀, Í} share; 2. *v.* {m̃, g̣, g̃} share (with s.o.).

kreó, 1. *v.* {m̀, Í, ṽ} replace.

kreō, 1. *v.* {m̀, m̃, Í} improve; 2. *v.* {m̀, m̃, Í} ameliorate.

kreọ, 1. *v.* {Í} form (come into shape); 2. *v.* {v́} form (into s.th.).

kreú, 1. *v.* {Í} seem (*propositions, compounds*); 2. *v.* {Í} appear (*propositions, compounds*).

kreỳ, 1. *v.* {m̀} explain.

kré, 1. *n.* game.

krémī, 1. *adj.* filled.

krésō, 1. *n.* replacement.

krè, 1. *n.* age.

krèkạ, 1. *adj.* popular.

krèkạclí, 1. *n.* popularity.

krèkạnuọ, 1. *v.* {m̀, Í} popularize.

krèkạnụkọ, 1. *n.* popularizer.

krèkạnụmọ, 1. *adj.* popularized.

krèkạrọ, 1. *adv.* popularly.

krèmy, 1. *adj.* explained.

krèra̱, 1. *n.* bomb.

krèsy̱, 1. *n.* explanation.

krèxú, 1. *adj.* aged (e.g. wine).

krēmō, 1. *adj.* improved.

krēnàsa̱, 1. *n.* royalty.

krēpī, 1. *n.* shelf.

krēsō, 1. *n.* improvement.

kre̱, 1. *n.* market; 2. *n.* economy.

kre̱fílè, 1. *n.* disaster; 2. *n.* catastrophe.

kre̱fílèxú, 1. *adj.* disastrous; 2. *adj.* catastrophic.

kre̱fílèxúrō, 1. *adv.* disastrously; 2. *adv.* catastrophically.

kre̱lí, 1. *n.* guitar.

kre̱líprà, 1. *n.* guitarist.

kre̱mo̱, 1. *adj.* formed.

kre̱na̱, 1. *n.* deer.

kre̱na̱na̱, 1. *n.* fawn.

kre̱so̱, 1. *n.* formation.

kre̱xó, 1. *n.* economics.

kre̱xóprà, 1. *n.* economist.

krē, 1. *comp.* since (temporal); 2. *prep.* since (temporal).

kriá, 1. *v.* {m̀, Í, ṽ} resurrect.

krià, 1. *v.* {m̀, ṽ} compare (contrast).

kriā, 1. *v.* {ḿ, m̀} attack.

krié, 1. *v.* {m̀, m̃} develop.

krimỹ, 1. *adj.* suggested.

kriò, 1. *v.* {m̀, Í} kick.

kripsacã, 1. *n.* dining room.

kripsã, 1. *n.* dinner.

krisỹ, 1. *n.* suggestion.

kriỹ, 1. *v.* {m̀, ñ} suggest; 2. *v.* {m̀, ñ} propose.

krí, 1. *n.* ice.

kríkē, 1. *n.* developer.

kríkrùprý, 1. *n.* octagon.

kríkrùprýxù, 1. *adj.* octagonal.

krímā, 1. *adj.* resurrected.

krímē, 1. *adj.* developed.

krínè, 1. *prep.* under; 2. *prep.* beneath.

krírē, 1. *n.* courtyard.

krírēcrō, 1. *n.* octahedron.

krírēcrōxù, 1. *adj.* octahedral.

krísā, 1. *n.* resurrection.

krísē, 1. *n.* development.

krísēxù, 1. *adj.* developed.

kríxù, 1. *adj.* icy.

krì, 1. *n.* park; 2. *n.* public garden.

krìkfi̱, 1. *n.* rectangle.

krìkfi̱xú, 1. *adj.* rectangular.

krìsa̱, 1. *n.* comparison.

krī, 1. *adj.* lax (not strict).

krīfō, 1. *n.* ruler (for measurement).

krīkā, 1. *n.* attacker; 2. *n.* assailant; 3. *n.* aggressor.

krīkè, 1. *n.* stage (theater).

krīlālē, 1. *adj.* aggressive.

krīlò, 1. *adj.* durable.

krīlòclí, 1. *n.* durability.

krīmā, 1. *adj.* attacked.

krīsā, 1. *n.* attack.

krīsè, 1. *n.* livelihood; 2. *n.* living.

kri̱, 1. *num.* eight.

kri̱kri̱, 1. *adj.* eighth.

kri̱kry̱, 1. *n.* ice cave.

kri̱pa̱, 1. *num.* eighty.

kri̱pa̱pa̱, 1. *adj.* eightieth.

kromū̃, 1. *adj.* settled.

krosū̃, 1. *n.* settlement.

krou̱, 1. *v.* {m̀, r̃} meet (on schedule).

kroū̃, 1. *v.* {m̀, Í} settle (resolve agreeably).

kròky̱, 1. *n.* pestle.

kròpí, 1. *n.* living room.

krō, 1. *n.* coat.

krōpsù, 1. *n.* disease.

krōpsùxú, 1. *adj.* diseased; 2. *adj.* pathological.

kro̤, 1. *adj.* brave.

kro̤clí, 1. *n.* bravery.

kro̤ro̤, 1. *adv.* bravely.

kro̤sṳ, 1. *n.* meeting (business, etc.).

kruâ, 1. *v.* {m̀, ṽ} cover.

kruè, 1. *v.* {ǹ, ṽ} base (s.th. on s.th.).

krukõ, 1. *n.* servant.

krulolerõ, 1. *adv.* obediently.

krulolē, 1. *adj.* obedient.

krulū, 1. *n.* mallet.

krumõ, 1. *adj.* obeyed; 2. *adj.* served.

kruó, 1. *v.* {m̀, m̃} arrange (prepare or plan).

kruõ, 1. *v.* {m̀} serve; 2. *v.* {m̀} obey.

kruô, 1. *v.* {ḿ, r̃} fight.

kruy, 1. *v.* {m̀, ĺ} freeze.

krúkò, 1. *n.* fighter.

krúmà, 1. *adj.* covered.

krúmō, 1. *adj.* arranged; 2. *adj.* prepared.

krúsà, 1. *n.* cover (e.g. a sheet).

krúsò, 1. *n.* fight; 2. *n.* battle.

krúsō, 1. *n.* arrangement (preparation or plan).

krùprý, 1. *n.* side.

krū, 1. *adj.* tight.

krūclì, 1. *n.* tightness.

krūnuō, 1. *v.* {m̀, ĺ, v́, ṽ} tighten.

krūnūmō, 1. *adj.* tightened.

krūrō, 1. *adv.* tightly.

krṳ, 1. *n.* boat.

krṳlyle̤, 1. *adj.* freezing.

krṳmú, 1. *n.* ocean.

krṳmúxēclù, 1. *n.* seascape.

krṳmúxù, 1. *adj.* oceanic.

krṳmy, 1. *adj.* frozen.

krṳpý, 1. *n.* military.

krṳpýprà, 1. *n.* soldier.

krýkō, 1. *n.* debate.

krýkōxù, 1. *adj.* contentious.

krỳ, 1. *n.* oil.

krỳpló, 1. *n.* opportunity; 2. *n.* chance.

krỳxú, 1. *adj.* oily.

krȳ̱, 1. *n.* back.

kry̱, 1. *n.* cave.

kry̱cu̱, 1. *n.* venison.

kry̱ro̱, 1. *n.* result.

kry̱ro̱xú, 1. *adj.* resultant.

krȳ̃, 1. *adj.* left (side or direction); 2. *adv.* left (to the left); 3. *n.* left.

kuà, 1. *v.* {m̀, ǹ} touch.

kuè, 1. *v.* {r̀} knock (on e.g. a door).

kuê, 1. *v.* {ḿ, m̀} discern; 2. *v.* {ḿ, m̀} tell.

kukfexuclĩ, 1. *n.* industriousness.

kukfexũ, 1. *adj.* industrious.

kukfẽ, 1. *n.* industry.

kukliclĩ, 1. *n.* value.

kuklĩ, 1. *adj.* valuable.

kumõ, 1. *adj.* surrendered.

kuó, 1. *v.* {ź} think; 2. *v.* {ź} ponder; 3. *v.* {z̃} think (about s.th.); 4. *v.* {ż} think (*propositions*).

kuõ, 1. *v.* {ḿ, m̀, ź} surrender; 2. *v.* {ḿ, m̀, ź} give up.

kusõ, 1. *n.* surrender.

kuý, 1. *v.* {m̀, Í} sting.

kuỳ, 1. *v.* {m̀, Í} punch.

kú, 1. *n.* case; 2. *n.* instance.

kúfū, 1. *adj.* giant.

kúkī, 1. *n.* zipper.

kúkō, 1. *n.* thinker.

kúkȳ, 1. *n.* stinger.

kúlōlē, 1. *adj.* contemplative; 2. *adj.* pensive.

kúlōlērō, 1. *adv.* contemplatively; 2. *adv.* pensively.

kúmō, 2. *adj.* thought out.

kúmȳ, 1. *n.* stung.

kúsō, 1. *n.* thought; 2. *n.* concept.

kúsōxù, 1. *adj.* pensive; 2. *adj.* contemplative.

kúsȳ, 1. *n.* sting.

kù, 1. *pn.* you (*singular*).

kùclu̱, 1. *n.* door.

kùkru̱, 1. *n.* crib.

kùmá, 1. *adj.* your (*singular*); 2. *n.* yours (*singular*).

kùmy̱, 1. *adj.* punched.

kùpe̱, 1. *adj.* straight.

kùpe̱nuo̱, 1. *v.* {m̀, í} straighten.

kùpe̱nu̱mo̱, 1. *adj.* straightened.

kùsy, 1. *n.* punch.

kū, 1. *adj.* sleepy; 2. *adj.* tired.

kūjì, 1. *n.* function.

kūrō, 1. *adv.* sleepily.

kūsū, 1. *n.* nightgown.

ku̱, 1. *adj.* shiny.

ku̱nuo̱, 1. *v.* {m̀, í, v́, ṽ} shine (make shiny).

ku̱nu̱mo̱, 1. *adj.* shined.

kyì, 1. *v.* {m̀, ǹ, í} dilute.

kysū, 1. *n.* pastime; 2. *n.* hobby.

ký, 1. *adj.* light (in color); 2. *n.* rent.

kýclō, 1. *n.* medal.

kýkfō, 1. *adj.* exact; 2. *adj.* precise.

kýkfōclì, 1. *n.* precision.

kýkfōrō, 1. *adv.* exactly; 2. *adv.* precisely.

kýnì, 1. *n.* paralysis.

kýnìxú, 1. *adj.* paralyzed.

kýnȳ, 1. *n.* boyfriend.

kỳ, 1. *n.* neck.

kỳmi̱, 1. *adj.* diluted.

kȳ, 1. *n.* saw.

kȳclù, 1. *n.* desk.

kȳmì, 1. *n.* apple.

kȳmìcifu̱, 1. *n.* apple tree.

ky̱, 1. *n.* map.

ky̱ci̱, 1. *n.* princess.

ky̱fi̱, 1. *n.* line.

kyfi̱xú, 1. *adj.* linear.
kyfi̱xúclì, 1. *n.* linearity.
kyri̱, 1. *n.* lettuce.
kỹ, 1. *adj.* busy.

L

laclẽ, 1. *n.* percentage.
lacrã, 1. *n.* abdomen.
laĭ, 1. *v.* {ź} breathe.
laprã, 1. *n.* artist.
laū, 1. *v.* {ḿ, m̀, Í, v́, ṽ} paint.
lá, 1. *pn.* it.
lákà, 1. *n.* stool (chair).
lámà, 1. *adj.* its 2. *n.* its.
lápsā, 1. *n.* earlobe.
lárì, 1. *n.* obstacle.
láxā, 1. *n.* melon.
là, 1. *intj.* no.
làkla̱, 1. *n.* scissors.
làsí, 1. *n.* respiration; 2. *n.* breath.
làsró, 1. *n.* gall bladder.
lā, 1. *adj.* purple.
lāfrà, 1. *n.* community; 2. **lāfrà cxèso̱** *n.* community center.
lāfràfra̱, 1. *n.* university.
lāfū, 1. *n.* vagina.
lākō, 1. *n.* purple.
lākū, 1. *n.* painter.
lāmēklī, 1. *prep.* according to; 2. *prep.* in s.o.'s opinion.
lāmū, 1. *adj.* painted.
lāpì, 1. *n.* meal.
lāsùcy̱, 1. *adv.* over there; 2. *n.* over there.
lāsū, 1. *n.* painting.
la̱, 1. *pn.* they (*neuter*); 2. *pn.* them (*neuter*).
la̱có, 1. *n.* data.
la̱cóxù, 1. *adj.* data-rich.

l**a**má, 1. *adj.* their (*neuter*); 2. *n.* theirs (*neuter*).

l**a**rósī, 1. *n.* grimoire.

L**a**rósī u càl**u**, 1. *n.* Necronomicon.

l**a**xé, 1. *n.* tiger.

lã, 1. *n.* art.

leclã, 1. *n.* interest (fiduciary).

leí, 1. *v.* {m̂, m̀, v̀, ṽ} smith.

leî, 1. *v.* {m̂, ń} go to sleep; 2. *v.* {m̂, ń} turn in.

lejã, 1. *adj.* hard-working.

lerõ, 1. *adv.* suddenly.

leū, 1. *v.* {m̂, m̀, m̃, l̂} investigate.

leû, 1. *v.* {m̂, m̀} blaspheme.

leỳ, 1. *v.* {m̀} access.

lé, 1. *n.* lock.

léfī, 1. *n.* pie.

léfrō, 1. *n.* distance.

léfrōxù, 1. *adj.* distant; 2. *adj.* far away.

lékī, 1. *n.* blacksmith.

lékù, 1. *n.* blasphemer.

lésī, 1. *n.* smithing.

lésù, 1. *n.* blasphemy.

lésùxú, 1. *adj.* blasphemous.

lè, 1. *adj.* wet.

lèclí, 1. *n.* wetness.

lèkf**u**, 1. *n.* kitchen; 2. **lèkf**u **nèkl**u *n.* kitchen sink.

lèlý, 1. *n.* wetland.

lèp**e**, 1. *adv.* too (overly); 2. *n.* too much.

lès**y**, 1. *n.* access.

lē, 1. *n.* spoon.

lēklȳ, 1. *n.* detail; 2. *n.* definition.

lēkū, 1. *n.* investigator.

lēlō, 1. *adj.* deliberate; 2. *adj.* intentional.

lēlōrō, 1. *adv.* on purpose; 2. *adv.* deliberately; 3. *adv.* intentionally.

lēmū, 1. *adj.* investigated.

lēmỳ, 1. *n.* army.

lēsū, 1. *n.* investigation.

lẹ, 1. *n.* stress.

lẹpá, 1. *n.* cabbage.

lẹxú, 1. *adj.* stressed.

lẽ, 1. *adj.* sudden.

li, 1. *conj.* or; 2. *conj.* nor.

lià, 1. *v.* {ĺ} wilt.

liâ, 1. *v.* {m̀, ĺ, v́, ṽ} link; 2. *v.* {m̀, ĺ, v́, ṽ} connect.

liă, 1. *v.* {m̀, m̃} bill (in business); 2. *v.* {m̀, m̃} charge (in business).

liē, 1. *v.* {m̀} call for (s.o./s.th.); 2. *v.* {ḿ} beckon; 3. *v.* {m̀} beckon for (s.o./s.th.).

liẽ, 1. *v.* {m̀, ĺ} knock (out s.o.).

likõ, 1. *n.* sufferer.

liniprã, 1. *n.* pianist.

linĩ, 1. *n.* piano.

liọcliạ, 1. *v.* {ĺ} die a painful death.

liõ, 1. *v.* {ź} suffer; 2. *v.* {z̃} suffer (from s.th.).

liô, 1. *v.* {m̀, m̃} design.

lisõ, 1. *n.* suffering.

lisỹ, 1. *n.* object.

liý, 1. *v.* {z̃} trust (s.o./s.th.); 2. *v.* {ż} trust (*propositions*).

liy̱, 1. *v.* {m̀, ǹ} require.

lí, 1. *n.* wall.

líkò, 1. *n.* designer.

lílȳlẽ, 1. *adj.* trusting.

límà, 1. *adj.* linked; 2. *adj.* connected.

límò, 1. *adj.* designed.

límȳ, 1. *adj.* trusted.

línò, 1. *n.* purpose.

lísà, 1. *n.* link; 2. *n.* connection.

lísò, 1. *n.* design.

lísȳ, 1. *n.* trust.

lì, 1. *n.* group.

lìcxạ, 1. *n.* rabbit.

lìcxạnạ, 1. *n.* bunny.

lìkfị, 1. *n.* crime.

lìkfịprá, 1. *n.* criminal.

lìkfị̀xú, 1. *adj.* criminal.

lìkfị̀xúrō, 1. *adv.* criminally.

lìkrý, 1. *n.* caliper.

lìlị̀xámà, 1. *n.* ambergris.

lìmạ, 1. *adj.* wilted.

lìmị, 1. *adj.* stubborn; 2. *adj.* obstinate.

lìné, 1. *n.* paper.

līkē, 1. *n.* beckoner.

līklē, 1. *n.* credit (financial).

līkù, 1. *n.* statue.

līkùnụ, 1. *n.* statuette.

līkùxú, 1. *adj.* statuesque.

līmē, 1. *adj.* beckoned; 2. *adj.* called.

līmī, 1. *n.* saddle.

lị̀lácī, 1. *n.* desert.

lịsy, 1. *n.* requirement.

lolulerõ, 1. *adv.* needily.

lolulẽ, 1. *adj.* needy.

lomã, 1. *comp.* except (for/that…); 2. *prep.* except for.

lomurõ, 1. *adv.* necessarily.

lomũ, 1. *adj.* needed; 2. *adj.* necessary.

losũ, 1. *n.* need.

loũ, 1. *v.* {z̃} need (s.o./s.th.); 2. *v.* {ż} need (*propositions*).

ló, 1. *n.* oven; 2. *n.* range.

lókfē, 1. *n.* girder.

lò, 1. *n.* shock (of hay).

lòlẹ, 1. *adj.* tough; 2. *adj.* chewy.

lòlẹclí, 1. *n.* toughness; 2. *n.* chewiness.

lònọ, 1. *n.* coffee.

lòrạ, 1. *n.* navel; 2. *n.* belly button.

lō, 1. *adj.* new.

lōkrē, 1. *n.* terrace (farming).

lōkrēxù, 1. *adj.* terraced (farming).

lōrū, 1. *n.* taiga.

lọ, 1. *n.* fat.

lọxú, 1. *adj.* fatty (of food, not lean).

luà, 1. *v.* {m̀, ĺ} curse.

lué, 1. *v.* {ḿ, v̀} beg.

luè, 1. *v.* {ź, z̃} believe (s.o./s.th.); 2. *v.* {ż} believe (*propositions*).

luē, 1. *v.* {m̀, ĺ} confirm.

luě, 1. *v.* {m̀} suppose.

lumĩ, 1. *n.* note (musical).

luò, 1. *v.* {j̃, ṽ} add (include, arithmetic).

luọ, 1. *v.* {m̀, j̃} leave (s.th. behind).

luploprã, 1. *n.* accountant.

luplõ, 1. *n.* accounting.

luxã, 1. *n.* status; 2. *n.* state; 3. *n.* condition.

lú, 1. *det.* either; 2. *det.* neither.

lúkē, 1. *n.* beggar.

lúmã, 1. *n.* era; 2. *n.* period; 3. *n.* time.

lúplȳ, 1. *n.* suit (formal clothing).

lù, 1. *n.* weight.

lùjọ, 1. *n.* fog; 2. *prep.* across.

lùjọxú, 1. *adj.* foggy.

lùjú, 1. *adj.* common.

lùjúclì, 1. *n.* commonality.

lùkẹ, 1. *n.* believer.

lùlẹlẹ, 1. *adj.* credulous.

lùlẹlẹclí, 1. *n.* credulousness; 2. *n.* credulity.

lùlẹlẹrọ, 1. *adv.* credulously.

lùmạ, 1. *adj.* cursed.

lùmẹ, 1. *adj.* believed.

lùmọ, 1. *adj.* added.

lùny, 1. *n.* lady (respectable woman); 2. *det.* Lady (respectful title).

lùprí, 1. *n.* analysis.

lùpríxù, 1. *adj.* analytical; 2. *adj.* meticulous.

lùsạ, 1. *n.* curse.

lùsé, 1. *n.* supposition; 2. *n.* assumption.

lùsẹ, 1. *n.* belief.

lùsọ, 1. *n.* addition.

lùsọxú, 1. *adj.* additional.

lùsọxúrō, 1. *adv.* additionally.

lùxú, 1. *adj.* heavy; 2. *adj.* weighty.

lū, 1. *n.* moon.

lūcìkrí, 1. *n.* sledgehammer.

lūfē, 1. *n.* brussels sprout; 2. *n.* sprouts.

lūmē, 1. *adj.* confirmed.

lūsē, 1. *n.* confirmation.

lu̧, 1. *adj.* large; 2. *adj.* big; 3. *adj.* great; 4. **prākfē lu̧** *n.* large intestines.

lu̧mo̧, 1. *adj.* left (behind).

lu̧nuo̧, 1. *v.* {m̀, Í} enlarge.

lu̧nu̧mo̧, 1. *adj.* enlarged.

lu̧ra̧, 1. *n.* cuff.

lu̧ro̧, 1. *adv.* mostly; 2. *adv.* largely; 3. *adv.* for the most part.

lyú, 1. *v.* {ḿ, m̀, m̃, Í} invade.

lyxū, 1. *adj.* vocal (speaking frequently or loudly).

lý, 1. *n.* land.

lýklū, 1. *n.* brick; 2. *n.* slab.

lýkū, 1. *n.* invader.

lýlūlē, 1. *adj.* invasive.

lýmū, 1. *adj.* invaded.

lýsū, 1. *n.* invasion.

lýxēclù, 1. *n.* landscape.

lỳ, 1. *adj.* empty.

lỳclí, 1. *n.* emptiness.

lỳnuo̧, 1. *v.* {m̀, Í} empty.

lỳnu̧mo̧, 1. *adj.* emptied.

lỳpru̧, 1. *n.* succulent.

lȳ, 1. *n.* ball.

lȳclà, 1. *n.* average; 2. *n.* mean.

lȳclàxú, 1. *adj.* average; 2. *adj.* mean.

lȳcȳ, 1. *n.* temperature.

lȳlù, 1. *n.* flute.

lȳlùprá, 1. *n.* flautist.

lȳnò, 1. *adj.* gray.

lȳnōkō, 1. *n.* gray.

lȳprù, 1. *n.* uterus; 2. *n.* womb.

lȳrū, 1. *n.* sheep.

lȳrūnū, 1. *n.* lamb.

lȳxò, 1. *n.* cannon.

ly̱, 1. *n.* god; 2. *n.* goddess; 3. *n.* deity.

ly̱fy̱, 1. *n.* beef.

ly̱jé, 1. *n.* windpipe; 2. *n.* trachea.

ly̱xú, 1. *adj.* godly; 2. *adj.* divine.

ly̱xúclì, 1. *n.* godliness; 2. *n.* divinity.

lỹ, 1. *n.* voice.

Í, 1. *aux.* hate to; 2. *dis.* {1: *Theme*}.

Ì, 1. *aux.* manage to; 2. *dis.* {2: *Location, Theme*}.

Ī, 1. *aux.* need to.

I̱, 1. *aux.* be willing to.

Ĩ, 1. *aux.* be afraid to (do s.th.); 2. *dis.* {3: *Theme, Beneficiary/Recipient, Cause/Instrument*}.

M

macaxuclī, 1. *n.* villainy.

macaxũ, 1. *adj.* villainous.

macã, 1. *n.* villain.

majẽ, 1. *n.* forest.

makfuxũ, 1. *adj.* rageful; 2. *adj.* furious; 3. *adj.* angry.

makfũ, 1. *n.* rage; 2. *n.* fury; 3. *n.* anger.

malẽ, 1. *n.* policy.

maú, 1. *v.* {Í} result; 4. *v.* {ǹ} result (in s.th.).

maū, 1. *v.* {m̀, m̃} tell (s.o. s.th.).

má, 1. *adj.* tepid; 2. *adj.* lukewarm.

mákrỹ, 1. *n.* cavity.

másū, 1. *n.* outcome; 2. *n.* result.

mà, 1. *n.* plant (organism).

mā, 1. *n.* site; 2. *n.* place; 3. *n.* location.

mākìprý, 1. *n.* facility.

mālī, 1. *n.* code.

māpè, 1. *n.* underwear.

māsū, 1. *n.* message.

ma̱cri̱ci̱, 1. *n.* religion.

mạcrịcịxú, 1. *adj.* religious; 2. *adj.* pious.

mạcrịcịxúrō, 1. *adv.* religiously.

mạfá, 1. *n.* trigger (e.g. of a gun).

mạjụ, 1. *adj.* evil.

mạjụclí, 1. *n.* evil.

mạplíjē, 1. *n.* satellite.

mạrí, 1. *adj.* fond (of s.th./s.o.).

mạsrá, 1. *n.* backpack.

mạsrạ, 1. *n.* area.

mã, 1. *conj.* but.

meclĩ, 1. *n.* fineness; 2. *n.* delicacy.

meî, 1. *v.* {z̃} want (s.o./s.th.); 2. *v.* {ż} want (*propositions*).

melafraxũ, 1. *adj.* labyrinthine.

melafrã, 1. *n.* labyrinth; 2. *n.* maze.

melỹ, 1. *n.* ribbon.

menẽ, 1. *prep.* over.

meprexũ, 1. *adj.* speedy; 2. *adj.* hasty; 3. *adj.* fast.

meprẽ, 1. *n.* speed.

meū, 1. *v.* {m̀} demand.

meỳ, 1. *v.* {m̀, Í, ṽ} order; 2. *v.* {m̀, Í, ṽ} sort.

meỹ, 1. *v.* {ḿ, r̀} run (jog).

mé, 1. *n.* top; 2. *prep.* on top of.

méclō, 1. *n.* clothing; 2. *n.* clothes.

mékìxú, 1. *adj.* desirous.

méklā, 1. *n.* pork.

mékrè, 1. *adj.* funny; 2. *adj.* humorous.

mémì, 1. *adj.* wanted; 2. *adj.* desired.

méràplỵ, 1. *prep.* in addition to.

mésì, 1. *n.* object of desire; 2. *n.* desire.

mè, 1. *n.* order (as opposed to chaos).

mènụká, 1. *n.* cauldron.

mèpụ, 1. *adj.* silvertongued; 2. *adj.* smooth.

mèsỵ, 1. *n.* order; 2. *n.* sequence; 3. *n.* sorting.

mèxú, 1. *adj.* orderly.

mē, 1. *prep.* for (*reason, goal*).

mēklì, 1. *adv.* right now.

mēkȳ, 1. *n.* runner (athletic).

mēlūlē, 1. *adj.* demanding; 2. *adj.* nagging.

mēmū, 1. *adj.* demanded.

mēplù, 1. *n.* lemon.

mēplȳ, 1. *n.* river.

mēsū, 1. *n.* demand.

mēsūxù, 1. *adj.* demanding; 2. *adj.* challenging.

mēsȳ, 1. *n.* run (athletic).

me̱, 1. *n.* fin.

me̱lo̱, 1. *n.* violin.

me̱lo̱prá, 1. *n.* violinist.

me̱rí, 1. *n.* evening.

me̱ró, 1. *adj.* patient.

me̱róclì, 1. *n.* patience.

me̱rórō, 1. *adv.* patiently.

me̱sri̱, 1. *n.* cuirass.

mē̃, 1. *adj.* delicate; 2. *adj.* fine.

miâ, 1. *v.* {ḿ, m̃, ǹ, ñ, r̀} count.

mie̱, 1. *v.* {ḿ, ź} laugh; 2. *v.* {m̀, ž} laugh (at s.th.).

miě, 1. *v.* {m̀, ĺ} memorialize.

miò, 1. *v.* {ḿ, m̀, ĺ} kiss.

mio̱, 1. *v.* {ḿ, j} go; 2. **mio̱ srō** *v.* {j} go home.

mí, 1. *n.* toy.

mì, 1. *n.* nose.

mìklá, 1. *n.* task; 2. *n.* piece.

mìko̱, 1. *n.* kisser.

mìku̱, 1. *n.* mansion.

mìmo̱, 1. *n.* kissed.

mìso̱, 1. *n.* kiss.

mī, 1. *adj.* sad.

mīclì, 1. *n.* sadness.

mīmā, 1. *n.* energy.

mīmāxù, 1. *adj.* energetic.

mīmāxùro̱, 1. *adv.* energetically.

mi̱, 1. *n.* snout.

mi̱lu̱, 1. *n.* lizard.

mirá, 1. *n.* father.

miráxù, 1. *adj.* fatherly (behaving as father); 2. *adj.* paternal.

miraprosu, 1. *n.* fatherhood; 2. *n.* paternity.

mise, 1. *n.* laughter.

mixy, 1. *n.* crystal.

mixyxú, 1. *adj.* crystal; 2. *adj.* crystalline.

mixyxúnuō, 1. *v.* {m̀, ǹ, Í} crystallize.

mixyxúnūmō, 1. *adj.* crystallized.

mixyxúnūsō, 1. *n.* crystallization.

mĩ, 1. *adv.* then; 2. *adv.* at that time.

moclã, 1. *n.* veranda.

moí, 1. *v.* {m̀} carry (support, e.g. a team).

moī, 1. *v.* {ź, ż} agree (with s.th./s.o.).

moî, 1. *v.* {m̀, ž} surprise (s.o.); 2. *v.* {ż} surprise (*propositions*).

moklỹ, 1. *n.* solstice.

monō, 1. *n.* wool.

moù, 1. *v.* {ḿ} meow.

moxurō, 1. *adv.* naturally.

moxũ, 1. *adj.* natural.

mó, 1. *n.* sound.

mófīnè, 1. *n.* syringe.

mólìle, 1. *adj.* surprising.

mólìlero, 1. *adv.* surprisingly.

mólō, 1. *n.* trunk; 2. *n.* chest.

mómì, 1. *adj.* surprised.

móplò, 1. *adj.* rough (not gentle).

móplòro, 1. *adv.* roughly.

mósì, 1. *n.* surprise.

mò, 1. *n.* war.

mòfre, 1. *n.* urchin.

mòkró, 1. *n.* helmet; 2. *n.* sallet.

mòprá, 1. *n.* warrior.

mòri, 1. *n.* bauble.

mòxú, 1. *adj.* warlike.

mō, 1. *n.* range (of numbers, options, etc.).

mōcìkrí, 1. *n.* war hammer; 2. *n.* maul.

mōpsò, 1. *n.* bronze.

mōpsòxú, 1. *adj.* bronze; 2. *adj.* made of bronze.

mōpūxà, 1. *n.* battleaxe.

mōrū, 1. *n.* talisman; 2. *n.* charm.

mo̲, 1. *n.* depth.

mo̲ci̲, 1. *n.* prince.

mo̲kló, 1. *n.* potion.

mo̲xú, 1. *adj.* deep.

mõ, 1. *n.* nature.

muà, 1. *v.* {ḿ, m̀, j̃} climb.

muā, 1. *v.* {m̀, m̃} shut (close s.th. vertically planar, e.g. a door).

mua̲, 1. *v.* {m̀, z̃} impress; 2. *v.* {z̀} impress (*propositions*).

mué, 1. *v.* {ǹ, Í} involve; 2. *v.* {ǹ, Í} concern; 3. *v.* {ǹ, Í} have to do with; 4. *v.* {ǹ} regard.

mue̲, 1. *v.* {m̀} support; 2. *v.* {m̀} be in favor of.

muě, 1. *v.* {v́} consist (of s.th.).

mufuxurõ, 1. *adv.* occasionally.

mufuxū, 1. *adj.* occasional.

mufū, 1. *n.* occasion.

mulukfĩ, 1. *n.* cosmos.

muō, 1. *v.* {m̀, m̃} permit; 2. *v.* {m̀, m̃} allow.

muô, 1. *v.* {ḿ, m̀, ñ, ǵ} lie.

mupĩ, 1. *n.* quarter (one-fourth).

murã, 1. *n.* role.

mureprã, 1. *n.* physician; 2. *n.* doctor.

murexū, 1. *adj.* medicinal.

murẽ, 1. *n.* medicine.

muý, 1. *v.* {m̀, ṽ} drive (in a nail, a screw, etc.).

muỳ, 1. *v.* {m̀} raise (children, etc.).

muŷ, 1. *v.* {m̀, m̃} wash.

mú, 1. *adj.* true; 2. *adj.* correct; 3. *adj.* right.

múclì, 1. *n.* truth.

múkò, 1. *n.* liar.

múlòle̲, 1. *adj.* deceitful.

múlòle̲ro, 1. *adv.* deceitfully.

múmē, 1. *adj.* concerned; 2. *adj.* involved.

múrō, 1. *adv.* truly; 2. *adv.* correctly; 3. *adv.* rightly.

mù, 1. *n.* soup.

mùcxe, 1. *n.* department.

mùka, 1. *n.* climber.

mùklú, 1. *n.* border (of a territory, etc.).

mùmy, 1. *adj.* reared; 2. *adj.* raised (e.g. a child).

mùrý, 1. *adv.* already.

mùxú, 1. *adj.* soupy.

mū, 1. *adj.* equal; 2. *adj.* equivalent.

mūclì, 1. *n.* equality; 2. *n.* equivalence.

mūfrè, 1. *n.* position; 2. *n.* location.

mūmà, 1. *n.* isle; 2. *n.* islet.

mūmā, 1. *adj.* closed.

mūmō, 1. *adj.* allowed; 2. *adj.* permitted.

mūnuō, 1. *v.* {Í} equalize.

mūnūmō, 1. *adj.* equalized.

mūnūsō, 1. *n.* equalization.

mūprè, 1. *n.* forehead.

mūpsā, 1. *n.* buffalo.

mūrō, 1. *adv.* equally; 2. *adv.* evenly (in distribution).

mūsā, 1. *n.* closure; 2. *n.* closing.

mūsō, 1. *n.* permission.

mu, 1. *prep.* on (*horizontal*).

muke, 1. *n.* supporter (of policy, etc.).

mulale, 1. *adj.* impressive.

mulalero, 1. *adv.* impressively.

muli, 1. *n.* oval; 2. *n.* ellipse.

mulixú, 1. *adj.* oval; 2. *adj.* elliptical.

muma, 1. *adj.* impressed.

mume, 1. *adj.* supported (position, legislation).

musa, 1. *n.* impression.

muse, 1. *n.* support (of policy, etc.).

mũ, 1. *adv.* hardly; 2. *adv.* barely.

mymajē, 1. *n.* rainforest.

myŭ, 1. *v.* {ź} menstruate.

mý, 1. *n.* rain.

mýxā, 1. *n.* scythe.

mýxù, 1. *adj.* rainy.

mỳ, 1. *n.* steel.

mỳcrisa, 1. *n.* overcoat.

mỳcxí, 1. *n.* lion.

mỳsú, 1. *n.* menstruation.

mỳxú, 1. *adj.* steel; 2. *adj.* made of steel.

mȳ, 1. *n.* spire.

mȳkfū, 1. *n.* challenge.

mȳkfūxù, 1. *adj.* challenging.

mȳpsī, 1. *n.* barrel.

mȳsrỳ, 1. *adj.* miserly.

mȳsrỳclí, 1. *n.* miserliness.

my, 1. *n.* way; 2. *n.* method; 3. *n.* means.

mylí, 1. *pn.* one another.

mȳ, 1. *n.* vein.

ḿ, 1. *aux.* must; 2. *aux.* have to; 3. *aux.* be supposed to; 4. *dis.* {1: *Agent*}.

m̀, 1. *aux.* like to; 2. *dis.* {2: *Theme, Agent*}.

m̄, 1. *aux.* try to.

m, 1. *aux.* love to.

m̃, 1. *aux.* will; 2. *aux.* shall; 3. *dis.* {3: *Theme, Beneficiary, Agent*}.

N

nacrõ, 1. *n.* brainstem.

naí, 1. *v.* {m̀, Í} defend.

nai, 1. *v.* {ż, ž} be used to s.th; 2. *v.* {ż, ž} be familiar with s.th.

nanã, 1. *n.* cerebellum.

naū, 1. *v.* {m̀, Í, v́, ṽ} equip.

naxexū, 1. *adj.* conic.

naxẽ, 1. *n.* cone.

ná, 1. *adj.* hard; 2. *adj.* firm.

náclì, 1. *n.* hardness; 2. *n.* firmness.

nákī, 1. *n.* defender.

nálīlē, 1. *adj.* defensive.

nálīlērō, 1. *adv.* defensively.

námī, 1. *adj.* defended.

nánuō, 1. *v.* {m̀, Í, v́, ṽ} harden.

nánūmō, 1. *adj.* hardened.

násī, 1. *n.* defense.

násrē, 1. *n.* cradle.

nà, 1. *n.* vine.

nàjoca, 1. *n.* wine.

nàmó, 1. *n.* imagination.

nàmóxù, 1. *adj.* imaginative.

nàprú, 1. *n.* breast.

nàpu, 1. *adj.* relevant.

nàpuclí, 1. *n.* relevance.

nācxì, 1. *n.* spider.

nākī, 1. *adj.* discreet.

nākīclì, 1. *n.* discretion.

nāklì, 1. *n.* necklace.

nāmū, 1. *adj.* equipped.

nāpā, 1. *n.* sorrow.

nāpāxù, 1. *adj.* sorrowful.

nāsù, 1. *n.* author.

nāsū, 1. *n.* equipment.

na, 1. *n.* chair.

nacri, 1. *n.* mead; 2. *n.* honeywine.

nakí, 1. *n.* palm (of hand).

nalý, 1. *n.* bra; 2. *n.* brassiere.

napra, 1. *n.* fruit.

naro, 1. *adj.* boring; 2. *adj.* dull.

naroclí, 1. *n.* dullness; 2. *n.* boredom.

nã, 1. *n.* brain; 2. *n.* mind.

necū, 1. *n.* nostril.

nemỹ, 1. *adj.* opened (e.g. a business); 2. *adj.* open (for business).

neú, 1. *v.* {z̃} wonder (about s.th.); 2. *v.* {ż} wonder (*propositions*).

neū, 1. *v.* {z̃} fear (s.th.); 2. *v.* {ż} fear (*propositions*).

neu, 1. *v.* {m̀, m̃, ŕ, j̃} include.

neū, 1. *v.* {Í, ì} fall.

neỳ, 1. *v.* {ḿ, m̀, Í} turn; 2. *v.* {ḿ, m̀, Í} rotate.

neỹ, 1. *v.* {Í} open (a business, etc.).

né, 1. *intj.* yes; 2. *adj.* far; 3. *adj.* far away; 4. *prep.* far from.

néfrō, 1. *n.* girlfriend.

nékfē, 1. *n.* maximum.

nékrī, 1. *n.* moustache.

nélī, 1. *adv.* otherwise.

nè, 1. *det.* every; 2. *det.* each; 3. *pn.* each.

nècu̱, 1. *pn.* anything.

nèklu̱, 1. *n.* sink; 2. *n.* basin.

nèmy, 1. *adj.* rotated.

nèni̱, 1. *pn.* anyone; 2. *pn.* anybody.

nèsy̱, 1. *n.* rotation.

nē, 1. *n.* leg.

nēclū, 1. *adj.* embarrassed.

nēclūclì, 1. *n.* embarrassment.

nēcrè, 1. *n.* legplates; 2. *n.* leg armor.

nēlūlē, 1. *adj.* fearful; 2. *adj.* afraid; 2. *adj.* scared.

nēmā, 1. *adv.* anyplace; 2. *pn.* anyplace.

nēmū, 1. *adj.* feared.

nērù, 1. *n.* pumpkin.

nēsū, 1. *n.* fear.

ne̱, 1. *n.* swamp.

ne̱fé, 1. *n.* shark.

ne̱mu̱, 1. *adj.* included.

ne̱pó, 1. *n.* winter; 2. *adj.* gentle.

ne̱póclì, 1. *n.* gentleness.

ne̱pórō, 1. *adv.* gently.

ne̱su̱, 1. *n.* inclusion.

nẽ, 1. *n.* horn.

niá, 1. *v.* {Í} differ; 2. *v.* {v́} differ (from s.th.).

nià, 1. *v.* {m̀, r̃} forgive.

nia̱, 1. *v.* {Í} sweat; 2. *v.* {Í} perspire.

niǎ, 1. *v.* {m̀} claim (e.g. as property).

niclī, 1. *n.* rarity.

niè, 1. *v.* {m̀, ñ} send (s.th. to s.o.); 2. *v.* {ĵ} send (s.th. s.w.).

nimuprā, 1. *n.* scientist.

nimũ, 1. *n.* science.

niò, 1. *v.* {z̃} love (s.o./s.th.); 2. *v.* {ż} love (*propositions*).

niō, 1. *v.* {m̀, ǹ} account (for s.th.).

ni̯o, 1. *v.* {m̀} report (on s.th. as in journalism, business, etc.).

niõ, 1. *v.* {g̀} pray (to s.o.); 2. *v.* {g̀} pray (for s.o.); 3. *v.* {m̀, ñ} pray (*propositions*).

niô, 1. *v.* {í, ì} happen; 2. *v.* {í, ì} occur.

nirẽ, 1. *n.* truss.

nirõ, 1. *adv.* rarely; 2. *adv.* seldom.

nisõ, 1. *n.* prayer.

niý, 1. *v.* {m̀, m̃, ǹ, í, v́, ṽ} light (e.g. a fire); 2. *v.* {m̀, m̃, ǹ, í, v́, ṽ} turn on (e.g. a light).

niỳ, 1. *v.* {Ø} storm.

ní, 1. *adv.* soon.

nícà, 1. *n.* trowel.

níprỳ, 1. *n.* aunt.

nísā, 1. *n.* difference.

nísāxù, 1. *adj.* different.

nísò, 1. *n.* occurrence.

nì, 1. *n.* key (for a door, etc.).

nìcxi̯, 1. *adj.* able-bodied.

nìke̯, 1. *n.* sender.

nìko̯, 1. *n.* lover.

nìla̯le̯, 1. *adj.* forgiving.

nìmá, 1. *adj.* claimed (e.g. as property).

nìma̯, 1. *adj.* forgiven.

nìme̯, 1. *adj.* sent.

nìpo̯, 1. *n.* eulogy.

nìsá, 1. *n.* claim (e.g. of property).

nìsa̯, 1. *n.* forgiveness.

nìso̯, 1. *n.* love.

nìsy̯, 1. *n.* storm.

nìxý, 1. *n.* responsibility.

nìxýxù, 1. *adj.* responsible.

nī, 1. *n.* year.

nīmō, 1. *adj.* accounted for; 2. *adj.* explained.

nīsō, 1. *n.* account; 2. *n.* explanation.

ni, 1. *n.* person; 2. *n.* people.

niclé, 1. *n.* olive.

nikfé, 1. *n.* nation; 2. *n.* country.

nilale, 1. *adj.* sweaty.

nisa, 1. *n.* sweat; 2. *n.* perspiration.

niso, 1. *n.* report (e.g. in journalism, business, etc.).

nixú, 1. *adj.* personable; 2. *adj.* good people.

nĩ, 1. *adj.* rare.

noí, 1. *v.* {m̀, Í} blind.

noì, 1. *v.* {Í} shine.

noklixũ, 1. *adj.* triangular.

noklĩ, 1. *n.* triangle.

nou, 1. *v.* {Í} matter (be important); 2. *v.* {z̀} matter (to s.o.).

nó, 1. *n.* wing.

nókè, 1. *adj.* pregnant.

nókèclí, 1. *n.* pregnancy.

nókènuo, 1. *v.* {m̀, Í} impregnate.

nókènumo, 1. *adj.* impregnated.

nómī, 1. *adj.* blind; 2. *adj.* blinded.

nómīclì, 1. *n.* blindness.

nóxù, 1. *adj.* winged (having wings).

nò, 1. *n.* meat.

nòclý, 1. *n.* location.

nòsi, 1. *n.* shine; 2. *n.* shining.

nòxú, 1. *adj.* meaty.

nō, 1. *adj.* rude; 2. *adj.* unkind.

nōclì, 1. *n.* rudeness.

nōfā, 1. *n.* fan; 2. *n.* enthusiast.

nōfāxù, 1. *n.* enthusiastic.

nōfò, 1. *n.* dale.

nōplā, 1. *n.* path; 2. *n.* trail.

nōplì, 1. *n.* clitoris.

nōrō, 1. *adv.* rudely; 2. *adv.* unkindly.

no, 1. *n.* plain; 2. *n.* prairie.

noklú, 1. *n.* parasite.

nọklúxù, 1. *adj.* parasitic.

nọlụlẹ, 1. *adj.* material; 2. *adj.* important.

nọsụ, 1. *n.* importance.

nọsụxú, 1. *adj.* important.

nọsụxúrō, 1. *adv.* importantly.

nõ, 1. *n.* month.

nuá, 1. *v.* {í, ì} arrive (s.w.); 2. *v.* {ì} reach.

nuclĩ, 1. *n.* fairness; 2. *n.* justice.

nuē, 1. *v.* {m̀, ǹ} damage.

nuẹ, 1. *v.* {ź} hiccough; 2. *v.* {ź} hiccup.

nuě, 1. *v.* {m̀, m̃} collect.

nunẽ, 1. *n.* nurse.

nurō, 1. *adv.* fairly; 2. *adv.* justly.

nuý, 1. *v.* {m̀, j̧, í, ì} return (oneself s.w.); 2. *v.* {m̀, j̧, í, ì} go back.

nuȳ, 1. *v.* {m̀, m̃} find.

núcē, 1. *n.* bank (on a river); 2. *n.* embankment.

núkfō, 1. *n.* arch.

núrù, 1. *n.* style.

núsā, 1. *n.* arrival; 2. *n.* destination.

núsȳ, 1. *n.* return (e.g. to a store).

núxē, 1. *adj.* favorite; 2. *n.* favorite.

nù, 1. *adv.* less.

nùcá, 1. *n.* shawl.

nùcạ, 1. *adv.* too; 2. *adv.* also.

nùké, 1. *n.* collector.

nùlé, 1. *n.* ethnicity; 2. *n.* people; 3. *n.* race.

nùmé, 1. *adj.* collected.

nùsé, 1. *n.* collection.

nùséxù, 1. *adj.* collective.

nū, 1. *n.* dye; 2. *prep.* by (*agent, experiencer*).

nūjè, 1. *adv.* very; 2. *adv.* really.

nūklè, 1. *n.* safety.

nūklèxú, 1. *adj.* safe.

nūkȳ, 1. *n.* finder.

nūmē, 1. *adj.* damaged.

nūmȳ, 1. *adj.* found; 2. *adj.* located.

nūnō, 1. *n*. thief.

nūsē, 1. *n*. damage.

nūsȳ, 1. *n*. found object.

nu̱, 1. *n*. tax.

nu̱ci̱, 1. *n*. tunnel.

nu̱jú, 1. *adj*. orange (color).

nu̱júkō, 1. *n*. orange (color).

nu̱pry̱, 1. *n*. coffin.

nu̱se̱, 1. *n*. hiccough; 2. *n*. hiccup.

nũ, 1. *adj*. fair; 2. *adj*. just.

nyfũ, 1. *n*. maw.

nyĩ, 1. *v*. {ḿ, m̀, ñ, ǵ} communicate.

nykã, 1. *n*. onion.

nykĩ, 1. *n*. communicator.

nynũ, 1. *n*. rate.

nysĩ, 1. *n*. communication.

nýrȳ, 1. *n*. column.

nỳ, 1. *adv*. therefore; 2. *adv*. so; 3. *adv*. thus; 4. *conj*. therefore; 5. *conj*. so; 6. *conj*. thus.

nỳkle̱, 1. *comp*. so that; 2. *comp*. in order that; 3. *comp*. for.

nȳ, 1. *n*. word; 2. *n*. term.

nȳlò, 1. *adj*. skinny.

nỹ, 1. *n*. blouse.

ń, 1. *aux*. doubt (*evidentiary*); 2. *dis*. {1: *Cause/Instrument*}.

ǹ, 1. *aux*. want to; 2. *dis*. {2: *Theme, Cause/Instrument*}.

ñ, 1. *aux*. start to; 2. *aux*. begin to.

n̠, 1. *aux*. used to.

ñ, 1. *aux*. look forward to; 2. *dis*. {3: *Theme, Recipient, Agent*}.

O

ó, 1. *prep*. to (*destination, recipient*).

ónō, 1. *adv*. least (*superlative*).

òcri̱, 1. *adv*. still; 2. *adv*. yet.

òcxé, 1. *n*. sapphire.

òcxéxù, 1. *adj*. sapphire; 2. *adj*. made of sapphire.

òlu̧, 1. *adj.* loyal.

òlu̧clí, 1. *adj.* loyalty.

òrȩ, 1. *n.* snack.

ōpī, 1. *n.* cancer.

ōpīxù, 1. *adj.* cancerous.

o̧kru̧, 1. *n.* parent.

o̧kru̧xú, 1. *adj.* parental (behaving as parents).

o̧líkì, 1. *n.* pickpocket.

P

pai̧, 1. *v.* {m̀, m̃, v̀, ṽ} play (music).

palỹ, 1. *n.* shoulder.

pamũ, 1. *adj.* known (facts).

pasũ, 1. *n.* knowledge.

paũ, 1. *v.* {z̃} know (facts).

pá, 1. *n.* tongue.

párò, 1. *n.* address.

pà, 1. *adj.* brief; 2. *adj.* short (not long).

pàclȩ, 1. *n.* shortstaff.

pàclí, 1. *n.* shortness; 2. *n.* brevity.

pàjé, 1. *n.* crab.

pàklȩ, 1. *n.* parabola.

pàklȩxú, 1. *adj.* parabolic.

pànuo̧, 1. *v.* {m̀, Í, v́, ṽ} shorten.

pànu̧mo̧, 1. *adj.* shortened.

pàpru̧, 1. *n.* shortsword.

pàpru̧ni̧, 1. *n.* shortswordsman.

pàro̧, 1. *adv.* briefly.

pācē, 1. *n.* glottis; 2. *n.* vocal cords.

pāklà, 1. *n.* shortbow.

pāklàni̧, 1. *n.* shortbowman.

pa̧cxa̧, 1. *n.* valley.

pa̧fri̧, 1. *n.* event.

pa̧ki̧, 1. *n.* musician; 2. *n.* player (of music).

pa̧klú, 1. *n.* earwax.

pale, 1. *n*. act.

pami, 1. *adj*. played (music); 2. *adj*. performed (music).

paprú, 1. *n*. banana.

pasi, 1. *n*. instrument (musical).

pã, 1. *n*. vest.

peí, 1. *v*. {ḿ, m̀, ñ} shout; 2. *v*. {g̀} shout (at s.th.).

pei, 1. *v*. {ḿ, m̀, m̃} can; 2. *v*. {ḿ, m̀, m̃} put by.

peprĩ, 1. *n*. wallet.

peú, 1. *v*. {m̀, m̃} buy; 2. *v*. {m̀, m̃} purchase.

peȳ, 1. *v*. {m̀} meet (encounter).

pé, 1. *det*. few; 2. *pn*. few.

pékū, 1. *n*. buyer.

pémū, 1. *adj*. purchased; 2. *adj*. brought.

pésī, 1. *n*. yell; 2. *n*. shout.

pésū, 1. *n*. purchase.

pè, 1. *n*. language.

pèxó, 1. *n*. linguistics.

pèxóprà, 1. *n*. linguist.

pē, 1. *adj*. young.

pēclì, 1. *n*. youth.

pēfà, 1. *n*. mace (bludgeon weapon).

pēsȳ, 1. *n*. encounter; 2. *n*. meeting.

pe, 1. *det*. both; 2. *pn*. both.

peclú, 1. *n*. mountain.

peclúxù, 1. *n*. mountainous.

peki, 1. *n*. canner.

pemi, 1. *adj*. canned; 2. *adj*. put by.

piā, 1. *v*. {m̀, m̃} prove.

pia, 1. *v*. {m̀, ǹ, Í, v́, ṽ} sink (e.g. a boat).

piã, 1. *v*. {m̀} follow; 2. *v*. {m̀} succeed; 2. *v*. {m̀} come after.

piéxeō, 1. *v*. {ḿ, m̀, r̃} experiment (on s.th. with s.th.).

piè, 1. *v*. {ḿ, j̀} wait; 2. *v*. {m̀} wait (for s.o./s.th.); 3. *v*. {m̀, m̃} await; 4. *v*. {m̀, m̃} hold.

pie, 1. *v*. {ź, ż} know; 2. *v*. {z̃} be familiar with (s.th.).

pikã, 1. *n*. successor.

piklarikoxū, 1. *adj*. two-dimensional.

pió, 1. *v.* {m̀, m̃} control.

piò, 1. *v.* {m̀, m̀, v̀, ṽ} aim (at s.th.); 2. *v.* {m̀, m̀, v̀, ṽ} take aim (at s.th.).

piō, 1. *v.* {ż} forget (s.o./s.th.); 2. *v.* {ż} forget (*propositions*).

piŏ, 1. *v.* {Í} transform; 2. *v.* {v́, ṽ} transform (into s.th.); 3. *v.* {m̀, ǵ} shrug (at s.o./s.th.).

pipapã, 1. *adj.* twentieth.

pipã, 1. *num.* twenty.

pipī, 1. *adj.* second.

pisã, 1. *n.* succession.

pícū, 1. *n.* edge.

píkēxēkō, 1. *n.* experimentalist.

píkō, 1. *n.* controller.

pímō, 1. *adj.* controlled.

pípà, 1. *n.* title.

písēxēsō, 1. *n.* experiment.

písēxēsōxù, 1. *adj.* experimental.

písō, 1. *n.* control.

písōxù, 1. *n.* controlling.

pì, 1. *n.* chicken.

pìcé, 1. *adv.* away; 2. *prep.* away from.

pìmó, 1. *adj.* transformed.

pìni, 1. *n.* chick.

pìpó, 1. *n.* commerce; 2. *n.* business.

pìse, 1. *n.* wait; 2. *n.* hold-up.

pìsó, 1. *n.* transformation; 2. *n.* shrug.

pìsóxù, 1. *adj.* transformative.

pìso, 1. *n.* aim; 2. *n.* goal; 3. *n.* objective.

pī, 1. *comp.* after; 2. *prep.* after.

pīklī, 1. *n.* crawlspace.

pīlōlē, 1. *adj.* forgetful.

pīlōlēclì, 1. *n.* forgetfulness.

pīmā, 1. *adj.* proven.

pi, 1. *adv.* dark (in color).

pīmō, 1. *adj.* forgotten.

pīsā, 1. *n.* proof.

pijé, 1. *adv.* somehow.

p**ij**ó, 1. *adv.* tomorrow.

p**ik**a, 1. *n.* benefit.

p**ik**axú, 1. *adj.* beneficial.

p**il**ele, 1. *adj.* knowledgeable; 2. *adj.* wise.

p**il**elero, 1. *adv.* knowledgeably; 2. *adv.* wisely.

p**im**a, 1. *adj.* sunk.

p**im**e, 1. *adj.* known; 2. *adj.* familiar.

p**in**uo, 1. *v.* {m̀, ǹ, Í, ṽ} darken (in color).

p**in**umo, 1. *adj.* darkened (in color).

p**ip**ro, 1. *n.* trouble.

pĭ, 1. *num.* two.

placlĭ, 1. *n.* shallowness.

plamõ, 1. *n.* question; 2. *n.* query.

plarõ, 1. *adv.* shallowly.

pláplỳ, 1. *n.* effect.

pláplỳxú, 1. *adj.* effective.

pláplỳxúrō, 1. *adv.* effectively.

plà, 1. *n.* problem.

plàlo, 1. *adj.* proper.

plàloro, 1. *adv.* properly.

plàxú, 1. *adj.* problematic.

plācxȳ, 1. *n.* picture; 2. *n.* depiction.

plācxȳxù, 1. *adj.* picturesque.

plāpỳ, 1. *adj.* usual.

plāpỳro, 1. *adv.* usually.

placra, 1. *n.* sweater.

plamó, 1. *adj.* perfect.

plamóclì, 1. *n.* perfection.

plamónuō, 1. *v.* {m̀, Í} perfect.

plamónūmō, 1. *adj.* perfected.

plamórō, 1. *adv.* perfectly.

plã, 1. *adj.* shallow.

pleò, 1. *v.* {ḿ, m̀, m̃} sing.

pleõ, 1. *v.* {m̀, m̃} hold (carry).

pleŭ, 1. *v.* {m̀} wear (clothes, etc.).

plé, 1. *n.* thumb.

pléfrō, 1. *n.* setting; 2. *n.* environs; 3. *n.* environment.

plémē, 1. *n.* equinox.

plè, 1. *num.* ten.

plèkọ, 1. *n.* singer.

plèmọ, 1. *adj.* sung.

plèplẹ, 1. *adj.* tenth.

plèsọ, 1. *n.* song.

plē, 1. *n.* beak.

plēkrùprý, 1. *n.* decagon.

plēkrùprýxù, 1. *adj.* decagonal.

plēnà, 1. *n.* camel.

plẹ, 1. *prep.* through.

plẹmá, 1. *n.* larder.

pliã, 1. *v.* {m̃, m̀, v̀, ṽ} barter.

pliâ, 1. *v.* {m̀, m̃, Í} manage (e.g. a business); 2. *v.* {m̀, m̃, Í} run.

pliè, 1. *v.* {m̃, m̀, m̃} eat.

plikã, 1. *n.* barterer.

plikfaxũ, 1. *adj.* philosophical; 2. *adj.* thought-provoking.

plikfã, 1. *n.* philosophy.

plikõ, 1. *n.* operator; 2. *n.* driver.

plimã, 1. *adj.* bartered.

pliõ, 1. *v.* {m̃, m̀, ń, ǹ} win.

pliõ, 1. *v.* {j̀, j̃} operate (a machine, e.g. a vehicle); 2. *v.* {j̀, j̃} drive (e.g. a vehicle).

plisã, 1. *n.* barter.

plisõ, 1. *n.* operation (e.g. of a machine).

pliỹ, 1. *v.* {m̃, Ì, ṽ} travel.

plí, 1. *num.* ten thousand; 2. *num.* myriad.

plíclī, 1. *n.* network.

plíkà, 1. *n.* manager.

plímà, 1. *adj.* managed (business, etc.); 2. *adj.* run.

plíplī, 1. *adj.* ten thousandth.

plísà, 1. *n.* management (of a business, etc.).

plìcị, 1. *n.* acid.

plìcịxú, 1. *adj.* acidic.

plìcịxúclì, 1. *n.* acidity.

plìkẹ, 1. *n.* eater.
plìkrị, 1. *n.* estate (property).
plìmẹ, 1. *adj.* eaten.
plī, 1. *n.* objective; 2. *n.* goal.
plīklē, 1. *n.* recipe.
plīkō, 1. *n.* winner.
plīkrè, 1. *adj.* lonely.
plīkrèclí, 1. *n.* loneliness.
plīkȳ, 1. *n.* traveler.
plīmō, 1. *adj.* won.
plīsō, 1. *n.* victory.
plīsȳ, 1. *n.* travel; 2. *n.* traveling.
plīxù, 1. *adj.* goal-oriented.
plịclý, 1. *n.* letter (orthographic); 2. *n.* character.
plịkrọ, 1. *n.* jumpsuit.
plịrí, 1. *adv.* forever.
plī, 1. *n.* while (period of time).
ploī, 1. *v.* {ṁ, ñ} say; 2. *v.* {ṁ, ñ} state.
ploǐ, 1. *v.* {ḿ, ǵ} talk (to/with s.o.); 2. *v.* {ḿ, ṁ, ǵ} speak (to/with s.o.).
plokroxũ, 1. *adj.* programmatic.
plokrõ, 1. *n.* program (computational).
pló, 1. *n.* mane.
plóklā, 1. *n.* gauntlet.
plò, 1. *n.* ear (external).
plòkí, 1. *n.* speaker.
plòlạ, 1. *adj.* suspicious.
plòlạrọ, 1. *adv.* suspiciously.
plòlílē, 1. *adj.* talkative.
plòmí, 1. *adj.* spoken.
plòsí, 1. *n.* speech.
plō, 1. *pn.* we; 2. *pn.* us.
plōmà, 1. *adj.* our; 2. *n.* ours.
plōmī, 1. *adj.* said; 2. *adj.* mentioned.
plōprù, 1. *n.* earring.
plōsī, 1. *n.* utterance.
plọ, 1. *n.* world.

plocló, 1. *n.* strategy.

ploclóprà, 1. *n.* strategist.

ploclóxù, 1. *adj.* strategic (calculated).

ploxú, 1. *adj.* worldly; 2. *adj.* cosmopolitan.

pluē, 1. *v.* {m̀, m̃, ĺ} end; 2. *v.* {m̀, m̃, ĺ} finish.

pluê, 1. *v.* {m̀, ĺ, ì} drop.

pluĕ, 1. *v.* {m̀, ĺ} con; 2. *v.* {m̀, ĺ} scam; 3. *v.* {m̀, ĺ} swindle.

pluklã, 1. *n.* ovary.

plukulaxū, 1. *adj.* precipitous.

plukulā, 1. *n.* precipice.

pluó, 1. *v.* {ǹ, ĺ} count.

pluò, 1. *v.* {ĺ, v́} rise.

pluô, 1. *v.* {v̀} use.

pluxū, 1. *adj.* heated; 2. *adj.* hot.

plú, 1. *n.* waist.

plúclì, 1. *adj.* savory.

plúkò, 1. *n.* user.

plúmò, 1. *adj.* used.

plúsō, 1. *n.* countdown.

plù, 1. *n.* glen.

plùje, 1. *n.* computer.

plùké, 1. *n.* swindler; 2. *n.* scammer; 2. *n.* conman.

plùsé, 1. *n.* swindle; 2. *n.* scam; 3. *n.* fraud; 4. *n.* con.

plùséxù, 1. *adj.* fraudulent.

plùso, 1. *n.* rise.

plū, 1. *adj.* white.

plūclì, 1. *n.* whiteness.

plūjē, 1. *n.* pig.

plūjēnē, 1. *n.* piglet.

plūkō, 1. *n.* white.

plūmē, 1. *adj.* finished.

plūnuō, 1. *v.* {m̀, ĺ} whiten.

plu, 1. *prep.* for (*beneficiary*).

plucla, 1. *n.* exit.

plufé, 1. *n.* leather.

pluféxù, 1. *adj.* leather; 2. *adj.* made of leather.

plukfá, 1. *adj.* truthful; 2. *adj.* honest.

plukfáclì, 1. *n.* honesty.

plukfárō, 1. *adv.* honestly; 2. *adv.* truthfully.

plumý, 1. *adj.* ugly.

plumýclì, 1. *n.* ugliness.

plũ, 1. *n.* heat.

plyì, 1. *v.* {Í} drool.

plyù, 1. *v.* {m̀, ṽ} fold.

plý, 1. *adv.* always.

plýsē, 1. *n.* focus.

plýsēxù, 1. *adj.* focused.

plỳlile, 1. *adj.* drooly.

plỳmu, 1. *adj.* folded.

plỳsi, 1. *n.* drool.

plȳ, 1. *n.* board (wood); 2. *n.* plank.

plȳcrò, 1. *n.* file.

plỹ, 1. *n.* reason; 2. *n.* impetus.

pojõ, 1. *n.* basis.

poú, 1. *v.* {ḿ, m̀} swallow.

pó, 1. *n.* stomach acid; 2. *n.* bile.

pócì, 1. *n.* finger.

pócīcò, 1. *n.* fingernail.

pócxā, 1. *n.* masonry.

pócxāprà, 1. *n.* mason.

pómū, 1. *adj.* swallowed.

póxù, 1. *adj.* bilious.

pò, 1. *pn.* I; 2. *pn.* me.

pòjo, 1. *n.* fame.

pòjoxú, 1. *adj.* famous.

pòjoxúrō, 1. *adv.* famously.

pòke, 1. *n.* cycle.

pòkexú, 1. *adj.* cyclical.

pòmá, 1. *adj.* my; 2. *n.* mine (*possessive*).

pòro, 1. *n.* cell (prison).

pòsre, 1. *adj.* previous.

pòsrero, 1. *adv.* previously.

pō, 1. *n.* hoof.

pōjōkfàpo̱, 1. *n.* infrastructure.

pōkrò, 1. *n.* mattress.

pōprù, 1. *adj.* weak (in flavor, etc.).

pōprùro̱, 1. *adv.* weakness (of flavor, etc.).

po̱, 1. *n.* time (in abstract).

po̱fó, 1. *n.* blanket.

po̱kfe̱, 1. *n.* waistband.

praí, 1. *v.* {m̀, m̃, Í, ṽ} solve.

praklũ, 1. *n.* company; 2. *n.* business.

pralõ, 1. *n.* sucker (organic).

prámī, 1. *adj.* solved.

prápē, 1. *n.* village; 2. *n.* town.

prásī, 1. *n.* solution (e.g. to a problem).

prànú, 1. *adj.* simple.

prànúclì, 1. *n.* simplicity.

prànúnuō, 1. *v.* {m̀, ǹ, Í, v́, ṽ} simplify.

prànúnūmō, 1. *adj.* simplified.

prànúrō, 1. *adv.* simply.

prā, 1. *n.* cap.

prākfē, 1. *n.* intestines.

prāmē, 1. *adv.* only; 2. *adv.* merely; 3. *adv.* strictly.

prāsòma̱, 1. *adj.* automatic.

prāsòma̱ro̱, 1. *adv.* automatically.

pra̱, 1. *n.* beard.

pra̱fí, 1. *adj.* opaque.

pra̱xú, 1. *adj.* bearded.

preclī, 1. *n.* width.

preì, 1. *v.* {ḿ} cower.

prenuõ, 1. *v.* {m̀, Í, v́, ṽ} widen; 2. *v.* {m̀, Í, v́, ṽ} broaden.

prerõ, 1. *adv.* widely; 2. *adv.* broadly.

preū, 1. *v.* {m̀, Í} sound.

preūjoū, 1. *v.* {m̀, ǹ, Í} shatter.

preu̱, 1. *v.* {m̀, ż} muster.

pré, 1. *adj.* clear; 2. *adj.* translucent.

préclì, 1. *n.* clarity.

prékfȳ, 1. *n.* advantage.

prékfȳxù, 1. *adj.* advantageous.

prèki̱, 1. *n.* coward.

prèki̱xú, 1. *adj.* cowardly.

prēmūjōmū, 1. *adj.* shattered.

pre̱, 1. *adj.* bad; 2. **pró pre̱** *adj.* worse; 3. **rà pre̱** *adj.* worst.

prepo̱, 1. *n.* satchel.

prero̱, 1. *adv.* poorly; 2. *adv.* badly.

prẽ, 1. *adj.* wide; 2. *adj.* broad.

priŏ, 1. *v.* {ž} hurt (s.o./s.th.); 3. *v.* {z̀} hurt (*propositions*).

prí, 1. *adj.* raw.

prì, 1. *adj.* ready.

prìclí, 1. *n.* readiness.

prìcy̱, 1. *adv.* here; 2. *n.* here.

prìjú, 1. *n.* barrier.

prìlólē, 1. *adj.* hurtful.

prìmó, 1. *adj.* injured; 2. *adj.* hurt.

prìnuo̱, 1. *v.* {m̀, Í} ready.

prìnu̱mo̱, 1. *adj.* readied.

prìro̱, 1. *adv.* readily.

prìsó, 1. *n.* pain.

prī, 1. *adj.* blue.

prīclì, 1. *n.* blueness.

prīfènú, 1. *n.* blueberry.

prīkō, 1. *n.* blue.

pri̱cxé, 1. *n.* shooting range.

pri̱fo̱, 1. *n.* island.

pri̱múkō, 1. *n.* brown.

pri̱mu̱, 1. *adj.* brown.

proí, 1. *v.* {m̀, Í} usure.

projũ, 1. *n.* newspaper.

prou̱, 1. *v.* {ž} experience (s.th.); 2. *v.* {ž} live (through s.th.).

pró, 1. *adv.* more (*comparative*).

prókī, 1. *n.* usurer.

prósī, 1. *n.* usury.

prò, 1. *adj.* distinct; 2. *adj.* different.

pròcó, 1. *n.* mortar.

pròkǫ, 1. *n.* cowl.

prònuǫ, 1. *v.* {m̀, Í} differentiate; 2. *v.* {m̀, Í} distinguish.

prònųmǫ, 1. *adj.* differentiated; 2. *adj.* distinguished.

prònųsǫ, 1. *n.* differentiation.

pròprí, 1. *n.* period; 2. *n.* time.

pròpríxù, 1. *adj.* periodic.

pròpríxùclí, 1. *n.* periodicity.

prō, 1. *adj.* smart; 2. *adj.* intelligent.

prōclì, 1. *n.* intelligence.

prǫ, 1. *n.* hill.

prǫkélò, 1. *n.* filament.

prǫkų, 1. *n.* experiencer.

prǫsų, 1. *n.* experience.

prǫsy, 1. *n.* factory; 2. *n.* plant (industrial).

prǫxú, 1. *adj.* hilly.

pruá, 1. *v.* {m̀, Í, ṽ} mark.

pruã, 1. *v.* {m̀, ṽ} divide.

pruǎ, 1. *v.* {m̀, m̃, g̀} refuse.

prukã, 1. *n.* divider; 2. *n.* divisor.

prumã, 1. *adj.* divided.

pruò, 1. *v.* {m̀, ñ} introduce.

prusã, 1. *n.* division.

prú, 1. *adj.* light (in weight).

prúmã, 1. *adj.* marked.

prù, 1. *n.* ring (jewelry).

prùnį, 1. *adj.* weird; 2. *adj.* strange; 3. *adj.* odd.

prùnįclí, 1. *n.* strangeness.

prùnįrǫ, 1. *adv.* strangely; 2. *adv.* oddly.

prùsá, 1. *n.* refusal.

prùsǫ, 1. *n.* introduction.

prùsǫxú, 1. *adj.* introductory.

prūrìprǫsų, 1. *n.* motherhood; 2. *n.* maternity.

prūrī, 1. *n.* mother; 2. *n.* moth (insect).

prūrīxù, 1. *adj.* maternal (behaving as a mother); 2. *adj.* motherly.

prų, 1. *n.* sword.

pruni, 1. *n.* swordsman.

pruxó, 1. *n.* swordsmanship.

prũ, 1. *n.* fang.

prymũ, 1. *adj.* revealed.

prysũ, 1. *n.* revelation.

pryũ, 1. *v.* {m̀, ǹ, Í} reveal.

pryxũ, 1. *adj.* scaly.

prỳ, 1. *adj.* taken (not single).

prỳcó, 1. *n.* detriment.

prỳcóxù, 1. *adj.* detrimental; 2. *adj.* deleterious; 3. *adj.* damaging.

prypé, 1. *prep.* with (*concomitant*).

prỹ, 1. *n.* scale (organic).

psaī, 1. {m̀} call (by telephone).

psaū, 1. *v.* {m̀} put away.

psá, 1. *n.* food.

psárì, 1. *n.* series (items in sequence).

psà, 1. *n.* sex.

psàxú, 1. *adj.* sexy.

psā, 1. *n.* eyelash.

psākī, 1. *n.* caller (by telephone).

psāmī, 1. *adj.* called (by telephone).

psāmū, 1. *adj.* put away.

psa̲, 1. *n.* week.

psa̲cí, 1. *n.* symmetry.

psa̲cíxù, 1. *adj.* symmetrical.

psa̲cíxùro̲, 1. *adv.* symmetrically.

pseí, 1. *v.* {ḿ, j} jump.

pseī, 1. *v.* {m̀, ñ} promise; 2. *v.* {m̀, ñ} swear.

pseī̀, 1. *v.* {m̀, Í} encourage.

pseĩ̀, 1. *v.* {ṽ} regard (s.o./s.th. as s.th.); 2. *v.* {ṽ} consider (s.o./s.th. as s.th.).

pselilẽ, 1. *adj.* encouraging.

psemĩ, 1. *adj.* encouraged.

psesĩ, 1. *n.* encouragement.

pseў, 1. *v.* {ḿ, m̀, m̃, ñ, g̀} write.

pséplō, 1. *n.* scarcity; 2. *n.* lack.

pséplōxù, 1. *adj.* scarce.

psè, 1. *adj.* on time; 2. *adj.* timely; 2. *adj.* punctual.

psèclí, 1. *n.* punctuality; 2. *n.* timeliness.

psèký, 1. *n.* writer.

psèmý, 1. *adj.* written.

psènó, 1. *n.* alchemy.

psènóprà, 1. *n.* alchemist.

psèpó, 1. *adv.* almost.

psèrọ, 1. *adv.* on time; 2. *adv.* punctually.

psèsý, 1. *n.* writing.

psēcrỳ, 1. *n.* pelvis.

psēmī, 1. *adj.* promised.

psēprò, 1. *n.* profit.

psēpròxú, 1. *adj.* profitable.

psēpròxúclì, 1. *n.* profitability.

psēsī, 1. *n.* promise.

psẹ, 1. *n.* bolt (building material, crossbow ammunition).

psejẹ, 1. *n.* contact (touching).

psẽ, 1. *n.* beam.

psiĕ, 1. *v.* {z̃} expect (s.o./s.th.); 2. *v.* {ż} expect (*propositions*).

psiĕkriā, 1. *v.* {ḿ, m̀} attack preemptively; 2. *v.* {ḿ, m̀} strike preemptively.

psiō, 1. *v.* {z̃} enjoy (s.o./s.th.); 2. *v.* {ż} enjoy (*propositions*).

psiŏ, 1. *v.* {m̀, m̃} check.

psiỳ, 1. *v.* {m̀, m̃} lead.

psiă, 1. *v.* {ḿ, z̃, ǵ} chuckle.

psí, 1. *n.* back; 2. *prep.* behind.

psíkrùprý, 1. *n.* heptagon.

psíkrùprýxù, 1. *adj.* heptagonal.

psì, 1. *n.* sheath.

psìky, 1. *n.* leader.

psìmé, 1. *adj.* expected.

psìsá, 1. *n.* chuckle.

psìsé, 1. *n.* expectation.

psìsékrīsā, 1. *n.* preemptive attack; 2. *n.* preemptive strike.

psìsó, 1. *n.* check.

psī, 1. *n.* idea; 2. *n.* image; 3. *n.* concept.

psīlè, 1. *n.* corkscrew.

psīsō, 1. *n.* enjoyment.

psīxù, 1. *adj.* conceptual.

psi̱, 1. *num.* seven.

psi̱pa̱, 1. *num.* seventy.

psi̱pa̱pa̱, 1. *adj.* seventieth.

psi̱psi̱, 1. *adj.* seventh.

psĩ̱, 1. *n.* bird.

psocreclĩ, 1. *n.* similarity.

psocrerõ, 1. *adv.* similarly.

psocrẽ, 1. *adj.* similar.

psoi̱, 1. *v.* {ḿ, m̀, ñ} murmur.

psoú, 1. *v.* {m̀, Í} sail.

psó, 1. *n.* pair.

psókū, 1. *n.* sailor.

psómū, 1. *adj.* sailed.

psósū, 1. *n.* sail; 2. *n.* sailing.

psò, 1. *adj.* clean.

psòxó, 1. *n.* physics.

psòxóprà, 1. *n.* physicist.

psō, 1. *n.* force (physics).

psōfrū, 1. *n.* sport; 2. *n.* sports.

psōfrūxù, 1. *adj.* sporty; 2. *adj.* athletic.

psōsrē, 1. *n.* target.

psōxù, 1. *adj.* forceful.

psōxùro̱, 1. *adv.* forcefully.

pso̱, 1. *n.* hut.

pso̱cí, 1. *n.* café.

pso̱ki̱, 1. *n.* murmurer.

pso̱si̱, 1. *n.* murmuring; 2. *n.* murmur.

psõ, 1. *n.* step; 2. *n.* footstep.

psuà, 1. *v.* {ḿ, m̀} exercise.

psuâ, 1. *v.* {m̀, Í} publish.

psuẽ, 1. *v.* {m̀, ǹ, Í} influence.

psuê, 1. *v.* {m̀, Í} beat; 2. *v.* {m̀, Í} batter.

psukẽ, 1. *n.* influencer.

psulelē, 1. *adj.* influential.

psumõ, 1. *adj.* understood.

psuõ, 1. *v.* {ź, ż, ž} understand; 2. *v.* {ź, ż, ž} comprehend; 3. *v.* {ź, ż, ž} get it.

psusexū, 1. *adj.* influential.

psusē, 1. *n.* influence.

psuxū, 1. *adj.* childish.

psú, 1. *adj.* sane; 2. *adj.* of sound mind.

psúclì, 1. *n.* sanity.

psúkà, 1. *n.* publisher.

psúmà, 1. *adj.* published.

psúmè, 1. *adj.* beaten; 2. *adj.* battered.

psúsà, 1. *n.* publication.

psù, 1. *n.* fork.

psùprẹ, 1. *n.* staff; 2. *n.* personnel.

psùsạ, 1. *n.* exercise.

psūlò, 1. *n.* theme.

psūxī, 1. *n.* system.

psūxīxù, 1. *adj.* systematic.

psūxīxùclí, 1. *n.* systematicity.

psụ, 1. *n.* port.

psụpá, 1. *n.* drought.

psụprọsụ, 1. *n.* childhood.

psụrá, 1. *n.* liver.

psũ, 1. *n.* child.

psyí, 1. *v.* {j} point (at s.o./s.th.).

psyì, 1. *v.* {ṁ, r̀} frown (at s.o./s.th.).

psyị, 1. *v.* {ṁ} acknowledge; 2. *v.* {ṁ} recognize.

psyī, 1. *v.* {ṁ, ń, ĺ} shake.

psyǐ, 1. *v.* {ź, ż, ž} remember; 2. *v.* {ź, ż, ž} recall; 3. *v.* {ź, ż, ž} recollect.

psylilē, 1. *adj.* shaky.

psymĩ, 1. *adj.* shaken.

psysĩ, 1. *n.* shaking.

psyụ, 1. *v.* {ṁ, m̃} confront; 2. *v.* {ṁ, m̃} face.

psyû, 1. *v.* {ṁ, ṁ, m̃} offer.

psyxũ, 1. *adj.* wood; 2. *adj.* wooden.

psý, 1. *n.* cape.

psýmù, 1. *adj.* offered.

psýplō, 1. *n.* standard.

psýplōxù, 1. *adj.* standard.

psýsù, 1. *n.* offering.

psỳ, 1. *adj.* tidy.

psỳclí, 1. *n.* tidiness.

psỳmí, 1. *adj.* remembered; 2. *adj.* recollected.

psỳni̱, 1. *n.* spinning wheel.

psỳplu̱, 1. *n.* car.

psỳpsu̱, 1. *n.* district; 2. *n.* county.

psỳro̱, 1. *adv.* tidily; 2. *adv.* neatly.

psỳsí, 1. *n.* memory; 2. *n.* remembrance; 3. *n.* recollection.

psỳsi̱, 1. *n.* frown.

psȳ, 1. *n.* dog.

psȳlȳ, 1. *n.* sand.

psȳlȳxù, 1. *adj.* sandy.

psȳnȳ, 1. *n.* puppy; 2. *n.* doggy.

psy̱, 1. *n.* shape.

psylu̱le̱, 1. *adj.* confrontational.

psymi̱, 1. *adj.* recognized.

psysi̱, 1. *n.* recognition; 2. *n.* acknowledgement.

psysu̱, 1. *n.* confrontation.

psỹ, 1. *n.* wood.

puá, 1. *v.* {m̀, m̃} accept.

puē, 1. *v.* {ḿ, m̀, ñ} complain (about s.th.).

pue̱, 1. *v.* {m̀, m̃} start (s.o./s.th.); 2. *v.* {m̀, m̃} begin (s.o./s.th.).

pujĩ, 1. *n.* couple (group of two).

pukõ, 1. *n.* planner.

pumõ, 1. *adj.* planned (in general).

puō, 1. *v.* {ḿ, m̀, Í} marry.

puõ, 1. *v.* {m̀, m̃} plan.

pusõ, 1. *n.* plan; 2. *n.* schedule.

puỹ, 1. *v.* {Í} alive (be alive); 2. *v.* {Í} live.

puy̌, 1. *v.* {m̀, j̱, ṽ} traverse; 2. *v.* {m̀, j̱, ṽ} cross.

pú, 1. *adj.* warm.

púclì, 1. *n.* warmth.

púmā, 1. *adj.* accepted.

púnuō, 1. *v.* {m̀, ǹ, Í} warm (up).

púsā, 1. *n.* acceptance.

pù, 1. *n.* bone.

pùkra̱, 1. *n.* riddle.

pùsry̱, 1. *n.* mouse.

pùxú, 1. *adj.* bony.

pū, 1. *adj.* lazy.

pūclì, 1. *n.* laziness.

pūlēlē, 1. *adj.* whiny.

pūmō, 1. *adj.* married.

pūnìxu̱, 1. *n.* remedy.

pūrī, 1. *adj.* yellow.

pūrīkō, 1. *n.* yellow.

pūrō, 1. *adv.* lazily.

pūsē, 1. *n.* complaint.

pūsō, 1. *n.* marriage (ceremony).

pūxà, 1. *n.* hatchet; 2. *n.* axe.

pu̱cí, 1. *adj.* holy; 2. *adj.* sacred.

pu̱cíclì, 1. *n.* holiness; 2. *n.* sacredness.

pu̱ke̱, 1. *n.* beginner; 2. *n.* neophyte.

pu̱me̱, 1. *adj.* started; 2. *adj.* begun.

pu̱se̱, 1. *n.* beginning; 2. *n.* start.

pycē, 1. *adj.* nightly.

pycxycō, 1. *adj.* governmental.

pyfifū, 1. *n.* authoritative.

pyfrī, 1. *adj.* piscine.

pyjecō, 1. *adj.* cellular.

pyjelō, 1. *adj.* epistolary.

pyjunē, 1. *adj.* musical (relating to music).

pykfū, 1. *adj.* manual (hand-related).

pyklarikō, 1. *adj.* dimensional.

pyklelō, 1. *adj.* uvular.

pykliprū, 1. *adj.* colonial.

pyklosī, 1. *adj.* digestive.

pyklujĩ, 1. *adj.* informational.

pykukfẽ, 1. *adj.* industrial.

pylã, 1. *n.* angle.

pylỹ, 1. *adj.* vocal (relating to voice).

pymulukfĩ, 1. *adj.* cosmic.

pynã, 1. *adj.* mental; 2. *adj.* cerebral.

pynimũ, 1. *adj.* scientific.

pynõ, 1. *adj.* monthly.

pynysĩ, 1. *adj.* communicative.

pyplikfã, 1. *adj.* philosophical (relating to philosophy).

pypluklã, 1. *adj.* ovarian.

pyplũ, 1. *adj.* thermal.

pypsĩ, 1. *adj.* avian.

pypylã, 1. *adj.* angular.

pyrẽ, 1. *adj.* work-related.

pyrỹ, 1. *adj.* cardiac.

pysipijõ, 1. *adj.* surgical.

pysrũ, 1. *adj.* anal.

pysumerĩ, 1. *adj.* nutritional.

pysũ, 1. *adj.* aerial.

pyū, 1. *v.* {ṁ, m̃} choose.

pyŭ, 1. *v.* {ṁ} visit (people); 2. *v.* {j} visit (locations).

pyxũ, 1. *adj.* lengthy; 2. *adj.* long.

pyxỹ, 1. *n.* pulmonary.

pý, 1. *n.* shin.

pỳ, 1. *n.* bowl.

pỳkú, 1. *n.* visitor.

pỳsú, 1. *n.* visit.

pȳ, 1. *comp.* whether.

pȳclūrū, 1. *n.* esophageal.

pȳcòclu̱, 1. *adj.* autumnal.

pȳcrū, 1. *adj.* late (dead).

pȳcxà, 1. *adj.* legal (relating to law).

pȳcxìká, 1. *adj.* causal.

pȳcxō, 1. *adj.* sectional.

pȳcxūnī, 1. *adj.* peninsular.

pȳfācỳ, 1. *adj.* disciplinary.

pȳfè, 1. *adj.* monetary.

pȳfōclù, 1. *adj.* testicular.

pȳfràfẹ, 1. *adj.* aural.

pȳfrùmí, 1. *adj.* estival.

pȳfrỳ, 1. *adj.* marital.

pȳfù, 1. *n.* skirt.

pȳjīlì, 1. *adj.* experiential.

pȳjò, 1. *adj.* lacustrine.

pȳkà, 1. *adj.* postal.

pȳkā, 1. *adj.* earthly.

pȳkfàpọ, 1. *adj.* structural.

pȳklìkró, 1. *adj.* distributional.

pȳkò, 1. *adj.* narrative.

pȳkòplỵ, 1. *adj.* muscular.

pȳkràsrú, 1. *adj.* political.

pȳkrōpsù, 1. *adj.* pathological (relating to disease).

pȳkūjì, 1. *adj.* functional.

pȳlàsí, 1. *adj.* respiratory.

pȳlāfrà, 1. *adj.* communal.

pȳlāfū, 1. *adj.* vaginal.

pȳlēsū, 1. *adj.* investigatory.

pȳlùprí, 1. *adj.* analytical (relating to analysis).

pȳlū, 1. *adj.* lunar.

pȳlȳprù, 1. *adj.* uterine.

pȳmà, 1. *adj.* botanical.

pȳmì, 1. *n.* nasal; 2. **mákrȳ pȳmì** *n.* nasal cavity.

pȳmùcxẹ, 1. *adj.* departmental.

pȳmū, 1. *adj.* chosen.

pȳmūfrè, 1. *adj.* positional.

pȳmỳsú, 1. *adj.* menstrual.

pȳnī, 1. *adj.* annual; 2. *adj.* yearly.

pȳnòclỵ́, 1. *adj.* locative.

pȳnōplì, 1. *adj.* clitoral.

pȳpācē, 1. *adj.* glottal.

pȳpè, 1. *adj.* linguistic (relating to language).

491

pȳpèxó, 1. *adj.* linguistic (relating to linguistics).

pȳpìpó, 1. *adj.* commercial; 2. *adj.* business-related.

pȳprākfē, 1. *n.* intestinal.

pȳprūrī, 1. *adj.* maternal (relating to mother, mother's side, etc.).

pȳpsēcrỳ, 1. *adj.* pelvic.

pȳpsūlò, 1. *adj.* thematic.

pȳpsūxī, 1. *adj.* systemic.

pȳpsȳ, 1. *adj.* canine.

pȳrēcrō, 1. *adj.* superficial (relating to surface).

pȳrēcrỳ, 1. *adj.* foundational.

pȳrēnù, 1. *adj.* penile.

pȳrìfro̱, 1. *adj.* evidential.

pȳrùlo̱, 1. *adj.* vernal.

pȳrūklò, 1. *adj.* skeletal.

pȳrūnà, 1. *adj.* societal.

pȳrỳsú, 1. *adj.* educational (relating to education).

pȳsècri̱, 1. *adj.* conditional (relating to a condition).

pȳsìfá, 1. *adj.* featural.

pȳsrì, 1. *adj.* paginal.

pȳsū, 1. *n.* choice.

pȳsȳ, 1. *adj.* book-related.

py̱, 1. *n.* chest (anatomy).

py̱cé, 1. *adj.* natal.

py̱ci̱ké, 1. *adj.* contextual.

py̱clípȳ, 1. *adj.* cultural.

py̱crésỳ, 1. *adj.* editorial.

py̱cro̱kfó, 1. *adj.* volcanic.

py̱cxású, 1. *adj.* ejaculatory.

py̱cxe̱psu̱, 1. *adj.* organizational.

py̱fi̱, 1. *adj.* amatory.

py̱fólū, 1. *adj.* palatal.

py̱fra̱, 1. *adj.* scholastic.

py̱frépȳ, 1. *adj.* definitional.

py̱fri̱ry̱, 1. *adj.* future.

py̱ji̱ní, 1. *adj.* rectal.

py̱jó, 1. *adj.* daily.

pyjokry, 1. *adj.* spatial.

pyjú, 1. *adj.* solar; 2. *adj.* stellar.

pyjúkā, 1. *adj.* coastal.

pyjýkrē, 1. *adj.* renal.

pyjypla, 1. *adj.* situational; 2. *adj.* circumstantial.

pykfilu, 1. *adj.* funerary.

pykfu, 1. *adj.* labial (relating to lip).

pykíprù, 1. *adj.* textual.

pyki, 1. *n.* ocular; 2. *n.* optical.

pykrakrí, 1. *adj.* technological.

pykre, 1. *adj.* economic.

pykrísē, 1. *adj.* developmental.

pykryro, 1. *adj.* resultative.

pyký, 1. *adj.* rental.

pykýnì, 1. *adj.* paralytic.

pylacó, 1. *adj.* data-related.

pylyjé, 1. *adj.* tracheal.

pymacrici, 1. *adj.* religious (relating to religion).

pymirá, 1. *adj.* paternal (relating to father, father's side, etc.).

pymy, 1. *adj.* methodical.

pynékfē, 1. *adj.* maximal.

pynékfērō, 1. *adv.* maximally; 2. *adv.* at most.

pynepó, 1. *adj.* hibernal.

pyni, 1. *adj.* personal.

pynikfé, 1. *adj.* national.

pyniro, 1. *adv.* personally.

pynúrù, 1. *adj.* stylistic.

pypá, 1. *adj.* lingual.

pypípà, 1. *adj.* titular.

pypísēxēsō, 1. *adj.* experimental.

pypléfrō, 1. *adj.* environmental.

pyplísà, 1. *adj.* managerial.

pyplo, 1. *adj.* global.

pyplocló, 1. *adj.* strategic (relating to strategy).

pypó, 1. *adj.* biliary.

pypo, 1. *adj.* temporal.

pyprokélò, 1. *adj.* filamentary.

pypsa, 1. *adj.* weekly.

pypuse, 1. *adj.* initial.

pypusero, 1. *adv.* initially; 2. *adv.* at first.

pyry, 1. *adj.* facial.

pysá, 1. *adj.* terminal; 2. *adj.* final.

pysárō 1. *adv.* inevitably; 2. *adv.* ultimately; 3. *adv.* finally.

pyséplālō, 1. *adj.* galactic.

pysemú, 1. *adj.* pancreatic.

pysici, 1. *adj.* minimal.

pysiciro, 1. *adv.* minimally.

pysó, 1. *adj.* health-related.

pysoju, 1. *adj.* scalar.

pysra, 1. *adj.* corporeal; 2. *adj.* bodily.

pysré, 1. *adj.* numerical.

pysréxō, 1. *adj.* mathematical.

pysró, 1. *adj.* dermal.

pysrucó, 1. *adj.* fecal.

pysrý, 1. *adj.* familial.

pysý, 1. *adj.* varietal.

pysyxó, 1. *adj.* literary.

pỹ, 1. *n.* length.

R

raclã, 1. *n.* plume.

rai, 1. *v.* {ḿ, m̀, ñ} serve (food, etc.).

raî, 1. *v.* {ḿ, v̀} succeed; 2. *v.* {ḿ, v̀} be successful.

rajã, 1. *n.* matter (physical).

rakajõ, 1. *n.* railroad.

rau, 1. *v.* {m̀, ǹ, Í, v́, ṽ} extinguish; 2. *v.* {m̀, ǹ, Í, v́, ṽ} turn off; 3. *v.* {m̀, ǹ, Í, v́, ṽ} put out (e.g. a fire).

rá, 1. *n.* curl.

rácxā, 1. *n.* goat.

rácxānā, 1. *n.* kid (infant goat).

rákfē, 1. *n.* member (of a group, etc.).

rálì, 1. *adj.* violent.

rálìclí, 1. *n.* violence.

rálìlẹ, 1. *adj.* successful.

rálìlẹrọ, 1. *adv.* successfully.

rásì, 1. *n.* success.

ráxù, 1. *adj.* curly.

rà, 1. *adv.* most (*superlative*).

ràkfị, 1. *n.* device; 2. *n.* gadget.

ràkfịprá, 1. *n.* gadgeteer.

ràkị, 1. *n.* server; 2. *n.* waiter; 3. *n.* waitress.

ràmị, 1. *adj.* served (food, drinks, etc.).

ràpsẹ, 1. *n.* media (news, entertainment).

rā, 1. *adj.* hot.

rāclì, 1. *n.* heat.

rāclī, 1. *n.* prostitution.

rāclīprà, 1. *n.* prostitute.

rācrū, 1. *n.* washer (building material).

rājì, 1. *n.* button (technology).

rākē, 1. *n.* snow.

rākēxù, 1. *adj.* snowy.

rākfè, 1. *n.* honey.

rānuō, 1. *v.* {m̀, ǹ, Í} heat up.

rạ, 1. *n.* wind.

rạfị, 1. *n.* cake.

rạkạ, 1. *n.* train (locomotive).

rạkrọ, 1. *n.* knee; 2. *n.* kneecap.

rạmụ, 1. *adj.* extinguished; 2. *adj.* turned off; 3. *adj.* put out.

rạnạ, 1. *n.* gust.

rạpí, 1. *n.* magnet.

rạpímīmā, 1. *n.* electricity.

rạpíxù, 1. *adj.* magnetic.

rạpíxùnuọ, 1. *v.* {m̀, ǹ, Ĩ, v́} magnetize.

rạpíxùnụmọ, 1. *adj.* magnetized.

rạpíxùnụsọ, 1. *n.* magnetization.

rạpsẹ, 1. *det.* how many; 2. *pn.* how many.

rạxú, 1. *adj.* windy.

rã, 1. *n.* claw.

recyclĩ, 1. *n.* continuity.

recỹ, 1. *adj.* continuous.

reī, 1. *v.* {m̀, m̃, í} steward.

rei̱, 1. *v.* {ż, z̃} please; 2. *v.* {ż, z̃} like (s.th. pleases s.o.).

reŏ, 1. *v.* {ḿ, m̀, m̃, ṽ} draw.

reȳ, 1. *v.* {m̀, m̃, í, ì} grow.

ré, 1. *n.* orb.

rékā, 1. *prep.* as much (*as much*... as s.th.); 2. *prep.* like.

rékfī, 1. *n.* wolf.

réklù, 1. *adj.* serious.

réklùclí, 1. *n.* seriousness.

réklùro̱, 1. *adv.* seriously.

rénā, 1. *n.* bayonet.

rècé, 1. *n.* weapon.

rèci̱, 1. *n.* stomach.

rèclý, 1. *n.* phase; 2. *n.* stage.

rèkó, 1. *n.* drawer (artist).

rèmó, 1. *adj.* drawn; 2. *adj.* sketched.

rèply̱, 1. *prep.* below.

rèsó, 1. *n.* drawing; 2. *n.* sketch.

rē, 1. *adj.* thin.

rēcōlỳ, 1. *prep.* beyond.

rēcrō, 1. *n.* surface.

rēcrōxù, 1. *adj.* superficial; 2. *adj.* shallow.

rēcrỳ, 1. *n.* foundation; 2. *n.* fundament.

rēcrỳxú, 1. *adj.* fundamental.

rēcrỳxúrō, 1. *adv.* fundamentally.

rēkī, 1. *n.* steward; 2. *n.* stewardess.

rēklà, 1. *n.* eyelid.

rēkȳ, 1. *n.* grower (e.g. of plants).

rēlōfò, 1. *n.* mystery.

rēlōfòxú, 1. *adj.* mysterious.

rēlōfòxúrō, 1. *adv.* mysteriously.

rēmȳ, 1. *adj.* grown.

rēnuō, 1. *v.* {m̀, í, v́, ṽ} thin.

rēnù, 1. *n.* penis.

rēnūkō, 1. *n.* thinner.

rēnūmō, 1. *adj.* thinned.

rēsī, 1. *n.* stewardship.

rēsȳ, 1. *n.* crop; 2. *n.* grow.

rẹ, 1. *n.* savings.

rẹsẹ, 1. *n.* venom.

rẹsẹxú, 1. *adj.* venomous.

rẹsú, 1. *prep.* ago.

rẽ, 1. *n.* work.

riá, 1. *v.* {ḿ, m̀, í} achieve.

riā, 1. *v.* {ḿ, m̀} answer.

rié, 1. *v.* {ḿ, m̀} work.

riè, 1. *v.* {ḿ, j̀, j̃} walk.

riŏ, 1. *v.* {z̃} see (s.o./s.th.); 2. *v.* {z̀} see (*propositions*).

risyxũ, 1. *adj.* orgasmic.

risȳ, 1. *n.* orgasm.

riỹ, 1. *v.* {ź} orgasm.

riŷ, 1. *v.* {m̀} take it (that...); 2. *v.* {m̀} presume; 3. *v.* {m̀} assume.

ríjà, 1. *n.* hairbrush; 2. *n.* brush.

ríkā, 1. *n.* achiever.

ríkē, 1. *n.* worker.

rílēlē, 1. *adj.* workaholic.

rímỳ, 1. *adj.* presumed.

rísā, 1. *n.* achievement.

rísē, 1. *n.* work.

rísrī, 1. *n.* sap.

ríxū, 1. *adj.* disgusting; 2. *adj.* sick.

ríxūrō, 1. *adv.* disgustingly.

rì, 1. *adj.* long.

rìclẹ, 1. *n.* longstaff.

rìfrọ, 1. *n.* evidence.

rìfrọxú, 1. *adj.* supported (i.e. by evidence); 2. *adj.* evidenced (well).

rìkẹ, 1. *n.* walker.

rìklạ, 1. *n.* coral; 2. **rìklạ kliprũ** *n.* coral reef.

rìmó, 1. *adj.* seen; 2. *adj.* observed.

rìnu̯o, 1. *v.* {m̀, ĺ, v́, ṽ} lengthen.

rìnu̯mo, 1. *adj.* lengthened.

rìpru̯, 1. *n.* longsword.

rìpru̯ni̯, 1. *n.* longswordsman.

rìpsa̯, 1. *n.* nightmare.

rìpsa̯xú, 1. *adj.* nightmarish.

rìsre̯, 1. *n.* monster.

rìsre̯xú, 1. *adj.* monstrous.

rīklà, 1. *n.* longbow.

rīklàni̯, 1. *n.* longbowman.

rīsā, 1. *n.* answer.

ri̯, 1. *adv.* where.

ri̯fe̯, 1. *n.* shovel.

ri̯kry, 1. *n.* gold.

ri̯kryxú, 1. *adj.* gold; 2. *adj.* golden; 3. *adj.* made of gold.

ri̯nu̯ký, 1. *n.* miracle.

ri̯nu̯kýxù, 1. *adj.* miraculous.

ri̯pri̯, 1. *n.* jade.

ri̯pri̯xú, 1. *adj.* jade; 2. *adj.* made of jade.

rocĭ, 1. *n.* jewelry.

rofrĭ, 1. *n.* lunch.

roì, 1. *v.* {ĺ} there is/are (*existential quantification*).

roi̯, 1. *v.* {ź} feel (*compounds*).

roú, 1. *v.* {ḿ} play (have fun); 2. *v.* {g̀} play (with s.o.).

roŭ, 1. *v.* {ḿ, m̀, m̃} make; 2. *v.* {ḿ, m̀, m̃} create; 3. *v.* {m̀, m̃} form.

ró, 1. *num.* zero.

rókū, 1. *n.* player (sports, games).

rólūlē, 1. *adj.* playful.

rólūlērō, 1. *adv.* playfully.

rò, 1. *adj.* heavy.

ròkú, 1. *n.* maker; 2. *n.* creator.

ròlú, 1. *prep.* about (*topic*); 2. *prep.* regarding.

ròmú, 1. *adj.* made; 2. *adj.* created.

rōkrà, 1. *n.* wisdom.

rōkràxú, 1. *adj.* wise.

rōkràxúrō, 1. *adv.* wisely.

rōprè, 1. *n.* buckle; 2. *n.* belt buckle.

rōsì, 1. *n.* lime.

ro̦, 1. *n.* jaw.

ro̦ko̦, 1. *adj.* hollow.

ro̦ko̦nuo̦, 1. *v.* {m̀, ǹ, Í, ṽ} hollow (out).

ro̦ko̦nu̦mo̦, 1. *adj.* hollowed (out).

ro̦lu̦, 1. *n.* plague.

ro̦pró, 1. *n.* mist.

ro̦xo̦, 1. *comp.* while; 2. *comp.* as long as; 3. *prep.* during.

ruá, 1. *v.* {ḿ, m̀} invest (e.g. money); 2. *v.* {g̀} invest (in s.th.).

ruă, 1. *v.* {m̀, ñ, ǵ} deliver.

ruē, 1. *v.* {Ø} thunder.

ruê, 1. *v.* {m̀} feel (touch); 2. *v.* {ẑ} feel (sense).

ruŏ, 1. *v.* {m̀, Í} engineer.

rurũ, 1. *adj.* millionth.

rú, 1. *adj.* clear (weather).

rúfrè, 1. *n.* option.

rúfrèxú, 1. *adj.* optional.

rúfrèxúclì, 1. *n.* optionality.

rúkā, 1. *n.* investor.

rúmā, 1. *adj.* invested.

rúmè, 1. *adj.* felt; 2. *adj.* touched.

rúsā, 1. *n.* investment.

rúsè, 1. *n.* sensation; 2. *n.* feeling.

rù, 1. *adv.* when.

rùkó, 1. *n.* engineer.

rùlo̦, 1. *n.* spring (season).

rùmá, 1. *adj.* delivered.

rùmó, 1. *adj.* engineered.

rùni̦, 1. *n.* gentleman (respectable man); 2. *n.* Lord (respectful title).

rùsá, 1. *n.* delivery.

rùsó, 1. *n.* engineering.

rū, 1. *n.* tooth.

rūklò, 1. *n.* skeleton.

rūsē, 1. *n.* thunder.

rūnà, 1. *n.* society; 2. *n.* civilization.

rūnàxú, 1. *adj.* sociable; 2. *adj.* social.

ru̱, 1. *n.* cat.

ru̱je̱, 1. *n.* clay.

ru̱je̱xú, 1. *adj.* clay; 2. *adj.* made of clay.

ru̱nu̱, 1. *n.* kitten.

ru̱pi̱, 1. *n.* cow.

ru̱pi̱ni̱, 1. *n.* calf.

ru̱si̱, 1. *n.* dessert.

rũ, 1. *num.* million; 2. *num.* one million.

rycrixū, 1. *adj.* exemplary.

rycrī, 1. *n.* example.

ryì, 1. *v.* {z̃} excite; 2. *v.* {ż} excite (*propositions*).

ryù, 1. *v.* {m̀, Í, z̃} confuse; 2. *v.* {ż} confuse (*propositions*).

ryŭ, 1. *v.* {Í} explode.

ryŭfīē, 1. *v.* {m̀, Í} demolish.

ryŭsriò, 1. *v.* {m̀, Í} launch (e.g. a rocket, a missile); 2. *v.* {m̀, Í} fire (e.g. a cannon, artillery).

rý, 1. *n.* flesh.

rýnì, 1. *n.* sister.

rỳ, 1. *det.* some; 2. *det.* any; 3. *pn.* some.

rỳcu̱, 1. *pn.* something.

rỳkúsrìko̱, 1. *n.* bombardier.

rỳli̱le̱, 1. *adj.* exciting.

rỳlu̱le̱, 1. *adj.* confusing.

rỳmi̱, 1. *adj.* excited.

rỳmúfīmē, 1. *adj.* demolished.

rỳmúsrìmo̱, 1. *adj.* launched (e.g. a rocket, a missile); 2. *adj.* fired (e.g. a cannon, artillery).

rỳmu̱, 1. *adj.* confused.

rỳni̱, 1. *pn.* someone; 2. *pn.* somebody; 3. *pn.* anyone; 4. *pn.* anybody.

rỳsi̱, 1. *n.* excitement.

rỳsú, 1. *n.* education; 2. *n.* explosion.

rỳsúfīsē, 1. *n.* demolition.

rỳsúsrìso̱, 1. *n.* launch (of e.g. a rocket, a missile).

rỳsúxù, 1. *adj.* explosive; 2. *adj.* educational; 3. *adj.* informative.

rỳsu̱, 1. *n.* confusion.

rȳ, 1. *n.* product; 2. *n.* goods.

rȳfrà, 1. *adv.* sometimes; 2. *adv.* at times.

rȳmā, 1. *adv.* somewhere; 2. *adv.* anywhere; 3. *pn.* somewhere; 4. *pn.* anywhere.

rȳmā prò, 1. *adv.* somewhere else; 2. *adv.* elsewhere.

ry̱, 1. *n.* face.

ry̱kfa̱, 1. *adj.* native.

ry̱me̱, 1. *n.* lute.

ry̱me̱prá, 1. *n.* lutist.

rỹ, 1. *n.* heart.

ŕ, 1. *aux.* be about to; 2. *dis.* {1: *Patient*}.

ř, 1. *aux.* (*progressive aspect*); 2. *dis.* {2: *Patient, Agent*}.

r̄, 1. *aux.* tend to.

r̠, 1. *aux.* (*inferential marker*).

r̃, 1. *aux.* should; 3. *dis.* {3: *Theme/Patient, Stimulus, Agent*}.

S

sa, 1. *conj.* and (non-exclusive).

saclī, 1. *n.* sickness; 2. *n.* illness.

saí, 1. *v.* {ż} have; 2. *v.* {ż} own; 3. *v.* {ż} possess.

salī, 1. *n.* suspenders.

sanumõ, 1. *adj.* sickened.

sanuõ, 1. *v.* {ż, z̃} sicken.

saù, 1. *v.* {Í} exist.

sa̱u̱, 1. *v.* {ṁ, m̃, ř} press (crush e.g. grapes).

saû, 1. *v.* {ḿ, ṁ, m̃, Í} create.

sá, 1. *n.* end (of a race, game, etc.).

sákù, 1. *n.* creator.

sálùle̱, 1. *adj.* creative.

sálùle̱clí, 1. *n.* creativity.

sálùle̱ro̱, 1. *adv.* creatively.

sámù, 1. *adj.* created.

sásù, 1. *n.* creation.

sà, 1. *n.* worm.

sàklé, 1. *n.* cactus.

sàpy, 1. *n.* rake.

sàsu, 1. *n.* existence.

sā, 1. *adj.* green.

sāclì, 1. *n.* verdure.

sājà, 1. *adv.* again.

sākō, 1. *n.* green.

sāprà, 1. *adj.* strong (in flavor, etc.).

sāpràro, 1. *adv.* strongly (in flavor, etc.).

saca, 1. *n.* cylinder.

sacaxú, 1. *adj.* cylindrical.

sakí, 1. *n.* tombstone; 2. *n.* gravestone.

salásā, 1. *n.* caravan.

sapó, 1. *n.* noodle.

sapru, 1. *n.* vegetable.

sã, 1. *adj.* sick; 2 *adj.* ill.

seó, 1. *v.* { m̀, Í} increase.

seù, 1. *v.* {m̀, m̃} copy.

seỳ, 1. *v.* {ź, ž} blush (at s.th.).

sé, 1. *n.* scalp.

sélī, 1. *n.* bell.

séplālō, 1. *n.* galaxy.

sésō, 1. *n.* increase.

sè, 1. *adj.* thick.

sèclí, 1. *n.* thickness.

sècri, 1. *n.* condition; 2. *n.* requirement.

sècrixú, 1. *adj.* conditional (subject to conditions).

sècrixúclì, 1. *n.* conditionality.

sèmu, 1. *adj.* copied (facsimile).

sènuo, 1. *v.* {m̀, Í, v́, ṽ} thicken.

sènumo, 1. *adj.* thickened.

sèsu, 1. *n.* copy (facsimile).

sèsy, 1. *n.* blush.

sē, 1. *n.* arrow.

sēkā, 1. *n.* broccoli.

sēklū, 1. *n.* relationship.

se, 1. *n.* sight; 2. *n.* vision.

sẹmú, 1. *n.* pancreas.

sẹpé, 1. *n.* church.

sẽ, 1. *adj.* expensive; 2. *adj.* costly.

siǎ, 1. *v.* {m̀} try; 2. *v.* {m̀} test.

siẹ, 1. *v.* {z̃} hear (s.o./s.th.); 2. *v.* {ż} hear (*propositions*).

siê, 1. *v.* {m̀} call (s.o. is called s.th.).

siě, 1. *v.* {m̀} lose; 2. *v.* {m̀} misplace.

sikõ, 1. *n.* reader.

simõ, 1. *adj.* read.

siõ, 1. *v.* {ḿ, m̀, m̃, ñ} read.

sipijoprã, 1. *n.* surgeon.

sipijoxũ, 1. *adj.* surgical.

sipijõ, 1. *n.* surgery.

sisõ, 1. *n.* reading.

siȳ, 1. *v.* {m̀, r̃} involve.

sí, 1. *n.* glove.

sírù, 1. *n.* carrot.

sìcrọcạ, 1. *n.* archipelago.

sìfá, 1. *n.* feature; 2. *n.* characteristic.

sìmá, 1. *adj.* tried; 2. *adj.* taste-tested.

sìmé, 1. *adj.* lost; 2. *adj.* misplaced.

sìnị, 1. *n.* needle.

sìný, 1. *n.* bracelet.

sìsé, 1. *n.* loss.

sī, 1. *adj.* wrong; 2. *adj.* false; 3. *adj.* incorrect.

sīclì, 1. *n.* falsity.

sīlēklū, 1. *adj.* vulnerable.

sīlēklūclì, 1. *n.* vulnerability.

sīmì, 1. *n.* pocket.

sīmìsrụjó, 1. *n.* pocket watch.

sīrè, 1. *n.* fly (on clothing).

sīrõ, 1. *adv.* wrongly; 2. *adv.* falsely; 3. *adv.* incorrectly.

sīsȳ, 1. *n.* involvement.

sị, 1. *prep.* as (*as* interesting as s.th.).

sịcị, 1. *n.* minimum.

sịkẹ, 1. *n.* hearer.

sįmę, 1. *adj.* heard.

sįpį, 1. *adj.* happy.

sįpįclí, 1. *n.* happiness.

sįpsý, 1. *n.* moment; 2. *n.* time.

sįpsýxù, 1. *adj.* momentary.

sįpsýxùrǫ, 1. *adv.* momentarily.

sįsę, 1. hearing (sense).

sĩ, 1. *det.* this; 2. *det.* these; 3. *pn.* this; 4. *pn.* these.

solyxū, 1. *adj.* balanced.

solỹ, 1. *n.* balance.

soxū, 1. *adj.* wealthy.

só, 1. *n.* health.

sófĩ, 1. *n.* king.

sómā. 1. *adv.* nowhere; 2. *pn.* nowhere.

sónĩ, 1. *adj.* even (numerically).

sópū, 1. *adj.* sufficient; 2. *adj.* pretty; 3. *adj.* handsome.

sópūclì, 1. *n.* sufficiency.

sópūrō, 1. *adv.* sufficiently.

sóxù, 1. *adj.* healthy.

sóxùrǫ, 1. *adv.* healthily.

sò, 1. *num.* hundred thousand; 2. *num.* one hundred thousand.

sòcló, 1. *n.* elbow.

sòklỵ, 1. *n.* pressure.

sòlá, 1. *n.* juice.

sòpǫ, 1. *adj.* constant.

sòpǫrǫ, 1. *adv.* constantly.

sòsǫ, 1. *adj.* hundred thousandth.

sōkỳ, 1. *n.* barricade.

sǫ, 1. *n.* rope; 2. *det.* no; 3. *pn.* none.

sǫjį, 1. *adj.* current.

sǫjįrǫ, 1. *adv.* currently.

sǫjų, 1. *n.* scale (for measurement).

sǫnį, 1. *pn.* no one; 2. *pn.* nobody.

sõ, 1. *n.* wealth.

sraĩ, 1. *v.* {m̀, ż} rely (on s.o./s.th.); 2. *v.* {m̀, ż} depend (on s.o./s.th.).

sraį, 1. *v.* {m̀, Í, Ì, j̃} roll.

sraĭ, 1. *v.* {m̀, ĺ} scratch.

sraū, 1. *v.* {m̀} spend.

srau̱, 1. *v.* {m̀, v̆} shoot; 2. *v.* {ñ} shoot (s.th. at s.o.).

sraû, 1. *v.* {m̀, ĺ} organize; 2. *v.* {m̀, ĺ} sort.

srámù, 1. *adj.* organized.

srásù, 1. *n.* order; 2. *n.* orderliness; 3. *n.* organization.

srásùxú, 1. *adj.* organized.

srà, 1. *adj.* secondhand; 2. *adj.* used.

sràlílē, 1. *adj.* scratchy.

sràmí, 1. *adj.* scratched.

sràplu̱, 1. *n.* material.

sràsí, 1. *n.* scratch.

srākī, 1. *n.* dependent.

srākīxù, 1. *adj.* dependent.

srākrà, 1. *n.* instance; 2. *n.* moment.

srākràxú, 1. *adj.* instant; 2. *adj.* instantaneous.

srākū, 1. *n.* spender (of money).

srālè, 1. *n.* bladder.

srāmū, 1. *adj.* spent.

srārè, 1. *n.* bracer.

srāsī, 1. *n.* dependence; 2. *n.* reliance.

srāsū, 1. *n.* cash; 2. *n.* money.

sra̱, 1. *n.* body; 2. *n.* corps (military, etc.).

sra̱ku̱, 1. *n.* shooter.

sra̱si̱, 1. *n.* roll (spin).

sra̱su̱, 1. *n.* shot (of a gun, etc.).

srã, 1. *det.* yonder; 2. *det.* that; 3. *det.* those; 4. *pn.* yonder; 5. *pn.* that; 6. *pn.* those.

sreclĭ, 1. *n.* strictness (in behavior).

sreî, 1. *v.* {m̋} groan.

srerõ, 1. *adv.* sternly; 2. *adv.* strictly (in behavior).

sré, 1. *n.* number.

srésì, 1. *n.* groan.

sréxõ, 1. *n.* math; 2. *n.* mathematics.

sréxõprà, 1. *n.* mathematician.

srè, 1. *adj.* west; 2. *adv.* west; 3. *adv.* westward; 4. *n.* west.

srèxú, 1. *adj.* western.

srē, 1. *adj.* deep.

srēlù, 1. *n.* estuary.

srēnuō, 1. *v.* {m̀, Í} deepen.

srērō, 1. *adv.* deeply.

srę̄, 1. *det.* many; 2. *det.* a lot of; 3. *pn.* many; 4. *pn.* a lot.

srē̃, 1. *adj.* strict (in behavior); 2. *adj.* stern.

sriă, 1. *v.* {v̀} apply (for e.g. recompense); 2. *v.* {m̀} apply (to e.g. a job).

srié, 1. *v.* {m̃, g̀} feed.

sriē, 1. *v.* {m̀, j̀, j̄} fly.

srió, 1. *v.* {m̀, Í, Ì, j̄} throw.

sriō, 1. *v.* {m̀} assert; 2. *v.* {m̀} claim; 3. *v.* {m̀} state; 4. *v.* {m̀} charge.

sriô, 1. *v.* {m̀} prevent.

srí, 1. *n.* risk.

srímē, 1. *adj.* fed (given food).

srínì, 1. *adj.* unique; 2. *adj.* original.

srínìrǫ, 1. *adv.* uniquely.

srísò, 1. *n.* prevention.

sríxù, 1. *adj.* risky.

srì, 1. *n.* page.

srìká, 1. *n.* applicant.

srìsá, 1. *n.* application (e.g. to a job).

srīkō, 1. *n.* claimant.

srīpȳ, 1. *n.* guide.

srīsē, 1. *n.* flight.

srīsō, 1. *n.* claim; 2. *n.* assertion.

srị, 1. *n.* foot (anatomy).

srịkry, 1. *n.* board (administrative).

srĩ, 1. *adj.* cool (cold).

sroclĩ, 1. *n.* blackness.

sroì, 1. *v.* {ḿ, m̀, Í, r̃} hunt.

sroī, 1. *v.* {m̃} treat (s.o. to s.th.).

srokē̃, 1. *n.* wrench.

sronumõ, 1. *adj.* blackened.

sronuõ, 1. *v.* {m̀, Í} blacken.

srosū̃, 1. *n.* discussion.

sroũ, 1. *v.* {m̀} discuss; 2. *v.* {ñ} discuss (with s.o.).

sró, 1. *n.* skin.

srómỳ, 1. *n.* practice (rehearsal).

srómỳxú, 1. *adj.* practiced.

srò, 1. *n.* reason; 2. *n.* logic; 3. *n.* gun.

sròki̧, 1. *n.* hunter.

sròmi̧, 1. *adj.* hunted.

sròni̧, 1. *n.* gunner; 2. *n.* gunman.

sròsi̧, 1. *n.* hunt.

sròxú, 1. *adj.* reasonable; 2. *adj.* logical.

srō, 1. *adv.* home; 2. *n.* home.

srōfènú, 1. *n.* blackberry.

srōfì, 1. *n.* message.

srōkō, 1. *n.* black.

srōnù, 1. *n.* geyser.

sro̧, 1. *prep.* on (*patient, theme*).

srõ, 1. *adj.* black.

sruā, 1. *v.* {m̀, m̃} correct.

sruě, 1. *v.* {m̀, ñ} describe.

sruò, 1. *v.* {j̧, z̧} defecate.

sruô, 1. *v.* {ḿ, ń} misbehave; 2. *v.* {ḿ, ń} act up.

srú, 1. *n.* cube.

srúkò, 1. *n.* miscreant.

srúsò, 1. *n.* misbehavior; 2. *n.* wrongdoing.

srúxù, 1. *adj.* cubic.

srù, 1. *adj.* pleasant; 2. *adj.* nice.

srùfú, 1. *n.* temple.

srùklu̧, 1. *adj.* flat.

srùklu̧nuo̧, 1. *v.* {m̀, ǹ, v́, ṽ} flatten.

srùklu̧nu̧mo̧, 1. *adj.* flattened.

srùmé, 1. *adj.* described.

srùsé, 1. *n.* description.

srùso̧, 1. *n.* defecation.

srū, 1. *adj.* slight.

srūfā, 1. *n.* ankle.

srūkūkù, 1. *n.* monolith.

srūkūkùxú, 1. *adj.* monolithic.

srūmā, 1. *adj.* corrected.

srūrō, 1. *adv.* slightly.

srūsā, 1. *n.* correction.

sru̠, 1. *adj.* low (requiring stock).

sru̠cí, 1. *n.* drum.

sru̠cíprà, 1. *n.* drummer.

sru̠có, 1. *n.* feces.

sru̠jó, 1. *n.* watch; 2. *n.* wristwatch.

sru̠se̠, 1. *adj.* obvious; 2. *adj.* apparent; 3. *adj.* clear.

sru̠se̠clí, 1. *n.* obviousness.

sru̠se̠ro̠, 1. *adv.* obviously; 2. *adv.* clearly.

srū̃, 1. *n.* anus.

sryí, 1. *v.* {ḿ, m̀} train.

srykfĩ, 1. *n.* family name.

sryxū̃, 1. *adj.* salty.

srý, 1. *n.* family.

srýkī, 1. *n.* trainer.

srýsī, 1. *n.* training.

srýsīklā, 1. *n.* training grounds.

srýsīxù, 1. *adj.* trained.

srỳ, 1. *adj.* smooth (surface).

srỳclí, 1. *n.* smoothness (surface).

srȳsè, 1. *n.* audience.

srȳxō, 1. *n.* saltwater.

sry̠, 1. *adj.* poor; 2. *adj.* impoverished.

sry̠clí, 1. *n.* poverty.

sry̠nuo̠, 1. *v.* {m̀} impoverish.

sry̠nu̠mo̠, 1. *adj.* impoverished.

srỹ, 1. *n.* salt.

suá, 1. *v.* {ḿ, ń} dance.

suklukū̃, 1. *n.* airplane; 2. *n.* plane.

sulõ, 1. *n.* bus.

sumerixū̃, 1. *adj.* nutritious.

sumerĩ, 1. *n.* nutrition.

suó, 1. *v.* reach {m̀} (for s.th.).

suo̱, 1. *v.* {m̀, ñ} ask.

suý, 1. *v.* {ż, z̃} witness.

suỳ, 1. *v.* {j̣, ź} sneeze (on s.th.).

sú, 1. *n.* test (academic); 2. *n.* exam.

súkā, 1. *n.* dancer.

súkȳ, 1. *n.* witness.

súmȳ, 1. *adj.* witnessed.

súsā, 1. *n.* dance.

sù, 1. *adj.* bright; 2. *adj.* light.

sùlyle̱, 1. *adj.* sneezy.

sùní, 1. *n.* screw (building material).

sùni̱múkȳ, 1. *n.* screwdriver.

sùnuo̱, 1. *v.* {m̀, ǹ, Í, ṽ} brighten.

sùnu̱mo̱, 1. *adj.* brightened.

sùro̱, 1. *adv.* brightly.

sùsy̱, 1. *n.* sneeze.

sū, 1. *n.* gown.

sūklā, 1. *adj.* additional; 2. *det.* another; 3. *det.* more; 4. *pn.* another; 5. *pn.* more.

sūrù, 1. *n.* tusk.

su̱, 1. *n.* bean.

su̱ko̱, 1. *n.* asker.

su̱kry̱, 1. *n.* paddy field.

su̱ku̱, 1. *adv.* there; 2. *n.* there.

su̱lo̱le̱, 1. *adj.* inquisitve.

su̱mo̱, 1. *adj.* asked.

su̱so̱, 1. *n.* question.

sũ, 1. *n.* air.

syi̱, 1. *v.* {ź} pass out; 2. *v.* {ź} go unconscious.

syIocã, 1. *n.* breakfast nook.

sý, 1. *n.* kind; 2. *n.* type; 3. *n.* variety.

sýcò, 1. *n.* intrigue; 2. *n.* interest.

sýcòxú, 1. *adj.* intriguing; 2. *adj.* interesting.

sýcòxúrō, 1. *adv.* interestingly.

sýnī, 1. *n.* turkey.

sýnō, 1. *prep.* between.

sýxù, 1. *adj.* typical.

sỳklú, 1. *adj.* relative.

sỳklúrō, 1. *adv.* relatively.

sȳ, 1. *n.* book.

sȳkfò, 1. *n.* sinew.

sȳkfòxú, 1. *adj.* sinewy.

sȳkrēpī, 1. *n.* bookshelf; 2. *n.* bookcase.

sȳprà, 1. *n.* printer (e.g. of books).

sȳxù, 1. *adj.* bookish.

sy̱, 1. *n.* house; 2. *n.* image (picture).

sy̱kro̱, 1. *n.* mutton.

sy̱lo̱, 1. *n.* breakfast.

sy̱mi̱, 1. *adj.* unconscious; 2. *n.* passed out.

sy̱pé, 1. *n.* sickle.

sy̱plá, 1. *n.* passion.

sy̱pláxù, 1. *adj.* passionate.

sy̱xó, 1. *n.* literature.

sỹ, 1. *det.* that; 2. *det.* those; 3. *pn.* that; 4. *pn.* those.

U

u, 1. *prep.* of.

uà, 1. *v.* {ź} be born; 2. *v.* {m̀} give birth to (s.o.).

úclū, 1. *adv.* even.

úprā, 1. *n.* despair.

úprāxù, 1. *adj.* hopeless.

úprāxùclí, 1. *n.* hopelessness.

ùma̱, 1. *adj.* born (given birth to).

ūcò, 1. *n.* daughter.

ūsū, 1. *prep.* as (function or character); 2. *prep.* like (function or character).

u̱nécèfy̱, 1. *n.* tar pit.

u̱ne̱, 1. *n.* tar.

V

v́, 1. *aux.* might; 2. *dis.* {2: *Instrument, Theme*}.

v̀, 1. *aux.* (*question marker*); 2. *dis.* {2: *Instrument, Agent*}.
v̲, 1. *aux.* (*frequentative marker*).
ṽ, 1. *aux.* have (*perfect aspect*); 2. *dis.* {3: *Theme/Patient, Instrument, Agent*}.

X

xalã, 1. *n.* cup; 2. *n.* mug.
xaū, 1. *v.* {ḿ, m̀, ń, ǹ} survive; 2. *v.* {ḿ, m̀, ń, ǹ} last.
xá, 1. *adj.* lucky; 2. *adj.* fortunate.
xáclì, 1. *n.* luck; 2. *n.* fortune; 3. *n.* chance.
xárō, 1. *adv.* luckily; 2. *adv.* fortunately.
xàmo̲, 1. *n.* knife.
xànu̲, 1. *n.* massif.
xā, 1. *adj.* cold.
xāclì, 1. *n.* cold.
xākū, 1. *n.* survivor.
xāsū, 1. *n.* survival.
xã, 1. *n.* half.
xekỹ, 1. *n.* performer.
xeō, 1. *v.* {m̀, m̃} test.
xesỹ, 1. *n.* performance.
xeý, 1. *v.* {Í} sleep (be asleep); 2. *v.* {ḿ} go to sleep.
xeỹ, 1. *v.* {ḿ, m̀, m̃} perform.
xé, 1. *adj.* red.
xéclì, 1. *n.* redness.
xéfènú, 1. *n.* raspberry.
xékō, 1. *n.* red.
xékỹ, 1. *n.* sleeper.
xénuō, 1. *v.* {m̀, Í} redden.
xénỹ, 1. *n.* sofa; 2. *n.* couch.
xésỹ, 1. *n.* sleep.
xésỹxù, 1. *n.* asleep.
xè, 1. *n.* mood.
xèclé, 1. *adj.* innocent.
xècléclì, 1. *n.* innocence.

xèclérō, 1. *adv.* innocently.

xèpsé, 1. *n.* chemical.

xèpsẹxó, 1. *n.* chemistry.

xèpsẹxóprà, 1. *n.* chemist.

xèxú, 1. *adj.* moody.

xēclù, 1. *n.* scenery.

xēsō, 1. *n.* test (experimental); 2. *n.* trial.

xẹ, 1. *adj.* full (filled).

xẹclí, 1. *n.* fullness.

xẹkli̯, 1. *n.* secret.

xẹklixú, 1. *adj.* secret; 2. *adj.* secretive.

xẹplu̯, 1. *n.* scrotum.

xẹro̱, 1. *adv.* fully.

xẽ, 1. *n.* sky.

xiakraĩ, 1. *v.* { m̀, m̃, Í} euthanize.

xià, 1. *v.* {ḿ, m̀, m̃} clean.

xiã, 1. *v.* {g̀} assist (s.o.); 2. *v.* {m̀} assist (with doing s.th.); 3. *v.* {g̀} help (s.o.); 4. *v.* {m̀} help (*propositions*).

xiâ, 1. *v.* {m̀, Í, ṽ} measure.

xiclĩ, 1. *n.* sharpness.

xiè, 1. *v.* {Í, Ì} settle (as powder, sediment, etc.).

xikã, 1. *n.* helper.

xilalaclĩ, 1. *n.* helpfulness.

xilalã, 1. *adj.* helpful.

ximakramĩ, 1. *adj.* euthanized.

ximã, 1. *adj.* helped; 2. *adj.* assisted.

xinukõ, 1. *n.* sharpener.

xinumõ, 1. *adj.* sharpened.

xinuõ, 1. *v.* {m̀, Í, v́, ṽ} sharpen.

xiō, 1. *v.* {ż} affect.

xiŏ, 1. *v.* {m̀, ñ} declare; 2. *v.* {m̀, ñ} state.

xisakrasĩ, 1. *n.* euthanasia.

xisaprã, 1. *n.* assistant.

xisã, 1. *n.* help; 2. *n.* assistance.

xiỹ, 1. *v.* {z̃} hurt; 2. *v.* {z̃} be in pain.

xí, 1. *n.* nail (used with hammer).

xímà, 1. *adj.* measured (on a scale).

xísà, 1. *n.* measurement.

xì, 1. *n.* leaf.

xìplạ, 1. *n.* prairie; 2. *n.* plain.

xìmạ, 1. *adj.* cleaned; 2. *adj.* clean.

xìmó, 1. *adj.* stated; 2. *adj.* declared.

xìnọmạ, 1. *n.* waterfall.

xìsó, 1. *adj.* statement; 2. *adj.* declaration.

xī, 1. *n.* brow.

xīmō, 1. *adj.* affected.

xị, 1. *adj.* near; 2. *adj.* nearby; 3. *adj.* close; 4. *prep.* near.

xịclí, 1. *n.* nearness; 2. *n.* closeness.

xịrạ, 1. *n.* beach.

xịrọ, 1. *adv.* nearly; 2. *adv.* closely; 3. *adv.* almost.

xịrú, 1. *n.* court; 2. **xịrú cxèsọ** *n.* courthouse.

xī̃, 1. *adj.* sharp.

xoī, 1. *v.* {ż} belong; 2. *v.* {ż} own.

xomũ, 1. *adj.* lifted (up); 2. *adj.* raised.

xọ nuọ, 1. *v.* {m̀, ǹ, Í, ṽ} darken (in light); 2. *v.* {Í} get dark.

xoú, 1. *v.* {m̀, m̃, Í} pick; 2. *v.* {m̀, m̃, Í} choose.

xoū, 1. *v.* {m̀, ż} gain (earn).

xoũ, 1. *v.* {m̀} lift (s.th. up); 2. *v.* {m̀} raise (s.th. up).

xoû, 1. *v.* {ż} burp.

xoxũ, 1. *adj.* opal; 2. *adj.* opaline; 3. *adj.* opalescent.

xó, 1. *n.* study (scholarly research); 2. *n.* research.

xójī, 1. *n.* thorax.

xóprà, 1. *n.* researcher.

xósù, 1. *n.* burp.

xósū, 1. *n.* pick; 2. *n.* choice.

xóxù, 1. *adj.* scholarly.

xò, 1. *comp.* unless.

xō, 1. *n.* water (in general).

xōcà, 1. *adj.* accurate.

xōcàclí, 1. *n.* accuracy.

xōkī, 1. *n.* owner.

xōlè, 1. *n.* llama.

xōmī, 1. *adj.* owned (as property).

xōpȳ, 1. *n.* proverb; 2. *n.* saying; 3. *n.* expression.

xōsī, 1. *n.* ownership; 2. *n.* possession; 3. *n.* belonging.

xōsū, 1. *n.* gain.

xōxù, 1. *adj.* watery.

xo̱, 1. *adj.* dim; 2. *adj.* dark (absence of light).

xo̱clí, 1. *n.* darkness.

xo̱jo̱, 1. *n.* corpse.

xo̱nuo̱, 1. *v.* {m̀, Í} dim.

xo̱nu̱mo̱, 1. *adj.* dimmed; 2. *adj.* darkened (in light).

xo̱pro̱, 1. *adj.* discrete.

xo̱pro̱clí, 1. *n.* discreteness.

xo̱ro̱, 1. *adv.* dimly.

xõ, 1. *n.* opal.

xuè, 1. *v.* {m̀, ǹ, v́, ṽ} cure.

xuē, 1. *v.* {m̀} signify; 2. *v.* {m̀} mean.

xuě, 1. *v.* {m̀} discover.

xukȳ̃, 1. *n.* pouncer.

xusȳ̃, 1. *n.* pounce.

xuȳ̃, 1. *v.* {ḿ, j̀, j̃} pounce.

xuŷ, 1. *v.* {ź} worry (about s.th.); 2. *v.* {z̃} worry (*propositions*); 3. *v.* {ź} be concerned (about s.th.); 4. *v.* {z̃} be concerned (*propositions*).

xúmỳ, 1. *adj.* worried; 2. *adj.* concerned.

xúnā, 1. *n.* quality.

xúnāxù, 1. *adj.* quality.

xúsỳ, 1. *n.* worry; 2. *n.* concern.

xùfi̱, 1. *n.* nipple.

xùké, 1. *n.* discoverer.

xùmé, 1. *adj.* discovered.

xùme̱, 1. *adj.* cured.

xùpli̱, 1. *n.* bench.

xùsé, 1. *n.* discovery; 2. *n.* finding.

xùse̱, 1. *n.* cure.

xū, 1. *n.* hope.

xūlēlē, 1. *adj.* significant.

xūlēlēclì, 1. *n.* significance.

xūlēlērō, 1. *adv.* significantly.

xūsē, 1. *n.* meaning.

xūsēxù, 1. *adj.* meaningful.

xūxù, 1. *adj.* hopeful.

xūxùrǫ, 1. *adv.* hopefully.

xųję, 1. *n.* empire.

xųjęxú, 1. *adj.* imperial.

xųká, 1. *n.* course; 2. *n.* route.

xųklų, 1. *n.* tundra.

xųplą, 1. *n.* butt; 2. *n.* buttocks.

xųrú, 1. *n.* vodka.

xyí, 1. *v.* {ḿ, ŕ, r̀} glare (at s.o./s.th.).

xyklarikoxū̃, 1. *adj.* one-dimensional.

xylỹ, 1. *n.* plateau.

xyū, 1. *v.* {ź} suffocate.

xý, 1. *adv.* on the one hand.

xýmà, 1. *adj.* actual.

xýmàrǫ, 1. *adv.* actually; 2. *adv.* in fact.

xýsī, 1. *n.* glare.

xỳ, 1. *adv.* on the other hand.

xỳfry̱, 1. *n.* mandible.

xȳ, 1. *num.* one.

xȳkrā, 1. *n.* telephone; 2. *n.* phone.

xȳsū, 1. *n.* suffocation.

xȳxȳ, 1. *adj.* first.

xȳxȳrō, 1. *adv.* firstly; 2. *adv.* primarily.

xy̱klǫ, 1. *adv.* particularly; 2. *adv.* especially.

xy̱prą, 1. *adj.* early; 2. *adv.* early.

xỹ, 1. *n.* lung.

Y

y̱fǫ, 1. *n.* cousin.

y̱rá, 1. *n.* gong.

Z

ź, 1. *aux.* (*past marker*); 2. *dis.* {1: *Experiencer*}.

ż, 1. *aux.* may; 2. *aux.* be allowed to; 3. *dis.* {2: *Theme, Experiencer*}.

ẓ, 1. *aux.* do (*emphasis marker*).

z̃, 1. *aux.* just (*recent past*); 2. *dis.* {2: *Stimulus, Experiencer*}.

WORKS CITED

Avelino, Heriberto. "The Typology of Pamean Number Systems and the Limits of Mesoamerica as a Linguistic Area." *Linguistic Typology* 10 (2006): 41–60.

Chomsky, Noam. *The Logical Structure of Linguistic Theory.* Plenum Press: New York, 1975.

Dambriunas, Leonardas, Antanas Klimas, and William Schmalstieg. *Introduction to Modern Lithuanian.* Brooklyn, NY: Franciscan Fathers Press, 1966.

De Haan, Ferdinand. "Evidentiality and epistemic modality: Setting boundaries." *Southwest Journal of Linguistics* 18, no. 1 (1999): 83–101.

Grice, H. P. "Logic and Conversation." *Syntax and Semantics* 3 (1975): 41–58.

Hammond, Robert M. *The Sounds of Spanish: Analysis and Application (With Special Reference to American English).* Somerville, MA: Cascadilla Press, 2001.

Hayes, Bruce, Kie Zuraw, Péter Siptár, and Zsusza Londe. "Natural and Unnatural Constraints in Hungarian Vowel Harmony." *Language* (2009): 822–863.

Itō, Junko, and R. Armin Mester. "Japanese Phonology." In *The Handbook of Phonological Theory*, edited by John A. Goldsmith, 817–838. Oxford: Blackwell Publishers, 1995.

Kabak, Bariş. "Turkish Vowel Harmony." *The Blackwell Companion to Phonology* (2011): 1–24.

Kittilä, Seppo. "Recipient-prominence vs. Beneficiary-prominence." *Linguistic Typology* 9, no. 2 (2005): 269–297.

Lamb, William. *Scottish Gaelic*. Lincom Europa, 2003.

Mazaudon, Martine. "Number Building in Tibeto-Burman Languages." *North East Indian Linguistics Society* 2 (2007).

McCarthy, John. "A Prosodic Theory of Nonconcatenative Morphology." *Linguistic Inquiry* 12, no. 3 (1981): 373–418.

Montrul, Silvina. "First-language-constrained Variability in the Second-language Acquisition of Argument-structure-changing Morphology with Causative Verbs." *Second Language Research* 17, no. 2 (2001): 144–194.

Propp, V. *Morphology of the Folktale*. Translated by Laurence Scott. Austin, TX: University of Texas Press, 1968.

Sharman, J. C., and A. E. Meeussen. "The Tabulation of Tenses in a Bantu Language." *Africa* 26, no. 1 (1956): 29–46.

Tomlin, Russell S. *Basic Word Order: Functional Principles*. Croom Helm, 1986.

Printed in the United States
By Bookmasters